Contents

Sacred art & architecture colour section following p.184

Traditional Cypriot food colour section following p.312

3
∎

Introduction to

Cyprus

Cyprus, the Mediterranean's third largest island after Sicily and Sardinia, only emerged as a notionally independent state on August 16, 1960. For the first time, following centuries of rule by whatever empire or nation dominated the eastern Mediterranean – including, from 1878 to 1960, Great Britain – the islanders seemed to control their own destiny. Such empowerment proved illusory: no distinctly Cypriot national identity was permitted to evolve by the island's Orthodox Christian Greek and Muslim Turkish communities. Within four years, tension between these two groups had rent the society asunder, followed in 1974 by a political and ethnic division of the island imposed by the mainland Turkish army.

 However, **calm** now reigns on the island, and for British visitors there's a persistent sense of déjà vu in Cyprus, perhaps more than with any other ex-Crown colony. Pillar boxes still display "GR" and "ER" monograms near zebra crossings; grandiose colonial public buildings jostle for space with vernacular mud-brick and Neoclassical houses; Debenhams, Next, Nando's, Starbucks, M&S, KFC, Pizza Hut and McDonald's are all present in the South's largest towns; and of course driving is on the left. Before the recent founding of universities in both South and North, higher education was pursued abroad, preferably in the UK, and **English** – effectively the second language in the South – is

Restoration accommodation

The rapid urbanization of Cyprus since the 1950s has led to the wholesale abandonment of many attractive hill villages, particularly in Páfos and Limassol districts. Since the late 1980s, a number of stone-built rural houses of different sizes have been restored as unique accommodation. Facilities range from small cottages with perhaps two studio units to rambling complexes, essentially small inns, around a shared courtyard with a pool. Traditional architectural features, such as fireplaces and soaring arches in the main room, are usually preserved. The idea is that guests will both interact socially with the remaining villagers and spend locally, rather than down at the coastal mega-resorts.

widely spoken. Despite the bitterness of the independence struggle against the UK, most is forgiven (if not exactly forgotten) a generation or so later.

Cyprus struggles to compete in allure with more exotic, airline-poster destinations, yet the place grows on you – as evidenced by the huge expat/immigrant population in the South, mostly British but also central and eastern European and south Asian. The **beaches**, which tend to be small, scattered coves on the south coast, or longer, dunier expanses on north-facing shores, are the focus of many trips, but there's more than enough to hold your interest inland. Horizons are defined by one of two **mountain ranges**: the convoluted massif of the Tróödhos, with numerous spurs and deep valleys, and the wall-like escarpment of the Kyrenia hills, seemingly sculpted of papier-mâché.

Archeology buffs, wine-tasters, flower-sniffers, bird-watchers and mountain bikers are particularly well catered for, though state-of-the-art nightlife and

cultural diversions can be thin on the ground outside Nicosia, Limassol and Ayía Nápa, in keeping with the predominantly forty-to-sixty-something clientele, and the island's enduring provincialism. This has both cause and effect in the overwhelming presence of the **package industry**, which has effectively put at least two of the bigger resorts plus numbers of hotels off-limits to independent travellers. But for an undemanding, reasonably priced and reliably sunny **family holiday** most months of the year, Cyprus is still a good bet.

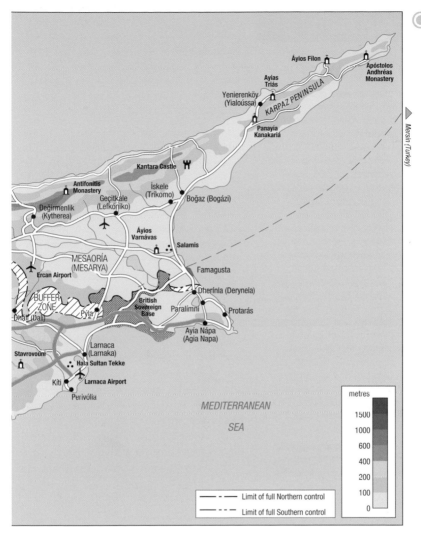

Áyios Filon

Apóstolos
Andhréas
Monastery

Ayías
Triás

Yenierenköy
(Yialoússa)

KARPAZ PENINSULA

Panayía
Kanakariá

Kantara Castle

Antifonítis
Monastery

İskele
(Tríkomo)

Boğaz (Bogázi)

Değirmenlik
(Kytherea)

Geçitkale
(Lefkóniko)

Áyios
Varnávas

Salamis

MESAORÍA
(MESARYA)

Ercan Airport

Famagusta

BUFFER
ZONE

British
Sovereign
Base

Dherínia (Derynela)

Dhali (Dali)

Pyla

Paralímni

Protarás

Ayía Nápa
(Agia Napa)

Larnaca
(Larnaka)

Stavrovoúni

Hala Sultan Tekke

Kíti

Larnaca Airport

Perivólia

MEDITERRANEAN

SEA

metres
1500
1000
600
400
200
100
0

––·–– Limit of full Northern control

––––– Limit of full Southern control

Where to go

ith the mutual isolation of South and North, you formerly had to choose which side of Cyprus to visit on any given trip. All this changed radically in April 2003, when the North suddenly opened the "border" (nobody in the South uses the term other than in inverted commas, as the present situation is viewed

Fact file

• Cyprus is the easternmost island in the Mediterranean, with a **surface area** of 9251 square kilometres (3572 square miles). The total **population** is about a million, with 650,000 Greek Orthodox, Greek-speaking islanders, 80,000 Sunni Muslim, Turkish-speaking natives, and roughly 250,000 foreign-born immigrants or seasonal residents, although there has been no island-wide census since 1960. After 1974 Cyprus was divided into two zones: the South, comprising 68 percent of the land and predominantly Greek Cypriot-inhabited, and the North, largely populated by Turkish Cypriots and an undetermined number of settlers from mainland Turkey. The **capital** of both regions is Nicosia.

• The **Southern republic** is a stable democracy, with regular, keenly contested elections, and since May 2004 a member of the EU. The president is head of state; there is no prime minister. The House of Representatives has 56 seats; 24 more are reserved under the 1960 constitution for Turkish-Cypriot deputies who have not, however, occupied them since 1963. Instead they sit in the North's 50-seat assembly.

Continued opposite...

as an interim one pending any definitive peace settlement). Disinformation is still promulgated by interested parties, but in effect EU nationals with proper ID are free to cross the line in either direction and stay as long as they wish; see p.35 for all pertinent details.

The package industry remains geared to taking you to one or other side of the island, and either portion has plenty to keep you occupied. When you've had your fill of the **South's** busiest beaches east of sleepy **Larnaca**, there's the popular hill village of **Páno Léfkara**, unique sacred art at the Byzantine churches of **Áyios Andónios** and **Angelóktisti** or the nearby Lusignan "**Chapelle Royale**", plus the atmospheric Muslim shrine of **Hala Sultan Tekke** to the west. **Ayía Nápa**, in the far southeast, briefly ranked as a Mediterranean clubbing destination second only to Ibiza, and is still the liveliest summer-spot on the island. Beyond functional **Limassol**, the Crusader tower of Kolossi guards vineyards as it always has, while ancient **Kourion** sprawls nearby atop seaside cliffs, which subside at the sandy bays of Pissoúri, Paramalí and Evdhímou. Inland, rolling hills shelter the **Krassokhoriá** or "Wine Villages", many of these attractively stone-built and little changed outwardly over the past century-plus.

[The Cypriot] is entering in thousands that trough – of how many generations? – between peasant honesty and urban refinement. "To be civilised," a Nicosia friend told me, "our people must first be vulgar. It is the bridge between simplicity and culture."

Colin Thubron

Of the main south-coast resorts, **Páfos** has most recently awoken to tourism, and with its spectacular Roman mosaics and early Christian relics has plenty to offer. The hinterland of Páfos district belies its initial bleak appearance to reveal fertile valleys and ridges sprinkled with brown-stone villages plus, to either side of the **Akámas peninsula**, the last unspoiled stretches of coast in the South. If you don't require lively nightlife, then **Pólis** and the coast flanking it makes a good, comfortable base in this area, serving too as a possible springboard into the foothills of the Tróödhos mountains. Magnificently frescoed ancient churches and monasteries abound, the best of these **Áyios**

Continues...

• The **Northern system** provides for both president and prime minister, and on paper has all requisite democratic trappings, but only since 2001 has the consolidation of power in the hands of an oligarchy been successfully challenged, and repression of their opponents relaxed.

• **Real estate sales** are the biggest foreign-currency earner across the island, with **tourism** slipping into second place just ahead of the general **service sector**, as the typically two million annual vacationers to the **South** has declined by over a third since 2005. British visitors make up roughly half the number, with Scandinavians, Germans, Greeks and Russians following, in that order. By contrast, the **North** gets 70,000–80,000 guests annually, with Brits again leading the way. Fresh produce, juices and wines are the principal **agricultural exports** of the South. Since 2000, the North's economy has effectively imploded, with its only significant money-spinners being higher education offered at small universities, and remittances from the thousands of Turkish Cypriots who commute to work daily in the South.

Divided Cyprus

Long-dormant rivalry between Cyprus's two principal ethnic groups was reawakened by the Greek-Cypriots' 1950s campaign for *énosis* or **union with Greece**. Following independence, disputes over the proper civic roles of the Greek- and Turkish-Cypriot communities, and lingering advocacy of *énosis*, or *taksim* (**partition of the island** between Greece and Turkey) by extremists in each camp, provoked widespread, ongoing communal violence.

Abetted by outsiders, these incidents – and a CIA-backed coup against the elected government – culminated in the Turkish army's 1974 invasion which partitioned the island, with Greek and Turkish Cypriots on the "wrong" side of the ceasefire line compelled to leave their homes. Nicosia, the capital, was divided like Cold War Berlin; much of Famagusta, formerly home to about six percent of the island's current population, still lies abandoned.

In the **aftermath** of 1974, the two zones of Cyprus nursed grievances against each other difficult for many outsiders to fathom, and for nearly three decades North and South remained mutually segregated, developing into parallel societies destined in the eyes of some never to converge again. The island's division was often compared to that of pre-1990 Germany, but Cyprus being a far more intimate place, the scale of human tragedy has been more poignant. Any sort of **reunification** will be hedged with conditions, and fraught with pitfalls like the German experience: while South and North are both avowedly capitalist, the current prosperity gap between them may prove difficult to bridge. Linguistic and religious differences are less likely to be problematic; many older people from each community still speak the "other" language, and Turkish Cypriot Islam must be one of the most easy-going variants in existence.

Negotiations between representatives of each community have recurred sporadically since before 1974, but have yet to bear fruit. The result of the April 2004 referendum on the UN-devised "Anan Plan" for reunification, approved by the Turkish Cypriots but rejected by the Greek Cypriots, dealt a serious blow to such efforts. However, the sudden **opening** of the "border" across the island in 2003 created its own, probably unstoppable momentum towards a settlement, and now the odds are that a solution will be cobbled together by the islanders themselves, with much less EU or UN input.

Neófytos and the **Paleá Énklistra** rock-cut rural shrine, **Ayía Paraskeví** in Yeroskípou, and **Áyios Kírykos** and **Ayía Ioulíti** in Letímbou.

Inland from Páfos or Limassol, the **Tróödhos mountains** beckon, covered in well-groomed forest, lovingly resuscitated from a nineteenth-century nadir. **Plátres**, the original Cypriot "hill station", makes a logical base on the south side of the range; to the north, more villagey character asserts itself at **Pedhoulás** or **Kakopetriá**. Scattered across several valleys, a dozen or so magnificently frescoed **late-Byzantine churches** provide an additional focus to itineraries here if the scenery and walking opportunities aren't enough. If time is limited, the most important churches are **Asínou**, **Áyios Ioánnis Lambadhistís**, **Áyios Nikólaos tís Stéyis**, **Panayía toú Araká** and **Stavrós toú Ayiasmáti**.

While not immediately appealing, southern **Nicosia** – the Greek-Cypriot portion of the divided capital – can boast an idiosyncratic old town in the process of revitalization, and, in the Cyprus Museum, one of the finest archeological collections in the Middle East. North Nicosia, on the other side of the now-porous 1974 ceasefire line, is graced with most of the island's Ottoman monuments – and also introduces the Gothic ecclesiastical architecture bequeathed by the Lusignan dynasty.

For the majority of tourists in the **North**, **Kyrenia** is very much the main event, its old harbour the most sheltered and charming on Cyprus. Mushrooming residential and resort development is outpacing the town's limited infrastructure, but despite this the Kyrenia area still (just) lags behind

▶ The Kyrenia hills

The Orthodox church

Southern Cyprus is one of the most religiously observant corners of the Orthodox world. Although women are more scrupulously devout, per head of population Cyprus sends more monks to Mount Áthos, the monastic republic in northern Greece, than any other Orthodox country. If you're used to the foul-mouthed blasphemies of metropolitan Greece, you'll notice that Cypriots for the most part keep a decorous tongue in their heads. Indeed, the Church used to all but run the show socially, ensuring that women kept to their allotted social place, that any other "creed" (this even meant yoga classes) was highly suspect, and that non-conformists – particularly communists in rural villages – soon sought exile in England or elsewhere. But two factors have steadily eroded clerical power since the 1980s: EU membership for Cyprus, which spelled the end of effective opposition to civil marriage and gay rights, and the Church's own involvement in a series of bizarre scandals (see p.404).

the South in that respect. The hills overhead support three medieval castles – **St Hilarion**, **Buffavento** and **Kantara** – whose views and architecture rarely disappoint. Add villages in picturesque settings north of and below the ridgeline, and it's little wonder that outsiders have been gravitating here longer than anywhere else on the island.

The **beaches** north of Famagusta are Kyrenia's only serious rival for tourist custom in the North, and hard to resist in tandem with **Salamis**, the largest ancient site on Cyprus. **Famagusta** itself is remarkable, another Lusignan church-fantasy wrapped in some of the most imposing Venetian walls in the world – though churches and ramparts aside there's little else to see or do, the town having lain devastated since the Ottoman conquest. North of the beach strip, the **Karpaz** (**alias Kırpada, Kárpas**) **Peninsula** points finger-like towards Syria, its fine beaches and early churches – most notably at **Áyios Fílon** and **Ayía Triás** – a favourite target of Greek-Cypriot weekenders since the "border" opened.

When to go

Because of a situation as much Middle Eastern as Mediterranean, Cyprus repays a visit in almost any month; the overall mildness of the **climate** allows citrus to grow at altitudes of 450m, grapevines to flourish up to 1000m and frost-tender cedars to sprout at 1500-metre elevations in the Tróödhos. Such plant-zone limits would be unthinkable even on nearby Crete, despite an identical latitude of

34 degrees north. There's a local saying in the South that the bad weather comes from Greece, arriving on the back of the prevailing west-southwest winds; the northerners say the same about Turkey, with cold midwinter storms trundling over from the mountains of Anatolia.

If you're coming for the **flora and birdlife** – as many people do – then **winter and spring**, beginning early December and mid-February respectively, are for you. Rain – rare of late – falls in sporadic bursts from December into April, leaving the spectacle of a green, prairie-like Mesaoría, the central plain which most tourists only know as a parched, stubbly dustbowl. March in particular is often very fine, if cool at night; you can get into the sea comfortably on the south coast at noon, and with global climate change it has become the peak spring-flower month, replacing April in this respect. You'll also **cut costs** significantly by showing up in the off-season.

As the months progress and the mercury climbs, you can either brave the multitudes – considerable in the South – at the seashore or follow the wild flowers inland and up the Tróödhos slopes, veritable havens of **coolness** and relatively uncrowded. In the coastal South, **midsummer** (specifically Aug) is too hot for many (though Páfos tends to be 1–2°C cooler than Limassol or Larnaca, and less humid, thanks to the prevailing winds), and of course incurs **high-season** prices. During July or August you're possibly better off in the **North**, along the seaward, damper slope of the Kyrenia hills, though humid heat here can be trying. Many North aficionados choose to show up in September or October, when hotel space is at a premium.

Autumn everywhere is delightful, with the sea at its warmest, forays into the hills benefiting from **stable weather**, and the air (around Limassol or Páfos especially) heavy with the fumes of fermenting grapes. And if you're after **resort life**, you'll find the coastal strips don't completely wind down until November, which – especially the latter half – can sometimes be wetter and gloomier than December. Christmas and New Year's breaks are popular, though in recent slack tourist years many hotels have been closed from December to mid-March.

Average temperatures and rainfall

	Jan	Mar	May	Jul	Sep	Nov
Nicosia						
Max °C	15	19	29	37	33	22
Min °C	5	7	14	21	18	10
Days of rain	14	8	1	0	1	6
Kyrenia						
Max °C	16	19	26	33	31	23
Min °C	9	10	16	22	21	14
Days of rain	13	7	2	0	1	7
Tróödhos foothills						
Max °C	10	15	23	29	25	15
Min °C	3	7	13	20	15	8
Days of rain	10	6	1	0	0	6

25

things not to miss

It's not possible to see everything that Cyprus has to offer in one trip — and we don't suggest you try. What follows is a selective and subjective taste of the island's highlights: superb ancient sites, outstanding buildings and natural wonders. They're arranged in five colour-coded categories to help you find the very best things to see, do and experience. All highlights have a page reference to take you straight into the guide, where you can find out more.

01 **Lara beach** Page **176** • On the northwest flank of the Akámas peninsula, this is one of the least-spoilt beaches in the South, with two separate coves divided by a headland.

02 Áyios Mamás Page 267 • The Gothic abbey-church at Áyios Sozómenos village is arguably the loveliest rural ruin in the South.

04 Lala Mustafa Paşa Camii Page 340 • Literally and figuratively over-the-top, the facade of the Lala Mustafa Paşa mosque – once the cathedral of St Nicholas – is the pride of Famagusta.

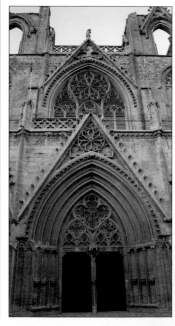

03 Avgás (Avákas) Gorge Page 174 • The narrows of the Avgás Gorge are a natural wonder of the uninhabited Akámas peninsula, and a popular trek-through venue.

05 **"Golden Beach"** Page **362** • Sea turtles and humans alike flock to Nangomí or "Golden Beach", one of the best on the remote Kırpaşa peninsula, and indeed the island.

06 **St Hilarion** Page **322** • Of the three Kyrenia range castles, St Hilarion conforms most closely to the archetype of the medieval fairy-tale citadel.

07 **Scuba diving** Page **95** • The wreck of the *Zenobia* off Larnaca is one of the best dives in the Mediterranean.

08 Büyük Han Page 286 •
This former tradesmen's inn in north Nicosia, meticulously restored, has reinvented itself as a successful crafts mall and café venue.

09 Tróödhos mountains
Pages **208–215** • Cross-island views, giant pines and other high-altitude flora and marked hiking trails make the Tróödhos a magnet for walkers and botanists.

10 Hala Sultan Tekke Page 95 •
Palm trees and this mosque near Larnaca combine in an orientalist's fantasy.

11 Roman mosaics, Káto Páfos Page 155 • The "House of Dionysos" shelters the largest group of Roman mosaics adorning Káto Páfos.

12 Paleá Énklistra Page 167 • The fifteenth-century ceiling frescoes of this rock-cut church are unique on the island for showing the Holy Trinity.

13 "Cyprus" delight See *Traditional Cypriot food* colour section • *Loukoúmi* to the Greek Cypriots, *lokum* to the Turkish Cypriots, this gooey, chewy comfort snack makes a popular gift to hosts island-wide.

14 Cyprus Museum Page 257 • This bronze nude statue of Roman emperor Septimius Severus is a highlight of the superb Cyprus Museum, the national archeological collection in South Nicosia.

15 **Events at Kourion** Page **140** • Ancient Kourion's amphitheatre comes to life again with music and drama performances in late June and early July.

16 **Salamis** Page **345** • The gymnasium colonnade is one of many highlights at ancient Salamis, just north of Famagusta.

17 **North Nicosia's Arabahmet district** Page **288** • This imposing mansion stands among terraces of well-restored vernacular houses in the Arabahmet district.

18 **Caledonian Falls** Page **210** • Named by nostalgiac British colonials, these are among the beauty spots accessible by maintained hiking trails around Mt Olympus.

19 **Sea turtles** Pages **175** & **332** • Green turtles (one shown hatching here) and loggerheads return every summer to lay eggs on remote beaches of Páfos district and the Kárpas peninsula.

20 **Ancient Soli** Page **294** • A swan mosaic is the main attraction at little-visited ancient Soli on the island's north coast.

21 **Abbey of Béllapais** Page **325** • This former Augustinian abbey forms the heart of the Kyrenian hill village which grew up around it.

22 **Kyrenia harbour**
Page **307** • Ringed with medieval buildings and flanked by a castle, this easily ranks as the most picturesque harbour on the entire island.

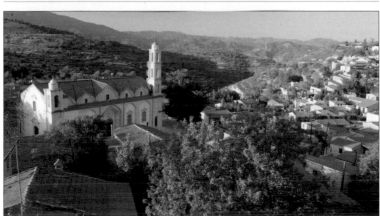

23 **Lófou** Page **130** • The best preserved of a score of stone-built villages in Limassol district's wine country.

24 **Mezé** See *Traditional Cypriot food* **colour section** • Tuck in to a multiple-platter *mezé* to get an idea of the full spectrum of Cyprus cuisine.

25 **Asínou (Panayía Forviótissa) church** Page **227** • One of nearly a dozen, vividly frescoed, UNESCO-recognized medieval churches in the Tróödhos foothills.

Basics

Basics

Getting there

Most UK short-stay visitors to Cyprus, South or North, arrive by air as part of an all-inclusive package; frequent scheduled and chartered flights operate year-round from London and several regional airports. There are at present no non-stop flights between North America and any point in Cyprus. The same is true for South Africa, Australia or New Zealand, despite the sizeable expatriate Cypriot communities in Australia and South Africa.

The South is accessible by air from most **neighbouring countries**, except Turkey, from where you can fly only to the North. Similarly, there is only passenger boat service between Turkey and the North at present. **Airfares** to Cyprus from Europe, North America and Australia always depend on the season. With minor variations for each market, "high season" means June to late September (plus Christmas/New Year week and October half-term) and "low season" means October to early December and January to late March, with "shoulder season" fares usually applicable otherwise, including around both Western and Orthodox Easter. When buying flights it always pays to **shop around**: check a few of the general travel websites listed on p.30, as well as the airlines' own, to get an idea of the going rates for the season. But remember that most general sites don't include charters or easyJet, and that all cheap tickets are restricted in some way – usually with stiff charges if you need to make any changes.

Flights from Britain and Ireland

Scheduled flights to anywhere in Cyprus are often overpriced for the distance involved; in season you might get better value from a **no-frills airline**, or a **charter** (available to the South only). Since the opening of the "border" in 2003, flying into Larnaca (in the South) for **access to either side** of the island has grown in popularity. **Indirect flights** via a European hub are unlikely to appeal except in high season when direct services fill; they tend to have long layovers and not be conspicuously cheaper, but are currently the only option travelling from the Irish republic.

Larnaca and Páfos, on the coast, are the southern Republic's two international airports, each some four and a half to five hours distant via UK-originated **direct flights**. **Cyprus Airways**, the national carrier, offers late March to late October services to **Larnaca** from London Heathrow (2–3 daily), London Stansted (4 weekly), Birmingham (3 weekly) and Manchester (5 weekly). Summer frequency to **Páfos** is markedly lower from London Heathrow (2 weekly), London Stansted (1 weekly), Manchester (2 weekly) and Birmingham (1 weekly). Winter frequencies are sharply reduced except on London routes. **British Airways** offers just a daily morning service from Heathrow to Larnaca year-round. Among no-frills operators, **easyJet** flies from Manchester (5 days weekly) and London Gatwick (2 daily) to Páfos, while **Thomsonfly** and **Avro** each call at both Cypriot southern airports from a variety of English airports.

Fares from the UK and Ireland to either southern airport have become somewhat volatile since the entry of budget airlines into the fray. However, from December to March (excluding the holiday period) you shouldn't have to pay over £200, and special offers in the region of £160–170 are common. Even in springtime fares hover at £180–230, and buying far enough in advance you can find high-summer fares for about £240 – though you'll typically pay £270, or even over £300 at short notice. Prices to Páfos and Larnaca are usually identical, as the airports are common-rated; with Cyprus Airways, it is also possible to fly into one airport and out of another for little or no extra charge (indeed planes out of Larnaca often touch down at Páfos to pick up more passengers). For fully

Travel and climate change

Climate change is perhaps the single biggest issue facing our planet. It is caused by a build-up in the atmosphere of carbon dioxide and other greenhouse gases, which are emitted by many sources – including planes. Already, **flights** account for three to four percent of human-induced global warming: that figure may sound small, but it is rising year on year and threatens to counteract the progress made by reducing greenhouse emissions in other areas.

Rough Guides regard travel as a **global benefit**, and feel strongly that the advantages to developing economies are important, as are the opportunities for greater contact and awareness among peoples. But we also believe in travelling responsibly, which includes giving thought to how often we fly and what we can do to redress any harm that our trips may create.

We can travel less or simply reduce the amount we travel by air (taking fewer trips and staying longer, or taking the train if there is one); we can avoid night flights (which are more damaging); and we can make the trips we do take "climate neutral" via a carbon-offset scheme. **Offset schemes** run by climatecare.org, carbon-neutral.com and others allow you to "neutralize" the greenhouse gases that you are responsible for releasing. Their websites have simple calculators that let you work out the impact of any flight – as does our own. Once that's done, you can pay to fund projects that will reduce future emissions by an equivalent amount. Please take the time to visit our website and make your trip climate neutral, or get a copy of the *Rough Guide to Climate Change* for more detail on the subject.

Ⓦ**www.roughguides.com/climatechange**

date-changeable or long-stay tickets you're looking at well over £500.

Charter companies such as First Choice, Eurocypria, Monarch and Thomas Cook also provide air links from Britain, but seats can be difficult to get on a flight-only basis. In addition to the major airports, charter flights leave from Bristol, Humberside, East Midlands, Cardiff, Luton, Glasgow and Newcastle. Although charters tend to have more family-friendly departure and arrival hours, such tickets are utterly inflexible and rarely available for more than two weeks' duration. They are usually, however, noticeably **cheaper** than scheduled flights: perhaps £169 London–Larnaca at Easter time, £179 Gatwick–Páfos in May, £188 Manchester–Páfos in June, £255 Birmingham–Páfos in July.

Because of the IATA boycott of north Nicosia's airport at Ercan, **North Cyprus** has direct air links only with Turkey, where northern European planes must first touch down (usually at İstanbul, İzmir or Antalya). Any reports of **"direct" flights** should be treated with healthy scepticism; this is permitted only during extreme weather conditions in Turkey, on an emergency basis,

though just occasionally a flight plan with a stopover in Turkey is filed, then disregarded (voiding the airline's insurance), much to the wrath of Greece, which monitors this air corridor. Even if a political settlement is reached, and Ercan declared licit, the economics of the situation will continue to dictate stopping flights. Despite the lengthening of travel time from five to seven or eight hours by the obligatory stopover, frequent scheduled flights start from several UK airports.

Cyprus Turkish Airways (*Kıbrıs Türk Hava Yolları*, KTHY), the official state airline, flies three days weekly from Heathrow to Ercan via İzmir; once weekly from Gatwick via Dalaman; at least daily from Stansted, usually via Antalya; twice weekly from Manchester via Dalaman; and once weekly from Birmingham via Dalaman. However, travellers' online forums are full of horror stories about KTHY and, despite an uncivilized return time from Ercan, many regulars reckon it worth paying the (often substantial) difference and flying with more professional **Turkish Airlines** (THY). They offer year-round daily services from Heathrow and Stansted to İstanbul, arriving in time to connect with the single daily evening flight to Ercan. Better yet, patronize **Pegasus**, which flies thrice weekly from Stansted to Ercan via İstanbul's minor Sahiba Gökçen airport and is often the least expensive carrier.

Fares from London to the North start at around £220 return during winter, with substantial hikes to about £280 in summer on Pegasus, and £330 and up on KTHY (£340–400 on THY) – though you can occasionally find last-minute deals for about £150. It is easiest to find THY tickets on UK travel websites – the Ercan airport code is ECN.

Airlines in the UK and Ireland

Avro ☎0871 423 8550, ⓦwww.avro.co.uk.
British Airways ☎0844 493 0787, in Republic of Ireland ☎1890/626 747, ⓦwww.ba.com.
Cyprus Airways ☎020/8359 1333, ⓦwww.cyprusairways.com.
Cyprus Turkish Airlines ☎020/7930 4851, ⓦwww.kthy.net.
easyJet ⓦwww.easyjet.com.
Pegasus ⓦwww.flypgs.com.
Thomsonfly ☎0871 231 4691, ⓦwww.thomsonfly.com.
Turkish Airlines ☎020/7976 1738, ⓦwww.thy.com.

Flights from North America

Because there are no direct flights between North America and any airport in Cyprus, you will find that **itineraries** will have at least one and sometimes two stops on route. Searches are most usefully directed towards Larnaca; entering the code for Ercan (ECN) in the North on North American booking websites will either draw a blank, or a ridiculously exorbitant quote.

The recent increase in direct flights **from the USA** to Athens in neighbouring Greece makes that an attractive initial first step, with a huge number of daily onward flights to Cyprus (allow $250 extra for that). Continental flies in from Newark daily between May and November (4–5 weekly otherwise), USAir daily from Philadelphia between May and September, Delta and Olympic each daily in summer from New York JFK (4–5 weekly off-season). From the USA, low season **fares** from the east coast

to Larnaca run about $750–800, high season $1200–1400; from the west coast, it's $1050 and $1600 respectively. For the **North via Turkey**, low-season New York–İstanbul direct flights on THY (4 weekly) cost about $700–850, or $1100–1350 (roughly daily) in peak season, with another $170 or so set aside for the final leg to Ercan in northern Cyprus, which is better purchased in İstanbul itself. From Los Angeles, add a couple of hundred dollars to each of these price bands.

From Canada, fares out of Toronto to Larnaca range from C$1300–1400 in low season to C$2250–2350 in peak season. The substantial Cypriot community in western Canada gets some joy from tickets out of Vancouver at just over C$1500 low season, C$2700 and up high season. Toronto–İstanbul runs C$1150 in winter, about C$1800 in summer, while Vancouver–İstanbul can be C$1300 low season, C$2200 peak season. Again, allow about C$200 for the final journey to Cyprus from İstanbul.

Flights from South Africa and Australasia

The sizeable Greek Cypriot community in **South Africa** prefers taking Olympic's overnight flight from Capetown and Johannesburg, with immediate connection on to Larnaca on either Olympic or Aegean, to the slightly cheaper service on Emirates via Dubai or Abu Dhabi, which involves a long layover – though a hotel stay might be included in the fare. Budget R7000 return as a minimum in low season.

Because of the way Australians and New Zealanders travel, most fares will be valid for either six months or a year. You may opt to get to Athens or İstanbul, and purchase an "add-on" fare from there; this depends, however, on the deals being offered at the time for through fares to Cyprus – for the South in particular this may not be necessary, with advantageous flights to Larnaca via the Middle East.

From Australia, the cheapest fares to Larnaca might be anything from just under A$2000 with Gulf Air (two stops via Singapore and Bahrain), to around A$2200 with Emirates via Dubai. Since the barriers came down it's no longer strictly necessary to fly into the North, and "ECN" (Ercan airport's code) may either not be recognized by websites or some crazy amount will be quoted. You'll pay somewhere between A$1900 and A$2500 to get to İstanbul, probably on Emirates, and will have to budget another A$250 or so for an onward flight to Ercan. **From New Zealand**, the best fares again tend to be two-stop relays on Emirates, with prices ranging NZ$2000–3000 depending on season.

Airlines in North America, Australasia and South Africa

Air Canada North America ✆ 1-888/247-2262, ⊛ www.aircanada.com.
Air France US ✆ 1-800/237-2747, Canada ✆ 1-800/667-2747; ⊛ www.airfrance.com.
Air New Zealand Australia ✆ 13 24 76, ⊛ www.airnz.com.au; New Zealand ✆ 0800 737 000; ⊛ www.airnz.co.nz.
American Airlines US ✆ 1-800/433-7300, ⊛ www.aa.com.
British Airways US ✆ 1-800/AIRWAYS, Australia ✆ 1300 767 177, New Zealand ✆ 09/966 9777; ⊛ www.ba.com.
Continental Airlines US domestic ✆ 1-800/523-3273, international ✆ 1-800/231-0856; ⊛ www.continental.com.
Cyprus Airways US ✆ 718/267-6882 (authorized agent, New York).
Delta Air Lines domestic ✆ 1-800/221-1212, international ✆ 1-800/241-4141; ⊛ www.delta.com.
Emirates Australia ✆ 03/9940 7807 or 02/9290 9700, New Zealand ✆ 05/0836 4728, South Africa ✆ 0861/364728; ⊛ www.emirates.com.
Gulf Air Australia ✆ 1300/366 337, ⊛ www.gulfairco.com.
Lufthansa US ✆ 1-800/645-3880, Canada ✆ 1-800/563-5954, Australia ✆ 1300 655 727, New Zealand ✆ 0800 945 220; ⊛ www.lufthansa.com.
Northwest/KLM US domestic ✆ 1-800/225-2525, international ✆ 1-800/447-4747; ⊛ www.nwa.com, ⊛ www.klm.com.
Olympic Airways US ✆ 1-800/223-1226 or 718/896-7393, South Africa ✆ 021 419 2502; ⊛ www.olympicairlines.com.
Qantas Australia ✆ 13 13 13, New Zealand ✆ 0800 808 767 or 09/357 8900; ⊛ www.qantas.com.
Singapore Airlines Australia ✆ 13 10 11, New Zealand ✆ 0800 808 909; ⊛ www.singaporeair.com.

Swiss US ✆ 1-877 FLY-SWISS, Australia ✆ 1300/724 666, New Zealand ✆ 09/977 2238; ⊛ www.swiss.com.
Thai Airways Australia ✆ 1300 651 960, New Zealand ✆ 09/377 3886; ⊛ www.thaiair.com.
Turkish Airlines US ✆ 1-800/874-8875, Australia ✆ 02/9299 8400; ⊛ www.thy.com.
United Airlines domestic ✆ 1-800/UNITED-1, international ✆ 1-800/538-2929; ⊛ www.united.com.
Virgin Atlantic US ✆ 1-800/862-8621, ⊛ www.virgin-atlantic.com.

Online booking

⊛ www.charterflights.co.uk (UK & Ireland). Charter flights from airports throughout the two countries.
⊛ www.cheapflights.co.uk (UK & Ireland), ⊛ www.cheapflights.com (US), ⊛ www.cheapflights.com.au (Australia) or www.cheapflights.ca (Canada). Fare-comparison site providing links to the airline or agent offering the deals.
⊛ www.ebookers.com (UK). ⊛ www.ebookers.ie (Ireland). Efficient, easy-to-use flight finder; scheduled flights only.
⊛ www.expedia.co.uk (UK & Ireland), ⊛ www.expedia.com (US) or www.expedia.ca (Canada). Discount airfares, all-airline search engine and daily deals.
⊛ www.lastminute.com (UK), ⊛ www.lastminute.ie (Ireland), ⊛ www.us.lastminute.com (US), ⊛ www.lastminute.com.au (Australia), or www.lastminute.co.nz (New Zealand). Good package and flight-only deals available at short notice.
⊛ www.opodo.co.uk Popular source of cheap UK airfares, run by a group of airlines.
⊛ www.orbitz.com (USA). Good generalist fare site.
⊛ www.skyauction.com (USA). Flight-only and travel packages up for auction.
⊛ www.travel.com.au and ⊛ www.goholidays.co.nz. Flight-only and holidays from Australasia.
⊛ www.travelocity.co.uk (UK & Ireland), ⊛ www.travelocity.com (US), ⊛ www.travelocity.ca (Canada). Long established for deals on car rental and lodging as well as fares.
⊛ www.travelonline.co.za (SA). Discount flights and information from South Africa.
⊛ www.zuji.com.au, ⊛ www.zuji.co.nz Antipodean sites with all the usual range of offers.

Flight and travel agents

Air Brokers International US ✆ 1-800/883-3273, ⊛ www.airbrokers.com. Consolidator and specialist in RTW tickets.

Airtech US ☎ 212/219-7000, ☻ www.airtech.com.
Last-minute and standby deals.

Andrews Travel UK ☎ 020/8882 7153. Long-established flight-only, fly-drives and tailor-made holiday specialists for Cyprus.

Best Flights Australia ☎ 1300/767 757, ☻ www.bestflights.com.au. Cheap flights and RTW deals.

Delta Travel UK ☎ 0161/273 7511, ☻ www .deltatravel.co.uk. Flight specialists to Cyprus, run by Cypriot travel agents.

Flightcentre US ☎ 1-866 WORLD-51, ☻ www .flightcentre.us; Canada ☎ 1-888 WORLD-02, ☻ www.flightcentre.ca; Australia ☎ 13 31 33, ☻ www.flightcentre.com.au; New Zealand ☎ 0800 243 544, ☻ www.flightcentre.co.nz. Rock-bottom fares worldwide.

Greece & Cyprus Travel Centre UK ☎ 0121/355 6955, ☻ www.greece-cyprus.co.uk. Competent flight consolidator with a myriad of fares to suit every need, including one-ways.

North South Travel UK ☎ 01245/608 291, ☻ www.northsouthtravel.co.uk. Friendly, competitive flight agency, offering discounted fares – profits are used to support projects in the developing world, especially the promotion of sustainable tourism.

Rosetta Travel Northern Ireland ☎ 028/9064 4996, ☻ www.rosettatravel.com. Agent specializing in deals direct from Belfast.

STA Travel UK ☎ 0870 160 0599, ☻ www .statravel.co.uk; USA ☎ 1-800/781-4040, ☻ www.statravel.com; Australia ☎ 1300/733 035, ☻ www.statravel.com.au; New Zealand ☎ 0800 474 400, ☻ www.statravel.co.nz. Worldwide specialists in low-cost flights for students and under-26s.

Trailfinders UK ☎ 020/7938 3939, ☻ www .trailfinders.com; Republic of Ireland ☎ 01/677 7888, ☻ www.trailfinders.ie; Australia ☎ 1300/780 212, ☻ www.trailfinders.com.au. One of the best-informed and most efficient agents for independent travellers; branches in all the UK's and Australia's largest cities, plus Dublin.

Travelers Advantage US ☎ 1-877/259-2691, ☻ www.travelersadvantage.com. Discount travel club, with cashback deals and discounted car rental. Membership required.

Travelosophy US ☎ 1-800/332-2687, ☻ www .itravelosophy.com. Good range of discounted and student fares worldwide.

Packages

Cyprus ranks as the **most packaged destination** in the Mediterranean after Malta, a status formerly mandated by a law in the southern Republic (until entry to the EU) which severely restricted flight-only allocations for charter companies. The message was clear – budget travellers need not apply – something reiterated by repeated hikes in package **prices** since the early 1990s. Expect to pay £650–800 per person in **the South**, assuming double occupancy, flight inclusive, for a two-week high-season package in a three-star hotel (the lowest grade now marketed as a package), or up to £1200 for two weeks at a four-star hotel; £1300–1600 for a detached villa with pool, including a rental car; £600–800 for a more traditional village house with or without a pool, again with a car provided; and a minimum of £220 for a week in a self-catering "hotel-apartment" studio in a less desirable area.

Peak season is reckoned as late June through late October, but each tour operator seems to have their own system of assessing this, and autumn departures in particular can be more expensive than spring or very early summer.

All brochures also heavily promote **activities** such as scuba diving, golf, wedding packages and (especially) 36- to 60-hour **cruises** to Egypt and/or Lebanon – you basically get a full day out in each country with the longer option. Except in high season when availability may be limited, it is always preferable (and cheaper) to arrange these after arrival in Cyprus. Sample per-person prices for a cruise to one country only start at £130, for both £200, and it's fun if you don't take it too seriously, with cheesy floor-shows on board, plenty of drinking, whirlwind tours of the sights (and souvenir bazaars), and a retinue of numerous, persistent touts.

Package prices in **the North** typically run £400–600 per person per week (often more for using Pegasus Airlines), depending on season and luxuriousness of the resort. Flight-only and hotel-only deals have become common. High season is nominally rated as early July to early October, subject to individual agency quirks. "**Winter specials**", whereby two weeks' half board, flight included, go for £299 (or less), with sometimes a few days' car rental thrown in for good measure, should be treated warily; at these prices, the hotels concerned have

NORTH CYPRUS
FLY DIRECT TO CYPRUS OR VIA TURKEY

"The strongest growing North Cyprus Tour Operator for 5 consecutive years."

Discover North Cyprus

A perfect haven for holiday makers, offering the purity of Cyprus twenty years ago. Enjoy the enduring echoes of its multicultural heritage, fairytale castles, abundance of history, quiet sandy bays, and 240 miles of crystal-clear waters.

For those looking for activity, there is plenty to enjoy; Paragliding, water sports, go-karting, horse riding, diving, hiking, bird & flower watching, golf.

The welcoming intimacy of the nightlife, with cosmopolitan café-bars, alfresco dining and local cuisines makes a perfect setting for couples, and families.

Direct Traveller offers holidays from 19 UK airports, with direct flights to Cyprus or via Turkey. Choose from a full range of hand selected hotels, and enjoy the service of our experienced team both in the UK and North Cyprus.
Please contact us for a brochure and details of our latest special offers.

Direct Flights

In May 2004 Cyprus joined the EU, this meant the borders were opened between North and South Cyprus. You can now travel freely between the borders. Direct Traveller was the 1st Tour Operator to pioneer the direct flight services through Larnaca. Today we are market leaders in North Cyprus holidays.

Direct Traveller

Your holiday starts here...

0845 123 5383
www.directtraveller.com

 ABTA
The Travel Association

Est. 2002: 1st & leading UK Tour Operator offering direct flight holidays in North Cyprus since 2004.

little incentive to provide service or decent meals, and you may find yourself, for example, without hot water for most of the day or confronting table d'hôte suppers that make airline meals seem gourmet in comparison. With a demonstrable oversupply of both hotels and restaurants in the North, there's absolutely no reason to tolerate shoddy service in either. The Famagusta area, except for one or two hotels, is no longer offered by UK operators. **Two-centre holidays** – a week on the Turkish coast or three nights in İstanbul, plus a week on Cyprus – are popular and heavily promoted, making a virtue of the necessity of stopping over in Turkey. Unless otherwise stated, operators are UK-based.

Package operators

General operators to the South

Amathus Holidays ☎0844 770 8095, ⓦwww .amathusholidays.co.uk. More comfortable hotels at all the usual beach resorts (including the northwest).
Argo Holidays ☎0871 902 7070, ⓦwww .argoholidays.com. Broad range of hotels at all the resorts; emphasis on four-star/luxury facilities.
Libra Holidays ☎0871 246 0446, ⓦwww .libraholidays.co.uk. Another generalist, focusing on the middle of the market.
Sun Island Tours Australia ⓦwww .sunislandtours.com.au. Fly-drives, a few hotels for the major resorts, cruises beginning and ending on the island.

General operators to the North

Anatolian Sky Holidays ☎0845 365 1011, ⓦwww.anatolian-sky.co.uk. Offering many of the better-quality complexes around Kyrenia, plus – almost uniquely – a selection of "private villas". Best bet for a two-centre holiday, as they're established Turkey specialists.
Cyprus Direct ☎0870 460 1234, ⓦwww .cyprusdirectholidays.com. Features some of the less commonly offered hotels around Kyrenia, and Famagusta.
Direct Traveller ☎0845 123 5385, ⓦwww .directtraveller.com. Broad selection of Kyrenia resort hotels in all classes; also flight-only specialists to Larnaca.
Green Island Holidays ☎020/7637 7338, ⓦwww.greenislandholidays.com. Established specialists with a broad mix of up-market and mid-range facilities around Kyrenia, plus İstanbul city-breaks.

Specialist operators

Cricketer Holidays ☎01892/664 242, ⓦwww .brocktravel.co.uk. Just two accommodation offerings, used in conjunction with springtime special-interest tours (wildflowers, Crusader castles).
Cyprus Villages Cyprus (South) ☎0357/24332 998, ⓦwww.cyprusvillages.com.cy. Accommodation in restored or traditionally built houses and flats in Tókhni, Kalavassós, Pendákomo and Psematisménos; also car hire, hiking, horse riding, mountain biking.
Sunvil Holidays ☎020/8568 4499, ⓦwww .sunvil.co.uk. By far the best operator for quality villas and restored village houses throughout Páfos district, plus a few elsewhere. Also restored village inns and (uniquely) small hotels in the Tróödhos Nicosia, fly-drives, watersports, plus selected larger hotels in Limassol and Larnaca.

Flights from neighbouring countries

Cyprus has air connections from most neighbouring countries, the vast majority of them **from Greece**, from where Olympic, Aegean and Cyprus Airways pile in year-round; Athens and Thessaloníki each have numerous departures daily for Larnaca, plus a couple weekly to Páfos. During summer, there are also several weekly flights between Iráklio (Crete) and Rhodes and Cyprus. Multiplicity of carriers does not mean especially cheap fares – budget €160 return from Athens. There are also several weekly links with Amman, Beirut, Cairo and Damascus, and daily flights in from Beirut and Tel Aviv.

Flying **from Turkey** to Ercan in the North, you can choose numerous routes from several major cities, including Antalya, Dalaman, İzmir, İstanbul and Ankara, though all of these can be fully booked far in advance at weekends. Principal carriers are KTHY, AtlasJet and THY. Return fares from İstanbul to the North run about €100 minimum – but if you don't have a car, this is still a far better option than the ferry from southern Turkey (see below).

By boat to the North

Despite Cyprus being an island, sailing there on scheduled ferry services (as opposed to a short cruise) is not a popular option. Only the North receives passenger services, and since only Turkey recognizes the Turkish Republic of Northern Cyprus, these leave from one of three **Turkish ports**: Taşucu, Mersin and Alanya. **Mersin–Famagusta** is the most reliable and weather-proof crossing, thanks to the larger ships employed, though it's longer and more expensive than the trip via Kyrenia (see below). The only company on this route is Kıbrıs Türk Denizcilik; departures from Mersin take place on Monday, Wednesday and Friday evenings, returning from Famagusta the next evening after a ten-hour journey. There's only one class of passenger fare on the dilapidated craft, at around £36 equivalent each way in pullman seats; transporting a car costs much the same.

Taşucu–Kyrenia looks temptingly short on a map but the standard of **car ferries** can be pretty poor (they've historically been demoted from more profitable lines in western Turkey). Crossing time for conventional boats is claimed to be four to five hours, but this sometimes stretches to six or seven owing to storms in the straits, Turkish navy manoeuvres, malfunctioning engines and the working hours of Kyrenia customs (captains are fined for docking before opening time). The more attractive alternative for the carless is a **catamaran** (*deniz otobüsü* in

Turkish), whose reported two-hour crossing time is more realistically three hours.

The two companies serving this route operate a joint cartel, with a conventional ferryboat carrying vehicles, and a catamaran or two. A slow ferry leaves Taşucu daily from Sunday to Thursday at midnight, arriving in Kyrenia the next morning, returning at noon (plus late-night return Fri). Only in peak season might there be Friday and Saturday crossings from Taşucu. By contrast, an "Express" **catamaran** (foot passengers only) leaves Taşucu every day at the nominal time of 11.30am, having first crossed from Kyrenia at 9.30am, plus there are two weekly (Mon, Thur) midday departures from Alanya.

Fares, no longer much subsidized by the Turkish government, can be dear for the distances involved. Figures below are converted from Turkish currency and are intended only as guidelines. One-way passenger fares on car ferries run about £22, with discounts for return trips or student status. A medium-sized car costs £52 to ferry, campers £63, with no return discount. Express catamarans from Taşucu cost £25 one way, £42 return, full fare; from Alanya (better value), £28/£49.

Shipping line agents

Akgünler
Taşucu ⓣ 324/741 4033
Alanya ⓣ 242/512 8889
Fergün Shipping
Taşucu ⓣ 324/741 2323
Alanya ⓣ 242/511 5565
ⓦ www.fergun.net
Kıbrıs Türk Denizcilik
Mersin ⓣ 324/231 2536

Moving between the North (or Turkey) and the South

Since April 23, 2003, when the Turkish Cypriot authorities opened several barred roads along the Green and Attila Lines without notice, it has been possible for most individuals to **cross between the two sectors of Cyprus** with little formality. All you need are a valid passport and (if you're bringing your own car) cash in hand to pay for supplementary insurance (see p.41).

At first both sets of authorities attempted to enforce "Cinderella" rules by which people had to return to "their" side by midnight, but this was quickly dropped in the face of massive civil disobedience, and the realization that such strictures were unenforceable. It is now routine for Greek Cypriots to take weekend breaks in the North, and (to a lesser extent, owing to economic factors) Turkish Cypriots to stay over in the South.

Although the Republic of Cyprus continues to describe Ercan airport, Kyrenia harbour and Famagusta harbour as "illegal ports of entry", under EU rules there is nothing they can (or will) do to **EU nationals** who land in the North and then head to the South – certainly on foot or by taxi; driving one's own foreign-registered car could prove trickier, and entry in a hire car with northern plates is not (yet) allowed, though ordinary northern Cypriot cars are allowed South. **Non-EU citizens** attempting the same could well be given a hard time, up to and including denial of entry or deportation depending on where they are detected, but we've yet to hear of any instances of this.

With this freedom of movement, many people fly into Larnaca, pay a round-trip taxi fare to Kyrenia or Famagusta, then fly out again at the conclusion of their holiday in the North; they reckon this worth it for the greater choice of flights and reduced flying time, though in fact they may save little money once the taxi fare is figured in. Conversely, Northern travel agents openly sell tickets out of Larnaca to all comers.

At time of writing there are **six legal crossing points** between the North and South. From west to east they are: Astromerítis–Güzelyurt (Mórfou), Áyios Dhométios–Ortaköy, Ledra Palace (pedestrians only), Lídhras (Ledra) Street–Girne Caddesi (pedestrians only), Pýla/Beyarmudu and the Four-Mile (Strovília) Crossing through SBA territory, between Famagusta and Xylotýmvou. More have been proposed, some highly likely to open during the lifetime of this edition, subject to funding for check-point staff. From west to east, they are: Pakhýammos–Káto Pýrgos direct via the Kókkina enclave coast road (set to open 2009), Káto Pýrgos–Limnítis (set to open 2009), Leofóros Athinás over Nicosia's Flatro Bastion (likely open 2010), Leofóros Kantáras–Mía Mília in the northeast of Nicosia, Dháli–Akıncılar (Louroujína) and Dherínia–Famagusta.

Although **Turkey** has no diplomatic relations with the South, since May 2003, **Republic of Cyprus passport holders** have been allowed to travel there after getting a visa at the Turkish embassy in north Nicosia. In a landmark case, a Greek-Cypriot man went to İstanbul on a weekend break, flying out of Ercan. He was prosecuted by his own authorities for using an "illegal" airport on his return; a conviction was duly obtained, and a fine imposed, but never enforced as the gentleman in question threatened recourse to the EU Court of Human Rights in Strasbourg, where he'd surely win his case – and compensation. Since then other **EU nationals** have imitated him.

Getting around

Cyprus has sparse bus services, augmented in the South by service (shared) taxis – even if "service" is often the last thing on drivers' minds. Private taxis are relatively expensive; there is no rail network. Car rental is very reasonable by European standards, making it the best option for visitors anywhere in the island – it's often the only way to reach isolated points of interest.

Local buses in the South

Principal inter-urban routes in **the South** are served by a number of private companies, whose terminals tend to be scattered at various points in the main towns: there's never anything that could be singled out as a central bus station, though a "reorganization" is being mooted for Nicosia. Except on Saturday afternoons and Sundays, when services can be skeletal to nonexistent, departures are fairly frequent during daylight hours. **Fares**, sold at kerbside offices or on board, remain affordable despite ever-increasing diesel prices; crossing the island from Nicosia to Páfos, for example, will set you back €8. If you make forays into the Tróödhos, however, you'll find frequencies dropping sharply; to explore up there it's far simpler to have a car.

Worth just a mention are the old-fashioned villagers' **market buses** – essentially a Bedford truck chassis with a multicoloured charabanc mounted on top. They are marvellously photogenic institutions, but with their typical once-daily, 6am-out-2pm-back schedules – plus school-bus seating – they're unlikely to be of much use, though lately numbers of them have been refurbished by adventure companies for use in back-country safaris – and by companies coordinating Cyprus weddings for foreigners.

Local buses in the North

In **the North**, local buses are consciously modelled on the Turkish system, with coaches gathered at a single vehicle park and often a ticket-sales/waiting building adjacent. With fewer cars in the economy, the poorest locals are dependent on buses and accordingly departures are more frequent: as much as quarter-hourly between north Nicosia and Kyrenia. **Fares** are marginally lower than in the South, but once again you'll find public buses inconvenient to do much adventuring. For the most part your fellow passengers will not be native Cypriots, but Anatolian settlers and soldiers returning to postings. Walking along roads, you may be tooted at by the drivers of oncoming buses in a bid to get your custom; wave them down if you want to ride.

Urban buses

Among island cities, Nicosia and Limassol (and to a lesser extent Larnaca and Páfos) support **urban bus networks.** With very few exceptions, however, these services run only from about 6am to 6pm (7pm in summer). Fares, distance-dependent, run €0.80–1.20, and route maps are available from the relevant tourist office. Routes of particular utility to visitors are detailed in the town accounts.

Service taxis and dolmuşes

Another Cypriot mode of transport is the shared minibus, called a **service taxi** in the South and a **dolmuş** in the North. Service taxis have been amalgamated into a single company, Travel and Express; their stretch limos and small transit vans, carrying four to seven passengers, can be booked by phone (☏77777474 South-wide, though we give local numbers in town accounts), and will pick up and drop off at any reasonable point (eg a hotel or private dwelling). That's the theory anyway; tales of ignored bookings abound, though reliability is claimed to have improved of late. Ticket prices are about double the bus fare for the same route, and journey times can be quick, though sometimes drivers' styles may have you fearing for your life. Drivers are famous for swearing fluently in Greek, English and Russian at other drivers (and passengers, especially those who delay them at all); local women scream at the drivers when they overtake on blind, hairpin curves – you'll be too petrified. Something to try once, perhaps.

In the North, there are no scheduled departures per se; **minibuses** dawdle, engines idling, in bus parks until they are full or nearly so, thus meeting the definition of *dolmuş* – "stuffed".

Taxis

Private taxis within urban areas in the **South** have rigidly controlled fares, sharply hiked since 2005. The meter starts at €3.07 (€4.01 between 8.30pm and 6am) and ticks over at a rate of €0.53 per kilometre (€0.59 per kilometre during night hours). Every piece of luggage weighing over 12kg incurs a €0.99 charge. Pets are paid for at €0.55 each, and they must travel in a cage or carrier.

Rural taxis provide service between Tróödhos resorts or foothill villages and nearby towns; for these trips you should know the going rate, as meters will not be used. The per-kilometre rate is €0.53 ordinarily, but €0.41 on an out-and-back trip, or €0.60 between 11pm and 6am; baggage over 12 kilos is charged at €0.53 apiece. As guidelines, Nicosia to Plátres will cost about

€40 per carful; from Limassol to the same place slightly less. From Larnaca airport to Kyrenia (an increasingly popular trajectory), budget at least €60. Over Dec 24–Jan 1, Good Friday–Easter Monday and May 1, a mandatory €1.96 tip is added to your fare on both urban or rural taxis.

In the relatively small towns of the **North**, there's less need for urban taxis. Moving between population centres, fares for the same distance are approaching those in the South, for example €33 from Ercan airport to Kyrenia.

Driving

Almost three-quarters of visitors to either part of Cyprus end up driving themselves around at some time during their stay, and this is really the best way to see the country. Either a licence from your home country or an International Driving Permit is acceptable in the North, though in the South, non-EU drivers are required to have an IDP in addition to their home licence.

Road rules

Traffic moves **on the left** throughout the island, as in the UK and most Common-wealth nations. **Front-seatbelt use** is mandatory on the open road but discre-tionary in towns; children under 5 years of age may not occupy the front seats, and kids aged 5 to 10 only if wearing seatbelts. As in most other countries, using mobile

---

Airport bus services

In summer 2008, bus services connecting Nicosia, Limassol and Páfos (but not yet Ayía Nápa) with **Larnaca Airport** were instituted. The service proved instantly popular, and bookings for the return trip from town are suggested. As we went to press some in-town departure points were still in a state of flux, but the following details (quoted fares include luggage carriage) were confirmed:

Nicosia 16 daily, 5.30am–1am from the airport, calling at the Filoxenia Tourism School car park; single fare €5; seat bookings on ☎7771477; information at ⓦwww .kapnosairportshuttle.com (Greek only but timetables legible).

Limassol 14 daily, 4am–1.30am from the airport, run by EAL (the Limassol urban bus company); calling at Khristofí Ergatoúdhi Street in Áyios Yeóryios Havoúzas district near the Polemídhia roundabout, and conceivably in future on the Yermasóyia tourist strip; single fare €7; seat bookings on ☎25370592 8am–5pm, ☎99444993 after hours; further information/timetables (in English) from ⓦwww.airportshuttlebus.eu.

Páfos regularly from around 6am–1am, calling in Káto Páfos and central Ktíma; single fare €14; no phone or website available.

phones while driving is forbidden, but rather unusually it's also illegal (in the South) to smoke while driving. **Drunk-driving laws** are strict, north and south, and if you're caught over the limit in the North, you'll pay a stiff fine *and* spend the night in a drying-out cell.

Speed limits in the South are 100km/hr (minimum 65km/hr) on dual carriageways – locals whiz by at 120km/hr – 80km/hr on other rural roads and 50km/hr in towns. Entry into urban zones is announced by big signs reading *"Katikómeni Periokhí"* (Built-up Area). In the North, limits are roughly the same, but may still be posted in miles per hour: 100kph/60mph on the Kyrenia–Nicosia–Famagusta highway, 60kph/40mph on smaller back roads and 50kph/30mph in built-up areas. Speed bumps and washboard ridging are ubiquitous traffic-calming measures both North and South.

Urban boundaries aren't explicitly signposted in the North, but dwindling numbers of khaki-drill-clad policemen maintain **speed traps** with hand-held radar devices at town outskirts. A particular stakeout, well known but still netting victims, is just west of Kyrenia, near the military camp, especially on weekend nights. **Speed cameras** – only one in ten actually functioning – are beginning to eclipse manned surveillance. You have fifteen days to pay **citations** at the district police station; if you don't, your name might pop up on the airport computer at departure. Fines are geared to local salaries and therefore seem risibly low to outsiders. Radar speed traps are now quite common on the motorways of the South, but they haven't yet made much of a dent on unsafe local driving habits, chief among which are tailgating and ambling down the centre of the road. On surface roads, beware of random controls for driving licence, insurance papers and blood-alcohol levels, especially at weekends.

In the larger Southern towns, use designated municipal lots for **parking**; they're not exorbitant – €2 for a half-day in Nicosia or Larnaca – though lots kept by private individuals can be much more. If you see a tempting-looking bit of waste ground and leave your car there, odds are that an attendant will appear as if by magic and dun you. Meters on main commercial streets require about €0.60 per hour, and yellow lines at kerbsides mean the same thing as in Britain: single, no parking during business hours; double, no parking or stopping at all. No-parking zones are poorly indicated in the North, though a policeman may appear and politely tell you if you're being blatantly illegal.

Road conditions

In the **South**, **roads** come in four grades: in descending order of quality, A, B, E and F, cited as such on maps and highway signs. "A" roads are the usually excellent, four-lane divided motorways linking Nicosia with Limassol, Larnaca, Páfos and Ayía Nápa, while "B" roads are major, undivided highways provided as a rule with verges. At the other end of the scale, "E" denotes a two-lane country road, while "F" can mean either a one-lane paved drive or an appalling dirt track fit only for jeep or mountain bike. Even when paved, many "F" or sub-F roads throughout the island are single-lane colonial relics with merely a thin layer of asphalt strewn over British cobbles. This makes them extremely bumpy, with very sharp edges over which you're forced to put two wheels by oncoming traffic. Lack of lane markings on "E" and "F" roads, and blind corners without mirrors, aggravate the effects of bad local driving.

The Limassol–Páfos A6 **motorway** and its flyover transition to the Limassol–Nicosia A1 was finally completed in 2009. The eastbound A3 from Larnaca was extended to Ayía Nápa in 2003 – surprisingly, the Cypriots had the right to take the highway across British Sovereign Base territory; in the event of a final federal settlement a spur will reach Varósha. Across the South, much of the road system, whether "A", "B", "E" or city-street, is apt to be dug up at any given moment, and there are plenty of busy uncontrolled intersections, so beware.

In **the North**, the **highways** between Kyrenia–Güzelyurt–Gemikonağı, Güzelyurt–Nicosia, Nicosia–Famagusta and Famagusta–Boğaz are comparable to an undivided British "A" route, and there are even stretches of four-lane, divided highway between the airport and Nicosia, or Nicosia and Kyrenia, built with Saudi funding.

Elsewhere, however, much of the road network has been essentially unimproved since 1974 and will be pretty slow going. The presence of unlit military lorries, lumbering along the Nicosia–Famagusta highway in particular, makes night driving in the North most inadvisable; there have been numerous fatalities, including Raif Denktaş, elder son of former Northern leader Rauf Denktaş, from drivers rear-ending such poorly visible **hazards**. Another danger in the North are cars with number plates beginning in ZZ, which should be treated with the utmost caution and deference. These temporarily imported cars usually belong to rich, spoilt Saudi, Gulf state and İstanbul Turkish students who rarely miss an opportunity to impress upon you – by running you off the road if necessary – just how flash and high-performance their buggies are. Involved in numerous smash-ups, these individuals have been the impetus for ongoing anti-drunk-driving campaigns in the North.

Signposting varies; village exits South or North are usually not obvious, so you'll get acquainted with the boys in the central café asking directions – otherwise you may well end up caught at the bottom of a steep cul-de-sac, with reversing the only way out. By contrast, the Tróödhos range forestry roads, despite their often horrific condition, are almost always admirably marked, with white lettering on a green background. In North Cyprus, however, many rural signs are badly faded, not having been repainted at all since 1974, though this has improved recently in the more visited parts of the Kyrenia hills.

All **road distances** are marked in kilometres in the South; accordingly, all rental car speedometers there indicate kilometres. Their signposting is often completely up the spout, however – yo-yoing up or down by several kilometres in the space of a few hundred metres, a consequence of marking not keeping pace with road regrading and straightening. In the North, kilometres are signposted along major highways, but distances appear – if at all – in miles on secondary roads or forest tracks, where you might have to keep a sharp lookout for old colonial milestones. A typical rental car speedometer in the North will show readings in both miles and kilometres.

Fuel

In **the South**, unleaded 95, 98 or 100 octane petrol, as well as diesel, has all passed the one-euro-a-litre barrier, though it's still cheaper than most neighbouring countries. Leaded fuel is extinct, though you can find lead-substitute fuel for those vehicles which need it.

Filling stations are normally open Monday to Friday 6am to 6pm (until 7pm Oct–March), with Saturday closure at 3pm, though they may also close on Tuesday at 2pm (or Wednesday at the same hour within Nicosia district). On Sundays and holidays only about ten percent of the South's stations are open, on a rota basis. To address this problem, large numbers of **automatic 24-hour stations** operate, with a consequent reduction in staffed stations; at these you feed euro-notes into a machine which then shunts that amount's worth of fuel to your pump. They generally work well, with instructions available in English. However, these machines don't actually give change; if your banknote exceeds the value of your fuel needs, hit the button marked "Receipt"; you'll get a sales slip showing the actual sale, which you can exchange for a refund of the difference at the same station during daylight staffing hours. You can avoid this by using plastic – most automats take the major **credit cards**, without surcharges, though readers are temperamental.

With the phasing out of Turkish subsidies, fuel costs in **North Cyprus** have risen to significantly more than in the South. Unleaded fuel is now widely, though not universally, available. Filling stations, especially in the Kyrenia area and Nicosia outskirts, are reasonably numerous and tend to be open until 9pm or even 10pm, with near-normal service on Sunday. Credit cards are now accepted at most stations, but those without online links to banks may demand a hefty commission.

Car rental

It's worth stressing that the **condition** of rental cars on either side of Cyprus can leave much to be desired, with bad brakes the most common fault; if possible, take the candidate car for a spin around the block before accepting it. Some rental cars in the North –

especially soft-top jeeps – have no radio-cassette/CD player; so many were stolen that they are no longer fitted. Reputable chains in the South will furnish you with a list of their branches Republic-wide, to be contacted in the event of a breakdown. Rental cars in both South and North have distinctive red **number plates** beginning with a single "Z", and their drivers have historically been accorded every consideration by police – for example, a warning instead of a ticket for not buckling up. For most of the year, a **three-day minimum rental period** applies in both parts of Cyprus; minimum age is generally 21, but sometimes 23 or 25 in the North.

Visitors may cross the Attila Line **from South to North** with a rental vehicle (but *not* at present from North to South), using one of the legal checkpoints (see p.35). All rental companies in the South will discourage you doing this because Republic of Cyprus insurance is not valid in the North. However, there is nothing to stop you turning up at one of the checkpoints and buying supplemental third-party insurance from a dedicated booth (€20 for 3 days, €35 for one month, longer terms available). The reason southern hire companies don't like you to do this is the low level of coverage furnished by these policies – €30,000 (though it's worth saying that remedial body work in the North is very cheap, should you biff a third party). There are also persistent, worrying reports that the companies involved don't pay out in the event of an accident. So the final word is, strictly at your own risk.

In **the South**, numerous agencies, including most international and several local chains, offer primarily A- and B-group Japanese and European compacts both at airports and in towns. Anything with an engine size of 1000cc or under (eg Chevrolet Matiz, Toyota Yaris) will have big trouble coping with grades in the Tróödhos. Summer rates start at €29/day for a week's rental, unlimited mileage and VAT included, a figure to keep in mind as a yardstick when pre-booking an A- or B-group vehicle from overseas. In or near high season you should reserve in advance – not difficult since so many fly-drive packages are offered. You are virtually obliged to accept an additional, on-the-spot fee for Collision Damage Waiver (CDW); venturing onto dirt tracks with a non-4WD vehicle will usually void your insurance cover if you damage the undercarriage. During winter, rates for saloon cars drop to as little as €20 per day, all inclusive (even sometimes the CDW).

If you intend to do any backroad exploration of the Tróödhos or Akámas areas, then some sort of **4WD vehicle** is highly advisable – such as a Toyota RAV4 or Honda HRV hardtop, though daily rates for these are high (from €75 in season). Otherwise, the lighter-weight, cheaper Suzuki Vitara or Jimny jeeps can just about take two adults with their luggage, though their soft tops make security problematic.

Credit cards are the preferred method of payment in the South. An irritating quirk of Cypriot rentals, both South and North, is that you may be asked to deposit an inflated sum (eg, €55 for a 40-litre tank costing €41 to fill), in cash or with credit card, covering the cost of a **full tank** of petrol; the idea is to return the car as empty as possible, rather than full as in other countries. In the South, if you return the car to a staffed office during normal working hours with a full tank, most companies will refund this deposit in full – though they may ask for proof of purchase near the airport. Because **the North** is unrecognized internationally, no overseas chain has been represented there in the past, leaving the field clear for local entrepreneurs. There are no car-rental booths at Ercan airport, so you'll be stranded unless you've pre-arranged to have a car meet your flight. Arrange a fly-drive package through a tour operator, or contact the agencies noted in Kyrenia, north Nicosia or Famagusta, directly from overseas – the latter strategy tends to be somewhat cheaper. They can also arrange advantageous taxi transfers from Larnaca airport straight to your hire car.

Available models, including automatic transmission option, have improved greatly – it's rare that you'll still be offered a bottom-end, left-hand drive Renault 9 made in Turkey. Rates for a more typical Opel Corsa, Fiat Panda, Ford Focus or VW Polo run about £20 per day in high summer (less any internet discount); expect to pay up to a third less out of season, maybe ten percent more if booking through a package agent. Given the state of many minor roads, you might prefer a 4WD – an adequate Suzuki Jimny hardtop costs about £23 a day in high season, fifteen percent less in low season. Credit cards or foreign cash are preferred payment methods, though be aware that most companies slap a **surcharge** on the use of cards, and many others require full advance payment of the estimated rental price in cash. A CDW premium is payable (typically £3/day), often in cash, on delivery of the car.

Bringing your own car

Cars brought over on boats **from Turkey to northern Cyprus** are allowed to stay for six months, and for the foreseeable future will very likely encounter difficulties in crossing the Attila/Green Line from North to South, irrespective of the nationality of their owner. No foreign insurance is valid in the North; you will be insured on the spot for basic, third-party cover as you roll off the boat, at the rates cited for the land-crossings from the South. It is much more economical to buy coverage for a month, or a year, like the Greek-Cypriots do. Should you be able to cross into the South, you will find your North policy inapplicable, and will have to buy another policy.

There are two cargo services a week from Keratsíni (a satellite port near Piraeus) in **Greece to Limassol in the South**, on which cars or motorcycles (but not their owners) can be put – you have to fly out to meet the vehicle. Cyprus is a signatory to the MGA (Multilateral Guarantee Agreement), whereby Cypriot cars can now circulate within the EU without customs formalities, with reciprocity for **EU cars** within Cyprus; this means that EU nationals with EU-registered vehicles should encounter no difficulties on docking. Green cards or EU-contracted insurance are recognized in the South, but only up to minimum statutory limits; you'll probably want supplementary coverage.

Non-EU drivers/cars, judging from past practice, can expect considerable hassle on arrival in Limassol, where you will only be granted up to twelve months' circulation in the Republic (beyond that you would have to officially import the vehicle). Entry controls tend to be strict, in the wake of stolen-vehicle scams; declaration forms may ask you to minutely document all accessories and extras.

Mechanics in the South are largely geared to the Japanese models that have virtually captured the market, but other European makes are represented. In the North, the more common Japanese or Italian makes have authorized spares outlets in north Nicosia for the flash sedans and 4WDs which have essentially replaced the antique British and Turkish models of yore.

Scooters and cycles

In the coastal resorts of the South, you can rent small **scooters** from €10 a day; few people will want to take them further than the beach, as you will get scant respect from four-wheeled motorists on curvy mountain roads. Crash helmets are compulsory in the South for anything over 50cc, a law systematically enforced. Rental motor-scooters and pedal-bikes have made a limited appearance in the North, restricted to a few outlets in downtown Kyrenia in the summer only.

By contrast, the uplands of either South or North are ideal for **mountain biking**. Both the Tróödhos range and the Kyrenia hills are crisscrossed by dirt forest tracks which would be extremely tedious for hiking but constitute a mountain biker's dream. With some planning or guidance (group bike tours are now advertised) you could cover either range from end to end in a few days. Mountain bikes are for sale in south Nicosia and Limassol, and for rent in the main Tróödhos resort of Plátres. Incidentally, few rented bikes are supplied with pumps or tyre repair kits. The CTO publishes a useful booklet detailing back-country road itineraries for cyclists.

Additionally there are less specialized, general bike sales and repair shops in most of the South's larger towns, which you will almost certainly take advantage of, if only to buy patches or replace a pump worn out from constantly inflating flat tyres. Plentiful thorns on the road ensure a steady incidence of punctures, and there's the usual hot-country problem of the sun melting the rubber solution, so repair jobs won't last if you leave the bike in full sun. Cypriot car drivers tend to regard cyclists as some lower form of life – on a par with the snakes found deliberately run over everywhere – and can be very aggressive, so pedal defensively.

Accommodation

The majority of visitors to Cyprus arrive on some sort of package that includes accommodation. That's not to say that independent travel is impossible: our listings favour establishments more geared for direct-booked trade by phone or internet, and not block-booked by foreign operators.

Following a run of slack seasons, **overbooking** in the South is pretty much a thing of the past, though the limited number of pensions and restoration inns in the Tróödhos or Páfos district remain heavily subscribed. Northern Cyprus, on the other hand, has only about seventy resort-standard hotels or self-catering establishments, which used to be rarely if ever full – not too surprising when you consider that scarcely seventy thousand English-speaking tourists show up in a typical year. However, since 1997 Turkish gambling tours have periodically placed some outfits off-limits to Europeans, and in September particularly there are rarely enough beds available at the quality outfits.

Most of the North's tourist industry was formerly based in **hotels** abandoned by Greek Cypriots and let out on a concession basis by the government-run Cyprus Turkish Tourism Development Corporation, but with one or two exceptions these inefficiently run and poorly maintained properties have now been "privatized" (ie, bought up by mainland Turks). Only after the late 1980s did numbers of privately funded, purpose-built and professionally managed **resorts** emerge under Turkish Cypriot ownership. Our accommodation listings show a preference for these.

Hotels and private rooms in the South

The CTO grades and oversees most accommodation in the South, be it hotels of zero to five stars, guest houses or "hotel-apartments" (self-catering units). Their names, locations and current prices are shown in the *Guide to Hotels*, issued yearly, but this does not distinguish between establishments which welcome independent travellers and the majority of lodgings, which are pitched at package bookings or are even all-inclusive resorts. Neither does it distinguish between the more modest listings geared for conventional tourist trade, and some which double up as brothels.

Hotels

All **hotels** of one star or over, and some unstarred ones, have en-suite baths. Hotel rooms are most frequently offered on a bed-and-(continental)-breakfast basis; charged separately, breakfast rarely exceeds €6 in humbler establishments, but frankly if you're having to pay extra, it's often better to go out and find a full English breakfast for about the same price. Desk **staff** are almost universally from central Europe or somewhere in the

---

Accommodation prices

All hotel and apartment-hotel prices across the island have been categorized according to the price codes given below. These categories represent the minimum you can expect to pay in the high season for a double room or a two-person self-catering unit. Single rooms will normally cost fifty to eighty percent of the rates quoted for a double room. While we quote price bands in euros for uniformity, pound sterling still tends to be a preferred currency of payment by overseas visitors in the North.

❶ €40 and under   ❹ €91–120   ❼ €201–250
❷ €41–60   ❺ €121–150   ❽ €251–300
❸ €61–90   ❻ €151–200   ❾ €301 and over

Real estate on Cyprus

Since the early 1990s, **property** all over Cyprus has been assiduously marketed to foreigners, especially Brits, interested in either a holiday/retirement home or an investment opportunity. Following the South's accession to the EU, a steady stream of purchases has become a flood. UK ownership numbers in the South are approaching six figures, with a purported 40,000 in Páfos district alone but a presence everywhere along the south coast; in the North, the total figure is estimated at about 25,000. **Real estate development** has drastically affected the landscape, infrastructure and society of both sides of the island, and in terms of money changing hands now far outstrips conventional tourism. There are scores of estate agents in every resort, though most projects are the work of the biggest half-dozen developers on each side of the island. In Páfos district, for example, almost every village – no matter how remote – has at least one cluster of villas built or under construction; the Brits in particular have set up a **parallel expat society**, with its own pubs, restaurants, parish halls and service provision (plumbing, pool maintenance, etc).

Infrastructure has not kept pace with construction; water shortages are set to become a permanent reality given chronic drought and climate change, rural roads are in a continual state of excavation, and ADSL internet is seldom available in remote areas. A market bubble is developing both North and South, with Cypriot real estate way overpriced compared to other popular Mediterranean destinations. A correction is well overdue as there are far too many properties for sale given the current levelled-off demand, yet developers are refusing to lower pricing for the moment. Properties, especially on coastal plains, are often **badly built**, beset by rising damp because they lack proper foundation pads. Developer greed has also created growing **social problems** on both sides of the island: prime agricultural land and olive groves have been given over to villa projects, and young Cypriot families can no longer afford to buy their first home anywhere, something strongly resented.

In the **South**, Larnaca is cheapest, Páfos the most expensive, with Limassol somewhere in between. It is assumed that many purchasers will engage in buy-to-let, though foreigners are restricted to one freehold piece of property up to 43,200 square feet. In the **North**, the bulk of development is in the Kyrenia area, though villas are sprouting near Salamis, on the Karpaz peninsula, and even around Cape Koruçam (Kormakíti). Isolated areas (plus cheap-and-nasty blocks in central Kyrenia) are the least expensive, Bellapais and the coastal plain immediately west of Kyrenia the priciest zones.

Indian subcontinent, the latter recruited for their English-language skills.

Single occupancy **prices** tend to be well over half the double rate, and maximum rates must be posted either in the room itself or over the reception desk on a CTO-validated placard. Generally there won't be any fiddling in this regard, and except between early July and early September you have some scope for bargaining, especially **booking** one of the larger outfits over the internet. Travelling **independently** outside peak season, it's usually possible to find comfortable if modest hotel rooms for less than €80 double; if you insist on a summer holiday, you're probably

wisest to book **in advance** from Britain on a package basis or (increasingly) online through the hotel's own website.

Agrotourism: restored inns and village houses

Faced with continued depopulation of the more attractive hill villages, the CTO during the mid-1990s established the **Cyprus Agrotourism Company** (CAC) to implement the restoration of old buildings, mostly in the Tróödhos foothills, as character accommodation. By staying in hitherto little-visited villages, guests confer

Comparing like for like, it appears initially that the North is about a third less costly than the South, but savings could well prove illusory and the strongest possible warnings apply about **security of title**. The overwhelming majority of apartment blocks and bungalow complexes here are built on what was, before 1974, Greek-Cypriot land. The titles issued since by the northern government to displaced Turkish-Cypriots, or Turkish settlers, using these properties, have never been recognized as valid outside the North – something reiterated by the European Court of Human Rights. When momentum for a settlement began to build in 2002–2003, these title-holders – many living abroad – sensed that the former Greek-Cypriot owners might demand some sort of compensation and/or that the post-1974 titles would soon be worthless. Deeds and property were quickly sold to mostly London-based developers, who overnight threw up the constructions now visible, flogging them just as rapidly (often over the internet and off-plan) to Brits (plus a few Germans and Israelis).

When the southern republic alone joined the EU in May 2004, affected Greek Cypriots were not slow in using **EU-wide law** to get satisfaction. One, Meletis Apostolidis, took a British couple to court over a house they'd built on land to which Apostolidis still has the original valid titles. In late 2004, a Greek-Cypriot court ordered the house demolished and the land returned to the plaintiff; because the edict was not enforceable owing to the Turkish military occupation of the North, there was a possibility that under EU law the couple's UK home could be seized and sold to compensate Apostolidis. The case eventually fizzled out without seizure, but even this inconclusive result has had a severe dampening effect on the Northern property market.

So the best advice when property-hunting in the North is to buy only where **pre-1974, Turkish-Cypriot titles** are demonstrable – these properties are in fact rare and relatively expensive (ie, at Southern prices), because such transactions will never be challenged in court. Otherwise, wait until a final political settlement permits the establishment of a property compensations board and an orderly, legitimate transfer of titles between North and South against payment. By the same token, you should not buy any property in the South which has a pre-1974 Turkish-Cypriot owner – unless they left the island before 1974, and they (or their heirs) can appear at your solicitor's personally with legitimate titles – or one that is still owned by the *vakıf* (Muslim benevolent fund). Already a number of resourceful Turkish-Cypriots have imitated their compatriots and taken the southern government to court for building refugee housing, roads, etc on their land, and they may well do the same to a private buyer or developer.

a bit of much-needed prosperity on these moribund communities scattered across Páfos, Limassol, Larnaca and Nicosia districts. There are now over seventy such properties, either entire houses or inns divided into conventional rooms or self-catering suites. It is a worthy and increasingly popular programme, if inevitably limited in numerical impact – and with greater expansion reportedly bogged down in bureaucratic muddles. There is some overlap in membership between the CAC and private initiatives such as the **Laona Foundation** (see p.176) and **Cyprus Villages** (see p.98). The CAC publishes its own useful booklet, *A Guide to Traditional Holiday Homes*, and you will find most of them – ie those that have gained official CTO certification – in the CTO's *Guide to Hotels and other Tourist Establishments,* in the section entitled "Traditional Houses". Few official double occupancy prices exceed €65 for one-bedroom apartments, and many studios or conventional doubles are about €50 – outstanding value for often exquisitely executed restoration facilities. Among package companies in the UK, Sunvil (see p.33) currently represents the best selection of these properties.

Private rooms

The CTO disavows all knowledge of, or responsibility for, **unlicensed rooms** in boarding houses and no-star hotels which have let their CTO certification lapse; similarly for those unofficial rooms in private rural houses, but the latter exist in some numbers, particularly in the villages of Páfos district and the Tróödhos foothills, both north and south slopes. The going rate currently is about €15 per person, and this often includes some sort of breakfast. They can offer quite a good look at country domestic life, and particularly welcoming families may lay on an evening meal at little or no extra cost, feeding you far better than at the nearest tourist grill. If there are no advertising signs out, the best strategy is to contact the *múkhtar* (village headman) and have him arrange something.

Hotels in the North

Choice is more limited in Northern Cyprus: the broad middle ground between luxury compounds and Turk-patronized dosshouses is so far thinly inhabited, and some establishments are block-booked by package operators, making just showing up on the off-chance a risky endeavour at Easter or between June and October. The North's tourism authority nominally exercises some control over hotel standards and prices, though in practice things tend to be pretty free-wheeling – proprietors have been known to quote double (or half) the "official" price for a given season without batting an eyelash.

Bed availability was complicated by the rise of North Cyprus as a Turkish **gambling** and **sex-tourism** destination, after the 1997 closure of Turkey's casinos prompted the organized-crime and money-laundering interests involved to shift their attentions to North Cyprus. Nightclubs near several hotels are also havens for prostitution, and many hotels see themselves obliged to accept patronage by the hour, especially during low season. Gambling weekends used to be all the rage; mainland Turks would have their flights, accommodation and meals laid on provided they wagered a certain amount per day. Under the circumstances, the management had little incentive to provide careful service or maintenance, and desk staff often spoke no foreign languages. With both the Turkish and North Cypriot economy still recovering from their 2000–01 crash, there is much less pressure of this sort on local accommodation, but several notionally luxurious complexes got the boot from most UK tour operator brochures in the late 1990s and never found their way back in. With Turks staying away, big resort-hotels in the North now actively tout for a Greek-Cypriot gambling clientele, something hoardings on the Nicosia–Kyrenia highway leaves in little doubt. Accordingly, with a few exceptions where the facility does not dominate the character of the hotel, this book does not recommend establishments with a casino on-site.

Apart-hotels, villas and longer stays

A good percentage of Cypriot accommodation, both the South and the North, is **self-catering** in so-called tourist apartments or **apart-hotels**, or the more appealing semi-detached **villas**. (Incidentally, you shouldn't utter the word "villa" to non-English speakers – it means the male generative organ in Cypriot Greek slang.) In the southern Republic most of these tend to be concentrated in Páfos district, with more scattered around Larnaca and Ayía Nápa; in Northern Cyprus they are almost exclusively in and around Kyrenia, though numbers have levelled out, as the latest wave of tourists – including Greek-Cypriot trippers – seems to want the full-service treatment of a hotel. The majority of villas have well-equipped kitchens and are well maintained by Mediterranean standards, the odd water shortage or power cut aside, though furnishings (in the North especially) tend to be spartan. See p.33 for specialists offering something out of the ordinary.

If you intend to **stay longer** in the South it's worth scanning adverts in one of the literally thousands of estate agency windows and in the real estate supplements of the two main English-language newspapers. In a reasonably desirable area, rents for one-bedroom furnished flats start at about €350 a month; two-bedrooms fall in the €450–800 range, with Larnaca and Páfos usually cheaper than Limassol or Nicosia. In Northern Cyprus such lettings are done almost exclusively through the dozens of estate agencies in Kyrenia, with rents at near-parity with levels in the South. With the new interest in hotels (and outright proprety ownership), many self-catering villas formerly marketed by overseas tour companies are being offered for rent medium-term.

"Guest houses", hostels and campsites

Neither the South nor the North was ever really on the backpackers' trail, something even truer since passenger ferry service between Greece and Israel (with the impecunious bound to or from a kibbutz) was suspended. In the South, "**guest houses**" are confined to Páfos, Limassol and Nicosia, and are frankly not recommended; hostels are also on the way out, while campsites (with one sterling exception) are grim caravan parks for Cypriots hankering after a cheap weekend residence.

In the **South**, for the record, there are spartan **hostels** in Nicosia, Larnaca and on Mount Olympus in the Tróödhos, and all have generated reader complaints ("condemnation-worthy" being a typical comment) at one time or another. Official IYHF cards are not required, and bunk-and-sheet charges won't exceed €10. There is also the extremely popular forestry lodge at Stavrós tís Psókas in the Tillyrian hills. In the **North**, scattered workmen's dosshouses in Kyrenia, Famagusta and (especially) Nicosia are pretty unsavoury and only for desperate solo males.

The South nominally has four licensed **campsites**, at Governor's Beach (near Limassol), Coral Bay and Yeroskipou (both near Páfos), and Pólis. Coral Bay and Yeroskipou were not functioning in early 2008, while Governor's Beach is a permanent caravan park pure and simple. That leaves only Pólis conforming to the American or west-European notion of a drive-up-and-pitch site. Additionally the forestry department runs over thirty more or less amenitied **picnic sites**, mostly in the Tróödhos; at most of these camping is expressly forbidden.

The North musters just a bare handful of **picnic grounds**, for example by ancient Salamis and in the Kyrenia hills, where overnighting would probably garner you the unwelcome attentions of the police or Turkish army; there are no authorized, maintained areas for **camping**.

Food and drink

Food throughout Cyprus is generally hearty rather than refined, and on the mainstream tourist circuit at least will get monotonous after a few days. In many respects resort food – especially in the South – is the unfortunate offspring of generic Middle Eastern, and 1960s British, cooking at its least imaginative. The (under)fried potato can be the tyrant of the table, resulting in a "chips with every-thing" cuisine. If all else fails, seek solace in the excellent beer, brandies and wine of the South. Restaurant fare in the North is a bit lighter and more open to mainland Turkish influence, but is still often heavily Anglicized.

All this is unfortunate, since once off the beaten track, or in a private home, meals are consistently interesting and appetizing, even if they might not ever rate a Michelin star. The less obvious, often vegetable-based delights of such cooking, and the stars of the Cypriot drinks cupboard, are featured below, and in both our *Traditional Cypriot food* colour section and the food glossary (p.460).

Breakfast

In the **South**, breakfast (*próyevma*) offered at less expensive hotels tends to be minimum-effort continental, with tea/coffee, cut-rate orange juice and slices of white toast with pats of foil-wrapped butter, jam and (if you're lucky) a slice of processed cheese or *halloúmi*. If you crave more, you'll have to pay extra for bacon-and-eggs-type English breakfasts, either at the hotels or at special breakfast bars in town. Comfortable hotels of three stars and above should provide a more substantial buffet breakfast.

Northern Cyprus has embraced the mainland Turkish breakfast of untoasted bread, jam, *beyaz peynir* or white cheese, *kaşar* (kasseri) cheese, olives and either tea or coffee plus inexpensive (typically orange) juice. In the better hotels, these will be presented as a buffet with hot or cold meats, some sort of egg dish, a choice of bread products and fresh fruit as well.

Snacks

Cypriots are not so prone to **eating on the hoof** as continental Greeks or Turks. Across the island small British-style cafés sell sandwiches and drinks, but local solutions are less common. Stuffed **baked goods** in the **South** include *eliópitta*, olive-turnover; *tashinópitta*, a pastry with sesame paste; and *kolokótes*, a triangular pastry stuffed with pumpkin, cracked wheat and raisins. Around Easter you'll be frequently offered *flaoúnes*, dough steeped in an egg-and-cheese mixture, then studded with raisins. Other dried seeds, fruits and nuts are easily available in shops.

In the **North**, **street vendors** offer *börek*, a rich, flaky layered pastry containing bits of meat or cheese. You'll have to sit down in a **pideci** or "pizza parlour" for a *pide* (Turkish pizza); usual toppings are *peynirli* (with cheese), *yumurtalı* (with egg), *kıymalı* (with mince), *sucuklu* (with sausage) or combina-tions of the above. Usually a small bowl of *çorba* (soup) is ordered with a *pide*. *Pidecis* may also offer *mantı* (central Asian ravioli, stuffed with mince) or *pirohu* (similar but stuffed with cheese), either of them topped with yogurt, garlic and chilli oil. *Tatar böreği*, broadly similar to *mantı,* is traditionally served with grated *helim* cheese and mint.

Food shopping

It's easy to find your way around the super-markets and corner stores in **the South**; product labelling is always in English as well as Greek. Local dairy products in all flavours and sizes are conspicuous, as are smoked breakfast and picnic meats; the best types are listed on p.461. In all of the major towns of the South (except Larnaca), central market halls are excellent sources of farm produce and meat. Because of Cyprus' many immigrant communities, it's fairly easy to find exotic spices and condiments on both sides of the island. **In the North** things aren't always so self-explanatory, but English labelling is on the rise, and largish markets in central Kyrenia are much like a medium-sized corner shop in North London – where many of the proprietors probably spent time. The biggest supermarket chain is Lemar, with particularly convenient ones at both the western and eastern edges of Kyrenia, plus another in nearby Karakum. The last surviving – and quite colourful – central market hall for produce is in north Nicosia.

Fruit

Cypriot **fruit**, especially from the South, has a well-deserved reputation, though in the North much comes from Turkey, since the orchard potential of the Kyrenia hills and the Mórfou plain is limited. Because of the long growing season, varieties tend to appear much earlier than in Europe – for example strawberries in April, watermelons in June. Until 2003, everything was grown locally in the South, since the government banned imported products – ostensibly to keep the island relatively pest-free but also to protect local farmers and specifically exclude smuggled-in goods from the North. As a result, subtropicals such as avocados, bananas, mangos, kiwis and starfruit have been grown in the warmer corners of Páfos district since the 1980s. In February 2005, restrictions on northern produce were relaxed, shortly after EU membership prised open the South's closed market.

Froutaría is Greek for a **roadside fruit-and-vegetable** stall, *manav* in Turkish. Big *froutaries* are apt to be far more satisfying than many southern supermarkets; besides an array of exotic tropical produce, they'll stock fish, meat, cheese and dairy products, plus frozen goods. For complete coverage of all available fruit varieties, and a calendar of their appearance, see p.463 and *Traditional Cypriot food* colour section respectively.

Restaurants

It takes diligence to avoid the bland, often over-fried stodge dished out to undiscriminating tourists at most restaurants. Generally this means going slightly upmarket, to restaurants with more imaginative or exotic menus, or to a mid-town *ouzerí* (Greek; often referred to as a **mezé-house**) or meyhane (Turkish), where local delicacies are served to accompany drink. Briefly defined, **mezé** (*meze* in Turkish) is a succession of around twenty small plates served in succession, along with a couple of grilled mains, until you're sated. (For full coverage of what these platters might be, see the *Traditional Cypriot food* colour section.) Unfortunately, many *mezé* houses opt for sick-inducing quantity over quality; another all-too-common failing of touristy *mezé/meze* is indiscriminate mingling of fish and meat platters. Such establishments have completely lost sight of the original Persian meaning of *meze*: "titbit" or "taste". All this acknowledged, such gargantuan **bouffes** are decent value at the €14–20 a head, drink extra, though in the South there is a minimum party of two (sometimes four) persons. Remote village tavernas, formerly the stars of the Cypriot eating scene, are going through a bad patch of late – sadly, expat tastes and require-ments have had their effect – though the **exokhiká kéndra** or country tavernas of the South cater more to native Cypriots, with limited but consistent-quality offerings.

As a rule **main-dish** portions are generous (if a bit too heavy on the chips), somewhat offsetting increasingly steep prices. Main courses cost between €9 (veg- or meat-based) and €19 (the priciest fish), with menu prices usually including a ten-percent service charge and VAT (fifteen percent). Prices in the North, except in the Karpaz, can be as much or more in whatever currency you reckon.

Restaurant hours are somewhat restricted compared to Greece or Turkey; **lunch** is generally available only from 12.30 to 2.30pm across the island, **dinner** from 7 to 10pm, even 9.30pm out of peak season From October to April, most village tavernas are likely to close from Sunday night through Friday noon, so ring ahead to avoid disap-pointment. The main exceptions to all of this are South/North Nicosia, and beachside tavernas, at which you can get lunch pretty much all afternoon. *Exokhiká kéndra* may be open most of the day or evening in summer, but tend to serve weekend lunch only in spring and autumn, and often close completely in winter owing to their outdoor seating.

Meat and fish

Meat–based mains predominate, both on and off resort menus. The most distinctively Cypriot ones are covered on p.462. Among more Greco-Mediterranean platters, lamb chops – *payidhákia* (Gr) or *pırzola* (Trk) – are small by British or North American standards but tasty. *Souvláki* or *şiş* is pork or lamb arrayed in chunks on a skewer and grilled; you'll be asked how many *smíles* (skewers) you want.

The Venetians introduced domesticated **pigeons** to the island, and they're much tastier than you'd imagine; **quail** (*bíldırcın/ ortíchia*) is the gamier alternative. In the North, you'll frequently encounter the set-price **full kebab**, where succulent grilled titbits – sausage chunks, lambs' kidneys, baby lamb chops – are relayed to your table piping hot. *Moussakás/musaka*, aubergine and potato slabs overlaid with mince and white sauce in its truest form, is better in the South; *karnıyarık* is a meatier Turkish aubergine dish without the potato or sauce.

Fish is not as plentiful as you'd think for an island, nor as cheap – typically €55/kilo in the South, on lucky occasions €45/kilo. The best places to get it are around Pólis in the South and on the Karpaz (Kárpas) peninsula in the North; otherwise you can safely assume, even at the most expensive restaurants, that almost all seafood has been flash-frozen and **shipped in** from elsewhere. Squid and cod, for instance, come from the North Sea, king prawns from farms in Thailand or Bangladesh, fraudulently passing off shark as swordfish is not unknown, and farmed bass and gilt-head bream are indistinguishable from those on offer in British supermarkets. If you want to be sure of having **fresh, local fare**, stick to humbler species such as *sorkós/sargoz* or *wóppes/woppa*. *Marídhes/ smirida*, the least expensive fish, are traditionally sprinkled with lemon slices, rolled in salt and then eaten whole, head and all. Barracuda and *sokan* are best grilled, and either full-sized grouper or its smaller cousin *lágos/lahoz*, usually batter-fried, must be well done to be appetizing. In North Cyprus, *sokan, mercan, karagöz* and *barbun* are the best-value species. Across the island, squid and octopus are standard budget seafood options.

Vegetarian food

Vegetarians may have limited options at times, especially in the South, where some restaurateurs think that overpriced plates of chips and tomatoes justify claims of catering to meat-avoiders. *Mezé* opening courses, fortunately, are largely meat-free, consisting principally of *húmmos/humus* (chickpea paté), *tahíni/tahin* (sesame purée), olives, fried *halloúmi/helim* cheese and other titbits; explicitly vegetarian *mezé* is now offered. Unfortunately, inferior rubbery *halloúmi* – full of added yeast and powdered (cow) milk, squeaking on the teeth when chewed – abounds; when you finally get the real thing (from sheep or goat milk, with the butterfat oozing out at the touch of a fork) you'll never willingly go back to the other.

Salads are offered with all entrees, usually a seasonal medley of whatever's to hand: lettuce, tomatoes, parsley, cucumbers, cheese and onions (the latter served on a separate plate). Chefs who try a bit harder may treat you with *rokka* (rocket) leaves, *koliándhros* (coriander) sprigs or purslane weed (*glystrídha*) – this last much tastier than it sounds. *Óspria* is the general term for any **pulse dish**, and what vegetarians should always ask for – it's often not written on the menu, considered too disgracefully peasanty to sell to foreigners. In the South, fava beans are pureed into *louvána* soup, not to be confused with *louviá* (black-eyed peas). In winter especially, *trakhanás/tarhana*, a soup of grain soaked in yoghurt, is prepared, though it is often made with chicken stock. Healthier **starch sources** than the ubiquitous potato include chunks of mild-flavoured *kolokássia/kolokasa* (taro root) brought to the island from Egypt or Syria over a thousand years ago, and *pourgoúri* (cracked or bulgur wheat). Lenten-tide **bread** is flat and unleavened, suspiciously like the Turkish *pide* served during Ramazan.

Desserts and sweets

Ice cream is everywhere, made by small local dairies, and far more prominent than the traditional Levantine sweets; Turkish- or Italian-style is invariably better than imitation British. In the South, P&P (Papaphillipou & Patisserie Panayiotis) and Iraklis are the best local brands; in the North there's Mr Bob's, sold on the main highway at Ortaköy in north Nicosia. Crème caramel and European-style pastries are also well represented. Again in the North, *firin sütlaç* (baked rice pudding) is delicious, and through Ramazan the novelty sweet *aşure* is very popular. In the South, *palouzé* (grape-must pudding with rosewater) is a common autumn treat.

Among oriental **sticky cakes**, you'll most often find *baklavás/baklava*, filo pastry layers alternating with honey and nuts; *galaktopoúreko/su böreği*, filo pastry filled with custard; and *kataïfi/kadayıf*, similar to *baklava* but in a "shredded wheat"-type winding. *Katméri/katmer* is a kind of crêpe filled with banana, honey and sometimes clotted cream, a common dessert in *mezé* houses/*meyhanes*.

Drinking

Traditionally Cypriots drink only as accompaniment to food, and prefer brandy or *raki*; inebriated, loud north Europeans staggering down the streets are apt to offend local sensibilities in either community.

Wine, sherry and brandy

Owing to near-ideal climate and soils, Cypriot wine-making history extends far back into antiquity, and the tradition has been continued with pride – indeed **wine-drinking** can be one of the highlights of a stay here, though with some exceptions the vintages aren't yet up to French, Italian or even Greek quality. The industry is based almost entirely in the South, and still dominated by four major wineries headquartered in Limassol: KEO, ETKO, LOEL and SODAP. However, there are a growing number of independent micro-wineries across the island whose products are usually superior; the best are cited below.

Cyprus Trade Centre booklets list over fifty labels of wine, sherry and brandy, quite a total for a medium-sized island, with more being added slowly as the result of research and new varietal planting. You would have to be a pretty dedicated toper to get through all of them during a short stay, so the following evaluations below should give you a head start.

Arsinoë is a very dry **white** from SODAP, while Danae (also SODAP) is slightly less dry, light white, though by no means fruity or sweet. LOEL's Palomino is a dry white, smoky in colour and taste; ETKO's White Lady is another contender in the dry-white market. Bellapais (KEO), a medium-dry, light sparkling wine a bit like Portuguese *vinho verde*, comes in white and **rosé** versions. Afrodhite (KEO), an acceptable medium-dry cheap white, and LOEL's Saint Hilarion, are about as sweet as you'd want to drink with food; Saint Panteleimon (KEO), essentially a dessert or mixer, is too sugary for most tastes. *Sódha* is the lingua franca for plain soda water – useful for making wine spritzers of those sweeter varieties.

KEO's Rosella is a very dry, dark rosé; the same company makes Othello, a full-bodied **red** not unlike a Cabernet Sauvignon. Hermes is for those who like a rough, dry red, while ETKO's Semeli is a bit more refined. LOEL's Mediterranean, made from actual Cabernet, isn't at all bad as a mid-range product. In Tróödhos foothill villages, it's worth asking for the local **bulk wine**: cheaper, often very good (if not decanted plonk from tetra-pak cartons) and sold in half- or full-litre measures.

Each major label produces dry, medium and sweet cream **sherries**, most famous being ETKO's Emva line. However, following objections from Spain, all the Cypriot players are going to have to call it something else, as "sherry" is now a protected AOC of the Jerez region.

Among **microwineries**, the Khrysorroyiátissa monastery bottles an excellent dry

Commandaria, a smooth, red dessert wine related to Madeira, has a pedigree going back to antiquity. Cyprus's first AOC wine, it's produced by just fourteen villages in the Limassol foothills, and made largely from white Xynisteri grapes, with dark Mavro added for colour and balance. These are sun-dried for a week, part-fermented, and then sent downhill to Limassol's major wineries (KEO and SODAP are reckoned to produce the best), who age it for a minimum of two years in oak barrels and then fortify it to 15 percent alcohol.

white, Ayios Andronicos, and a pale red, Ayios Elias. Most wine from the Fikardos winery in Mesóyi is worthwhile, though not easily available outside Páfos district. Their products include the Amalthia Xynisteri, a very crisp but easy-drinking white, the Ayia Irini white, the Ravanti red from Mataro grapes, and a Cabernet Sauvignon. Other proven products to keep a lookout for include Pampella rosé and Alina white, from Vouni in Panayía; Agravani and Ambelidha, two organic wines from Oekologiki Oenotechnia in Áyios Amvrósios village; Ayios Onoufiros, a dry blended red from Vasilikon in Káthikas; Cava Rotaki, from the Linos winery; anything from Perati, in the Limassol foothills; the Yiaskouris blended red or Shiraz from the eponymous winery in Pákhna; the Domaine Nicolaides rosé, from Anóyira; and the Kilani Village red or white, from the Ayia Mavri winery. Among newer players, the Domaine Vlassides (Kiláni) Shiraz and Cabernets are excellent, while almost anything from the Kyperounda, Vasa and Tsiakkas wineries is worthwhile.

In the **North**, the only quality winery, family-run and worth supporting, is Chateau St Hilarion, based at Geçitköy, making a decent Cabernet Shiraz red and a rosé. All other wine at North Cypriot restaurants is imported from Turkey; Turasan and Peribacası, two quality labels from Cappadocia, are about the best of those commonly available.

Beer

In **the South**, Carlsberg is the best-selling locally brewed **beer**, available in small 333ml or large 645ml bottles at 4.6 percent alcohol content. The same brewery's Leon label is hoppy and not at all bad. Rival KEO's pilsener comes in the same sizes and alcohol strengths, though some slam it as watery and insubstantial. In **North Cyprus**, your choices are the Turkish mainland Efes label; Gold Fassl, an Austrian lager made locally under licence; or the stronger (5.2 percent) local pilsener, Altınada. There is now a wide variety of imported beers across the island, especially at theme pubs in Ayía Nápa and Páfos.

Spirits and liqueurs

Stronger local **firewater** includes *zivanía/ zivaniya*, nearly pure grape alcohol produced

far in excess of local requirements, essentially identical to the *marc* of France, the *tsípouro* of Greece and the arak of the Arab world. Some is flavoured with botanical agents for home use; the rest is sold to the southern government or exported to fortify weak drink as far away as Russia. **Oúzo**, as in Greece, is increasingly popular in the South, mostly KEO but also made by a few smaller labels.

KEO also makes a range of rather dubious **hard liquor**, though imported booze is easily available. As for **brandy**, independently bottled Peristiany 31 and KEO VSOP 12 are fine, though locals prefer to tipple either KEO's Five Kings, Hadjipavlu Anglias or VO 43, all historically smuggled into the North (along with Peristiany). The North's 1975 edict outlawing Greek-Cypriot-produced brandy was deeply unpopular, as brandy-drinking was (and is) one of the few enthusiastically shared tastes of the two communities – with the "border" porous such trade is less furtive now. "**Brandy sour**", brandy spiked with lime or lemon juice and Angostura bitters, is effectively the national aperitif in both communities and beloved of holiday-makers; unfortunately, use of premixed citrus base, which can't really substitute for fresh ingredients, is prevalent. Among the more bizarrely flavoured **liqueurs** are Filfar, a sickly sweet orange aperitif, and Mosphilo, made from hawthorn fruit.

Tea, coffee and soft drinks

Tea in both communities comes in somewhat expensive packs of bags, though in the North, Anatolian settlers have introduced, in the villages at least, the practice of brewing loose tea in a double-boiler apparatus called a *çaydanlık*. The favourite island-wide **herbal** tea is *spadjá*, a variety of sage.

Traditional Middle Eastern **coffee**, fine-ground, boiled without filtration and served in small cups, comes in three grades: plain, medium-sweet and very sweet. Rombout's may be preferable to Nescafé in the South, but if you're in a villa with drip-filter coffee-making apparatus, packs of pre-ground are widely available. Incidentally, except at our top-drawer listings for North Nicosia and Famagusta, it's all but impossible to get a proper espresso or cappuccino in the North – it will likely be made with instant coffee!

Juices throughout the island come in a rainbow of flavours and are usually excellent, available at markets in either litre cartons or bottles. Fresh citrus juice goes briskly at most resort bars. *Aïráni/ayran* is a refreshing street-cart/market-stall drink made of diluted yoghurt flavoured with dried mint or oregano and salt, though the dwindling number of vendors seems restricted to Larnaca and Nicosia. Among brands of **mineral water** in the South, Agros has more ecological packaging in 665ml glass bottles, but Ayios Nikolaos is considered the best and purest. **Tap water** in carafes is not usually offered at restaurant tables except in the Tróödhos mountains.

Health

You're unlikely to experience health problems in Cyprus other than a spell of constipation brought on by initial contact with stodgy food. Water is fit to drink almost everywhere except Famagusta and environs (where the sea has invaded well bore-holes), though not always so tasty; bottled water is widely available. No inoculations are required for any part of Cyprus, though it's wise to keep your tetanus booster up to date.

Health hazards

Most routine threats to your health concern overexposure, the sea and flying insects. To avoid the danger of **sunstroke** wear a hat and drink plenty of fluids during the hot months. **Jellyfish** are rare, **sea urchins** more common. If you are unlucky enough to tread on, or graze, one of the latter, a sterilized sewing needle, scalpel and olive oil are effective aids to removing spines; left unextracted, they will fester. A pair of swim goggles and footwear for walking over tidal rocks should help you avoid both. In sandy-bottomed bays, **rays** and **skates** are fairly common; they have a barbed tail which is capable of inflicting nasty wounds with one swat. When entering such waters, make a bit of commotion so as to send on their way these creatures who have a habit of burrowing in the sand, with just the eyes visible.

In terms of dry-land beasties, there are **scorpions** about – tap out your shoes in the morning – and one stubby, mottled species of **viper**; antivenins for it are available at local pharmacies. Those enormous, two-metre-long black **whip** or **Montpellier snakes** which you'll see on the road are usually harmless to humans, and were in fact imported by the British to hunt both rodents and other venomous serpents. **Mosquitos** (*kounoúpia* in Greek, *sivrisinek* in Turkish) can be troublesome in summer, especially between Famagusta and the Karpaz (Kárpas) peninsula; solutions offered by hotels include pyrethrum incense coils, electrified vapour pads, and air-conditioned rooms with closed windows. In the South, insect-repellent-vaporizing units with a 30ml refill bottle on the bottom (eg, Aroxol brand) are popular and effective, allowing you to sleep with the windows ajar on hot nights. **Sand flies** are almost invisible, but their bites pack a punch, and itch nearly as badly as mozzies – insect repellent is the answer.

There are few stray animals on Cyprus and thus (uniquely for this part of the world) **rabies** is not much of a danger. Indeed one of the few things the Greek- and Turkish-Cypriot communities agreed on before 1974 was to round up and put down most stray dogs, since many carried **echinococcosis**, a debilitating liver fluke which can spread to humans. Adherence to the practice is laxer now in the North, but overall the canine population is still not up to previous levels.

Medical attention

The standard of **health care** is relatively high in Cyprus, with many English-speaking and -trained doctors; indeed provision of health care to residents of surrounding Middle Eastern nations has become a highly successful hard-currency earner. The fancier hotels can generally recommend local practitioners, and may even post lists of them. General **hospitals** in both sectors of the island have walk-in casualty wards where foreigners can have cuts sewn up and broken bones set at no, or low, cost. Be sure to bring your European Health Insurance Card (valid in the South only).

Minor ailments can be dealt with at **chemists** (*farmakío* in Greek, *eczane* in Turkish); pharmacists are well trained and often dispense medicines which in Britain would only be available on prescription. In the South, dial the operator on ☎192 to ask for the rota of night-duty chemists; in both North and South, this is also published in the English-language newspapers.

Maps and place names

There are various complimentary and commercial maps available for Cyprus, but no single one is entirely satisfactory and most handle the island's division awkwardly. The changes in nomenclature introduced by both North and South further complicate matters.

Many island-wide maps have limited usefulness owing to international non-recognition of the **Turkish Republic of Northern Cyprus** (TRNC) and poor documentation of the **Attila/Green Line**, the ceasefire line marking the Turkish Army's furthest advance in August 1974, and the attendant **buffer zone** just beyond it. This zone, also called the "dead zone" or No-Man's Land, is off-limits to everyone except UN personnel and local farmers, and varies in width from a few paces in Nicosia and at the Strovília corridor to a few kilometres at the old Nicosia airport and the Nicosia–Larnaca expressway. Greek-Cypriot depictions of the "border" tend to be optimistic, placing it at the limit of the Turkish advance rather than at the southern Republic's edge of the buffer zone. All chapter maps in this guide show the correct extent of the buffer zone, into which you should not venture unless (as at Pýla) specifically allowed or invited to do so by the authorities – despite an ongoing recent mine-clearing programme since April 2003, there are still plenty of "live" fields laid by both the Turkish Army and the Cypriot National Guard.

Road maps

It's wisest to get an overall touring map of the island before leaving home, since the better ones are banned for sale in the South for political reasons. The best small-scale commercial **road map** is the **GeoCenter** (formerly Marco Polo/Shell) 1:200,000 folding one, which alone of currently available commercial products shows almost all paved (and many unpaved) roads accurately, including the South's motorway system. There are two similarly priced products at the same scale; you want the one which cites both Turkish and Greek names for places in the North, and gives Greek lettering (but no stress accents) plus "official" transliteration for spots in the South. It is also one of the very few commercial maps to depict the buffer zone accurately, but has no town plans on the verso. Nearly as good is the **Freytag and Berndt** product at 1:250,000, which shows the motorways fairly accurately, Turkish names in the north and Greek script with accents, with the lesser road network up to

2002 currency. The official *Survey of Cyprus Administration & Road Map* (1:250,000), revised in 1996, shows contours, district boundaries and fairly accurate road tracings, though in many cases surfaces have been improved in the interim. No other currently in-print product merits serious consideration.

For detailed **town plans**, the **Selas** series, locally sold in the South, are the most accurate available for Limassol, Nicosia, Páfos and Larnaca (though annoyingly no scales are provided). Their countrywide sheet at 1:250,000 lacks detail, has no Greek script or Turkish aliases, and is only adequate for journeys on major roads.

The **CTO** gives out a number of **free maps**: *A Visitor's Map of Cyprus*, the entire island at 1:400,000; Nicosia city centre and suburbs; Limassol town and environs; Larnaca town and environs; Ayía Nápa and environs; Páfos and environs; and the Tróödhos. These are all reasonably current and accurate, having been last revised in 2006–07.

Topographical maps

Unless you plan to do some hard-core, cross-country exploration, the walking maps in this book are adequate to take you around safely. Otherwise, **topographical maps** are prepared in the South by the Department of Lands and Surveys. The availability of the 1:25,000 series from 1982 seems to depend on your face and how the folk responsible are feeling that day, and it's obtainable (if at all) only through special petition directly to the DLS in south Nicosia (corner Alásias and Dhimofóndon streets, ☏22304120). However, the 1:25,000 issue

International English forms

Throughout the book the **internationally accepted forms** for five of the six largest towns – Nicosia, Limassol, Larnaca, Famagusta and Kyrenia – are used in preference to the official vernacular renditions, which are given just once for reference at the beginning of accounts.

from 1969 is still on sale in the Republic of Cyprus – albeit featuring dense, highly coloured cartography, and Roman-alphabet lettering in the pre-1995 transliteration scheme (see p.56). Also available, curiously, is the 1981 series at 1:5,000, covering the entire island in 59 sheets and a joy to behold, though much more practical for archeology and geology than hiking. At present, none of these maps is sold abroad. More easily found, both in the South and overseas, is the 1:100,000 DLS 18 series, last revised in 1997, which covers the whole island in four sheets, or the K717 series at 1:50,000, covering the island in forty sheets but unavailable overseas (and possibly, depending on security jitters, in the South). Each of these series should cost about €9 per sheet.

Unsurprisingly, the Turkish military occupying **the North** do not make anything they have prepared available to the public.

Place names in the North

A major problem in **the North** is that all available maps, except the TRNC's tourist handouts, and the GeoCenter, Freytag and Berndt or Rough Guides commercial products, continue to show **only Greek place names** in the North as it existed pre-1974, despite the fact that all Greek signposts (except outside Koruçam/Kormakíti) have long since vanished there. The southern Republic considers this **Turkification** just one aspect of the "cultural vandalism and falsification of history", as they put it, which has taken place in the North since 1974. Even the Turkish Cypriots in the North, whether native or resettled refugees, are often nonplussed by the official village names imposed on them, since virtually every place had a Turkish form from Ottoman times – often phonetically related to the Cypriot Greek one – which is still used conversationally in preference to the often clumsy official name. Only certain villages which had always borne Turkish names were exempted from the Turkification campaign.

In "The North" section of **this guide**, first the "new" name as it appears on road signs is cited, followed by the pre-1974 Greek name and finally (if known) any Ottoman

Turkish names in brackets. Maps also show first the post-1974 name, and then the internationally recognized name in brackets immediately following. This convention is intended to help readers find their way about, and should not be construed as an endorsement of the North's official nomenclature.

Place names in the South

As in the North, so in the South: the orthography of place names has become hostage to **ethno-political correctness**. Considerable dismay was prompted, both on Cyprus and abroad, by the arbitrary introduction in late 1994 of a **new nomenclature and transliteration** system for all place names in the South. Despite the misgivings of then-Mayor Lelos Demetriades, the name "Nicosia" was officially abolished by a vote of councillors, to be replaced by Lefkosía even in English literature; those concerned believed that Nicosia was a colonial imposition of the British, though in fact the word dates back to Lusignan times. Similarly, Larnaca officially became Lárnaka on tourist bumph, Limassol woke up to Lemesós, and Paphos ended up as Páfos (the only instance this book conforms to, to distinguish it from ancient Paphos). Street names were also re-transliterated, wholesale, and in many cases renamed after EOKA heroes; political correctness truly disappeared up its own backside with such Roman-alphabet street-sign renditions as "Tzon Kenenty" and "Fragklinou Rousvelt". Even Cypriot personal names were affected, with individuals being effectively commanded to change the Roman-alphabet spellings of a lifetime to the new "legal" forms (eg, Yiannis to Giannis). The changeover was largely the work of two Helleno-fanatic incumbents in the Ministry of Education and Culture, convinced of the manifest inferiority of Cypriot dialect compared to that of "Mother Greece", though Cypriot is arguably more venerable and truly "Greek" in retaining extensive vocabulary and pronunciation apparently unchanged since ancient times. It seems further ironic that the South's government should, on the one hand, castigate the North for its forcible name-changes, and then engage in a similar mutilation of cultural heritage on its own turf.

Barring a major political upheaval (or some clause of whatever federal settlement occurs), the new system is here to stay. But most foreign residents and native islanders alike remain strongly opposed to the new rules, not least because the old system gives non-Greek speakers a reasonably phonetic rendition of the local-dialect pronunciation. Organizations **opting out** of the new scheme include many UK tour operators, Friends of the Earth, the Laona Foundation, most wildlife conservation bodies, most foreign archeologists (who continue to produce works in the old scheme), the *Cyprus Mail*, estate agents, and several municipalities. Latchí refused to be rechristened Lakki, but had to settle for Latsi; the Nicosia borough of Eylenjá ("too obviously Turkish", they were told) wasn't having Aglangeia, but as a concession only got "Aglantzia" in brackets after the "official" signposting.

In **this book**, we place the new forms in brackets following the old form, where different (they aren't always).

Phones and internet access

Cyprus has good-to-excellent phone service, though call boxes are fewer than in the UK or North America across the island, verging on non-existent in the North. Southern callboxes are based on UK prototypes; those in the North were until recently duplicates of mainland Turkish ones, though now there are models apparently imported from the US and UK.

The South

Phones in the Republic of Cyprus are administered by the Cyprus Telecommunications Authority, CYTA for short. Town- and village-centre **call boxes** should have detailed calling instructions in English, but if not, to **phone overseas from Cyprus** dial ☎00 – waiting for changes in tone – and then the country code. There are automatic direct-dial connections with just about everywhere, including the North, which however is treated as a separate country – dial ☎00 392 before the ten-digit number (see p.38 for a discussion of northern phone schemata).

All (often noisily situated) call boxes are **card-operated**; you may have to keep your thumb on the back end of the card to keep it from popping out. You can purchase telecards in various denominations from CYTA offices, certain banks, post offices, corner kiosks and wherever you see the telecard logo displayed. Counter-top **coin-op** phones are found in some hotel lobbies and restaurants. Rates for card or coin-phones are slightly higher than from fixed phones, but calls **from hotel rooms** attract a minimum surcharge of a hundred percent on the basic long-distance rates – luxury hotels bump up overseas rates by factors of four or five.

Almost all Southern **phone numbers**, whether fixed or mobile, are a uniform eight digits, with previous internal area codes having become mere prefixes (consult the box on p.58 for prefixes which still show where your callee resides). All numbers starting with 2 are fixed lines; those beginning with 99 are mobiles; 8000 for the first four digits means a free-phone service; while 900 or 909 signals a premium-rate service. Six-digit numbers beginning with 77 are so-called "universal access" numbers, analogous to the UK's 0845 or 0870 codes. To **ring the Republic of Cyprus from overseas**, dial the country code ☎357, followed by all eight digits.

It's possible to bring your home-country **mobile SIM** and roam while in the South, but with a price-fixing cartel applying within the EU (€0.51/min to make or €0.26/min to receive calls), and Cyprus offering some of the cheapest mobile rates in the world, you'd be mad to do this for any stay of over a week. On arrival, pop your home SIM card out – having the apparatus unblocked if necessary at any corner telecoms shop – and buy one of the two local **pre-paid plans** available. Cytamobile-Vodafone's "So Easy" costs under €26 VAT inclusive to get started, with about €5 worth of call-time included and top-ups valid for a year, so you can re-use your SIM if you return to the island next season. Rates for any other phone on the island are about €0.07/min – vs €0.10 for using a call box – while ringing a UK mobile is about €0.26 per minute. The alternative is MTN-Areeba Pay as You Go, with comparable connection fee (€25 VAT inclusive) and €5 call time included (valid one month) but top-ups of €10 and €20 valid for a year. Calling charges are comparable to Cytamobile, and given grumblings about unreliable service, it's much less popular.

If you're planning to stay quite a long time, you might consider a **contract plan** with either Cytamobile-Vodafone or MTN-Areeba: €17 for the number, plus monthly subscription from €7, with call tariffs ranging from €0.02–0.06 depending on subscription and/or time of day.

The North

Fixed phones in the Turkish Republic of Northern Cyprus are handled by the

Useful numbers and codes

The South

International operator (reverse-
  charge calls, from private or hotel
  phones only) ☎198
Inland directory assistance ☎192
Overseas directory assistance ☎194
Speaking clock ☎193
Police, fire and ambulance ☎199
  or 112
Forest fire reporting ☎189 or 1407
Fixed-phone numbers in ... start
  with: Nicosia district ☎22
  "Free Famagusta" district ☎23

Larnaca district ☎24
Limassol district ☎25
Páfos district ☎26

The North

Directory assistance ☎118
International operator ☎115
Police ☎155
Ambulance ☎112
Fire ☎199
Forest fire reporting ☎177

Telekomünikasyon Dairesi or Telecom Division. **Call boxes** accept *telekarts*, available only from the *Telekomünikasyon* offices. Such (noise-plagued) call boxes are so rare that we've pinpointed them in the guide; working ones tend to have long queues of soldiers and students.

You may get more joy from a **kontürlü telefon** (metered counter phone), which costs about double the *telekart*-phone rates but still about half as much as using a hotel-room phone (see below). These phones are prominently signposted and fairly common in central Kyrenia – you pay after completing your call. Alternatively, there are a bare handful of peaceful booths or counter phones in the equally scarce (and limited-hours) **Telekomünikasyon offices** themselves, where again you pay after you've finished.

Despite outrageous surcharges (at least quadruple the basic *telekart* rate), some prefer to place calls from their **hotel room**, reckoning it worth the extra convenience and privacy. Once clear of the hotel circuitry, dial ☎00 to get an **international line**, followed by the usual repertoire of country and area codes.

Mobile phone users can roam with the local subsidiary of Turkey-based Telsim or Turkcell, and coverage is excellent, but tariffs to dial anywhere in the EU (including the South) are exorbitant, as bad as or worse than hotel surcharges, and fees for dialling locally to either fixed or mobile lines are still grossly inflated. Not being subject to intra-EU controls, any sort of roaming is a blatant

rip-off, especially dialling overseas; locals who need to do this a lot simply buy a Cytamobile-Vodafone or MTN-Areeba subscription. From anywhere on the Mesarya with a clear line of sight to the South's antennae – almost half the country – you too can take advantage by just selecting Cyta-moibile or MTN as your network and roam at EU capped tariffs. Better yet, just cross the "border" and get a plan as described above, or (if you're stuck behind the Kyrenia range) subscribe to one of the North's **pay-as-you-go** mobile plans: either Telsim's "Kolaykart", 100 units plus a SIM for YTL 17.50, or Türkcell's identical offering for 20YTL.

It is also now a simple matter to call **the South** from a fixed line; simply precede the eight-digit number in the South with 00 357. As with calling in the opposite direction, it's charged as an international call, though negotiations are under way to get this down to something like local CYTA rates.

Since 1993, North Cyprus has shared the ten-digit Turkish phone number convention: a three-digit area code, ☎392, which applies to fixed phones in the entire country, followed by a seven-digit subscriber number. Mobile numbers are prefixed with ☎0542, 0533 or 0535. When dialling a land line within North Cyprus, omit the ☎392, but when ringing mobiles you must include ☎0542, 0533 or 0535. If **ringing from overseas**, preface these ten digits (leaving off the initial zero of mobile codes) with the international code for Turkey, ☎90; as in matters postal (see p.73), Turkey effectively "fronts" for North Cyprus in the international arena.

Internet access

With about half the adult population in the South owning a computer, and a growing proportion in the North, **internet cafés** are not big on either side of the island. If you have a lightweight laptop, consider bringing it; although **wi-fi** is not universal in hotels, Cytanet has various wi-fi zones in the South

which can be used with a pre-paid or credit card. If instead you choose the modem-cable route, bring any necessary plug adaptors; South hotel phone sockets tend to be flat, UK-type, while those in the North are either RJ11-type – or an antiquated triple-pin variety for which no adaptor is available. Cytanet offers a subscription-free **dial-up** programme called Cytanet for All, at €0.056/min (see ⓦ www.cytanet.com .cy/onthemove/cytanetforall/).

The media

For a modest-sized island, Cyprus is served by a disproportionately large number of printed publications and TV/radio channels. This is partly due to non-market factors, such as sponsorship of print media by political groups, and also to its critical position in the eastern Mediterranean, enabling the island both to tap the airwaves from, and beam to, neighbouring countries.

Newspapers and magazines

While the vernacular-language print media will be inaccessible to most visitors, there are a number of informative, locally produced English-language publications aimed primarily at expats. A very few foreign newspapers are available – at a price.

Nearly a dozen **Greek-language newspapers**, many toeing a particular party line, cater to native readers in **the South**; *Politis* is considered the best written and most editorially consistent, not changing its politics for every fad. Two **English-language papers**, *The Cyprus Weekly* (Fri, ⓦ www.cyprusweekly .com.cy) and the daily (except Mon, ⓦ www .cyprus-mail.com) *Cyprus Mail* are both part-colour but design-challenged. The *Mail*, one of the oldest publications in the Middle East and considered a paper of record, is more intelligent, worth a read for Patroclos's Sunday-only "Tales from the Coffee Shop" scandals-and-corruption column alone. More native Cypriots than care to admit are known to take a peek at it, and at the paper overall. The standard of journalism at the *Weekly*, a

Turkophobic, nationalist fishwrap, is far lower. Editorial content aside, both have news, extensive small ads, chemist rotas, real estate pullouts, and daily/weekly programmes for most radio and TV stations. The *Mail* has brief weekday sections for films and exhibitions and airport timetables, though the Sunday edition is more esteemed for its "Seven" pull-out section listing the week's film, TV, radio and live events. The *Weekly*'s extensive, pull-out "Lifestyle" arts-review section includes TV and cinema listings. **Foreign newspapers** are generally limited to *The Times*, the *International Herald Tribune*, the *Guardian* and the *Daily Mail*.

You'll see only occasional, overpriced copies of the *Financial Times* or *Sunday Times* in **the North**, the rather turgid *Turkish Daily News* from the mainland, plus the Asil-Nadir-owned weekly *Cyprus Today* (Sat) in English (with radio and TV listings, plus the rota of late-night chemists and Ercan airport flight info), and its slightly cheaper competitor the *Cyprus Observer* – of passable quality, unlike the daily bird-cage liner *Cyprus Times*.

One of the best publications for an objective overview is the annual (autumn) **Report of** the Friends of Cyprus, a British lobby of parliamentarians, Euro-MPs and other public figures pushing for an equitable settlement for the island's division. In addition to a summary of the previous year on Cyprus, it has a mix of technical articles on law and statecraft along with memoirs, poetry and book reviews. To subscribe (£5 plus postage per issue), contact Mary Southcott ☎0117/924 5139, ℮marysouthcott@hotmail.com.

Radio and TV

The advantages of having your own **electronic media** for propaganda purposes were not lost on either of Cyprus's two main communities. **Bayrak**, the North's radio voice, dangles lengthy Greek-music and -language programming to reel in Southern listeners (plus the latest UK styles), as a prelude to news broadcasts presenting the South as overrun with mafiosi, corruption, terrorism and unreconstructed *énosis*-ists. For its part, the Southern station **CyBC** (Cyprus Broadcasting Corporation), even in its Turkish-language programming, studiously refers to the North as "Turkish-occupied territory", and President Talat as "leader of the Turkish-Cypriot community". In recent years, broadcast hours have lengthened and (at last count) two dozen **private stations** have emerged, mostly on FM, a sharp break from the past where meagre advertising revenues and a limited audience dictated just a few hours' broadcasting per day on public-only stations.

Radio

On the **radio**, CyBC's strictly Greek Programme 1 can be found at 97.2 and 90.2FM and/or 693 AM, 6am to midnight. CyBC's Programme 2, at 91.1, 92.4 and 94.2 FM during the same time slot, has a more cosmopolitan line-up with news in English at 1.30pm and 8pm, and all-English programming from 6pm to midnight. The BBC World Service broadcasts at 1323 AM more or less around the clock; reception is usually very strong, since the transmitter for the whole Middle East sits on the coast between Larnaca and Limassol. The British Sovereign Bases operate the British Forces Broadcasting Service (BFBS), in English with

Western (mostly rock, pop and country) music programming, on Programme 1 (24hr) at 92.1 (Limassol), 89.7 (Nicosia) and 99.6 (Larnaca) FM, and features, news and serials (including almost-daily doses of *The Archers*) on Programme 2 (6am to 9pm) at 91.7 or 95.2 (Nicosia), 85.3 (Larnaca) and 81.9 FM (Limassol). Skipping along the dial you'll also find several private, local English-language stations, such as Radio Napa at 90.9FM and Kiss at 89FM – as well as 2008 entrant Ⓦwww.nationalradio1.com, the first online-only all-English-language pop station. Among Cypriot channels, Kanali 6 at 107.1FM is excellent for quality Greek music, especially on Sunday.

In **the North**, the official Bayrak Radyo (87.8 and 105 FM) functions 6.30am–midnight; there tends to be quality Western music at night, also listened to by numbers of folk in the South. Most people listen to Metro at 104 FM, with a good range of Western pop, and widely available as it's beamed in by powerful transmitters from Turkey. The most reliable BFBS-2 frequencies are 95.2, 91.7 (Nicosia) and 89.9FM, and 1089 or 1503AM.

Television

CyBC 1 and 2 (RIK 1 and RIK 2 in Greek) beam TV from **the South** daily 7am–1am and 8am–3.30am respectively (subject to variations); programming is a mix of soaps, films, music, sports, talk shows and documentaries. There's a lot of foreign material with its original soundtrack, and most Greek transmissions have English and Turkish subtitles. Otherwise people tune in to the Greek stations ET1, Mega and Antenna from Rhodes, Paphos TV in Páfos district, or private local stations Logos, Sigma, Lumiere (alias LTV, mostly films; subscriber only), Alfa or Fred-TV. Satellite dishes pick up BBC World and CNN.

In **the North**, Kıbrıs TV will have at least one foreign film nightly, starting between 8.30 and 10.40pm, with original soundtrack; BRT2 has films and variety shows, plus occasional news in English, from 5.30pm until almost midnight. Otherwise people make do with TRT from Turkey, or a host of private Turkish channels such as ATV, Show, Star, Kanal Altı, NTV and Kanal D. The better hotels have foreign cable channels.

Archeological sites, museums, churches and mosques

Archeological sites and museums across Cyprus have user-friendly opening times, though you may find certain Northern museums and monuments shut (when they're supposed to be open) without explanation owing to staffing problems. Admission fees have risen of late, especially in the North, where they are noticeably more than in the South. Churches and mosques of interest to visitors have less established visiting hours and operate on a "donation" basis.

Opening times and admission fees

The more popular ancient sites in **the South** are fenced but accessible from roughly 9am to near sunset all year, though even during long-day months they're never open past 7.30pm. Most major museums shut weekdays at 4.30 to 5pm, and by 1pm on Saturday and Sunday. On most public holidays outdoor sites are unaffected, but many museums keep short – or no – hours, and everything closes on Easter Sunday, Christmas and New Year's Day. No entrance fee for state-run facilities exceeds €3.50, and most are currently €1.70 (set to rise to €2 in

2009); children under 10 usually get in free, but student discounts are not the rule. Since Cyprus's entry to the EU, many (though not all) sites are free to EU nationals on Sundays.

Operating hours at the limited number of museums and sites in **Northern Cyprus** are vaguely similar; admission fees run a hefty 4–9 YTL, depending on the attraction, though properly identified students almost always get a two-thirds discount.

Churches

Most of the South's famous **frescoed/mosaiced churches** are still used in some sacred capacity, and kept locked to protect

Churches in the North

Since the events of 1974 only a bare handful of **churches in the North** continue to function as houses of Christian worship. The rest have been either converted into mosques or museums, or desecrated in various ways, mostly by the Turkish army but also by Anatolian settlers or Turkish Cypriots.

This behaviour is seized on by the outraged Greek Cypriots as further proof of (mainland) Turkish barbarism, and used to good effect in their sophisticated "public relations" efforts. The Southern government pointedly contrasts the treatment of these buildings with the relative consideration accorded to mosques in the South, which are held in trust by a Religious Affairs Department, provided with a tiny budget to maintain the buildings.

For their part, northerners either won't even acknowledge that injury has been done or justify it as the understandable venting of frustration and aggression on the most tangible, helpless reminders of the atrocities perpetrated on the Turkish Cypriots by EOKA, which included the dynamiting of mosque minarets on occasion. Moreover, it is claimed that the ringing of church bells often signalled the start of an anti-Turkish-Cypriot pogrom in formerly mixed villages.

What this means to a visitor is that Northerners can be touchy about requests to visit churches not specifically prepared for public viewing. You will often find abandoned churches off-limits as military depots, and/or appallingly vandalized, sometimes with their entrances bricked up to prevent access. It is a depressing exercise visiting these battered buildings, empty of the devotion which the Greek Cypriots lavished on them, and something most people will only do once or twice.

them from thieves and the elements; they don't always have set visiting hours. Often, part of the experience is locating the key-keeper, not always a priest, who may live or work some distance away. A donation (of €1–2) to the collection box, if not the person himself, is required; some wardens can be impatient with the non-Orthodox, and will begin fidgeting or muttering if in their view too much time is spent in gawping irreligiously at the frescoes. Since all but one or two of these churches are still consecrated, men may not usually enter in shorts, nor women in trousers or culottes of any sort, and neither sex in sleeveless tops – wraps for the indecently attired are not provided. Photos, especially with flash or tripod, are usually not allowed. At the more noteworthy, "first-division" churches there will be some sort of formal schedule (noted in this guide) and more relaxed caretakers.

Mosques

Most **mosques** in the South are now kept locked, presumably awaiting the hypothetical return of their Turkish-Cypriot users. Several still function in south Nicosia, Limassol and Larnaca, meeting the spiritual needs of the Republic's sizeable population of Arabs, Pakistanis, Bangladeshis, Egyptians, Lebanese and Iranians – as well as slowly growing numbers of remaining (and returning) Turkish Cypriots in the South. The Hala Sultan Tekke near Larnaca is also still an active place of pilgrimage for both island and foreign Muslims.

The same **etiquette** applies to any mosque on the island. Contrary to what you may read elsewhere, shoes must be removed at the entrance, and one does not enter scantily clad – this in effect means the same guidelines as for churches. Native Cypriot Muslims are remarkably easy-going (with tolerant attitudes, for example, towards drinking and dogs) so you would have to do something fairly insensitive to irk them. As a minimum, don't enter mosques when a service is in progress, and try not to walk in front of a praying person.

Crime and personal safety

Cyprus was long one of the safest Mediterranean travel destinations, with low assault and theft rates, but sadly this is changing – gone are the days when one routinely left cars (rental or otherwise) unlocked. Organized rings target parked cars of part-time residents in the South, driving them north to be resold in Turkey or beyond. Statistically, most crime still rates as fraud, extortion and smuggling, plus periodic grisly killings inside the Cypriot underworld, though none of these doings are likely to affect visitors.

Civilian authorities and police in both communities usually go out of their way to make tourists feel welcome, and the most likely occasion for misunderstandings will be the various **military zones** – far more numerous in the North than in the South. Give any military installation in the North a very wide berth; do not park or halt cars, "loiter" (walk slowly past), read, write or photograph *anything* within sight of a command post, barracks, officers' apartments, military hospital, canteen, etc. Sentries are apt to be twitchy and over-zealous, especially since the September 11 incidents and the İstanbul UK consulate bombing (Turkish forces are considered lackeys of the US by al-Qaeda and thus a tempting target). The Turkish army is a law unto itself – no civilian authority will intervene on your behalf – and you could find yourself detained for an hour or more by a trigger-happy conscript, until a commanding officer and interpreter are found to help ascertain that you are not in fact a suicide bomber.

Unless you are actually visiting someone living in the **buffer** (demilitarized, "dead") **zone**, or are escorted by authorized UN personnel, you'll at least raise an eyebrow or two by driving into it and could provoke a major incident by using any roads marked as blocked-off on our maps. With more legal crossings expected to open shortly, you'll have little excuse for being found in such places.

Do heed the **"no photography"** signs near military bases either side, as well as along the Attila Line (called the Green Line in Nicosia). If you are caught photographing, even inadvertently, a military installation anywhere in Cyprus, your film or memory disk may be confiscated – politely, and possibly returned after processing and screening, in the South; more brusquely by the Turkish army in the North. In the southern Republic monasteries are now partly or wholly off-limits to cameras, since the monks grew tired of being zoo-animal-type attractions. Similarly, don't sneak snaps of the interiors of the South's frescoed churches – caretakers accompany you inside to prevent this, among other reasons.

For years, casual visitors were unlikely to see much evidence of **organized crime** on the island. But as of the mid-1990s spectacular scandals implicated the higher ranks of the South's police force in a spate of gangland shootings, car bombings, apartment arson and torture of suspects in detention with UK-supplied stun-batons. Things have not let up much since then, as mafia dons – now disproportionately *Russopóndi* or Caucasians of Greek ethnic origin – fight turf wars for control of lucrative vice-ventures. Though it all sounds lurid, if you steer clear of cabarets, massage parlours, gambling dens and purchases of drugs, you'll avoid being caught in crossfire or getting on the wrong side of the police.

The influence of organized crime has become equally pervasive in the brothels and casinos of the North, but violent scores tend to be settled in mainland Turkey, where most of the big bosses remain. An exception – and the most "illustrious (Cypriot) corpse" to date – was Sabri Tahir, dubious (anti)hero of Lawrence Durrell's *Bitter Lemons*, who in 2001 was gunned down (on the second attempt) at the helm of his Orient Brothel-Casino, ironically just opposite the Ministry of Tourism. It seems he had not made payoffs to associates in a timely manner.

Sexual harassment and prostitution

Both Greek- and Turkish-Cypriot men are more reserved than their mainland counterparts, though as throughout the Mediterranean, resort areas support a few underemployed Romeos. Told to desist in no uncertain terms, Cypriot men usually will. In the more traditional inland areas, unescorted women will generally be accorded village courtesy.

The traditional, home-grown red-light districts of Limassol and Nicosia may have been (mostly) wound up since the millennium, but they were long since eclipsed in any case, on both sides of the line, by veritable armies of eastern European prostitutes. Over 1500 "natashas" who work the brothels and "nightclubs" of the **North** pay large "sureties" against future taxes, plus fees for residence permits, to the governing regime which is in effect pimping from them. Since the "border" opened in April 2003, their former Turkish mainland clientele has been mostly replaced by a Greek-Cypriot one.

In the **South**, the focus of the industry is Limassol, where an undetermined number of Russians, Moldavians, Bulgarians, Ukrainians and Romanians staff the "gentlemen's/night clubs" or patrol the hotel strip. **Cabarets** are to be avoided as a nightlife option; the bill for three or four beers can run to €600–700, and reluctant payers will be frog-marched by bouncers to the nearest cash dispenser to withdraw the necessary funds – or have their credit cards cloned and repeatedly charged to rub salt in the wound.

Festivals and public holidays

Generally the South's public holidays have a religious focus, reflecting the Greek Orthodox Church's (formerly) pre-eminent position in its culture, while the North – technically a secular society – has more commemorations of salient events in Turkish communal history. In recent years special events have been developed by the Southern tourism authorities, with a view to a foreign audience, to supplement the bedrock of traditional religious festivals.

Public holidays in the South

In the South, there is near-complete overlap between religious and bank **holidays**, so of the dates in the box opposite, official business is only conducted (after a fashion) on *Kataklysmós*. When these dates fall on a Sunday, the subsequent Monday is usually a public holiday – in the case of Easter, the following Tuesday is also a bank holiday, as is Good Friday and part of Maundy Thursday. Shops stay open on Good Friday and Holy Saturday morning, but then remain shut until Wednesday morning except in tourist areas, so beware.

Religious holidays in the South

New Year's Day in Cyprus is the feast day of Áyios Vassílios (St Basil), and the evening before, most homes bake a *vasilópitta* or cake containing a coin bringing good luck to the person finding it in their slice. The saint is also the Orthodox equivalent of Santa Claus, and gifts are exchanged on this day, though see opposite about Christmas.

In the Orthodox Church, **Epiphany** (Jan 6) marks the baptism of Christ in the Jordan, and the conjunction of the Holy Trinity; the Greek name *Ta Theofánia* refers to the resulting inner illumination. Holy water fonts in churches are blessed to banish the *kalikándzari* demons said to run amok on earth after Christmas. As a finale at seaside or reservoir locations, a local bishop hurls a crucifix out over the water, and young men swim for the honour of recovering it.

Clean, or "Green", Monday – marked by picnics in the countryside – comes at the end of the ten days of **Carnival**, the occasion for fancy-dress balls and float-parades, most notably in Limassol on the Saturday. The Thursday eleven days previous used to signal the beginning of a strict seven-week abstention from meat, but in an indication of how low in esteem the Orthodox Church as fallen, said picnics now feature the ostentatious grilling of meat as a two-fingers-up to the clergy. March 25 is usually billed as "Greek National Day", but is more properly the feast of *Evangelismós* or the **Annunciation**.

Observance of **Easter** starts early in **Holy Week**, and the island's small Catholic and Armenian communities celebrate in tandem with the Orthodox majority. The most conspicuous customs are the dyeing red of hard-boiled eggs on Maundy Thursday, the baking of special holiday cakes such as *flaoúnes*, and on Good Friday eve the solemn procession of the *Epitáfios* or Christ's funeral bier in each parish, whose women provide its elaborate floral decoration. In Páfos town, for example, at least two of these are paraded solemnly through the streets, preceded by an intimidating military escort and youth bands playing New-Orleans-ish cortège themes, until they meet near the central park at about 10.30pm, where the local bishop conducts a brief service.

On Saturday evening, huge bonfires (*lambrádjia*) are set – giving rise to the word **Lambrí**, the alias for Easter in Cypriot dialect – before the spectacular midnight *Anástasi* or Resurrection mass. Not everyone will fit into the confines of a typical village church, so crowds gather in the courtyard, around the embers of the fire. Observance is pretty casual, even by Greek rural standards; the noise of high-decibel fireworks set off by teenagers – everything from Roman candles to dynamite left over from the Límni mine in Tillyría – all but drowns out the liturgy.

Things calm down temporarily at midnight, when the officiating priest appears from behind the altar screen bearing a lighted candle and the news of eternal life for believers, and soon church interiors and courtyards are ablaze with the flame passed from worshipper to worshipper. The skyline of the larger towns will be illuminated by spectacular fireworks displays – the wealthier the municipality the better. It is considered good luck to get your candle home still alight, to trace a soot-cross over the door lintel; then the Lenten fast is broken with *avgolémono* soup, and family members crack their red-dyed eggs against each other (owner of the last unbroken egg "wins").

Kataklysmós or the **Festival of the Flood**, fifty days after Easter, is unique to Cyprus; elsewhere in the Orthodox world it is merely Whit Monday or the Feast of the Holy Spirit, but here it's a pretext for several days of popular events. At all coastal towns people crowd into the sea and sprinkle each other with water; the festival ostensibly commemorates the salvation of Noah and his family from the Flood, but it's likely a vestige of a much older pagan rite in honour of Aphrodite's birth, or perhaps her purification after sleeping with Adonis.

Christmas (*Khristoúyenna*) is relatively subdued in Cyprus, though European-style commercialization – including house illuminations and plastic Santas – has made inroads. The most durable old custom are the *kálanda* or carols, sung by children going door-to-door accompanying themselves on a triangle. It's worth noting that many establishments seem to shut down between Christmas and New Year, and then open only sporadically between January 1 and 6.

Other events in the South

In addition to the strictly ecclesiastical holidays, municipalities and tourist boards lay on a number of other events. The most reliable of these include the May *Anthistíria* or **Flower Festivals**, best in mid-May at Larnaca and Páfos; the **Shakespeare Festival** preceding **Cyprus Music Days**, at Kourion's ancient theatre during June/July; the Limassol and Larnaca municipal festivals in July; the **Páfos festival** of music, theatre and dance staged in the ancient *odeion* and medieval castle from July to September; the **Ayía Nápa festival** in September; and the **Limassol Wine Festival,** with free tasting sessions in the central park, during late August/early September. If you're determined to coincide with any or all of these, get a copy of the CTO's monthly summary of events, produced at each local tourist office.

Public holidays in the North

In the **North**, the holiday calendar is again a mix of religious holidays and official, patriotic

Public holidays in the South

2009	2010	2011	
1 Jan	same	same	Áyios Vassílios (New Year's Day)
6 Jan	same	same	Theofánia (Epiphany)
2 March	16 Feb	7 March	Clean (Green) Monday
25 March	same	same	Annunciation
1 April	same	same	Southern Republic Day
27 April	2 April	22 April	Orthodox Good Friday
29 April	4 April	24 April	Orthodox Easter Sunday
1 May	same	same	Labour Day
18 June	24 May	13 June	Kataklysmós (Flood Festival)
15 Aug	same	same	Assumption of the Virgin
1 Oct	same	same	Cyprus Independence Day
28 Oct	same	same	Greek National Day
25/26 Dec	same	same	Christmas/Sýnaxi tís Panayías

Public holidays in the North

2009	2010	2011	
1 Jan	same	same	New Year's Day (Yılbaşı)
27–30 Nov	16–19 Nov	6–9 Nov	Kurban Bayramı
9 March	26 Feb	15 Feb	Mevlûd (Muhammad's Birthday)
23 April	same	same	National Sovereignty & Children's Day
1 May	same	same	Labour Day
19 May	same	same	Youth and Sports Day
20 July	same	same	Peace Operation Day
1 Aug	same	same	TMT Day
30 Aug	same	same	Zafer Bayramı (Victory Day)
29 Oct	same	same	Turkish Republic Day
21–23 Sept	10–12 Sept	31 Aug–2 Sept	Şeker Bayramı
15 Nov	same	same	TRNC Foundation Day

commemorations, many imported from Turkey. All religious feasts recede approximately eleven days yearly in the western calendar (twelve in a leap year) because of the lunar nature of the Muslim calendar; however future dates of festivals as given on Islamic websites are provisional, owing to factors such as when the moon is sighted and the international dateline, so expect variance of up to a day in the ranges given in the box above. Unlike in the South, there's just not the budget or inclination for laying on big-theme secular bashes. Surviving, reliable and prestigious **cultural festivals** include the Bellapais (classical) Music Festival (late May to late June), with performances by name artists in the eponymous abbey; the Famagusta International Festival, featuring more varied acts from late June to mid-July; and the International Music Festival in late summer, in Famagusta and around Kyrenia. Additionally, there are festivals on the Mesarya (Mesaoría) linked to the harvest of various crops, especially the Güzelyurt Orange Festival in mid-May.

The official holidays of the North are fairly self-explanatory, though a word on the movable **religious feasts** is in order. **Şeker Bayramı** marks the end of the fasting month of **Ramazan** (Ramadan), and is celebrated with family get-togethers and the distribution of presents and sweets to visitors. At the northern outskirts of Nicosia, there's a fun-fair on purpose-built grounds, with "luna-park" rides for kids, and traditional foods and crafts on sale. **Kurban Bayramı** commemorates the thwarted sacrifice of Ishmael by Abraham – a Koranic version of the Abraham and Isaac story – and used to be distinguished by the dispatch and roasting of vast numbers of sheep; the custom is now on the wane among native-born Turkish Cypriots.

By their own admission, Turkish Cypriots are among the laxest Muslims world wide in terms of observance – few set foot in a mosque on any given Friday – but almost everybody makes some effort to observe Ramazan by swearing off booze for the duration (a major sacrifice, given some pretty hard drinking habits) and food during daylight hours, which means outside of Kyrenia many restaurants shut at midday, especially if the fasting month falls during the tourist off-season. This, and the fact that everyone eats in to save up money for expensive nights out on **Arife**, the first evening of the Şeker Bayramı festivity, makes Ramazan a rather dull time to travel. Restaurants are particularly empty on the fifth evening before Şeker Bayramı, known as **Kadir Gecesi** or the night the Koran was revealed to Muhammad. Most people stay home then, reading the Koran and praying; it's believed that prayers on this night have a special efficacy. During the day of Arife, it is customary to go to cemeteries and pay respects to departed ancestors. Many, if not most, Turkish Cypriots do attend mosque services on Şeker Bayramı and Kurban Bayramı.

Sports and outdoor activities

Because of its mild climate, Cyprus is a good venue for assorted open-air athletic activities. In terms of spectating, football and tennis – for which the South hosts major international tournaments yearly – are the big events.

Water sports

Virtually all resorts in the South cater to any conceivable water sport, from kayaking to parasailing by way of water-skiing. **Windsurfing** boards are available everywhere, but you only get strong breezes around the island's capes: in the far southeast, between Ayía Nápa and Protarás; around Páfos; and occasionally on the exposed coast west of Pólis. Small sailcraft can be rented from the marinas at Larnaca, Limassol and Páfos. In North Cyprus, windsurfing and sailing facilities concentrate west of Kyrenia, and at the luxury hotels near ancient Salamis.

Perhaps the biggest attraction is underwater; unusually for the eastern Mediterranean, where submerged antiquities are prone to theft, **scuba** is promoted by the tourism authorities and numerous dive operators – we've listed at least one in each major resort. In the North, at least two (in some years three) scuba schools operate in or near Kyrenia, plus there's a worthwile operator in the Karpaz. As a general rule, diving off the island's north coast – whether from Greek Cypriot or Turkish Cypriot territory – tends to be more exciting, and sheltered, than off the south coast, with the outstanding exception of the *Zenobia* wreck near Larnaca. This may, however, change if plans to imitiate Malta – by scuttling several carefully stripped boat-hulks at various spots off the southern republic's coast – come to fruition. A two-dive day around Latchí will cost €65–72 depending on the centre; on the busier south coast budget €80. PADI or BSAC Open Water certifications run €370–400 at most centres – try not to pay more. In the North, on the Karpaz, Open Water courses are a bargain at £195.

On land – and overhead

Horse-riding, especially during the cooler months, has grown hugely in popularity since the millennium. There are a dozen riding clubs in the South, distributed fairly evenly over Nicosia, Larnaca, Famagusta, Limassol and Páfos districts, plus at least one in the North.

Mountain biking has already been noted as a possibility on p.42, but there are also some bona fide marked trails – as opposed to vehicle tracks – in the Tróödhos, prepared expressly for **hiking** by the CTO in conjunction with the forestry division. The guide covers most of them, though the longest itinerary will fill just a single day. The only long-distance, GR-type route, between the Akámas and Ayía Nápa, is the European long-distance trail E4, though much of it is a bad joke, relying extensively on jeep tracks and even stretches of paved road – hardly the point of such a route. It's possible to walk in the steeper Kyrenia hills as long as you steer clear of military areas, but again there are very few paths as opposed to dirt or paved tracks, and the forest around Kyrenia has never properly resprouted after a catastrophic fire in 1995.

Southern Cyprus can boast the exotic attraction, for the Middle East, of a **ski resort**. A single complex of four lifts serves seven runs on the northeast face of Mount Olympus, the island's summit. The season lasts at best from January to late March, though there's been no snow since 2006.

Since 1995 **golf**, focused on the new golf courses at Tsádha, Secret Valley and Aphrodite Hills in Páfos district (plus the Elias and Vikla clubs near Limassol), has been heavily promoted to visitors. The North's first course opened in 2007, near Esentepe (Áyios Amvósios). Most package-tour operators offer the option of pre-booking green fees, which, depending on the company and time of year (high summer is cheapest) vary from €30–55 per day. The continued viability/sustainability of such facilities, however, must be questioned in light of the island's ongoing water crisis – greens are soon likely to be browns – and falling short-stay visitor numbers.

Finally, you can **tandem paraglide** above the Kyrenia area, taking off from points in the hills behind; details on p.310.

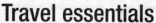

Travel essentials

Addresses

In **the Greek-Cypriot sector**, addresses are written either in Greek or in English. When in Greek, the number follows the street name, for example "Leofóros Faneroménis 27". The same place in English is cited as "27, Faneromenis Avenue". Postcodes exist but are not yet used much; more often a district within the municipality is cited.

In **Northern Cyprus**, addresses are generally given bilingually (Turkish/English) on visiting cards and bumph, but if not, *Caddesi*, abbreviated to Cad, means avenue; *Bulvarı* (Bul) is boulevard; *Meydan/Meydanı* (Meyd) is plaza; *Sokak/Sokauı* (Sok) means street; and *Çıkmazı* (Çık) is a dead-end alley. *Karşısı* means "opposite from", as in *PTT karşısı*, "opposite the post office".

Bargaining

Not a regular feature of Cypriot life, except for **souvenir purchases** where price is not marked. Don't expect the vendor to come down more than twenty percent from their opening bid, however. At off-peak times you can often get **accommodation** in the South for twenty to forty percent less than posted rates; the same applies to car rental, at least with local chains and one-offs. In the North things are more flexible; written rates and prices are not so conspicuous, but again expect only small discounts.

Children and babies

Sacred in both communities, and should present few problems travelling; in most resorts geared for the package trade on either side of the island, **family-sized suites** are easy to come by. Many southern hotels offer child-friendly programmes, and such outfits are usually clear about this in brochures/websites. Baby formulas and **nappies** are available in pharmacies and supermarkets everywhere. Fresh, full-fat milk is easy to get in any supermarket; organic and salt-free products can be found in the South with some diligence. Child seats, not necessarily up to UK standards, are available in rental cars if booked well in advance.

Cigarettes and smoking

In **the South** ashtrays are ubiquitous in clubs and cafés, but despite this locals are light puffers compared to all surrounding countries, and non-smoking areas and campaigns are gaining ground under EU pressure – including all hotel diners, airports and on Cyprus Airways, to the consternation of native island passengers. Nicotine habits are a bit more pronounced in **Northern Cyprus**, based almost entirely on rough Anatolian brands, but again you won't die of asphyxiation if you're a non-smoker.

Contraceptives

The Greek for **condoms** is *profylaktiká*, the Turkish is *preservatif*.

Costs

The main Cyprus travel season begins early in spring and extends well into autumn, with July/August visits somewhat unappealing for a number of reasons. Obviously you'll save a lot on lodging in either part of Cyprus if you're willing to go **outside midsummer** (though September is also reckoned peak season), a sensible strategy whatever your budget. Some form of **student identification** is useful for discounted admission to archeological sites and museums.

The South

The southern Republic of Cyprus has a partly deserved reputation for being expensive, accentuated since entry into the EU; food and lodging are a good fifteen to twenty percent higher than in neighbouring Greece, for instance, and marginally (if at all) cheaper than in France. Travelling independently in the South, you should budget a **minimum** of around £40 per person a day. This assumes, however, exclusive reliance on bicycles or public transport, staying in one of the limited number of basic village pensions or no-star hotels and only one modest meal out at about £14 per person, with the balance of food bought from shops.

To travel in some **comfort** and style, though, you'll want at least £65 disposable per person, which should let you book a mid-range hotel on double-occupancy basis and share the cost of a **rental car** (and petrol – slightly less than in Britain), as well as two full main meals. **Beer and wine** are good, and affordable at €2.50–3.50 and €12 per large bottle respectively at restaurants; village wine from the barrel goes for as little as €5 per litre, while brandy sours run about €2.

Winter visits – or even extended residence, a popular strategy with British senior citizens – offer considerable savings. One-bedroom apartments can be found starting at €350 per month, two-bedroom ones from €450. Car rental can be 35 percent cheaper than normal, and hotels nearly as much less. If you wear out your wardrobe,

January–February sales for shoes and clothing take place as in northern Europe.

The North

The economy of **Northern Cyprus** has lagged behind that of the South, but paradoxically it can often be as or more expensive to travel around. It's also slightly harder to travel independently here given the limited number of hotels geared to a walk-in trade; at package-oriented hotels, theoretical over-the-counter prices are often higher than those granted to advance bookings and agencies. There are just a handful of small, attractive **pensions and hotels** in and around Kyrenia, plus a few small inns on the Karpaz peninsula, charging £7–17 per person a night, and hardly any restoration projects along the lines of the South's agro-tourism programme. Elsewhere, you're squarely in three-star resort territory, though prices for equivalent facilities are a bit less than in the South at £60–85.

Eating out can be more expensive than in the South, especially around Kyrenia, where you can easily spend £18–20 per head on a **meal**; head for the Karpaz, and bills can drop as low as £10 apiece. **Car rental** is often slightly less than in the South, though this is offset by more expensive fuel costs. **Overall**, budget £55–60 a day per person (including mid-range accommodation) to live in **comfort**.

Customs limits

Previous bans on importing perishable produce into the South have been substantially relaxed. However, when transitting **from the North to the South**, you are limited to €135 worth of gifts and personal purchases, 40 cigarettes and a litre of spirits. Car boots will be opened and inspected at most crossings by Cypriot customs officials (who

---

Tipping and taxes

Since a ten-percent **service charge** is included on virtually all restaurant bills in the South, no extra amount need be left unless table-waiting was exceptional; in the North, where only the fancier places will tack on an identical fee, use your discretion. Taxi-drivers, especially in the South, expect a gratuity.

VAT (Value Added Tax) is levied at fifteen percent in the southern Republic; in the North it's also fifteen percent, often charged separately in fancy restaurants.

often can't be bothered late at night and/or in off season), but at Pýla/Beyarmudu or the Four-Mile Crossing by SBA police deputizing for the Republic – who are looking not so much for booze and fags as for illegal immigrants and pickled songbirds (banned in the EU). In a reciprocal measure, the **Northern authorities** continually threaten to impose low limits on the value of routine shopping that Northern residents bring back from trips to the South.

Electric current

Throughout the island, this is **220–240 volts AC**, with triple, rectangular-pin plugs: hence British visitors won't need any sort of adaptor to run electrical appliances. In very old buildings, you may still encounter the closely spaced, triple, round-pin, Chelsea system sockets. **Two-to-three-pin adaptors** are often furnished in better hotels and villas for use by continental European (ie Greek or Turkish) customers; if not, they are easily purchased in corner shops.

Visitors from North America will want to come equipped with their own two-to-three adaptor suitable for dual-voltage hair dryers or irons, as they are expensive and not as easily found. Continental plug-owners can easily and cheaply prepare one by replacing the 1-amp fuse in a two-to-three unit marked "for shaver only" with a 5-amp fuse.

Entry regulations

Most foreign nationals require only a valid **passport** for entry into either the southern or northern sectors of Cyprus. Canadian, New Zealand, Australian and US nationals do not require a **visa** for either side, and get a three-month tourist-visa stamp in passports on arrival. EU nationals no longer have passports stamped on arrival in the South at either of the two airports. On **arrival in the North**, however, whether at a seaport, airport or land-crossing, a free visa will be stamped on a separate, loose slip of paper, so as to avoid spoiling one's passport with a "visa" from an unrecognized state.

The **southern Republic** has long declared all seaports and airports in the North "prohibited ports of entry and exit", but since the Republic joined the EU in May 2004 there is in fact nothing they can do to stop EU nationals

entering the South if they've entered the North first (see our fuller remarks on p.35).

Gay life

This is apt to be furtive and underground in the tight-knit, family-oriented Cypriot society. In **the South** homosexual acts between men used to be illegal, with offenders liable in theory to five years in prison; even "attempts to commit" homosexual acts (ie cruising) potentially earned a sentence of three years. During the EU membership application process, various European authorities noted that this was at major variance with standards in other member countries; initially the South only undertook not to prosecute "overt" acts, rather than decriminalizing homosexual behaviour on the statute books, though in the face of staunch opposition from the Orthodox Church, formal repeal of the offending laws took place in 1998. **The North**, while having no specific legislation, shares the same attitudes, and both communities will often be hostile to any public display of gay affection. Contact is thus still low-key: the few bars, clubs and beaches, in and around Larnaca, Limassol or Páfos, that have reputations as gay meeting places are mentioned in the text.

Insurance

The southern Republic at least is an EU member, which means provision of public **health care** to other EU nationals on the same basis as locals on presentation of the European Health Insurance Card. The surplus of doctors drives down private clinic consultation fees, and virtually halves the cost of even fairly major surgical procedures compared to northern Europe or the US. All that said, it's still essential to take out some form of travel insurance.

Just about any travel agent, bank or insurance broker will sell you **comprehensive cover**, which includes not only medical expenses, but also loss or theft of belongings and trip curtailment/cancellation. Rough Guides offers its own insurance policy, details of which are given in the box below. If you intend to rent an off-road vehicle or motorbike, or engage in **special activities** such as paragliding, horse-riding or scuba diving, be sure to advise your insurers when getting cover.

Rough Guides travel insurance

Rough Guides has teamed up with Columbus Direct to offer you **travel insurance** that can be tailored to suit your needs. Products include a low-cost **backpacker** option for long stays; a **short break** option for city getaways; a typical **holiday package** option; and others. There are also annual **multi-trip** policies for those who travel regularly. Different sports and activities (trekking, skiing, etc) can be usually be covered if required.

See our website (ⓦ www.roughguides.com/website/shop) for eligibility and purchasing options. Alternatively, UK residents should call ☏ 0870/033 9988; Australians should call ☏ 1300/669 999 and New Zealanders should call ☏ 0800/55 9911. All other nationalities should call ☏ +44 870/890 2843.

When taking out medical coverage, ascertain whether **benefits** will be paid as treatment proceeds or only after return home, whether there is a **24-hour medical emergency number**, and how much the deductible is (sometimes negotiable). When securing baggage cover, make sure that the **per-article limit** – typically well under £500 in the UK – will cover your most valuable possession. Otherwise, it may have to be claimed on using your household effects policy (if any).

If you have anything **stolen**, go to the nearest **police station**, report the theft and get a copy of the report or the identification number under which it has been filed: you will need this when **making a claim** back home. Incidentally, following a spate of fraudulent claims, the police in the South are extra-vigilant for funny business, and will prosecute offenders.

Money

Cyprus's relatively low crime rate – South and North – and EU membership make notes or plastic far preferable to traveller's cheques as a way of carrying funds, and in the North you can pay for almost anything directly with euro or sterling.

The South adopted the **euro** in early 2008, at a fixed exchange rate of €1.7086 to the old **Cyprus pound** (C£). Euro notes exist in denominations of 5, 10, 20, 50, 100, 200 and 500 euros, and coins in denominations of 1, 2, 5, 10, 20 and 50 cents, plus 1 and 2 euros. Avoid getting stuck with counterfeit euro notes (€100 and €200 are the most common); genuine notes all have a hologram strip or (if over €50) patch at one end, there's a watermark at the other, plus a security thread embedded in the middle.

From 1983 until 2004, the legal tender in **the North** was the **old Turkish lira** (TL) – a policy informed more by ideological than economic reasons, and one with which few inhabitants were happy, thanks to its habitual devaluation/inflation rate of close to eighty percent per year. Given this imported hyperinflation, prices in old TL were fairly meaningless, so all northern prices tended – and still tend – to be quoted in pounds sterling. Following the 2002–03 stablization of the TL, a long-mooted currency reform took place, whereby the six final zeros of the old lira – ultimately worth over two million to the pound sterling – were knocked off at the new-currency launch on January 1, 2005.

The **new Turkish lira** (YTL or *yeni türk lira*) comes in paper notes of 1, 5, 10, 20, 50 and 100 YTL. One YTL is subdivided into one hundred kuruş, and there are also coins in various denominations between one kuruş and one YTL inclusive. Beware of getting passed 1YTL coins – the same size, weight and colour as the €2 coin – or 50-kuruş coins, similarly identical to the €1 coin, in the South: check your change carefully, as the disparity in value is small consolation for their working nicely in southern phone boxes and parking meters.

With any durable federal settlement, the euro will be introduced as the uniform currency throughout the island. At the moment both, along with the pound sterling, are accepted as payment across the North. Sterling tends to be given a fair exchange rate, but the euro is generally discounted about ten percent off its true value. As almost everywhere in Europe of late, US dollars are disdained.

There are no strict **controls** on the amount of cash or traveller's cheques imported into the North, but you should leave with as few YTL as possible, for the simple reason that – despite their newfound stability – they're poorly regarded outside Turkey or North Cyprus.

Banks and exchange facilities

Southern banks are open 8.30am–12.30pm, Monday to Friday, plus 3.15–4.45pm on Monday in winter; however, many branches in well-touristed areas offer a supplemental afternoon service, Tuesday to Friday, 4–6pm (May–Sept) or 3.15–4.45pm (Oct–April). Banking and exchange facilities in the two airport arrival lounges are open for all flights; however, experience has shown that airport ATMs can seize up without warning, so have some sterling notes handy to exchange at the staffed booths. Plan funding needs ahead at Orthodox Easter, a popular time to visit: all banks will be shut from Holy Thursday noon until the following Wednesday morning, with most ATMs running out at some point during this period.

Cash can be changed easily (with no commission), while **traveller's cheques** are subject to hefty fees. Plastic (especially a debit card) is also extremely useful, as **ATMs** are ubiquitous: most machines accept at least one from among Visa, Visa Electron, MasterCard, Maestro, Cirrus and Plus system cards. Screen instructions are given in English on request. **Credit cards** are widely accepted for purchases, but sometimes attract surcharges of three to five percent; chip-and-PIN routines are not much used.

The various banks operating in **North Cyprus** are inconvenient as tourist facilities, with few banks outside the three largest towns, an off-putting amount of red tape and hopelessly short working hours for foreign exchange (8.30am–noon Mon–Fri).

A much better bet, one used by virtually everyone involved in tourism, are the *döviz bürolari* (**money exchange houses**), several of which function in each of the major towns. Open 8.30am–1pm and 2–5pm Monday to Friday (6pm in summer), plus Saturday 8.30am–1pm, they give speedy service and top rates for foreign cash and traveller's cheques without taking commission.

Foreign-currency notes are in many ways the best form in which to bring funds to the North. You can pay directly for hotel bills, car-rental surcharges, souvenir purchases, restaurant meals and hotel extras such as sauna or phone fees with overseas cash (in order of preference as noted above) – and you may well *have* to pay the airport cabbie in sterling, so keep some £5 and £10 notes ready. Even UK one-pound, and sometimes even fifty-pence, coins are accepted at exchange houses, as well as at many shops and hotel receptions. The only things that you must pay for in YTL are such "official" purchases as postage stamps, museum admissions and phone cards; when you buy articles with pounds sterling, you'll be given change in YTL on a near-as-dammit basis.

Finally, **plastic** is very handy, both for large transactions such as car rental or buying petrol, and for use in the growing number of ATMs scattered across the North. Ones with foreign-language greeting messages accept some or all from among the same array of card types as in the South. Locations are detailed in the guide. Chip-and-PIN protocol is often enforced for credit cards.

Movies

In **the South**, prints are generally in the original language, with Greek subtitles. Screening times are usually given in the foreign-language press. Producing a student ID nets a small discount. For details of where cinemas are, see individual town accounts. In **the North**, movies tend to be up to a year old, but of reasonable projection quality. Programmes are given on the "What's On at the Cinema" page of *Cyprus Today*'s centre pullout section.·

Naturism

Unisex topless is the rule in the busier resorts of the South, and with some discretion in North Cyprus. And that's about as far as you'll prudently go, except at the most isolated beaches (such as Lára in the South and certain Karpaz coves in the North).

Opening hours

Business hours throughout the island are scheduled around the typical Mediterranean midday siesta. Town shops in **the South** are meant to be open daily in summer (June to mid-Sept) 8am–1pm and 4–7.30pm, except for Wednesday and Saturday when there are no afternoon hours. During spring (April–May) and autumn (mid-Sept to Oct), afternoon hours end at 7pm. Winter (Nov–March) hours are daily 8.30am–6pm, except for Wednesday and Saturday when everything shuts at 2pm. Office-based private professionals work nominally 8am–1pm and 3–6pm (mid-Sept to May), 8am–1pm and 4–7pm (June to mid-Sept). Both mountain village stores and establishments in tourist resorts are likely to keep longer hours. Food shops along roads leading to dormitory/suburb villages around major towns are open beyond 7pm, often until 9.30pm. In August, all filling stations close down for a week, with a rota in place ensuring that at least a few are open at any given time.

In **the North**, summer hours are supposedly 8am–1.30pm and 2.30–6.30pm Monday to Friday, plus a morning session on Saturday, with mandatory closure on Wednesday afternoon and all Sunday, although supermarkets (defined, controversially, by size) may elect to open on Sunday. In winter, shops are meant to operate continuously 8am–6pm Monday to Saturday. Observance of schedules may be haphazard, with midday summer closures extending until 4pm. Some office-based professionals are taking to closing by 5pm, especially in winter.

Post

Post offices in **the South** are generally open Monday to Friday 7.30am–1.30pm plus Thursday 3–6pm except in July and August; in the four largest towns, a limited number of branches, listed in the guide, are open every weekday afternoon except Wednesday 3–6pm (4–7pm May–Sept; 3–5pm only in Plátres), as well as Saturday 8.30–10.30am.

Outgoing mail is reliable and invariably travels faster than incoming, though postage is not especially cheap. Stamps can also be purchased from newsagents, but they may not know exact rates for your destination. Count on five to seven days for post to arrive in the UK. Numbers of quaint colonial pillar-boxes survive, the royal monograms "GR" and "ER" still visible through coats of fresh yellow paint. The same central post offices which have afternoon services also usually have **poste restante** and **parcel** facilities.

In **Northern Cyprus**, most post offices are open in summer 7.30am–2pm and 4–6pm Monday to Friday, 8.30am–12.30pm Saturday, while in winter hours are 8am–1pm and 2–5pm Monday to Friday, 9am–noon on Saturday. **Outgoing mail** is tolerably quick (five to eight days to the UK), considering that it has to be shuffled through Turkey to get around the international postal union boycott; despite this, North Cyprus issues its own stamps. As in the South, look for red or faded yellow kerbside pillar-boxes. **Parcels** are easily sent from Nicosia, Famagusta or Kyrenia. **Poste restante** service is theoretically available in these three towns.

Shopping

Cyprus is not a souvenir hunter's paradise, but there are certain items worth looking out for. See also the note on bargaining on p.68.

The **South** is most famous for **lacework**, produced principally at Páno Léfkara, equidistant from the three largest towns, but

---

Sending mail to North Cyprus

Because of the international postal union boycott of North Cyprus, all mail is initially routed through Turkey. When sending anything to North Cyprus, you must add a special qualifier – **Mersin 10, Turkey** – to the last line of the address (this designates the tenth county of Mersin province – further support for the contention that North Cyprus has been subject to creeping annexation by Turkey). If you fail to do so, the item may be misdirected to the South or more likely to the "addressee unknown" bin.

it's worth bearing in mind that this drawn-thread work no longer uses local materials (preferring Irish linen) and can be presented alongside "hand-made" tape lace from the Far East that's actually machine-produced. Léfkara **silverware** is more reliable and affordable, while attractive, colourful **loom-woven items** are available in Páfos district.

Basketry is the Cypriot craft and souvenir par excellence. Traditionally women's work, products are hand-made from various grasses, grain straws and palm fronds, with only an awl as a tool. Of particular interest are the almost Amerindian-looking, bi- or tri-colour circular mats (*tséstos* in Greek, from Italian *cesta*), which adorn the walls of many tavernas, or are used as shallow trays (*panéri*). You can find them at the central markets of Nicosia, Páfos and Limassol, as well as at Yeroskípou and Liopétri villages. Another taverna-decor staple which can be purchased are *kolótzia* or **etched gourds**, their designs either painted or burned on.

Urban specialities include **shoes**, **silver jewellery** and (in particular) **optical goods**. High-quality sunglasses at the numerous opticians cost about the same as in North America, owing to direct importation, and thus much less than in Britain. Moreover, speciality products such as high-diopter plastic lenses for registered blind persons can be obtained reasonably and quickly from warehouse stock (often within 24hrs), as opposed to a month on special order in Britain.

The government-run **Cyprus Handicraft Service** has several fixed-price retail outlets, which gather together under one roof "approved" examples of each craft. It's worth stopping in to gauge quality and cost at the very least; addresses are given below.

Cyprus handicraft centres

Larnaca Kosmá Lysióti 6
℡24630327
Limassol Themídhos 25 ℡25330118
Páfos Apostólou Pávlou 64
℡26240243
South Nicosia Athalássas 186
℡22305024; Laïkí Yitoniá
℡22303065

There is rather less on offer in the **North**, though Léfkara-type **lace** is made, while the basketry products (*sesta* or *paneri* in Turkish) seem more refined, and comparatively expensive. You can find very strong, large **baskets** suitable for clothes hampers in north Nicosia and the village of Edremit, though as in the South items tend to be made elsewhere, in the remote villages of Serdarlı, Gönendere and Görneç. Junk and antique dealers in Nicosia and Famagusta have a limited and expensive stock of **old copper and household implements**. The North's answer to the Cyprus Handicraft Service, opposite the Ali Ruhi Efendi fountain in North Nicosia, is the **Folk Arts Institute** (🅦www.hasder.com/last/).

Otherwise you are faced with the task of sifting through abundant second-rate **kitsch** (garish backgammon sets, thin-gauge copper lanterns, onyx eggs, ceramic ashtrays, frankly bad carpets), imported from Syria and Turkey, lying in wait for tourists insisting on something "Oriental".

Time

Two hours ahead of GMT, and seven hours ahead of EST. Clocks go forward one hour for summer time at 2am on the last Sunday in March and back again at 2am on the last Sunday in October. A recorded time message can be heard by dialling ℡193 in the South.

Toilets

In the South, these are found in parks, on coastal esplanades, etc; sometimes there's a small fee. They tend to close by 5pm from October to April. In the North, pay toilets are well signposted in strategic crannies of Kyrenia harbour, Famagusta old town and Nicosia, but you'll prefer to use restaurant and hotel loos. When present, bowl-side baskets are for collecting paper which would block temperamental drains.

Tourist information

Before leaving home it's worth stopping in at the tourist office of whichever part of Cyprus you intend to visit, since their stock of brochures and maps is often better than what's to be found once you're on the island. The **Cyprus Tourism Organisation** (CTO, www.visitcyprus.com) of the internationally recognized Republic of Cyprus (the South), with longer experience of such things, not surprisingly showers you with an avalanche of professionally presented and often useful material on every conceivable topic; the **North Cyprus Tourist Office**'s offerings (www.northcyprus.cc), are less slick and far less substantial, though the website itself is quite professional.

Among **CTO brochures** to look out for are the *Guide to Hotels and Other Tourist Establishments*, a massive compendium of virtually every licensed hotel and hotel-apartment in the South, plus travel agencies and car-rental firms, published each March but often delayed; *A Guide to Traditional Holiday Homes*, for restored, high-standard houses in the interior; the not necessarily annual *Cyprus Travellers Handbook*, containing nuts-and-bolts facts, rules and handy addresses; *Cyprus: Follow the E4 and other Nature Trails*, a summary (with maps) of all prepared hiking routes; and *Domestic Transport Services*, a complete tally of bus and taxi schedules and fares between the major towns and resorts, appearing annually between February and May.

The CTO has **tourist offices** in the Republic of Cyprus at Nicosia, Limassol, Larnaca, Páfos, Ayía Nápa and (March–Oct) Plátres. Hours are typically Monday to Friday 8.15am–2.30pm, plus Monday, Tuesday, Thursday and Friday 3–6.30pm, and Saturday 8.15am–1.30pm, with small local variations; exact addresses and schedules are given in the text.

Essential **North Cyprus publications** include a folding map, which in addition to showing all villages as renamed in North Cyprus, also indicates most of the southern villages from which the refugee Turkish Cypriots came. There's also the annual *Hotel Guide of Northern Cyprus*, produced by the hoteliers' association, which however isn't necessarily exhaustive. At the time of writing no detailed city plans for Girne, Lefkoşa and Gazimağusa, as Kyrenia, Nicosia and Famagusta are called in Turkish, were available other than rather crude ones on the tourism website.

North Cypriot **tourist offices** are found only in Kyrenia, Famagusta, Nicosia and

(seasonally) Yenierenköy; theoretical hours are given in the guide but, especially during the off-season, they are often shut when they shouldn't be. It's wise to call at their closest overseas branch before departure.

Cyprus tourism offices abroad

The Republic of Cyprus

UK CTO, 17 Hanover St, London W1S 1YP ☎020/7569 8800, ✉ctolon@ctolon.demon .co.uk
USA CTO, 13 East 40th St, First Floor, New York, NY 10016 ☎212/683-5280, ✉gocyprus @aol.com
Netherlands Cyprus Verkeersbureau, Prinsengracht 600, 1017 KS Amsterdam ☎020/624 4358, ✉cyprus.sun@wxs.nl
Sweden Cypriotiska Statens Turistbyrå, Norrlandsgatan 20 103 86 Stockholm ☎08 10 50 25, ✉info@ctosweden.org

North Cyprus

UK North Cyprus Tourist Office, 29 Bedford Square, London WC1B 3ED ☎020/7631 1930, ✉info @northcyprus.cc
US 1667 K St NW, Suite 690, Washington DC, 20006 ☎202 8876198, ✉trncdc@verizon.com

Useful websites

With the exception of sites under "General and bicommunal", the division of Cyprus is reflected as starkly in its internet representation as in its print and broadcast media (see p.59), with many websites propagandizing (subtly or otherwise) on behalf of one side or the other.

The South

www.**kypros.org** aka Kypros-Net; news, music downloads, live radio streams, online Greek lessons, and other titbits from the southern Republic.
www.**moi.gov.cy/moi/pio/pio.nsf/index_en /index_en?opendocument** The official web page of the southern Republic, maintained by the Public Information Office; essentially the utterances, and comings and goings, of officialdom.
stravara.blogspot.com/ Aka "Stavaramas". Very funny, irreverent blog-site on all things Cypriot, much of it in English – probably the best online read for news and culture, though it helps to know a bit about the island beforehand.

Ⓦ www.mcw.gov.cy/mcw/da/da.nsf
/DMLindex_en/DMLindex_en?OpenDocument
The Department of Antiquities; excellent for
potted summaries of museum collections and
archeological sites.

The North

Ⓦ www.trncwashdc.org The official voice of the
North, though US-originated and maintained, with
good general information.
Ⓦ www.hamamboculeri.org The main
alternative online forum in the North, with blogs and
articles in English and Turkish.

General and bicommunal

Ⓦ https://www.cia.gov/library/publications
/the-world-factbook/geos/cy.html The
online *CIA World Factbook* entry, with statistical
information on the geography, population, economy
and political situation of both halves of the
island; an astonishing amount of trivia, much of it
interesting and useful.
Ⓦ www.friendsofcyprus.org.uk/ Displays most
contents of the recommended FoC annual report,
but there's usually a lag of some months before the
most current issue is digitized.
Ⓦ www.cyprus-conflict.net/www.cyprus
-conflict.net/intro%20page.html Far and away
the best and most objective site on how Cyprus
got to the state it's in, with collected articles by
recognized experts.

Travellers with disabilities

Hotels in the South are excellent for the
wheelchair-bound, with plenty of ramps and
lifts; the North is less equipped, but many of
the low-rise bungalow complexes are intrin-
sically well suited for people with mobility
problems. Both sides rate less well in
catering for those with sight problems: too
many shiny marble bank floors, not enough
stripes at stair edges, or audio-pips at
pedestrian crossings (themselves nonexistent in the North).

Weather reports

Ⓦ www.cyprus-weather.com has five-day
forecasts for five points in the South, while
Ⓦ weather.yahoo.com/regional/CYXX.htm
includes two stations in the North as well.

Weights and measures

The southern Republic went completely
metric in 1987, while in North Cyprus a few
imperial units (eg miles) still linger. There are
two Ottoman holdovers on both sides of the
Line: the *dönüm* (Tr)/*skála* (Gr), a measure of
land equal to about a third of an acre, and
the *oka* (same in Gr/Tr) equal to 2.8 pounds
in weight and still used in food markets.

Work

Planning to work for someone else is pretty
much a non-starter anywhere on the island;
employers can only hire foreigners (except as
bar-girls) after satisfying the authorities that
the help cannot be recruited locally. Any
labour shortages in **the South**'s tourism,
construction or agricultural sectors are filled
by either EU nationals from countries which
joined 2004–07, Turkish Cypriots who cross
the Line in huge numbers daily, and South
Asians (typically Sri Lankans and Bangladeshis) hired on short-term contracts and
treated miserably, paid one-fourth the
statutory minimum wage and deported
instantly if they make any fuss. There are also
numbers of Russians, Moldovans, Ukrainians, Lebanese and Egyptians, to name the
most conspicuous other nationalities. Brits at
work in resorts are invariably **tour-group
couriers** recruited and paid from abroad, or
those with special skills (eg, scuba-diving
instructors). Generally, expats are self-
employed in the service sector (pet sitting,
villa maintenance, "consultancy", etc).

Opportunities for work in **Northern Cyprus**
are even more limited; again your only chance
is to start a business with imported capital,
such as a windsurfing or ballet school, where
locals can't or won't compete.

The South

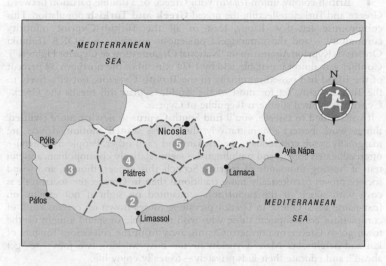

Introduction

The foundation of the island-wide **Republic of Cyprus** in 1960 was a compromise solution to a Gordian knot of imperial, regional, Cold War and ethnic problems. Independence was the alternative to remaining a British colony, union (*énosis*) with Greece or a double partition between Greece and Turkey, reflecting the mixed **Greek and Turkish** population. This compromise left few happy, least of all the Turkish-Cypriot minority community – and the intransigent pro-énosis guerrillas in EOKA (Ethnikí Orgánosis Kypríon Agonistón or "National Organization of Cypriot Fighters"). Conflict was almost inevitable, and by 1974 control of the northern 38 percent of the island had passed nominally to the Turkish Cypriots, but effectively to the Turkish army. Yet for most of the world, Cyprus still means the Greek-Cypriot-inhabited southern Republic of Cyprus.

If you're used to Greece, you'll find South Cyprus somewhat more civilized: things work better; administratively, there's less wasted motion; drivers are marginally more courteous to pedestrians and each other. People in general – often educated abroad and multilingual – seem relatively cosmopolitan, a useful trait if hosting thousands of tourists. Scratch this veneer, though, and island society proves paradoxically more traditional than in Greece: the social scale is cosy, with much of the population acquainted on sight if not exactly on first-name basis. Unlike in Greece, prevailing mores frown on certain kinds of conspicuous consumption; those who wish to gamble or spend a night on the town go to Greece or northern Cyprus, away from the censorious tongues of kin and neighbours. Many Cypriots are too busy working two jobs – to "get ahead", and educate their kids privately – to really enjoy life.

Until the 1980s Cyprus was very much like Ireland, both in its bipolar ethno-religious conflict and its suffocating provinciality. The village was the core social unit; women were expected to "know their place", which meant never working for non-family members; and, until recent scandals disgraced it, the **Orthodox Church** remained enormously influential, tapping a vein of uncomplicated, fervent faith co-existing with the worldliness.

Despite a politically motivated Hellenization campaign in the South since the early 1990s, and the dominance of Greek franchises in banking, petrol stations and fast-food outlets, there is little love lost between Greek Cypriots and continental Greeks. The latter are generally referred to in Cyprus as *kalamarádhes*, and the mainland dialect as *kalamarístika*. These terms arose in the 1800s, when schoolmasters from peninsular Greece first introduced "proper" Greek to the island; these purveyors of linguistic rectitude were dubbed *kalamarádhes* (quill-wielders), after the main tool of their trade. Over time, the word came to apply, in a mixture of opprobrium and affection, to all mainlanders, especially Greek army officers on the island during the 1960s. Some wear the label as a badge of honour, but it's most often prefixed indivisibly by *poústi* (literally "sodomite", in effect "untrustworthy bastard").

The troubled republic

Both parochialism and internationalism were exhibited to destructive effect over the **fourteen turbulent years** between independence in 1960 and the

1974 catastrophe. Power-sharing between the two communities, regulated by a meticulously detailed constitution, had by 1964 collapsed in an orgy of recriminations and violence orchestrated by EOKA and its Turkish counterpart **TMT** (*Türk Mukavemet Teskilati* or "Turkish Resistance Organization"). The island was further destabilized with meddling by "mother" countries Greece and Turkey; soon the superpowers and the UN were inextricably involved.

Cyprus limped along as a unitary state for ten more years, albeit with a thoroughly poisoned civic life: Turkish Cypriots withdrew into a series of TMT-defended **enclaves**, while the Greek Cypriots retaliated by severely restricting traffic in goods or persons in or out. Feeble reconciliatory overtures alternated with fresh incidents, but Cypriot society was already split, with Turkish Cypriots relegated to second-class citizenship in their laagers.

When **all-out war** erupted in July 1974, only the exact timing and details came as a surprise. At the instigation of the military junta then ruling Greece, **EOKA-B**, successor to EOKA, staged a coup aimed at effecting *énosis*; in response the Turkish army, technically acting as guarantor of the island's independence, landed on the north coast and instead presided over de facto **partition**. The Greek Cypriots fled, or were expelled, from the North, the population of the scattered Turkish-Cypriot enclaves soon replacing them.

In the **aftermath of the war**, all Cyprus was prostrate, with both ethnic communities demoralized and fearful, and the economy in tatters. The South was particularly hard hit: about 160,000 Greek Cypriots had immediately fled the North, to be followed within a few years by 20,000 more. The Turkish army held the most productive portions of the island, assiduously developed since 1960: the Greek Cypriots lost the fertile citrus groves around Mórfou, busy Famagusta port with its bulging warehouses, and lucrative tourist facilities in Kyrenia and Varósha. Southern unemployment stood at forty percent until 1976, with the added burden of providing emergency shelter for the refugees.

South Cyprus today

Since 1974, the South has wrought an **economic miracle** – at a price. Developing the hitherto untouched southern coast for tourism, with few zoning restraints and maximum financial returns, was seen as the quickest fix for a dire predicament. Until around the millennium, **tourism** was the country's biggest foreign-currency earner, with all-too-plain results: hideous unbroken strips of low-to-medium-rise blocks around Larnaca, Limassol, Ayía Nápa and Páfos.

Inland, crash programmes rehoused refugees in often shoddily built **housing estates**, with only a rising standard of living diminishing the appeal of a return to the North. The relocation of nearly a third of the Orthodox population meant overcrowding (artificial, given the relative emptiness of North Cyprus) and inflated property prices. Private, speculative development took precedence over delayed, underfunded public works. Much of the countryside is now for sale to the highest bidder, and phalanxes of **villas** sprout anywhere passingly desirable. Since 1998, road-improvement works have reached the remotest corners of the South, either serving villas already there or encouraging more to take root. The momentum for this is the huge indebtedness of developers – sales of apartment and villa developments assist cash-flow during recent years of sluggish conventional tourism, and indeed **residential tourism** is seen as the future as ground-breaking for hotels slows or even stops.

All this threatens not just how Cyprus looks, but its basic **environment**. On an island permanently short of water – indeed rationed by 2008, and imported from Greece – supplies no longer suffice for residential or agricultural needs, let alone tourism, yet somehow enough is found for "water-parks" at Limassol and

Ayía Nápa, and golf courses near Limassol and Páfos. There are periodic signs of a token rethink, as conservationists organize to protect remaining unspoiled landscapes and to promote human-scale tourism; a single Green MP, the island's first has served from 2001 onwards. The government has provided muddled direction: while one agency proposed national parks, the tourism authority long adhered to a policy of encouraging five-star, high-impact tourist installations. In 1995, a moratorium was imposed on new accommodation construction, essentially freezing the number of licensed tourist beds in the South at just over 80,000 – though this had been rescinded by 1998. Cut-rate package tourism is seen as damaging the social and environmental fabric, but since 2004 there have not been enough customers at luxury facilities to justify their multiplication. The compromise – "**agrotourism**", mostly in Páfos district and the Tróödhos foothills, comprising just a few hundred beds – has had merely symbolic impact. Many long-standing Cyprus fans are staying away, as the "product" goes increasingly mass-market despite protestations of "quality" from the Cyprus Tourism Organization. The new wave of clients often opt for one-week stays rather than two – or make a beeline for one of the thousands of estate agents and join the ranks of part-time residents.

Offsetting this dependency on volatile tourism patterns, the demise of nearby Beirut as a business centre provided a welcome windfall for Cyprus. The South is now established as a popular venue for **international conferences**, and – thanks to its taxation policies and reliable infrastructure – as a base for **offshore companies**, though EU membership put a stop to the dodgier among these. Liaisons begun in the heyday of the non-aligned movement, and the traditional importance of AKEL (the local Communist Party), continue to pay dividends in relations with eastern Europe, Africa and the Middle East. Starting in the 1990s, Russian "investment" – mostly **money** in need of **laundering** – flooded into Cyprus, reflected in a rash of Cyrillic-alphabet restaurant menus, estate agent signs and tourist literature. For the most part, Cypriots welcome these big spenders, no questions asked; tales abound of Russians buying villas off-plan with a suitcase full of $100 bills. High-quality **medical care** is pitched at neighbouring countries as a reliable earner; it has also been developed as a matter of local need, since – like many isolated island populations – Cyprus is a massive incubator for debilitating genetic diseases such as thalassaemia, and the expat population here is on the elderly side, who (in part) chose Cyprus because of its medical facilities.

While all credit is due to the Greek Cypriots for reviving their part of the island, there's no denying that much of the recovery was subsidized by **foreign aid**. Only the southern Republic belongs to such multinational bodies as UNESCO, the EU and the World Bank, and has thus been eligible for direct assistance from those organizations. Light **industrialization** resumed after 1976, mostly geared towards export markets. General economic growth has been impressive, resulting in an unskilled **labour shortage**. As a result, the South is one of the most cosmopolitan places on earth, its huge (and growing) foreign workforce a veritable Tower of Babel. It's possible to holiday here and never meet a native Cypriot, since front-of-house staff at hotels and restaurants are ninety percent Sri Lankan, Pakistani, Indian, Georgian or from various central European newer EU nations. Largely unrepresented by local unions, they're often treated appallingly, with sexual harassment and other abuse common – none more so than legions of cabaret *artistes* (a code word for **prostitutes**), brought here on six-month renewable visas. The lucky ones save enough for down payments on property back home, or escape the brothel system by marrying (or becoming the mistress of) a Cypriot.

Despite retaining its original name, the contemporary Republic of Cyprus is a fundamentally different country: all but mono-ethnic (disregarding the burgeoning foreign population), yet *énosis* having been completely eclipsed by the quasi-*énosis* with Greece afforded by joint EU membership; its 1960 constitution a dead letter; and public life preoccupied with *Tó Kypriakó* (**Cyprus Question**) – the imposed partition of the island. Until the dramatic events of 2003–04 (see p.82 & p.407), posters and graffiti referred obsessively to the 1974 events, as did periodic demonstrations, heartfelt enough to need little stage-managing (though they were inevitably exploited by nationalist ideologues). The theore-tical right of Greek Cypriots refugees to return to the North has been the most emotionally charged issue, though it seems that very few would actually do so. Nostalgically named refugee clubs attempt to link the generation born in exile with ancestral towns, and maintain community solidarity for a possible day of repatriation. Telephone directories still list numbers in the North as they were before July 1974, and the official hotel guide pointedly cites Famagusta and Kyrenia hotels as named before the Turkish intervention, without, however, giving any practical details.

The South on the defensive

Lacking the military means to expel the Turkish army, the South instead exploited its monopoly in world forums to launch a relentless propaganda campaign against, and **boycott** of, the Turkish Republic of Northern Cyprus (TRNC) in an attempt to bring it to heel. Ire has been directed at Turkey, too, in overseas court cases demanding that vanished property or persons be accounted for. When advised this was unlikely to create a favourable climate for reconciliation, the South retorted that giving North Cyprus more breathing space would remove any incentive for it to come to terms.

With the benefit of hindsight, some Greek Cypriots have belatedly recognized the wisdom of generous gestures towards the Turkish Cypriots, initiatives unthinkable before 1974. Despite the official campaign against the TRNC, many (in private, anyway) willingly **admit past errors**: in particular, there's widespread revulsion at the activities of EOKA-B, which during its brief 1974 reign killed more Greek Cypriots than Turkish Cypriots. A retrospectively rosy view of intercommunal relations before 1960 prevails, but whether this is genuine or promulgated to counter Northern pessimism is debatable.

Officially the southern Republic is still **bicommunal**, though fewer than three thousand island-born Turkish Cypriots – less than half a percent of the population – still live there (albeit significantly increased since the late 1990s, and dwarfed by the estimated 15,000 Turkish Cypriots who now commute daily from North to South to work). Many public signs remain trilingual in Greek, Turkish and English; radio and TV broadcast Turkish-language programmes; the official languages of university instruction are Greek and Turkish (not English, as in the North); the eighty-seat parliament currently functions with only 56 deputies, the balance reserved for hypothetical Turkish-Cypriot representatives as per the 1960 constitution. Pre-2008 official negotiating proposals envisioned generous constitutional concessions on condition that Turkish Cypriots embrace federation and drop their insistence on separate states. But the model put forth – that of Belgium – is hardly one to emulate, given the simmering ethnic tensions and governmental paralysis there.

The Southern government tried to prevent the South's 44,039 **Turkish Cypriots** from **departing** – voluntarily or otherwise – to the North in early 1975, correctly fearing that Turkey would deem this a quid pro quo for the involuntary expulsion of Northern Greeks. It is increasingly common for Turkish Cypriots to **return**, which they do as much to escape misery in the North as out of any "patriotic" feeling. Once in the South, their reception can be ambivalent: while theoretically welcomed as a tiny reversal of the island's apartheid, they are also distrusted as potential spies, and many end up living on the margins of society, involved in off-the-record or low-prospect work with little job security, and smuggling contraband to the North.

All immovable **property** of Southern Turkish Cypriots is technically held in trust by the government, which stands accused of not adequately protecting the interests of their owners. Current Greek-Cypriot occupiers have only rental agreements with departed Turkish-Cypriot owners, but commercial rents especially are at risibly low levels, and many city-dwellers illegally renovate and squat Turkish-Cypriot country houses as weekend retreats. In several instances Turkish-Cypriot land was built over by the government to house refugees, and court cases have been filed by aggrieved Turkish-Cypriot owners, mirroring the more famous suits pursued by dispossessed Greek Cypriots.

Events since 2003

All existing parameters were in part overtaken by the milestone events of April 2003 to February 2008. In order of occurrence if not significance, they were the sudden **opening of the "border"** dividing the island, on April 23, 2003, to pretty much unrestricted travel; an island-wide **referendum** on April 24, 2004, on the UN-promulgated **Annan Plan** for a federal solution; the Republic of Cyprus's **joining the EU** on May 1, 2004; and obstructionist President Tasos **Papadopoulos' surprise defeat** in the February 2008 election. Freedom of movement permitted a reality check for all concerned, after years of nostalgia and demonization; vast numbers of people (on both sides) went back to look at their ancestral properties and consider "what to do if ...", while interaction between Greek and Turkish Cypriots as "tourists" in the others' territory was remarkable for its civility. However, despite reconciliation on a personal level, this did not translate into a political solution. For reasons analysed on p.409, the Annan Plan was approved in the North by a 2:1 margin – but defeated in the South by a thumping 3:1 (both communities had to vote "yes"). EU officials, hoping to welcome a Cyprus en route to a solution, were incandescent, feeling the Republic had manoeuvred itself into the "Europe of 25" on Papadopoulos' insincere assurances that he would guarantee a "yes" vote in the referendum. As the Turkish Cypriots had often complained about in the past, the South would yet again speak for the whole island in an important multinational body – a prime example of the long-running gap in understandings as to what constitutes the appropriate roles of communities and central government on Cyprus. Indeed, many opined that EU membership came prematurely for the Republic, which somewhat awkwardly toed the line on myriad matters ranging from the trivial to the fundamental: no more eating songbirds (in public), tormenting homosexuals, or making Turkish Cypriots queue separately from Greek Cypriots when crossing from North to South. With the election of AKEL-affiliated President **Demetris Christofias** in early 2008, prospects for a comprehensive political settlement – and application of EU norms to the entire island – seem more promising than ever.

1

Larnaca and around

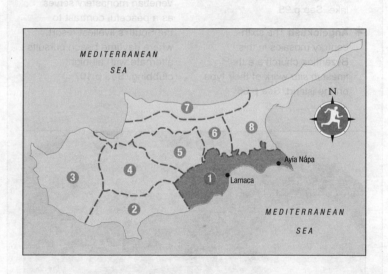

CHAPTER 1 # Highlights

✳ **Pierides Museum** The collection at this privately run museum in central Larnaca overshadows those at many state-run archeological museums. See p.91

✳ **Hala Sultan Tekke** A stereotypically Middle Eastern tomb and mosque further enlivened after wet winters by flamingos in the adjacent salt lake. See p.95

✳ **Angelóktisti** The sixth-century mosaics in this Byzantine church are the finest *in situ* work of their type on the island. See p.96

✳ **Khirokitia** The largest and most completely excavated Neolithic town on Cyprus. See p.100

✳ **Áyios Andónios, Kelliá** This hilltop church contains some of the oldest and most unusual Byzantine frescoes on the island. See p.105

✳ **Ayía Nápa** A central Venetian monastery serves as a peaceful contrast to the South's liveliest resort, where daytime beach pursuits alternate with all-night clubbing. See p.107

▲ Mosaic of the Virgin, Angelóktisti

Larnaca and around

The southeastern flank of Cyprus, centred on Larnaca, is still the most touristed portion of the island: a result of the 1974 Turkish invasion, and the subsequent conversion of hitherto sleepy Larnaca airfield into the southern republic's main international airport. Aside from its hilly western part, the district isn't particularly scenic – not that this bothers most patrons of the burgeoning resorts, who seldom venture far from the clear, warm sea and their self-contained hotels.

Despite being a short motorway drive from two mega-resorts at the island's southeastern tip, the district capital of **Larnaca** still claims its share of local tourism, though increasing industrialization – and the possibility that Varosha (see p.344) might soon be rehabilitated – shadows its future as a holiday destination. However, just southwest of town lie two of the most appealing, and most easily accessible, monuments in the area: the Muslim shrine of **Hala Sultan Tekke** by Larnaca's salt lake, and the mosaic-graced Byzantine church of **Angelóktisti** at Kíti. **Perivólia**, on the approach to **Cape Kíti**, is perhaps the last human-scale resort in this part of the island. The coast beyond rewards only determined explorers; at the end of the line, little **Zíyi** port with its famous fish tavernas is just as accessible from the main Nicosia–Limassol expressway.

Inland and west in Larnaca district, attractions are scattered to either side of this highway. Neolithic **Khirokitia** is one of the oldest known habitations on Cyprus, and a visit can be easily twinned with one to **Páno Léfkara**, a picturesque village in the Tróödhos foothills, renowned for its handicrafts. More directly approached from Larnaca along a secondary road, the **Chapelle Royale** at Pýrga houses a rare example of Lusignan sacred mural art, and nearby **Stavrovoúni** is an equally unusual instance of a strictly penitential Cypriot Orthodox monastery. **Tókhni** and nearby **Kalavassós** on the inland side of the A1 expressway are among the district's more attractive villages, both now popular holiday bases thanks to some imaginative accommodation schemes taking advantage of their traditional architecture.

East of Larnaca, there is little specifically to recommend along the coast: the sandy crescent of Larnaca Bay and the British Sovereign Base Area of Dhekélia are each compromised in their own way. Things only look up at the two overgrown resorts to either side of **Cape Gréko**: though by no means the largest permanent community, **Ayía Nápa** mushrooms in season to become the busiest clubbers' resort in the area, while the strip at **Protarás** to the northeast is slightly more upmarket and Cypriot-orientated.

With Larnaka as a base, it's easy to make several full- or half-day trips to surrounding attractions. But to do this with any degree of flexibility, you'll need

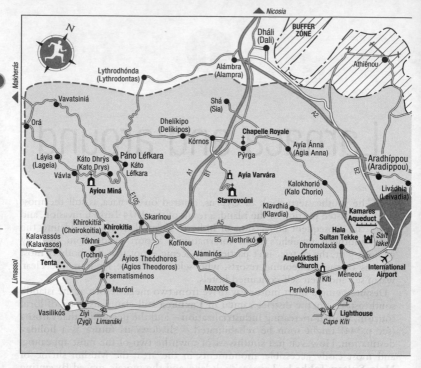

a car, for while public transport links the city with most of the sites detailed, there are few connections between them. Outside Larnaca, Ayía Nápa and Protarás, **accommodation** can be found at Perivólia, Kalavassós, Tókhni, Vávla, modern Khirokitiá and Páno Léfkara.

Larnaca (Larnaka)

LARNACA (officially **LARNAKA** since 1996) retains little tangible evidence of its eventful history, and today presents a somewhat uneasy combination of commercial port, yacht marina and second-division tourist centre, most popular with Scandinavian and Arab visitors. Gone is the romantic town depicted in eighteenth-century engravings, with only furnace-like summer heat, an adjacent (often dry) salt lake and palm trees imparting a nostalgic Levantine touch.

Such growth as has occurred in recent decades is primarily due to regional catastrophe; numbers were first swelled by Greek refugees from Famagusta in 1974, and a year or two later by Lebanese Christians fleeing the strife in their homeland. Perhaps the most bizarre recent arrivals – given Cyprus's ban on Jewish settlement from Roman times to the early British era – is a community of Lubavitcher Hassidic Jews. With a permanent population of about 75,000, Larnaca is just half the size of Limassol, and more characterized by town-based tourism, though this is still dwarfed by the coastal resort zone at Voróklini just to the northeast.

Some history

The site of Larnaca was originally colonized by Mycenaeans in the thirteenth century BC, but had declined, like many other Mediterranean towns, by about 1000 BC. It emerged again as **Kition** two centuries later, re-established by the Phoenicians, and resumed its role as a port shipping copper mined at Tamassos and elsewhere in the eastern Tróödhos. A subsequent period of great prosperity was complicated by the city's staunch championing of the Persian cause on Cyprus: Kimon of Athens, heading a fleet sent in 450 BC to reduce Kition, died outside the wall in the hour of what proved to be a transient victory. Persian influence only ended with the Hellenistic takeover of the whole island a century later, a period which also saw the birth of Kition's most famous son, the Stoic philosopher **Zeno**.

Christianity came early to Kition, traditionally in the person of **Lazarus**, the man resurrected by Christ at Bethany. Irate Pharisees tried to dispose of the evidence of this miracle by casting Lazarus adrift in a leaky boat; he supposedly landed here to become the city's first bishop and, following his (definitive) death, its patron saint. After an otherwise uneventful passage through the Roman and early Byzantine eras, Kition suffered the same seventh-century Arab raids as other Cypriot coastal settlements. It didn't really recover until the fifteenth century and the end of the Lusignan era, when the Genoese appropriation of nearby Famagusta prompted merchants to move here to take advantage of the small port; by now the anchorage was called **Salina** or **Les Salines**, after the salt lake just inland.

The name **Larnaca**, derived from *larnax* (a sarcophagus or urn, of which there were plenty to hand from various periods of the town's past), only gained wide

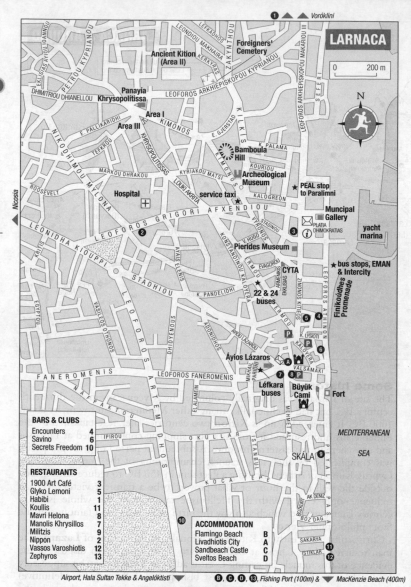

Voróklini

LARNACA

0   200 m

N

Foreigners'
Cemetery

Ancient Kition
(Area II)

Panayía
Khrysopolítissa

Area I

Area III

Bamboula
Hill

Archeological
Museum

Hospital

service taxi

★ PEAL stop
to Paralimni

Muncipal
Gallery

PLATIA
DHIMOKRATIAS

yacht
marina

Pierides Museum

CYTA

★ bus stops, EMAN
& Intercity

22 & 24
buses

Finikoúdhes
Promenade

Áyios Lázaros

Léfkara
buses

Büyük
Cami

Fort

MEDITERRANEAN
SEA

SKÁLA

BARS & CLUBS

Encounters	4
Savino	6
Secrets Freedom	10

RESTAURANTS

1900 Art Café	3
Glyko Lemoni	5
Habibi	1
Koullis	11
Mavri Helona	8
Manolis Khrysillos	7
Militzis	9
Nippon	2
Vassos Varoshiotis	12
Zephyros	13

ACCOMMODATION

Flamingo Beach	B
Livadhiotis City	A
Sandbeach Castle	C
Sveltos Beach	D

Airport, Hala Sultan Tekke & Angelóktisti ▼   B, C, D, 13, Fishing Port (100m) & ▼ MacKenzie Beach (400m)

currency at the start of Ottoman rule. By the eighteenth century Larnaca was the premier port and trade centre of the island, briefly eclipsing Nicosia in population, with numerous foreign consuls in residence. Around the consuls gathered the largest foreign community on the island, leading lives of elegant and eccentric provinciality, the inspiration for countless travel accounts of the time. In 1878 the British landed here to take over administration of Cyprus, and it was not until after World War II that Larnaca again fell behind Famagusta and Limassol in importance.

Arrival, orientation and information

Landing at busy Larnaca **airport** (set to have a new terminal 500m west of the existing one by 2011), you'll find a **CTO** office open for all arrivals – usually around the clock – and ample exchange facilities, including two **ATMs**. If you don't have a rented car awaiting you as part of a fly-drive arrangement, there are a half-dozen rental booths in the arrivals area. **Municipal buses** #22 or #24 (the former labelled "Makenzy-Tekkes-Airport") run into town up to seven times daily in season (Mon–Sat 8am–5pm; Wed & Sat till noon only), dropping you on Ermoú. Alternatively, a taxi into town shouldn't cost much more than €10 at day rates – a placard in arrivals lists legitimate rates to common destinations.

Larnaca's street plan is confusing, with numerous jinks, one-ways and name changes, though the sea is always due east, with two north–south boulevards paralleling it. The palm-tree esplanade of **Finikoúdhes**, officially **Leofóros Athinón**, has always been the focus of the tourist industry and, towards its north end, hosts a few important inter-city **bus terminals**. **Platía Dhimokratías** (formerly, and still occasionally mapped as Platía Vassiléos Pávlou) is home to the not wildly helpful **CTO office** (Mon–Fri 8.15am–2.30pm, Sat 8.15am–1.30pm, plus Mon, Tues, Thurs & Fri 3–6.30pm). From here, **Leofóros Grigóri Afxendíou** runs out to the Nicosia and Limassol roads. Running parallel to the sea front, **Zínonos Kitiéos** leads south to the diagonal junction with **Ermoú** and, via the alleyways of the bazaar, indirectly to **Platía Ayíou Lazárou**, home to its ornate namesake church and more bus stops. **Ayíou Lazárou**, later **Stadhíou**, reaches the roundabout that gives onto both the Nicosia road and **Leofóros Artemídhos** to the airport and beyond along the coast.

Comprehensive one-way systems can prove a nightmare for drivers. Moreover, **parking** in the centre, on a pay-and-display basis, is pretty well confined to a large purpose-built structure on Valsamáki, about 200m inland from the Finikoúdhes, plus a few apparently unattended open-air lots nearby – where wardens appear as if by magic to demand fees.

Accommodation

The **accommodation** situation in Larnaca for those showing up on spec is not great, though slightly better than in Limassol or Ayía Nápa. Budget lodgings are unsavoury to non-existent; for a bit more you'll get a relatively quiet sleep and some sea breeze (maybe a sea view) south of the town centre along Piyale Pada towards Mackenzie Beach, the rather meagre strip of sand preceding the airport. Larger resort hotels (from three–five stars) are located at Voróklini, 5–8km along the coast to the northeast (see p.106).

Flamingo Beach Piyale Paşa 152, 400m past the fishing port, just opposite the start of Mackenzie Beach ☎ 24828208, ⓦ www.flamingobeachcyprus .com. One of Larnaca's better in-town three-star hotels, under new management in 2008; there's a rooftop pool, air con, lobby wi-fi and on-site cafeteria, while all rooms have an oblique balcony view of the sea. Frequent internet discounts. From ❸

Livadhiotis City Hotel Nikoláou Róssou 50 ☎ 24626222, ⓦ www.livadhiotis.com. Unbeatably located businessmen's hotel, renovated in 2007, with medium-sized, veneer-floored rooms and suites in a bright colour scheme. Internet in lobby; dataports in rooms. ❹

Sandbeach Castle Piyale Paşa, past the fishing port ☎ 24655437, ⓦ www.castlehotel.com.cy. Larnaca's only town hotel with its feet (and lovely dining terrace) in the sea, this small, mock-castle outfit was originally built in the 1930s as the colonial district commissioner's residence. Half the main-wing rooms face the sea, as do four newer bungalow units adjacent, with shared terrace. Open April–Nov. ❸

Sveltos Beach Hotel Apartments Piyale Paşa, south of the fishing port ☎ 24657240, ⓕ 24658334. Beachfront hotel apartments just south of the city limits; no pool. Studio ❷, two-bedroom apartment ❸

The City

Larnaca's minuscule old town is gamely struggling to reverse a long decline epitomized by the 1997 demolition of its old covered market to make way for an open-air car park – only the gateway and one external gallery of shops remains. Local boosters tout the Finikoúdhes esplanade with its over-pruned washingtonia palms as an echo of the French Riviera; viewed squintingly, after a few drinks, there might be some resemblance, but most will be hard pressed to find it among the mess of mediocre pubs, estate agents, billiard halls and fast-food outlets lining the shore. Between the two, a bar-crammed, pedestrianized "Laïkí Yitoniá" is optimistically modelled on the one in Nicosia. The only relatively upmarket post-millennium development is the restoration of several former customs warehouses on harbourfront Platía Evrópis as the **Larnaca Municipal Gallery** (Tues–Fri 9am–1pm & 4–6pm, Sat 10am–1pm, plus Oct–April Sun 10am–1pm; free), which has a changing programme of exhibitions by local and overseas artists.

The remaining sights – a much-revered church, a handsome mosque, two museums and an archeological zone – can be seen in a leisurely day, preferably a cool one, as they're scattered in such a way as to make use of the minimal city bus service difficult and a walking tour appealing.

Áyios Lázaros (Agios Lazaros) church

The most obvious start to a tour is landmark **Áyios Lázaros** (daily: April–Aug 8am–12.30pm & 3.30–6.30pm; Sept–March 8am–12.30pm & 2.30–5pm). Poised between the former Turkish and bazaar quarters, it was erected late in the ninth century to house the remains of Lazarus, fortuitously discovered here. The church is distinguished by its graceful Latinate belfry, part of a thorough seventeenth-century overhaul and a miraculous survival of Turkish rule; the Ottomans usually forbade such structures, considering their height a challenging insult to the minarets of Islam, and (more practically) fearing they would be used to proclaim insurrection. Indeed the church had to be ransomed from the conquerors in 1589, and was used for joint worship by Roman Catholics and Orthodox for two centuries after – as evidenced by Greek, Latin and French inscriptions in the Gothic-influenced portico, in addition to the earlier Byzantine and Lusignan coats of arms near the main south door.

The spare stone interior (consequence of a fire in 1970) contrasts with the busy decoration of many Cypriot churches; three small domes are supported on four double pillars, with narrow arches springing from wedged-in Corinthian capitals. The ornate carved *témblon* (altar screen), partly restored after the fire, and a Rococo pulpit on one pillar are some three hundred years old; on another pillar hangs a filigreed icon of Lazarus emerging from his tomb, an image reverently paraded every Easter Saturday evening.

The low-ceilinged crypt under the altar supposedly housed the relics of Lazarus only very briefly – they were taken to Constantinople by the Byzantine emperor Leo VI in 901, from where they were stolen, turning up later in Marseilles. But his purported tomb eventually formed part of a catacomb of general use, as witness several sarcophagi lying about. In the northeast corner of the outside compound are more graves in an enclosure – this time of foreign consuls, merchants and family members who died in Larnaca's unhealthy climate during the sixteenth to nineteenth centuries.

Skála, Finikoúdhes and the bazaar

Stretching from Áyios Lázaros almost to the fishing port, the extensive **Turkish quarter of Skála** has retained its old street names, but is now home to Greek

Orthodox refugees from Famagusta and the Kárpas villages. To judge from some impressive houses and bungalows, it seems the local Turks have been wealthier than in Páfos – but there are "chicken shacks" as well. Originally the late medieval church of the Holy Cross, the porticoed, flying-buttressed **Büyük Cami** (Cami Kebir), at the north end of the quarter, now sees regular use by the local Egyptian/Syrian/Iranian population. The mosque is open for visits during daylight hours, except at prayer hours, allowing you a glimpse of its arcaded, three-aisled interior, complete with wooden gallery. The minaret is now visibly cracked and scaffolded against imminent danger of collapse. The nearby **fort** (June–Aug Mon–Fri 9am–7.30pm; Sept–May Mon–Fri 9am–5pm; €1.70), a 1625 Ottoman refurbishment of a Lusignan castle, stands mostly empty at the south end of the Finikoúdhes, but its upper storey hosts a small medieval museum of armaments and pottery. The courtyard is also the occasional venue for summer evening events, when you can ponder the fact that before World War II the British used the fort as a prison. Immediately north of the fort stretches the **Finikoúdhes** promenade, with some more upmarket cafés at its north end. This in turn is fronted by the town beach – some 800m of gritty, hard-packed sand, well patronized despite its condition; you'll find somewhat better beaches either side of town, at Perivólia and Voróklini. The bulk of the **bazaar** sprawls north of Áyios Lázaros, though shopping options of most interest to visitors are discussed on p.94. Spare a glance for the unusual nineteenth-century **Zuhuri Cami** (literally, "Clown Mosque") with its double dome and truncated minaret at Nikólaou Róssou 27, now occupied by a not especially recommended youth hostel.

The Pierides Museum

Just off Platía Dhimokratías, the **Pierides Museum** (Mon–Thurs 9am–4pm, Fri & Sat 9am–1pm; €1.70) shares an old wooden house at Zínonos Kitiéos 4 with the Swedish consulate, and was reorganized in late 1994, though there are still a few unsorted, unlabelled display cases. The building was originally the home of Dhimitrios Pierides, who began his conservation efforts in 1839, using his wealth to ransom what archeological treasures he could from tomb plunderers, including the infamous Luigi Palma di Cesnola, first US consul at Larnaca.

Unlike Cyprus's state-run archeological museums, the well-lit collection, expanded by Pierides' descendants, ranges across the entire island, and is the best and most digestible ensemble for a complete overview of Cypriot culture through the ages. That said, it's strongest on Archaic terracottas, plus other unusual small objects that have escaped the attention of the official district museums. The half-dozen exhibition rooms are arranged both by theme and by period, with the earliest artefacts to the left as you enter.

Among the oldest items is the famous Chalcolithic (c.3000 BC) "**Howling Man**" from Souskiou, in the first gallery to the left. Liquid poured through his hollow head pees out of a prominent member; the mechanics give little clue as to whether he had a religious or secular function. Less unexpected are Archaic female statuettes brandishing drums and other votive offerings, left in shrines as "permanent worshippers".

There are numerous notable examples of painted **Archaic pottery**, especially one decorated with a so-called "astronaut" figure (beloved of extraterrestrial-visitation enthusiasts), bouncing on what appear to be springs or other mechanical devices, described here as a "stool". Among imported **painted Attic ware**, you'll find Theseus about to run the Minotaur through with his sword, while on another pot in the same glass case, two centaurs, emblems of lust, flank a courting couple. The collection of relatively rare Classical and Hellenistic **terracottas** includes a funerary reclining man from Marion, in perfect condition down to the fingers, and a model sarcophagus with three pull-out drawers; other oddities include a surprisingly delicate spoon among a trove of Early Bronze Age black incised ware. A room to the right of the main corridor – itself containing a superb collection of **antiquarian maps** of Cyprus and the Aegean – is devoted to **Byzantine and Lusignan pottery**, in particular brown- or green-glazed *sgraffito* ware. Perhaps the drollest etched-in design is a rampant Lusignan anthropomorphized lion, prefiguring Picasso.

In the "folklore" wing on the right at the rear, you'll find jewellery, embroidery and household utensils, as well as a finely carved polychrome desk and *armoire*. There are also numerous works by "naive" painter **Mikhaïl Kashalos**, killed aged 89 by the Turkish army at his village studio in 1974, including a canvas of the Green Line in 1964, complete with UN personnel.

The Archeological Museum

Larnaca's other significant collection, the **Archeological Museum**, stands a ten-minute walk away, north of Grigóri Afxendíou (Mon–Fri 9am–2.30pm, Sept–June also Thurs 3–5pm; €1.70). It's purpose-built, with excellent labelling, but you get a feeling that the collection comprises pickings and leavings compared to Nicosia's Cyprus Museum or the nearby Pierides – in the entry hall, for example, the curators have been reduced to displaying copies of a famous Artemis statue and funerary stele (the originals in Vienna and Berlin respectively).

Pre-eminent in the early exhibits is a reconstructed **Neolithic tomb** from Khirokhitia, complete with a stone atop the corpse's chest indicating a fear of revenants from the dead. Later exhibits illustrate how Late Bronze Age pottery, especially the so-called "white slip ware", prefigured the decorated dishes of the Geometric era. The fact that the latter were painted only on the outside (unless any inside designs were worn off by use) may indicate that they were meant to be hung up by their handles as decoration, like today's woven *tsésti* or trivets.

Vast amounts of **Mycenaean pottery** in the so-called "Rude" (ie rustic) Style, dug up at adjacent Kition, demonstrate Argolid settlement around 1200 BC; the prize exhibit is a fish *krater* (large wine goblet) from Áyios Dhimítrios near Kalavassós. Cypriot literacy dates to at least two centuries earlier, as evidenced by a display of Cypro-Minoan inscriptions (so far undeciphered), while a case of items imported towards the end of the Bronze Age demonstrates trade links at the same time. Among indigenous ware, there's an unusual clay torch from Pýla, and a clay brazier-pan from Athiénou – perhaps meant to heat bedclothes or a small room. Terracotta highlights in the Archaic section include a horse and rider with emphasized eyes, plus a couple – possibly royal or divine – in a horse-drawn chariot.

Ancient Kition

Most of **ancient Kition** lies under modern Larnaca, and thus cannot be excavated, though Einar Gjerstad's Swedish team made attempts during the 1920s. The British had complicated matters in 1879 by carting off much of what had survived above ground as "rubble" to fill malarial marshes. Their depredations were worst at the ancient acropolis on fenced-off Bamboúla hill, directly behind the Archeological Museum; consequently there's little to see except for a nearby excavation – possibly the Phoenician port, well inland from today's shoreline – next to the municipal tennis courts on Kilkís street. So-called Areas I and III, opposite the weird, top-heavy belfry of Panayía Khrysopolítissa, are Late Bronze Age holes in the ground, of only specialist interest now that they have disgorged their treasures.

The only accessible zone is **Area II**, beyond Arkhiepiskópou Kypriánou, from which you turn up Kérkyras to reach the entrance (Mon–Fri 9am–2.30pm, Sept–June also Thurs 3–5pm; €1.70), where a wooden catwalk allows an overview of ongoing excavations. The Phoenician resettlement sits atop Late Bronze Age foundations, abutting the mixed mud-brick and stone wall which bounded Kition to the north. The main structures are a large shrine, rededicated to the fertility goddess Astarte in Phoenician times, and four smaller, earlier temples, one of them linked to smelting workshops found here, suggesting – if not worship of a copper deity – then at least a priestly interest in copper production. In another of the shrines, probably that of a masculine seafaring god, a pipe for ritual opium-smoking was discovered. Few Hellenistic or Roman artefacts were found, making the site unusual and archeologically important – as well as politically delicate, since Greek Cypriots are often less than enthusiastic about remains indicating Asiatic cultural origins.

Eating and drinking

It doesn't take much nous to work out that you're going to dine poorly along the Finikoúdhes, with its multiple chain-snack outlets and handful of overpriced restaurants. However, a little foraging inland will turn up various good, reasonably priced eating and drinking venues in Larnaca. If you're keen on being beside the seaside, head south along Piyale Pasha to the cluster of decent seafood tavernas near the fishing harbour.

1900 Art Café Stasínou 6 ☏ 24653027, ⊛ www.artcafe1900.com.cy. Housed on two levels of an early twentieth-century mansion, and run by local radio-journalist Marios and his artist partner Maria. Upstairs, the civilized restaurant with its wall-art and winter fireplace attracts a mix of locals and foreigners. A fusion of Cypriot and western bistro food is on offer, based mostly on lamb, chicken, with a few *mezés* and veggie platters, washed down by an international wine list and Belgian beer, followed by apple cake *à la mode*. Downstairs, the classy bar – with a decor of old film posters and a largely local clientele – offers a hundred whiskies, a similar number of wine labels and 27 beers. Throughout there's a soundtrack of classic jazz or 1950s rock and roll. Open 6pm–late; closed Tues.

Glyko Lemoni Zínonos Kitiéos 105. Certainly the most pleasant café/snack bar in the bazaar, inside a lovingly restored premises. Coffees, novelty hot chocolates, fresh juices, milk shakes, sandwiches, *calzone* and sweet pastries are the stock in trade. Closes 8pm.

Habibi Efessoú 7, 3km north of the centre in Livádhia. The best surviving Lebanese diner in the area, with a gut-busting 27-platter *mezé* for about €18 – arrive hungry and be prepared to take a

couple of hours over your meal. Open daily lunch/dinner.

Koullis Piyale Paşa 5, corner of İstıklar. Reliable taverna specializing in fish and catering predominantly to a local clientele. €18 will get you a starter, octopus and a beer, €24 a grilled fish meal, while two can eat well on less glamorous species (cuttlefish, *marídhes*) for €38. May closed Wed–Thurs.

Manolis Khrysillos Faneroménis, opposite Áyios Lázaros. Workers' and shoppers' hole-in-the-wall *mayirió* doing home-style dishes like rabbit stew, bean dishes, *afélia* at budget prices. Lunch only.

Mavri Helona (Black Turtle) Mehmet Ali 11, near Áyios Lázaros ☏ 24650661. Most of the rough edges of this durable little upstairs *ouzerí* have been filed smooth over the years, and the menu has got blander and more expensive (€16 per person, drink extra). However, it remains popular with nearly as many locals as tourists, and in season you'll probably have to book. On Fri and Sat nights there's *bouzoúki* and accordion music of indifferent quality. Dinner only Tues–Sat.

Militzis Piyale Paşa 42, 250m south of the fort. Limited menu, and sometimes offhand service, but what they do – baked or grilled meat, casserole dishes – they do well, generously and without grease.

Nippon Grigóri Afxendíou 57, opposite the American Academy. Just a handful of tables in predictably minimalist surroundings, where some of the best Japanese fare on the island is dished up. Expensive, unless you go for the Sun/Mon all-you-can-eat specials. Open daily lunch and dinner.
Vassos Varoshiotis Piyale Paşa 7 ☎24655865. More plushly appointed than rival *Koullis* next door, with terracotta floors, wall-to-wall aquariums and swishing fans. Excellent, if slightly pricey, fare: salad, their famous seafood soufflé, a dessert and wine comes to about €30. It's always crowded,

especially at weekend lunchtimes when service gets erratic under pressure.

Zephyros Piyale Paşa 37 ☎24657198. Arguably the best-value of this street's fish purveyors, though beware their pricing policy – a "portion" is notionally 250g, though most specimens are much bigger and charged by the kilo (reckon €23 a head plus drink). Your fish comes with excellent chips and *çayırı* (raw greens) but mezé platters not included. Service copes well with typical weekend-lunch crowds attesting its popularity. Closed Wed.

Nightlife and entertainment

Visitors in search of a musically accompanied drink head towards the half-dozen **bars** in Laïkí Yitoniá, the most long-standing of these being *Savino*, with both classic and contemporary rock music. *Encounters*, by McDonalds at Finikoúdhes 73–76, is a two-in-one **club** – *Topaz* (lounge bar with chill-out tunes) and *Club Deep* (R&B, house) – both with a smarter-than-casual dress code, opening at midnight. The most ambitious club, however, has to be *Secrets Freedom* out at Artémidhos 67 (the airport road; ⓦ www.secretsfreedomclub .com for upcoming events), the island's largest **gay venue**.

Watch the municipal hoardings for details of more formal events, especially during **Kataklysmós**, the five-day Festival of the Flood, usually in June (see p.65). Most years, one of the commercial sponsors or the *Cyprus Weekly* publishes a full programme of events; the evening singing, dancing and verse competitions are heavily subscribed.

Two local **cinemas** show first-run "family entertainment": the central *Othellos 1 & 2* (☎24657970) at Ayías Elénis 13, and – a short drive out of town by the Kamáres aqueduct – the six-screen *K-Cineplex* at Peloponnísou 1 (☎24819022). Best check English-language newspapers or on-site posters for screening times, as phone numbers have Greek-only recordings.

Shopping

In Skála quarter, just inland from Piyale Paşa and in adjoining lanes five blocks south of the fort, are the studios of several leading Cypriot **ceramicists**, all of Famagusta origin. The workshops of Efthymios Symeou, Akdeniz 18 (☎24650338), Stavros Stavrou, Akdeniz 8 (☎24624491), and Fotini Kourti-Khristou, Bozkurt 28 (☎24650304), turn out a range of thin stoneware and *raku* ware, either practical or decorative, in both traditional and innovative designs. In what remains of the tradesmen's bazaar on Kaloyéra there are a few coppersmiths, wood-restorers and **antique dealers**, plus another shop (Antique Emporium) on Valsamáki near the enclosed car park.

Listings

Airport flight information ☎24643000.
Bookshop Academic & General, Ermoú 41, is one of the best in Cyprus, with a large English-language stock on all subjects, including travel (some Rough Guides), magazines and Cypriana.
Bus companies Principal outfits include Intercity, to Nicosia, Limassol, Ayía Nápa and Protarás, and

EMAN, to Ayía Nápa, both departing from terminals on the Finikoúdhes. Municipal PEAL buses to Paralímni leave from a stop on Arkhiepiskópou Makaríou, near the police station, but to Voróklini hotels from Kaloyéra Street; services to Páno Léfkara, Kíti (for Hala Sultan Tekke and Angelóktisti church) and Perivólia go from Platía Ayíou Lazárou.

The wreck of the Zenobia

Far and away the best **scuba** destination in Cyprus is the 1980 wreck of the **Zenobia**, an enormous car ferry 1400m outside Larnaca commercial port. She was brand-new when a computer malfunction flooded a ballast tank as she was leaving the harbour; the *Zenobia* listed fatally to port, constituting a stationary navigational hazard, and the decision was made to tow the ship out to the present locale and scuttle her. Over a hundred lorries are still trapped on board, along with an aquarium's worth of resident sea-life. Water temperature varies from 16°C to 27°C by season, and visibility in calm conditions can approach 50m.

The wreck depth ranges from 16m to 42m, so this isn't a beginner's dive; some of the chains holding the lorries in place are also distinctly corroded, so caution must be exercised. The former local monopoly on diving the *Zenobia* has been broken, and several island operators anchor in orderly and fairly amicable fashion at various points along the 172-metre length of the wreck. Usually you'll have a two-dive day, the first to about 35m, the second (after lunch taken on board the dive boat) shorter and shallower. Some local outfitters, such as Larnaca's Dive-In, offer "Four Wrecks in a Day", including a sunken private yacht, the *Alexander* (scuttled in 30m of water near the *Zenobia*) and the British patrol boat HMS *Cricket*, as well.

Car rental Agencies at the airport include Andreas Petsas, GDK/Budget, Hertz, Sixt and Thrifty/U-Drive. In-town outlets are limited to GDK/Budget, Arkhiepiskópou Makaríou 59 ☎ 24822666, and Theodoulou Self Drive, Leonídha Kiouppí 13 ☎ 24627411.
Internet Alto, Grigóri Afxendíou (daily 10am–2am); Replay, Finikoúdhes (daily 10am–1am).
Post offices Main post office is next to the CTO on Platía Dhimokratías (Mon–Fri 7.30am–1.30pm, also Mon, Tues, Thurs, Fri 3–6pm in winter, 4–7pm in summer, plus Sat 8.30–10.30am); also a small branch opposite Áyios Lázaros church (Mon–Fri morning hours only, plus Thurs 3–6/4–7pm).

Scuba school Best in-town outfit is Dive-In, Piyale Paşa 132 ☎ 24627469, ⊛ www.dive-in.com.cy, with the considerable advantage of their own boat moored at the nearby fishing marina rather than at the main port. They're normally open March–Nov (plus winter by arrangement), offering triox and nitrox programmes in addition to the usual PADI/BSAC courses, and welcome disabled and underage divers. Octopus Diving Centre, opposite *Palm Beach Hotel* on the Voróklini strip ☎ 24646571, ⊛ www.octopus-diving.com, also comes recommended. See also the box above.
Service taxis Services to Limassol and Nicosia run by Travel & Express operate from a terminal at Kímonos 2 ☎ 24661010.

Southwest of Larnaca: the coast

Larnaca is conveniently situated at the centre of its administrative district, with archeological sites, handicraft-producing villages and less popular resorts scattered in a broad arc all around. The main expressways to Limassol and Nicosia pass well inland west of the city, leaving the coastal plain to the southwest relatively untravelled except for local village traffic.

Hala Sultan (Umm Haram) Tekke

The **Hala Sultan (Umm Haram) Tekke**, 5km southwest of Larnaca just past the airport, is quite possibly the first thing of note you'll see as you touch down in Cyprus. According to the foundation legend, Muhammad's paternal aunt, accompanying her husband on an Arab raid of Cyprus in 649, was attacked by Byzantine forces here, fell from her mule, broke her neck and was buried on the spot. A mosque grew up around the grave on the west shore of a salt lake, surrounded today by an odd mix of date palms, cypress and olive trees. Rainfall permitting, a tank and a series of channels water the grove, adding to the oasis feeling of this peaceful, bird-filled place.

Tekke literally means a dervish convent, but this was always merely a *marabout* or saint's tomb. Despite the events of 1974, heavy-gauge fencing and a nocturnal police guard against vandalism, it's still a popular excursion destination for Greek Cypriots and **place of pilgrimage** for both Cypriot and foreign Muslims, for Hala Sultan ranks as one of the holiest sites of Islam, after Mecca, Medina, Kairouan and Jerusalem. The twin name is Turkish/Arabic: *Hala Sultan* means "the Ruler's paternal aunt", while *Umm Haram* or "Sacred Mother" seems an echo of the old Aphrodite worship.

Having left your shoes at the door, you're ushered inside the present nineteenth-century mosque (daily: May–Sept 7.30am–sunset, Oct–April 9am–sunset; may close an hour earlier; donation) to the **tomb recess** at the rear, behind the *mihrab*. Beside the presumed sarcophagus of the Prophet's aunt, there's a 1930 tomb of the Turkish wife of King Hussein of the Hejaz. Above, shrouded in a green cloth, you'll see three slabs of rock forming the dolmen that probably marked the grave until the mosque was built. The horizontal slab, a fifteen-ton meteorite chunk, is said to have been suspended miraculously in mid-air for centuries, before being forcibly lowered into its present position to avoid frightening those praying underneath.

Flamingos and other migratory birds stop over at the **lake** during winter and early spring (see p.430), though they've been absent in recent drought years. Like the *tekke*, the lake has a foundation legend: the resuscitated Bishop Lazarus, passing by, asked a woman carrying some grapes for a bunch; upon her rude refusal, he retaliated by turning her vineyard into the salty lagoon, now three metres below sea level. Post-resurrection Lazarus certainly comes across in legend as a rather grim figure; it is said that he never smiled while he was bishop, a result of what he'd seen during his brief sojourn in the realm of the dead.

The Kíti-bound PEAL municipal **bus** from Larnaca (Mon–Fri 8 daily 8am–7pm, Sat 5 daily 8am–1pm, reliable summer only) brings you to within 1km of the *tekke*; alight at the signposted side road, just the far side of the causeway over the salt lake. On the north shore of the lake near the Limassol-bound road is the so-called **Kamares** ("Arcade") **aqueduct**, built in 1747 by Abu Bekir, the only popular Ottoman governor of the island. The 75 surviving arches, illuminated at night to good effect, carried water until 1930.

Angelóktisti church

The PEAL bus continues to **Kíti**, 10km from Larnaca, where at a prominent three-way junction in the village, the Byzantine **church of Angelóktisti** (daily 9.30am–noon & 2–4pm; donation) stands amid flagstones and lawn, shaded by a giant terebinth. If necessary, the key can be fetched from the nearby snack bar, and smocks are provided for the "indecently" dressed. Most of the church dates from the eleventh and twelfth centuries, having replaced an original fifth-century sanctuary destroyed by the Arabs. What today serves as a narthex and display area for old icons began life as an apsed, rib-vaulted Latin chapel in the thirteenth or fourteenth century. The main nave has three aisles, a single apse, a large *yinaikonítis*, and painted-on, all-seeing eyes either side of the *témblon*.

But the highlight of Angelóktisti is the **mosaic** (illuminated on request) in the conch of the apse, probably the last surviving section of the original building. Inside a floral/vegetal border, the Virgin – labelled unusually as *Ayía María* or "Saint Mary" – lightly balances a doll-like holy infant on her left arm as she gazes sternly to a point just left of the viewer. The pair are attended by two dissimilar archangels – Gabriel, on the right, is fleshier and more masculine than the damaged portrayal of Michael – proffering celestial orbs and sceptres in the direction of the infant. The date of the mosaic is controversial, but the Ravenna-esque artistic conventions, especially Mary's stance on a jewelled pedestal and inclination to the left, would suggest the sixth century. Yet it is far more refined than the purportedly contemporaneous mosaic in the North Cyprus church of Kanakariá (see p.255), which was the only other complete Cypriot ecclesiastical mosaic *in situ* until its desecration.

Perivólia and Cape Kíti

Just 2km southeast of Kíti, **PERIVÓLIA** has become a resort because of its proximity to the beaches on **Cape Kíti**, almost 3km further in the same direction (and also reachable from Meneoú – follow signs for "Meneoú Beach"). These beaches, to either side of the lighthouse, are mostly scrappy, narrow and sharply shelving, with large pebbles on a sand base. Nonetheless, self-catering hotel apartments jostle at the outskirts with ever-multiplying villas and apartments for sale, and "Flats to Let" signs abound in the village.

If you have a rented car, Perivólia or its beach annexes could be a good, relatively quiet base, less tatty than Larnaca itself. Out by the lighthouse, there are two moderately priced beachfront **hotels**, both with tennis courts, pool and similar facilities: *Three Seas* (℡24422901, ⓦwww.3seashotel.com.cy; ❷), with an international clientele, and *Faros Village* (℡24422111, ⓦwww.farosvillage .com; ❸), a plusher, landscaped bungalow complex represented by a few UK package companies. A restored sixteenth-century **Venetian watchtower** looms on a knoll 1km north of the modern lighthouse. Dirt tracks converge there from all directions, and it's always in sight – though not especially compelling once you get there.

Westwards to Maróni and Zíyi

Returning to Kíti village, it's possible to follow the coast **westwards** by forking left, away from Mazotós. Despite the good paved road running alongside, the shore thus far remains relatively undeveloped except for farms, Cypriots' weekend villas and one hotel complex, though frankly there's little to justify any exploitation; the few beaches are rocky and difficult to reach, though once you are in the water the seabed is sandy.

If you persevere along this road, you eventually return to civilization at either Zíyi or **MARÓNI**, a major hothouse-vegetable centre spread appealingly over several hills. Its atmospheric old town, like that of Psematisménos, 2km north, is home to numerous expatriates as well as agrotourism **accommodation**, and a taverna or two. The larger of the two restored complexes is *Teacher's House* (℡24332132), comprising three studios (❶) and two one-bed apartments (❷). Although a mixed village before 1974, its Greek-Cypriot inhabitants were among the most virulently nationalist in the district, and, in the words of one former resident, "made Nikos Sampson (see p.393) look like a Communist sympathizer". When local Turkish Cypriots left in late 1974, the remaining villagers bulldozed their houses and claimed their fields, rather than distribute them to refugees from the North.

ZÍYI (Zygi), 3km southeast of Maróni, sprang up in the nineteenth century as the first Cypriot port dedicated to shipping carob pods; the Greek name means "weighing scales", the Turkish moniker *Terazi*, "carob". The Cypriot republic inherited two military bases here from the British, their radar masts still overshadowing the regional BBC transmitter – and acting as a magnet for would-be spies, with two Israelis (allegedly paid Turkish agents) arrested and jailed for several years in 1998.

Today, Zíyi has a newer role as a minor local resort, with seaside villas for Cypriots and up to ten (in season) fish **tavernas** drawing in crowds even from Nicosia. ✳ *Santa Elena* (limited seating, book ☎2433223) in a converted warehouse on the pedestrian zone opposite the church is the most atmospheric and cheapest, with abundant portions; seaside *Loizos Koumbaris* is dearer but also popular. That said, at all establishments much of the seafood is frozen.

The lack of nearby beaches hasn't deterred day-trippers or weekenders. The nearest approximation of one is **Limanáki**, about 3km east of Zíyi: look for a side track (signposted as "Maroni Beach") to seaward just west of the turn-off for Maróni. This little bay has the only patch of sand for miles around, but the cove is jetsam-prone.

Western Larnaca district

Compared to the parched, rather barren land close to Larnaca and the low-rise excesses of outer Limassol, the gently rolling country of western Larnaca district presents a welcome change, with trees, streams and a hint of the Tróodhos foothills further west. Several points of interest flank the Limassol–Nicosia expressway, suitably provided with exit roads across and onto the old highway, which in many respects is better for travelling short distances here.

Kalavassós

If you're seized by an urge to stay in the area – and it has the considerable virtue of being roughly equidistant from Nicosia, Larnaca and Limassol – cross the expressway from either Maróni or Zíyi to ravine-nestled **KALAVASSÓS** (Kalavasos), where a night-time chorus of frogs croaking in the stream-bed is the only thing likely to disturb your sleep. Until 1972, the village lived off copper mines just up the valley, their profits funding the extravagantly ornate north portal of the church. One of the little locomotives which used to haul ore-cars out of the hills to the coast has been poised on an isolated stretch of narrow-gauge track over the Vasilikós River.

Kalavassós – along with adjacent Tókhni – is the main focus of an admirable **accommodation** scheme based in a dozen or so well-adapted village houses, plus a few new stone-clad structures, run by ✳ *Cyprus Villages* (☎24332998, 𝕎www.cyprusvillages.com.cy). Studio, one- and two-bedroom units are available at daily rates (❷–❹ by size; advance bookings essential), but they're generally let as part of one-week packages with car rental and airport transfers included, arranged directly or through various British, German and Scandinavian tour companies. Cyprus Villages is affiliated with Drapia Farm (☎99437188), a **horse-riding centre** just north of the village; **mountain bikes** are available to rent from an office on Kalavassós' central square. At or near the scheme's Tókhni headquarters, there's more bike hire, a sauna, *hamam* and therapeutic massage available.

Accommodation in Kalavassós that's not part of Cyprus Villages includes the *Kontoyiannis House* (☎25580306, 𝕎www.kontoyiannis.com; 1-bed ❸, 2-bed ❹), with four modernized units in an old building, and *Stratos House* (☎24332293 or 25346588, 𝕎www.stratoshousecyprus.com; ❷), three units just north of the square, more sympathetically restored. Kalavassós has two all-year **tavernas**: *Romios* just off the central square, and *Bridge House* at the village entrance providing standard, inexpensive Cypriot meals, the premises doubling as a convivial bar with both indoor and outdoor seating.

Tókhni

TÓKHNI (Tochni), in the next valley east, is even more appealing scenically, but it's as well to know that this was the site of a particularly ugly inter-communal atrocity in summer 1974, when all of the Turkish-Cypriot men over 16 were killed by an EOKA–B detachment (see pp.392–393 in Contexts). The Turkish quarter was on the easterly hillside; besides many derelict houses, slowly being restored, the only traces of it are a sturdy mosque (without minaret) and the old graveyard near the turning for the Cyprus Villages office. Down in the central ravine, the arcades of a coffeehouse frame the belfry of the church straddling the ravine.

Among the eight separate Cyprus Villages properties (see "Kalavassós" opposite), the *Myrto* complex of five studios and one-beds at the southwest edge of the village is worth singling out for its high standard of restoration, peaceful setting and private pool. Up by the *Tokhni Taverna*, there's an eponymous cluster of stone-clad studios and one-bedroom apartments with another, less private pool. As at Kalavassós, there are also several "independent" **accommodation** options, though a few don't operate outside peak season. The most conventional is *Socrates House* (☎24333636, ⓕ24332536; closed Nov–March; ❸), on the slope west of the central church, though the rooms are small. **Self-catering** outfits include *Vasilopoulos House* (☎24332531, ⓕ24332933, ⓔavasifa@spidernet.com.cy; ❷), a courtyard complex of studios and one-bedroom units on the east side of the village; and *Niovi Traditional Villas* (☎99468446, ⓦwww.tochnivillas.com; ❷), three restored units from studio to two-bedroom size with a shared pool.

For **eating out**, *Tokhni Taverna*, managed by Cyprus Villages, offers adequate if somewhat unadventurous fare, with the setting (balcony in summer, fireplace

▲ Locals relaxing in Tókhni

in winter) being the biggest plus. Other options like *Nostos*, opposite the church, are not always open outside peak season.

Tenta (Ténda)

Near Kalavassós and Tókhni are two important excavated ancient sites. Closest is the Neolithic village of **Tenta** (Mon–Fri 10am–4pm; €1.70, guidebook €6 extra), smaller than roughly contemporary Khirokitia (see below), but sharing its cultural features. To get here head south out of Kalavassós, then bear right (west) onto "Tenta Street", which leads up to an unmissable teepee on a hillock next to the expressway. The canopy protects mud-and-stone-rubble structures culminating in the largest **roundhouse**, "Structure 14", at the summit, just glimpsing the sea; there are smaller round huts immediately east, with a ditch and **perimeter wall** at the edge of the settlement. This appears to have numbered some 45 to 50 dwellings, both flat- and dome-roofed, sheltering at most 150 people. Burial practices were a bit more casual than at Khirokitia, with about half the skeletons found outside dwellings, mixed with rubbish. The original name of the place is unknown; the modern one arises from a legend asserting that Saint Helena, mother of Constantine the Great, pitched her tent (*ténda*) here on returning from Jerusalem with a portion of the True Cross, en route to founding the monastery of Stavrovoúni.

Khirokitia

Some of the earliest traces of human settlement in Cyprus, from around 6800 BC, are found at Neolithic **Khirokitia** (Choirokoitia), roughly halfway between Larnaca and Limassol on the modern expressway. The proper name of the site is Khirokitia-Vouni, but it's usually called simply Khirokitia after the modern village to the northwest.

Khirokitia ranks among the most rewarding of Cypriot ruins, despite noisy distraction from the motorway, with ongoing excavations likely to increase its allure. The excavated area forms a long ribbon on a southeast-facing slope dominating a pass on the age-old highway from the coast to Nicosia. It's not always open during the prescribed **admission hours** (Oct–April Mon–Fri 9am–5pm; May–Sept until 7.30pm, Sat & Sun 9am–5pm; €1.70, pamphlet available for a small extra charge), and at weekends at least it's unwise to show up after 1pm. The only nearby amenity is a taverna on the access road from the main highway, on the east side of the bridge over the Maróni creek.

The site

The combination of arable land below and an easily defensible position proved irresistible to the settlement's founders, apparently hailing from the Levantine coast or Anatolia. Archeological investigations continue in the earliest inhabited sector, a saddle between the two knolls at the top of the slope; despite the limited area uncovered to date, it seems that most of the hillside was inhabited.

What's visible so far are housing foundations – most substantial and recent at the bottom of the slope – and a maze of lanes, dictated more by the placement of dwellings than any deliberate planning. You walk up on what appears to be the main street, in fact a defensive **perimeter wall**, something that becomes more obvious at the top of the hill; the very few houses built outside it were later enclosed by a secondary outer wall.

The sixty-plus circular *tholos* (beehive-type) **dwellings** exposed to date are single-storey structures that probably had a mixture of domed and flat roofs. Interior walls were lined with stone benches doubling as sleeping platforms, with scanty illumination through slit windows. The largest dwelling, an egg-shaped chieftain's "**mansion**" with an inner diameter of just under six metres, had two rectangular piers supporting a loft. As the structures deteriorated, they were flattened into rubble and built over by the next generation (this practice prompted the now-discarded theory that the perimeter wall was in fact the main street, its elevation constantly raised to keep pace with the level of the new houses). This "urban-renewal" method has greatly complicated modern excavations, which began in 1936, two years after the site's discovery; these have yielded vast troves of small Neolithic objects, now kept at the Cyprus Museum in Nicosia. Several concrete replicas have been erected to give an idea of how claustrophobic life in one of the original houses must have been.

Estimates for the maximum **population** of Khirokitia run as high as two thousand, an astounding figure for the time. Wheel-less pottery techniques were known only in the local culture's latter phases; during the so-called **Aceramic** period, the inhabitants worked strictly in stone, turning out relief-patterned grey andesite bowls and schematic idols. Flint sickle blades, grinders hollowed out of river boulders, and preserved cereal grains provide proof of the community's largely agricultural basis, though hunting, particularly for deer, and goat herding were important too.

The Khirokitians **buried their dead** in the fetal position under the earth floor, or just outside the entrance, of some of the round-houses – a rather convenient, if unhygienic form of ancestor reverence; beneath one dwelling, 26 graves on eight superimposed levels were discovered. The deceased were surrounded by offerings and personal belongings, exquisite stone-and-shell necklaces being found in female graves; more ominously, the corpses usually had their chests crushed with a grinding quern to prevent the dead returning. As at Tenta, infant mortality was high, and adult skulls show evidence of ritual deformation – surviving infants would have been tightly bound on a cradle-board to flatten the back of the head.

Hill-villages: the long way to Páno Léfkara

En route to Páno Léfkara, a rewarding detour can be made through some little-visited hill-villages. The first of these, **KHIROKITÍA**, straddles a ridge 2km west of the ruins and offers both high-quality restored **accommodation** at the three-bedroom *House of Achilles* (UK ☎07909 538844, ⓦwww.thehouse ofachilles.com; €130), plus a foretaste of **VÁVLA**, a depopulated village 9km to the northwest, whose array of beautiful old houses is slowly being restored. Families and groups may stay in the baronial, two-bedroom *Papadopoulou House* (☎99451246; ❸); at weekends snacks are offered at the lone *kafenío* here.

Vávla marks the turning for **Ayíou Miná (Agios Minas) convent** (Oct–April Sun–Fri 9am–noon & 2–6pm; May–Sept 9am–noon & 3–6pm), one of several convents functioning in the South, but among the least visited despite its proximity (7km) to Páno Léfkara. The Byzantine-Gothic church, probably founded by the Dominicans during the fifteenth century and reworked two hundred years later, provides the main focus of interest, especially its elaborately carved and painted *yinaikonítis*; the friendly nuns produce icons and honey, both offered for sale.

The main valley road from Vávla continues up through less distinguished Láyia (Lageia) and Orá, then over a saddle towards **VAVATSINIÁ**, nestling in a fold of Mount Kiónia at the top of the valley that drains towards Ayíou Miná. Above the central church, an *ayíasma* (holy spring with curative powers) issues from a deep shaft; below the church the *Pefkos* taverna, packed out at weekends, looks across the gorge towards a typical peaked-roof hill-country chapel: fresco-less but with a carved-wood interior. As you leave the village in the direction of Páno Léfkara, you pass two more enormous **tavernas** on the outskirts, also jammed at warm-weather holidays with Cypriot day-trippers.

Páno Léfkara

PÁNO LÉFKARA, 700m above sea level on the fringes of the Tróödhos, is reached along an easy climb from the motorway onto the well-made E105. A retreat of the Orthodox clergy in Lusignan times, it's now almost a small town and a very handsome one to boot: arches make veritable tunnels in the streets, and fine door-frames and balconies complete the picture. Many of the old houses are being bought and restored by Cypriots and foreigners at high prices, owing to equidistance from the South's three largest towns. There was a small Turkish quarter here, too, down at the low end of the village by the mosque.

Casual visitors come to sample the **lace and silver** for which the place is famous; it is claimed, somewhat apocryphally, that Leonardo da Vinci purchased a needlepoint altarcloth for Milan cathedral when he came to Cyprus in 1481. The silver jewellery and silverware, men's work, are more reasonably priced than the women's lace. Both are sold in over half a dozen shops devoted to each craft, mostly on the main commercial street.

Constant "shopping tours" have had their effect, and everyone from petrol-pump attendant to café owner will happily trot out the work of relatives at the first opportunity – be prepared to be almost ceaselessly hassled (having parking fees waived in exchange for "just a look" is a common ploy). It's also useful to know that the "lace" to be embroidered is actually imported Irish linen. On the whole, lace prices are inflated in Páno Léfkara, so bargain hard, or seek out better deals in surrounding villages. The **Patsalos Museum of Traditional Embroidery and Silver** (Mon–Thurs 9.30am–4pm, Fri & Sat 10am–4pm; €1.70), devoted largely to the two crafts, might be a useful first stop before going on a shopping spree.

Practicalities

As you approach, it's best not to take the first signposted turn-off into the village – there's no **parking** on this side and it leaves you with a fair hike into town. Instead, leave a vehicle at the northeast end of the village by the **post office** (there's also an **ATM** nearby), where a line of arched, wooden-floored *kafenía* opposite the school offers a marvellous tableau of the village elders playing at cards or dice. The preferable of Páno Léfkara's two **hotels** is the simple but pleasant *Lefkarama Village* (℡24342154, ⓦwww.lefkarama.com; closed Jan; ❷).

Káto Léfkara and Kátho Dhrýs

Páno Léfkara's lower neighbour, **KÁTO LÉFKARA**, 1500m down the road, is also architecturally of a piece, but less frequented – here too, however, there is a snack bar and several trinket shops. The real sight in Káto is the largely twelfth-century **Arkhángelos church** (unsigned, always unlocked), by itself in a scruffy piece of ground 200m southwest of the village car park. Although the condition and quantity of its **interior frescoes** cannot rank it with the best examples of painted churches in the high Tróödhos, what remains is well worth the slight detour. The oldest and best surviving images decorate the apse, with *Christ's Communion with the Apostles* (six of whom are missing) above five early Fathers of the Church. Over the south door, the *Mandylion* (*Holy Kerchief*) is essentially a *Pandokrátor* superimposed on a shawl, just below a badly deteriorated *Baptism*.

A much later (fifteenth-century) *Resurrection* in the arch of the west vault looks suspiciously like the *Healing of the Leper*.

Lace-making endeavours are also evident 2.5km to the southwest at **KÁTO DHRÝS** (Kato Drys), on the road between Káto Léfkara and the convent of Ayíou Miná. There are a few shops here, **accommodation** at two agrotourism members (for example stone-built *Gabriel's House*, ☎24655164, ❷), plus two **tavernas**, including the *Platanos* at the outskirts, with seating under the namesake trees.

Pottery villages: Kofínou and Kórnos

Back on the route towards Nicosia, you can detour almost immediately to **KOFÍNOU**, which has a single pottery workshop near the ugly prefab church producing urns and other practical wares alongside souvenir-sized items. The present villagers are refugees from the North; this was among the largest, nearly all-Muslim villages in the South, attacked on scanty pretext by EOKA on November 15, 1967. Before a truce was arranged two days later, 25 local Turkish Cypriots had died, and the incident nearly precipitated a Greek-Turkish war. Scars of the battle are still evident in the old Turkish quarter, now boarded up and signposted as "Government Property"; the incoming Greek Cypriots were housed in a prefabricated development just west. Kofinou is well known locally for its **kléftigo** houses, for example *Pentadaktylos Kleftigo House*, one of several such adjacent to the Larnaca-bound motorway; just under €12 should see you to a small beer, a very creditable *kléftigo* with not much gristle, and a caper-garnished salad. The closest alternative with vegetarian dishes 3km southwest along the B1 at **SKARÍNOU**, where Pauline's and Achilleas' *Happy Valley House* (☎24322544) offers such delights as bean soup, or just coffee and dessert, to a mostly expat clientele in what was originally a staging-post on the old Larnaca–Limassol road. Sunday lunch is particularly popular and must be pre-booked.

KÓRNOS, 11km north of Kofinou in a stream valley on the other side of the highway, is a more cheerful place, and also occupies itself with pottery (*kórnos* means "clay" in Cypriot dialect). Again there's just one "proper" shop, with a phone number to call in the (likely) event they're shut. Several informal kilns also operate in back gardens.

Stavrovoúni monastery

Proportionate to its small population, Cyprus contributes more monks to the monastic enclave of Mount Áthos in northern Greece than any other Orthodox country. You can get an inkling of why at **Stavrovoúni monastery**, perched atop an isolated, 689-metre crag dominating this corner of the island.

Its foundation legend ranks it as the oldest religious community on Cyprus: Saint Helena, mother of the eastern Roman Emperor Constantine, supposedly came by here in 327 on her way back from Jerusalem, leaving a fragment of the True Cross (plus the entire cross of the penitent thief). Previously home to a temple of Aphrodite, the peak took its modern name from this event (*Stavrovoúni* means "Cross Mountain"), and a religious community quickly grew around the holy relics.

In Lusignan times, Benedictine monks displaced Orthodox ones, but despite an imposing fortified design, both monastery and revered objects were destroyed after the 1426 rout of King Janus nearby (see "Pýrga" below). Today's silver reliquary crucifix, which supposedly encases the venerated sliver of the True Cross, dates only from the late fifteenth century; perhaps the contents are identical with the purported cross of the penitent thief which a wandering Dominican friar claimed to have seen here, still intact, by the altar in 1486.

After the Ottoman conquest the monastery was burned again, and only during the nineteenth century was Stavrovoúni rebuilt, on the old foundations, and repopulated – by both monks and dozens of cats, the latter a scourge of snakes here as at the Cape Gáta nunnery at Akrotíri. But by the late 1970s the place was in decline again, with just two elderly monks besides the abbot. It had given up its once-extensive holdings to surrounding villages, a process doubtless completed by the pressure of refugees from the 1974 invasion, though it retained the convent of Ayía Varvára at the base of the hill as a dependency.

Monastery life

Today about twenty very committed, mostly young monks follow a rota: six or seven up in the citadel, the rest down at Ayía Varvára at any given time. They are on an **Athonite regimen** (as on Mount Áthos in Greece), the strictest on the island, which entails a day divided into roughly equal thirds of prayer and study, physical labour, and rest. "Rest" means only two frugal, meat-less meals, just before midday and an hour or so before sunset, plus sleep interspersed between the nocturnal devotional periods. There are at least four communal liturgies each day in the courtyard church: matins before dawn, the main liturgy after sunrise, vespers before the evening meal and compline afterwards.

Life has been eased somewhat since the 1980s by the paving of the steep, twisty road up and provision of mains water and electricity, but winters on top are severe, and the monks still do a full day's work on the surrounding agricultural terraces in addition to their devotions. Honey and sultanas, the latter legendarily having their first Cypriot cultivation here, make up some of the harvest. The icon-painting studio of the elderly Father Kallinikos at well-restored **Ayía Varvára** (closed noon–3pm) is well signposted; he is claimed to be one of the finest living practitioners of the art – although some consider him vastly overrated – and his work is accordingly expensive.

Visits

Strict conditions apply for **visiting the upper monastery**. In accordance with Athonite rules, no women are admitted at all, not even children or babies; no entry is allowed from noon to 3pm (11am–2pm in summer – the monks don't observe daylight-saving time – or noon–2pm winter); and photos are forbidden – cameras must be left at the guard house at the foot of the long stairway up from the car park. In short, you don't come here to gawp – except perhaps at the amazing views, since there's little left of artistic or architectural merit after the pillaging, fires and a ham-handed 1980s restoration – but on pilgrimage, possibly to stay the night on invitation.

A Greek sign in the entry hall sums up the monastic creed: "If you die before you die, then when you die you won't die." In other words, he who has renounced the world gains eternal life. When a monk *does* die bodily, he is interred for the five years prescribed by Orthodoxy and then exhumed for display in the ossuary, his religious name emblazoned across the forehead of his skull.

Pýrga: the Chapelle Royale

Near the centre of **PÝRGA** village, just 3km from Kórnos and east of the expressway, stands the **Chapelle Royale** (signposted as "Medieval Chapel"), a small, frescoed Lusignan shrine actually dedicated to Saint Catherine (open daylight hours according to keeper's whim; €1.70). It owes its alias to a fine wall-painting of **King Janus**, who, together with his queen, Charlotte of Bourbon, built the chapel in 1421. "Good King Janus" was among the last of Cyprus's Crusader monarchs, as respected as he was ineffective; just a few kilometres south, below Khirokitía village, his armies were defeated by the Mamelukes in 1426. Janus was held prisoner in Cairo for two years before being ransomed, and this little church is his only surviving legacy.

The plain building itself is merely a single-vaulted structure with three doorways. By 1426 all the inside surfaces had been decorated by a Greek-Cypriot painter effecting a unique synthesis of Byzantine and Latin iconographic elements; sadly only a small fraction of the paintings survive. Janus appears, along with Queen Charlotte, as a tiny, kneeling figure at the foot of a fragmentary *Crucifixion* on the east wall. On the northeast ceiling you can make out *The Raising of Lazarus* and a *Last Supper*, the latter the best-preserved image here and – unusually in Cyprus – identified in medieval French. Opposite, also with French inscriptions, an *Ascension* and *Pentecost* are just recognizable.

Kelliá: the church of Áyios Andónios

The Byzantine **church of Áyios Andónios**, a mere 5km north of Larnaca via Livádhia, makes a satisfying complement to the two preceding sites. It's just west of **KELLIÁ**, formerly wholly Turkish Cypriot and named after the hermits' cells which existed here long before the village. The originally ninth-century church enjoys a commanding position atop a man-made knoll, though what you see now is an engaging amalgam of eleventh- to fifteenth-century styles, plus an eighteenth-century west arcade. The building's current ground plan is a multi-vaulted cross-in-square, with three aisles and apses, plus a fifteenth-century narthex. Since whitewash and extraneous buttressing were removed, the value of Áyios Andónios's early Byzantine **frescoes** has been recognized and the church is now kept scrupulously locked; to gain entry (donation to the offerings box) – and it's well worth it – you must track down genial caretaker Mikhalis, who lives in the white house with a vast courtyard, opposite the main *kafenío*.

The paintings exposed thus far decorate four interior pillars and the west wall. On the right front (southeast) pier, the faces of the *Crucifixion*, the earliest known fresco on the island, are strangely serene and wide-eyed in the Middle-Eastern, paleo-Christian manner; just above this, a surviving fragment of the eleventh-century *Betrayal* clearly shows Peter lopping off the ear of the high priest's servant. On the rear left (northwest) pier, the figure of an equestrian Saint George is twelfth century, but the slightly mismatched legs of his horse date from the tenth century; from the south face of the same pier, another, tenth century, George gazes out, a heavy-lidded, slightly foppish Byzantine prince. Facing this pier, on the west wall, is a figure of Saint Pandelímon (often misidentified as either saint Kosmas or Damian), from the early eleventh century, with his gaze averted to his right. On the southwest pier, facing the narthex, a *Virgin Enthroned*, thought to date from the tenth century, is superimposed on a geometric background, the latter possibly a holdover from the Iconoclastic period. Immediately opposite this on the west wall are two versions of the Sacrifice of Isaac, from the early eleventh and twelfth centuries; the later, lower rendition, is more intact, complete with the angel admonishing Abraham not to do the deed.

East of Larnaca: the resort coast

As you head out of the city, the bight of Larnaca Bay bends gradually from north to east. It takes nearly 5km along the B3 road to outrun oil refineries and tankers to reach the paragliders and hotels of **VORÓKLINI** (Oróklini) shore annexe. The beach here is acceptable for a dip, but nothing to rave about: the tidal zone is often reefy, the water interrupted by rock jetties and breakwaters. Most of the ten or so **hotels** clustered south of the motorway rate three or four stars; the most consistently well regarded is the lushly landscaped ✤ *Palm Beach* (℡24846600, Ⓦwww.palmbeachhotel.com; standard ❺, studio ❻ internet rate), a mix of standard doubles and garden studios with indoor/outdoor pools, gym/sauna and all other typical amenities of a four-star resort complex. Others worth considering include the well-priced, four-star *Sandy Beach*, 7km out of town (℡24646333, Ⓦwww.sandybeachhotel.com.cy; ❺); and the five-star *Golden Bay* (℡24645444, Ⓦwww.goldenbay.com.cy; ❼), three self-contained complexes with beachfront locations.

Special uses for the Dhekélia Sovereign Base

The existence of the **Dhekélia Sovereign Base** (see box, p.136), and its inviolability during and after the 1974 invasion, gave rise to some anomalies in the supposedly hermetic, pre-2003 separation of Cyprus north and south. Both Turkish and Greek Cypriots continued to hold jobs on the base; access from the South was unrestricted, and with the right paperwork from their own authorities Northerners could enter along the so-called "Four Mile (Strovília) Crossing" from Famagusta, or (more usually) at the Beyarmurdu/Pérgamos–Pýla crossing. Turkish Cypriots wishing to make clandestine visits to the South, especially for nightlife, merely left their northern numberplate cars in the base or at Pýla, where Greek-Cypriot friends with suitable cars awaited them.

Pýla, entirely within the buffer zone near a point where the boundaries of the North, the South and the Dhekélia base meet, acquired notoriety as one of only two remaining bi-ethnic villages in the southern Republic (the other is Potamiá, near Nicosia, though only about thirty Turkish Cypriots remain there now). Preserved here is an approximate microcosm of 1963–74 island life: Greek (67 percent) and Turkish (33 percent) Cypriots live in proximity but segregated, with two coffeehouses (one – guess which – called *Iy Makedhonia/Macedonia*), two flagpoles and separate communal schools. Disputes over property boundaries or vandalism of respective national symbols often require the mediation of the local UN post; in theory the writ of neither North nor South runs here. A **medieval tower**, restored in 2006–07 for a yet-undisclosed purpose, looms beyond the minaret, both overlooked by a ring of modern Turkish army watchtowers on the crags just above – hence no photos anywhere in the village.

Before April 2003 the only tacit intercommunal co-operation involved the high-volume **smuggling** of goods from the North, just 5km away across Sovereign Base territory at Pérgamos (Beyarmudu). This loophole made a mockery of the Republic of Cyprus's prohibition on "foreign" agricultural produce, with even fruit and seafood from hated Turkey entering via this corridor. Mostly on the access road in from Larnaca, shops did a roaring trade in "duty-free" jewellery and designer clothing, though by the late 1990s official clamp-downs and price-cutting elsewhere had shut them down. Since the two-way opening of the checkpoint at the southern edge of Pérgamos/Beyarmudu, there is in fact nothing much to distinguish this road from the other legal routes between North and South – though Base personnel are especially keen to search your car for contraband (see p.70) when returning from the North.

Beyond the hotel strip, there's even less to stop for on the B3, and halting is awkward once inside the **Dhekélia Sovereign Base**, home to the British Forces and an enormous, ugly power station between the highway and the sea. The only real bright spot is the *Kantara Taverna* (☎24645783) near Dhekélia village, popular with Cypriots for fish, steak and unusual starters, served in an upmarket environment and priced accordingly.

Once clear of the Sovereign Base, your first detour might be to **Potamós Liopetríou**, a long, narrow creek-inlet that's a genuine, rare fishing anchorage. The only facilities are two **tavernas**, the *Potamos* and the *Demetrion*, both mobbed for weekend lunches, despite slightly bumped-up prices and average-to-good fare. At *Demetrion*, closer to the mouth of the inlet, fresh grilled squid, a salad and a beer will leave you change from €20. The place itself is attractive, if beachless, though some sand has been hopefully strewn at a suitable bathing spot near the mouth of the inlet. French poet Rimbaud stopped here, too, working as a quarry foreman in 1879 before supervising the construction of the governor's residence in the Tróödhos.

Ayía Nápa

In his *Journey into Cyprus*, Colin Thubron describes cooking a fish, in the summer of 1972, on empty Krýo Neró beach below the then-fishing village of **AYÍA NÁPA** (Agia Napa), and later being awoken by sandflies. Were he today to find an unpoliced stretch of sand, he'd be lucky to sleep at all over the thump of nearby clubs. Any local identity has been utterly swept aside, with Ayía Nápa press-ganged into service as one of the South's largest package resorts, replacing the lost paradises around Famagusta. The beach is still obvious enough, a crescent swath extending east hundreds of metres from the fishing harbour, but it's packed to the gills in mid-summer. You don't really need a guidebook to get around here – all is pretty self-explanatory – but rather a fat wallet, a large liver capacity and boundless stamina for physical and/or nocturnal exploits.

Channel 4's "Fantasy Island" series, by tracing the rise of **UK garage** in Ayía Nápa during 1999, kept Ayía Nápa ranked as the Med's second hottest clubbing destination (after Ibiza) until 2001. That's now history; by 2004 visitor numbers had dropped precipitously, a pattern repeated in subsequent years. Most premier clubs from the resort's heyday survive (just), but the local listings mag has folded for lack of advertising revenue, and venues now make do with local DJs rather than the high-salaried international-circuit personalities of old.

The bursting of the bubble had other causes besides a notoriously fickle scene simply moving on. Ayía Nápa always had a reputation for testosterone-fuelled brawls (including a fatal stabbing in 2000) among holidaying lager-louts, their numbers sometimes augmented by British servicemen. Following their involvement in various instances of rape, affray and murder, squaddies from both Dhekélia and the UN contingent were periodically banned from bars and clubs here, only to misbehave (most recently in 2008) when allowed back in. But the biggest factor, perhaps, in Ayía Nápa's decline was locals' racist hostility to large numbers of black visitors, many from South London, and a dim view of drug use. Although controlled substances were never as common as on Ibiza, a "zero tolerance" narcotics policy was instituted, undercover agents abounded, and being caught with even a spliff or a few ecstasy tablets earned many people a few months in the slammer.

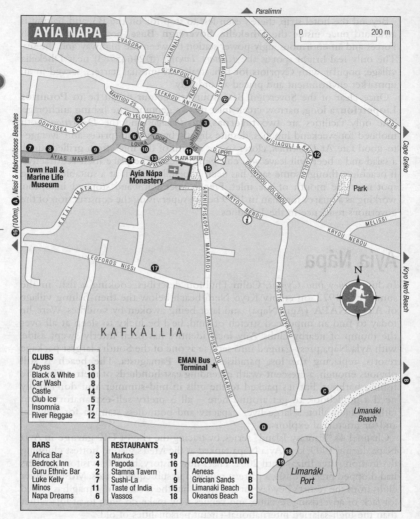

The Town

Around central **Platía Seféri** and its pedestrian zone, notional centre of the old pre-tourism village, anything not related to nightlife is likely to be a clothing boutique or overpriced fast-food outlet. Aside from the monastery, don't expect any other manifestations of high culture in Ayía Nápa. By day the place can seem eerily quiet, since most visitors (predominantly British and Scandinavian, few of them over 35) sleep until noon, then soak up some sun on the beach before a long evening nap. People next emerge for dinner, before partying until dawn.

The monastery of Ayía Nápa

The beautiful Venetian-style **monastery of Ayía Nápa** (always open) comes as a surprise after the commercialization of the adjacent *platía*. The monastery's arched cloister encloses an irregularly shaped, flower-decked courtyard, in the middle of which sits an elegant octagonal **fountain**, its sides decorated with reliefs and the whole surmounted by a dome on four pillars. Across the way burbles a boar's-head spout, the terminus of a Roman **aqueduct** whose spring-fed waters were the impetus for sporadic settlement here since Hellenistic times – and the focus of the monastery's foundation legend.

During the sixteenth-century Venetian period here, some hunters had a mangy dog whose coat improved markedly after visits to a hidden spring. Curious, the hunters followed the wet dog, finding not only the source of the abandoned aqueduct but also an icon of the Virgin hidden here for seven hundred years since the Iconoclastic era, when Byzantine zealots outlawed the adoration of such images. News of the waters spread, with humans availing themselves of its healing powers, and soon a monastery was founded near the lower end of the refurbished aqueduct. Work was scarcely completed when the Turks conquered the island, expelling the Catholics from the complex and replacing them with more tractable Greek Orthodox monks; they too soon departed, but a village sprang up around the abandoned monastery.

The **church**, right (west) of the sloping courtyard, is partly subterranean and has a magnificent fanlight-cum-rose window over the door. In the gloom at the base of the stairs down is a supplementary Latin chapel, from the time of the monastery's original dedication, though the miraculous icon has long since vanished. Back outside you can look from the south façade towards the sea over a cistern brimming with carp, and two giant sycamore figs said to be six centuries old. The Venetians built the hefty **perimeter wall** to keep pirates out; it now has the happy effect of protecting the place from drunken revellers.

The monastery was restored during the early 1970s and made available, ironically in light of Ayía Nápa's eventual fate, to the World Council of Churches as a conference centre; delegates, and a few Arab Christians acting as volunteer co-ordinators, are the only people in residence now. From April to December the church itself see heavy Sunday use: Anglican services at 11am, Catholic vespers at 5pm, followed by local baptisms (prestigious monastic churches are highly popular for this purpose among Cypriots).

The beaches

Some 2km west of central Ayía Nápa along its namesake avenue, **Nissí Beach** is for once as attractive as touted – but in high season it's hopelessly crowded as several hotels here disgorge their occupants onto the few hundred metres of sand, or into the handful of snack kiosks. At such times you can retreat by wading out to the islet which lends the beach both definition and its name (*nissí* means "island"). The rocky shore between Nissí and "Sunny Bay" is a popular gay hangout. Nissí and the adjacent **Makrónissos Beach**, some 5km from the centre, are both linked to Ayía Nápa proper by cycle paths, of which (to its credit) the resort has many.

Otherwise, the big attraction at Nissi is **bungee-jumping**, organized by Bungee Downunder (June–Sept daily 10am–6pm; bookings on ☎99605248). As the outfit's name implies, they're Australian-based and -trained, with one of the sport's pioneers still involved; a fifty-metre plunge, with the option of dipping your hair in the sea, will set you back €85. For more water and less air, there's **Waterworld**, a waterpark at the west end of town (March–Nov daily 10am–6pm; adults €27, children €13.50).

Arrival, information and accommodation

Orientation is straightforward: **Nissí** is the initial name of the main E309 avenue west to Nissí and Larnaca, 39km distant; **Arkhiepiskópou Makaríou** links the central square, **Platía Seféri**, with the harbour; and **Krýou Neroú** heads out east-southeast towards Cape Gréko. Above Platía Seféri, winding streets eventually lead to the big roundabout at the top of town funnelling traffic towards Paralímni.

EMAN **buses** from Larnaca will drop you down at the main ticket office near the base of Arkhiepiskópou Makaríou. The none-too-enthusiastic **CTO** (Mon–Sat 8.30am–2pm, plus Mon, Tues, Thurs & Fri 4–6.30pm) is around the corner at Krýou Neroú 12. The central **post office** keeps limited afternoon and Saturday morning hours, while **ATMs** abound. **Car-rental** franchises near the town-centre end of Nissí avenue include Andreas Petsas at no. 20 (☎23721260) and GDK/Budget at no. 46 (☎23724416). Best of several **internet** cafés is IntenCity Media Networks, at Belloyiánni 10 (24hr), with 32 terminals.

Nowadays, you won't necessarily arrive on a package, as most local hotels offer substantial direct internet-booking discounts. **Hotels** to go for include the five-star *Aeneas* behind westerly Nissí beach (☎23724000, Ⓦwww.aeneas .com.cy; ❻), with a huge pool and excellent sports facilities, or the four-star *Grecian Sands* (☎23721616, Ⓦwww.grecian.com.cy; ❻), set in tiered gardens behind easterly Krýo Neró beach. If you want a beachfront but still fairly central location, the two-star *Okeanos Beach* (☎23724440, Ⓦwww.okeanoshotel .com.cy; ❸) and three-star *Limanaki Beach* (☎23721600, Ⓦwww.ayianapa hotels.net; ❷) are both small-scale operations with reasonable amenities, just northeast of Limanáki harbour. Most other affordable on-spec accommodation in Ayía Nápa is **self-catering**, with studios and one-bedrooms starting at €45–60, two-bedroom units at €75; the CTO office keeps complete lists of licensed premises.

Eating

Despite its ostensible range – everything from Japanese to Mexican, by way of Italian and Danish – Ayía Nápa cuisine can mostly be summarized as hot, abundant and looking vaguely like the glossy picture on the menu outside. Perhaps the most authentic **dining** is at the fish tavernas down at pedestrianized Limanáki port, where Cypriots can be found dining at off-season weekends despite the bumped-up prices.

Markos Limanáki Port. The "right-hand" taverna, the first (1955) established here; open all day, all year, with an ever-popular courtyard.

Pagoda Nissí 29. Part of the chain which first brought Chinese food to Cyprus in 1969, this serves reliable Szechuan and Peking dishes such as chicken in black bean sauce and shredded beef in chilli sauce.

Stamna Tavern Stone's throw from Platía Seféri. Authentically rustic, and grumpy service actually highlights the excellence of the food, with remarkable *loúntza* jostling for attention next to succulent *halloúmi*, jumbo-size local olives and sweet tomatoes.

Sushi-La Bar & Lounge Ayías Mávris 8 ☎23725125. Good value, intimate (bookings advised), 2007-opened Japanese venue, emphasizing good-value sushi. Open 5.30pm–midnight.

Taste of India Arkhiepiskópou Makaríou 8, just below Platía Seféri. The best surviving Indian in town, with an intriguing *mezé* including prawn *puri* and butter chicken with *roti* and Kashmiri rice; one of a local island chain.

Vassos Limanáki Port ☎23721884. Among several local fish tavernas, this (adjacent to *Markos*) is the second oldest (1962), one of the most reliably open (all day until 10.30pm) and typically the busiest (weekend bookings essential) – always a good sign.

▲ Hitting the town at Bedrock Inn, Ayia Napa

Drinking and nightlife

Most of the brashest watering-holes congregate just uphill from the town's monastery, around Platía Seféri and the pedestrian zone above it and to the west, particularly along Louká Louká (universally nicknamed "The Look" Street). **Bars** are licensed between 9am and 2am, with half-hour extensions at weekends – but the music must be shut off at 1.30am, which sees these outfits empty rapidly in favour of the **clubs**, which can hold over two thousand revellers. Clubs open at 1.30am and mostly close at 4am; entry in these lean times averages around €7, subject to increases for special events. Garage and house are not, contrary to image, the sum total of Ayía Nápa; they have long since made room for trance, R&B and nostalgia tracks from the 1960s to the 1980s.

Bars

Africa Bar Eleftherías, just uphill from the *platía*. A mother-and-daughter team have a late licence until 6am and triple-for-double-measure deals on their spirits which render mixers largely irrelevant.
Bedrock Inn Louká Louká, corner of Ayías Mávris. Check out this hilarious Flintstones-themed bar for karaoke and its feet-through-the-floor car.
Guru Ethnic Bar Odhysséa Elýti 11. Occupying an old house with terraced gardens, this is the most upmarket spot in town (ie, smart dress code), vaguely hankering after the Parisian *Buddha Bar*; gourmet snacks, flavoured tobaccos in chillled hubble-bubbles, three outdoor bars, mood-enhancing "global" music.
Luke Kelly Ayías Mávris 28, opposite town hall. Irish brews on tap, live music and sports on the big screen make this a perennially crowded success. Open until 3.30am Fri/Sat.

Minos Platía Seféri. One of the most established bars, with excellent resident DJs playing hip-hop, R&B and garage – an ideal vantage point from which to survey the madness, if you arrive early.
Napa Dreams Louká Louká. Rivals *Minos* for quality, but adds tropical decor and poles to the mix. Pounding house music will keep you on your feet until closing time.

Clubs

Abyss Grigóri Afxendíou 17. Housed in a sumptuous four-level setting, Ayía Nápa's "first purpose-built superclub" lodges DJs in a pulpit and caters to all tastes, from 1970s sounds to R&B.
Black & White Louká Louká 6. Ayía Nápa's oldest and possibly smallest, most crowded outfit, a spartan but intense underground venue perfect for hip-hop, soul, funk and smouldering R&B. Open most of year.

Car Wash Ayías Mávris 24. Popular with an older crowd who bop to a 1970s/1980s soundtrack, including (of course) music from the eponymous film. Still busy thanks partly to unsurpassed sound system and lighting effects; open most of the year.

Castle Grigóri Afxendíou. Merits a look for its ridiculous drawbridge/moat decor, and is ideal if you're part of a larger group with different tastes, as R&B rubs shoulders with drum 'n' bass, house and trance in this three-room club (plus outdoor chill-out area). At 3000 capacity, it's one of the largest clubs, but often fills up since tour reps steer their charges here.

Club Ice Louká Louká 14. Fake icicle and snow decor, as the name suggests. One of the few venues still organizing foam and popcorn parties, the latter supplied in 200-kilo quantities by air cannons.

Insomnia Nissí 4. Late (4–7am) operation ensures the most popular old skool house and garage after-parties. Cuban cigars and a bottle of champagne are mandatory accessories.

River Reggae Access via Rio Napa Apartments on Mishaoúli ke Kavazóglou. The best pre-dawn venue in Ayía Nápa. Its spectral "Apocalypse Now" jungle setting boasts two winding pools for night-swimmers and beaten-up pool tables. A mix of reggae and trance is played against a backdrop of hidden alcoves and sweeping rock faces, where exhausted clubbers can sit on a ledge and watch the sun rise in each others' arms. Open 1–7am.

Around Ayía Nápa

Inland from Ayía Nápa and the south coast, the gently undulating terrain is dotted with the **Kokkinokhoriá** or "Red Villages", so called after the local soil, tinted by large amounts of iron and other metallic oxides. This is the island's main potato-growing region, the little spuds irrigated by water drawn up by dozens of windmills – the only distinguishing feature of an otherwise featureless region – and harvested in May. (Since 1990 the overdrawn aquifer has been invaded by the sea, and fresh water must be brought in by pipeline from the Tróödhos.) Less savoury is the area's tradition of trapping songbirds for food, particularly at Paralímni; *ambelopoúlia* are small fig-eating blackcaps (often known by their Italian name, *beccafico*), pickled whole and mostly exported to the Middle East. The practice is now illegal under EU law, but continues.

Other than this, there is little to be said for or about the hinterland, and even the CTO admits as much in its earnest, rather desperate promotion of a handful of second-division, late medieval churches scattered in or near various relent-lessly modern villages. Despite their inland location, however, they're too close to the seashore fleshpots to have entirely escaped the notice of visitors and expatriates, so **Dherínia** and **Paralímni** in particular have a smattering of necessary infrastructure and recommendable restaurants. East of Paralímni, tiny coves flank **Pernéra** resort, dwarfed by the massive development of **Protarás** extending south towards **Cape Gréko**, which enjoys some protection as a natural reserve.

Dherínia

DHERÍNIA (Deryneia) is visited mainly for its hilltop setting just south of the Attila Line overlooking the "dead zone" towards Famagusta and its modern suburb Varósha. Disconnected windmills spin aimlessly, or stand devaned and idle in the abandoned fields just north. A cluster of cafés, installed in the last Greek-Cypriot-civilian-occupied buildings before the dead zone, charge small sums for the privilege of using their binoculars or telescopes to take in the sad tableau of **Varósha** crumbling away, its rusty construction cranes frozen in their August 1974 positions. Videos and posters at the viewing platforms sensation-alize the violent nearby incidents of 1996 (see p.402).

In the event of a settlement and the reoccupation of Varósha by its original inhabitants, these cafés will doubtless lose most of their *raison d'être*. Much more likely to survive is an excellent *mezé*-format **taverna** between the main old church and a little chapel, ※ *Misohoro* (aka *Makis*) at Dhimokratías 32 (☎23743943; open all day but may close Tues).

Paralímni and nearby beaches

After the events of summer 1974, **PARALÍMNI**, a few kilometres south of Dherínia, became the de facto administrative capital of "Free Famagusta" district, and thus offers banks, petrol pumps, shops and cultural venues – as well as the most northerly access to the strip of Greek-Cypriot-controlled coast below Famagusta. Beachfront development extends well northwest of Ayía Triádha cove, past the roundabout funnelling traffic west to Paralímni, becoming more low-key before fizzling out just before the buffer zone. There are some fine, more or less normally priced **tavernas** here too: *Ikaria* at Prótou Aprilíou 210, featuring metropolitan Greek (as opposed to Cypriot) fare, and *Tony's* (aka *O Xenykhtis* – "Night Owl" because it's open until 3am; closed Mon) near the CYTA telecom tower, purveying great bean dishes, snails, fish, imported game and home-made dips, and boasting one of the largest wine cellars on the island.

The coast itself has a number of sandy beaches, divided by little headlands. Working southeast from **Ayía Triádha** (Agias Trias), there's tiny **Mouzoúra** (taverna) and then larger, protected **Loúma** (water sports offered) at **PERNÉRA**. The most unusual **accommodation** is Elena Koumoulli's peaceful *Sirena Bay* Hotel (☎&⒡23823502; closed Dec–Feb; ❸), an eight-room B&B outfit right on the water near Ayía Triádha, with a pool and on-site taverna.

Protarás

Pernéra merges south into **PROTARÁS**, a developmental disaster of some fifty wall-to-wall hotels and self-catering facilities, packed out from mid-May onwards with relatively well-behaved Scandinavian and British families. The rather narrow sandy beach is not even indicated from the inland bypass road – only the hotels themselves are signposted. Thus if you don't know that the *Salparo Apartments* mark the north end of the bay, and the *Louis Nausicaa Beach Apartments* the southern extreme, it's quite easy to drive right past the resort without ever seeing the sea. Once you do figure it out, you'll find that big shoreline lawns and swimming pools, substantial enough to accommodate the crowds, supplement the lack of sands – conveying a clear message that, unless you're actually staying at one of the behemoths or using their manifold recreational facilities (water-skiing, paragliding, etc), you're not exactly welcome here. At least the sea, if you do manage to reach it, is as clear and warm as you'd hope for.

It's difficult to imagine a setting less appropriate for non-package visitors, but Nicosians come here in some force at weekends, and (unlike Ayía Nápa) much of the resort stays "open" in winter. A good bet for anyone showing up on spec is the three-star *Pernera Beach* (☎23831011, ⓦwww.pernera.com .cy; ❹). The area's commercial hub is **Eden Square**, a mini mall of bars and restaurants. Other worthwhile, scattered places to eat include *The Raj* (dinner only April–Dec; closed Mon Nov–Dec) on the main drag in Protarás, with tandoori dishes a strength, and fish-and-steak specialists *Nissiotis Beach* at so-called Flamingo Bay.

Cape Gréko

Chances for a quiet, free-access swim are better south of Protarás, where the road along the mostly rocky shoreline threads through a brief patch of forest en route to **Cape Gréko** (Gkreko), Land's End for this corner of the island. Tiny beaches offer good snorkelling in the vicinity of Kónnos Bay, though excursion boats tend to arrive by noon. **Kónnos** itself is the only stretch of sand south of Protarás, but it's tiny and ridiculously gently shelving; a water-sports centre and café also means it's not exactly peaceful.

Despite the area's status as a national reserve, the cape-tip remains off-limits owing to a lighthouse, British military installations and the Radio Monte Carlo International relay station. A favourite landlubbers' activity in the area involves **hiking the coastline** from Protarás to Ayía Nápa (or vice versa), following a dirt track running parallel to the shore; this three- to four-hour outing will take you past impressive cliff-scapes, sea caves (with the local rubbish tip scandalously adjacent), a natural rock arch and a Roman quarry. You'll also see lots of cross-country racers and mountain bikers using the same rough path, notionally part of international trail E4. All told, however, the area's intrinsic merits are sufficiently limited to make you wonder just how developed for tourism it would be had the rather better beaches from Famagusta northwards remained under Greek-Cypriot control.

Travel details

Buses

Ayía Nápa to: Nicosia (Mon–Sat 1 daily, early morning, on EMAN; 1hr 30min); Paralímni via Protarás (May–Oct Mon–Sat, half-hourly 9am–8pm, hourly 8–11pm; Sun service half-hourly 9am–noon & 4–8pm, hourly noon–4pm; Nov–April Mon–Sat 7 daily; 20min).
Larnaca to: Ayía Nápa (May–Oct Mon–Sat 9 daily 8.30am–5.30pm, Sun 5 daily 8.30am–4.30pm, otherwise Mon–Fri 5 daily, Sat 4 daily, Sun 2 daily,

on EMAN; 40min); Limassol (Mon–Fri 4 daily 8am–4.30pm, Sat 2 daily 8am–1pm, on Intercity; 1hr 15min); Nicosia (Mon–Fri 7 daily 6.15am–4.15pm, Sat 2 daily 7.30–11am, Sun 4 daily 9am–4.30pm, on Intercity; 1hr); Protarás via Ayía Nápa on Intercity (summer Mon–Sat 4 daily 9am–5pm, winter 2 daily 10am–3pm; 50min); Protarás via Paralímni on PEAL (Mon–Fri 4 daily 8am–4.30pm, Sat 3 daily 11am–3pm, Sun 1 daily; 1hr).

2

Limassol and around

MEDITERRANEAN
SEA

7

6

8

5

3

4

1

2

Limassol

MEDITERRANEAN
SEA

N

CHAPTER 2 # Highlights

* **Limassol** The old town attracts visitors with its contemporary shopping, restored nineteenth-century architecture and cutting-edge restaurants. See p.122

* **Lófou** One of the most perfectly preserved, yet least commercialized, hill-villages in the foothills of Limassol's wine country. See p.130

* **Panayía Iamatikí** An intriguing hybrid Byzantine-Lusignan church in Arakapás village. See p.132

* **Kolóssi** The single, imposing legacy of the crusading Knights of St John. See p.137

* **Kourion** Extensive Roman and early Christian structures enjoy a magnificent setting atop coastal cliffs. See p.138

* **Beaches** Koúrion, Paramáli, Evdhímou and Pissoúri are four fine beaches in the western half of Limassol district. See p.141 & p.144

▲ Eating out at Limassol's Lanitis Carob Mill complex

Limassol and around

L imassol, the island's second largest city, is a brash, functional and grittily authentic place, redeemed by a wide range of dining options and sophisticated nightlife. More than anywhere else in the South, it has acted as a magnet for extensive urban drift from the impoverished hill-villages just north, and was a major focus of Greek-Cypriot refugee resettlement after 1974.

The city continues to expand a hundred or so metres annually to the east along the coast (westward growth is blocked by a British Sovereign Base), and a similar distance up into the barren, shrub-clad foothills of the Tróödhos, whose nearer settlements are now merely commuter dormitories. The most interesting spots, such as **Ayía Mávra**, **Ómodhos**, **Vouní** and **Lófou**, are easily visited en route to the high Tróödhos. Other half-inhabited hill-hamlets, like **Arakapás** with its fine Italo-Byzantine church, **Akapnoú** and **Odhoú**, see few outsiders from one week to the next. Reaching any of these spots requires your own vehicle, as there's effectively no public transport in the backcountry.

Along the coast east of Limassol, you have to outrun some fairly horrific hotel and apartment development before the tower-blocks halt a little past the small but evocative ancient site of **Amathus**. Just before the coast road veers inland towards Nicosia, there's access to **Governor's Beach**, the last remaining (relatively) unspoilt stretch of sand east of town, though the adjacent bay of **Áyios Yeóryios Alamánou** is better for dining.

Heading out of Limassol in the opposite direction holds more promise. A long beach fringing the **Akrotíri peninsula**, home to one of the island's three British Sovereign Bases, ends near the legend-draped convent of **Ayíou Nikoláou tón Gáton**. On the far side of the lagoon, orange and eucalyptus groves soften the landscape en route to the atmospheric crusader castle of **Kolossi** and the clifftop ruins of **Kourion** – together with its associated **sanctuary of Apollo Hylates**, one of the most impressive ancient sites in the South. You can swim at the beach below the palisades, but it's probably best to continue to the more secluded bays at **Evdhímou** and **Pissoúri**, both favourite hideouts of British expats.

Limassol (Lemesós)

Although its old centre of Levantine stone buildings and alleyways lends the city some charm, **LIMASSOL** (*Lemesós* in Greek, now the official name) is primarily the industrial and commercial capital of the southern coast, specializing in

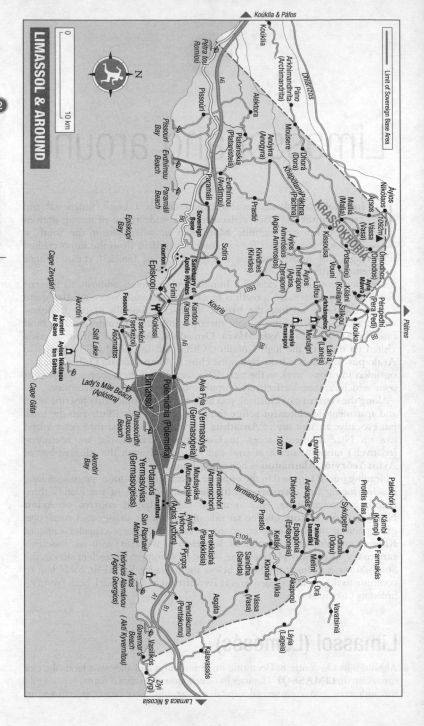

wine-making, citrus processing and canning. Since 1974 and the loss of Famagusta, it has also become the South's largest port, with container ships anchoring all year just offshore.

Limassol (population c.160,000) basks in its reputation as a mini-Texas of conspicuously consuming, gregarious nouveaux riches – and this was true even before a massive, mid-1990s influx of Russian *biznismen* who briefly dominated the "offshore banking" industry here. Along with the laundering of money smuggled out of the Russian Federation, prostitution and topless "gentlemen's clubs" are major local enterprises which have spilled out from the confines of the traditional central red-light zone.

Most of the conventional tourist industry is ghettoized in a long, unsightly ribbon of development east of town, in the areas of **Potamós Yermasóyias** (Potamos Germasogeias) and **Amathus** (Amathous). This consists of 16km-plus of intermittent roadworks, faded, rabbit-warren hotel and apartment buildings, neon bars, naff restaurants and "waterparks", all abutting a generally mediocre beach. Jewellery and furs are assiduously pitched at the Russian market – every fourth sign is in the Cyrillic alphabet – while many (though by no means all) of the hotel entrances are closely patrolled by eastern European prostitutes.

All is not frowsiness and vulgarity, however; since the millennium, extensive areas of the old commercial centre have been rehabilitated. The giant Anexartisías mall just off the eponymous main street, the refurbished central market and the Lanitis Carob Mill project constitute the main foci of this urban renewal. Native Lemessans do their utmost to uphold the city's reputation as the island's party town – something abetted by the recent establishment of a technical university – with live music venues, quality restaurants and stylish cafés. And if you're considering a winter-sun break, Limassol (or at least its environs) makes an excellent base – as a "real" town, it definitely doesn't close down off-season the way Ayía Nápa does.

Some history

A near-complete lack of significant monuments attests to the relative youth of the town. Limassol hardly existed before the Christian era, being for centuries overshadowed by Amathus to the east and Kourion to the west. It burst into prominence in 1191, when Richard the Lionheart's fiancée, Berengaria of Navarre, and his sister were nearly shipwrecked just offshore. Isaac Komnenos, self-styled ruler of the island, refused to send them provisions. Hearing of this insult to his intended, Richard landed nearby in force, married Berengaria on the site of the present-day Limassol castle, and went on to claim the island after defeating Isaac in battle.

Two centuries of prosperity followed, with both the Knights Hospitallers and Knights Templars having extensive holdings around Limassol after the loss of the Holy Land. However, an earthquake and devastating raids by the Genoese, Mamelukes and finally the Turks combined to level the settlement by the beginning of the Ottoman era; it's only since the end of the nineteenth century that the town has grown again.

Arrival, orientation and information

Since 2002, passenger-ferry services to Limassol have been suspended and show no sign of resuming; Cyprus was unwilling to terrorist-proof the port terminal, 4km southwest of the town centre, to the satisfaction of Israel, which shared the boat-line. Bus #30 still runs into town from the port via the seafront, its route extending along the coastal boulevard the entire 16km to the marina and last hotel (every 15min 6.25am–5.50pm; half-hourly only from old port 6–8.30pm).

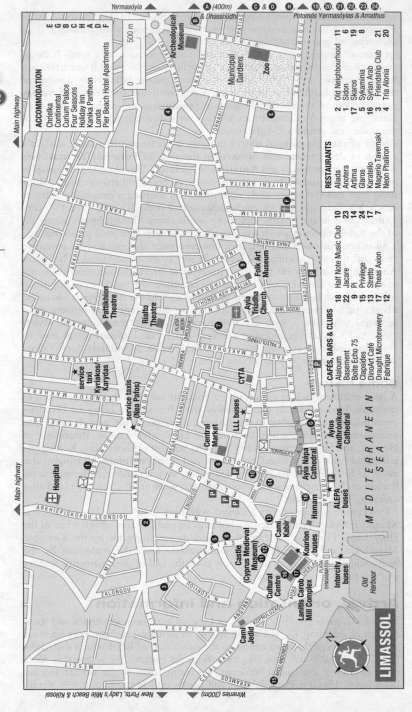

LIMASSOL

ACCOMMODATION

Chrielka	E
Continental	G
Curium Palace	B
Four Seasons	C
Holiday Inn	H
Kanika Pantheon	A
Londa	D
Pier Beach Hotel Apartments	F

RESTAURANTS

Aliada	2	Old Neighbourhood	11
Anotera	1	Sidon	6
Artima	17	Skaros	19
Glaros	15	Sykaminia	8
Karatello	16	Syrian Arab	21
Magerio Tavernaki		Friendship Club	
Neon Phaliron	4	Tria Alonia	20

CAFÉS, BARS & CLUBS

Alaloum	18	Half Note Music Club	10
Basement	22	Jacare	23
Boîte Echo 75	9	Pi	24
Clapsides	15	Privilege	17
DinoArt Café	13	Stretto	17
Draught Microbrewery	17	Theas Axion	12
Fabrique	7		

Yermasóyia

Potomós Yermasóyias & Amathus

Archeological Museum

Municipal Gardens

Zoo

Pattikhion Theatre

Rialto Theatre

Folk Art Museum

Ayia Triádha Church

CYTA

service taxi Kyriakos/Karydas

service taxis (Néa Pafos)

Central Market

LLL buses

Hospital

Ayios Andhronikos Cathedral

Ayia Nápa Cathedral

Hamam

Castle (Cyprus Medieval Museum)

Cami Kabir

Kourion buses

ALEPA buses

Cultural Centre

Lanitis Carob Mill Complex

Cami Jedid

Intercity buses

Old Harbour

MEDITERRANEAN SEA

New Ports, Lady's Mile Beach & Kolossi

Wineries (300m)

Main highway

Arriving by **long-distance bus** or **service taxi**, you'll be dropped at one of the terminals shown on our map and detailed in "Listings" (p.126). If you're driving, make for the public pay-and-display **car parks** on the seafront promenade, or various privately operated ones inland along Elládhos. There are a very limited number of uncontrolled spaces around the municipal gardens.

The town centre is defined by four main thoroughfares: the coastal boulevard, which changes its name first from **Spýrou Araoúzou** to (very briefly) **Khristodhoúlou Hadjipávlou**, then to **28–Oktovríou** as you head northeast; the main shopping street, **Ayíou Andhréou**, which runs roughly parallel to it just inland up to the Municipal Gardens and Archeological Museum; and **Anexartisías**, which bisects downtown to meet up with **Gládstonos**, which bounds the centre to the northwest. To its considerable credit, the municipality has laid out a continuous **shoreline promenade** for bikers and walkers only, linking the entire coast from the old port to the new marina.

The main **tourist information** office (Mon, Tues, Thurs & Fri 8.15am–2.30pm & 4–6.30pm, Wed 8.15am–2.30pm, Sat 8.15am–1.30pm) sits on the ground floor of the *Continental Hotel* building at Spýrou Araoúzou 115, but their stock of leaflets is not great – English-language material in particular can disappear quickly. There's also a branch near Dhassoúdhi beach at Yeoryíou toú Prótou 22, which keeps the same hours.

Accommodation

Moderately priced **accommodation** in Limassol is scarce, with little between the shabby "guest houses" of the bazaar and the luxury digs of the resort strip. Certain no- or one-star hotels, near the old harbour or the red-light district, are best avoided. However, there are some decent hotel-apartments within the town limits.

Chrielka Olymbíon 7 ☎ 25358366, ⓦ www.chrielka.com.cy. These superbly appointed A-class hotel-apartments are the best in the city centre. Units, pitched at a business clientele, have large bathrooms and kitchens, though breakfast is also available on the ground floor. Limited sea views, but there's a pool, and front rooms face the Municipal Gardens. Studio ④, 1-bed ④

Continental Spýrou Araoúzou 115 ☎ 25362530. Rather faded two-star relic that's the best budget option by default; get a sea-view room and overlook the fug of decades of cigarette smoke, the poor breakfasts and the lack of a lift. ②

Curium Palace Výronos 11 ☎ 25891100, ⓦ www.curiumpalace.com. One of Limassol's first, 1930s, orientalized Art Deco hotels, this was refurbished in 2002 to four-star standard, without altering the listed exterior. Vast common areas make it a popular wedding and conference venue; there's also a pool, sauna, gym and tennis court tucked away in the deceptively large back garden. Three grades of rooms, all with tubs in the baths and somewhat low ceilings. Standard ④, executive suite ⑦

Four Seasons Amathus, 9km east of centre ☎ 25858000, ⓦ www.fourseasons.com.cy. The dominant motif at this five-star resort is "oasis", with a jungle-like atrium and koi ponds outside. The in-house *Mavromatis* supper-only diner, sister to the Paris one, is well regarded. Main-wing units aren't huge (though bathrooms are decent) – the beachside garden studios, popular with families, are preferable. Internet rate standard rooms ⑦, garden studio ⑨

Holiday Inn City/Potamós Yermasóyias boundary, 2km east of town centre ☎ 25851515, ⓦ www.ichotelsgroup.com. Four-star beachfront outfit with water sports, indoor outdoor pools, gym and better-than average hotel food. You'll get higher standards further out of town, but this is the most comfortable choice closer in. Best rates through the corporate website. ⑥

Kanika Pantheon 28-Oktovríou, corner of Ioánni Metaxá, 400m from the Municipal Gardens ☎ 25591111, ⓦ www.kanikahotels.com. Along with the *Curium Palace*, the most comfortable digs within the city limits. Not seafront – that's 5min distant – but a well-priced three-star with two pools and health club. Rooms have oblique sea views, and for a little extra you can get an "upgraded" room with desk and wi-fi. ④

Londa Yeoryíou toú Prótou, about 5km east of centre ☎ 25865555, ⓦ www.londahotel.com. The blank, narrow façade of this 2006-redone, self-dubbed boutique hotel – Limassol's first – gives nothing away. Once inside, the white, beige and wood-panelled common areas are echoed in the individual rooms, their designer furnishings on a vaguely Asian theme. There's not much of a beach, but a nice deep terrace pool, and the in-house *Caprice* restaurant offers Italian and seafood dishes to a business clientele. Well-trained staff, a big gym and a spa complete the picture. Internet discounts on rack rates of ❽ standard, ❾ suite.

Pier Beach Hotel Apartments 28-Oktovríou 261A ☎ 25749000, ⓦ www.pierbeachhotel.com. High-quality B-class studios and one-bedroom units, most with sea view. Run more like a standard hotel, with an on-site restaurant, roof terrace with jacuzzi and pavement terrace bar; parking at the rear. ❸

The City

Limassol presents isolated points of interest rather than a townscape to savour: from 1974 until it was outstripped by Ayía Nápa in 1994 this was statistically the number-one tourist base in the South, but you won't need more than a full day to take in all there is to see. After looking in at the **castle**, the **carob mill** area and several **museums**, perhaps taking a stroll around the **bazaar** or a **winery tour** and having a good meal or two, many visitors will probably be ready to move on, at least in summer.

Limassol castle

Unassuming from the outside, **Limassol castle** stands in a pleasant garden immediately north of the old port. What you see today is a careful restoration of Byzantine foundations, Venetian and Ottoman miliatry adaptations and British colonial-prison architecture. Somewhere under the existing walls stood the long-vanished Byzantine chapel of Saint George in which, tradition has it, Richard the Lionheart married Berengaria on May 12, 1191. Anticipating his rout of Isaac, Richard also had himself crowned king of Cyprus and his bride queen of England, in the presence of assorted Latin clerics and nobility.

The castle shelters the **Cyprus Medieval Museum** (Mon–Sat 9am–5pm, Sun 10am–1pm; €1.70), though the building, with its musty, echoing vaults, air shafts and masonry ribs, is as interesting as the exhibits, most of which are on the upper floor. The emphasis is on metalware, heraldry and sacred art, including bas-reliefs and pottery with Christian designs; the best bits are silver Byzantine plates showing events in the life of David, part of the Lambousa Treasure (see p.314), and a suit of armour from the Lusignan period. When open, the roof terrace and secondary tower afford excellent views over the town.

The Lanitis Carob Mill development

In 2002, the row of stone-built industrial and commercial premises bounding the castle on two sides was rescued from long-standing dereliction by its owners, the Lanitis Foundation. The **Lanitis Carob Mill** on the northwest side was restored both as a free museum to the processing of the pods into syrup, animal feed-pellets and culinary powder, which only ceased in the 1970s, and also as a **cultural centre** for changing exhibits and conferences. The warehouses occupying the southwesterly row of buildings have, without exception, been colonized by trendy bars, cafés and restaurants, for which see p.124.

The bazaar

The neighbourhood surrounding the castle was once the Turkish commercial district, as street names will tell you. The **Cami** (pronounced "Jami") **Kabir**, its minaret visible from the castle roof, is still used by Limassol's Arab and remaining Turkish-Cypriot population, though the **Cami Jedid** (aka the Köprülü Hacı İbrahim Ağa mosque), at the far end of Angýras nearer the former Turkish residential quarter, is firmly locked. The apses of a much older

Lusignan church which once stood here have been excavated and left exposed in the lane immediately east of the Cami Kabir, while immediately south the Ottoman **hamam**, with a calligraphic inscription over the door, still functions daily from 2 to 10pm. Immediately around the castle, fast-food joints alternate with tacky souvenir stalls; the covered **central market**, a recently refurbished, late-nineteenth-century stone-built structure, appeals more, especially the pedestrianized square and its cafés out front.

Winery tours

The city's four **wineries** – ETKO, KEO, LOEL and SODAP – are strung out in a row on Franklin Roosevelt, west of the old harbour; each lays on a free tour (Mon–Fri) at 10am, though **ETKO** also has a somewhat broader schedule (9.30am–1.30pm). Parking is available in front of the wineries, but the brief walk from the castle or a bus #30 ride along Franklin Roosevelt are perhaps better options after the final tasting session. Incidentally, do the tours on your own, since group coach tours have to be paid for (and are exactly the same).

To join the daily tour at **KEO**, the largest drinks manufacturer on the island, just show up at 9.50am (except in summer when you should book on ✆25362053) in the reception area of the administration building. Over half an hour you're rather perfunctorily shown the cellars for the heavy, sweet Commandaria (see p.51) where a third of each barrelful is retained as the *mána* or "mother" ferment for the next cycle; the distillery for *zivanía* (grape-mash spirit), used to fortify KEO's liqueurs; the 40,000-litre oak ageing barrels for brandy; and barrels of sweet and cream "sherry" – no longer allowed to be labelled as such, owing to objections from Spain – ageing out in the sun.

Other musuems and the municipal gardens

At the opposite end of Ayíou Andhréou, near the corner of Óthonos kéh Amalías at no. 253, the **Folk Art Museum** (June–Sept Mon–Wed & Fri 8.30am–1.30pm & 4–6.30pm; Oct–May Mon–Wed & Fri 8.30am–1.30pm & 3–5.30pm; €0.80) has filled a grand old mansion with rural and domestic knick-knacks, woodwork, traditional dresses and jewellery. The lighting and labelling aren't good, however, and you're virtually obliged to buy the guide booklet to make much sense of the exhibits.

A little way beyond the Folk Art Museum spread the **Municipal Gardens** (daily 8.30am–7/8pm), an extent of well-tended greenery fronting the sea. The gardens are the venue for the annual **Wine Festival** (10 days in late Aug to early Sept); there's also a **mini-zoo** (daily: May–Sept 9am–noon & 3–7pm; Oct–April 9am–6.30pm; €0.80), mostly comprising an aviary, though it has a zebra and a few cheetahs.

The district **Archeological Museum** (Mon–Fri 9am–5pm, Sat 10am–1pm; €1.70), just north of the gardens, is strongest on Archaic, Geometric and Bronze Age artefacts. The left-hand gallery is ninety percent pottery, best of which are the Geometric-era dishes – an obvious inspiration for the modern *tsésti* or woven circular wall-hangings you see everywhere in tavernas. Archaic terracotta figurines also abound, with presumed toys scattered amongst animal-drawn chariots and other votive offerings. Highlights include a *rhyton* in the form of a bull, and a headless torso with unusually detailed hands holding a bird to its chest. Female figures, possibly offerings for fertility, clasp their breasts or a mirror (a symbol of Aphrodite/Astarte), and one plays a frame-drum. A column capital in the guise of Hathor demonstrates the introduction of Egyptian gods to the island.

The smaller, central Classical room is sparsely stocked except for some gold and precious-stone jewellery; there's also a curious anthropomorphic lampstand, with ears for an oil wick and the head hollowed to accommodate a candle or incense. The Roman section on the right contains painted and multi-coloured glass; the rainbow/oil-slick effect is the result of sodium and potassium ions leaching into the alkaline soils in which the objects were buried.

Eating and drinking

The steak-and-chips eateries interspersed among *McDonald's*, *Starbucks* and *KFC* along the waterfront and in Potamós Yermasóyias are pretty dismissible, but a brief drive or even just a short walk will be amply rewarded. Bear in mind also that as in metropolitan Greece Lemessans **eat** late, from about 9.30pm onwards – though this is much less true on the tourist strip.

Restaurants: centre

Aliada Irínis 117 ☎ 25340758. One of the more consistent and best-value of several "old house" tavernas hereabouts. For a set price (around €23) you get soup, cold self-service buffet, a hot main course and the run of the fancy (Western) sweet trolley, plus *zivanía* as an aperitif (wine extra). Dinner only; closed Sun; reservations essential at weekends.

🎭 **Anotera** Gladstonos 5. Probably the best traditional Cypriot *mezé* in the city limits, with fish, meat and vegetable choices, served in either a summer garden or lovely old-house interior. Also good à la carte seafood platters garnished with chips, salad and broad beans. Closed Sat noon & Mon.

Artima Lanitis Carob Mill buildings, Vassilíssis St. Generic Mediterranean-cum-Italian fare in stylish surroundings. Antipasti, pasta and fish or meat mains for about €30 per head, plus drink. Open daily.

Glaros Eleftherías 50. Seafood restaurants are generally overpriced in Limassol; this one, formerly near Áyios Andónios but relocated in 2006 to the Old Town, has long been favoured by locals for reasonably priced if not stellar mains (humbler fish species from around €12/portion). The extensive seating includes a secluded rear garden. Lunch and dinner daily except Mon.

Karatello Lanitis Carob Mill buildings, Vassilíssis St. An upmarket take on the traditionally *mezé* house (though there are also à la carte mains), in industrial-minimalist surroundings. Tick off your choices on the menu and eat well (wine extra) for about €25 a head.

Magerio Tavernaki Eleftherías 121. Homestyle lunchtime fare (meat-and-veg stews) is average-to-good in quality, at average prices, yet this spot is enduringly popular and cosier than *ly Sykaminia*. There's live *rebétika* music at night, when the menu offers more typically Cypriot *mezédhes* and grills.

Neon Phaliron Gládstonos 135 ⊕ www .neonphaliron.com. Considered one of the top, and top-priced "nouvelle Cypriot" restaurants in Limassol, founded in 1960. Arguably best in winter, when duck, quail and other game (mostly imported) comes to the fore; otherwise seafood is a strength. Closed Sun dinner.

Old Neighbourhood Angýras 14. Looks like a tourist trap, in a touristy area, but proprietor "Mr Nick" purveys some of the best, freshest fish in Limassol. Supper only.

Sidon Saripólou 71–73, opposite covered market. Quite a cavernous interior behind a small storefront at this elegant Cypro-Lebanese eatery. Decent appetizers (turnovers, chicken livers) precede a mains list strong on lamb and chicken dishes, topped off by increasingly rare *mahallebías* dessert. Count on €30 per person with a modest intake of local drink – imported wines much pricier. Dinner only; closed Mon.

Sykaminia Eleftherías 26. Classic working-man's *mayirío* which got a 2005 refit – reflected in somewhat higher prices. The stock-in-trade remains lamb with spinach, assorted *ospriá*, small fried fish and other home-style dishes. Open Mon–Sat lunch only.

Restaurants: Yermasóyia/ Potamós Yermasóyias and Áyios Týkhon

Skaros North end of Yermasóyia village, opposite municipal car park ☎ 25325080. Fish and seafood here is fifty percent dearer than the norm but the quality is high, with an attractive environment for both indoor and outdoor seating. Ring for reservations and opening hours.

🎭 **Syrian Arab Friendship Club** Iliádhos 3, opposite *Apollonia Beach Hotel*, Potamós Yermasóyias, 5km east of the centre. The same, outstanding, 15-platter Arabic *mezé* and hubble-bubbles as its sister branch in Nicosia (see p.261), which is recommendation enough. Open daily all year; outdoor summer dining.

Tria Alonia Village centre, Áyios Týkhon ☎ 25323913. Not much for vegans in their copious, 15-platter *mezé* encompassing spinach-egg, *kouloúmbra*, liver and pasta with cheese among more usual options; if meaty quantity sometimes overshadows quality, it's still worth the short trip inland from the resort strip. Large parties should book tables at the stone-clad interior or conservatory. Dinner only, Mon–Sat.

Cafés and bars

Draught Microbrewery Lanitis Carob Mill buildings, Vassilíssis St. Very popular in the early evening for its own-brewed beer, and later on for DJ-spun sounds, but the international bistro food is overpriced.

DinoArt Café Irínis 62–66. The latest entrant in this street's renaissance, with flavoured coffees, decadent cakes and snack platters in cutting-edge surrounds. Open till midnight every day.
Pi Kitíou Kyprianoú 27. Arty stone-clad lounge-café that also offers impressive salads, sandwiches and other light meals to a jazz soundtrack, as well as the occasional art exhibit.
Stretto Lanitis Carob Mill buildings, Vassilíssis St. Ultra-trendy café with light snacks as well as drinks, exposed stonework, squishy sofas, fat candles and a long wine list.

Nightlife and entertainment

The resort strip of Potamós Yermasóyias, defined by its main drag Yeoryíou toú Prótou, has the expected complement of foreign-orientated **bars and clubs**, most closed during low season – many permanently in the wake of the tourism slump. Town-centre venues have much greater patronage from locals, and stay open all year. There's a scattering of **gay**, or at least gay-friendly, clubs among them.

As part of the revival of downtown Limassol, the **Rialto Theatre** (℡25343900, ⓦ www.rialto.com.cy) at Andhréa Dhroushióti 19, on the corner of Platía Iróön, has been gloriously refurbished and pressed into service as the city's main venue for serious musical, dance and dramatic acts, both Greek and foreign names, plus film festivals. The restoration has partially reclaimed Platía Iróön, the traditional heart of Limassol's red-light district, from the sin merchants – there are now even "respectable" places for theatre patrons to have a coffee before or after performances. The 1930s Internationalist-style **Pattikhion Theatre** at Ayías Zónis 2 (℡25343341) is the city's other (and slightly bigger) quality music and drama venue, and still offers a crowded programme.

Limassol has several **cinemas**, including Othellos, Thessaloníkis 19 (℡25352232); the Rio at Elládhos 125, corner Navarínou (℡25871410), also

▲ Beach life, Limassol

with outdoor summer premises; and the five-screen K–Cineplex at Ariádhni 8 in Potamós Yermasóyias (☎77778383). There's also the cheaper **Limassol Film Society**, housed in the Praxis Theatre on Mikhaïl Mikahelídhes (☎25357570), which shows art-house movies on Mondays at 8.30pm (not July/Aug).

Centre

Alaloum Loutrón 1. Limassol's longest-running gay club, housed in stone-built, arcaded premises, with proprietor Stelios laying on a mixed Greek/European soundtrack and making an older mixed clientele (including transvestites and lesbians) feel at home.

Boite Echo 75/Ikho Evdhomindapende Ayíou Andhréou 259. Pub-like atmosphere, enhanced by a pool table. The place also does duty as the headquarters of GAIA, an "ancient culture club". Occasional live music; open 6pm to midnight.

Clapsides End of Ayíou Andoníou; ☎25747511. Long-running, come-as-you-are café/bar, with an open-air dancefloor in summer. Live Greek and foreign music most evenings from 10pm; Fri is "retro" night.

Fabrique Angýras 18, by castle. Occupying a former workshop (thus the name), this stone-built club is bigger than it looks from the outside; mainstream Greek and overseas tunes, younger crowd.

Half Note Music Club Sokrátous 4, corner with Saripólou ☎25377030. Busiest on Fri and Sat nights, when it acts as a straightforward club, but comes into its own with regular live name acts

(Brazilian, Greek mainland, trans-Atlantic rock) which will set you back €15–18 cover.

Theas Axion Elénis Paleoloyínas 40. Reasonably priced, classy wine (and beer) bar, with large snack platters available, imbued with the personality of ex-actor owner Kostas, who has set up shop in his parents' former house, a round-fronted 1930s-vintage structure. An excellent choice before or after attending an event at the nearby Rialto Theatre.

Potamós Yermasóyias

Basement Yeoryíou toú Prótou 91. Small but recently overhauled and usually busy with a young clientele, playing mainstream club tunes (with occasional specific house or trance nights through a state-of-the-art sound system). Open nightly.

Jacare Pópiland 67. Tucked away in an alley off the main drag, this is the "other" local gay bar, more frequented by a younger clientele.

Privilege By the St Raphael hotel, 18km east of the centre. The largest and most locally patronized of the clubs here, with lots of different dance areas (mostly outdoor), and a mix of mainstream Greek and north-European hits. Fri–Sun only.

Shopping

Central Limassol is in the grip of a restoration craze, as fine Neoclassical buildings are steadily rehabilitated for business and residential use. This has created a market for **antiques and furniture** to furnish the interiors, and central dealers abound. The plushest, installed in a former candy factory, is Hermal's Auction House at Gládstonos 48 (☎25340104).

More affordable, locally produced art – primarily **painting** – is on view at Morfi Gallery, Angýras 84 (Tues–Sat 10am–1pm & 4–7pm, Mon 10am–1pm; Ⓦ www.morfi.org). For **ceramics**, Kerameas, nearby at no. 55, has a selection of portable, yet unusual, objects. At Ergastiri Keramikis Tekhnis (Workshop of Ceramic Art) at Khrístou Sózou 15, between Ayíou Andhréou and Spýrou Araoúzou, you'll find highly idiosyncratic, often eerie, large-scale work by Pambos Michlis, displayed in an old house just behind the seafront.

Listings

Bookshops Try Ioannidhes, Athínon 30–32, the best in town for books on Cyprus and also for Department of Lands and Surveys maps, or Kyriakou, an English-oriented general-purpose bookstore at Gríva Dhigyení 3. For used paperbacks, head for Marilyn's Book Swap at Kitíou Kyprianoú 51, where you're given forty percent credit on returning your original purchase.

Bus companies/terminals Useful long-distance outfits include Intercity ☎24643492, from the old port, for Larnaca; ALEPA ☎99625027, by Panikos Kiosk on Spýrou Araoúzou, for Páfos; LLL ☎22665814, from the central market for Nicosia; PEAL ☎25552220, from Dhassoúdhi beach (also stopping at the market) for Plátres in the Tróödhos. Buses for Episkopí village and the turning for Kourion ruins depart from beside the castle.

Car rental Andreas Petsas, Yeoryíou toú Prótou, Sea Breeze Court, Suite 1, Potamós Yermasóyias ☎ 25323672; Leos, LeOfóros Ámathus, White Arches Block L, Shop 1, ☎ 25320000, ⓦ www .leoscy.com; St George's, Arkhiepiskópou Makaríou 62 ☎ 25562077, ⓦ www.stgeorges-carhire.com; Sixt, Yeoryíou toú Prótou, Belmar Complex, Shop 5, Potamós Yermasóyias ☎ 25312345.

Post offices The main branch, with late afternoon hours and parcel/poste restante service, is inconveniently located at the west end of Gládstonos; there's a more central branch for outbound letters on Kyprianoú in the bazaar, open standard morning hours, plus Mon, Tues, Thurs & Fri 3–6pm & Sat 9–11am.

Scuba schools Dive-In has a branch operating out of the *Four Seasons Hotel* (☎ 25311923); see Larnaca "Listings" for details (p.95).

Service taxis Travel & Express is the corner of Kavagóglou and Mishaoúli (☎ 25877666).

Travel agent Becky's Travel at Arkhiepiskópou Makaríou 95, Shop C ☎ 25386032, ⓦ www .beckystravel.com, are tops for advantageous air fares at very short notice.

The Limassol foothills

Inland from Limassol, the Tróödhos foothills nurture a substantial fraction of Cyprus's commercial **vineyards**, set amid infertile terrain covered in maquis vegetation. Given little other significant economic activity, however, many local villages are moribund, with futures only as weekend retreats for city-dwellers, holiday homes for foreigners or artists' colonies.

The rise to the highest peaks of the Tróödhos is not uniform: roads going inland roller-coaster past the first set of barrier ridges into hollows and hidden valleys that contain most local attractions. Many of these places were fiefs of the Hospitallers or other Lusignan nobility; they lie primarily between 600 and 800 metres above sea level, resulting in a pleasant climate even in high summer. Outsiders will probably pass through the various settlements just off the two main highways up towards the Tróödhos, the **E601** and the **B8**, which begin at Erími and Polemídhia respectively on the Limassol coastal plain. The British first opened a "Wine Road" (later the E601) as far as Ómodhos early in the twentieth century to facilitate the shipping out of the grape harvest.

The westerly Tróödhos approach: the Krassokhoriá

The large villages clustered near the top of the westerly route towards the Tróödhos are collectively labelled the **krassokhoriá** (wine villages) in tourism promotion, but as "Commandaria villages" on some maps; in any event, they are renowned for both their dry and sweet-dessert wines. At autumn vintage time, huge lorries groaning with grapes lumber along the narrow roads, and signs warn of grape-juice slicks on the pavement, while many of the villages have autumn *palouzé* (grape-must pudding) festivals.

Vouní

Your first likely detour from the E601 is just beyond Áyios Amvrósios, a seven-kilometre drive towards part-abandoned but highly picturesque **VOUNÍ**, where the remaining elders sit at a few *kafenía* on the Paliostráta or old high street. The village has been long a protected architectural showcase, and is striking seen against its hillside from the southwest, though some jarring Hellenic-blue balustrades and a few illicit brickings-up have crept in among the traditional materials and methods supposed to be used for renovations.

127

Vouní (or rather the Stená ravine, well signposted just west) is home to the **Vouní Donkey Sanctuary** (Mon–Sat 10am–4pm; €1.70), which plays host to 127 beasts who can no longer be cared for by their former owners. Today the animals are only used at grape-harvest time to work terraces inaccessible to farm machinery, and instances of abuse and abandonment have increased sharply. The aim of the sanctuary is not only being a "retirement home", but to provide veterinary care to donkeys elsewhere, and a bank of strong, healthy animals which can be hired out for a few weeks yearly during the vintage season. There is also a café, visitors' centre and gift shop on site.

The better of the two village-centre **tavernas** is *Iy Orea Ellas* (June–Oct daily not Mon; Nov–May Fri dinner to Sun lunch only; ☏25944328), which stresses metropolitan Greek rather than Cypriot food, presented in *mezé* format, though portions are small and prices have climbed since discovery by a trendy Limassol clientele – reckon on €20 a head plus drink. An alternative lies 6km south towards Áyios Amvrósios, where *Ohyro* (same opening hours) offers a more abundant, traditional *mezé*.

Kiláni and Ayía Mávra

KILÁNI (Koilani), 5km northeast of Vouní, is architecturally less of a piece but a bit livelier in its central pedestrianized area with several *kafenía*. If you're taken with the place, **stay** at one of two apartments in the *Mavrikios House* (☏99642763; €61) near the square. There are also several excellent local **wineries**, visitable by appointment only: Erimoudes (☏99625826), Vardalis (☏25470261), Ayia Mavri (☏25470225) and Domaine Vlassides (☏99441574), the latter perhaps the most renowned for the sake of its excellent Cabernet Sauvignon and Shiraz reds.

Inside the church of Monoyénis, the Limassol archbishopric has set up an **ecclesiastical museum** (☏99302086 24hrs in advance for admission), a better-than-average collection of icons and other sacred objects salvaged from nearby insecure churches. The Kiláni location was chosen because of its past importance in church affairs; several bishops of the sixteenth to eighteenth centuries hailed from here, and indeed the archbishopric of Limassol itself was based here during the seventeenth century, when Limassol was at its nadir.

Continuing a kilometre up the valley of the Krýos stream from Kiláni, past the Ayia Mavri winery on the village's outskirts, you can't miss the twelfth-century chapel of **Ayía Mávra** (or Ayía Mávri; always open), set in the river gorge by some trees and a handful of rural weekenders' **tavernas**. The little church is all that remains of a much larger monastery, and a spring still burbles from the apse; according to legend the water flows from a cleft in the rock created when Mavra, pursued by her father and unwanted fiancé, appealed to the Virgin to preserve her vow of chastity – and was promptly swallowed by the low cliff. This tale, told with variations around the Greek Orthodox world, is a reworking of the pagan legend of Daphne pursued by Apollo; in fact, the historical Mavra is supposed to have married Saint Timothy.

Inside are some engaging, if smudged fifteenth-century frescoes. Áyios Timothéos (Saint Timothy) and Mávra herself have been cleaned, and face you as you enter; just above are the remains of the Dormition. A *Virgin Enthroned* graces the conch of the apse, flanked by the *Ascension* (left) and *Pentecost* (right). The central vaulting is occupied by indistinct scenes from the Life of Christ, with the Pandokrátor in the dome.

Potamioú and Vássa

A right turn off the E601 after Kissoúsa leads up to **POTAMIOÚ**, nearly the equal of Vouní in architectural distinction and graced by the sixteenth-century

Ayía Marína church with octagonal dome. The ruins of Byzantine Áyios Mnáson lie down in the valley of the Khapótami.

Staying with the E601 brings you to VÁSSA (Vasa), 35km from Limassol and, like its neighbours, a hive of renovation activity. Spare a moment for fifteenth-century, roadside Áyios Yeóryios church, in the ravine just north of the village, with slightly later frescoes. Of special note are the *Evangelists* on the squinches, including Saint John the Divine with his disciple Prohoros, an *Annunciation* over the main door, and a *Deposition* on the central arch.

There is no short-term accommodation here, but two **tavernas** operate in the cobble-paved village centre during the warmer months. However, much the best and most reliable local eating is well south of town near the bypass road: 🍴 *Iy Ariadhni* (☎25944064; closed Tues off-season). This offers excellent homestyle fare such as *koupépia* with farm-fresh sheep's yoghurt, *keftédhes*, *louviá* with celery, *bourékia* with *anári* cheese, good grills and a couple of dishes of the day, all washed down by decent bulk wine – or the products of the local **Vasa winery** (☎25945999 to visit), particularly their Cabernet Sauvignon.

Ómodhos

Three kilometres beyond either Potamioú or Vássa is the more heavily promoted **ÓMODHOS** (Omodos), unusually laid out around its **monastery of Timíou Stavroú** (the Holy Cross), with a vast cobbled square fronting it – probably an instance of Lusignan town planning, since rarely in the Greek world is a monastery the core of a settlement. Although of Byzantine origin, what you see now dates entirely from the early and mid-nineteenth century. Dositheos and Khrysanthos, sponsors and abbots of the monastery during its late eighteenth-century revival, were hanged by the Ottoman authorities in 1821 on the outbreak of the mainland Greek rebellion. Since 1917 the monastery has been empty of monks, and Orthodox pilgrims visit principally to revere purported Crucifixion relics kept inside the otherwise undistinguished church. The gallery of the upper storey is sporadically open, worth the climb up for its intricate woodwork. This includes carved lattice railings along the walkway past wooden cell doors, and – at the northeast corner of the enclosure – the bishop's room with its carved ceiling and cabinets lining the east wall.

The **village** itself is pleasant enough, if very commercialized, with touts inveigling you to visit rather bogus traditional houses. Much the best interior is that of the originally Lusignan *linós* or old **wine press** (free, always open) just north and downhill from the monastery; find the light switch to view the mammoth boom of the press, embedded *kioupiá* (urns) for holding the grape mash, and the copper *zivanía* still. The best buys are bottles of the red and white local wine – Linos is particularly recommended – or *loukoúmia* ("Turkish" delight); only some of the basketry and lace displayed here are locally crafted. There are about a half-dozen **tavernas** in or just outside Ómodhos – none especially recommended; a few simple **cafés** alternate with the souvenir displays on the main plaza. On September 14, the monastery church becomes the focus of the Holy Cross festival, which spills out onto the square outside.

Malliá, Ársos and the ridge route to Páfos

MALLIÁ (Malia), overlooking a major junction near the end of the E601, once had the largest Turkish-Cypriot population in the Limassol hills; the graves of six original villagers, killed in the early-1964 troubles, lie by the mosque in the western clifftop neighbourhood, its houses slowly being squatted and renovated as weekend retreats (dwellings lower down have been sparsely occupied by Greek-Cypriot refugees). Malliá is the highest in altitude of the Commandaria-producing villages – there's a large KEO plant at the outskirts – and before 1974 the inhabitants used to barter their dessert wine for dry wine from Ársos. Just at the main entrance to the village an old 1940s Internationalist-style *kafenío* has been refurbished as a **taverna**, the *Platanos Malias* (℡25944944; closed Sun night & Mon winter), featuring good Ársos wine, though their *mezé* is better than their *kléftiko*.

ÁRSOS, 3km north, is much the biggest of the wine villages, but while it's an imposing, stone-built place, there's nothing in particular to see other than the **Nikolettino winery** (℡99437137 to visit). There are two **tavernas** and restoration **accommodation** at *Dia's House* (℡25372368; ❶ assuming four sharing), a nineteenth-century arcaded stone dwelling at the northwest edge of "town"; *Moustos* (℡99679788, Ⓔadonis.sh@cytanet.com.cy; 1-bed unit ❸, 2-bed ❹) with a huge salon; and central *Cornaro House* (℡25358836, Ⓔcornaro@cytanet .com.cy; studio ❷,1-bed unit ❸), most suitable for couples.

From Ársos you reach Áyios Nikólaos, near the head of the Dhiárizos valley (see p.201), or backtrack slightly to follow an interesting ridge route along the eastern flank of the valley into Páfos district, with spectacular views west. **DHORÁ** (Dora), remotest of the *krassokhoriá*, is an attractive place on the brow of a ridge whose narrow, stone-paved lanes repay exploration; there are two **tavernas**.

The road continues to Arkhimandhríta in Páfos district, from where it's plain sailing down to Koúklia on the main Limassol–Páfos highway; entirely paved, often two-lane, and one of the fastest ways to Páfos from the Tröödhos.

The easterly Tröödhos approach

The more heavily used of the two main roads to the Tröödhos, the B8 up from Exit 28 of the coastal expressway, is less immediately appealing than the western route, but off the pavement some attractive old villages and monastic churches cling to the vine-clad hillsides.

Lófou

The first worthwhile detour, 18km out of Limassol, is the side road up to **LÓFOU** (it can also be reached from Perá Pedhí to the north, Áyios Amvrósios to the west, or Monágri via Áyios Yeóryios to the east). It's an extraordinarily photogenic village built on several hills, as its name (*lófos* is "hill" in Greek) implies – though the outskirts straggle untidily with modern villas. Over 800m up, so cool in summer, it was once one of the wealthiest hill villages, with lands down to the sea. The best of three well-signposted **tavernas** is Kostas Violaris' central 🍴 *Iy Lofou* (reservations usually needed on ℡25470202 or 99468151; open lunch/dinner Tues–Sun, may close Sun pm). Small (€13) or large (€16) *mezé* will include less usual dishes like ravioli, spinach-egg, *stifádho* and *pourgoúri*, served with quaffable bulk wine in a converted arcaded house, best in the cooler months when a hearth fire blazes while Kostas and friends provide acoustic musical accompaniment. Just down the street is the affiliated *Lofou Wine Cellar*, featuring their own *loúntza* and serving as one of the main venues for **Music in the Mountains** (advance booking needed; Ⓦwww.cyprusvillagelink.com, "Events" button), which organizes intimate concerts of all sorts of music several nights monthly. Kostas also offers **accommodation** in surrounding houses both meticulously restored and built traditionally to highest standards (Ⓦwww .lofou-agrovino.com; ❹), with breakfast provided in the taverna.

Monágri, Arkhángelos and Panayía Amasgoú

There's little to prompt another halt until the short turning left to **MONÁGRI**, about 21km out of Limassol. Immediately beyond the village stands

Arkhángelos monastery, surrounded by vineyards overlooking the Koúris river valley. Originally founded in the tenth century atop an ancient temple, it was rebuilt following a disastrous 1735 fire and, after 1989, both church and grounds were restored by the now-dissolved Monagri Foundation and the Department of Antiquities. The Limassol archbishopric has re-appropriated the premises and the basis of future visits remains uncertain; should you gain entry, you'll be allowed into the **monastic church**, whose fine eighteenth-century frescoes (including some by Filaretos, who painted the interior of Áyios Ioánnis in Nicosia – see p.253) have been cleaned by London's Courtauld Institute. Uniquely in Cyprus, the interior retains geometric *mihrab* decoration over the south window from the church's time of use as a mosque (Monágri was once a Linovamváki village – see box, p.380 – which later openly espoused Christianity), while the front porch is supported by two Corinthian columns recycled from a Roman temple. The main outbuilding incorporates a **Roman olive mill**, the only one on the island.

The twelfth-century monastic **church of Panayía (Panagia) Amasgoú**, 3km downriver from Monágri on the west bank, has fine if only partly cleaned fresco fragments from four periods up to the sixteenth century; the nuns of the surrounding convent will admit you (Tues, Thurs & Sat mornings only).

Silíkou and Lánia

A little further up the Koúris valley and the B8 are two other villages of interest. Attractive **SILÍKOU**, west of the B8 and also reachable from Monágri, can offer an **olive-press** and Evro and Zina's creditable *Silikou Taverna*, the other main venue for Music in the Mountains events.

East of the B8, via a one-kilometre side road, stands **LÁNIA** (Laneia), another atmospheric village popular with expats (a third of the population), including a few artists; one, Michael Owen, runs the Mediterranean Bookshop. There's one **taverna**, the *Lania*, whose good cooking makes up for somewhat limited opening hours (lunch only weekdays, plus dinner Fri–Sat; closed Mon); otherwise the **kafenío** *Platanos* (closed Mon pm) does decent snacks and *mezé*.

Eastern hill-villages

The area bordering Larnaca district contains some of the most isolated and forlorn villages in the Limassol foothills – which in today's Cyprus is an attraction in itself, though the region isn't quite the miniature Tuscany the CTO pitches it as. The main problem, from a tourism-attraction standpoint, is that enough cash has trickled in to finance unsightly "improvements" ruining the architectural homogeneity of these places. Easiest access to this area is via either the Yermasóyia (Germasogeia, Exit 24) or Parekklishá (Parekklisia, no. 21) exits of the Limassol–Nicosia expressway.

Kelláki to Eptagónia

The road in from Parekklishá emerges after 16km on a knoll at **KELLÁKI**, with a grand view of the Pitsylian ridges across the valley. A few villas have gone up, with more local land for sale. But otherwise neither Kelláki nor its neighbour Prastió to the west offers much to casual visitors. You'll get a fair idea of the original vernacular architecture by detouring some 6km east to **KLONÁRI** hamlet with its pitched-roof church of Áyios Nikólaos, bare inside, but the tenants of the smelly dovecotes far outnumber the remaining humans. The dozen houses of **VÍKLA**, 2km further, are largely abandoned despite a fine setting, though this will change now that the informal, 18-hole **Vikla Golf Club** (Ⓦ www.vikla-golf.com) has opened adjacent.

Dirt roads continue north to **AKAPNOÚ**, on a hillock surrounded by relatively fertile and well-watered land. This has retained about thirty friendly inhabitants and a few attractive houses, many now restored, as well as some flagstoned pedestrian lanes. Besides the *kafenío* by the square, there's also an *exokhikó kéndro* in the fields west of the village, near the small chapel of **Panayía toú Kámbou**. Among the sixteenth- and seventeenth-century frescoes inside high up on the south wall are an *Annunciation* and part of a *Nativity*: worth seeing if the key is in the door, but not worth a special detour.

You return to the main road at **Eptagónia** (Eptagoneia), a relatively busy place, from where a road climbs impressively and scenically through Melíni and crag-set Ódhou, just over the border in Larnaca district, to a 1100-metre pass in the Pitsylian ridges; once onto the watershed, you've a view down onto handsomely spread-out Farmakás and Kámbi (see p.236).

Arakapás and Panayía Iamatikí

Using the road from Exit 24, you'll run quickly through Yermasóyia, then past its eponymous dam, before slowing down for some scenic ridge-driving until Dhieróna (Dierona) and Arakapás (22km from the highway). Along with Eptagónia, they're the closest things to going concerns hereabouts, with olive and mandarin orchards providing a partial living. Low-lying **ARAKAPÁS** sits in a natural depression, lower and warmer than its neighbours (thus the citrus), with plenty of cafés and snack bars in its centre. Heading north towards Pitsyliá from here, a narrow but paved road threads through ravine-hugging Sykópetra and Profítis Ilías, improbably set amid bare, rocky spurs and just 7km shy of Palekhóri on the main Tróödhos ridge route.

The big local attraction is Arakapás' much-modified cemetery **church of Panayía Iamatikí**, on the eastern outskirts. Originally a sixteenth-century Latin foundation, it was rebuilt in 1727, preserving only the westernmost transverse arch of the original, plus two fine triple arcades which divide the present church into three aisles. Architecturally, it is almost unique in southern Cyprus, having only the ruined Gothic church at Áyios Sozómenos (see p.267) as a peer.

▲ Interior arcading, Panayía Iamatikí

The wonderful, mysterious interior repays the small effort of getting access; the presiding priest appears every evening, or seek him out at one of the cafés.

The Italo-Byzantine style of the interior **frescoes** is similarly rare in Cyprus. In the soffit of the arches closest to the west door are some finely sketched angels, inside roundels. Images on the north arcade, dating from the 1600s, include the four Evangelists in the spandrels, plus Áyios Ioánnis Dhamaskinós (Saint John Damascene) attended by a miniature figure of the Virgin. Frescoes on the damp-damaged south arcade are a bit earlier; these include the monk Zozimas spoon-feeding the withered desert ascetic Osia Maria, a former courtesan who repented of her ways, and Áyios Mámas riding on his trademark lion, a flowing robe giving a tremendous sense of motion.

East of Limassol: the coast

The town beach at Limassol, stony and flanked by intermittent breakwaters and stationary tankers, is pretty forgettable; recognizing this, the CTO has improved a beach at **Dhassoúdhi (Dasoudi)**, about 4km east of town near the edge of Potamós Yermasóyias. But you really need to travel further towards Larnaca before reaching any patches of natural coastline.

Amathus (Amathoús, Amathoúnda, Amathounta)

Some 13km east of Limassol town centre along the resort strip, **ancient Amathus** (daily: April–May & Sept–Oct 8am–6pm; June–Aug 8am–7.30pm; Nov–March 8am–5pm; €1.70) lies just inland from the coast road. Low-lying Amathus isn't the most evocative ruin in Cyprus, but its presence has kept resort hotels at a healthy distance, and as excavations proceed there may eventually be more to see. Limassol city **bus** #30 passes the site, but the nearest official stop is about 800m west; some find it more enjoyable to follow the coastal promenade on foot or bicycle, with an underpass allowing site access.

Some history

Amathus is among the oldest of Cyprus's city-kingdoms, supposedly founded by a son of Hercules, revered as a god here. In some versions of the myth, Ariadne, fleeing from the Cretan labyrinth, was abandoned here and not on Aegean Naxos by Theseus; she then died in childbirth, and was buried in a sacred grove, where her cult melded easily with that of Aphrodite. Lightly Hellenized, and prone to worshipping Egyptian gods like Bes as well as Asiatic ones, Amathus sided with Persia against Salamis and the other Cypriot kingdoms during the fifth- and fourth-century BC revolts, though it later declared for Alexander the Great.

The Romans made it capital of one of the four administrative districts of the island; this anticipated a bishopric in Byzantine times. But decline and destruction followed the repeated Arab raids of the seventh century, and a vandalistic visit from Richard the Lionheart in 1191, and the city was largely forgotten until the eighteenth century, when its west necropolis was looted. Shortly after, some of its dressed stone was taken to Egypt to line the locks of the new Suez Canal, though the contractors mostly used fresh-cut stone from a nearby quarry. The first systematic excavations occurred in 1862, 1893 and 1930, though there was no lack of plundering and pilfering in between.

The site

The remains of the city are dominated by a vast paved **agora**, studded with a dozen restored and re-erected columns, three of them spirally fluted. In the middle of the area there's a square foundation filled with rubble and masonry fragments; its original function is uncertain, though it was probably a fountain. To make any sense of the place, consult the site plan on the raised viewing dais near the Hellenistic baths at the agora's seaward end.

Backed into the bluff at the northwest end of the marketplace is an elaborate **waterworks system**, terminus of an aqueduct which supplied the city from the north. The flow of a niche-spring was diverted through tunnels to sluices, feeding a small basin at the head of more channels running to a pair of large, roofless **cisterns**. Some water appears to have run through open gutters, but you can still see a conspicuous large water-main which, exposed, leads out into the marketplace. A stepped street leads up the partly excavated slope past rows of Hellenistic-era **houses**.

Up on the bluff is the ancient **acropolis**, with stretches of defensive **walls** to seaward, the remains of Amathus's main **temple**, jointly dedicated to Aphrodite and Hercules, plus one of the more important of the Byzantine city's **Christian basilicas** superimposed upon this, retaining extensive patches of *opus sectile* and *champlevé* flooring. Across the road, towards the sea, are more sections of wall and traces of the ancient port. Richard the Lionheart supposedly landed here in May 1191 to begin his march on Limassol.

Áyios Yeóryios Alamánou and Pendákomo

Beyond Amathus, you can continue east along the old B1 road or take the A1 motorway to Exit 18, which allows access to both the bay of Áyios Yeóryios Alamánou and the inland village of Pendákomo.

As you head seawards down the pleasant, narrow valley here, unlikely to ever be much developed, you might shun the turning up and right to the convent of **Ayíou Yeoryíou (Agiou Georgiou) Alamánou**, an uninteresting modern construction and a "working" institution, not a tourist attraction. Fork left instead; soon the narrow lane dwindles to dirt surface, and some 1600m from the junction you'll arrive at the bay of **Áyios Yeóryios (Agios Georgios) Alamánou**. The short beach here sports coarse pebbles verging on melon-size, and to either side is some of the most impressive white-cliff scenery in Cyprus, with the occasional sea-cave or small-pebble inlet to explore. At road's end a single, popular **taverna**, *Paraliako Kentro* (T99624376), features sustaining seafood grills and fry-ups without airs or graces.

Some 2.5km inland, **PENDÁKOMO** (Pentakomo) is the last village before the border with Larnaca district and the first community east of Limassol with an existence other than that of a dormitory suburb. It supports a restoration **accommodation** complex, *George's Houses* (W www.palmerovillas.com; no phone), eight villas sleeping two to six available only by the week. In the centre, just up from the church, is the *Iris Music Taverna* (evenings only; closed Mon). Food is offered, but the emphasis is on **musical and theatrical events** held regularly in the covered courtyard; call T25633733 for the current programme.

Governor's Beach (Aktí Kyvernítou)

More appealing beaches can be found 29km east of Limassol at **Governor's Beach (Aktí Kyvernítou)**, just a few kilometres off the expressway at Exit 16. Here several coves of fine dark sand contrast dramatically with the low chalk cliffs that back them. The shore fills quickly on warm weekends, and each cove is dominated by spruced-up **tavernas**, their manicured lawn-gardens sloping down to the sand, and a few flats to rent – though these are now vastly outnumbered by villas proliferating just inland.

The road from the expressway forks almost immediately, and where the right-hand turning splits again (actually either bearing joins to form a loop), a signboard locates the various, expensive tavernas. Bearing right first leads to the broadest, cleanest, most sheltered stretch of sand and sunbeds, with the *Akti Sofroniou*, *Kamintzis*, *Adamos* and *Faros* tavernas clustered around. From the lighthouse cape beyond, looking towards the eyesore industrial installations at Vasilikós, one can walk west over white-rock cliffs, which have a reputation as a gay hangout. The coves on the far left are narrower and more secluded, served by the *Panayiotis* taverna (which rents flats).

The Akrotíri peninsula

At the southwest end of Limassol, near the entrance to the new port, two routes leave the city: the minor road, paved part way only, that parallels the **Akrotíri peninsula**'s east shore, and the better, paved road heading roughly west across the base of the peninsula to the Fassoúri plantations.

Lady's Mile Beach (Aplóstra)

Officially signposted as **Aplóstra**, but still popularly known as **Lady's Mile Beach** in honour of a mare named Lady that a British officer used to exercise here, the east shore is, in fact, closer to four miles of grey, hardpacked sand. No permanent development has taken place since it remains the property of the British Ministry of Defence and also because, with a mosquito-plagued salt lake behind, it's not very good as a beach. The barely sloping tidal flats are better for jogging (and dune-buggying, popular with locals) than sunbathing. Every few hundred metres there's a shack-like café or taverna catering for the weekend crowds, but, as signs warn you, various activities, including camping, are prohibited since parts of the beach are supposedly a turtle-nesting area.

Ayíou Nikoláou tón Gáton and Akrotíri

At the south end of Lady's Mile, the dirt track takes a bend inland to follow the southern shore of the salt lagoon; after about a kilometre a signposted driveway on the left wiggles through a gate and past hedgerows to the grounds of the convent of **Ayíou Nikoláou tón Gáton** (St Nicholas of the Cats).

The peculiar name springs from a Byzantine **legend** according to which Saint Helena imported hundreds of cats from Egypt or Palestine, at the time of Saint Nicholas's fourth-century foundation, to control the poisonous snakes which infested the place. The monks (at what was originally a monastery) would summon the cats to meals by the tolling of a bell, and another bell would send them out into the surrounding fields to battle the serpents.

The habit of keeping cats to combat the island's numerous snakes spread quickly to most other Cypriot monasteries, and also to Rhodes; when the Knights Hospitallers of Saint John moved there, they are said to have taken a whole shipload of cats with them. More recently, the Greek Nobel laureate **George Seferis** used the inter-species struggle as a metaphor for opposition to the dictatorship then in power in Greece, in one of his last published poems "The Cats of Saint Nicholas":

Wildly obstinate, always wounded,
They wiped out the snakes, but in the end they were lost,
They couldn't endure so much poison...

The contemporary reality of Ayíou Nikoláou is not so lofty: a working cloister, it was brashly remodelled since 1990 and of little architectural interest other than a fine coat of arms over the door of the thirteenth-century church; an enormous, brick-paved forecourt dwarfs the buildings. Today the convent is home to a handful of aged nuns and – still – dozens of cats. They stalk about like denizens of a temple to the Egyptian cat-god which may once have stood here; Cape Gáta (She-Cat), beyond the Akrotíri airfield's runway, is named after them.

The road to Kolossi

From near Limassol's modern harbour, the good E602 road signed towards Asómatos and Fassoúri runs west to the Crusader castle of Kolossi and beyond to the stunningly sited ancient city of Kourion (see p.138). The route is scarcely longer, and far less dangerous, than either of the inland highways, the steep, winding B6 and the high-speed A6. It's also the most scenic: giant cypresses, planted long ago as windbreaks, have grown to form lofty tunnels over the road; eucalyptus clumps drained the swamps here and allowed extensive **orange groves** to flourish, most of them originally planted by Jewish settlers at the end of the nineteenth century. About a dozen families stayed on after independence

The British Sovereign Bases

One of the conditions of Cypriot independence in 1960 was the retention of a certain percentage of the island as a British military reserve, known as the **Sovereign Base Areas** or SBAs for short. Indeed, the date of nationhood was delayed by disputes over the SBAs' exact aggregate size, eventually fixed at 99 square miles. Most of this area consists of the Episkopí Garrison, adjoining Akrotíri Air Field and the Dhekélia Base between Larnaca and Ayía Nápa. Base borders were drawn in such a way as to exclude almost all private land and villages – the only exception being Akrotíri village (whose inhabitants have dual Cypriot and British nationality), and Áyios Nikólaos hamlet near Famagusta. In addition to these main bases, fifteen "retained sites" (annexes) lie scattered across the South; the most conspicuous of these include the RAF/NATO radar domes on Mount Olympus and Cape Gréko, radio masts at Zíyi and an artillery range (now unused) on the Akámas peninsula.

Technically the bases form **British Dependent Territories** administered by a military governor, though the population of about eight thousand (about half servicemen, the rest their dependants and other civilians) is subject to a civil legal code based closely on Cypriot law – provided alleged offence(s) occurred on SBA territory, and not in Cyprus proper. Thanks to periodic Greek-Cypriot-nationalistic protests against the continuance of the SBAs, internal security is quite tight; vehicles are liable to be stopped and checked by the distinct SBA police force, and photography is strictly forbidden. Otherwise, there is no formal border control: the main indications that you've entered a base are a sudden outbreak of UK-style street signs, with names like Mandalay Road, Suffolk Road or Agincourt Lane. Southern Cypriots as well as foreigners circulate freely in the SBAs, and over two thousand Greek Cypriots have jobs on the two largest bases.

About three hundred Turkish Cypriots also continue to work at the Dhekélia Base; before the thaw of April 2003, they entered strictly via the "Four Mile Crossing" and now live in Nicosia. At roadside stalls near the Red Seal Phassouri Plantation, you can buy giant sacks of the fruit, the cheapest in the South. One particular, old-fashioned variety to look out for are the sweet *sherkérika* or sugar oranges, the name derived (say some) from Tserkézi (Tserkezoi) village en route, but equally likely from the Turkish *shekerli*.

Long before citrus arrived, sugar cane and grapes were cultivated in this area; the **castle of Kolossi** (daily: June–Aug 8am–7.30pm; Sept–May 9am–5pm; €1.70), just south of the eponymous village, still stands evocatively amid the vineyards that helped make it famous. Frequent #16 or #17 **buses** run here from Limassol's central market (Mon–Sat only; journey time 20min).

The story of Kolossi is inextricably linked with the **Knights Hospitaller**, whose *commanderie* it was – the name later accrued to the rich dessert wine, Commandaria, still made from vines in the Limassol foothills. The Knights were first granted land here in 1210 by the Lusignans, and the local castle became their headquarters after the Crusaders' final loss of the Holy Land. Even after the order shifted to Rhodes exactly a century later, the Knights kept Kolossi as the headquarters of their local fiefs, which included dozens of foothill villages. Mameluke raids of the fifteenth century virtually levelled the original castle, later rebuilt on a smaller scale; in 1488 the Venetians appropriated it, along with the Order's other holdings. The Ottomans allowed the place to slowly deteriorate until a British restoration of 1933.

Today's three-storey keep-structure stands among the ruins of a much larger castle; from the **coat of arms** of Grand Master Louis de Magnac, set into the

(Strovília), a thin sliver of British territory abutting the outskirts of Famagusta and the Attila Line. After August 1974, almost 10,000 Turkish Cypriots from the Limassol area, escaping reprisal attacks by EOKA-B, sought refuge in the Episkopí base for six months, until they were airlifted out to Turkey – and from there to the North.

The justification for the bases' establishment and continued existence posits their vital **strategic value** as listening posts, east Mediterranean airfields and warm-winter training areas. Indeed Britain's 1878 acquisition of Cyprus, and stubborn retention of the island in the face of nationalist agitation, was premised on such logic. Ironically, it is only since the late 1950s, with the winding-up of empire and successive Middle Eastern crises, that the SBAs have come to play the role originally envisaged for the whole island.

It is often asserted that the USA has a secret base somewhere on Cyprus. This is half-true, since Americans in fact get total co-operation from the British and do not require their own facilities. The US Air Force still flies U2 surveillance missions over the Middle East out of Akrotíri airfield, and formerly sent supplies to the US embassy in Beirut on low-altitude Blackhawk runs which touched down momentarily, for reasons of protocol, at Larnaca. The conspicuous sixty-metre-wide electronic dish beside the Four Mile Crossing gathers information shared among the NATO allies, while emitting dangerous levels of radiation. Indeed, construction of a new, 190-metre-high radio mast at Akrotíri stirred long-simmering Cypriot resentment to boiling point in early July 2001. Incensed by the arrest of ultra-nationalist MP Marios Matsakis on charges of trespass and criminal damage, over a thousand violent demonstrators trashed the Episkopí police station, set 35 British military vehicles alight and caused over £300,000 of damage in a single night. In fact, base sources claim that the new antennae would emit far less radiation at ground level than the ones being replaced.

east wall, a date of approximately 1450 has been deduced for the earlier restoration. Modern stairs have replaced a retractable defensive ramp up to the door; the ground level with its vital well, a three-chambered storage basement, originally had no entrance from outside. In the left-hand, vaulted room of the middle storey, probably the kitchen, are the first of several huge **fireplaces**, more appropriate to northern European chateaux and not equalled on the island since. By the spiral stairway in the other room, a glass plate protects a damaged **fresco** of the Crucifixion. The upper storey has thinner walls, and two grand halls at right angles to those below – presumably the quarters of de Magnac, as his heraldry again appears on one of two back-to-back fireplaces. The stairway continues to the flat roof, where machicolations over the gate permitted the pouring of noxious substances onto uninvited guests.

The other building (off-limits) adjacent is the **sugar factory**, a barn-like vaulted structure. The millstone was powered by sluices fed in turn by a huge aqueduct, now shaded by a giant pepper tree, at the northeast corner of the grounds. The springs still ran until recently, as modern, metal-sheathed extensions of the spillways snake through the landscaping. A bit northeast of the castle, the usually locked twelfth-century church of **Áyios Efstáthios** was the Knights' place of worship.

Kourion (Curium)

Perched dramatically on a sheer bluff overlooking the sea, **Kourion** (Latinized as "Curium") is easily the most spectacular of the South's archeological sites – even though close up some of its individual attractions may be roped off or dimly lit owing to overhead canopies. Kourion consists of two sites, entirely contained within the Episkopí Sovereign Base: the ancient city, closer to Kolossi, and the sanctuary of Apollo Hylates, a few kilometres west – you'll need half a day to see them both. The ruins lie about 5km west of Kolossi, but are served by a separate **bus service** from Limassol castle.

Some history

Despite discouraging water-supply problems, this easily defensible clifftop may have been occupied in Neolithic times, but a recognizable city only emerged following Mycenaean colonization between the thirteenth and twelfth centuries BC. Kourion played a leading – negative – role in the **Cypriot rebellion** against Persia; at a critical moment its king Stasanor defected to the enemy with his troops, guaranteeing the island's resubjugation. Like Amathus, it later championed Alexander against the Persians, and remained an important town throughout the Roman and early Byzantine periods; most of what can be seen today dates from those two eras. The city was utterly destroyed in a cataclysmic earthquake in 365AD, and only tentatively rebuilt and resettled. After the seventh-century Arab raids, Kourion, like many other coastal settlements on Cyprus, was abandoned for good, and its bishop moved to nearby Episkopí.

The notorious American consul-turned-antiquarian **Luigi Palma di Cesnola** began excavating (or rather plundering) in 1865, and eleven years later claimed to have unearthed several untouched hoards of gold, silver, bronze and objects inlaid with precious stones, suggesting Kourion had been far wealthier than anyone imagined. Even back then many doubted his story, accusing him of doctoring the evidence and assembling the collection from various sites across the island. Whatever the truth, the troves were shortly sold

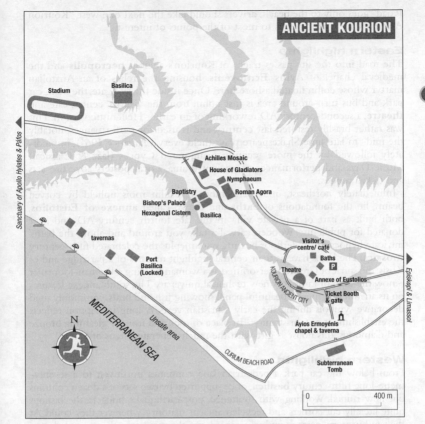

ANCIENT KOURION

Stadium
Basilica

Sanctuary of Apollo Hylates & Páfos

Achilles Mosaic
House of Gladiators
Nymphaeum
Baptistry
Roman Agora
Bishop's Palace
Hexagonal Cistern
Basilica

tavernas

Port
Basilica
(Locked)

Visitor's
centre/ café
Baths
P
Theatre
KOURION ANCIENT CITY
Annexe of Eustolios

Episkopi & Limassol

Ticket Booth
& gate

MEDITERRANEAN SEA

Unsafe area

N

Áyios Ermoyénis
chapel & taverna

CURIUM BEACH ROAD

Subterranean
Tomb

0   400 m

en bloc to the New York Metropolitan Museum and became known as the **Curium Treasure**.

Between 1933 and 1954, George McFadden of the University of Pennsylvania carried out rather desultory **archeological excavations** at both the ancient city and the nearby sanctuary of Apollo. While popular locally, he was not a particularly systematic or effective archeologist, and after his untimely death by drowning just below the site, more important work was undertaken by a Cypriot team. In the early 1980s they were succeeded by David Soren's American expedition, who dramatically established not only the exact date of the mid-fourth-century quake which had levelled Kourion, but also – from jewellery found on several victims – that its population was already substantially Christian.

The ancient city

It's imperative to visit the site of the **ancient city** (daily: June–Aug 8am–7.30pm; Nov–March 8am–5pm; April–May & Sept–Oct 8am–6pm; €1.70) early or late, since coach tours of cruise-ship patrons clog the walkways between 10am and 3pm, making it physically impossible to see (or even move about) the place. The more prominent turn-off signed as "Curium Beach

Road" goes only to the beach; drivers should take the next one west, "Kourion Ancient City", which leads to most of the points of interest.

Eastern highlights

The road into the site passes traces of Kourion's ancient **necropolis** and the medieval chapel of **Áyios Ermoyénis**, housing the relics of an Anatolian martyr whose coffin floated ashore here. Once inside the site gate, the main car park and bus turn-around area is just uphill from the visitors' centre/café and **theatre**, a second-century AD reworking of an earlier Hellenistic version. This was rather brashly restored last century, and is used for performances, notably the mid- to late June Shakespeare plays (held every year since 1961), immediately followed by the more recently inaugurated Cyprus (Jazz & Classical) Music Days and performances of ancient drama. Local posters advertise acts and ticket venues.

Immediately northeast, under enormous tarpaulin roofs upheld by curved beams, lie the foundations of **baths** and the so-called **annexe of Eustolios**, both built as part of a private villa in the late fourth century AD, and later donated for public use. Wooden catwalks take you around and above the baths' intricate hypocaust (underfloor heating system), plus the celebrated fifth-century **mosaics**. The baths have as their central highlight mosaics of a partridge and of Ktisis, the spirit of Creation personified as a woman holding a Roman-foot ruler – now the logo of Limassol's new technical university. The south annexe features on its atrium pavement a beautiful panel showing fish and birds, commonly used decorative symbols during the early Christian years. A long inscription reflects the establishment of Christianity: "In place of rock and iron, or gleaming bronze and diamonds, this house is girt with the much-venerated signs of Christ."

Western highlights

From below the car park a pedestrian lane continues northwest to a seventy-metre-long fifth-century **basilica**, once supported by two sets of a dozen columns but now ruined. Working with straitened, post-earthquake budgets, the bishops quite literally cut corners and recycled ancient masonry wherever they could. At the southwestern, narthex end you can admire the view over the sea and also an unusual, deep hexagonal **cistern**, which presumably held the water for baptisms.

These, it is assumed, took place next door at the smaller **baptistry**, of a slightly later date and in better condition, with more complete geometric floor mosaics plus the odd standing column. In the middle yawns another hexagonal pool for holy water, and on the south side of the nave a marble-lined, cruciform font shows signs of having been modified for infant baptism. At the seaward end of the building, surviving arches are thought to be part of a **bishop's palace**.

Beyond the baptistry lie the late Roman **House of Gladiators** and the **Achilles Mosaic**, both hidden under the same wood-and-tarpaulin roofs as the Eustolios annexe. The former takes its name from a floor mosaic of two pairs of gladiators in combat, one set attended by a referee; all the figures are named with inscriptions, and presumably were stalwarts of contests in the nearby theatre. The badly damaged but still recognizable *Achilles Mosaic* shows Odysseus detecting Achilles disguised as a maiden on Skyros, by tempting him with weapons which Achilles has rushed to try; the same building also has a panel of Ganymede being kidnapped by Zeus in eagle form.

Now that excavations have been completed, there should be no access problems for the Roman **agora**, with its stretch of re-erected second-century colonnade. This is flanked by the **nymphaeum** (fountain-house), once fed by an aqueduct which also supplied some conspicuous **baths**.

The beach

The **beach** southwest of the ruins is reachable either by the link road past Áyios Ermoyénis, or "Curium Beach Road" proper. Once clear of the prominently marked unsafe area, the water is cleaner and deeper (beyond the pink buoys) than the 800m of hard-packed sand suggests. The swimmable end of the beach is dotted with three impromptu **tavernas**, all unabashedly commercial and much of a muchness. Immediately inland from road's end are prominent remains of the sixth-century, so-called **port basilica**, which presumably served those working in the ancient port near here and is currently off-limits.

The sanctuary of Apollo Hylates

About 2km west of Kourion proper, at the large sacred complex (same hours as Kourion; separate €1.70 admission) surrounding the **sanctuary of Apollo Hylates** – sometimes cited as Ylatis or Ylatou. Apollo was worshipped as the god of the surrounding woodland and protector of the pre-Christian city. Today a huge RAF antenna farm just west detracts somewhat from the atmosphere, but it remains an attractive archeological site.

The sacred precinct was consecrated during the eighth century BC, but the present buildings are early Roman, flattened by the great earthquake of 365 AD. The two ancient **gates**, Paphos on the west and Kourion on the east, are no longer intact, though the path from the ticket office passes the stumps of the former. On the right, before reaching the Kourion gate, you'll see the **palaestra** area, with a large water jug in one corner used by ancient athletes to cool off. Beyond, to the northeast, the **baths** sprawl under a shelter.

A **processional way** starts at the extensive **xenon** or inn for pilgrims, with its restored Doric colonnade, and passes the presumed **priests' quarters** and precinct walls as it climbs a slight slope to the partly restored **temple of Apollo**. Two columns, a wall corner and an angle of the pediment enclose the altar area, open to the sky even in its day, and most holy; unauthorized individuals profaning it even with an inadvertent touch were hurled off the Kourion cliffs to appease the god's wrath. On the west side of the grounds, near the site of the Paphos gate, are the foundations of the **display hall** for votive offerings; between it and the processional way hides a curious round structure or **vothros**, not yet completely excavated, where it is surmised the priests discreetly disposed off old and surplus gifts to the god.

A curious and ubiquitous sanctuary feature is a series of broad **stone channels** hacked out of the rock. Once thought to be aqueducts, current theory identifies them as planter boxes used by the priests of Apollo for landscaping the grounds in a manner befitting a woodland god.

Little is left of the imperial Roman **stadium** (access unrestricted), 500m to the east; it once seated six thousand, but now only a few rows of seats, and three gaps where the gates were, can be distinguished. On a knoll still further east, a sixth-century **basilica** has a huge well in the floor and traces of floor mosaic in the altar area. Much of the flooring, however, was found in 1974 to be marble plaques pilfered from the city's nymphaeum, laid face down so that bas-reliefs of pagan mythological scenes would not offend Christian sensibilities.

Episkopí and Erími

The **Kourion site museum** (Mon–Fri 8am–4pm except Thurs 8am–5pm; €1.70) is 2.5km from the old city, in the large village of **EPISKOPÍ**, which shares the same bus service from Limassol as the site. Follow signs through Episkopí to the church of Ayía Paraskeví; the museum, in the rambling mud-brick house built for archeologist George McFadden, stands opposite. The collection, occupying two wings, consists largely of terracotta objects from Kourion, the sanctuary of Apollo and two minor sites nearby.

Episkopí has become a popular overnight base, especially for Brits visiting relatives in the military here, though beware Saturday nights, when the village centre serves as the venue for loud bands of variable quality accompanying wedding celebrations. The best-value local **accommodation** is *Antony's Garden*

▲ Apollo Hylates temple

House (☎25933910; may close Jan–Feb; ❸), a well-converted old-house pension with a lovely courtyard and pool.

Some 2km northeast towards Kolóssi, **ERÍMI** is home to the private **Cyprus Wine Museum/Kypriako Inomousio** on the through road (daily 9am–5pm; €4.25), which chronicles the purported five millennia of wine-making on the island with displays and archeological artefacts from the owner's collection and also loans from other museums. Selected winery products are on sale.

West towards Páfos: the coast

The limits of the Episkopí Sovereign Base extend almost to the boundary of Páfos district, again having the happy if unintended side effect of protecting the local coast. Some 27km west of Limassol on the old road, a sign points seawards to **Evdhímou Bay**, not to be confused with inland Evdhímou village (Avdimou; own motorway exit), which like its three western neighbours was Turkish-Cypriot-inhabited before 1974. A paved side road from either the old B6 road or the motorway exit leads towards the sand-and-pebble **beach**, one of the best in the South, with little inland other than ruined carob warehouses just behind the site of the long-vanished jetty. Long, quiet **Paramáli** beach is just east, reached from the eponymous village on the B6.

Two **restaurants** overlook respective ends of Evdhímou beach, each with separate road access through unsullied vineyards and grain fields: the long-hours, more Cypriot *Melanda* on the west (March–Nov, closed Mon eve) has savoury seafood-and-chips-with-everything lunches, and the *Kyrenia* to the east, more of an expats' hangout (daily March–Nov), featuring Cypriot and British dishes and Western puds (sticky toffee pudding, strawberries and cream).

Anóyira

The closest **accommodation** to Evdhímou is in **ANÓYIRA** (Anogyra), some 10km inland at *Nicolas and Maria's Cottages* (☎99525462, ✉nmcottages @cytanet.com.cy; studios ❸), a restored old house surrounding a courtyard. The escarpment-top village itself is attractive, with stone-paved lanes, old houses and medieval niche-fountains, and is waking up to tourism. Anóyira was once the district hub of **carob production**, and in the very centre a two-room **Pastelli Museum/Workshop** details the industry and offers *teratsómelo* (carob syrup) for sale. Other local attractions include, on the southerly approach road, the restored monastic church of **Tímios Stavrós** (fourteenth-century frescoes); a well-regarded winery, Domaine Nicolaides (☎25221709 to arrange visits), now in its third generation, and Oleastro (daily 10am–7pm, €2.50, ⊕www.oleastro.com .cy), a combination olive mill, restaurant and museum featuring everything to do with the quintessential Mediterranean product. Anóyira has two central **tavernas**, though the central *mezé* house in nearby **PLATANISKIÁ** (Platanisteia), 10km distant by roundabout roads, gets top reports.

Pissoúri

The only significant coastal settlement between Episkopí village and the Páfos border is **PISSOÚRI**, draped over a ridge a bit south of the motorway, though disfigured by too much new construction to be really attractive up close. Owing to easy access and proximity to the sovereign bases, it's a favourite with service families, and has several places to **stay** and **eat**. Among these, modern

Hillview (☎ 25221972, ⓦ www.hillview.ws; studio; ❷, 2-bed ❸) at the north-western edge of the village lives up to its name, its popular restaurant (closed Mon) serving the inevitable Sunday-lunch carvery. More traditional, and central, is long-established *Bunch of Grapes Inn* (☎ 25221275, ⓔ bogpisouri @hotmail.com; ❷) installed in a converted 1700s farmhouse, its rooms upstairs from the courtyard restaurant where token Cypriot dishes jostle the "continental" fare. **Nightlife** is provided by a cluster of café-bars on the small pedestrianized square.

Pissoúri's **beach**, 3km below the village, is longer (nearly 1km) than it appears from above, well protected and sandy, with **windsurf** rental through Surfcyprus (ⓦ www.surfcyprus.com). You could do worse than base yourself here, though as it's outside SBA territory, real-estate development crowds the winding access road. Modest **accommodation** includes wood-ceilinged *Kotzias Apartments* (☎ 25221014; 1-bed ❷, 2-bed ❸), set in well-maintained gardens, but indisputably the best-standard local digs are the beach-side, 2005-refurbished *Columbia Beach Hotel* (☎ 25833333; €235 standard, €360 garden poolside studio, €490 suite, ❾) and adjacent ⚘ *Columbia Beach Resort* (☎ 25833000; junior suite from €330, executive €455, ❾; ⓦ www.columbia-hotels.com for both), available through most UK tour operators. The four-star hotel wing has good-sized, well-appointed rooms (though baths are small); the mock-traditional five-star bungalow-suite complex flanks its pool, with gardens down to the beach and every amenity you'd expect for the category, including a stunning spa. Several bars and a like number of **restaurants** surround the central beachfront car park; much the best eatery is *Limanaki*, purveying slightly pricey Mediterranean fare with a Lebanese twist, reflecting proprietor Sam Kazzaz's origins; book at weekends (☎ 25221288).

Pétra toú Romíou

Beyond Pissoúri, both motorway and old road run through desolate countryside until, just over the boundary in Páfos province, the imposing shoreline monolith of **Pétra toú Romíou** breaks the monotony. Most parking off the B6 is beside a small kiosk selling ice cream and drinks, with access to the beach via an underpass (or a gap in the guard-rail).

In legend Aphrodite, ancient patron goddess of Cyprus, emerged here from the sea foam (there's a wish-bush – see p.157 – here, resorted to by the lovelorn), though the formation actually takes its name (Rock of Romios) from Byzantine folk-hero Dhiyenis Akritas, aka Romios, who used this and other boulders as missiles against pirates. A longish **beach** of pebbles and coarse sand extends either side of the largest rock and its satellites, though its popularity is arguably due mostly to the mythic associations and easy access; traffic whizzing by just overhead hardly makes it alluring, though this has lessened since the expressway opened just inland. Inland looms the five-star *Intercontinental Aphrodite Hills* resort-cum-golf-course-and-villas-for-sale, largest development on the island.

Travel details

Buses

Limassol to: Agrós (Mon–Fri 1 daily at 12.20pm with Agros Bus, from the market square; 1hr); Kourion (Mon–Fri 3 daily via Episkopí village at 10am, 12.30pm, 1.30pm, returns 11.50am, 2.50pm; 20min); Larnaca (Mon–Fri 4 daily, Sat 2 daily with Intercity; 1hr); Nicosia (Mon–Fri 19 daily, Sat & Sun 4 daily, with LLL, Mon–Sat 1 daily with ALEPA; 1hr 15min); Páfos (Mon–Sat 1 daily with ALEPA; 1hr 15min); Plátres (Mon–Fri 1 daily at 9.15am with PEAL; 1hr 30min).

Páfos and the west

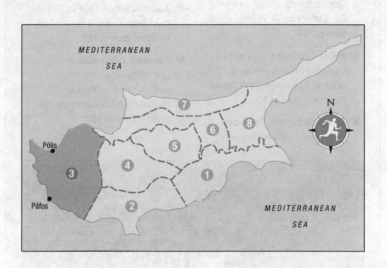

MEDITERRANEAN
SEA

Pólis

Páfos

MEDITERRANEAN
SEA

N

CHAPTER 3 # Highlights

✳ **Roman mosaics, Páfos**
These extensive Roman mosaics are among the best in the eastern Mediterranean.
See p.155

✳ **Tombs of the Kings, Páfos**
A subterranean tomb complex carved from living rock.
See p.158

✳ **Koúklia, La Cavocle**. Attend a chamber concert in the Gothic banquet hall of this Crusader manor house.
See p.167

✳ **Paleá Énklistra** This remote cave-hermitage shelters unique if damaged medieval frescoes. See p.167

✳ **Áyios Neófytos** Secluded monastery with its superb hermitage of St Neophytos.
See p.170

✳ **Avgás (Avákas) gorge** Walk through this spectacular gorge on the west coast.
See p.174

✳ **Lára Turtle Hatchery** On summer nights you may witness turtles laying or hatching at the protection station at Lára. See p.176

✳ **Asprókremos** One of the best beaches the South has to offer. See p.188

✳ **Akámas peninsula** An uninhabited wilderness, popular with walkers, mountain bikers and scuba divers. See p.189

▲ Walking on the Akámas Peninsula

Páfos and the west

Since Cyprus passed out of Byzantine control late in the twelfth century, the western end of the island has been its most **remote** and **least-developed** region. Following the Ottoman conquest, the district of Páfos also became the most **Turkified** part of the island, and close to a third of the population were Turkish Cypriot before the events of 1974. These conditions inevitably had a profound effect on local customs and speech, with the accent and dialect of both communities strongly influencing each other – and becoming all but incomprehensible to outsiders. Another result of the area's relative **isolation** was the Greek community's retention of a large vocabulary of Homeric Greek, a heritage of the original Mycenaean colonization that further complicated the linguistic profile.

Other Cypriots disparaged the Pafiots as backward, mongrel bumpkins and told (and still tell) scurrilous jokes about them; the Pafiots retorted that this was simply jealousy at work, since they were cleverer than the other islanders. With the departure of the Turkish community in 1975, and the opening of Páfos international airport in 1983, local idiosyncrasies have inevitably diminished, and the level of touristic development matches that of the other coastal districts. But big chunks of the region are still exhilaratingly wild, its villages characterful, and the beaches arguably the best in the South.

The district capital of **Páfos** is showing all the signs of too-rapid growth, but still makes a comfortable base and has much to offer in the way of antiquities and sophisticated dining. Strike out in any direction and rolling, well-tended hills or deep river valleys provide relief from the occasional tattiness of the town, as do the tantalizing ruins of its ancient predecessor **Palea Paphos** and the middle- and late-Byzantine monuments of **Yeroskípou**, **Émba**, **Áyios Neófytos** and **Paleá Énklistra**.

Northwest of Páfos, the **coast** is surprisingly deserted once past the last gasp of resort and villa development; the beaches leading up to the **Lára** area, itself protected, remain the focus of battles between developers and conservationists, the latter steadily losing ground as the former buy up every scrap of available private land. The recent growth of tourism, both short-term and residential, on the coast has halted the depopulation of the closer hill villages, but chances of traditional livelihoods surviving in the remoter settlements are slim, especially when selling up your marginal fields will get you more income than thirty years of goat-grazing. Accordingly, the rural areas are favourite targets for foreign second-home hunters, and it's estimated that there are about 30,000 Brits residing full- or part-time in the entire district – as well as a considerable number of eastern European immigrants, legal or illegal – an astonishing proportion in a total population of just over 80,000, a figure itself doubled since the late 1990s.

PÁFOS & THE WEST

BUFFER ZONE

Káto Pýrgos

Khaléri

Páno Pýrgos

Mansoúra

Mosfiléri

Aléyga

Pakhýammos (Pachyammos)

Kókkina (Erenköy)

Pómos

Ayía Marína

Yialiá

Georgian Monastery

T I L L Y R Í A

Kýkko

Tripylos (1362m)

CEDAR VALLEY

Zakharoú (1214m)

Stavrós tís Psókas

Psíkas

Stavrós tís

Argaka

Kinoússa

Lysó (Lysós)

Filoússa (Fjlousa)

Skárfos Bridge and Mill

Saramá

Lássa (Lasa)

Fýti

Panayía Horteni

Pelathoússa

Steni

Peristeróna

Evréfou

E712

Simou

Dhrýmou

Khrysokhoú Bay

Pólis

F733

Khrysokhoú (Chrysochou)

Skoúlli

Ayía Ekateríni

Káto Akourdháilia (Akourdaleia)

Páno Akourdháilia

Miliou

Yiólou

Thelétra

Goúdhi (Goudi)

Khóli (Choli)

Térra (Tera)

Krítou Térra (Tera)

Ayii Anáryiri Miliou (Agia Anargyroi)

Asprókremos

Latchí (Latsi)

Ttákkas Bay

Prodhrómi (Prodromi)

Dhroúsha (Drouseia)

Fasli

Inia (Ineia)

Káto Aródhes (Arodes)

Páno Aródhes

Kathikás

E709

Potámi Chiftlik

Loutrá Afrodhítis

Fontána Amoróza

Cape Arnaoútis

Khrysokhoú Bay

Neokhorió (Neo Chorio)

Andhrolíkou (Androlikou)

Ayios Yeóryios (668m)

Avgás Gorge

Kouklia

White River

Áspros

A K Á M A S   P E N I N S U L A

Jóni

Koudhounás

Turtle Station

Cape Lára

Toxeftra

Ayios Yeóryios (Agios Georgios)

Yerónissos (Geronissos)

Cape Dhrépano

E701

F704

Ávios Stavrós

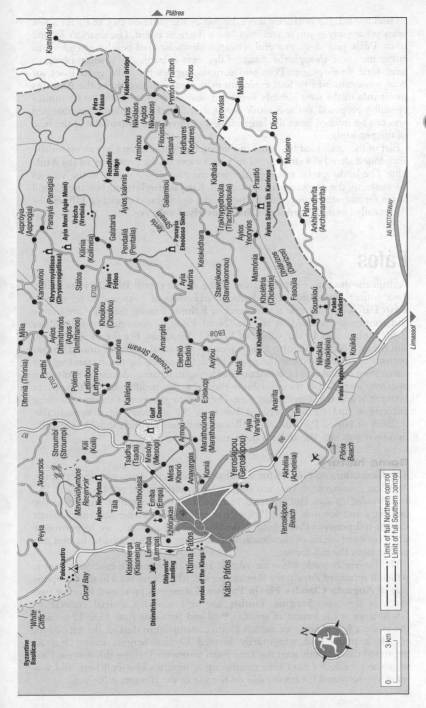

▲ Plátres

Kaminária

Kélefos Bridge

Péra Vássa

Ároos

Pretóri (Praitori)

Áyios Nikólaos (Agios Nikólaos)

Filoússa

Mallá

Yerovása

Dhorá

Moúsere

Roudhiás Bridge

Arminou

Kédhares (Kedares)

Mesaná

Páno Arkhimandhríta (Archimandrita)

A6 MOTORWAY

Aspróyia (Asprogia)

Panayiá (Panagia)

Vrécha (Vretsia)

Ayía Moní (Agie Moni)

Áyios Ioánnis

Galatariá

Kídhasi

Prastió

Trakhypédhoula (Trachypedoula)

Ayios Sávvas tis Karónos

Khrysorroyiátissa (Chrysorrogiatissa)

Kannavioú

Státos

Kiliínia (Koilineia)

Pendaliá (Pentalia)

Panayía Eleoússa Sindí

Áyios Yeóryios

Áyios Fótios

Salamioú

Kelokédhara

Khoúlou (Choulou)

Ayía Marina

Stavrókono (Stavrokonnou)

Mamónia

Mílía

Áyios Dhimitriános (Agios Dimitrianos)

Amargéti

Mesána

Dhiárzos (Diarzos)

Dhrinïá (Thrinia)

Psathi

Lemóna

Khelétria (Choletria)

Fasoúla

Polémi

Eledhió (Eledio)

Old Kholétria

Souskioú

Paleá Énklistra

Letímbou (Letymvou)

Axýlou

Natá

Nikóklia (Nikokleia)

Koúklia

Dhriniá

Kallépia

Anarítá

Koniá

Ayía Varvára

Paleá Páphos

E703

Eledió

Enískopi

Tsádha (Tsada)

Golf Course

Armoú

Marathoúnda (Marathounta)

Ayía Varvára

Tímí

Fóría Beach

Peyia

Akoursós

Stroúmbi (Stroumpi)

Kíli (Koili)

Mavrokólymbos Reservoir

Áyios Neófytos

Mésa Khorió

Anavargos

Yeroskípou (Geroskipou)

Akhélia (Acheleia)

Tála

Trimithoússa

Mesóyi (Mesogi)

Paleókastro

Kissónerga (Kisonerga)

Émba (Empa)

Lémba (Lempa)

Khlórakas

Ktíma Páphos

Yeroskípou Beach

Byzantine Basilicas

"White Cliffs"

Dhimítrios wreck

Dhiyenís' Landing

Tombs of the Kings

Káth Páphos

Coral Bay

B7

B8

B6

Limassol ▶

N

0   3 km

--- Limit of full Northern control
----- Limit of full Southern control

3

149

Head towards the northerly shore, lapped by Khrysokhoú Bay, and – for a few years yet anyway – you're seemingly on a different island. The district's second town, **Pólis**, provides a peaceful retreat, with uncluttered beaches stretching in either direction, though the coast to the west in particular is succumbing to large-scale development. Pólis and surrounding resorts make good bases for boat, mountain-bike or foot explorations along the rugged tip of the **Akámas peninsula** to the west – thinly vegetated, slashed by ravines, and (so far unsuccessfully) proposed as the South's only national park. This almost uninhabited area can be reached from the large villages of **Péyia** and **Dhroúsha** at the base of the peninsula.

East of the main road lies some of the emptiest country on Cyprus, essentially abandoned after 1974 or reduced to a backwater by the proximity of the Attila Line. The landscape becomes gentler and the pace of life slower in the villages en route to the showcase monastery of **Khrysorroyiátissa**, but there's still scope for adventure (and good hiking) in the uninhabited forests of **Tillyría**, or the equally isolated **Xeró** and **Dhiárizos river valleys**.

Páfos

Perhaps the most noteworthy feature of the district capital **PÁFOS** is its layout. Two distinct settlements – the harbour, archeological zone and hotel strip at **Káto Páfos**, and the true town centre of **Ktíma**, 3km up the hill – are jointly and confusingly referred to as Néa (New) Páfos, to distinguish it from Palea (Old) Paphos, now by the village of Koúklia, 16km east. For the moment, Káto and Ktíma together still form a fairly pleasant provincial capital of around 45,000 permanent inhabitants, but the upper town, first settled by the Byzantines as a haven from coastal attacks, is in danger of losing its separate identity, as ready-mix concrete lorries and their medium-rise offspring steadily fill in the spaces between it and the lower resort area. The only bright spot of the inconvenient excavations and traffic diversions has been the discovery of a considerable quantity of buried Roman and Hellenistic antiquities, which should eventually find their way into the archeological museum.

Some history

The foundations of **Néa Páfos** are obscure; in legend Agapenor, leader of the Arcadian contingent to Troy, was shipwrecked nearby in the twelfth century BC and decided to stay. But it seems to have been only a minor annexe to the sanctuary and town at Palea Páphos (see p.165) until Hellenistic times, when the last independent Pafiot king, **Nikoklis**, laid out a proper city. Its perimeter walls enclosed much of the headland behind the harbour, which shipped out timber from the hill-forests.

The Ptolemies made Páfos the island's rather decadent administrative centre, which it remained during the Roman period, when it rejoiced in the pompous title of **Augusta Claudia Flavia Paphos**. Cicero was proconsul here for two years, as was one **Sergius Paulus**, the first recorded official convert to Christianity, at the behest of apostles Paul and Barnabas. Acts 13:6–12 records the event: a Jewish sorcerer named Elymas attempted to distract the proconsul, at which point Paul temporarily blinded Elymas. Sergius Paulus was so impressed that he embraced the True Faith forthwith. Despite this success, Paul seems to have had a hard time combating Aphrodite's love-cult here, and was reputedly scourged for his trouble on the site of the Byzantine basilica.

Successive earthquakes, including two in the fourth century, relegated Páfos to a backwater, and the Cypriot capital reverted to Salamis (Constantia), though Páfos was designated – and has since remained – an important bishopric. The **Arab raids** of the seventh century completed the process of desolation, however, and for more than a millennium afterwards visitors were unanimous in characterizing the shabby port as a hole – if they were lucky enough to survive its endemic diseases and write about it.

Under **British administration** Páfos's fortunes perked up: the harbour was dredged and the population began to climb from a low point of less than two thousand to about nine thousand at independence. During the late 1950s, when Páfos district was a hotbed of EOKA activity, the British ran a major interrogation and detention centre in the town. But when **Archbishop Makarios** (see p.196) took refuge here following the 1974 EOKA-B coup, it was the British who saved his bacon by airlifting him into exile.

Arrival and information

There is no bus service to or from the **airport**, 15km southeast of Káto Páfos (though there is a service to and from Larnaca airport – see p.37); taxi fares to various points in Páfos are around €28–30, considerably more than a day's car rental from one of the three or four booths in the arrivals hall (best arranged in advance). There's also an ATM and a staffed bank, but all logistics will change drastically by 2009 or 2010 when a new, desperately needed terminal with unified arrivals/departures comes into use.

Long-distance **buses** and **service taxis** arrive at the points detailed on the Ktíma Páfos map and on p.163. **Driving** into Káto Páfos, you'll probably end up **parking** in the enormous, free, paved lot behind the waterfront by the mosaics, or the dirt lot immediately behind this; in high season the narrow streets of the hotel "ghetto" will be out of the question. All other lots are **pay-and-display**; the cheapest, up in Ktíma, lies at the foot of the bluff on which the bazaar and old Turkish quarter of Moúttalos are built.

Páfos's main **tourist information office** (Mon–Fri 8am–2.30pm, plus Mon, Tues, Thurs & Fri 3–5.45pm), which has a fairly complete stock of maps and handouts, can be found in Ktíma on Pávlou Melá (still cited as Gládstonos on many maps). There's also a Portakabin tourist office in Káto Páfos (same timings) opposite the *Almyra Hotel*.

Municipal bus services

The main car park below Ktíma's market is the central stop for ALEPA **municipal bus services** (fares about €1.50), with several useful lines along the main drags: Káto Páfos and Ktíma (often cited as "Agorá" on schedules) are linked during daylight hours by bus #11, which plies Leofóros Apostólou Pávlou, connecting the two districts, and Posidhónos, the shorefront road of Káto's southerly hotel ghetto. The #10 bus goes further afield, diverging from Apostólou Pávlou at Leofóros Táfon tón Vasiléon and heading out past the northwesterly resort strip en route to Coral Bay; the #10A variant includes Áyios Yeóryios; the #15 plies a similar route to the #10 every 15–20 minutes, beginning from Yeroskípou beach.

Other numbered ALEPA routes to the **suburb villages** of Yeroskípou, Khlórakas (Chloraka), Lémba, Kissónerga (Kisonerga), Émba, Tála, Péyia, Tsádha, Anavargós, Mesóyi (Mesogi) and Trimithoússa (Trimithousa) begin at the Karavélla parking lot off Andhréa Yeroúdhi in Ktíma. Ask at the central kiosk here for your bus, as they may not have their route numbers or destinations prominently displayed.

Accommodation

Páfos, upper and lower, has outstripped Limassol as the South's second-largest resort and there are now over 20,000 guest beds available. However, aggravated by a recent wave of apartment conversions and mandatory full-board rates, little decent accommodation remains, especially in Káto Páfos, that is not part of the pre-booked package scene. The places below are no exception, but at least are geared up to accepting independent web bookings. To the municipality's credit, hotels are not allowed to monopolize the shoreline – a **public walking/cycling promenade** extends all the way southeast to Yeroskípou beach.

Káto Páfos

Alexander the Great Leofóros Posidhónos ☎26965000, ℮alexander1@kanika.com. Cosier, less daunting and less pretentious (eg cheaper drinks) than some neighbours, this four-star resort has a prime setting just above a semi-natural beach (and incorporating an archeological site). It has all the expected facilities including spa and conservatory pool. ❼

Almyra Leofóros Posidhónos, seaward side ☎26888700, ⓦwww.thanoshotelscom. Smallish designer four-star hotel – room and common-area décor very Japanese/minimalist – that's especially good for families; there's a children's club, and all perishable needs are supplied locally inclusive or for a small extra charge, thus saving on air luggage allowance. ❻

Annabelle Near northwest end of Leofóros Posidhónos, seaward side ☎26938333, ⓦwww.theannabellehotel.com. Páfos' most established five-star option, looking to the sea over exotic terraced gardens (including a "swim-in" grotto at the end of a serpentine – there's a standard rectangular pool too). Several on-site restaurants, a spa, a gym and a range of rooms from standard to family studios complete the picture. Discounts often available. ❾

Pioneer Beach Leofóros Posidhónos, 3km southeast of central Káto Páfos ☎26964500, ⓦwww.pioneer-cbh.com. The beach of the name is okay, but the distinctive features here are a lush garden setting and the fact that this four-star outfit is now for adults only (over age 16). ❻

Ktíma Páfos

Axiothea Ívis Malióti 2, a stair-street off Apostólou Pávlou ☎26232866, ⓦwww.axiotheathotel.com. Strategically located on Moussalás hill, the ancient acropolis, the bar/breakfast lounge and terrace of this congenially run two-star hotel have unbeatable views over the town and coast. The rooms themselves are on the small side, and furnished to a higher standard in the preferable new wing. ❸

Kinyras Arkhiepiskópou Makaríou 91 ☎26941604, ⓦwww.kiniras.cy.net. The town's only surviving restoration inn, seven of whose high-ceilinged rooms have balconies – all have fridges, a/c and clock radios. There's a well-regarded courtyard restaurant on the ground floor, where breakfast is served. ❺

Káto Páfos

The main resort strip in **Káto Páfos**, east of Apostólou Pávlou and the harbour, consists of opticians, estate agents, ice-cream parlours, fast-food franchises, more estate agents, indistinguishable restaurants, nightclubs, still more estate agents, clothes shops, souvenir kiosks, banks and excursion agencies, the characterless pattern repeating itself every couple of hundred metres along **Leofóros Posidhónos**, the shoreline boulevard. The only "sight" on this lacklustre sequence is the **Paphos Aquarium**, at Artémidhos 1 (daily 10am–8pm; €7 adults, €4 children, or €18 family ticket) with 72 tanks containing sea creatures (including a few alligators).

A better place to begin a tour of the lower town is the **harbour**, a few hundred metres west, near traces of the ancient and medieval town, as so often in Cyprus placed cheek by jowl or converted for use by later occupiers. The harbour-mouth **castle** and its inland counterpart **Saránda Kolónes** are originally Lusignan, while the early churches of **Ayía Kyriakí** and **Ayía Solomóni** both show signs of previous use, and the Hellenistic **Tombs of the Kings** eventually served as Christian catacombs. But the glory of Káto Páfos is the series of

KÁTO PÁFOS

0 ——— 200 m

N

MEDITERRANEAN SEA

▲ Tombs of the Kings   ▲ Ktíma

ACCOMMODATION

Alexander the Great	A
Almyra	D
Annabelle	C
Pioneer Beach	B

Carob warehouses

Airport

Fabrica Hill

Classical Theatre

Áyios Agapitikós

Ancient perimeter wall

Áyios Lambrianós

Ayía Solomóni tree

Roman Odeion

Lighthouse

PLOUTARKHOU

Agora

Lusignan Baths (ruin)

Ottoman Baths (ruin)

Áyios Yeóryios

House of Dionysos

Saránda Kolónes

Ayía Kyriakí

Early basilica foundations

BAR ZONE

House of Aion

House of Orpheus

House of Theseus

Entrance

Aquarium

Panayía Limeniótissa

Old Customs House

Taxi rank

POSIDHONOS

half-submerged ancient breakwater

Municipal beach

Castle

East Tower base

RESTAURANTS

Artio	1	La Piazza	9
Atlantida	11	La Sardegna	2
Cavallini	10	Nicos Tyrimos	3
Hondhros	4	Taste of India	12

BARS

La Boite 67	14
California Beach Bar	8
Different Bar	5
Flintstones	7
Notos	13
Rainbow Club	6

Roman mosaics found northwest of the harbour; having been buried and forgotten over centuries, they were never subsequently modified or adapted.

Local **beaches** extend east of the little port, fronting the row of resort hotels (and the newer walkway) that has sprung up since 1983. They are serviceable at best and have to be artificially supplemented with sand from elsewhere.

The harbour and castle

The **harbour** area was "improved" during the early 1990s, with the quay pedestrianized and the old customs warehouse (now used for rather naff art exhibits) restored. A half-dozen indifferent waterfront patisseries and tavernas trade largely on their position, as do numbers of persistent time-share touts. **Cruises** in glass-bottomed boats are also on offer, varying from a short hop to a wreck, or all the way along the Akámas peninsula. Many, however, are as dubious as the time-shares, especially the so-called "fishing trips" – departing in choppy seas is an expensive way of seeing your breakfast again, and little is visible by day.

The diminutive **castle** (daily Nov–March 8am–5pm; April–Oct 8am–6pm; €1.70) guarding the harbour entrance is reached by a small stone bridge across a narrow moat. You can climb up to the roof for unrivalled views over the port and town, though the building itself is currently empty – it's the occasional venue for events like the early September opera evenings during the Pafos Aphrodite festival. The existing structure is merely the reworked western tower

153

Most four- and five-star hotels have an in-house dive school, but Páfos harbour is still home to a few independent scuba operators. In theory, there are up to fifty **dive sites**, near and far, from which to choose. Many are morning-only dives, since much of the year prevailing winds from the southwest pick up after noon and make conditions unpleasant, if not downright nauseating; ensure that any boat you're boarding is of sufficient size, ideally with a stabilizer or prominent keel. Dive sites are jealously preserved trade secrets, with preferred ones changing from season to season in accordance with storm damage, oversubscription from competing outfits, or divemaster boredom. The following, more common, destinations are likely to continue in use.

Shore dives

These include transfer to the site by transit van (or even on foot from Páfos waterfront).

Cynthiana, near the eponymous hotel. A novice favourite (10m).

The Maze, near "White River" beach. A labyrinth of gullies at 11m maximum.

Moray Cove, north of Coral Bay. Especially good as a night dive (15m).

Roman Wall, in the harbour. The usual beginners' training site at under 6m depth.

Boat dives

Janchor Reef A popular morning dive with an old anchor and (often) groupers seen near the 27-metre bottom.

Manijin A classic multilevel site (6–22m) with a drop-off, caves (one covered in pink-and-purple algae) and an archway. The sea must be calm for this one, as a forty-minute boat transfer each way is involved.

Mismaloyia A "reef" (gentle drop, no real wall) at 26–32m for the moderately experienced, where amberjack and (with luck) loggerhead turtles can be glimpsed.

The Valley of the Caves Rather underwhelming as the grottoes barely rate as overhangs (9–15m).

Wreck dives

Of the two local **wreck** dives touted, the *Vera K*, some 25min east-southeast of the harbour, is a feasible afternoon dive at 10–11m and more exciting than the *Achilleas* at the same depth west-southwest of the port; be warned that both ships are well broken up and don't remotely compare to the *Zenobia* near Larnaca (see p.95). Another potential future wreck dive is the *Dhimitrios*, a lumber freighter which ran aground off Khlórakas during a violent storm in March 1998. It is in imminent danger of breaking up (though the oil has been pumped out); local dive schools are trying to get permission to work it free and scuttle it properly as an underwater attraction.

Dive operators

CyDive, in the Myrra Complex shopping centre at Posidhónos 1, Káto Páfos ☎26934271, ⓦwww.cydive.com, the longest-established school in the district, has a good reputation and operates most of the year out of their own boats. They offer morning or afternoon shore and boat dives, mostly quite shallow but including archeological remains, caves and some wrecks, as well as full days out. For qualified divers, €50 per dive (€85 2-tank dive) for all equipment, transport and dive master; basic PADI courses €400, Advanced Open Water certification €290. Alternatively, for a less formal approach try Latvian-Russian-run **ABC Dive** at Ikárou 21, ☎99819529, ⓦwww.abcdive.info.

of a much larger Lusignan castle dating from 1391, which the Venetians demolished nearly a century later. The stump base of the easterly tower is still visible about seventy metres along the modern mole, itself pointing towards the ancient breakwater, now half submerged. The Ottomans repaired what was of use to them in 1592; the ground floor served as their dungeons, which the British used as a salt warehouse till 1935.

The Paphos mosaics

Whatever else happens in Páfos, the entire headland between the harbour and the lighthouse will remain a fenced-off "archeological park", as it's suspected that as much archeological wealth lies buried as has so far come to light. The most spectacular finds unearthed to date are the **Roman mosaics** (daily: April–Oct 8am–7.30pm; Nov–March 8am–5pm; €3.40 includes odeion and Saránda Kolónes), discovered accidentally by a ploughing farmer in 1962. Subsequent Cypriot and Polish excavations revealed an extensive complex of Roman buildings with exquisite floor mosaics, showing ancient mythological episodes and considered among the best in the eastern Mediterranean. Nowhere is the wealth and opulence of imperial Roman Paphos better suggested than in these vivid panels. Mosaics have always been an expensive medium, far more so than frescoes, requiring not just master craftsmen and several assistants, but often the application of gold leaf as well as paint to the tiny glass cubes or tesserae which make up the images. (Other, less costly, tesserae were chipped from stones of the appropriate colour.) Modern shelters protecting many of the mosaics are naturally lit and provided with catwalks for viewing – though often the colours are far from dazzling, since the tesserae are not kept polished as they were when new.

The Houses of Dionysos and the Four Seasons

The largest building in the mosaics complex is the **House of Dionysos**, so called because of repeated representations of the god, and probably built in the late second or early third century AD as the villa of a wealthy merchant. However, a much earlier Hellenistic pebble-mosaic, showing the monster Scylla, has been relocated to a previously undecorated floor, and is the first thing you see on entering. Towards the rear of the building Zeus as an eagle abducts Ganymede, while Dionysos frolics with Ariadne, attended by Cupid and a hunting dog.

But the most famous panels ring the main atrium, on the west side of which Apollo pursues Daphne, while her father, the river-god Peneios, reclines below; in a nearby panel Poseidon chases after the nymph Amymone with more success, as evidenced by Cupid hovering over the sea-god's quarry. The *Triumph of Dionysos*, with the god riding in a chariot pulled by two she-leopards and flanked by satyrs, slaves and bacchantes, reflects the decadence of the Roman town.

Another long panel shows first Dionysos proffering a bunch of grapes to the nymph Akme – as her name implies, the personification of perfection (in this case a good vintage); next is King Ikarios, legendary first manufacturer of wine, with a bullock-drawn cart of the new elixir; and on the far right, two lolling, inebriated shepherds are rather redundantly labelled "The First Wine-Drinkers". The First Piss-Up apparently ended badly – in the unshown sequel, friends of the shepherds, thinking them poisoned, murdered Ikarios. Left of this group the tragedy of Pyramus and Thisbe unfolds, the lion escaping with Thisbe's mantle, and Pyramus shown erroneously as the god of the eponymous river in Anatolia.

Around the other three sides of this atrium there is fine animal detail in a series of hunting scenes; elsewhere a peacock dominates the central square of one of several excellent geometrical floors. At the edge of several panels, including that of the Four Seasons personified (near the entrance), visitors are exhorted to "Rejoice" (*Khairei*), presumably with liberal quantities of wine – from these inscriptions it's deduced that these panels formed the floor of a banqueting hall or a reception room.

The **House of the Four Seasons**, an area discovered early in 1992, is named after personifications of the seasons, though only Autumn has survived. It is contiguous with the House of Dionysos but unfortunately not open to the public at the moment; should this change, you'll see engagingly realistic hunting scenes, and various animal portraits.

The House of Aion

In the **House of Aion**, uncovered in 1983, the mosaics are later (mid-fourth century) and more sophisticated in theme and execution. In the lower right panel, Apollo sentences the silenus Marsyas, who dared challenge him to a musical contest, to be flayed. In the next scene above, the result of a beauty contest between Cassiopeia and several nereids is depicted; the latter, the losers, ride sulkily away on an assortment of sea monsters. Still on the right, the topmost frame shows Hermes offering baby Dionysos to the centaur Tropheus for rearing, surrounded by nymphs preparing a bath. The left-hand scenes are less intact; of the god Aion, from whom the building takes its name, only the head is visible, and a version of Leda preparing to meet the swan is somewhat damaged. Except for the statue niche in the west wall, the building itself is a purpose-built reconstruction from old masonry.

The Houses of Theseus and Orpheus

The next precinct, the unroofed **House of Theseus**, takes its name from a round mosaic of coarse tesserae that portrays Theseus brandishing a club against the (vanished) Minotaur, while Ariadne and personifications of Crete and the Labryrinth look on. In the next area west, a very late (fifth-century) mosaic, *The First Bath of Achilles*, is shown: a nursemaid carries him firmly in the presence of the three Fates and his parents. Its arrangement strongly prefigures the iconography of early Christian portrayals of the Nativity, wherein the Virgin reclines in the same way as the nymph Thetis, and the three Magi replace the Fates. It is speculated that this building, or a vanished adjacent one, was the location of Sergius Paulus's interviews with the apostles.

At the west edge of the archeological zone, the **House of Orpheus** features Orpheus charming a naturalistic bestiary with his lyre, in an exceptionally large floor panel, currently alas under a protective layer of sand and dirt.

The Roman odeion and lighthouse

From the northerly access path to the mosaics, a short lane leads up to the **Roman odeion**, a workmanlike 1970s restoration of the theatre and not very compelling except during summertime ancient drama evenings. Just south of the contemporary agora, beyond the stage to the east, extensive ancient building foundations await excavation. From the odeion a pedestrians-only dirt track leads west to the picturesque **lighthouse**, beyond which are the most intact stretches of the city's **perimeter wall**.

Saránda Kolónes

Just north of the exit road from the municipal car park, the fortress of **Saránda Kolónes**, signposted as Byzantine, is actually a Lusignan structure built atop its predecessor. Almost as soon as it was completed, it was destroyed by a 1222 earth tremor, and until excavation (1957–83) the only objects visible above ground were numerous tumbled columns – hence the Greek name, "Forty Columns".

It's still a confusing jumble of moat-ringed masonry. Some well-worn latrines, near the remaining arches, are the only obvious items – they were fitted with doors, in deference to Christian modesty; the pavement is riddled with sewer tunnels, vaults and stables, some interconnecting. For a supposed stronghold, an improbable number of sally ports fitted with stairs breach the roughly square walls. The ramparts were originally entered by an easterly gateway, and sported eight mismatched towers.

Ayía Kyriakí (Khrysopolítissa)

Crossing busy Apostólou Pávlou, pedestrianized Stassándhrou leads directly to **Ayía Kyriakí (Khrysopolítissa)**. This eleventh- or twelfth-century Byzantine church, with a later belfry, is dwarfed by the vast foundations of an earlier, seven-aisled basilica and archiepiscopal palace, both destroyed by the all-destroying Arab raids. What's left are extensive fourth-century floor mosaics, mostly geometric, and a scattering of probably contemporary columns, including one dubbed "St Paul's Pillar" after the apocryphal tradition that the apostle was tied to it and scourged.

Though still being excavated, much of the fourth-century zone, considerably below modern ground level, is now open to close-up viewing. Highlights include a **figural mosaic** of a brimming wine *krater* accompanied by an inscription: "Wisdom Inside This (Vessel)" – not, as in the pagan villas, an exhortation to drunkenness, but part of a series of allegories in this vehemently Christian terrain. Nearby panels show a deer (today with its head missing) drinking under the remains of the opening to Psalm 42: "As the hart panteth after the springs of water, so panteth my soul after thee, O Lord...", and, just above some grape clusters, the intact inscription "I am the True Vine" (John 15:1).

A catwalk gives access to Ayía Kyriakí itself. The small **church** is completely bare inside, and was ceded early during the 1990s by the Orthodox bishop of Páfos to the Catholic and Anglican expatriate communities for their use – perhaps the first time that heterodox rites have been celebrated here since the Lusignans displaced the Orthodox with a Catholic diocese in 1220. To the north are scattered the domed **Ottoman baths, on the map these are referred to as Turkish baths** and the **Lusignan baths**, which the Turks heavily modified, as well as a Byzantine church converted to a mosque and a tiny, cottage-like modern mosque used by local Turkish Cypriots until 1975.

Ayía Solomóni catacombs and Fabrica Hill

Ayía Kyriakí lies near the easternmost circuit of ancient walls, and other points of historical interest lie up Apostólou Pávlou. The **catacombs of Ayía Solomóni**, just east of the pavement, are overshadowed by a huge **terebinth tree** festooned with knotted-together votive rags or kerchiefs, a practice common to both Christians and Muslims throughout the Middle East and similar in efficacy to the prayer flags of the Buddhists. Steps lead down to a multi-chambered, sunken sanctuary honouring one of those obscure, weirdly named saints in which Cyprus specializes – here a Jewish woman whose seven children were martyred by one of the Seleucid kings of Palestine. It's thought that the subterranean complex was once the synagogue of Roman Paphos, and doubtless a pagan shrine before that. Most curious is a sacred well, accessed by a separate flight of stairs, with water so clear that you'll step into it unintentionally even though you've been warned. Just up Apostólou Pávlou is the similar catacomb-shrine of **Áyios Lambrianós**.

The rock outcrop just north, known as **Fabrica Hill**, contains more tunnelled-out tombs and churches, including those of **Áyios Agapitikós** and **Áyios**

Misitikós. These two shrines honour saints even more shadowy than usual, and pointedly unrecognized by the Orthodox Church. According to legend, dust gathered from the floor of the former can be used as a love charm (*agápi* means "love" in Greek), but from the latter has the opposite effect (*misós* means "hate"): useful magic that presumably ensures the saints' long-running veneration. Ongoing Australian excavations since 1995 on the south slope of Fabrica hill have uncovered most of a **Classical theatre** – hacked, like everything else here, out of the living rock, and bidding to rank as the largest on the island.

The Tombs of the Kings

From Fabrica Hill, a well-signed major road, Leofóros Táfon tón Vasiléon, leads 2km northwest to the so-called **Tombs of the Kings** (daily: summer 8.30am–7.30pm; winter 8am–5pm; €1.70). Rock outcrops blanketed in pink spring cyclamens near the shore – called *Paleokástra* ("Old Citadels") for their similarity to castles – conceal dozens of tombs hacked out of the soft strata, since this was a permissible distance outside the city walls for a necropolis. There's no evidence of royal use, merely that of the local privileged classes, starting in the third century BC. Their design is not strictly indigenous but heavily indebted to Macedonian prototypes, passed on from Alexander's legions to the Ptolemies who ruled Cyprus.

Eight complexes of tombs are singled out by number (nos. 3, 4 and 8 are the most elaborate), and include several reached by stairs down to sunken courts, ringed by peristyles of rough square, or round fluted, Doric rock-columns. Beyond the colonnades, passages lead to rooms with alcoves or niches provided for each corpse. At anniversaries of the death of the deceased, relatives would troop out to the tomb for a *nekródhipno* or ceremonial meal, with the leftovers deposited near the actual sepulchre; a variant of this custom – the *kóllyva* – still prevails in Greek Orthodox observance. Carved crosses and residual fresco pigment in some tombs suggest their use as catacombs in early Christian times. Later they were systematically looted, and scholarly excavations only began in 1977. Today it's still an eerie place, the drumming of the distant sea and chirps of nesting birds the only sounds.

Ktíma Páfos

Looking down from the edge of the escarpment on which **Ktíma Páfos** is built, you can appreciate the Byzantines' defensive reasoning: it's nearly a sixty-metre elevation drop to the coastal plain, with the harbour castle assuming toy-like dimensions at this distance. The main thoroughfares of Pávlou Melá and Pallikarídhi subdivide the upper town: to the east lies a cantonment of broader avenues containing the courts, police station, archbishop's house, various schools with their grand Neoclassical facades, the municipal gardens, tourist facilities and **museums**, while on the west, a warren of narrower, denser-gridded streets encompass the bazaar and the old Turkish quarter of **Moúttalos**.

The bazaar and Moúttalos

Heading northwest on Agorás, the continuation of Makaríou, you soon reach a relatively ornate, early twentieth-century building – the **covered market**, where souvenir schlock and trinkets have replaced the former vendors of fresh produce. South of this, over the edge of the palisade, you'll spy a medieval **"Turkish" hamam** down by the car park, restored early in the 1990s (open only for special events/exhibits); in fact it appears to have originally been a

▲ Tombs of the Kings

Latin, or even Byzantine church before its use as a bathhouse, which only ended during the communal troubles of the 1960s.

Further northwest lie the narrow alleys of **Moúttalos**, before 1974 a guarded Turkish-Cypriot enclave, with refugees from outlying Pafiot villages. The sole monument here is the **Cami Kebir** or "Great Mosque" (locked), once the Byzantine church of Ayía Sofía and still a handsome building. Near the end of the clifftop neighbourhood, where the original street signs in Turkish still survive, there's a *platía* flanked with kebab houses and clubs used by the locals, all Orthodox refugees from the North. After the often conspicuous wealth of urban Greek Cyprus, the meanness of the bungalows here may come as a shock – you are not merely looking back nearly forty years in time, but also at the consequences of both a TMT-enforced prohibition on doing business with Greek Cypriots, and retaliatory government measures against the enclaves, whereby a long list of materials deemed "militarily strategic" were forbidden to be brought in.

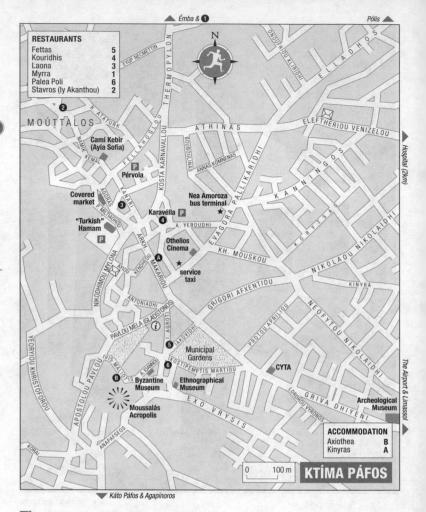

RESTAURANTS

Fettas	5
Kouridhis	4
Laona	3
Myrra	1
Palea Poli	6
Stavros (Iy Akanthou)	2

MOÚTTALOS

Cami Kebir
(Ayia Sofía)

Pérvola

Covered
market

"Turkish"
Hamam

Karavélla

Nea Amoroza
bus terminal

Othellos
Cinema

service
taxi

Municipal
Gardens

Byzantine
Museum

Ethnographical
Museum

Moussalás
Acropolis

CYTA

Archeological
Museum

ACCOMMODATION

| Axiothea | B |
| Kinyras | A |

0   100 m

KTÍMA PÁFOS

Hospital (2km)

The Airport & Limassol

▼ Káto Páfos & Agapínoros

The museums

The southeastern cantonment of Ktíma is home to three important museums, collectively worth a half-day of your time. First stop might be the privately run **Ethnographical Museum** at Éxo Vrýsis 1, south of the municipal gardens, occupying two floors of the Eliades family mansion (Mon–Sat 9am–6pm, Sun 9am–1pm; €1.70). Although the rooms are labelled after a fashion, snag the guide booklet available at the entrance to make complete sense of the ground-floor rural collection, which intermingles priceless antiques with recent cast-offs like aluminium cheese-graters. Some of the best bits include basketry, especially straw trays (*tsésti*), sieves and irons, and devices pertaining to the processing of cotton, now a vanished livelihood on Cyprus. One of the four rooms is mocked up as a bed-chamber, with lace and clothing; another contains a comprehensive display of nineteenth-century island pottery. Larger items, of the sort now often pressed into service as taverna decor, include *pinakótes* (dough-moulding boards), *dhoukánes* (flint-studded threshing sledges) and three wagons parked on the flagstones of the cruciform passageway. In the sunken garden, a wood-fired bakery stands near a genuine third-century rock-tomb hewn from the cliff.

The **Byzantine Museum** (Mon–Fri 9am–5pm, Sat 9am–1pm; €1.70) occupies part of the bishopric's premises on Andhréa Ioánnou, near the church of Áyios Theódhoros. The collection consists mostly of sixteenth-century, post-Byzantine **icons** rescued from local country chapels; though of consistent artistic merit, few really stand out. Exceptions include an eighth- or ninth century image of Ayía Marína, the oldest icon known on the island; a late twelfth-century icon of the Panayía Eleoússa from the monastery of Áyios Sávvas tís Karónos in the Dhiárizos valley; and a curious double-sided icon of the thirteenth century from Filoússa.

Ktíma's **Archeological Museum**, well east of the town centre (Tues, Wed & Fri 8am–3pm; Thurs 8am–5pm; Sat 9am–3pm; €1.70), requires a special detour and sufficient time for the extensive, interesting exhibits. The chronological displays begin with Chalcolithic figurines and rather wild abstract pottery, which becomes recognizably zoomorphic by the time the Bronze Age is reached; this exotic trend continues, in a more refined manner, in the Archaic display case. The Hellenistic-Roman room features myriad glass objects, as well as more figurative representation, though colourful glazed pottery does not appear again until the Byzantine and Lusignan section, much of it from Saránda Kolónes fort. Perhaps the strangest items are Hellenistic clay hot-water bottles, moulded to fit various afflicted body parts, and a finely wrought crouching lion of the same era.

Eating and drinking

Contemplating the identikit **restaurants** that clutter Káto Páfos, you might well despair of any characterful, good-value choices. Yet even in Káto there are many finds, while Ktíma has a few stand-outs by virtue of its status as a "real" town, and the area between the two holds a number of surprises. Overall, traditional Cypriot eateries are losing ground to foreign cuisine – aficionados of Italian, Indian, Thai, Chinese and French food are well catered for.

Káto Páfos

Atlantida Yeroskípou "Tourist Beach", at the southeast end of Káto Páfos' hotel row ☏26964525. Upmarket seafood specialist with good service set behind the lawn of its "private" strand, serving a wide variety of palpably fresh fish and shellfish, with salad included. Cheaper species like squid or cuttle-fish around €45/kilo; scaly fish is more expensive. **Cavallini** Leofóros Posidhónos 65, corner of Dhanaïs ☏26964164. Fairly authentic northern Italian cuisine, in formal surroundings. Antipasti, meat dishes and pasta all feature in sizeable portions, though service can be uneven. Reckon on €23–29 apiece for two courses and dessert, plus booze. Dinner only; closed Sun.

Hondhros Apostólou Pávlou 96. Consistently well-executed, moderately priced Cypriot standards, plus fish; allow €14–16 each if you stay away from seafood, and always ask about the off-menu specials. Pleasant outdoor seating, especially at lunch, and a congenial bar indoors, decorated with old photos, customer graffiti and the murals of Andy Adamos (his widow Jenny and changing shifts of four children run the place). Closed mid-Jan to mid-Feb. **La Piazza** Alkminís 11–12, just off Posidhónos ☏26819921. Very upmarket Italian with a Venetian flair, its menu and recipes vetted once yearly by a north-Italian professor. A good balance between seafood, pasta and meat dishes, and you can eat well (and drink, sparingly) for about €35 each.

Taste of India Posidhónos, by Aliathon Hotel ☏26961700. The best of three outlets of an island North Indian chain, with pretty authentic standards: tandoori gobi, naans, parathas, birianis, prawn dishes and curries. Four can dine with copious lashings of Cobra beer, popaddoms, pickles and *kulfi* for about €150.

Between Káto and Ktíma

Artio Pyrámou 6, off Táfos tón Vasiléon ☏26942800. Chic without being snooty, with cutting-edge decor and well-trained staff, this brasserie is the most exclusive see-and-be-seen spot in town. The cuisine is nouvelle Mediterranean, accompanied by a wide-ranging Cypriot/French/New World wine list. Three courses and Cypriot wine will set you back over €50 each. Dinner only Mon–Sat.

Nicos Tyrimos Agapínoros 71, behind the old carob warehouses on Apostólou Pávlou ☎26942846. This is arguably Páfos's best in-town fish restaurant, as the owner has a contract to have first crack at whatever the local fleet brings in. Offers a wide selection, preceded in spring by unusual, abundant *mezédhes* like *agrélia* (wild asparagus – may be charged extra), *kírtamo* (rock samphire) and fried baby crabs. About €17 per head *mezé* format, plus wine from a good list, and service charge; going à la carte, budget €30 for two fair-sized fish, plus another €22 for assorted extras (garnish, drink, service) per couple. Open noon–midnight, dinner reservations advised; closed Mon.

La Sardegna Apostólou Pávlou 70, Shops 6–7 ☎26933399. Excellent wood-oven-fired pizzas are the big hit here, purveyed by native Sardinian Gino Sechi. On the menu, small means medium by most standards, medium means large – you have been warned. About €20 a head with salad or starter, drink extra (curiously, there are no desserts); booking suggested at busy times. Dinner only; closed Tues.

Ktíma Páfos

Fettas Corner Iakovídhi and Ioánnou Agróti, opposite the fountain roundabout ☎26937822. A classic evening-only eatery that's had a thorough facelift and tarted-up (so priced-up – allow €18–20 each) menu, but basically the same top-flight salad, *halloúmi*, *loúntza*, *tahíni*, grills, superior chips or *pourgoúri*, and a few oven dishes (or *mezé* platters) still packs the locals in. Thus it's a bit

noisy, with reservations suggested, especially weekend nights when there's live music. The only black mark is a tendency to "creative accounting" – check bills carefully.

Kouridhis Haralámbou Moúskou 1, corner Kósta Karnavállou. A high turnover guarantees freshness at the town-centre outfit specializing in *mezé* and roasts, best at lunchtime. Don't go expecting a scenic or quiet location, though.

🏃 **Laona** Vótsi 6. This *kafestiatório* is the best venue in town for an inexpensive, traditional cooked lunch (Mon–Sat 10am–4pm) in salubrious surroundings – a 110-year-old terrazzo-floored room, plus summer pavement seating. Bank employees packing out the place on Mon particularly tell you you're on the right track; plenty of bean-based dishes, plus stews like pork with *kolokássi*, and home-style sweets including *kalopráma* and *palouzé*, plus decent bulk wine from Statós.

Myrra Neapóleos 37, corner of Lámbrou Sépi ☎26936009. Established in 1988 by a refugee family, this ramshackle old-house taverna (also with outdoor seating) does a decent 15-course €15.50 *mezé* (own-label wine extra), or grills à la carte. Dinner only except Sun/hols; good atmosphere; reservations in season don't hurt.

Palea Poli Ikostipémptis Martíou 4. Metropolitan Greek dishes – *spetzofäï*, lamb liver, *fáva* – outnumber Cypriot platters (the owner is Greek) at this *mezedhopolío* installed inside an old house. Relatively pricey, especially the drinks – budget €40 for two plus booze.

Stavros (ly Akanthou) Platía Mouttálou. A well-loved local where the busy, focal-point bar is on an equal footing with the food service; not many foreigners come here, especially off-season. The *mezé* is good value at about €15 each, and meat platters in particular are top-notch.

Nightlife and entertainment

Conventional local nightlife is concentrated down in the hotel district of Káto Páfos, with most **bars and clubs** found along Posidhónos, just inland as it intersects Ayíou Andoníou, and the lanes around. One word of warning: stretches of Táfon tón Vasiléon with cabarets and attendant pimps, touts and street hassle are worth avoiding, especially by unescorted women. Among **cinemas**, the Cine Orasis two-plex at Apostólou Pávlou 35 tends to have more first-run foreign fare than Othellos at Evagóra Pallikarídhi 41; there's an art–film club on Thursday nights. The **Pafos Aphrodite Festival** (early Sept) and the **Akamas Festival** (late March) see concerts and other events in the larger hotel venues or Páfos castle. Other classical performances are regularly staged at the Markidion Theatre, on Andhréa Yeroúdhi in Ktíma.

La Boite 67 Káto Páfos harbour. Students from the Lemba art school and Páfos trendies tend to be found drinking between or after

meals at this durable pub, though its heyday – despite the "artists' pub" sign outside – has passed.

California Beach Bar Ayíou Andoníou. Run by a returned California Cypriot named Jimmy, this features DJs on rotation playing various sounds; get hammered with "fish bowl" cocktails and vodka slush puppies.

Different Bar Ayías Nápas 6–7, near corner of Ayías Anastasías. The local gay bar, but gets a mixed clientele for the sake of its tasteful soundtrack, cool interior and friendly, informative owner.

Flintstones Dhionysíou, off Ayíou Andoníou. Run by three brothers as an annexe of their house, this attracts a mix of locals and tourists, with music at a level to permit conversation, and a good atmosphere engendered by the landlords.

Notos Bar Old port. One of the more locally orientated clubs, with frequent DJed theme parties.

Rainbow Club Ayíou Andoníou. Káto's oldest and most prestigious dancehall, with R&B, hip-hop, house and trance spun by big-name DJs typically poached from London, Ibiza or Ayía Nápa.

Listings

Airlines Cyprus Airlines is at Gládstonos 37–39, Ktíma ☎ 26933556.

Airport flight information Ring ☎ 77778833 and ask for the extension of your airline.

Backcountry expeditions Guided hiking excursions have effectively died out around Páfos – thanks to track-bulldozing and a change in clientele – and jeep safaris offered are all much of an (environmentally destructive) muchness; they won't take you anywhere that your own rental jeep, used in conjunction with this book, can't visit. For a sterling exception to the above, contact either David Pearlman, naturalized Cypriot, archeologist extraordinaire and certified tour guide (☎ 99603513, ✉ taramas@cytanet.com.cy) or Simon Demetropoulos (☎ 99427152, ✉ chelonia @logos.cy.net), one of the top naturalists in Cyprus; they can arrange hiking trips and quality bespoke jeep safaris to less frequented areas.

Bookshops Terra Books, in two premises in the arcade at Ayíou Kendéa 31 in the heart of town, has a good mix of Greek and English titles, both new and (especially) second-hand, as well as large-scale DLS maps. Moufflon Books, Kinýra 30, has a large stock of new books on Cyprus (both coffee-table and guides), fiction and fine art.

Bus companies Long-distance companies in Ktíma are limited to ALEPA at the Karavélla car park ☎ 26934410, with services to Limassol and Nicosia; and Nea Amoroza at the same location ☎ 26936740, to Pólis and Pomós.

Car rental ASG/Europcar, Leofóros Posidhónos, Natalia Court, Shops 19–20 ☎ 26936944; Andreas Petsas, Apostólou Pávlou 86, Green Court ☎ 26935522; Budget/GDK, Leofóros Táfon tón Vasiléon, Dora Complex ☎ 26953824; Sixt, Leofóros Táfon tón Vasiléon 58, Aristo Royal Complex Shop 8 ☎ 26936991; Thrifty/U-Drive, Leofóros Posidhónos, opposite Cypria Bay Hotel ☎ 26813181.

Internet Most central are the two branches of Maroushia (Mon–Sat 9am–11pm, Sun 3–11pm), in Káto at the Myrra Complex Shop no. 15 on Posidhónos, and up in Ktíma at the central junction, above the Hellenic Bank.

Motorbike rental Shikkis, Leofóros Posidhónos 2, ☎ 26965349; Pentaras, Ikárou corner Agapínoros ☎ 26952151.

Post offices The nominal main branch, in an old colonial building on Nikodhímou Myloná (Mon–Fri 7.30am–1.30pm, plus Thurs 3–5.30pm), has been effectively supplanted for things like parcels and poste restante by the district sorting office on the corner of Eleftheríou Venizélou and Vassiléos Konstandínou (Mon–Fri 7.30am–1.30pm, plus Thurs 3–5.30pm; Sat 9–11am).

Shopping The Cyprus Handicraft Service showroom is at Apostólou Pávlou 64, Ktíma. Mikis Antiques, Fellahoglou 6, Klíma, displays some wonderful Belle Epoque phonographs, rural impedimenta and furniture.

Taxi Travel & Express is at Evagóra Pallikarídhi 8, Ktíma ☎ 26933181. Direct service to Limassol only; journeys to Nicosia or Larnaca are via Limassol.

Southeast from Páfos

The A6 motorway has siphoned off much of the traffic heading southeast from Páfos, making the B6 road far more manageable, and a better bet for short-haul touring: it passes over a trio of rivers, the lower reaches of streams beginning far up in the Pafiot corner of the Tróödhos range (exploring the Xéros and Dhiárizos valleys is described on pp.199–202). The resulting fertility (notably in melons) softens the usual mineral, parched yellowness of the south Cypriot coast, seemingly in sympathy with the age-old worship of the island's patron goddess, Aphrodite, at **Yeroskípou** and **Palea Paphos**. Little tangible remains of her shrines, but her worship continues faintly in Christianized forms. One emphatically Byzantine site which doesn't owe much to pagan antecedents is the remote painted cave-shrine of **Paleá Énklistra**.

Eastern beaches

The Páfos town beaches, specifically those fringing the eastern hotels, aren't up to much; to reach anything moderately attractive you have to get a little way out of town. The first substantial strip is the maintained beach in **Yeroskípou**, between the *Atlantida* seafood restaurant and the last hotel, though most locals content themselves with the kilometre or so of natural shingle shore just east from the *Ricco Beach* snack bar. The bottom's sandy, the water's clean, and there's a well-established gay nude-bathing scene here after dark in summer, especially around the full moon. Onshore across the road, on any warm night, the *Barrio del Mar* is one of the better **nightspots** in the region. The other easterly beach is **Flória**, seaward of Tími village, about halfway along the airport spur road – follow signs pointing to the dirt drive that leads to some ramshackle tavernas and the first hints of development.

Yeroskípou

YEROSKÍPOU village (Geroskipou, pronounced "Yerostchípou") is now virtually a suburb of Páfos, beginning just a kilometre or so beyond the district archeological museum, and linked with Ktíma (Karavélla parking lot) by ALEPA **bus** #1. The name is a modern rendition of the ancient *Hieros Kipos* or "Sacred Garden and Grove", consecrated to Aphrodite, which grew in the fertile plain below towards the sea.

The Folk Art Museum and Ayía Paraskeví

These days, Yeroskípou has a reputation as a **crafts centre**, as reflected by numerous stalls on the main road peddling basketry, "Cyprus" delight (they bristle if you call it "Turkish" delight) and pottery (Savvas at the east edge of the village is considered tops for that). The craft theme is highlighted in the Yeroskípou **Folk Art Museum** (Mon–Fri 9am–2.30pm, plus Sept–June Thurs 3–5pm; €1.70). This, on Leondíou just south of the through road, is lodged in the former house of a certain Andreas Zoumboulakis, the early nineteenth-century British vice-consul here, better known as Hadji Smith, having adopted his sponsor's surname. The museum is among the best of its kind on the island, emphasizing domestic implements on the ground floor and local costumes upstairs, plus decorated gourds, including one fashioned into a stringed instrument.

Despite its name, the village is probably of Byzantine origin, the best demonstration of this being the renowned church of **Ayía Paraskeví** (nominal hrs May–Oct daily 8am–1pm & 2–5pm; Nov–April closes 4pm; free), now marooned amid a hideous pedestrianization project.

The damaged frescoes in the altar dome are non-representational, dating construction to the ninth century, when the Iconoclasts held sway in the Byzantine Empire. The church is unique on the island in having six domes, including that of the reliquary under the nineteenth-century belfry. Most of the surviving frescoes date from the fifteenth century and were cleaned in the 1970s, but unfortunately many are now prevented from sloughing off only by temporary protective gauze. Up in the central cupola hides a crude but engaging *Virgin Orans*; opposite the south door, and the first images seen upon entering, are the Last Supper, the Washing of the Feet, the Betrayal – where figures in Lusignan armour date the images – and Pilate washing his hands. Across from these you see the Birth and Presentation of the Virgin, complete with a set table in the former scene, plus the Raising of Lazarus and the Entry into Jerusalem. Back on the north wall arch, between the western and central domes, there's an unusual representation of Simon carrying the Cross for Christ while a Roman soldier drags Jesus along by a rope, with a Nativity and Baptism diagonally opposite, in the niche closest to the altar screen. The church itself was originally cruciform with a single nave, but had an ungainly narthex added to the south side in the nineteenth century (though a *yinaikonítis* or women's gallery in the rear was removed in the late 1990s).

Eating and drinking

Among a handful of **tavernas and snack bars** around, or just off, the central square, most distinctive – doubling as a butcher's shop – is *Khristos Pitsillis Ofton Kleftiko*, some 80m east of the square on the north side of the highway. You can enjoy some of the best *kléftigo* on the island (with the traditional raw-onion-and-lemon garnish) at a few rickety outdoor tables, for around €7 plus drinks.

But the most celebrated *mezé* house in the district, with a loyal following, is off Dhanaïs at Anthypolohagoú Yeoryíou M Sávva 37, on the Ktíma Páfos-Yeroskípou boundary: *Efta Aï-Yiorkidhes/Seven St Georges* (☎99655824, ⓦwww.7stgeorgestavern.com; reservations advised; closed Mon & random weeks Jan–Feb). It's named for an episode when seven lads named George battled Saracens scaling the cliffs here; they were all killed, but their resistance allowed the villagers to escape. The set *mezé* (€25 per head with house wine and coffee) encompasses imaginative dips, seasonally changing pickled veg- or meat-based platters which might include flash-fried *agrélia*, *ospriá*, forest mushrooms, Armenian *pastirma*, *moúngra*, bladder campion sautéed with eggs, *tsamarélla*, roast lamb, wild greens and goat-and-cumin *tavás*, plus preserved fruit and home-made liqueurs to finish off. All vegetables are either organically grown or self-gathered by proprietor George and son Ben, who also offer wonderful taped music at this converted old house with indoor/outdoor seating.

Koúklia and Palea Paphos

Approaching the boundary of Limassol district, some 11km southeast of Yeroskípou, you can't help noticing a large, solidly built structure on a prominent rise. This is **La Cavocle**, a fourteenth-century manor that's the inevitable marker-cairn and introduction to both the ancient city site of **Palea Paphos** and the large village of **KOÚKLIA** just to the north. Once an ethnically mixed community, Koúklia remains a pleasant if unremarkable place of low houses (overlooking the inevitable villa project), whose meandering lanes converge on a small *platía* with a church and some coffeehouses. Indifferent to the trickle of tourists visiting the adjacent ruins, the centre has changed little – except for the departure of its Turkish Cypriots – since independence. Of three **tavernas** in the village centre, the most accomplished (and renowned for its *mezé*) is *Dhiarizos* (closed Mon), though you may have to contend with a constantly blaring TV.

Incidentally, the **road** from Koúklia over the district border via Moúsere to Dhorá (see p.130) is the shortest, easiest and best-condition route from Páfos to the high Tróödhos – as well as giving access to the Paleá Énklistra (see p.167).

PÁFOS AND THE WEST | Southeast from Páfos

165

The archeological site

The ancient temple stood on a knoll about 2km inland, overlooking the sea but probably not the orchards and fields which have appeared since. Despite the hoariness of the cult here, there's little above-ground evidence of it or of the city which emerged around, and the archeological site itself is really of specialist interest. The courtyard-type **sanctuary of Aphrodite** (June–Aug Mon–Fri 8am–7pm, Sat & Sun 8am–5pm; Sept–May daily 8am–4pm, until 5pm Thurs; €3.40), with rustic, relatively impermanent buildings, was common in the pre-Hellenic Middle East; thus, little has survived other than low foundations to the north as you enter. Matters were made worse for posterity when a wealthy Roman built a private villa (bits of its mosaic floor still visible) next to the Archaic shrine in its last years, and the medieval placement of sugar-milling machinery atop the convenient stone foundations was extremely destructive to anything remaining above knee level. Finally, the nearby villagers, from Byzantine times onwards, treated the ruins as a quarry – most old buildings in Koúklia incorporate a cut stone or two from the shrine area.

In one corner of the precinct a short path leads to the "**Leda Mosaic House**", where the central image, Leda baring her behind to the lustful Zeus-swan, is a copy. The replica was installed here after the second- or third-century AD original was stolen by art thieves, then luckily recovered, to be lodged in Nicosia's Cyprus Museum.

Outside the sacred precinct, there's even less to see until excavations are completed. To the northeast, off the road towards Arkhimandhríta, are the remains of a **city gate**, and a **siege ramp** built by the Persians in 498 BC to breach the city walls. The defenders burrowed under the ramp in a vain attempt to collapse it and thus the Persian war-engines atop; two of the tunnels are now

The Paphiot cult of Aphrodite

The cult of the Cypriot patron goddess **Aphrodite** is of considerable antiquity; it was already established in a hilltop temple at Palea Paphos in about 1500 BC, and a town grew up around it, becoming capital of one of the original island kingdoms. Foundation legends credit the hero Kinyras as the first king and consort of Aphrodite, who supposedly emerged from the sea nearby at Pétra toú Romioú. Their beautiful daughter Myrrha was turned into a fragrant bush by the jealous goddess, and Adonis, born of its wood, completed the cycle by becoming Aphrodite's lover.

All this reflects historical facts about the Kinyrid dynasty, who not only "wedded" the goddess through her temple prostitutes, but married their own daughters on the death of their wives – royal descent was reckoned through the women of the line. Despite the incest, it was a relatively civilized observance, considering that neighbouring Asiatic love-goddesses, to whom Aphrodite owed much in pedigree and ritual, used to demand the sacrifice of their consorts after the rite of love-making.

The sacred prostitutes were apparently island matrons and damsels obliged by custom to give themselves at least once to strangers in the temple precincts. The business of prostitution was invariably brisker at the spring festivals for Aphrodite and Adonis, when separate processions of garlanded men and women made their way from Nea Paphos to the shrine, via the site of modern Yeroskípou. The rituals survive in a modern spring flower festival, the *Anthistíria*, which is celebrated with special enthusiasm in Ktíma Páfos, and in *Kataklysmós*, the Flood Festival in June, where the participants' obligatory sea-plunge seems to commemorate Aphrodite's emergence from the waves. Worship here continued until the Byzantine emperor Theodosius proscribed paganism late in the fourth century, nearly eight hundred years after the foundation of Nea Paphos.

open for public inspection. The **necropolis** (still under investigation) lies to the southeast of the hill, and appears to have escaped the notice of tomb robbers.

Just east of the precinct stands the usually locked twelfth- to sixteenth-century church of **Panayía Katholikí**, new goddess of the local cult. Should you gain admission (best chance weekdays 10am–noon), there are traces of fourteenth-century frescoes inside, the most curious being gargoyle-like personifications of the rivers Tigris and Euphrates on the west wall. Until recently Koúklia village women used to light candles nearby in honour of the Panayía Galaktariótissa – the Virgin Who Gives Milk to Mothers.

La Cavocle and the local museum

The most obvious, worthwhile item in the main archeological zone is the four-square Lusignan "Royal Manor House" of **La Cavocle**, whose name is a rendition of (take your pick) the Greek *kouvoúkli*, "canopy"; *kovoukuleris*, the royal bodyguard; or more likely the Latin *cubiculum*, "pavilion" – corrupted in whichever case to Koúklia, the name of the modern village. La Cavocle was the headquarters of the Crusaders' surrounding sugar plantations, and continued to serve as the "big house" of a large farm in Ottoman times. Only the east wing survived the Mameluke raid of 1426; the rest, including a fine gate tower, is a Turkish reconstruction. Because the courtyard level has risen over the centuries, you descend slightly to the ground floor of the east wing, where a Gothic thirteenth-century banquet room sports a rib-vaulted ceiling. This is now an acoustically superb venue for early summer **chamber music concerts** – see Ⓦ www.thepharostrust.org.

The **local museum** (same timings as the site) is housed upstairs from the concert venue. Among the few exhibits in Gallery I is one of several existing *betyls* or phallic cult monoliths (the biggest one is in Nicosia), which, not unlike Hindu Shiva *lingams*, used to be anointed with olive oil by local women well into modern times. Gallery II contains finds of all eras from the site, in chrono-logical order. Best is the huge chalk bathtub of the eleventh century BC, complete with a soap dish. Most of the other items are painted pottery, with some bronze work, much of which was found in the rubble piled up by the Persians to support their siege ramp.

Paleá Énklistra

Just outside Koukliá, hollowed out of a cliff, is the Byzantine cave-hermitage of **Paleá Énklistra**, so-called (*énklistra* means enclosure) by locals who mistook it for St Neophytos's (see p.169) first hermitage. The grotto and its frescoes are in fact mid-fifteenth century, 250 years too late to have sheltered Neophytos. Although the faces of the figures were mutilated during the 1960s by shepherds from the nearby village of Souskioú, it's still emphatically worth the trip out (first get the key from the Palea Paphos museum, daily 8am–3pm, in exchange for piece of ID). From the centre of Koukliá, drive 3.5km east–northeast on the F612 road towards the Tróödhos, then turn left onto a dirt track to the visible chapel of Áyios Konstandínos (signposted in blue-on-white Greek lettering with a red arrow), 500m further. Leave cars here, then continue on foot along a narrower track which drops briefly to the stream-valley floor before climbing to the cave in the north-facing cliff opposite.

The **iconography** of the Paleá Énklistra is quite unusual, dictated in part by the irregular surfaces, but even more so by the doctrinal conventions of the time, which help date its frescoes to shortly after 1439, when the eastern and western Churches were briefly united and the Holy Ghost held to proceed from the Son as well as the Father. Accordingly, instead of the expected

▲ Paleá Énklistra cave-hermitage

Pandokrátor on the ceiling, there's a rare late-Byzantine depiction of the Holy Trinity, ensconced in two diamond-shaped mandorlas. All three figures bear a ICXC monogram, including the Holy Spirit, perching as a dove on the Gospel; of the pair of lower figures each labelled "OΩN" (Being, or Existence), the rather hairier figure on the viewer's right, with ethereally delicate hands, is God the Father. Around them are arrayed the heavenly guardians: cherubim (with eyed, sextuple wings), seraphim shown abstractly as winged rings, and the Archangels, including the seldom-shown Rafael and Uriel in addition to the usual Gabriel and Michael. In the next circle out, evangelists Mark and Luke share a desk, while opposite sit John the Divine, his scribe Prokhoros and Matthew with their respective scrolls. Still lower down, Saint Anastasía east of Mark and Luke holds her fabled antidotes to poison.

To vary a return to Páfos, take – shortly before the turning for Paleá Énklistra – the signed, stabilized-dirt-then-cobble track bound for **Souskioú** in the Dhiárizos valley; it's a scenic 3km there, with partridges dashing every which way. The village itself is ex-Turkish Cypriot and abandoned save for goat pens and a modern mosque, but lies just east of the F616 road.

North from Páfos

North of Páfos the landscape is initially flattish and uninspiring, dotted with large villages that are essentially dormitories for the district capital, or venues for expat residence. Only as the terrain begins tilting gently up at the first outriders of the Tróödhos mountains does development diminish and the mystique of the country reassert itself. Most of these settlements can boast some late-Byzantine church or remains, but with the exception of the following two monuments, all have had their appeal compromised by ill-advised additions or renovation.

Panayía Khryseléoussa

In the middle of **ÉMBA** (Empa), 3km north of Páfos, twelfth-century **Panayía Khryseléoussa** church sits in a small park just uphill from a horrible, hangar-like modern church. A dome perches at each end of the double-cruciform ground plan, and the narthex with stairs up to vanished monks' cells on the mortared roof is an eighteenth-century addition. For admission, enquire in the arcaded municipal office building opposite, or in the *kafenía* up the road. ALEPA urban **bus** #4 passes through Émba en route to Tála.

Inside, late fifteenth- or early sixteenth-century frescoes were cleaned during the 1970s, but they'd been badly retouched during the late nineteenth century, and some were damaged by the quake of 1953. Anything that remained out of reach of the "restorer", however, is still worth scrutiny: the Apocalypse and the Second Coming on the right of the main nave's vault, for example, is very fine high up but mauled below. Funds permitting, the cruder overpainting will eventually be removed by the archeological services.

The *témblon* (altar screen) dates from the sixteenth century, and the eyes of St John the Divine (on the panel left of the main icon) seem to follow you around the room. The revered icon of the Virgin is unique in that both she and the Child are crowned; there is also a sixteenth-century icon of the apostles.

The monastery of Áyios Neófytos

Nine kilometres from Páfos and five from Émba, at the head of a wooded canyon, the **monastery of Áyios Neófytos** (Agios Neofytos, sometimes Ayíou Neofýtou) appears suddenly as you round a curve. On weekdays at 9.30am and noon ALEPA **bus** #4 extends its route beyond Tála to call here.

The hermit Neophytos, born in 1134 near Léfkara, moved here aged 25 from a monastery near Nicosia, seeking solitude in this then-desolate region. His plan backfired badly; such was Neophytos's reputation that he became a guru to numerous disciples who gathered around his simple cave-hermitage, founding the monastery here long before his death in 1219 or 1220. Unusually for a "desert ascetic", Neophytos was a scholar and commentator of some note, and a few of his manuscripts have survived. Among these are the *Ritual Ordinance*, a handbook for monastic life, and a historical essay on the acquisition of Cyprus by the Crusaders in 1191, deeply disparaging of the two protagonists Isaac Komnenos and Richard the Lionheart. That he could write this with impunity is perhaps a measure of the respect in which he was held during his lifetime.

The katholikón

The enormous monastery compound, home now to just seven monks, consists of a square perimeter cloister enclosing a garden and aviary, with the **katholikón**, or central church, on its own terrace. At the rear of the vaulting over the *katholikón*'s south aisle, the best remaining among early sixteenth-century frescoes is a pensive Prayer of Joachim in the Wilderness, where an angel descends with the tidings that Anna shall bear the Virgin. Westernized decoration above the north aisle is much more fully preserved, consisting of a complete cycle of the Akathistos Lenten hymn (each stanza beginning with one of the 24 letters of the Greek alphabet), glorifying the Virgin and Christ. Especially noteworthy and well lit, are the Nativity (stanza G), with unusually no bath for the Holy Infant but plenty of shepherds and angels in attendance; the Adoration of the Magi (stanza I); and the Flight into Egypt (stanza K); opposite these are Christ Minded to Save the World, leading a troupe of angels (stanza R) and near the end, Christ Enthroned (stanza T). But interesting as they are, the *katholikón* frescoes are not the main reason visitors visit here.

The énklistra of Neophytos

On the far side of the car park with its café (lively during the feasts of Jan 24 & Sept 27), at the very head of the ravine, cave-niches form the **énklistra (hermitage) of Neophytos** (daily: April–Sept 9am–1pm & 2–6pm; Oct–March 9am–4pm; €0.85). This has obvious parallels with the roughly contemporary man-made cave-shrines of Cappadocia, and of course the much later Paleá Énklistra; the hermit supposedly dug many of the cavities himself, and it's conceivable that a few of the oldest frescoes are by Neophytos, though most were merely done under his supervision. At least two other painters, one signing his work as that of Theodore Apseudes, were involved.

Visits begin with stairs mounting to a pair of chambers on the left comprising a chapel, dedicated to the Holy Cross and completely decorated by 1196. These frescoes, of a "primitive" Syrian/Cappadocian style, were redone in 1503 and cleaned in 1992, so in the **outer nave** it's easy to make out a complete, clockwise cycle of Passion scenes such as the Last Supper (where Judas reaches over the carrots and radishes of the Hebrew Passover to snatch the fish of the Believers), the Washing of the Feet (with various disciples undoing their sandal-straps) and Roman soldiers portrayed as Crusaders in the Betrayal, and in the Descent from the Cross the figure of Joseph of Arimathea, thought to be a portrait of Neophytos himself, about to wrap the dead Christ in a shroud.

In the **ierón** or inner sanctuary, the Ascension behind the hanging lamp is cleverly hacked from the soft rock so that Christ seated on his trademark mandorla (borne by two angels rather than the usual four) appears to be disappearing up a small hole in the ceiling, through which Neophytos, from his quarters upstairs, used to hear confessions and issue edicts (he only emerged once a week to preach). On the west wall, two archangels seem like celestial policemen (as they indeed are in Orthodox belief), escorting Neophytos to the ranks of angels in a ceiling painting done in the more fashionable Constantinopolitan style. Flanking the north door to the hermit's cell is an exceptionally fine Annunciation, with the Archangel Gabriel's cloak swept back in his own wake as he delivers the good news to a visibly startled Virgin.

The third chamber to the right (north) was Neophytos's earlier private **cell**, with benches, niches and a desk carved for his use, as well as his sarcophagus – appropriately presided over by an image of the *Anastasis* or Resurrection, complementing a slightly later one on the nave's east wall, unusual for including the Hebrew kings David and Solomon, plus John the Baptist with a prophetic scroll. The hermit left instructions that his quarters be walled over at his death "that none may know where I have been buried; there my worthless body shall stay in quietness until the common Resurrection". This command was predictably disregarded in 1756, when the sarcophagus was prematurely emptied so that Neophytos's bones might serve as relics; today pilgrims to the *katholikón* kiss his skull in its silver reliquary.

The upper caves of the cliff-face are undecorated and currently inaccessible. Neophytos retreated there in 1197 after the lower levels became unbearably busy with his followers, ensuring his privacy with a retractable ladder.

Northwest along the coast

Leaving Páfos heading **northwest**, the avenue beyond the Tombs of the Kings continues as a fairly broad road for some kilometres, passing phalanxes of modern hotels and villa projects. During the 1950s this rugged coast was so deserted that EOKA chose it as a landfall when smuggling in arms and men from Greece. Today, signs for Chinese and Indian restaurants lend the only exotic touches, along with the banana plantations just inland. But while this route seems to offer little promise of seclusion or beauty (other than the "**Baths of Adonis**" at the head of the Mavrokólymbos valley), you are heading towards one of the most unspoiled stretches of shoreline in the south, past **Áyios Yeóryios** with its small basilica, and up towards the **Akámas peninsula**. The latter offers excellent beaches at **Toxéftra** and **Lára**, just beyond the sculpted **Avgás** gorge. **Buses** run as far as Coral Bay and less often to Áyios Yeóryios, but there's no public transport any further along the coast.

Lémba

An inland route from Ktíma brings you, after 4km, to **LÉMBA** (Lempa); ALEPA bus #3(7) shows up sporadically. An outrageous (and controversial) roadside *objets-trouvés* sculpture, the 45-metre-long (and growing) "Great Wall of Lempa", indicates the approach to the **Cyprus College of Art** (ⓦwww .artcyprus.org). Visitors are welcome at the dozen or so studios, and there is a small gallery of finished work for sale. Two independent **potteries** nearby, particularly George and Sotiroulla Georgiades' *Lemba Pottery* (ⓣ26943822), are also well worth calling in at.

Conspicuously signposted at the downhill end of town, the Lémba **prehistoric site** (unrestricted entry) was founded in about 3500 BC and flourished for over a thousand years, courtesy of the nearby spring and stream. The well-labelled **Lemba Experimental Village**, a thorough reconstruction by the University of Edinburgh excavation team of a half-dozen Chalcolithic dwellings, lends considerable interest, and in terms of architectural appeal compares favourably with the appalling tower blocks seaward. Most of the finds from the prehistoric site can be found in the Páfos archeological museum (see p.161).

The only local **taverna** is *Lemba* (ⓣ26271451), out on the Khlórakas-Kissónerga bypass road. Their speciality is *soúvla* and *gourounópoulo*, and despite an emphasis on quantity over quality, and zero atmosphere in the shed-like conservatory (softened in winter by a fire in the central hood), it's moderately priced and popular with locals.

The Dhiyenis' Landing museum

Some 4km out of Páfos along the coast road, the site of George "Dhiyenis" Grivas's disembarkation on November 10, 1954, to begin the EOKA uprising is now prominently marked below Khlórakas as **"Dhiyenis' Landing"** (for more on Grivas, see p.254). Right by the sea at Rodhafiniá cove, just south of the enormous *St George Hotel* and eponymous church (the latter constructed by the bishopric of Páfos to commemorate the landing), a purpose-built **museum** houses the gun-running caïque *Áyios Yeoryios* (open daily all day; free). This was captured by the British along with its Greek crew of five, and eight local EOKA activists who had come to meet them, on January 25, 1955. On the walls are archival photos of the capture and trial of the thirteen, along with their deadly cargo, though British testimonials to the bravery of these men during the recent world war – subtly reiterating the long-standing Greek-Cypriot position that they were essentially owed independence in return for their faithful service to the Allies – have vanished since the millennium.

Mavrokólymbos Reservoir and the Baths of Adonis

About 1km before Coral Bay (see below), signs point inland to the **Mavrokólymbos (Mavrokolympos) Reservoir**, a popular picnic and angling spot, especially in the heat of summer – though in these drought years the water level is likely to be pathetic. Swimming is not an option; for that, and for more alluring scenery, there are the so-called **Baths of Adonis** upstream, though their much-touted connection with Adonis and Aphrodite is utterly spurious.

There's a choice of two **access** routes to the Baths: for jeeps, the more direct but steep (and in spring, muddy) dirt track taking off from the Akoúrsos road, or the longer (10.7km) but well-signposted way in from Kissónerga via Tála and the Leptos Kamara housing estate, the only sensible choice for cars. However you arrive, just beyond the car park lies the attractively restored **watermill** and snackbar of actor and self-styled arts personality Pambos Theodhorou (his grandfather was the last miller here). There's an admission charge of €7.50, not strictly legal since rivers and the shore for a width of 12 feet are public land in Cyprus. Once inside the grounds, you'll find two sets of impressive **waterfalls**, each feeding sizeable **pools** with water temperature at a brisk 17°C. The lower one, fitted with a rope swing, is about 6m deep at the centre; daredevils jump in from the ledge above (strictly at your own risk). The upper pool is shallower (2–3m) but more secluded, with discreet skinny-dipping tolerated. From Kíli (Koili) village further upstream it's possible to walk in direct and "free" to the upper pool, but you will probably be detected and ejected if you venture down to the lower one.

Possibly the best method of visiting the area is with the reputable Paddocks Horse Farm in Kissónerga (☎99603288). On offer is a three-hour ride to the dam for moderately experienced **horse riders**, and a six-hour all-day trip to the Baths of Adonis for veterans.

Coral Bay

With the coast hitherto inaccessible, unsafe (see below) or overrun by hotels, the first place that might prompt a stop is **Coral Bay** (officially Kólpos Koralíon in Greek), 11km out of Páfos and blessed with a public-access beach, for once not dominated by hotels. A fine-sand, gently shelving, 600-metre crescent is bracketed by a pair of headlands, with three snack bars and sunbed-rental places behind, packed out in summer. The only sight, on the northwesterly headland, is vestigial **Paleókastro** (Máa), a Bronze Age settlement excavated before 1985 and claimed to be the Myceneans' first landfall in Cyprus. Although the site itself is somewhat neglected, there's an adjacent **Museum of the Mycenean Colonization of Cyprus** (daily: 8.30am–5pm; €1.71), housed in an Italian-designed "beehive" intended to mimic the tholos tombs at Argolid Mycenae in Greece.

Down on the main bay, the water is not always the cleanest, but the bay is at least safe from currents, which can't be said for the tempting-looking, cliff-backed beach, with anglers and a few sunbeds, at **Pótima** 2km south. Almost every summer there are drownings here owing to strong undertow and lateral currents.

Practicalities

Coral Bay is the end of the line for the ALEPA #10 and #15 **bus** routes from town. Atop the promontories and along the access road is an estate of summer homes for wealthy Cypriots and expats, a cluster of hotels, and a single commercial high street.

Accommodation overlooking the other sandy bay beyond the northwest headland includes the five-star *Coral Beach Resort* (☎26621601,

Ⓦwww.coral.com.cy; rooms ❼, studio ❽, suites ❾), set in extensive gardens. Its common areas are in better taste than many, with arts and crafts exhibitions and other concessions to traditional Cypriot culture, though the 1993-vintage standard rooms themselves are overdue for a refit. A little marina, shared with the few fishermen who've been allowed to stay, serves as base for water sports. Adjacent stands the ⚓ *Thalassa Hotel* (☎26623222, Ⓦwww.thalassa.com .cy; ❾), sharing the headland with Paleókastro. It's not much to look at from outside – it was originally planned as a three-star hotel – but impressions change dramatically once inside Cyprus's first self-styled boutique hotel, one of the few "butler-concept" lodgings in the Mediterranean (a member of the multinational staff is dedicated to gratifying every whim of guests in the higher-grade units). All units have at least a partial sea view, from standard doubles (€300) to true suites of 60 square metres and above (€580 and up), though the most popular option is a two-bedroom, two-bath suite (€930). Public areas include the main restaurant and several bars, plus the spa (every conceivable treatment on offer), yoga studio and gym. The rock lido immediately east is not that appealing, but guests may use the co-owned *Coral Beach* beach and its facilities.

Villas are a popular option around Coral Bay; one of the best (book via Ⓦwww.sunvil.com) is spacious *Villa Hilarion* – there's no pool, but there are many terraces and it's walking distance to the beach. **Restaurants** on the main strip are generally pretty forgettable; much the best local eating is at south-Indian-run *Keralam* (☎26622877) northwest of the main beach in the Aristo Coral Bay Complex. As the name suggests, Keralan food is featured; portions aren't huge, and it's not cheap, but the fare is deceptively rich and quality high. The less expensive Sunday-lunch buffet (drink extra) has a rather limited choice.

Áyios Yeóryios

Just past Coral Bay, developments begin to taper off amid vineyards, banana groves and isolated villas; the road, while still asphalted, dwindles too. The Roman town on **Cape Dhrépano**, 8km beyond, has been supplanted by a modern Christian church at **ÁYIOS YEÓRYIOS** (Agios Georgios), with a nearby offering-tree next to a medieval chapel dedicated to Saint George. Prayers are still said here for the recovery of lost objects and people (hence the tree). Some 200m southeast of the modern church sprawls an enormous Byzantine sixth-century **basilica complex** (summer daily 9am–1pm & 2–6pm; winter Mon–Sat 9am–3.45pm; €1.70) with extensive panels of geometric and animal floor mosaics, not as vivid as those in Káto Páfos but still worth a stop. In the nave, behind the *synthronon* or semicircular bishop's throne (on the left as you face it), an octopus is surrounded by birds, fish and even a turtle; two panels right of this, a crustacean and a snail appear. Such bestiaries are common enough in pagan art, but rare in Christian iconography; it has been theorized that they evoke the pre-lapsarian Golden Age detailed in Isaiah 11:6–9. The most vivid geometric mosaics, a trellis pattern of interlocking curved squares, are at the southwest corner, in the baptistry.

Aside from the basilica mosaics, and a few rock-cut tombs (accessible by footpath down the cliff), the headland has little allure other than spectacular sunsets, and serving as a base for exploring the Akámas peninsula. American-sponsored archeological digs on **Yerónissos (Geronisos)** islet offshore have discovered a stone inscribed to Apollo at the bottom of a sacred well, and Byzantine-era remains. This is explained by **Moudhális**, the little port opposite still used by modern fishermen, being an important halt on the trade route between Byzantium and Egypt; if you follow the road down to modern

Moudhális, you'll find artificially strewn (and often littered) sand, and water hardly more salubrious.

There's more secluded and attractive shoreline south along the dirt track beginning from the "STOP" sign on the curve of the road down to Moudhális. Spurs off the main track lead to the so-called "**White Cliffs**", sculpted chalk formations offering good sunbathing and concealing miniature sandy coves as far down as Manijín islet. They're well known to locals, however, and getting into the water can be problematic, with reef underfoot. It's also possible to **walk** back to Coral Bay, 6km through countryside rapidly being filled with villa projects; however the coastal track is a public right of way.

Practicalities

Several **hotel-tavernas** are scattered about the cape within walking distance of each other. Two to try are one-star *Yeronissos* (℡26621078; ❷), slightly inland by the access road, with friendly British-Cypriot co-management; and *West End Rooms & Restaurant* (℡26621555; ❷), opposite, the best value here, with immaculate en-suite doubles. *Saint George* (℡26621306; ❷), the sea-view establishment, has a limited number of basic rooms and a lovely terrace **restaurant** serving fresh fish, straight from the anchorage just below. It's always packed at weekends (booking advised); with starters and a beer, the bill won't be much more than €24 a head.

Beaches and gorges: Avgás and around

At the intersection 500m inland from Áyios Yeóryios, the northbound option signposted "Akámas Peninsula, 18km" takes you towards the finest **canyons** and **beaches** on this coast. The road is paved only until "White River Beach", and beyond that point is apt to be badly chewed up; you can usually wrestle an ordinary car as far as the junction 8km beyond Cape Lára (see p.176), but for guaranteed passage, you really need a 4WD vehicle.

"White River" and Toxéftra beaches

The first attractive bay, signposted as "**White River Beach**" (Áspros Pótamos in Greek), lies about 1km north of the junction, at the mouth of the Áspros gorge; access from the road is controlled with a chain, locked at dusk, to prevent folk absconding with the "sunbets" and "ubmrellas" (sic). Just inland of the road here stands *White River Snack Bar*, whose proprietor has seen to the illicit paving of the road to his doorstep (but no further, of course). Most drivers will press on another 1500m towards unamenitied **Toxéftra Beach**, far sandier and lonelier.

The Avgás (Avákas) and Koufón gorges

Toxéftra beach is essentially the mouth of the Avgás gorge system, "Avákas" in dialect and increasingly signposted as such, or officially as Argaki tis Avgas. With your own vehicle, bear right away from the beach, following a wooden forestry department sign, to the point where the valley, initially given over to grapefruit and banana plantations, splits into the two ravines. After parking near the more spectacular left-hand (northerly) one, which is the **Avgás/Avákas Gorge** proper, you can start off on the trail that quickly appears. The canyon walls soar ever higher, and before May at least there's water, duly tapped by irrigation piping for the thirsty orchards downstream. Some fifteen minutes along, the gorge narrows into a spectacular gallery where the sun rarely penetrates, before opening again, about half an hour along, at the foot of a scree-and-boulder slope loosened further by a 1996 earthquake.

Avoid this, continuing straight upstream through the canyon, where **stream-side vegetation** abounds: juniper, plane and pine trees, terebinth, mastic, oleander and fragrant storax shrubs, plus (at ground level) orchids, cyclamen and a rare endemic centaury. The receding cliffs to either side are alive with birds, and you might spy Savigny's tree frog on nearby foliage. Just over an hour later, you emerge in the Lípati pastures just below the vineyards of Aródhes.

Sea turtles and their conservation

The west coast of Páfos district is one of the last Mediterranean nesting grounds of **green** and **loggerhead turtles**, both endangered species. Although ocean-going reptiles, the turtles require shoreline to lay eggs, navigating late at night towards long, fine-sand, gentle-surf beaches.

In Cyprus, the turtles **nest** every two to four years from late May to mid-August, laying clutches of one hundred round eggs 50–70cm deep every two weeks during this period. The hatchlings emerge after dark seven weeks later, instinctively making for the sea, which they recognize by reflected moon- or star-light. Any artificial light sources (flashlights, bonfires, hotels, etc) disorientate baby turtles, who head in the wrong direction to die of dehydration. Similarly, if the females are disturbed by light or movement, they will return to the sea without depositing their eggs properly. Because of these factors, green turtles no longer breed on most of Cyprus' south coast; loggerheads still attempt to nest on beaches fringed by light sources, which usually results in death for the hatchlings.

Sea turtles apparently reach maturity between fifteen (for loggerheads) and thirty years (greens) after hatching, and through a not-yet-understood imprinting process return to their natal beach to breed. Perhaps one in a thousand hatchlings survives to adulthood. Predators, particularly foxes, dig up the eggs; a high surf can literally drown the eggs; and until they attain sufficient size at about ten years of age the juveniles are easy prey for sharks, seals and large fish.

Surveys first taken in 1976–77 showed an alarming drop in turtle populations, to barely a hundred green turtle females in the Lára region, and a few more loggerheads (also found in the Pólis area). Accordingly, in 1978 the **Lara Turtle Conservation Project** and its field station were established in an attempt to reverse this decline. Each summer since then, volunteers search local beaches for the telltale tracks that females leave behind when returning to the sea; nests are assessed for viability, and if poorly sited, the eggs are dug up and transferred to Lára for reburial within anti-fox mesh. Turtle gender is determined by incubation temperature, which in turn is a function of nest depth: 29–30°C results in an even sex balance, with males thriving in lower temperatures and females in higher. The programme has quadrupled the yearly survival rate for hatchlings, and staff scientists have begun raising young turtles in tanks to further reduce mortality.

Despite financial support by the government's Department of Fisheries and the EU, the turtle conservation project may ultimately be futile if **development battles** raging over this deceptively peaceful place go the wrong way. The designation of the entire coast from Asprós to a point several kilometres north of Lára as a "specially protected area" in 1989 did not prevent 25 lorry-loads of sand being illegally carted away from Toxéftra Beach by minions of the bishop of Páfos in 1995, for use on the Tsádha (Tsada) golf-course; the archdiocese still hopes to put up a luxury resort within sight of Lára, and has refused a generous compensation offer from the World Bank in exchange for dropping opposition to the establishment of a national park here, which would incorporate some of its property. Almost the only entities opposing such development are Friends of the Earth, the Cyprus Conservation Foundation and the Green Party. The news is not all bad, however; sand-filching has stopped, and in 2003 turtle-hatching beaches around Pólis gained some statutory protection.

The right-hand (southerly) gorge of **Koufón (Argaki ton Koufon)** seems initially less impressive, but after about twenty minutes past weirdly eroded rocks you reach a point where rock-climbing and/or abseiling skills are required. You eventually reach the Lípati tableland, which separates Koufón from Avgás.

Cape Lára and beyond

The symmetrical cape at **Lára**, just over 5km north of Avgás and nearly 28km from Páfos, shelters large sandy beaches on either side. The slightly overpriced but beautifully set **café-restaurant** overlooking the kilometre-long southerly beach is the sole facility (March–Nov).

The smaller northerly bay, signposted as "**Lara Turtle Hatchery**", is one of several local nesting grounds for green and loggerhead sea turtles. Gently shelving, and thus warm enough for dips early in spring, this is even more scenic than its neighbour, backed by low cliffs and buffeted by the surf, which wafts the turtles in on midsummer nights to lay their eggs. Accordingly most of it is fenced off to vehicles (there are pedestrian-sized gaps), with no access to the coast allowed on peak nesting-season evenings (June to early Oct).

Beyond Lára, the coastal track continues past more tiny coves on its way to Jóni and a former British Army firing range (see p.189). Rather than completely retracing steps to Páfos, there are three alternative ways out of the Lára area. The most adventurous involves heading 8km north to **Koudhounás junction**, then climbing for 5km more through thick forest to the ridge track above the Smiyiés picnic grounds. Some years this is feasible in an ordinary car, but most seasons you'll need a jeep – always enquire locally before committing yourself. Otherwise, the more northerly ("Ineia 13km, Drouseia 13km") of two signposted dirt tracks heading inland from behind the southerly Lára Beach winds up to a point on the main ridge road between Faslí and the two named villages. The southerly track ("Ineia 8km"), mostly cemented now, is an easier climb **up to Ínia village**, a rise in altitude of 500m past the outcrops of Áyios Yeóryios peak, presenting no problems to an ordinary car.

Villages of the Akámas heights

The Akámas peninsula begins north of a line joining Áyios Yeóryios and Péyia village. Named after a legendary lover of Aphrodite, this is the most desolate, and (except for Tillyria) the most thinly populated portion of Cyprus. An inclined plane of sparsely vegetated chalk and reef limestone atop sharp volcanic peaks, it drops off sharply to the east and north but falls more gradually west towards the sea, furrowed by ravines hiding precious water. At its centre the land climbs to a spine of hills nearly 700m high, now supporting the bulk of permanent habitation in the area.

Several of the **villages of the Akámas heights** were partly or wholly Turkish Cypriot before 1974, and either the prior troubles or the subsequent exodus left them almost empty: their lands, however extensive, were generally too poor to attract refugees from the North, and silk-cocoon culture – the major traditional earner – had already withered away by the 1960s. Other, wholly Greek-Cypriot communities have shrunk as well – thanks to the usual emigration overseas or to Cypriot towns. Mostly the old remain, some wondering why the "miracle" of Ayía Nápa shouldn't be repeated here.

Virtually the only organization to suggest otherwise is the **Laona Foundation** (PO Box 50257, 3602 Limassol, ⓦ www.conservation.org.cy) which endeavours to protect the wildest parts of the Akámas, and to revive the dying villages by introducing "sustainable tourism" – specifically the restoration of selected old properties for use as visitor accommodation, and the involvement of tourists in the day-to-day village economy. Sunvil Travel (Ⓦwww.sunvil.com) is currently the exclusive UK representative for several Laona-restored properties between Páfos and Pólis; if already in Cyprus, you can contact the Foundation directly (Ⓣ25358632 or website) to book any of the several properties available in Milioú, Páno and Káto Akourdhália, Krítou Térra and Káthikas.

Péyia

Some 4km above Coral Bay along the well-graded E709, the large village of **PÉYIA** (Pegeia) tumbles down a hillside overlooking the sea. Its identity has shifted considerably since it became a dormitory community for vast numbers of expats buying purpose-built villas or renovating old houses. The villagers themselves had already become wealthy from selling off land closer to the shore early in the Pafian tourist boom, reflected in not always sympathetic "updating" of Péyia dwellings.

Most **accommodation** around Péyia is between the village and Coral Bay, in expensive, purpose-built villas with pools. For longer-term (by the month) lodging in the village, try the local Agridiana Company (Ⓣ99696956). A few decidedly carniverous **tavernas** are grouped around the cistern-fountain square; *Peyia* is one of the most consistent and popular, the cheap-and-cheerful option where meals run about €12 whether *mezé* or à la carte. The *Jail Pub*, just downhill from these, was the regional British police station, magistrate's court and prison from 1916 to 1953; prison decor abounds, along with billiards, darts and a steady expat clientele. Péyia rates its own ALEPA **bus** connection on line #7.

The E709 road from Péyia curls west, then east as it climbs scenically through dense pine forest, and then photogenic vineyards, on its way to Káthikas, up on the Akámas watershed at the very edge of the commercial grape-growing zone. However, if you're starting from Coral Bay, the minor F704 is shorter (though not faster) and more relaxing, threading en route through the goatherds' village of **AKOÚRSOS**, which has one seasonal taverna – and a small Turkish-Cypriot population who refused to leave in 1975.

Káthikas

KÁTHIKAS has long been noted for its wine, particularly any that's not sent downhill to the mass-market wineries; the best local **micro-winery** is Vasilikon (Ⓣ26633237) on the western bypass road, noted for its Ayios Onoufrios red and Vasilikon white. Káthikas has ample short-term **accommodation**, including *Chelidona* (Ⓣ26233358, Ⓔioloarch@spidernet.net; ❶), three one-bedroom apartments in a restored house; *Loxandra's House* (Ⓣ99608333 or 25336673; studio ❶, 1-bedroom ❷), a smart complex with four one-bedroom or studio units; and *Anogia tou Mikhali* (Ⓣ26944229 or 99667888; ❷), at the start of the road to Akoúrsos, with a walled courtyard and two split-level units.

Among several **tavernas**, the best is ✷ *Taverna Imoyeni/Imogen's Inn* (Ⓣ26633269 or 26632954; closed Dec–Feb), 100m west of the church on the through road, where Marina and Greek husband Apostolos offer à la carte *mezé* platters with a bit more spice and flair than usual; good recorded music, wine and home-made desserts complete the picture. There's attractive courtyard seating in summer, while during the cooler months the engraving-adorned interior can be crowded with a loyal following. Former classic *Araouzos* (Ⓣ26632076), 50m further west, is resting on its laurels under new management and now offers a fairly humdrum 24-plate *mezé* for €17.

The ridge route to Pólis

At Káthikas the E709 turns north to track the spine of Akámas; it's a drive worth doing for its own sake, as opposed to the main valley route (the B7) which is in fact no quicker (and far more dangerous). All the **villages** along here require slight detours off the main ridge route.

PÁNO ARÓDHES (Arodes) is still mostly inhabited, despite being rocked by an earthquake on February 23, 1995; sensitive restoration of damaged buildings around the square and church include **accommodation** at *Karydhia Cottage* (☏99659928 or 24634680; ❹), a three-bedroom house with pool, available through ⓦwww.sunvil.com. **KÁTO ARÓDHES** was also badly hit by the quake, but before that was a sad casualty of 1963–74; a few cracked houses emblazoned with the Turkish star and crescent still stand empty, the fields and vineyards around largely abandoned, their terrace walls slowly being toppled by vaulting goats. But such is the pressure of tourism and second home hunger that here, too, many dwellings have been renovated, though there are no villa projects yet on the largely Turkish-Cypriot-owned fields around.

Humble **ÍNIA** (Ineia), in the shadow of craggy Áyios Yeóryios peak, once cultivated cotton, flax and winter wheat all the way down to the Lára shore; now the villagers only concern themselves with goats and a few vines. The Laona Foundation has helped establish a private **basket-weaving museum** here (☏26332562 for information). The sole surviving **taverna**, working only in season, is *Zornas*.

Dhroúsha

DHROÚSHA (Drouseia), with its sturdy stone dwellings, magnificent views and winding streets, is still perhaps the best place to visit beyond Káthikas, despite incipient gentrification. There are just four hundred current inhabitants in this, the largest Akámas village, but supposedly fifty times that many loyal emigrants and descendants live abroad. The three-star **hotel** *Cyprotel Dhroushia Heights* (☏26332351; ❹) has sweeping views, plus a small pool and tennis court, but was never terribly comfortable and is getting a bit long in the tooth. The usually unstaffed *Sappho Manor House* in the centre (☏26332650 or 99604010; ❷ studio, ❸ 1-bed) is a more characterful restoration, with a swimming pool. Both above and below the central junction are half-a-dozen *kafenía* and **tavernas**, though none is especially memorable and many only operate in summer; *Phinikas* at the bottom has the longest season (April–Sept). **Beyond Dhroúsha**, head north to rejoin the main ridge road, which brings you to Prodhrómi, just west of Pólis. Alternatively, you could cut eastwards from Dhroúsha across the main ridge road, to reach **Krítou térra** and its ex-Turkish-Cypriot neighbour, **Térra**, a kilometre north down the same valley.

Krítou Térra and Térra

KRÍTOU TÉRRA (Kritou Tera) – supposedly dating from Roman times – is far bigger and more handsome than initial impressions suggest, with old houses lining the lush, upper banks of the ravine and covering the ridge beyond. Best among places to **stay** are the *House of Anastasia* on the east side of the village (☏26332209; ❷), or *Makrynari* (☏26232522 or 99603603; ❶), at the west entrance to Krítou Térra. By the trough spring at the village entrance, the *Kefalovryso* café-taverna intends to work year-round under new management. On the same plaza, an **Environmental Studies Centre** (☏26332532, ⓦwww.esc.com.cy) organizes conservation activities and runs courses for both local and overseas students. The village also marks one possible approach to the late Byzantine church of Ayía Ekateríni (see p.180): proceed through the village, past the single central *kafenío* and the *House of Anastasia*, exiting on to a cement drive descending south into a canyon; follow this paved track as it bends north-northeast to reach the isolated church after 4km.

Ex-Muslim **TÉRRA** (Tera), 1km down the hill, was long occupied by about ten Greek-Cypriot refugee families but many more of its fine dwellings have recently been squatted by Nicosians keen on a weekend retreat. It's worth seeking out the handsome, buttressed, eighteenth-century mosque and the arcaded (but now dry) fountain just south and down the hill.

Along the Páfos–Pólis highway

The busy **B7** route north out of Páfos to Pólis, the district's second town, climbs to a saddle near Tsádha (Tsada) and then rollercoasters through the gentle hills around Stroumbí (Stroumpi) and Yíolou (Giolou), two of several local villages devoted to wine-grapes. The hummocky terrain is softened, too, by fruit trees and the occasional hedge of artichokes, budding until May. Don't get too distracted by the beauty of the surroundings, though – the road is dangerous, with bends, sharp grades and plenty of slow trucks; the motorway is set to be extended from Páfos to Pólis by 2011.

Milioú and the Akourdhália villages

Beginning the gradual descent to Pólis, a detour 2km west leads to the calcium-sulphate spa of **Áyii Anáryiri Milioú (Agioi Anargyroi Miliou)**, set in a secluded, citrus-planted valley. The monastery here is being restored as a luxury spa, ready for 2011. **MILIOÚ** village itself, 1km further, was badly hit by the February 1995 quake (the two fatalities were recorded here) but still has an oasis feel; there's a single taverna-coffee-shop which – if it's open – may be persuaded to prepare good-value meals.

A direct onward road from Milioú to Páno Akourdhália shown on most maps does not really exist. You actually emerge at **KÁTO AKOURDHÁLIA** (Kato Akourdaleia), with its "Folk Art Museum" in the former school 300m west of the village centre (headman Mr Sofokleous has the key and can often be found at his farm a little way down the track to Ayía Paraskeví). Just before the folk museum, a signposted cement – later dirt – track leads west 1500m to the jewellery box-like chapel of **Ayía Paraskeví**, perched opposite a ruined watermill on the flank of the Kyparísha gorge. Restored in 1991, its original construction date is uncertain – estimates vary by nearly a thousand years – but some time between the twelfth and fifteenth centuries seems likely. Though completely bare of decoration, it's worth the special trip, not least for its magical setting above the ravine.

Káto has ample **accommodation**: the eccentrically managed *Amarakos Inn* (☎26633117 or 22313374, ⓦwww.amarakos.com; ➍), whose en-suite rooms are furnished to a high standard. There's an attractive breakfast courtyard, though the restaurant itself is not up to much. Nearby there's the family-oriented *Olga's Cottage* (☎99571065; ⓦwww.olgascottage.com; ➍ for up to 4 people). **PÁNO AKOURDHÁLIA** (Pano Akourdaleia), when you finally reach it by continuing southwest on the main road through Káto, has a sixteenth-century church as attractive as its modern replacement is hideous, and a Laona-instigated herb centre in the old school.

Ayía Ekateríni

About 1km short of Skoúlli village on the B7, a sign points up towards **Ayía Ekateríni**, the best-preserved late-Byzantine church in the Akámas, 1500m along a side road to the left (which continues to Krítou Térra). Set amid vineyards, the church is unusual for its southwest-to-northeast orientation, its lofty central cupola and (betraying Lusignan influence) an arcaded, domed narthex of the sixteenth century. There was apparently once another structure like the narthex on the north side, also with three domes, hence Ayía Ekateríni's local nickname of "Seven-Domed" (counting the central one). Currently, the existing domes are brightly plastered, and visible from afar. Since the 1953 earthquake, only fresco traces remain, but the masonry is largely intact, and the setting, looking across the Stávros tís Psókas stream valley to the Tillyrian Tróödhos, is enchanting – especially towards evening, as the sun sets on the hills opposite. Inside, the church (unlocked) is triple-aisled, these set apart by delicate arcades of three pointed arches; recently stone floor-tiles, electric light and pews have domesticated what was long an essentially abandoned shrine.

Khóli, Goúdhi and Khrysokhoú

Just before the Skoúlli bridge, a narrow, inconspicuous road leads west towards **KHÓLI** (Choli), remarkable for two beautiful post-Byzantine churches. The late fifteenth- or early sixteenth-century **Arkhángelos Mikhaïl** is actually predated some fifty years by its belfry, built by James II as a watchtower to monitor the Ottoman threat. Inside the barrel-vaulted, single-ribbed church a number of rather Italianate frescoes survive. The north side of the vault is devoted to the life of the Virgin, with a particularly good Blessing of the Infant Mary by the High Priests on the lower right. Below this is a recognizable fragment of Osia Maria being spoon-fed by the abbot Zozimadhos; Maria was an Alexandrine courtesan who, repenting of her ways, fled to the desert and performed extreme penances, being found at the point of starvation by the good abbot. The south wall was reserved for the Life and Passion of Christ; particularly vivid scenes include the *Transfiguration* behind the altar screen, with one apostle covering his mouth in awe, and a well-preserved Crucifixion at the far west end, with the Virgin and friends on the left of the Cross, and St John and the Good Centurion on the right. There are also frescoes in the nearby fifteenth-century chapel of the **Panayía Odhiyítria**; the keys for both churches are found in the combination *kafenío*-dwelling of the priest and his wife, just uphill from the phone box. You're expected to donate a candle, and the keepers may get tetchy if, as a non-Orthodox, you linger too long.

In the adjacent hamlet of **GOÚDHI** (Goudi) there's the popular **hotel** *Kostaris* (☎99626672 or 26270440, ✉kostaris@cytanet.com.cy; 2-bed ❹, 3-bed ❺), with a terrace-pool. Approaching Pólis, you can't help but notice the forlorn mosque, once a Byzantine chapel, of **KHRYSOKHOÚ** (Chrysochou) village, abandoned like many other Turkish settlements to the south and east of Pólis in 1975. In this case the surrounding farmland was fertile enough to attract a full complement of Greek-Cypriot refugees. The disused mosque was fenced off and locked after its stone minaret was restored in 1998–99.

Pólis

Set back slightly from the Stavrós tís Psókas stream as it enters Khrysokhoú (Chrysochou) bay, **PÓLIS** is still the most easy-going of the island's coastal resorts, and the only one that makes much provision for independent travellers.

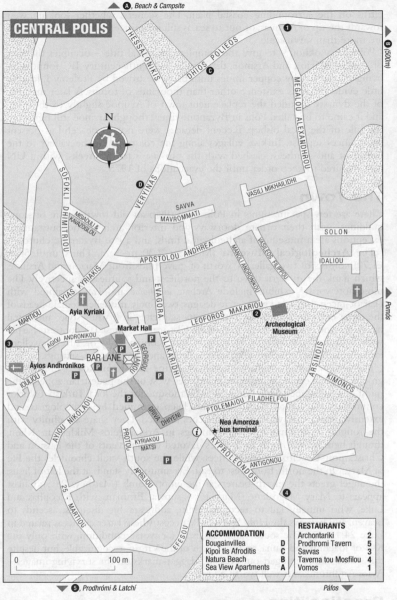

CENTRAL POLIS

Ⓐ, Beach & Campsite

THESSALONIKIS

DHIOS POLIEOS

Ⓒ

Ⓑ (500m)

MEGALOU ALEXANDHROU

N

SOFOKLI DHIMITRIOU

VERYINAS

Ⓓ

VASILI MIKHAILIDHI

SAVVA

MAVROMMATI

MISAIOU & KAVAZOGLOU

APOSTOLOU ANDHREA

MANOLI ANDRONIKOU

VASILEOS FILIPPOU

SOLON

IDALIOU

AYIAS KYRIAKIS

EVAGORA

LEOFOROS MAKARIOU

Ⓟ Pomos

25 - MARTIOU

Ⓐ Ayia Kyriaki

AGIOU ANDRONIKOU

Market Hall

Ⓟ

GEORGIOU

STYLIANOU

PALIKARIDHI

Ⓟ

Archeological Museum Ⓟ

ARSINOIS

KIMONOS

IOULIOU 9

Ⓟ Ⓐyios Andhrónikos

BAR LANE

Ⓟ

Ⓟ

GRIVA DHIYENI

PTOLEMAIOU FILADHELFOU

AYIOU NIKOLAOU

PROTOU

KYRIAKOU MATSI

ⓘ

Nea Amoroza
★ bus terminal

KYPROLEONDOS

ANTIGONOU

APELLOU

Ⓟ

25 - MARTIOU

Ⓟ

Ⓐ

EFESOU

| 0 | 100 m |

ACCOMMODATION
Bougainvillea   D
Kipoi tis Afroditis   C
Natura Beach   B
Sea View Apartments   A

RESTAURANTS
Archontariki   2
Prodhromi Tavern   5
Savvas   3
Taverna tou Mosfilou   4
Vomos   1

Ⓐ, Prodhrómi & Latchí

Páfos ▼

The Berlin backpacker-hippies who "discovered" the place in the early 1980s have long since moved on, traded up or been supplanted by Dutch, and gentrification (and commitment to the package industry) have set in. Pólis is now growing at a rate of knots, and extensive road works and building sites are perennial constants. Gone is the small, strictly linear town straggling along a ridge and the road down to the shore – now a huge, featureless extension sprouts in the flatlands to the east, and apartments and villas slowly displace citrus on the surrounding coastal plain. The scenery, whether looking west towards the tip of Akámas, or out to sea, is still magnificent, and nearby beaches are more than serviceable.

Pólis Khrysokhoú – to give the complete historical title – occupies the sites of ancient Marion and Arsinoë, the former a seventh-century BC foundation living off the nearby copper mines until being destroyed by Ptolemy I, leaving little evidence of its existence other than thousands of tombs. A later member of the dynasty founded the replacement town of Arsinoë slightly to the west, and it came to be called Pólis in Byzantine times, though Arsinoë still figures in the title of the local bishop. Recent decades were not so peaceful as present appearances suggest; Turkish villages along the coast and in the valleys to the northeast and southeast clashed with the pro-*énosis* town Greeks, with a UN post required to keep order until the evacuations of 1975.

The Town

There are few specific sights in Pólis other than an old town centre of stone buildings, with their ornate doorways and interior arches. The outstanding exceptions are a museum of archeological finds, and a late Byzantine church.

The **Archeological Museum** (Mon–Sat 7.30am–3pm, Thurs until 5pm; €1.70) consists of two galleries' worth of grave finds from Marion and Arsinoë, which flank the modern town to the northeast and southeast respectively. The most noteworthy exhibits include Archaic *amphorae* and *kraters* painted with chariot-racers, birds and geometric designs; two finely modelled female heads of the same era, plus slightly later terracotta statuettes in "Attic" style; and spiral hair-rings and plaque-like earrings of the Classical era. These last contrast sharply with a limited quantity of Hellenistic and Roman gold or silver jewellery, looking startlingly modern with its fine detail and careful stone-settings.

The little sixteenth-century church of **Áyios Andhrónikos** (admission in groups only, escorted by museum guard) lies west of the pedestrian zone, in the midst of a landscaped park. Long the main mosque for the local Turkish-Cypriot community, since their departure it has been examined by archeologists, and extensive, previously whitewashed frescoes revealed. They share an affinity with the roughly contemporary wall paintings in Arkhángelos Mikhaïl in Khóli, though here it's the north vault that's devoted to the events of the Passion and Christ's post-Crucifixion appearances, while the south vault chronicles the life of Mary. On the north, from west to east, Eve unusually stands at the left of Jesus; the angel greets the myrrh-bearers at the empty tomb (Matthew 28:5); Christ appears to Mary Magdalene (Mark 16:9), sups at Emmaus with Kleophas and Luke, who initially fail to recognize him, addresses his disciples, ascends to heaven, and bestows the Holy Spirit at Pentecost (these latter events as related in Luke 24:13–35). The south vault, alas, is in far worse condition, with only the Kiss of Joachim and Anna, and the Birth of the Virgin, recognizable, but despite this – and sundry gouged-out eyes and dagger-marks on the surviving images – Áyios Andhrónikos is well worth a visit.

Practicalities

The town is well provided with pay-and-display **car parks** – or you can park for free in the streets north of the archeological museum. **Minibuses** from Ktima Páfos stop at the Nea Amoroza booking office (℡26321114) near the southern edge of town on Kyproléondos. There's a **CTO office** more or less opposite, at the entrance to the town centre (Mon–Fri 9am–3.30pm, Sat 9am–2pm), plus a well-stocked second-hand **bookshop** opposite the museum. Other amenities include a **post office**, several **ATMs** and the municipal **market hall**, the best place to buy fruit and meat for miles around. There are about five **scooter-rental** agencies (such as Petrides, near the pedestrian zone; ☎26321578, ⓦwww .cyprus-rent-a-car.info), often doubling as mountain-bike outlets – a popular activity in spring or autumn.

Accommodation

One used to be able to drive up and find **accommodation** on spec, but this is no longer a good idea in peak season. There are plenty of "rooms/flats to let" signs lining the highway, especially towards Latchí, though many remain unlicensed by the CTO. As an alternative to "urban" Pólis, the "suburb" of **Prodhrómi** (Prodromi), just 1km west, makes a good base with its abundant self-catering accommodation. Few are especially worth singling out and many are in thrall to package operators.

Within the town itself, **self-catering** choices include the *Sea View Apartments* (☎26321276; ❷), on a small turn-off from the access road to the campsite; the fancier sea-view studio or one-bedroom units at *Bougainvillea* (☎26812250, ⓦwww.bougainvillea.com.cy; ❸), also partway along the campsite road; and, best located of all, overlooking (aside from one villa project) peaceful fields, the *Kipoi tis Afroditis* at Dhiós Póleos 8 (☎26322219; ❷).

Among very few bona fide **hotels**, the best is 1km east of town between citrus and olive groves – the three-star, low-rise *Natura Beach* (☎26323111, ⓦwww .natura.com.cy; ❹), separated from a turtle-nesting beach by a broad sweep of lawn. It's nothing special architecturally, but the rooms (two-thirds ocean view, one-third mountain) are large and tasteful, if rather spartan. There's an annexe of five, higher-standard self-catering, three-bedroom villas, lobby wi-fi and on-site bicycle and scooter rental.

The **campsite** (April–Oct), the only proper one left in Cyprus (as opposed to caravan parks), is magically set in a jungle of eucalyptus and calamus 1500m north of town, at the east end of the long beach (and paved coastal walkway) stretching all the way from Latchí. It can't be faulted except for its relative remoteness, though it has a very popular on-site snack bar.

Eating and drinking

Just about all the **restaurants** in the compact town centre are on the expensive or touristy side; for value and salubriousness you're better off further afield, for example at *Savvas* (*The Fisherman*), with well-priced fish if expensive drink served in a pleasant indoor/outdoor environment by the park, or 1km west on the highway at glade-set *Prodromi Tavern*, doing vegetarian starters, casserole dishes, roast chicken and once-weekly suckling pig roasts at moderate prices. Carnivores are also well seen to at friendly, homely *Vomos* (end March–Nov), well northeast of the centre, with the best *kléftigo* in town. For a special blow-out, try *Archontariki* (☎26321328), next to the museum, set in an old mansion, with attentive service and good food – most nights, especially Saturday when there's live music, you'll need to book. However, much the best and best-value traditional eating in Pólis – if uninspiringly located at a junction by a filling station – is ⚜ *Iy Taverna tou Mosfilou*, offering either a superior *mezé* (ca. €13) or à la carte platters of assorted beans, spinach, *kolokássi*, superior *loúntza*, rabbit, *moussakas* and grilled meat, washed down by good bulk wine and served in a lovely old building with Belle Époque tiles, high ceiling and archival photos on display.

Nightlife – such as it is – revolves around the triangular, pedestrianized central plaza, where a half-dozen self-styled "café-bar-snacks" vie for your attention (one or two pitching wi-fi access).

Northeast of Pólis

There's rather less traffic up the coast towards Káto Pýrgos, partly because its backwater status was reinforced in 1974 by the ceasefire line just beyond – the former direct route to Mórfou and Nicosia could no longer be used, though it's almost certain that the Káto Pýrgos–Limnítis crossing point will be opened by the time you read this. The area only comes alive in summer, when the environs of **Pomós** and **Pakhýammos** become retreats for Cypriots who haven't the appetite for the purpose-built hotel strips and restaurants elsewhere in the South. Public transport is rare along this stretch, so you really need your own wheels, and a fair bit of spare time for the arduous detour around the **Kókkina enclave** – though this too may soon open to through traffic.

The first twenty-odd kilometres towards Pomós parallel the little-developed, exposed shoreline, though villas are multiplying here, too. One **taverna** of note, on the highway near **Argáka**, is the *Half Way House* grill, with a mixed Cypriot/expat clientele – the former order *kebab* or *sheftaliá* in *pítta* with salad, the latter succulent pork chops with chips; the outdoor-only seating is lovely despite the adjacent road.

The Georgian monastery

Beyond Argáka, a side road leads through the straggly streamside village of ex-Turkish **YIÁLIA** (Gialia) village, with a single **taverna** (*Mylos*), 6km to a well-signposted twelfth-century **Georgian monastery** in the dense Tillyrian forest. Shown erroneously on some maps as Áyios Mámas, it's actually dedicated to the Panayía Khyrsoyialiótissa, and was uncovered over three seasons of excavations by a Georgian team. The shaded setting threatens to outshine the sparse ruins (fenced but gate always open), but enough remains above ground to make out the typically domed Georgian ground plan. There are fresco fragments on one pier under a tent-like shelter, plus Georgian inscriptions on another's masonry.

Pomós and Pakhýammos

POMÓS has a few self-catering apartments and an **ATM**, but the village is quite featureless, and the main beach not up to much. Indeed, the best pretext for a visit is a few **tavernas**, including *Kanali*, on the promontory east of the village centre, overlooking the fishing anchorage, which serves no-nonsense seafood at reasonable prices, with views from the terrace across to the Kormakíti peninsula and the Kyrenia hills. It was, though, being redone at the time of writing, in which case the more seasonal *Sea Cave* up on the main road is your fallback, straddling access to a small, sheltered beach.

Both, however, defer to ⅞ *Paradise Place* (in theory open all year, 10am–late, no set meal hrs; ℡99516932 to check), about 1km west of the village centre (look for the unmissable veranda). Sokratis the proprietor lived and worked in Greece for 23 years, which has a salutary effect on the dishes, such as chicken, lamb, aubergine *imám* and a one daily special; budget €16 a head plus booze. You could also just have a drink, listening to perhaps the largest and most sophisti-cated music collection – blues/gospel/African/salsa/jazz/Greek – on the island. The "Place" hosts periodic events and live sessions, culminating in an annual three-day, late-July **jazz festival** (Ⓦwww.paradiseplaceproductions.com). The promisingly named "**Paradise Beach**" (shown on the restaurant's business card) is well hidden and just downhill from some greenhouses across the road; the final trail approach is slippery, so wear sturdy shoes.

Sacred art & architecture

Cyprus, which adopted Christianity late and was seldom an important enough imperial possession to merit lavish endowment, might seem an unlikely home for sumptuous religious art. Yet it boasts an improbable number of churches in every conceivable style, as well as a few mosques. While Christian mosaics here followed conventions set at Ravenna and Constantinople, churches themselves were simpler than continental models. Interior frescoes developed in a unique direction, similar only to those found in nearby Rhodes and Crete.

Mosaics and churches

Cyprus' specifically Christian mosaics date from the fourth to the sixth centuries, when most of the population was converted. In large basilicas – notably at Páfos, Kourion and Ayías Trías – mosaic floors relied on Roman and Hellenistic artistic techniques and conventions, with refinements. For example, animals were shown in profile in pagan art, while only humans were depicted frontally; the side view was soon also used for wicked non-believers, face-on for the righteous faithful.

Ayia Paraskeví, Yeroskípou ▲

 Áyios Mámas, Louvarás ▲
Vaulting, Selimiye Camii (Ayía Sofía) ▼

Surviving Byzantine churches on Cyprus are concentrated in Páfos district and the Tróödhos foothills. They're humble affairs, reflecting the straitened economy of a backwater province of the empire: a half-dozen basic designs appear, all stonebuilt, with no elaborate brickwork as found in the Balkans or Italy. The simplest, such as the little churches at Khyrsókhou and Pólis, have just a single, apsed aisle, with a vaulted roof; such structures were occasionally elongated and elaborated with a single dome, as at Tími. More ambitious churches at Yeroskípou and Peristeróna exemplify the triple-aisled basilica, with five domes forming a cross. Domed cross-in-square shrines as at Peléndhri and Kelliá are rare on the island; a simple cruciform floor-plan is more common.

Tróödhos chapel frescoes

If church floor-plans tended to be basic, this was rarely true of interior decoration, especially in frescoed Cypriot churches. Certain departures from conventional Orthodox iconography were caused by the many pitched, domeless roofs of the famous Tróödhos chapels; there were often no cupolas, pendentives or vaults for the standard hierarchical placement of the *Pandokrátor* (Christ in Majesty), cherubim, evangelists and so on. However, a cartoon-strip, story-telling format, chosen to teach the Gospel to illiterate parishioners, was enhanced in these small rectangular churches. The usual arrangement is a fairly complete life-cycle of the Virgin and Jesus on the south and north upper walls, with emphasis on their crucial dedications to God and various events of Christ's ministry. Over the west door, the donor/builder typically appears in a portrait, presenting the church in miniature to Christ or the Virgin, below an inscribed request for mercy at the Last Judgement.

Gothic and hybrid styles

The **Lusignan dynasty** imported both their feudal order and their notions of monumental splendour from northern France; the great Gothic cathedrals at Nicosia and Famagusta, plus several smaller churches in both towns as well as Bellapais abbey, are based on thirteenth-century prototypes such as Reims cathedral. These employ the full Gothic stylistic vocabulary: tracery, rose windows, rib vaulting and buttressing. Less obvious and bombastic, and often more interesting, are later churches in a **hybrid style**, like Stavrós toú Misirkoú in Nicosia – with Byzantine ground plans and domes but Latin traits such as short Gothic columns and pointed arches. In the villages, Lusignan influence is indicated by subtle details such as relief ornamentation, coats of arms and external buttressing. Subsequently, the **Venetians** added their fillips, resulting in churches with Byzantine cores, Lusignan era narthexes and interior arcades, plus Venetian loggias or fountains.

▲ Tracery, Béllapais Abbey

▼ Fountain-house, Ayía Napa monastery

Sacrifice of Abraham, Áyios Mámas ▲

Arabahmet mosque ▼

Styles and quirks

The oldest Cypriot Byzantine frescoes are of the hieratic or monastic style, with roots in Syria and Cappadocia; later work was influenced by Constantinopolitan artisans arriving in the twelfth and thirteenth centuries. As Lusignan rule progressed, building and decorating churches or cave-shrines became a rural, rearguard action, since the Orthodox were banished from larger towns. The naïve, post-Byzantine style of the fifteenth and sixteenth centuries takes liberties with Orthodox conventions in its frequent echoes of Renaissance art and fascinating period details such as aristocratic and military dress, or shepherds playing rustic instruments. Old Testament personalities or episodes like the Sacrifice of Abraham, rarely seen elsewhere, recur in late fifteenth-century Tróödhos churches, and act as the signature of Philip Goul – perhaps a Latinized Greek – or one of his apprentices.

Cypriot mosques

Following the sixteenth-century **Ottoman conquest**, Cyprus – one of the sultan's less prestigious realms – acquired few imposing mosques. Instead, Muslims appropriated key churches, adapting them for worship by adding minarets and whitewashing frescoes, following the Quranic ban on imagery. There are scarcely a dozen purpose-built mosques on the island predating the twentieth century: a few in Larnaca, Nicosia and Limassol, plus a handful of village mosques. Town mosques mirror Anatolian models, with a central dome over a square plan and a portico in front, while village mosques, some from the early 1900s, tend to be small and square, with round-topped windows, vernacular arcades of pointed arches, and stubby minarets.

Things improve scenically as you round the prominent cape and bounce along the deteriorating road into aptly named **PAKHÝAMMOS** (Pachyammos) – "Broad Sand"; here the settlement tilts downhill towards the huge (if occasionally wave-battered, seaweed-littered) beach. Amenities here are limited to a taverna at the local pilgrimage shrine of Áyios Rafaélos.

The Kókkina enclave to Káto Pýrgos

Beyond Pakhýammos the narrow road climbing sharply inland through forested hills is paved, but it's still a tedious twenty-kilometre, 45-minute detour around the problematic enclave of **KÓKKINA** (Erenköy). Along the way, Greek-Cypriot and Turkish-Cypriot watchtowers face each other a few hundred metres apart; the single **UN post** towards Pakhýammos is currently manned by Argentines, often to be seen jogging along the road. You'll pass

The Kókkina enclave

The **Kókkina enclave** was off-limits to Greek Cypriots years before the Turkish Army occupied it in 1974. Beginning in 1962, the Turkish-Cypriot TMT made it a beachhead for off-loading supplies from Turkey, just as their EOKA counterparts had previously used the then-empty westerly Páfos coast for receiving shipments from Greece. Over 500 TMT fighters – mostly young students, some of them returning from life in London – filtered into the handful of Turkish-Cypriot villages here, to stiffen morale; the Greek Cypriots not surprisingly sealed the area off from further land approaches. Effectively besieged, the civilians and young garrison did without bathing and subsisted on stale bread and wormy olives as 1964 wore on.

Matters came to a head on August 3, 1964, when 3000 National Guard troops under the command of General George Grivas (see box, p.254) attempted to throttle the only tenable coastal landing-point from Turkey by attacking Kókkina and several surrounding Turkish hamlets. Archbishop Makarios, communicating by field telephone from Káto Pýrgos, attempted to dissuade Grivas from proceeding, but was rebuffed. The outnumbered Turkish-Cypriot defenders were forced back into Kókkina itself; on August 8, as they were at the end of their tether, dozens of Turkish jets appeared from the mainland, bombing, napalming and strafing nearby Greek villages (including Pólis) for two days, with heavy casualties. Among these were coachloads of Greek students being bused in to gloat over the impending TMT surrender. One of the jets was shot down; the pilot bailed out, but on landing was beaten to death by outraged Greek-Cypriot villagers.

Outright war between Greece and Turkey was only narrowly avoided through UN intervention, but the Kókkina episode marked a double turning point. Had EOKA succeeded in overrunning the place, all further Turkish-Cypriot militancy would probably have collapsed; in any event, the estrangement of the two island communities, which had begun the previous year, was now complete. Until 1974, Turkish Cypriots from the hills around continued to enter the fortified enclave; after the invasion, all civilians were relocated to Yenierenköy on the Kárpas peninsula, and Kókkina became strictly a military base, and remains so today – there's one Turkish Army garrison, and one UN contingent in the buffer zone towards Pakhýammos. Annually on August 8, the villagers and surviving members of the TMT garrison make a pilgrimage (by boat, of course) from the rest of the North, and visit the graves – tended as shrines – of the thirteen students who fell. Whatever the other details of a final peace settlement, the North is unlikely to give Kókkina up gracefully; it's too potent a symbol of Turkish-Cypriot resistance, despite its current lack of any strategic significance – other than hosting a powerful transmitter for Bayrak, the north Cypriot television and radio station.

through long-abandoned Turkish-Cypriot hamlets such as Alévga and Áyios Yeorgoúdhi, and surviving Greek Mosfiléri, before reaching the coast again at ex-Turkish-Cypriot **MANSOÚRA**, its houses being renovated by squatters as weekend retreats. Otherwise, there's just a Greek-Cypriot military outpost here, a good, sandy if exposed beach with an indifferent taverna and the beautiful medieval bridge that carries the old road just upstream.

Set among peach orchards beside the buffer zone, **KÁTO PÝRGOS** is a surprisingly large place, which, despite mediocre beaches to either side and a certain scruffiness, is well equipped for guests, with numerous self-catering units pitched mainly at Nicosians eagerly awaiting the opening of the nearby "border" crossing. Among three overpriced **hotels**, *Pyrgos Bay* is the most reasonable (☎2652001; ③). Other than going swimming and eating fish, however, there's little to do here, but the potential for excursions inland is greater since the paving of a road through the forested Tillyrian mountains towards Kámbos (at a lower contour than the one described on p.219), opened to service Greek-Cypriot military posts. Although the route is broad and paved, it's steep, twisty and 50km/hr maximum speed – eighty minutes from Káto Pýrgos to the first of several roads descending from Kámbos, twenty minutes more to Astromerítis. There's no mobile reception nor any facilities en route, so don't have a mishap.

West of Pólis

Once beyond Prodhrómi, the road west (with a shoreline promenade for walkers and cyclists in parallel) hugs the so far little-developed (aside from sunbed concessions) beach on its way to the emphatically developed resort of **Latchí**. Beyond here, you've a choice between excursions inland to **Neokhorió**, one gateway to the Akámas region, or following the coast to the excellent beaches at **Asprókremos** and **Ttákkas**.

Latchí

The most celebrated "fishing village" of Páfos district, **LATCHÍ** (Latsi, Lakki) has acquired a distinctly tatty air, as seen from the through-road with its succession of souvenir shops, groceries, banks and accommodation. Latchí's seaward aspect is rather more appealing, with half a dozen fish tavernas jostling to be close to the picturesque harbour – extended to encompass a yacht marina. At Latchí's pebble **beach**, windsurfing or canoeing are on offer; the beach itself improves as you head east towards Pólis, or west towards Loutrá tís Afrodhítis.

Practicalities

The best-value local **accommodation** is the two-star *Souli Beach* (☎26321088, ⓦwww.soulihotel.com; ④), just west of Latchí overlooking a clean patch of beach; there's a pool, too, as well as an attached restaurant serving decent if not terribly adventurous food. For a well-executed self-catering complex, try the *Elia Latchi Village* (☎26321011, ⓦwww.eliavillage.com; studio ④, 1-bed ⑤, 2-bed ⑥), with two pools, lush gardens and fun activities for kids.

Restaurants along the improved Latchí waterfront promenade are much of a muchness, with little consistency in quality; per-kilo fish prices should be bargained. *Yangos and Peter's*, the oldest one with mostly local clientele, has suffered since a management change; on the opposite (east) end esplanade, the *Seafare* is more often hit than miss. Family-run *Psaropoulos Beach Restaurant*

Scuba diving near Latchí

Latchí Watersports Centre, on the waterfront and with a beach annexe at the Anassa Hotel (☎26322095, ⓦwww.latchiwatersportscentre.com; Easter–Nov at a minimum), offers motorboat and sailboat rental, as well as windsurfing hire and tuition. Most of their energies, however, are devoted to **scuba-diving**; the main sites are around Áyios Yeóryios island, a protected marine reserve, and further out towards Cape Arnaoútis. Conditions are typically better here than on the Páfos side, as the coast is sheltered from prevailing southwesterly winds. Just southwest of **Áyios Yeóryios** there's a forty-metre wall, with lots of schooling fish and scorpionfish to see, plus a cave (12m) that often contains octopuses. Even shallow beginners' dive classes are likely to see brilliant orange moray eels, groupers and perhaps a ray. Remoter (25-min boat transfer) but shallower dives (9–15m) around **Cape Arnaoútis** include Pláka reef and Mazáki island, with caves, gullies and even an arch or two, and grouper holes, wrasse and baby barracuda during the summer.

Two introductory dives cost €79. PADI-certification courses start at €367 (BSAC and nitrox tuition also available), or qualified divers can dive twice daily over five days for €341 (all equipment included). Unusually, Latchi Watersports will accept paraplegics, and children aged 8 to 14, on its courses and dives, and their equipment/instruction standard is excellent.

(all year), about 1km east with heated premises for the cooler months, has good-sized salads and well-presented if variable fish – what they do best. *Zouk Bar*, overlooking the marina, offers less geriatric **nightlife** than the area's norm, especially at weekends.

Neokhorió and around

At the junction 1500m beyond Latchí, the inland turning leads to **NEOKHORIÓ** (Neo Chorio), with a dramatic hillside setting for its attractive stone houses overlooking the **Petrátis Gorge**, famous for its bat cave (one of two caverns here) filmed by David Attenborough in 1985. There's abundant self-catering **accommodation**, most of it fairly high standard; much the best of this is the very friendly ⚑ *Tavros Hotel Apartments* at the outskirts (☎26322421, ⓦwww.tavroshotel.com; ❸; March 25 to Christmas). About two-thirds of the large, airy rooms have seaviews; others overlook the pool. Among a few tavernas, look no further than ⚑ *Kouppas Stone Castle*, with very reasonable home-made fish soup, *afélia*, *sheftaliá* and roast chicken served in a stone-clad diner. Neokhorió is also known for its lively **Easter Sunday festival**, with traditional games such as tug-of-war, street snacks and evening live music.

Once clear of Neokhorió, if you bear left and down at the first junction, a scenic dirt track (4WD only if any mud present) crosses the shallow top of the Petrátis Gorge before reaching the former Turkish-Cypriot villages of Andhrolíkou and Faslí. Goat-patrolled **ANDHROLÍKOU** (Androlikou) is now uninhabited except for a few Greek-Cypriot shepherds, plus Hasan Mustafa (a "star" of the film *Our Wall*; see Contexts) and his wife. Abandoned houses are being done up as weekend retreats by Nicosians, and for their benefit a paved road arrives directly up from Prodhrómi, passing two quarries. A short, good dirt road leads from Andhrolíkou to **FASLÍ**, which has a sheltered position out of the prevailing winds; it too is served by a paved road from the south, along which you wind, under the antenna-and-radar-crowned crenellations of Áyios Yeóryios peak, summit of the Akámas, en route to Ínia.

The signposted road, bearing straight ahead just outside Neokhorió, leads, after about 3km of occasionally rutted track (passable in a two-wheel-drive), to the picnic grounds at **Smiyiés (Smigies)**, a pleasant, pine-forested spot, with a slightly mineral spring at one end of the eponymous nature trail (see p.192). Another 500m of careful driving brings you out onto the summit ridge; turn left and go another 500m or so to the well-signed top of the five-kilometre link road down to Koudhounás and eventually Cape Lára.

③ The coast: Asprókremos and Ttákas Bay

The shoreline west of Látchi is dominated, just beyond the turning for Neokhorió, by the five-star **Anassa Hotel**, erected in stark contravention of the government's "master plan" for the Akámas area. Although scaled down from its original plans, it has served as the thin end of the wedge for villa projects which will soon fill in all empty coastal space between the Anassa and Loutrá tís Afrodhítis (see p.191). There is a potential for cesspit leakage affecting water quality, but the beaches here remain excellent and – despite Anassa facilities implying otherwise – public.

Immediately west of the hotel lies a (currently) empty field with both a dirt-surface vehicle track, and – inconspicuous at the Anassa's western boundary – a concreted pedestrian lane, which they've been obliged to provide down to **Asprókremos beach**, among the best in Páfos district. Beyond this public access is the turning for the modest, two-star *Aphrodite Beach Hotel* (☎26321001; ④); the site is superb, and the hotel decent value. The affiliated snack bar and sunbed-rental booth down on the beach is thus far one of only two developments actually at sea level.

The other, reached by the next side-turning, is the friendly *Ttakkas Bay Restaurant* (☎26321087; closed Nov–March), whose good seafood (bream and little crabs for €30) and unbeatable setting attracts a return clientele. Table capacity is limited so booking is advisable in high season. The little fringing **bay**

▲ Asprókremos beach

of the name has a serviceable beach of coarse sand and pebbles, with showers and more rental sunbeds/umbrellas, but carry on east around some rocks to the west end of Asprókremos's two- to three-kilometre extent – which ends more or less under the *Anassa*.

The Akámas peninsula

Neokhorió is the last bona fide village before the final, tapering tip of the **Akámas peninsula**. Except for dense pine groves along the summit ridge, the region is largely deforested, though springs and tiny streams are tucked into relatively lush hollows and gorges. The coast drops off fairly sharply, especially on the northeast, and there's very little sandy shoreline anywhere. It's a starkly impressive rather than calendar-page beautiful landscape, much of its appeal residing in the near-absence of human activity (except during the hunting season); spring and autumn appearances of migrating cranes, herons and storks add to the allure.

The Akámas is often best explored from a boat, in a 4WD or on some sort of very sturdy two-wheeler (mountain biking is popular). The few marked trails are summarized below, but a plethora of fitfully signposted jeep tracks go almost everywhere else. The often shadeless terrain is not conducive to aimless wandering on foot, especially between June and September.

A national park for the Akámas?

Despite years of international expert reports and lobbying by Cypriot environmental groups, the **Akámas peninsula** still has no comprehensive protection regime, but remains a crazy quilt of private land (both Greek- and Turkish-Cypriot-owned) and state forest. A 1995 World Bank/EU study recommended that isolated patches of state forest be joined up, land-owners compensated, and buffer zones created, with land uses incrementally restricted to those compatible with the aims of a natural reserve. Hunting is barely, if at all, controlled, with Wednesdays and Sundays from autumn to spring the designated (and thus hazardous to walkers) shooting days.

The only positive subsequent developments were a ban on goat-grazing within state forest land, the prohibition of motor rallies, a moratorium on new licences for "jeep safaris", and the cessation of British military exercises at their artillery firing range west of the Akámas watershed. An unlikely coalition of environmentalists and nationalists agitated for years to get the British to leave, exploiting lingering resentment against the UK for failing to do more to stop the invasion of 1974, though ironically the British military presence may have helped keep the area in a relatively pristine state.

After the millennium, the governmental Council of Ministers instead proposed the extension of the "tourist development zone" for several kilometres northwest beyond Loutrá tís Afrodhítis, thus allowing Carlsberg brewing magnate and developer Photos Photiades to realize his ambitions of building a major holiday complex, complete with paved-road access. Since Cyprus's accession to the EU in May 2004 (and the extra funding available for infrastructure and compensation), discussions with Mr Photiades continue, with a possible outcome of him being offered a deal he can't refuse – prime beachfront land near Pólis – in exchange for quitting his holdings on the north Akámas coast. This isn't, however, an option available to local villagers, who stand to lose extensive land upon the declaration of any sort of park, and thus oppose it. Financial compensation would be inadequate, and in the current climate of intense real estate pressure around the island, actual land is all they have to bequeath newlywed offspring for building on. Thus they, and professional developers, are racing to nibble at the edges of proposed park territory, compromising its final value.

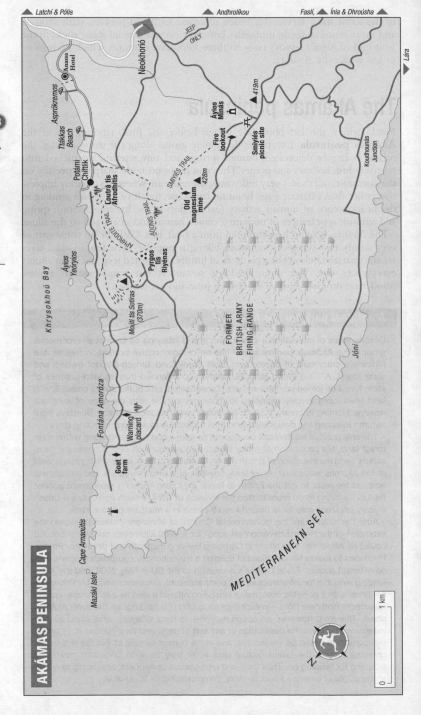

AKÁMAS PENINSULA

MEDITERRANEAN SEA

FORMER
BRITISH ARMY
FIRING RANGE

Khrysokhoú Bay

Fontána Amoróza

Cape Arnaoútis

Mazáki Islet

Goat
farm

Warning
placard

Moútti tís Sotíras
(370m)

Áyios
Yeóryios

Pýrgos
tís Rigénas

Loutrá tís
Afrodhítis

Potámi
Chiftlík

ADONIS TRAIL

AFRODHÍTE TRAIL

Old magnesium
mine

SMIYIÉS TRAIL

428m

Smiyiés
picnic site

Fire
lookout

Áyios
Minás

419m

Neokhorió

JEEP
ONLY

Anassa
Hotel

Asprókremos

Thákkas
Beach

Koudhounás
Junction

Jóni

▼ Lára

0   1 km

N

Loutrá tís Afrodhítis (Baths of Aphrodite)

The paved road along the northern side of the peninsula from Pólis and Latchí ends at a large car park and **CTO pavilion** just past the few houses of Potámi Chíftlik hamlet. Here, the named "Aphrodite" nature trail begins with a three-minute walk to **Loutrá tís Afrodhítis** (Loutra tis Afroditis), the "Baths of Aphrodite". In legend the goddess retired here to bathe before (and after) entertaining assorted lovers; today's reality is a flagstoned area beside an attractive pool about four metres across, the headspring of the irrigated oasis below, fed by rivulets off the rock face of a grotto smothered in wild fig trees. Signs forbid you to bathe in the shallow water, to drink it or to climb the trees.

Akámas trails and tracks

A combination of the "Aphrodite", "Adonis" and "Smiyiés" trails described below would give you the best possible transect of the Akámas watershed, though when you reach the Smiyiés picnic grounds you face an additional 45-minutes' walk to Neokhorió, the closest habitation. The dirt road between the two can be rough and/or muddy after rainy winters – starting from the village, an ordinary car will make it, but a taxi-driver might refuse or charge you dearly.

The best commercial **map** available is Marengo Publications' "Akámas Walkers' Map", packaged as part of their pocket guide *Walks in the Akamas Area* (see p.444). To access the various trails from the Baths of Aphrodite pool, proceed downstream through the gate to rejoin the coastal track, past placards announcing entry to northern Akámas.

The Aphrodite trail

Just before the latter placard, you head up the **Aphrodite trail**, climbing from carob, mastic and eucalyptus near sea level up to juniper, pine and other species labelled in Greek and Latin; in May, white *Cistus* (rock rose) is everywhere, while in March *Cyclamen persicum* predominates. At the top of the first hard climb you get views east over the Pólis coastal plain and nearby offshore islets, before a trail heads west through an old firebreak. There are some waymarks, plus lots of shotgun shell-casings: game birds love the phrygana (scrub biome). Some 45 minutes above the "baths" you'll arrive at a picnic area in a hollow shaded by a gigantic oak tree. The adjacent **Pýrgos tís Riyénas (Rigainas)** – the remains of either a Byzantine monastery or Lusignan fort – is self-explanatory.

Walk five minutes west-northwest along a dirt track from the ruins and oak tree, before bearing right onto the trail's signposted continuation, and again right onto a dirt track. The path is finally subsumed into the narrow, sharply climbing track, which ends some twenty minutes above the oak with an opportunity to detour left five minutes on a path to the 370-metre summit known as **Moúti tís Sotíras (Páno Vakhínes)**. There's a suicide leap out towards Cape Arnaoútis, the tip of Akámas, so retrace your steps down to the signed junction for the descending, onward footpath to the coast. Ingeniously engineered into the seaward slopes, this offers one more viewpoint before meeting the coastal track within twenty minutes. You can avoid a fair amount of track-walking on the return to the car park by keeping to the slightly higher path system until it ends a few minutes before some smelly goatpens. Allow approximately two and a quarter hours for the entire loop out of the CTO pavilion.

The Adonis and Smiyiés trails

From **Pýrgos tís Riyénas**, another nature trail, the **Adonis**, initially climbs south for thirteen minutes over a saddle, then meets a wider track heading southeast. After six minutes on this, you bear left (east) again onto the resurgent trail, which shortly reaches the currently unpotable **Kefalovrýsia** spring in a forested dell at the head of a canyon.

There's also an important marked junction here: northeast down the canyon back to Loutrá tís Afrodhítis along the Adonis trail – also marked as the E4 – or south onto the **Smiyiés** path. Following the latter for just over five minutes brings you to the kiln stack and tunnels of a derelict magnesium mine, also accessible by jeep track along the ridge to the west. The path continues briefly east, then heads south again on a fairly level course before reaching the Smiyiés picnic site just over an hour from Pýrgos tís Riyénas.

From Kefalovrýsia, the Adonis trail back towards the CTO pavilion descends along the canyon, following a water pipe at first, before curling east. Next you bear north, then east again, across what is now a plateau along a much-widened track through scrub and spring-blooming anemones. Suddenly there's a zigzag plunge down towards the coastal road, the route debouching under a wooden nature trail canopy beside E4 street furniture, about 500m southeast of the Loutrá tís Afrodhítis car park. From Kefalovrýsia down to the car park, allow 45 minutes.

The Fontána Amoróza coastal track

The most straightforward – if least exciting – Akámas walk is the one leading 6km to **Fontána Amoróza**, almost at Cape Arnaoútis. Despite the track forming part of the E4 trail, it's actually more enjoyable on a mountain bike. If you insist on walking, arrange a boat transfer from Latchí to drop you at Fontána Amoróza, and then walk back towards Loutrá tís Afrodhítis – it's pretty tedious done both ways. A simple tramp back to the CTO pavilion takes about ninety minutes; just keep to seaward at every option. Some path shortcuts are possible, especially those mentioned above at the base of Moúti tís Sotíras. Vegetation en route is mostly juniper and mastic, with scattered pines. The coast itself is disappointing; the sea is quite clear, but a northern exposure means there is lots of debris in the coves of mixed sand and pebbles.

The celebrated **spring** at Fontána Amoróza is a crashing non-event – nothing more substantial than a tiny, covered well on the cliff overlooking the protected bay. Mythological hype surrounding the "fountain of love" stems from the sixteenth-century Italian traveller-poet, Ludovico Ariosto, who confused it with Loutrá tís Afrodhítis, to the frustration of all who followed him. On the bright side, the best swimming along the route is just below, where a small sand-and-gravel beach at the base of the cliff lies out of the wind. The closest proper spring – after a rainy winter, at least – is up a canyon just before the *fontána*, accessed by a track starting from an obsolete artillery range warning sign. About 400m along this, in a stream gully, **drinkable water** trickles amid the greenery.

Eastern Páfos district

East of the main Páfos–Pólis road, the starkness of the Akámas yields to more forgiving, stereotypically beautiful countryside planted in vineyards and almond groves. The most promoted target here is **Panayiá**, birthplace of Archbishop (and first Cypriot president) Makarios, and the historic monastery of **Khrysorroyiátissa** just south, but there are arguably more worthwhile halting points beforehand, including a frescoed church in **Letímbou**, a winery at **Lemóna**, the **Skárfos bridge/mill** near Filoússa, and the crafts village of

Fýti. Beyond Panayía, it's possible to reach the Tillyrian wilderness (see p.198) and, with some hard driving, the coast northeast of Pólis; or, more easily, to turn south to explore the valleys of Xerós and Dhiárizos.

Routes from Páfos

You've a choice of **approach roads** into the hills. Coming from Páfos initially on the B7, the quickest route – on the broad E703 – is through Polémi, descending to Kannavioú, a negligible place except for the chance to pause at tree-shaded tavernas, before the final climb to Panayiá. Alternatively, leave the B7 at Tsádha for the F719, then turn east on the E702, via **Letímbou** (Letymvou).

Letímbou, Khoúlou and Lemóna

LETÍMBOU's pride and joy is its twelfth-century **church of Áyios Kírykos and Ayía Ioulíti**; the key is kept in the house opposite the newer central church of Áyios Theodhóros. The Byzantine church is 350m away; beside the paved plaza with a double fountain, turn left (there may be a faded sign), and then almost immediately bear right – Áyios Kírykos should be visible on the brow of a hill just ahead. The building is strikingly unusual, with the apse facing northeast rather than east, the transept far longer than the nave in a modified cross-in-square plan; the dome is supported by four low symmetrical arches rather than piers. Late fifteenth-century frescoes are fragmentary and in need of cleaning, but enough remains to see that they were once remarkable and in many cases rare in subject matter.

The west side of the south transept hosts scenes from the birth and life of the Virgin, in particular Joachim reading to Anna from the scriptures (written in cod-Hebrew script), kissing lip-to-lip in a very un-Orthodox manner, and the blessing of young Mary by three high priests at a table elaborately set with utensils and foodstuffs. Evangelists Mark and Matthew occupy their customary places up on the pendentives, while the northeast vault (in the *ierón*) is devoted to Christ's post-Crucifixion (dis)appearances. There the Angel at the Tomb surprises the Myrrh-Bearers, the Pentecost includes a rare personification of the World (*Kosmos*) holding the twelve scrolls over the assembled Nations, and – next to this – an almost unique portrayal of Christ "in another form" (Mark 16:12), standing in a six-pointed mandorla and raising his right hand in blessing, showing the nail-wound.

Beyond Letímbou, it's easy to get to Panayiá via Khrysorroyiátissa, leaving the E702 at Áyios Fótios. The route passes through handsome **KHOÚLOU** (Choulou) village with its old mosque and central **tavernas**, and the side road from there to **LEMÓNA**, home to the **Angelos and Loukia Tsangarides micro-winery** producing award-winning Mattaro- and Cabernet Sauvignon-based reds (Sat–Sun 9am–6pm, otherwise by appointment on ☎26722777; Ⓦ www.tsangarideswinery.com).

Routes from Pólis

From Pólis two initially parallel roads look as if they would be the quickest ways going southeast; however, the option for Pelathoússa dwindles to dirt track after that village. Just under 4km from town a marked side track veers 300m left for domed and vaulted **Panayía Hortení**, picturesquely perched at the mouth of a ravine, overlooking the sea. Of the sixteenth-century frescoes in this restored medieval country chapel (always open), only a ring of seraphs and angels in the dome, and part of the Assumption of the Virgin on your left as you enter, remain recognizable; damp and vandals have seen to the rest.

The next side road south, the F733, is more rewarding, leading eventually to both Panayiá and Stavrós tís Psókas. Stení isn't up to much; **PERISTERÓNA**, the next village, has a single taverna, a nearby gorge (signposted as a 1950s EOKA lair) and the rather optional **Byzantine Museum of Arsinoë** (April–Oct Mon–Fri 10am–1pm & 2–6pm, Sat 10am–1pm; Nov–March Mon–Fri 10am–4pm, Sat 10am–1pm; €1.70). Forking left above Peristeróna, the road carries on to Lysó and then 17km more to Stavrós tís Psókas.

Lysó

③

On a terrace just below the centre of **LYSÓ** (Lysos), the largest village in the Pólis foothills, stands the handsome fifteenth-century **church of Panayía Khryseléoussa** (usually locked), overawed by a surpassingly hideous free-standing belfry. In keeping with Lysó's importance, it was probably the place of worship for the Lusignan overlords of the area, and the building shows strictly Gothic features rather than the Byzantine-Latin hybrids seen elsewhere in Cyprus. There's lovely tracery over the north window, a blind Gothic window at the apse, and the coats of arms of the Gourri and Neville clans above the north and south doors respectively. The interior is not so distinguished, but does have an elaborate wooden *yinaikonítis*, and behind the altar screen, in the niche of the blocked apsidal window, a post-Byzantine *Panayia Glykofiloussa*, the Virgin Kissing the Child, probably executed not long before the Ottoman conquest.

About 1km east of the village is an impeccably located **hotel**, ⚔ *Paradisos Hills* (☎26322287, ⓦwww.paradisoshills.com; ❹; all year). The stone-clad, tile-floored rooms, some interconnecting, have rustic-modern furnishings, wood trim and (often) sea views from the balconies; the in-house **restaurant** offers a sustaining if not wildly exciting Sunday buffet lunch.

Skárfos bridge and mill

Forking between Peristeróna and Lysó takes you through deserted Filoússa (Filousa), with the one-lane road beyond continuing 2.5km south to the floor of the lush Stavrós tís Psókas stream valley, popular with birdwatchers in spring-time (and unfortunately also, even in this remote spot, with villa developers). Here also are the well-signed remains of the Lusignan, single-arched **Skárfos bridge**, which carried the medieval Páfos–Pólis road. Once over the modern bridge downstream from this old one, bear left along the south bank to the indicated start of the short but faint path leading down to the bridge. The **watermill** visible beyond, easiest reached along the north-bank track, is equally picturesque and unusually still retains its millstone.

From the bridge turning it's another 2.6km south, up to the E712 just below Símou; you can also visit Skárfos from this direction, with the turning off the E712 well marked for both the bridge and Filoússa ("5.5km").

Starting from the B7, the E712 threads through the villages of **Símou**, **Dhrýmou**, **Lássa** and **Dhriniá**, all scattered on the south-bank ridge of the Stavrós tis Psókas stream canyon, before linking up with the E703 at Áyios Dhimitrianós, just below Kannavioú. Closer to the B7 than the Skárfos turning, the isolated, stone-clad *Sa Buneri* **taverna**, overlooking the reservoir and abandoned Turkish-Cypriot village of Evrétou, makes a good touring halt. The kindly managing family provides simple fare: bean soup, *halloúmi*, salads at any hour and grilled meat when there are sufficient customers.

Fýti

At Lássa (Lasa) it's worth detouring 1km east up to **FÝTI,** the most architectur-ally distinguished of this string of villages along the E712, where locally woven

lacework and *plakotó* **wall hangings** are sold. While there's little of the hustle that accompanies the trade in Páno Léfkara (see p.102), and it's commendable to see production (and buy) at source, you won't save much over Páfos town prices. Before buying, you might want to have a look at the free, privately run **Weaving Museum** (℡26732126 for information). The stone-clad *Phiti Village Taverna* (℡26732540; may close part of winter) across from the church is a *mezé* house, where Maria provides many vegetarian offerings and excellent home-made *loúntza* (smoked pork loin).

Panayiá

PANAYIÁ (Panagia, Pano Panagia on some maps) is the largest of several settlements near the headwaters of the Ézousas stream. Here, 750m up, you're at the fringes of the Tróödhos mountains, with walnut trees and tufts of forest on the ridge behind. The village is famous as the birthplace of late Archbishop and President Makarios III (see box, p.196) honoured by two small museums and an enormous statue in the main square. Behind this sits the grandiosely named **Makarios Cultural Centre** (Tues–Sun 9am–1pm & 2–4pm; free), displaying photos and paraphernalia of the great man's activities. While the mock-up of the radio set over which Makarios broadcast his defiance of the July 15, 1974, coup is of some interest, other displays are pretty feeble, padded out with such items as the slippers and alarm clock of a cousin.

More atmospheric is **Makarios's Childhood House**, well signposted south of and below the central *kafenío* crossroads (same timings as, & key from, Cultural Centre). With a pleasant garden and two interior rooms, it seems surprisingly large for a peasant house of the early twentieth century – until you realize that the livestock occupied the back room, with two adults and four children up front. Photos of moments in Makarios's life – some duplicates of those in the Cultural Centre – and assorted household knick-knacks make up the exhibits.

Practicalities

Ample **accommodation** exists in Panayi, with several "agrotourism" facilities clustered on the lane between the two Makarios museums: the *Palati tou Xylari* (℡99614673, @palati@hotmail.com; studio ❷, one-bedroom ❸) comprises four self-catering units sharing a wood-and-stone lounge. The one-unit *Stelios House* (℡99433094; ❷) has a large courtyard, while the combined two-bedroom (❸) and studio (❶) units of the *Liakoto* just opposite (℡26235597) are very family-friendly. *Arhontiko tou Meletiou* (℡26935011; studio ❶, two-bed ❸) is almost a small inn, with a range of accommodation formats.

There's a line of **tavernas** across from the statue *platía*, though they all appear to be owned by the same family and we've received repeated complaints of assorted rip-offs. Your best bet for **food** is *Kentron Avramis*, outside Asproyiá (Asprogia) on the main road up from Kannavioú, with good salads and *halloúmi*. In the same direction from the village, partway along, the **Vouni Panayia Winery** (daily: winter 8am–5.30pm, summer 8am–7pm) gives free tours and samples of its Pampela rosé, Alina white and Maratheftiko red.

Khrysorroyiátissa

Just 3km south of, and slightly higher than Panayiá, the **monastery of Khrysorroyiátissa** (officially, Moni Chrysorrogiatissa; in church Greek, Khrysorroyiatíssis) stands at a shady bend in the road, overlooking terraced valleys to the west. Revisionist derivation of the strange name, "Our Lady of

President-Archbishop **Makarios III**, the dominant personality in post-independence Cyprus until 1974, was a contradictory figure. For a start, there's the apocryphal tale that he was really the illegitimate son of a Turkish-Cypriot father; in reality Makarios' perfect Anatolian Turkish was the result of his studies at the Hálki (Heybeliada) Orthodox seminary near Istanbul. Both a secular and a religious leader, his undeniable charisma and authority were diminished by spells of arrogance and naivety, plus a debilitating tendency to surround himself with yes-men. Many observers found it difficult to understand the fusion of his two roles as spiritual and political leader of the Greek Cypriots, in what was nominally a secular republic; they failed to recognize that this ambiguity had been institutionalized in Greek history since the fall of Byzantium. Cyprus is still ambivalent about him: officially (though by no means universally) revered in the South, resented when not detested in the North, a balanced, homegrown appraisal of his life – including his alleged numerous relationships with women (and, more often, men) – seems unlikely, especially since Makarios kept no diary and left no memoirs.

Early career

One among four children of Christodhoulos and Eleni Mouskos, he was born **Michael Mouskos** in Panayiá on August 13, 1913. He herded sheep in the surrounding forest before spending his adolescence as a novice at nearby **Kýkko monastery** (see p.218). The monks paid his fees at the prestigious Pancyprian Gymnasium in Nicosia; after graduating in 1936, Mouskos proceeded to Greece, where he attended university and survived the harsh wartime occupation. Postgraduate work in Turkey and Boston was interrupted in April 1948 when he was chosen as Bishop of Kition (Larnaca).

Adopting the religious name **Makarios (Blessed)**, he turned his attention to island politics. Soon after coordinating a plebiscite in early 1950 showing 96 percent support among the Greek Orthodox population for *énosis* (union) with Greece, he was elected Archbishop of all Cyprus, which made him the chief Greek-Cypriot spokesman in future negotiations with the British. With George Grivas (see box, p.254), in 1952 he co-founded **EOKA** (Greek Organization of Cypriot Fighters) to struggle for *énosis*. But Makarios initially balked at the violent methods proposed by Grivas, and for various reasons the rebellion did not begin until April 1955. Makarios's contacts at Kýkko proved essential, as both he and Grivas used the monastery as a hideout, recruiting centre and bank.

It didn't take the British long to determine who was lending moral if not material support to the revolt, and Makarios plus three other clerics were **exiled** to the Seychelles, but released after a year on condition they didn't return to Cyprus. So Makarios continued his tactic, evolved since 1948, of touring overseas capitals watching the strategies of others and drumming up support for his cause – particularly among the newly independent portions of colonial empires. Among tactics emulated were accepting help from whatever quarter offered – including AKEL (the Cypriot Communist Party) and the Soviet Union. In the short run this helped unite polarized Greek-Cypriot society and much of world opinion behind *énosis*, but in the more distant future would generate accusations of unscrupulousness – and earn him the undying, and ultimately catastrophic, enmity of the overwhelmingly right-wing membership of EOKA.

Énosis vs independence

The last straw, as far as EOKA extremists were concerned, was his acceptance in 1959 of the British offer of **independence** for the island, rather than *énosis* (faced with Makarios's hesitation, the British secret services apparently confronted him with compromising photographs from his seminary days; the archbishop signed on the dotted line). Grivas returned to Greece, soon to plot more mischief, while Makarios was elected first president of the new republic. He faced an unenviable task, not least convincing suspicious Turkish Cypriots that his abandonment of the cause of *énosis* was genuine. This he failed to do, most signally in 1963–64, by first showing considerable tactlessness in proposing crucial constitutional changes to the Turkish-Cypriot Vice-President, then by failing to restrain EOKA appointees in his cabinet and EOKA gunmen in the streets, and finally by outright threats of violence against the Turkish-Cypriot community both before and during the Kókkina incident (see p.185).

It's arguable that, during the Republic's early years, Makarios was backpedalling towards *énosis*, but following the colonels' coup in Greece of April 1967, he again saw the advantages of non-aligned independence, especially if the alternative were union with a regime he openly despised – and his own relegation to a backwater bishop. By early 1968 he had proclaimed the undesirability of *énosis* (in favour of two "Greek" voices at the UN) and began looking for ways out of the impasse, specifically by reopening negotiations with the Turkish Cypriots and opting for an assimilationist approach to the "problem" they represented. But these talks, which continued intermittently until 1974, were never marked by any sufficiently conciliatory gestures – which would have exposed him to danger from EOKA extremists, these shortly materializing anyway.

American and EOKA-B vendetta

To these vacillations on the relative merits of *énosis* and independence, and Makarios's continued espousal of the Non-Aligned Movement (not to mention his relations with communists at home and abroad) can be traced to the roots of growing **US opposition** to the archbishop. US President Richard Nixon vilified him as "Castro in a cassock", while Secretary of State Henry Kissinger sought a discreet way to remove this obstacle to more malleable client-states in the Mediterranean. The Greek junta's views on Makarios matched his opinion of them, so they needed little encouragement to begin conspiring, through cadres planted in the National Guard and EOKA-B (a Grivas revival), for his overthrow. Despite repeated **plots**, instigated by the junta and the CIA, to assassinate him between 1970 and 1974 – including the downing of his helicopter – Makarios dithered over how to handle their proxies, EOKA-B; by the time the archbishop and his supporters decided on firm suppression, in April 1974, it was too late.

On **July 15, 1974**, the EOKA-B-infiltrated National Guard, commanded by junta-appointed Greek officers, stormed the archiepiscopal palace in Nicosia – Makarios's residence – inflicting comprehensive damage with clearly lethal intent. Makarios, actually in the nearby presidential palace at the time, escaped, being spirited away by loyalists first to his old refuge at Kýkko and later to the Páfos archiepiscopal palace, where he broadcast a message disproving announcements of his death. From here his old adversaries, the British, airlifted him onto the Akrotíri airfield and thence to London and exile. Neither the British nor the Americans initially bestirred themselves much to reinstate a leader whom they felt had received his just desserts for years of intriguing.

Yet Makarios's long career as emissary to and of the Third World paid off, particularly at the UN, and late in 1974 he was able to **return to Cyprus**, addressing a huge rally in Nicosia with the consummate showmanship which came so naturally to him. He resumed office as president, but the multiple attempts on his life and the depressing fact of the island's partition must have weighed on him. On August 3, 1977, Makarios suffered a fatal heart attack, and five days later was buried in an artificial grotto near Kýkko. Controversy surrounded even the unseasonable downpour at his funeral: Greek-Cypriot eulogists characterized the rain as the tears of God weeping for his servant, while Turkish Cypriots – watching the proceedings on television in the North, making sure their bogeyman was really dead – retorted with their folk belief that the sins of the wicked deceased were washed away by the rains before burial.

the Golden Pomegranate", from an epithet of the Virgin as Golden-Breasted, seems to point suspiciously back to Aphrodite's similar attribute. A twelfth-century foundation legend relates how the hermit Ignatius retrieved a glowing icon from the Pafiot shore and, as so often when miraculous images make their wishes known, heard a celestial voice commanding him to build a home here. Over the years this particular manifestation of the Virgin became the patroness of criminals, who prayed to avoid arrest or for a light sentence – probably a holdover of the safe haven granted to fugitives in certain pagan temples. Dating like the rest of the structure from 1770, with 1967 repair of fire damage, the *katholikón* is plunked down in the middle of a triangular cloister. Its most interesting feature is not the *témblon* or the hidden icon, but the carved and painted wood-panel *yinaikonítis* in the rear of the nave.

Khrysorroyiátissa is ostensibly a working monastery – the reasonably priced products of the basement **Monte Royia winery**, including some selected aged vintages, are on sale in the shop, and the current abbot Dionysios is meticulously involved with icon restoration. But the few monks are chary about tourists, and the guest quarters are reserved for religious pilgrims. The courtyard seems open all day, but the shop and *katholikón* close during summer from 12.30 to 1.30pm. Outside the walls a panoramic snack/drink bar comes alive at the time of the local February 1–2 and August 14–15 **festivals.**

The Tillyrian wilderness

North of Panayiá extends a vast, empty, wooded tract of hills, historically known as **Tillyría** (pronounced *Dillyrgá* in dialect), though strictly speaking the label doesn't apply until you're past the Stavrós tís Psókas forestry station. Unlike the Tróödhos proper, the region is not and never has been very populated, frequented in the past mainly for the sake of its rich copper mines (now redundant). Until the 1960s, what Tillyians there were (both Orthodox and Muslim) lived either as charcoal-burners or professional beggars who followed the annual festival circuit. If you're staying anywhere on the Pólis coast, a drive through here, and a ramble along the nature trails, satisfactorily completes a day begun in the Páfos hills.

Cedar Valley

Leaving Panayiá on the paved route signposted for Kýkko monastery (head towards Kýkko at the well-marked junctions), continue for 22km until the paving ends abruptly on arrival at **Cedar Valley** (Kiládha tón Kédron in Greek). This is exactly that, a hidden gulch with thousands of specimens of *Cedrus brevifolia*, an aromatic cedar indigenous to Cyprus. At a hairpin bend in the track, there's a picnic area and a spring, while a sign points to another track – wide but not suitable for vehicles – that leads 2.5km up to **Trípylos peak** (1362m). Strangely, the hike passes few of the handsome trees; they're mostly well downstream, and (perhaps intentionally) inaccessible.

Kýkko itself (see p.218), some 20km further along, is more usually and easily approached from Pedhoulás in the Tróödhos. If you're heading on to Stavrós tís Psókas and the coast, backtrack 4km from the picnic site to the junction marked "Stavros". Follow the sign right and you'll pass, after 6km, a labelled jeep track coming down from the Trípylos summit.

Stavrós tís Psókas and beyond

Some 7km further along the paved road, there's another important junction: right goes down and north to the coast, left and south descends 3km more to the colonial-era forestry station and rest house at **Stavrós tís Psókas**. The name recalls the monastery, abandoned in the nineteenth century, which once stood here, and is usually politely translated as "Cross of Measles"; it actually means "Cross of the Mange", and in the days before pesticide lotions a spontaneous cure of scabies must have seemed well-nigh miraculous.

Facilities at Stavrós include a small, fairly useless **café** with overpriced snacks, the local **forestry headquarters** and the extremely popular **hostel** (℡ 26332144; €20 each), where space must be reserved in advance from June to August. Bunks are in simple rooms with en-suite bathrooms. The rangers may proudly assure you that this, 950m up in deep shade, is the coolest spot in the district. Most visitors drive up the easiest ways, either on the wide, surfaced road taking off between Kannavioú and Panayía or (in 45min) along the equally broad route from Lysó.

The nature trails

Some 200m along the road west towards Lysó stands an enclosure for Cyprus **moufflon**, only just saved from extinction – one is now the tail-fin logo of Cyprus Airways. Wild members of the small herd also wander the surrounding ridges, but you're exceedingly unlikely to see any roaming free while hiking one of the two circular **nature trails**. The first, called Chorteri, begins about 1.7km along the seven-kilometre stretch of paved road north of Stavrós towards Trípylos and takes about two hours, looping around a fire lookout station; the second, hour-long Moúti toú Stavroú, begins and ends further uphill towards Zakhárou peak (1214m) at the three-way saddle-junction called Selládhi toú Stavroú, where paved roads go either to the Cedar Valley and Kýkko, the coast or back down to the station.

Out to the coast

The route **to the coast** is well signposted and paved, but curvy, slow going and littered with rockfall after rainstorms. You'll end up in Pomós, west of the Kókkina enclave (35km from Selládhi toú Stavroú) in an hour, or Káto Pýrgos (39km) via the inland salient of the Kókkina detour (25km) in well over an hour. En route you'll notice how the careful husbandry of the British and Republican forestry services was set back considerably by the Turkish Air Force, which set the trees alight with napalm during summer 1974; patterns of reafforestation terraces are still some years from fully reversing this act of sabotage. The forest is, in fact, very monotonous; the fine views over successive ridges and down to the sea are the point of the drive.

The Xerós and Dhiárizos valleys

The far southeast of Páfos district is taken up the major river valleys, of the **Xerós** and the **Dhiárizos**. They offer not only exciting landscapes and walking opportunities, but abandoned monastic churches on the riverbanks and two ancient bridges over the streams. The latter formed an integral part of the **Venetian camel-caravan route**, the beasts transporting copper ore from the Tróödhos down to Páfos or Pólis. Not being as durable as the cobbled, round-island Roman road, the Venetian path can scarcely be traced any longer, but the bridges are still there. Most of the villages hereabouts, however, lack the distinction of those further west, having been devastated by a great earthquake in 1953 and repaired in a utilitarian manner, if at all.

The upper Xerós valley

The upper reaches of the **Xerós valley**, which contain the more interesting monuments, are easily reached from Khrysorroyiátissa (see p.195). From here it's 10km south, via Statós, to the ruins of old Áyios Fótios, abandoned in 1969; the ground is unstable and its houses are literally heading south. Here you turn east and then north for **Galatariá** (*Galatargá* in dialect), whose central taverna-*kafenío* is inoperative at the moment.

Vrécha and the Roúdhias bridge

The narrow but still-paved road continues through Kilínia (Koilineia) to ex-Turkish **VRÉCHA** (Vretsia). Before 1974, this constituted a major enclave, as borne out by an empty UN post and abundant graffiti in favour of "Taksim" (partition of Cyprus between Turkey and Greece) and "Volkan" (the pre-TMT Turkish-Cypriot militants' organization); accordingly, the Republican administration never provided the place with electric current. Though it's one of the most beautiful spots in the district, with ample water and land, Vrécha remains abandoned except for a few sporadically occupied houses and a seasonal **taverna**.

From the lower, south end of Vrécha it's under an hour's descent on foot to a derelict, single-arched **watermill** near the river bank; the valuable millstone has been filched, recycled for use in modern olive presses. The medieval **Roúdhias** (*Roúthkias* in dialect) **bridge**, a simple, round-arched span hidden by trees, lies a ten-minute walk upstream from here; nearby you'll find a deep, swimmable pool, which retains water most years into July. The bridge is also accessible by a more direct jeep track from Vrécha, leaving the obvious track by the mosque, which crosses a modern bridge just above the older one. Once you're past this point, the track can be followed east, via Péra Vássa and the Kélefos bridge, for about 20km to Áyios Nikólaos (see p.202); walkers can use a 17-kilometre **nature trail** from Vrécha to Kaminária village.

Panayía Eleoússa Síndi

Retracing your route through Kilínia and Galatariá, proceed south to attractive Pendaliá (Pentaleia), sadly plagued by landslips. From the old village centre, a southeasterly dirt track (passable to cars depending on mud levels) just over 6km long heads to the lonely monastery of **Panayía Eleoússa Síndi** (Panagia tou Sinti), at the mouth of a side stream on the west bank of the Xerós valley. The main watercourse is flanked by defunct watermills, which once ground the monastery's corn. Síndi, a dependency of Kýkko monastery, was restored in 1994–97; in a proposed next phase (indefinitely postponed), wings of cells around the courtyard will be reconstructed with an eye to monastic rehabitation. The most striking feature, once inside the walled precinct (always open; free), is a wonderful fieldstoned courtyard; the very plain, high church with its octagonal lantern dome and new *témblon* dates mostly from the early sixteenth century.

Out to the coast

From Pendaliá, it's easy to continue southwest towards the coast on the high-standard E606 road, via Amargéti, Eledhió and Axýlou. **AMARGÉTI** could be a touring base: the *Exohiko Kendro Zoodhohos Piyi* (☏26723212; ❷) has a few rooms to let upstairs, but food and atmosphere are rather sanitized, and you'll probably have to settle for steak Diane and chips unless you ring ahead to arrange for their *mezé*.

From Amargéti or Axýlou (both grid-plan bungalow replacements for nearby, destroyed villages) you can either proceed straight to the coast at Akhélia, or detour down directly or via Natá to **cross the Xerós River** just above the Asprókremos reservoir. The area is good for bird-watching, and this route – the only partially paved one to the far side of the valley – is a handy shortcut for getting to the Dhiárizos valley via old Kholétria, but the river could be too high to ford in very early spring; enquire in Natá before proceeding. Old **KHOLÉTRIA** (Choletria) is slowly being reoccupied by the renovation-minded, and has a swish, riverview **taverna**, *Choletria* (closed Tues), a few hundred metres north of the attractive, possibly sixteenth-century village **church of Áyios Pandelíomonas** (usually open, signposted from the eastern ridge road near new Kholétria).

The Dhiárizos valley

The easiest introduction to the **Dhiárizos (Diarizos) valley**, if you haven't got a jeep or haven't crossed the Xerós as described above, is via the turning from the B6 southeast of Páfos for **NIKÓKLIA** (Nikokleia). Here, the *Vasilias Nikoklis Inn* (T 26432211, W www.vasilias.nikoklis.com; ❷) – inconspicuously tucked east of the main highway, above the village – is a restored medieval roadside hostelry with tiled and beamed rooms. It has a pool, plus characterful bar/restaurant on the ground floor, serving the last prepared food you'll see for a while heading up stream.

Immediately downstream from Nikóklia, the road divides; the more westerly option, which traces the ridge dividing Xerós from Dhiárizos, is one of the quicker ways up towards the Tróödhos. Among several villages en route, only **Kholétria** early on – built to replace quake-shattered old Kholétria (see above) – plus **Salamioú** and **Armínou**, near the top of the valley, show many signs of life. From Armínou, the road swoops in well-graded arcs to cross over to the more scenic east bank of the river via Filoússa.

Heading upstream from Nikóklia to Áyios Nikólaos via the easterly road, you wind past **MAMÓNIA**, the only local Orthodox village at independence; roadside *Mylos* tavern just north of the village serves good, light meals. Old Prastió, on the east flank of the increasingly sheer valley, was, like Souskioú and Fasoúla downstream, shattered by the 1953 quake; the replacement, a roadside prefab grid opposite, had hardly been occupied before communal troubles dictated its abandonment.

Áyios Sávvas tís Karónos

Prastió (Prasteio) is the closest place to the intriguing monastic Byzantine-Latin church of **Áyios Sávvas tís Karónos**, easiest reached from just downstream. Some 3km east of Áyios Yeóryios, watch for a black-on-white Greek-lettered sign reading "Pros Eklisaki Ayiou Savva", pointing to an initial cement track crossing the river (maybe not passable late winter/early spring), which heads initially towards a modern chapel on a hillock. Go past this, on a well-surfaced dirt road, for 2km to reach the walled former monastery in its lovely setting. At first the rectangular, gable-roofed church, first erected in 1120, seems more like a carob warehouse than a monastery *katholikón*, but then you notice the Gothic arches over the north and south doors, the plaque over the west door commemorating the Venetian restoration of 1501, and the little grinning gargoyle just above this. Inside (one door always open), the double-ribbed vault is bare except for an intricately worked *témblon* with naive polychrome painting on the lowest level in geometric and floral designs. At both the west wall and apsidal end are small round windows, with delicate tracery. Outbuildings, ruined since the nineteenth century, include an arcaded meeting hall.

Pretóri, Áyios Nikólaos and the Kélefos bridge

Beyond Kidhási, the last valley-bottom settlement of yet another former Turkish-Cypriot enclave, the road crosses the Dhiárizos River and skims the district border as it climbs through more prosperous and scenic Kédhares and **PRETÓRI** (Praitori), which has tasty and abundant **snacks** in its coffee house. In an exquisitely microscopic bit of regional rivalry, the east-bankers of the Dhiárizos used to reproach the west-bankers, regardless of ethnic affiliation, with excessive stinginess – a grave insult in a peasant society. The worst, apparently, were the pre-1974 inhabitants of Áyios Ioánnis, a Turkish-Cypriot village descended from the peculiar Linovamváki sect (see p.380). Just beyond Pretóri is the worthwhile **Nelion Winery** (daily: summer 9am–7pm, winter 9am–5pm; ⓦ www.cyprusvines.com/nelion.htm).

Some 26km from Nikóklia, **ÁYIOS NIKÓLAOS** (Agios Nikolaos) is one of the highest of the Dhiárizos villages. Beautifully set amid orchards and irrigation ditches, it boasts most of the few **tavernas** in the Dhiárizos valley – the best being *Rumeli* on the bypass road, where you can lunch on *louvána* and *kléftigo* for about €12 per person, finishing with their own candied fruits or *palouzé*. The village is also the easiest access point for the graceful **Kélefos bridge** ("*Tzílefos*" in dialect, and lately even on signage), which spans the upper Dhiárizos and is reached along a six-kilometre paved (after a fashion) road northwestwards; with its pointed arch, it's more photogenic than the Roudhiás bridge. It is also possible to reach Kélefos directly from Roudhiás via a dirt track passing **Péra Vássa** forestry station.

From the Kélefos bridge, with a decent map to navigate by, you can either carry on 3km east, on a wide, paved road, to the Elía bridge (and thence to Kaminária village in the Tróödhos); retrace your steps to Áyios Nikólaos and cross the district border heading southeast to Ársos to visit the *Krassokhoriá*; or proceed from Áyios Nikólaos to Mandhriá and thence Plátres.

Travel details

Long-distance buses

Ktíma Páfos to: Limassol (Mon–Sat 1 daily on ALEPA; 1hr 15min); Nicosia (Mon–Sat 1 daily on ALEPA; 2hr 30min); Pólis (Mon–Fri 11 daily, Sat 6, with Nea Amoroza; 45min); Pomós (Mon–Sat 2 daily, via Pólis, with Nea Amoroza; 1hr 45min). **Pólis** to: Latchí/Loutrá tís Afrodhítis (June–Sept 3 daily Mon–Fri; 15min).

Local buses (ALEPA)

Káto Páfos to: Coral Bay (summer daily 8am–6pm every 20min, 6–11pm every 15min; winter daily 8am–6.30pm every 20min; 40min).

Ktíma Páfos (Karavélla terminal) to: Áyios Neófytos (Mon–Fri 2 daily; 20min); Émba (Mon–Fri 4 daily, Sat daily; 15min); Lémba (Mon–Fri 3 daily, Sat 1; 15min); Péyia (Mon–Fri 2 daily, Sat daily; 30min); Yeroskípou (Mon–Fri 6 daily, Sat 2 daily; 10min).
Ktíma Páfos (market car park) to: Áyios Yeóryios (8 daily 9am–4pm, change at Coral Bay; 50min); Coral Bay (Mon–Sat every 15–20min 7.30am–5.40pm; 30min); Káto Páfos (summer Mon–Sat 6.15am–7pm every 10–15min; winter Mon–Sat 6.15am–6.30pm every 15–20min, Sun 6.15am–6.30pm every 30min all year; 20min).

The High Tróödhos

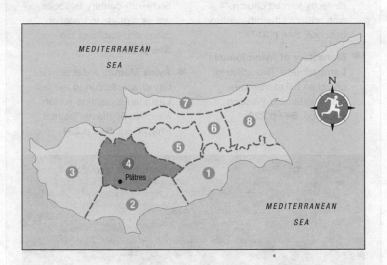

MEDITERRANEAN SEA

Plátres

MEDITERRANEAN SEA

N

CHAPTER 4 # Highlights

❋ **Tróödhos mountains**
The high-altitude flora
encompasses everything from
spring cherry blossoms to
orchids. See pp.208–217

❋ **Mount Olympus** Nature trails
provide good hiking around
the summit of the island's
highest mountain. See p.211

❋ **Arkhángelos Mikhaïl,
Pedhoulás** A small but
perfectly formed church,
with brilliant fifteenth-century
frescoes. See p.217

❋ **Monastery of Áyios Ioánnis
Lambadhistís** Two adjacent
churches full of frescoes
reflect extensive Western
influence. See p.222

❋ **Linos Inn, Kakopetriá** In
the heart of the old quarter,
one of the best executed
restoration inns on the island.
See p.224

❋ **Asínou (Panayía Forviótissa)**
Isolated country church with
some of the oldest, clearest
and most vivid frescoes in
Cyprus. See p.227

❋ **Arkhángelos Mihaïl, Vyzakiá**
Sixteenth-century frescoes
act as a guide to Venetian
dress and habits of the era.
See p. 228

❋ **Áyios Mámas** A deceptively
tiny chapel featuring the last
Lusignan-Byzantine-fusion
frescoes by master painter
Philip Goul. See p.234

▲ Frescoes at Asínou

The High Tröödhos

Rising to nearly 2000m, the **Tröödhos** mountains (pronounced as three syllables, "*Tro*-o-dhos", not "True-dhos") – form the backbone of the southern Republic and occupy nearly a quarter of the island's surface area. This dense mass of igneous rock is thrust-up primordial sea bed, allowing rare glimpses of geological strata normally hidden beneath lighter continental landmasses. It's also extraordinarily rich in mineral deposits and metallic ores, mined until recent decades. Too low and hummocky to be stereotypically alpine this far south, the Tröödhos still acquit themselves as a mountain resort area, and their western part supports what is touted as the best-managed island forest in the Mediterranean. But this is by no means virgin, first-growth woods: ancient miners felled all of that to feed nearby copper-smelting furnaces, and after centuries of neglect under the Lusignans, Venetians and Ottomans, the British found scarcely more trees growing when they arrived.

In every era the range has been a barrier as well as a resource, and during the Christian era especially, a refuge for Hellenic culture. The devastating Arab raids of middle Byzantine times left the hills untouched, and during nearly four centuries of Lusignan rule, when the Orthodox Church was humiliatingly subordinated elsewhere, the Tröödhos provided a safe haven for a minor renaissance in its fortunes – most strikingly evidenced in the famous collection of **frescoed rural churches** here. The Ottomans didn't bother to settle the region, and when the mainland Turks returned in 1974, the obstacle the mountains represented may, as much as any ceasefire agreement, have kept them from overrunning the entire island. Among foreign occupiers, only the British, homesick and sweltering down in the flatlands, realized the recreational potential of the mountains, building roads and assorted architectural follies.

From the south, the usual gateway to the region is the functional, though beautifully set, resort of **Plátres**, which has the largest concentration of hotels on that side of the watershed. Its higher neighbour **Tröödhos** has no village character whatsoever, but is the jump-off point for a day's walking around the highest summit, **Mount Olympus**. Good roads lead from either place to **Pedhoulás**, chief village of the Marathássa valley – and also your introduction to the painted churches of the Tröödhos, both here and downstream at **Moutoullás** and **Kalopanayiótis**. Pedhoulás also offers the easiest access to **Kýkko monastery**, out by itself at the edge of the Tillyrian wilderness.

The next area east of Marathássa, **Soléa**, has as its "capital" the resort of **Kakopetriá**, with its preserved old quarter and unusually accessible concentration of frescoed churches, up-valley at **Áyios Nikólaos tís Stéyis** and downstream at the adjacent village of **Galáta**. Slightly less convenient are the magnificent churches of **Asínou** and **Arkhángelos Mihaïl** in the Kannávia

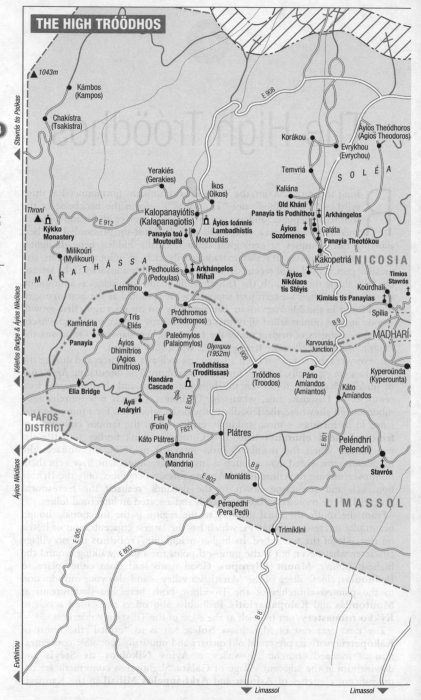

▲ 1043m

Kámbos
(Kampos)

Chakístra
(Tsakístra)

Korákou

E 908

Áyios Theódhoros
(Agios Theodoros)

Evrýkhou
(Evrychou)

Yerakiés
(Gerakies)

Temvriá

S O L É A

Íkos
(Oikos)

Kaliána

Throní

▲

Kýkko
Monastery

E 912

Kalopanayiótis
(Kalapanagiotis)

Áyios Ioánnis
Lambadhistís

Old Kháni

Panayía tís Podhíthou   Arkhángelos

Áyios
Sozómenos

Galáta

Panayía toú
Moutoullá

Moutoullás

Panayía Theotókou

Milikoúri
(Mylikouri)

M A R A T H Á S S A

Kakopetriá   N I C O S I A

Pedhoulás
(Pedoulas)

Arkhángelos
Mihaíl

Áyios
Nikólaos
tís Stéyis

Tímios
Stavrós

Lemíthou

Koúrdhali

Kímisis tís Panayías

Trís
Eliés

Pródhromos
(Prodromos)

Spilia

B 9

MADHARÍ

Kaminária

Panayía

Áyios
Dhimítrios
(Agios
Dimitrios)

Paleómylos
(Palaiomylos)

▲ Olympus
(1952m)

E 908

Karvounás
Junction

Kyperoúnda
(Kyperounta)

Troödhítissa
(Troditissas)

Tróödhos
(Troodos)

Páno
Amíandos
(Amiantos)

Káto
Amíandos

Elía Bridge

Handára
Cascade

E 804

Áyii
Anáryiri

Finí
(Foini)

F 821

Plátres

Peléndhri
(Pelendri)

Káto Plátres

E 801

Stavrós

Mandhriá
(Mandria)

Moniátis

B 8

L I M A S S O L

E 802

Perapedhí
(Pera Pedi)

E 805

Trimíklini

E 803

▼ Limassol   Limassol ▼

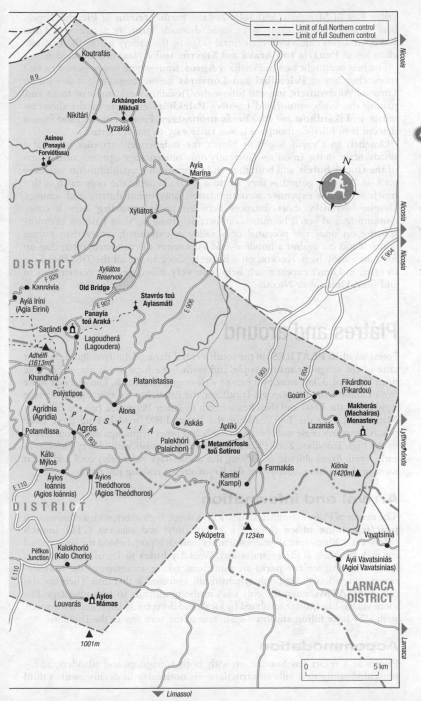

valley. East of Marathássa and Soléa lies the harsher terrain of **Pitsyliá**, largely bare of trees but in many ways more dramatic than its neighbours. From Kakopetriá you climb over the central ridge to the valleys where the first-rate churches of **Panayía toú Araká** and **Stavrós toú Ayiasmáti** are hidden.

The best overnight base in Pitsyliá is **Agrós**, from where you're poised to visit more churches at **Peléndhri** and **Louvarás** before beginning a descent to Limassol. Alternatively, you can follow the Tróödhos peak line east to its end, passing the lively, untouristed town of **Palekhóri** en route to the showcase village of **Fikárdhou** and **Makherás monastery**. From here, the most logical descent is to Nicosia, though it is also fairly easy to reach Larnaca.

Uniquely in Cyprus, South or North, the independent traveller is not at a disadvantage in the Tróödhos. Currently only one package operator offers some of the fancier **hotels**, and both they and more modest establishments welcome walk-in business, geared as they are to a local clientele; the only catch is that much of the less expensive accommodation only opens during mid-summer. Despite nominally short distances between points, **touring** here is time-consuming, and you'll be more comfortable changing your base on occasion, moving on once the potential of a valley is exhausted, rather than pitting yourself and car against a hundred-odd kilometres of contorted, often dug-up road on a daily basis. Reckon on a leisurely week to see all the Tróödhos have to offer, and don't expect much help from very infrequent bus connections to and from Limassol or Nicosia.

Plátres and around

Forest-swathed **PLÁTRES** on the south-central flank of the Tróödhos is the first taste of the range for many people, and easily – perhaps too easily – accessible from Limassol, 37km away, by a pair of well-engineered roads. The quickest route from Limassol, the B8, goes via Trimíklini; the other, more scenic option starts at Episkopí as the E601 and then heads north to either Perapedhí (via the E805) or Mandhriá (along the E803). Above the lateral E802 road linking these three points, vineyards cease and cherry orchards and pines begin, signalling your arrival in the high Tróödhos; Káto Plátres in particular is awash with cherry blossom in early April. At an altitude of 1150m, the resort stays (relatively) cool and green most of the summer, courtesy of the Krýos stream rushing just below.

Arrival and information

The extent of Plátres' commercial district is a single high street, with a combination **post/telephone office** (Mon–Fri 3–5pm only) and adjacent **CTO branch** (Mon–Fri 8.30am–4pm all year, sometimes 9am–3.30pm), behind the large central car park doubling as the central square. Weekday **buses** to Limassol depart from here. Municipal fee **car parks** are numerous, taking advantage of the summer-season congestion, though only systematically enforced at that time. There are also two **bank ATMs**, about the only ones in the mountains, so take advantage. The more village-like quarter, inhabited by locals and deceptively large, lies to the south, with a 24-hour **filling station** – again one of the very few in the Tróödhos.

Accommodation

Plátres as a resort has lost favour with both foreigners and islanders, and – notwithstanding new villa construction – is noticeably in decline, with a third the number of **hotels** compared with the late 1980s. Surviving local accommodation – just six establishments have retained their CTO certification – is scattered away from the high street; however, many of these places only operate at peak summer season.

Forest Park At the southwest end of the upper through road ℡ 25421751, Ⓦ www.forestparkhotel .com.cy. Four-star modern hotel offering every comfort, including indoor/outdoor pools, tennis court and fitness centre, avoid the restaurant. ❺

Minerva On the upper through road ℡ 25421731, ⒺⒺ minerva9@cytanet.com.cy. Two-star, currently for sale but will likely continue as accommodation with some involvement by the original managing family, including ace botanist Yiannis Christofides. All rooms are heated, and some have balconies, some full bathtubs; there's also an annexe of six superior wood- or tile-floored rooms with antique furnishings, gabled ceilings and large bathrooms – the best-value facilities in the mountains. ❸

New Helvetia Above the river at the north end of the resort ℡ 25421348, Ⓦ www.minotel.com. Magnificent period piece from 1929 (renovated in 2005), offering mountain bikes, car rental and vouchers for the Plátres public pool. ❹

Semiramis On the upper through road ℡ 25422777, Ⓦ www.semiramishotel.com .cy. The pick of the hotels, an Edwardian-era folly restored and reopened in 2006. The ground floor has a fireplace lounge contiguous with the breakfast area; among the rooms, with wood-and-tile floors and pastel colour schemes, nos. 8 and 9 have jacuzzis in the bathrooms. Half board is available through the affiliated *Village Restaurant*. Open all year. B & B ❷

The Town

Long after independence, Plátres remains a weekend haunt of **expats** and enlisted men – you can watch UK footie in one of several pubs, and many tavernas are tuned to British Forces radio. Comparisons with Indian hill-stations were doubtless inspired by a few remaining **villas** with whimsical turrets and rooflines (all built, incidentally, by wealthy native Cypriots), but a staggering quantity of modern development pitched at locals and *nouveau riche* foreigners (especially Russians) is dwarfing the "Raj days" architecture, especially at Plátres' south end. During summer the main drag becomes an unenticing uproar of double-parked buses, strolling day-trippers and tacky souvenirs. The myriad wide dirt tracks in the surrounding hills can be explored with rented **mountain bikes** – look for the sign behind the main square.

Eating and drinking

Restaurant prices are nearly identical across the board, often for mediocre fare. Honourable exceptions include *Skylight* on the main drag, doing good trout with al dente vegetables and a starter for about €19, plus less successful typical Cypriot dishes; the interior's pleasant, and includes a swimming pool (free use with meal). *The Village Restaurant*, towards the western end of the same street, has salubrious food in *mezé* format: ten starter platters plus a couple of mains for about €30 per couple, in an equally savoury environment. Alternatively, just north of the developed area, the more brazenly touristy Psilódhendhro **trout farm** has heated indoor premises and outdoor seating under the trees, and claims to work daily year-round (but 11am–5pm only); budget €15 for a trout-based meal. Káto Plátres has its own **microwinery**, Lambouri (℡ 25421329 to arrange visits), which makes a very decent white, worth asking for in local restaurants.

Easy walks around Plátres

Two popular, fairly easy if lengthy walks start from Psilódhendhro, 300m north of Plátres. If you're not up for an outing of several hours, the **Myllométri trail,** a half-hour stroll down to the base of the eponymous waterfalls, starts halfway between the central church and Plátres' central plaza. Other excursion destinations are all shown on the map on p.212.

Walk to Caledonian Falls

The most popular walk from Psilódhendhro leads up to **Caledonian Falls**, designated as the "Kaledonia Nature Trail" by CTO signage. Begin on the wide track passing left of the trout farm as you face it; after 300m this dwindles to a marked trail, with the distance to the falls given as 1km. The impressive eleven-metre cascade, the highest on the island, indeed beckons twenty minutes later, in a pleasantly wooded ravine. En route you must change sides of the stream several times, and you'll get your feet wet in the springtime; more water crossings are involved in continuing upstream along the path.

Some 45 minutes beyond the falls you emerge at the opposite trailhead, marked by a typical canopied notice board, about 1km from the Tróödhos resort (see "Mount Olympus" below). If you do this walk in the opposite direction, the access slip road off the Tróödhos-bound highway, just below that serving the "Katoikiai/Residences" of the president, is also well signposted, with yet another wooden nature-walk sign. Hiking downhill to the falls also takes about 45 minutes, owing to the roughness of the trail at some points – those with trainers beware.

The walk is short enough that retracing your steps is not arduous; if you're vehicle-less, it's worth noting that this trail, despite its steepness, is much the quickest way of getting up to the Tróödhos resort on foot. Alternatively, combine it with one of the Pouziáris trails, following the description below in reverse, to make a loop.

Before British administration began in 1878, the area was little visited except for shepherds based at Plátres and gatherers of snow (used for refrigeration), but shortly afterwards a military training camp was established near the site of present-day Tróödhos, and a **summer residence** built for the British High Commissioner. Now the retreat of the president of the southern Republic, this stands just above the high end of the Caledonian Falls trail, and is also a touch-down point for one leg of the Pouziáris trail. Signs by the driveway-start discourage entry, but you may want to stop in to read the rather startling plaque by the door of what looks like an ordinary Highland shooting lodge. Written in French, it declares: "Arthur Rimbaud, French poet and genius, despite his fame contributed with his own hands to the construction of this house, 1881." Rimbaud's two visits to Cyprus were sandwiched between time with the Dutch colonial army in Java, recuperation from typhoid in France and a stint in the Horn of Africa; he in fact merely supervised a work party here and did no actual manual labour – nor was he yet famous.

Pouziáris trail

The **Pouziáris trail** system, which starts on the east bank of the Krýos stream by the trout farm, offers meatier hiking and the possibility of loops, though at least one leg is probably worth avoiding for its dreary surface. You've an initial quarter-hour climb (signed as "1km") east-northeast through some oaks – and severe landslide damage from 2004, which should now be repaired – to a divide in the path and beginning of the loop system. At this junction bear left (north-northwest), crossing a firebreak-cum-jeep-track just over twenty minutes along. Continue climbing steadily in zigzags, east then north, up onto the shoulder of Pouziáris; here the trail narrows, and you've your first views west to Páfos, and south to the sea. There's less shade now, though the basic vegetation profile of mixed pine and oak remains the same. Just under an hour from the start, veer

Since 1981 the CTO, together with the forestry department, have prepared a growing number of **nature trails** in the high Tróödhos. Actually, most of these paths existed long before then, used for travel between the highest villages and monasteries, but since the 1950s many had become overgrown and forgotten, while others were bulldozed or even paved. Almost all the survivors have been cleared and rehabilitated as **hikers' routes**.

The 1981-vintage 1:5,000 topographic maps (see p.55) show many of them correctly; guests at the hotel in Plátres can ask to see map sets, kept by the management for consultation. The nature trails have also been fitted with numbered wooden markers calling walkers' attention to selected natural features. Labelling, however, is pretty perfunctory, with only Latin species names given – if at all – and often specimens are embarrassingly dead or missing. To enjoy the trails as they were intended, it's essential to pick up folding leaflets which contain number keys for four of the more popular trails in the Tróödhos/Plátres area. These are variably available; if you intend to follow the markers, scour tourist offices for English-language leaflets long before you reach Plátres or Tróödhos; otherwise you may have to settle for French- or German-language versions – or nothing at all.

Of the four fully documented local trails in the Tróödhos, most with Greek mythological names, the **Atalante** nearly completes a circuit of Mount Olympus; the **Persephone** leads to a viewpoint known as Makriá Kondárka (Makrya Kontarka); **Kaledonia** links the presidential forest lodge with Caledonian Falls; while **Artemis** executes a complete loop of Khionístra summit at a higher contour than the Atalante. In addition to the still undocumented Pouziáris trail, there are also several other trails, thus far sparsely labelled, along and across the Madharí ridge between Spília and Agrós, some kilometres east of Tróödhos. All of the South's prepared trails are described in a glossy booklet, *Follow the E4 and Other Nature Trails*, but this is strictly schematic, far from error-free and not suitable for navigation.

onto what looks like a minor trail hairpinning back and right (straight on leads to the top of the Kaledonia trail, as described opposite); over the next ten minutes, the side turning zigzags east-southeast through more imposing pines to the secondary, 1629-metre summit of Pouziáris hill (signed as the "shoulder"), with its small radar reflector, two benches and superb views south.

At the marked intersection here, left or north leads more or less levelly towards the British radar "golf balls" and the Makriá Kondárka path, for a longer loop returning via Tróödhos resort and the Caledonian Falls; or you can head down and right ("Kaminoudia 2km, Psilon Dendron 6km"), though the latter option isn't particularly recommended as it's poorly routed (mostly on track) and signposted.

Mount Olympus

At 1952m (6404ft), the Khionístra (lately Chionistra – "snow-pack" or "chilblain") peak of **Mount Olympus** (Olympos) is the highest point on Cyprus. It does not rise particularly dramatically from the surrounding uplands, which are cloaked in dense forest of hardy black and Austrian pine, plus a few Cypriot cedar and junipers. The trees keep things cool except in high summer, and provide much of the justification for five marked nature trails (two of them already mentioned above). In (increasingly rare) snowy winters, the northeast-facing slopes host the island's only ski resort. The area merits a visit at any season; however, the altitude and terrain can act as traps for sudden storms in most

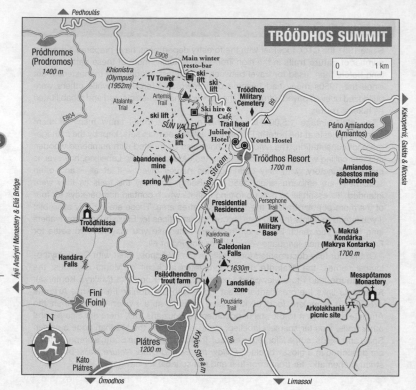

TRÖÖDHOS SUMMIT

Pródromos
(Prodromos)
1400 m

E908

Khionístra
(Olympus)
(1952m)

TV Tower

Main winter
resto-bar

ski-
lift

ski
lift

0   1 km

Atalante
Trial

Artemis
Trail

Tröödhos
Military
Cemetery

E804

ski lift

Ski hire &
Café

SUN VALLEY

P

Trail head

ski
lift

Jubilee
Hotel

Youth Hostel

Páno Amíandos
(Amiantos)

abandoned
mine

Tröödhos Resort
1700 m

Amíandos
asbestos mine
(abandoned)

spring

Kakopetriá, Galáta & Nicosia

Presidential
Residence

Persephone
Trail

Tröödhítissa
Monastery

UK
Military
Base

Makriá
Kondárka
(Makrya Kontarka)
1700 m

Kaledonia
Trail

Caledonian
Falls

Handára
Falls

Psilódhendhro
trout farm

1630m

Landslide
zone

Mesapótamos
Monastery

Finí
(Foini)

Pouziáris
Trail

Arkolakhaniá
picnic site

N

Plátres
1200 m

Káto
Plátres

▼ Ómodhos

▼ Limassol

4

months, so don't step off unprepared onto the paths. When you do, you'll find them relatively empty, except perhaps on Thursdays, which is the designated "walk day" for large groups of German coach tours.

The Tröödhos resort

The only thing resembling permanent habitation in the alpine zone is a strip of development, called **TRÓÖDHOS** (Troodos), flanking the main road junction about 1750m above sea level. By no stretch of the imagination is this a village, merely a resort complex, beset all day long in high seasons by tour coaches whose clients barely venture off the single flagstoned parade with its landscaped park (and fee car park). Public **buses** to and from here operate weekdays out of Limassol via Plátres, and also from Nicosia; the uphill morning leg of the Limassol-based bus is an excellent way for walkers to get from Plátres to here, though the downhill journey starts early, at 3.30pm.

There seems little to recommend an overnight stay here other than the pine-scented air, with just one **hotel**, the two-star *Jubilee* (℡25420107, ⓦwww .jubileehotel.com; ❹) and its attached mountain-bike rental facility. Just north of the major T-junction stands the ten-bunk **youth hostel** (closed Nov–April); alternatively, the exceedingly basic **campsite** (May–Oct), 1km northeast of the intersection on the road to Nicosia, functions primarily as a caravan park for Cypriots. Just off the "high street", the **Tröödhos Visitor Centre** (daily 10am–4pm; €0.80) justifies its admission fee with well-planned displays on the geology and (natural) history of the region, plus a ten-minute film showing; the

Skiing on Mount Olympus

No one comes to Cyprus to ski, but if you're around between New Year and the end of March, you might consider the slopes for their novelty value. Four T-bar lifts serve eight runs of 200 to 600 metres in length, none rated as difficult except one north-facing one, dubbed "Jubilee". **Snow** tends, alas, to be slushy or icy owing to warmish, sunny days alternating with freezing nights, even in the pit of winter – and there's been little skiiable snow at all in recent years. That said, on a good day immediately after a snowfall, you can get proper powder. The shorter, more southerly Sun Valley runs are considered beginners' areas, and this is where **equipment** is rented and **lessons** given; the more advanced north-facing runs are sometimes reserved for competitions, with the main **restaurant/café** at the base well poised to watch the action. For current information, contact the Ski Club in Nicosia (℡22675340) or the ski station itself for a **weather report** (℡25420104). If you're planning way in advance, ⊛www.skicyprus.com is worth a look, containing current lift ticket prices, lesson fees and equipment hire rates among other information – as well as organizing expeditions to ski in Lebanon with its more reliable snow cover.

free nature trails leaflets are most likely to be available here, as well as commercial guidebooks and postcards.

Spare a moment also for a look at the **Tróödhos Military Cemetery**, a wonderful spot on the hillside just above the road between the campsite and the youth hostel. Most of the fatalities – infants and children as well as military personnel – date from the peacetime summers of 1879 and 1885, a reminder of just how unhealthy Cyprus then was.

A summit loop-hike

Perhaps the **best high Tróödhos hike** is the circuit made possible by combining parts of the Atalante and Artemis nature trails. It can be done in half a day – slightly more if you detour towards the actual summit – and in clear weather offers among the best views of the island, as well as an attractive plant (and bird) community en route. The walk is most enjoyable in May or June, when numerous streams (and the one improved spring) are still likely to be flowing.

Itineraries **begin** at the archwayed trailhead for the Atalante trail west of the resort parade, behind the Visitor Centre. A signpost reading "Chromio 8km" is somewhat misleading: the labelled path is approximately that distance, but you never actually end up at the abandoned chromium mine in question. Your first fork is some twelve minutes out; go left, following red-dot waymarks. The proper trail skims the 1750-metre contour with little elevation change. Some forty minutes along, there's a three-way junction; ignore a wide track up the ridge to the right but not the onward trail taking off behind a wooden bench. Within ten more minutes there's a masonry fountain, running much of the year. An abandoned chromium mine shaft about ninety minutes out is often flooded and probably dangerous to explore; here shun wider tracks in favour of the narrower path hairpinning back left along the far side of the creek valley. Just under two hours along, you've a first view of Pródhromos village far to the west, and its giant, derelict Hotel Berengaria. Soon a TV tower looms overhead, then the trail becomes a track through mossy pines about ten minutes before ending, two-and-a-half hours into the hike, on the Tróödhos–Pródhromos road.

Rather than emerging onto the road, bear up and right along a **link trail** for just three minutes to the intersection with the Artemis trail, a true loop closer

▲ Walking near Mount Olympus

to the summit. It's possible to follow this to the right (anti-clockwise), but for the quickest way back to the original trailhead, take a left turn, crossing the courses of two T-bar ski lifts. Once past the second lift, there's a fine view northeast over northern Cyprus, as you progress roughly parallel to the paved road to Tróödhos. You soon meet the tarmacked side road up to Khionístra peak; cross to the nature-trail canopy opposite to stay with the path. At the next track junction bear left, keeping to path surface; three minutes along this bear left again at trees tacked with a yellow arrow and a red dot, forsaking both a track ahead down the ridge and the onward nature trail in favour of an older track dropping down into the valley on your left.

Rocks here are splashed with a few **blue dots**; followed in reverse up the hill, this blue-marked route passes a giant, labelled black pine and the top of the Sun Valley ski lift on its route to the summit area. Resuming the descent, you drop through a defile, and then the narrowing track curls back to join the Atalante trail just below the *Jubilee Hotel*. You should be back at the starting point roughly an hour and fifteen minutes from the "Chromio" end of the same path (not counting any detours to the peak), for a total walking time of well under four hours.

In recent years the Atalante trail has been properly extended on the other side of the main Tróödhos-Pródhromos paved road, so the less adventurous can opt out of all the foregoing, and follow the lower trail for a true circuit in slightly less time.

Khionístra summit

If you're intent on **visiting the peak**, it's better to arrive by car, a ten-minute drive from the resort. Scant ruins of a Venetian watchtower and an ancient temple of Aphrodite are all but invisible; what draws the eye are various electronic/surveillance installations on the very summit, which have always figured prominently in the island's geopolitical status. The right-hand (easterly) compound is one of the UK "retained sites", with its famous RAF radar "golf ball", visible for miles around (there used to be two more but they've been moved to Makriá Kondárka). The left-hand (westerly) compound is Cypriot, comprising civilian telecom and TV towers, plus a small "golf ball" built to guide the Russian SS-300 missiles (see p.403) which never arrived. There's a narrow corridor between the two bases, all of 100m long, which can be traversed for the view north, but this is sullied by electrified barbed wire and more military installations down the slope; no photography is allowed.

The Makriá Kondárka (Persephone) trail

This additional short walk is just the thing if you haven't had enough for the day, and can be extended to get you back to Plátres, as you will have almost certainly missed the afternoon bus down the hill. The path begins inconspicuously at the southeast end of the Tróödhos resort, beyond the police station; if you end up at an off-limits British base, you'll know you've missed the trailhead. At a moderate pace, the out-and-back route should take just over ninety minutes; the destination is the viewpoint of **Makriá Kondárka** (Makrya Kontarka) at 1700m, allowing unobstructed views southeast over the Limassol foothills and coastal plain. On the way back you get to look at the incongruous radar domes and telecom tower on Khionístra, as well as the huge scar of the **Amíandos (Amiantos) open-pit asbestos mine**, largest in the world, to the northeast. Owned by the Limassol bishopric, it is not exhausted but has shut down owing to a sharp drop in demand for this carcinogenic material; the site was supposed to be filled with topsoil and planted with trees, but never has been. From the viewpoint, a path heads southeast towards Plátres, joining the track to Mesapótamos about 2.5km shy of Psilódhendhro.

West of Plátres and Tróödhos

Rather than proceeding directly from Plátres or Tróödhos to the Marathássa valley, it's worth detouring slightly along one of three more roundabout, westerly routes, all converging at the alpine settlement of **Pródhromos**. The quickest of the three options, an entirely paved route from Plátres, passes above venerable **Troödhítissa monastery**, now closed to the non-Orthodox. Closer to Plátres lies workaday **Finí** village, with a dwindling crafts tradition. Rather than proceeding due north from Finí via the pleasant but nondescript hamlets of Áyios Dhimítrios and Paleómylos, veering west along partly dirt roads is justified by a trio of minor **medieval monuments** along the way.

Troödhítissa monastery

Nestled in orchards and pines 8km northwest of Plátres at about 1200m elevation, **Troödhítissa** (Panagia tis Trooditissas) is the highest working monastery in the land. It owes its thirteenth-century foundation to a wonder-working icon of the Virgin Enthroned which floated mysteriously over from Asia Minor at the height of the eighth-century Iconoclast controversy. Two hermits guarded it in a nearby cave for some years; after they had died and the memory of the relic faded, an unearthly glow alerted a succeeding generation to its presence, and a suitable home was built for the image. A marked three-minute trail up to the hallowed **cave** begins 300m east of the turn-off for the monastery; a sign in Greek reads, "to the cave in which the icon of the Virgin Troödhítissas was found". On arrival, you'll find the diminutive grotto has little palpable air of mystery, though at least it's not tastelessly gaudy; in the cascade-lashed gorge below, British forces often hone their abseiling techniques.

The present monastery buildings date mostly from 1730, and since 1996 have been out of bounds to the non-Orthodox; there's a notice to this effect at the start of the access road, and a gatehouse to vet visitors. A dozen monks live here, following the same austere regime as at Stavrovoúni (see p.103). In the **katholikón** monks traditionally encircle young women with a medallion-studded girdle, said to induce fertility – in the old days any resulting boy-child had to become a monk, or be "ransomed" from the church with a generous donation.

Finí

A paved side road just 1km up the Troödhítissa-bound highway, the F821, mysteriously never shown on maps, provides easy, fairly direct access to **FINÍ** (Foini), just 4km from Plátres. Unlike its near neighbour, this is a "normal" village with a functioning primary school, and its semi-arid landscape and domestic architecture attract few visitors. There is, however, a surviving crafts heritage, in the shape of two elderly female potters turning out an assortment of practical and kitsch wares, and the privately run **Pivlakion Museum** (daily 9am–noon & 2–5pm; donation). This is run by Theofanis Pivlakis, who personally escorts visitors through his collection of rural oddments while talking the hind legs off a donkey for up to two hours – you have been warned. Though enormous *pithária* (olive-oil jars) are no longer made commercially here, a number of older specimens, with date stamps just above their middle, are exhibited. Fashioned by a wheel-less method, they were built upwards from a knob at the base, like a swallow's nest. The only other local "sight" is the **Handára** (Chantara) **waterfall**, 2km uphill along a dirt track; follow signs towards the trout farm.

In the village centre are a few simple grills and *kafenía*, and Finí also has a famous producer of **loukoúmi** ("Cyprus" Delight) – claimed the best in the region – but both the full-service restaurants are unmemorable or worse.

Áyii Anáryiri and Elía bridge

Some 2km west of Finí on the narrow paved road to Paleómylos, a sign by a small cement wayside shrine points down a dirt track towards **Áyii Anáryiri** (Agioi Anargyroi) a fifteenth-century monastic church, in a lovely setting surrounded by orchards. An eerie legend attaches to the place, specifically that on Saturday at dusk a ghostly horseman emerges through the dog-toothed west portal, the oldest surviving portion of the building. A new, locking door has been fitted, presumably resistant to spectral dashes, yet Áyii Anáryiri seems an altogether unlikely spot for hauntings. It is probably not worth hunting down the key to glimpse the few surviving, late-medieval frescoes within.

Just past the Áyii Anáryiri wayside shrine, bear left (west) onto a rough but passable dirt track; after 7.5km, you'll reach another junction on the paved Kaminária–Kélefos road. Very nearby stands the single-arched **Elía bridge** (signposted as "Gefyri tis El(a)ias"), the easterly link in the Venetian caravan route (see p.199). Though smaller and less impressive than the Kélefos and Roúdhias bridges to the west, the little bridge enjoys a fine position amid dense forest, with a perennial brook flowing underneath.

Kaminária and Pródhromos

From the Elía bridge, a broad paved road leads west towards Kélefos and Áyios Nikólaos village (see p.202); going north, the road – still paved but narrower – reaches within 5km the friendly, surprisingly large village of **KAMINÁRIA**.

On a knoll west of the village is the early sixteenth-century **chapel of Panayía**, with contemporaneous frescoes. Ask at the central *kafenío* or the *soúvla* taverna opposite for the priest-with-key, and expect to return here for a post-viewing coffee.

Although it cannot compare with the best painted churches of the Tróodhos, Panayía is compelling enough. The most interesting surviving paintings include, on the north wall, the donor family in Lusignan-influenced dress; *The Sacrifice of Isaac* inside the *ierón*; Saint Mamas on his lion on the west wall; and, as part of *The Crucifixion*, a weeping, crouching Virgin, with two friends standing behind – entirely western imagery imported into late-Byzantine iconography.

Along with Páno Amíandos, **PRÓDHROMOS** (Prodromos) is the highest true village in the country at 1400m elevation. It's also noted for its apples and cherries, the trees ablaze with blossom in spring, but they're being uprooted and replaced (lower down the mountain) with olives, a move subsidized by the government in its desire to fall in line with EU policy, with the result that Cyprus now has to import apples. The most interesting item here is the rambling, hilltop **Hotel Berengaria**, built as one of the first "modern" Cypriot lodgings during the 1920s but abandoned in 1980. A foreign consortium intended to convert it to a casino, but accomplished little other than repeatedly reroofing it after arsonists set fires; the general dereliction of the place, now all but a write-off, makes it an oddly haunting relic of the British empire. The village itself has little more for casual trade, with just one or two shops and a **petrol pump** at its top end. **Eating** opportunities comprise a handful of carniverous *exokhiká kéndra* near the main ridgetop crossroads, strategically placed to cater for pilgrims to Kýkko.

Marathássa

Directly north over the ridge from Pródhromos yawns **Marathássa** (Marathasa), a deep canyon of Asiatic grandeur. Like most watercourses on the north side of the Tróodhos, the Setrákhos stream draining it runs into North Cyprus, and a dam has been built to rescue the water that would otherwise go unharnessed into "enemy" territory. Marathássa is famous for its cherry orchards, from which it makes a partial living (though as noted above, their days may be numbered); tourism, while catered to, is not the be-all and end-all that it is at Plátres. The valley can boast a respectable concentration of frescoed churches, and though not strictly speaking within Marathássa, the prestigious **Kýkko monastery** is easiest reached from here.

Pedhoulás

At the top of the Marathássa valley, 1100m up, compact **PEDHOULÁS** (Pedoulas) is amphitheatrically laid out in tiers, though close up most of the buildings are not so attractive, even if a vogue for pointing their stonework has begun. Somewhat unusually for a Tróodhos village, it has an unobstructed view of the sea to the north on clear days. As a base it's a viable alternative to Plátres, both for convenience to Marathassan sights and for the range of choice in eating and sleeping.

Arkhángelos Mihaïl church and Byzantine Museum

The main sight, and quite possibly your first frescoed church of the Tróodhos, is **Arkhángelos Mihaïl** (Archangelos Michail), well signposted in the lower quarter of the village (admission through key-keeper, phone number posted on door). The core of the church dates from 1474, so the images (cleaned in 1980 and again in 2008) depart from the austerity of earlier work in favour of the naturalism of the post-Byzantine revival. The archangel Michael himself looms left (north) of the minimalist *témblon*; inside the *ierón*, or priestly quarters, is *The Sacrifice of Abraham*, with the principals of the potentially gruesome drama radiating a hieratic serenity. Starting on the south wall, there's a clockwise life-cycle of the Virgin and Christ. *The Baptism* features the River Jordan stylized like a throw-rug with fish embedded in it; in *The Betrayal* a miniature Peter lops off the ear of the high priest's servant, here in Crusader dress, while two apostles cense the Virgin's bier in *The Assumption*. Over the north door, donor Basil Khamadhes and his family, in noble costume of the period, hand a model of the church to the archangel, who emerges from a curtain-like fold of cloud next to the dedicatory inscription. Above *The Virgin Orans* in the apse looms a smudged *Ascension*, in lieu of the usual *Pandokrátor*.

A **Byzantine Museum** just opposite (daily: April–Oct 9.30am–1pm & 2–6pm; Nov–March closes 5pm; €1.70) contains a fine collection of local icons and ecclesiastical artefacts.

Practicalities

There are two **banks** (but no ATMs). The daily market **bus** on the Nicosia–Plátres line passes through here very early in the morning heading downhill, returning at lunchtime. Three modest **hotels** in the village centre, all on the main through road, all comparably priced, vie for your custom. *Christy's Palace* (☎22952655; ❷) is spartan rather than palatial, though centrally heated for all-year operation. *Two Flowers* (☎22952372; ❷), more or less opposite *Christy's Palace*, and *Mountain Rose* (☎22952727; ❷) have also had good reader reports. However, when **dining**, it's best to avoid the unseemly lunchtime scrums of the coach-tour and jeep-safari groups at *Mountain Rose* and *Two Flowers*, where microwaving or serving independent travellers the leftovers are common ploys. Top choice, at midday at least, is perennial *To Vrysi* (alias *Harry's*), a shady and authentic *exokhikó kéndro* on a minor road up to the main highway, open daily most of the year. This features Arsos red wine, home-style dishes such as pickled wild mushrooms, occasional white-fleshed wild trout (as opposed to the pink farmed variety) and a full spectrum of candied fruits and vegetables. It's not rock-bottom cheap, but portions are generous, so show up hungry.

Kýkko monastery and around

Nineteen paved but twisty kilometres west of Pedhoulás sits the enormous, fabulously wealthy **monastery of Kýkko** (Panagia tis Kykkou, *Tchýkou* in dialect), one of the most celebrated in the Orthodox world. Here Michael Mouskos, better known as Makarios III, began his secondary education, and later served as a novice monk, prior to using the monastery as a hideout during his EOKA days (when Grivas's headquarters were nearby). Thus Kýkko is inextricably linked with the Cypriot nationalist struggle.

Despite these hallowed associations, the place is of negligible artistic or archi-tectural interest; repeated fires since Kýkko's twelfth-century foundation by the hermit Isaiah have left nothing older than 1831, and the garish mosaics and frescoes lining every corridor and the *katholikón*, however well intentioned, are workmanlike and of recent vintage, some as new as 1987. Isaiah had been given an **icon** of the Panayía Eleoússa, the Most Merciful Virgin, by the Byzantine emperor Alexios Komnenos in gratitude for curing the latter's daughter. The monastery grew up around this relic, claimed to have been painted by

Luke the Evangelist, which now has pride of place in a rather gaudy shrine in front of the *témblon* or altar screen. Considered too holy for the casual glances of the impious and unworthy, who would run the risk of a most unmerciful instantaneous blinding, the original image has been encased in silver for almost four centuries now. Nearby in the *katholikón* is a brass arm, said to be that of a blasphemous Turk who had it so rendered by Virgin while sacrilegiously attempting to light his cigarette from a lamp in the sanctuary.

On weekends Kýkko is to be avoided (or gravitated towards, according to your temperament), when thousands of Cypriots descend upon the place. A ban on photos or videoing inside, enforced against the heterodox, is cheerfully ignored by proud relatives snapping the relay baptisms which dominate Saturdays and Sundays; lottery ticket-sellers circulate out in the courtyard as howling babies are plunged one after another into the steaming font. Monks at more austere monasteries ridicule the practice – what's the matter with one's local parish church for christening your child, they say – but this ignores the tremendous prestige of Kýkko, and the ease of access from Nicosia.

Besides the pilgrimage activities, there's a worthwhile **museum** of ecclesiastical treasures adjoining the inner courtyard (daily: Oct–May 10am–4pm; June–Sept 10am–6pm; €2.55). At Room 13, to the right of the main gate of the outer courtyard, you can request a room in the enormous *xenónas* or **guest quarters** if you're Orthodox Christian. The overpriced, listless fare in the nearby "tourist restaurant" is eminently avoidable; eat in a mountain village en route, or bring your own snack.

Thróni and the EOKA hideouts

The longish, scenic trip in from Pedhoulás to Kýkko is much of the attraction; it can be prolonged by another 2km to a final car park below **Throní**, a hill topped by the **tomb of Makarios**, a bunker-like capsule, with the main opening to the west and a National Guardsman keeping a permanent vigil. A modern **shrine** just south adorns the true summit, which allows comprehensive views of the empty Tillyrian hills to the west, and Mount Olympus to the east; in many ways it's a better vantage point than the latter. On the yearly festival (Sept 7–8) the icon of Kýkko is paraded to the shrine and back amid prayers for a rainy winter. The stark concrete design of the chapel is further offset by a **wish-tree** (more accurately, wish-bush) on which the faithful have tied votive hankies, tissues and streamers as petitions for more personal favours from the Virgin.

About 3km before arrival at Kýkko, a small brown-and-white sign by the roadside points right (north) to "EOKA hideouts, 2km". A curvy, one-lane track – just negotiable in a saloon car – leads to a clearing where some of the EOKA bunkers have been preserved, more or less in their original state. Still further uphill is the main HQ, reached by a steep path with a loose shale surface – take care on the descent in particular. All this glorification of EOKA and its doings is part and parcel of the tide of Hellenic nationalism which has engulfed the South since the early 1990s.

Wilderness road to Pólis

Just before Kýkko, where the E912 peels off to the north, signs beg you to head north 9km to visit **Kámbos** (Kampos), the only substantial habitation in Tillyría, poised in isolation about halfway down the slope towards the Attila Line. It's a scenic, untouristed spot, with the locals fairly unused to foreign visitors – you'll have celebrity value at the single café. **Chakístra** (Tsakistra), 2km before, lives primarily from its sawmills, while in spring the valley floor here is a mass of white cherry blossom. However, at the time of writing, there was no licensed accommodation or working full-service tavernas in the area.

Between Kýkko junction and Chakístra, about 3km below the former, there's another prominently signposted forking for the paved **road** west, then north, towards various attractions in Tillyría. As per the placard, it's 10km to the Cedar Valley, 22km to Stavrós tís Psókas, 52km to Káto Pýrgos, and 56km to Pólis. But don't let the asphalt and nominal distances lull you into taking the drive lightly; the forestry department forbade straightening of the bends when the road (still subject to rockfalls) was surfaced, and howling wilderness prevails between the destinations cited, so be prepared for up to two hours of fairly strenuous driving. Another route, marginally faster, from beyond Kámbos to Pomós via Káto Pýrgos, is described on p.186.

South to Milikoúri and the Eliá/Kélefos bridges

Much the most enjoyable return from the Kýkko area to Plátres is via remote **Milikoúri** (Mylikouri; no facilities) village, near the head of the beautiful Platýs valley. One of the wildest in the Tróödhos, alive with springs and rivulets (a picnic area takes advantage of these), the valley has been saved from a proposed dam but is now threatened by a planned E-standard road up from Áyios Nikólaos in Páfos district, as this is the most likely route. After about 14km of fairly easy driving, you emerge on the paved road between the two historic bridges of Eliá and Kélefos, a bit closer to the latter.

Moutoullás: Panayía toú Moutoullá

The earliest surviving example of the Tróödhos pitched-roof church, **Panayía (Panagia) toú Moutoullá** (constructed in 1280), stands next to the cemetery at the highest point of **MOUTOULLÁS** village, 3km below Pedhoulás. A stone-paved ramp leads up from the end of the marked, dirt-surface side road to the church. The warden is Kostas Grigoriou, contactable by phone on ☎99337572, or in his **kafenío/taverna** on the main road, the only facility here. You enter via two sets of doors, the outer pair piercing the protective structure grown up around the original church, the inner ones (and the altar screen) very fine, carved antique pieces. The village is still renowned for its carved feed-troughs and other utilitarian objects, as well as its spring water, bottled down in the canyon.

On the original exterior wall of the church, now enclosed by the L-shaped "narthex", Christ is enthroned over the inner doors, flanked by Adam and Eve, Hell and Paradise (with the saints marching into the latter). Inside, the cycle of events is similar to that of Arkhángelos Míhaïl in Pedhoulás, but less complete, and stopping with the Assumption rather than the Ascension; it seems that the British, while engaged in an anti-EOKA raid, damaged many scenes. An unusual Nativity on the south wall shows the Virgin rocking the Christ Child in his cradle (she's usually still reclining after having given birth), while Joseph sits on a wooden donkey saddle much like ones that were formerly produced in the village. An equally rare martial Áyios Khristóforos (Saint Christopher) stands opposite Áyios Yeóryios (Saint George) on the north wall, slaying a dragon with the torso and crowned head of a woman. On the west wall, the Raising of Lazarus includes the obligatory spectator holding his nose against the reek of the tomb; on the north wall, there's a rather stiff portrait of donor Ioannis Moutoullas and his wife. Overall, the images don't rank as the most expressive in the Tróödhos, but are the earliest, unretouched frescoes around.

Frescoed churches of the Tróödhos

Indisputably the most remarkable monuments in the Tróödhos, if not the whole island, are a group of lavishly **frescoed Byzantine churches**, predominantly on the north slopes of the range. Almost every mountain village has such a pitched-roof church – but only a very few are still painted inside. Strictly speaking, few of the **paintings** were actually executed with true fresco technique (in which pigment is applied while the plaster is still wet), so they should more accurately be termed wall paintings or murals; this guide refers to them as frescoes for convenience. The earliest date from the eleventh century, with church construction continuing until the early 1500s; murals were applied sporadically over the whole period and serve as a chronicle of changing dress styles and artistic tastes, often juxtaposed in the same building. For further analysis of these images, and their relationship to the idiosyncratic form of the buildings sheltering them, see the colour section *Sacred art and architecture*.

Architecturally, most of the churches were originally simple rectangular structures about the size of a small barn; later they often developed domes, less frequently narthexes. If it didn't originally exist, an all-encompassing, drastically pitched roof would eventually be added to shed heavy snow, with ample allowance for protruding domes if necessary. Most importantly, by extending down to the ground on one or both sides, they enclosed L- or U-shaped spaces which *de facto* served as narthexes, so that many frescoed exterior walls were now afforded some protection.

The way to most of these churches is **well signposted** from the main roads, and many are proudly identified on wall plaques as being listed on the UNESCO World Cultural Heritage roster – and kept firmly **locked**. Thus hunting down the key is an integral part of your visit; usually the contact name and number for the key-keeper and permissible visiting hours are posted (and repeated in this guide). Sometimes the **caretaker** is a layman who lives nearby, otherwise a peripatetic priest who can take some time to arrive, as he could be responsible for conducting liturgies at several neighbourhood churches. The most noteworthy churches now have set hours during which they are supposed to be open. Caretakers vary in terms of knowledgeability (none is a trained guide, few speak much English) and cordiality; while there is usually no set admission fee, a **donation** is expected, especially in cases where you've taken the key-keeper miles out of his (sometimes her) daily routine. Usually a box is provided in the church; otherwise you should tip the responsible person at the conclusion of your visit. A euro per person is sufficient for a small church where the guard lives next door, two to three euro per small group for a large monument off in the woods. In most churches **photography** of any sort is strictly forbidden, though enforcement of this rule varies – videoing tends to be looked on with more favour than still cameras with flash, which degrades the pigments. Accordingly, **lighting** is often feeble, and keepers can be reluctant to switch it on (much less open doors) for heathens.

If you're keen, you can see all of the churches in a few days. If your interest is more casual, three or four will suffice – the most important are reckoned to be Asínou, Áyios Ioánnis Lambadhistís, Áyios Nikólaos tís Stéyis, Panayía toú Araká and Stavrós toú Ayiasmáti. Should you develop a compulsive interest in the subject, an indispensable **specialist guide** is *The Painted Churches of Cyprus*, by Andreas and Judith Stylianou. Currently out of print, it's set to be reissued; Moufflon Books in Nicosia (see p.263) or rare-book websites should have current information. For a glossary of theological, artistic and architectural terms, see p.464.

Kalopanayiótis and around

Just over 1km further down the Setrákhos valley from Moutoullás, **KALOPA-NAYIÓTIS** (Kalopanagiotis) seems a bit less concrete than Pedhoulás and more geared to tourists, and is the most compact of the three villages – though it has a suburb hamlet, Íkos (alias Níkos, officially Oikos), downstream and across the river. Many old handsome houses have retained their tiled roofs, and there are fine views up-valley to Pedhoulás. The village is thought to be the successor of ancient Lampadhou, which produced the saints Iraklidhios and Ioannis (see below for the latter). There are also two fine old **bridges** in the area: one next to the local sulphur springs, the other just upstream from the local reservoir and below Íkos, still serving a little-used medieval trail descending from Íkos to the west bank of the valley. A marked trail leads within thirty minutes from the monastic church to Íkos, making a loop-hike possible. Some 4km west of Íkos and Kalopanayiótis lies **YERAKIÉS** (Gerakies), a quiet, traditional village with two **kafenío-restaurants** in the centre, and a short-loop **nature trail**, the "Ariadni", taking off just west from the brow of a ridge.

Three no-star **hotels** here function, if at all, in high summer only. More reliably open is the agrotourism offering just down the access road to the monastic church, *Olga's Katoi* (℡22952432 or 22350283; ❷), where the original main house provides the lounge and self-catering facilities for the annexe rooms. For **meals**, you're restricted to two main-road kebab houses.

Áyios Ioánnis Lambadhistís

Plainly visible from Kalopanayiótis across the river, and accessible by a one-kilometre side road or a more direct footbridge (or by paved lane from Íkos), the rambling **monastery of Áyios Ioánnis Lambadhistís** (Agios Ioannis Lampadistis; Tues–Sun 9am–noon & 1–4pm) is probably the successor to a pagan shrine, owing its foundation to some cold sulphur springs just upstream. The saint in question is not John the Evangelist, but a local eleventh-century ascetic who died young, and to whose tomb were ascribed healing powers. This is one of the few Tróödhos monasteries to have survived relatively intact from foundation days – many of the painted churches are lonely *katholiká* bereft of long-vanished cloisters, and those monasteries that still exist have been renovated beyond recognition over the centuries. If the courtyard and church doors are not open during the stated hours, ring the caretaker-priest Father Andhreas on ℡99476149 – though at weekends, even off-season, he's likely to be on-site.

Huddled together under a single, huge, pitched roof are three **churches** built to an odd plan, their aggregate south-to-north width much greater than their lengths. The double main nave, one part dedicated to Iraklidhios during the eleventh century, the other to Ioannis a hundred years later (though redone after a collapse in the mid-1700s), is entered from the south side; other doors lead beyond to a later narthex and a northerly Latin chapel added towards the end of the fifteenth century.

By virtue of the building's sheer size, there is room for nearly complete coverage of the synoptic gospels, including a number of duplications as a result of the **frescoes** having been added in stages between the thirteenth and fifteenth centuries. The *Pandokrátor* in the dome of the nave dedicated to Iraklidhios, and panels over the side entrance, are the oldest frescoes.

The earlier subjects are the usual locally favoured ones, with slight variations: in the Resurrection, Christ only lifts Adam, and not Eve, from Hell, and the Sacrifice of Abraham is idiosyncratic in its position on the south wall rather than in the *ierón*. There are several versions of Christ before Pilate, and two versions of the Raisings of Lazarus from obviously different eras, both on the south side of the nave. As so frequently in Tróödhos frescoes, children – here wearing black gloves – shimmy up a date palm for a better view of *Vaïofóros* or Entry into Jerusalem, where Christ rides side-saddle on a rather grouchy-looking ass.

The later frescoes of the northerly Latin chapel constitute the most complete Italo-Byzantine series on the island, and it seems almost certain that the native Cypriot painter had stayed for some time in Italy. Most panels take as their theme the *Akathistos* hymn in praise of the Virgin, with 24 stanzas (and thus 24 scenes) beginning each with a letter of the Greek alphabet. By the small apse, the naturalized Arrival of the Magi shows the backs of all three galloping off, on horses turned to face you, as if part of the background to a Renaissance canvas, not the main subject. The Roman soldiery in several panels not only wear Crusader armour, but fly pennants with a red crescent, apparently a Roman symbol, and then a Byzantine one, before being adopted by the Turks. In *The Hospitality of Abraham*, one of a few exceptions here to the *Akathistos* theme, the patriarch washes the feet of three decidedly Florentine angels prior to serving them at table.

Also in the monastery grounds is a **Byzantine Museum** (Tues–Sun: March–May & Sept 9.30am–5pm; June–Aug 9.30am–7pm; Oct–Feb 10am–3.30pm; €0.80), containing many rare and high-quality icons, the best and oldest (twelfth to thirteenth century) – for example the Virgin and Child by the door of the first gallery – from the monastery itself.

Soléa

The region of **Soléa**, centred on the Karyótis stream valley, was the Tróödhos' most important late-Byzantine stronghold, as witnessed by its large concentration of churches. The terrain is much less precipitous than adjacent Marathássa on the west, from which Soléa is accessible by a steep but completely paved road, taking off from the main highway between Pródhromos and Pedhoulás. **Kakopetriá** is Soléa's chief village and showcase, conveniently close to several frescoed churches, but a number of small hamlets, in varying states of preservation, are scattered downstream and worth a visit.

Kakopetriá

KAKOPETRIÁ, "Wicked Rock-Pile", takes its name from a rash of boulders which originally studded the ridge on which the village was first built. Most were removed, but some had to stay, including the **Pétra toú Andhroyínou** (Couple's Rock), a particular outcrop on which newlyweds used to clamber for good luck – until one day the monolith heaved itself up and crushed an unlucky pair to death. Low enough at 660m elevation to be very warm in the summer, Kakopetriá was formerly a wine- and silk-production centre, but is now a fashionable resort, the closest Tróödhos watering hole to Nicosia (from where regular buses call). Kakopetriá is busy enough to support two **bank ATMs**, a **post office** (Mon–Fri 9.30am–1.30pm & Thurs 3–6pm) and a 24-hour **petrol pump**.

The village straddles the river, which lends some character, as does the officially protected (and not yet too twee) old quarter. This was built on a long ridge splitting the stream in two; a preservation order was slapped on it in 1976, but a few new buildings apparently got in after it went into effect. Derelict traditional dwellings were salvaged by the Department of Antiquities between 1979 and 1986, and subsequently bought up at premium prices and further done up by Nicosians and foreigners, a process continuing briskly today. Down in the western streambed, across a medieval bridge, hides an old water-powered grain mill, also refurbished with an adjacent drink stall.

Accommodation

A half-dozen ordinary **hotels** are grouped east of the river on Gríva Dhiyení and Ayíou Mámmandos, but they are relatively poor value and have little character. Unlicensed **rooms** are available at *Dimos* (☏22922343; ❷), up past the old quarter on the minor road to Áyios Nikólaos tís Stéyis (see opposite), or in the old quarter itself on the single "high street" under the *Kafenio Serenity*, overlooking the stream ravine (☏22922602 or 22922810; ❷).

If money's no object, much the best choice in town is the 22-unit ✻ *Linos Inn*, at the heart of the old quarter (☏22923161, ⓦwww.linos-inn.com.cy; B&B rooms ❹, suites/studios ❺; reservations essential weekends & summer). Opened in 1997, this rambling restoration complex of knocked-together houses comprises a mix of standard doubles, suites and self-catering studios, all with antique furnishings, plus mod cons such as jacuzzis (there's also a communal sauna). The five newest units occupy a restored annexe a few paces towards the river and are probably the best-appointed on the island, with original architectural features preserved where possible.

The only thing comparable to Linos comfort-wise is the 2001-inaugurated *Mill Hotel* (☏22922536, ⓦwww.cymillhotel.com; closed mid-Nov to mid-Dec; ❸ standard, ❺ suites), an enormous, mock-trad multistorey building across the river. A lift whisks you from the riverbank to the three grades of lodging; accommodation consists of either standard rooms, junior suites or full suites, the latter two generous-sized and suitable for three or four, with balconies and tasteful furnishings running to terracotta tiles and marble trim.

Eating and drinking

There's a pleasant bar-café (noon until late) between the two lodging units at the *Linos Inn*, while the in-house **restaurant** is massively popular at weekends, when diners spill out onto the garden terrace. It's been somewhat eclipsed by the affiliated *Mesostrato* (weekends only off-season), just up the lane at no. 47, a *mezé* house with excellent fare (home-made sausages, *kolokýthia me avgá*, ravioli) at set-price (allow €30 for 2 plus drink), and a welcome fire during winter.

▲ Linos Inn, Kakopetriá

However the best, and best-value old-town eatery is ✗ *To Tziellari* at no. 70, with another fireplace and Olde Worlde interior, a pleasant lane-side terrace, and excellent starters complemented by Argentine-style grilled chops and sausages (the ex-UN chef is Argentinian). Reservations are advised on ☎ 22463738 (Fri–Sun winter, Tues–Sun otherwise).

Áyios Nikólaos tís Stéyis

The engaging church of **Áyios Nikólaos tís Stéyis** (Agios Nikolaos tis Stegis) stands 3km above Kakopetriá, just off the paved road over to Marathássa. Once part of a monastery, it is now isolated at the edge of the archdiocese's YMCA-type camp and recreation centre. You cannot drive up to it, but must walk through a gate and turnstile, then along a path skirting the playing pitch. When the church is open (Tues–Sat 9am–4pm, Sun 11am–4pm; donation), the charming, English-speaking warden, Spyridhoula, will give an informative tour.

The core of the church, with some of the oldest frescoes in the Tróödhos, dates from the eleventh century. A dome and narthex were added a hundred years later, and during the fifteenth century an unusually extravagant protective roof (*tís Stéyis* means "of the Roof") was superimposed on the earlier domed cross-in-square plan. As so often, the frescoes are dated to various periods from the eleventh century to (in the south transept) the fourteenth and fifteenth, thereby spanning all schools from the traditional to post-Byzantine revival.

The most unusual, later images are found in the transept: the north side has a Crucifixion with a personified sun and moon weeping, and an unusual *Myrrofóri* (spice-bearers at the sepulchre), with the angel sitting atop Christ's empty tomb, proclaiming Christ's resurrection to the two Marys (Magdalene and the mother of James) and Martha. The Nativity in the south transept vault shows the Virgin breast-feeding the Child with a symbolic, anatomically incorrect teat – icons of the subject (*Panayía Galaktotrofoússa*) abound but frescoes are rare, mostly confined to Coptic Egypt. Around her goats gambol and shepherds play bagpipe and flute, while a precociously wizened duplicate infant Jesus is given a bath by two serving-maids.

Opposite the Nativity unfolds the locally more favoured ordeal of the Forty Holy Martyrs, Christian soldiers in the Roman army tortured by immersion in a freezing lake at Anatolian Sebastaea. One, weakening in resolve, heads for the shore, but a Roman guard, overcome with admiration for the Christians, is seen shedding his tunic to join them. At the top of the image are rows of martyrs' crowns, descending from heaven to the condemned. The tale of the Forty Martyrs, with its moral of solidarity, constancy and endurance of pain, was a favourite among the officers of the Byzantine army. The warrior saints Yeóryios and Theódhoros (George and Theodore), in Crusader dress, brandish their panoply of arms on one column of the nave.

On the ceiling of the main vault, the Transfiguration is juxtaposed with the Raising of Lazarus on a single panel; in the former, three disciples cower in fear at the base of strange mountains reminiscent of volcanic Cappadocia, while in the latter scene Mary, the sister of Lazarus, is clutching Christ's foot.

Galáta

Around 1500m north of Kakopetriá, **GALÁTA** is a more aesthetic village, the through road lined with handsome old buildings sporting second-storey balustrades. Just 2km further down the valley, the best example of these is an old **kháni** or wayfarers' inn, between the turnings for Kaliána and Temvriá.

Keep an eye peeled for a modern *kafenío*; the old inn is three buildings beyond, on the same side of the road. Galáta's notable **churches** are numerous, scattered and – as usual – locked. You'll need a vehicle to chauffeur yourself and the current key-keeper, Kostas Papakonstandinou, around (☎99985049; 9am–noon & 1–4pm only).

Arkhángelos and Panayía tís Podhíthou

The road from the east side of the bridge leads north about a kilometre to the adjacent sixteenth-century churches of Panayía tís Podhíthou and Arkhángelos, the most notable of several in and around Galáta. The former was once part of a monastery, but today both stand alone, amid springtime beanfields, on the east bank of the river.

Dating from 1514, **Arkhángelos** (Archangelos), the first and smaller church, is also known as Panayía (Panagia) Theotókou, but referred to here by the former tag to avoid confusion with a nearby namesake (see below). The interior adheres to local conventions as to style and choice of episodes, featuring an unusually complete life of Christ, with such scenes as the Agony in Gethsemane, the Washing of the Disciples' Feet and Peter's Denial, with crowing cock; fish peer out of the River Jordan in the Baptism. The chronological sequence begins with the Prayer of Joachim (the Virgin's father) near the door, finishing with the Redemption of Adam. Most unusually the signature of the painter, Simeon Axenti, can be seen in the panel depicting the donor Zacharia family, who were of Hellenized Venetian and Lusignan background, the women following the Catholic rite, the men adhering to Orthodoxy. Such arrangements were not uncommon in formerly Byzantine territories captured by the West.

The unusual shape of **Panayía tís Podhíthou** (Panagia tis Podythou), built in 1502, dictates an equally unconventional arrangement of its cartoon-like panels, which were never completed. Abbreviated lives of the Virgin and Christ are relegated to the *ierón*. In the apse, Solomon and David stand to either side of the Italo-Byzantine Communion of the Apostles; at the top of the pediment formed by the roofline, the Burning Bush is revealed to Moses. The walnut *témblon* itself, complete with gargoyles from which lamps are hung, is magnificent despite its icons having been variously stolen or taken to Nicosia for restoration.

Above the west entry door, its favoured position, there's a very detailed, Italianate *Crucifixion*, complete with the two thieves, the Virgin fainting, Mary Magdalene with loose hair at the foot of the Cross and the soldier about to pierce Christ's side. Indeed the sense of tumult and vulgar spectacle is totally un-Byzantine; onlookers' dress, demeanour and facial features are highly differentiated, and approach caricature at times (for similar treatment, see the church at Vyzakiá, p.228). Out in the U-shaped "narthex", created by the later addition of the peaked roof, the donor Dhimitrios de Coron and his wife stand left of the Redemption; above this the Virgin Enthroned appears in the company of various Old Testament prophets, rather than with the usual Fathers of the Church as at neighbouring Arkhángelos.

Áyios Sozómenos and Panayía Theotókou

If you wish, the same key-keeper will accompany you to **Áyios (Agios) Sozómenos**, 50m behind and uphill from Galáta's big modern church. Its iconography is very similar to that of Arkhángelos – hardly surprising since the artist (Axenti) and construction date are identical. The frescoes are numerous but relatively crude, and can't compare with those at Podhíthou or Arkhángelos.

However, there are some wonderful touches: in the lower echelons of saints on the north wall, the dragon coils his tail around the hind legs of Saint George's charger as he's dispatched; a maiden chained at the lower right demonstrates how the tale is a reworking of the Perseus and Andromeda myth. Saint Sozomenos himself, a fifth-century Syrian hermit, appears in a niche over the north door. On the south wall, Saint Mamas holds his lamb as he rides an anthropomorphized lion (see p.235 for an explanation). Overhead, the original painted wooden struts are still intact (they've rotted away in most other churches); behind the *témblon* is a *Pentecost* on the left, in addition to the typical episodes of Abraham's life to either side of the apse. Out in the U-shaped narthex, there's a damaged Apocalypse left of the door, while various ecumenical councils (complete with heretics being banished) meet on the other side.

The early sixteenth-century **Panayía (Panagia) Theotókou** flanks the road up to Kakopetriá opposite a butcher's, where the key is kept; the interior preserves an unusually large panel of the Assumption, with Christ holding the Virgin's infant soul, plus a Pentecost and a fine Angel at the Sepulchre. Behind the handsome *témblon*, the Hospitality of Abraham is offered on the right, with a cow lowing for its calf, and his vivid attempted Sacrifice opposite. In the apse conch, the Virgin Enthroned reigns over the six *Ierárkhi* (Fathers of the Church) below, while over the entrance, the donors, Leontios and Loukretia, huddle with a half-dozen others.

Asínou (Panayía Forviótissa)

Arguably the finest of the Tróödhos churches, **Asínou** (Panayía Forviótissa) lies out in the middle of nowhere, but emphatically justifies the detour off the B9 Kakopetriá–Nicosia road. Unless you have a 4WD vehicle, don't be tempted by the twelve-kilometre "shortcut" from Áyios Theódhoros village to Asínou – this forest track is pretty rough, and you won't save much time in any case. The key-priest, Father Kirykos, lives in the nearby village of **NIKITÁRI**, reached via Koutrafás or Vyzakiá; you can ring him on ☎ 22852922 or 99689327, or call in at Nikitári's central *kafenío*, though he will probably be at the **church**, 4km above Nikitári, during its formal opening hours (Mon–Sat: Jan & Feb 9.30am–1pm, March–Dec 9am–1pm; also March & April 2–4.30pm, May & June 2–5.30pm, July & Aug 2–6pm, Sept & Oct 2–5pm, Nov–Feb 2–4pm; plus all year Sun 10am–1pm & 2–4pm; donation).

The popular, less formal name of the church stems from the ancient town of Asinou, founded by Greeks from Peloponnesian Asine but long since vanished; the same fate has befallen any monastery which might have once stood here, leaving only a half-dozen *exokhiká kéndra* in the immediate vicinity – surely surplus to requirements, though the beautiful countryside does make for an ideal Sunday outing. *Panayía Forviótissa* may mean "Our Lady of the Pastures", though only the church-crowned hilltop is treeless, with forested river valley all around; another derivation has it as "Our Lady of the Milkwort" – botanical epithets of the Virgin are common on Cyprus. A barrel-vaulted nave, remod-elled during the fourteenth century, dates originally from 1105; an unusual narthex with dome and two bays was added a century later, giving the church a "backwards" orientation from the norm. The frescoes span several centuries from 1105–06 to the early 1500s.

The interior

Many of the myriad **panels** in the nave were skilfully redone in the fourteenth or fifteenth century, while the nave's vaulted **ceiling** is segmented into recesses by two arches: one at the apse, the other about two-thirds of the way west towards the narthex door. In the westernmost recess, the Forty Martyrs of Sebastaea on the north curve seem more natural than those at Áyios Nikólaos tís Stéyis, despite their crowns floating down from Heaven; the Holy Spirit also descends at the Pentecost overhead, and Lazarus is raised on the south of the same curve. In the middle recess, the life of Christ from the Nativity to the Resurrection is related; here the Crucifixion is treated as just one panel of many, not as in higher, barn-like churches where it often dominates the triangular pediment over the door. Generally, the fresco style is highly sophisticated and vivid: Saint Tryphon on one arch could be a portrait from life of a local shepherd, while the three *Myrrofóri* in the north recess recoil in visible alarm from the admonishing angel. In the apse, an almost imploring twelfth-century Virgin raises her hands in benediction, flanked by the two archangels, while to either side Christ offers the wine in the Communion of the Apostles (save for Judas, who slinks away). Over the south door, the builder Nikiforos Mayistros presents a model of the church to Christ in a panel dated 1105 by its dedicatory inscription, while a fine Dormition of the Virgin hovers over the west door of the nave.

The **narthex frescoes** are of the fourteenth century, with wonderful whimsical touches. On the arch of the door to the nave, a pair of hunting hounds tied to a stake and their moufflon quarry make an appearance, heralds of the Renaissance as Byzantine iconography has no place for dogs. In the shell of the north bay, Earth (riding on a lion) and Sea (upon a water monster) are personified; in the opposite bay, the donors appear again, praying in period dress before a naturalistic Virgin and Child, above an equestrian Saint George and the lion-mounted Saint Mamas. Below the Earth and the Sea, Saint Peter advances to open the Gates of Paradise, while the patriarchs Abraham, Isaac and Jacob wait to one side. In the cupola the *Pandokrátor* presides over the Twelve Apostles, with the Blessed and the Damned depicted on arches to either side.

Vyzakiá: Arkhángelos Mikhaïl

It's well worth continuing down-valley to **VYZAKIÁ**, 6.5km away in total via Nikitári, to see the crude but vividly unique images in the little post-Byzantine church of **Arkhángelos Mikhaïl**. This stands just west of the stream running past the village, on the north side of the road, but you'll have to go into the centre for the key from the priest, Papa Savvas, who lives in the house right opposite the modern church of Ayía Ekateríni.

Both church and frescoes date from 1502, with the latter exhibiting pronounced Venetian influence despite their rustic, even deformed execution. On the upper zone of the south wall, from east to west, a squat, stubby angel figures in the Annunciation; in the Nativity, one shepherd plays a shawm, and another, wearing an extraordinary patchwork sheepskin, converses with Joseph; while the personi-fied river god lolling about in the Baptism is so distorted as to appear club-footed. On the same level of the west wall, the food in the Last Supper (with multiple fish, not just one as customarily) is being consumed with two-pronged wooden forks, a habit introduced by the Venetians and found in no other Cypriot depiction of the scene; in the Betrayal, the massed Roman soldiery are all hooded, undifferentiated grotesques with beaky noses, and in the Deposition the dead Christ is almost floppy in the Virgin's arms. Above these scenes, in the west pediment, is a remarkable Crucifixion, where a youth in Venetian carnival dress is lancing Christ's side, while on the right of the cross, another youth in noble attire proffers the sponge with vinegar on a spiral wand.

Pitsyliá

Southeast and uphill from the Soléa valleys, the region of **Pitsyliá** (Pitsilia) is a jumble of bare ridges and precipitous valleys forming the east end of the Tróödhos range. Instead of forests, groves of hazelnut and almonds grow, though there are pines on the north slopes. Grapevines flourish, too, but for local use, not the vintners' co-ops; in some villages they're guided on elaborate trellises over streets and houses.

The easiest roads into Pitsyliá head east from Tróödhos resort (the B8) or southeast from Kakopetriá (the B9), converging at the crossroads in the central Tróödhos known as Karvounás, 1200m above sea level (just south of which, on the E801, is a 24hr petrol station). From there you are within easy reach of Kyperoúnda and the several walks above and west of it, or the vast church of **Kímisis tís Panayías** at **Koúrdhali**, actually a short way off the road up from Kakopetriá.

From Vyzakiá, the F929 heads up the Kannávia valley past Ayía Iríni (with its diminutive church of **Tímios Stavrós**) and **Spília**, emerging on the B9 just downhill from the Karvounás junction. However, about 3km above Vyzakiá, a minor paved road veers east to Ayía Marína (Agia Marina) village, just off the E907, which gives direct access via a scenic, forested canyon to two of the finest churches in Pitsyliá: **Panayía tou Araká** in Lagoudherá village, and **Stavrós toú Ayiasmáti** outside Platanistássa. About halfway between Ayía Marína and Lagoudherá, you pass the pine-set **Xyliátos reservoir**, the last known habitat of the aquatic "grass" snake, which is endangered by the practice of stocking the water here with trout (the fish eat the juvenile snakes). Just above the reservoir, at the start of a minor but marked jeep track to Stavrós toú Ayiasmáti, a Venetian-era **caravan bridge** (see p.199) is prominently signposted.

Pitsyliá is less frequented than Marathássa or Soléa, though three surprisingly large villages – almost small towns – are strung along near the ridge line: **Kyperoúnda**, **Agrós** and **Palekhóri**, the latter with its worthwhile church of **Metamórfosis toú Sotírou**. Kyperoúnda and Agrós, while excellent start-points for **hikes**, have no painted churches of their own; the closest are below Agrós, at **Peléndhri** (Stavrós) and **Louvarás** (**Áyios Mámas**). Roads, though improved on the main trunk routes, are still challenging and slow-going for the most part.

Panayía toú Araká

The large, single-aisled church of **Panayía (Panagia) toú Araká** ("Our Lady of the Pea") enjoys a wonderful setting amid trees – and the wild peas of the name – on a terrace 500m northwest of the village of **LAGOUDHERÁ** (Lagoudera), about halfway to Sarándi village. Both villages have tavernas, the closest about 200m from the church. The warden is supposedly inside during opening hours (notionally daily: Dec–Feb 9am–noon, also 2–4pm & March–Nov 3 6pm), or you can try ringing the priest, Pater Khristodhoulos, on ☏99557369.

The **interior frescoes** (of 1192 vintage, save for a few fourteenth-century ones on the north wall) are not as numerous as they might be, since the original west wall, presumably with a Crucifixion and/or Apocalypse, was removed when the existing narthex was built late in the seventeenth century. They are exceptionally clear, however, having been cleaned between 1968 and 1973, and include, unique in the Tróödhos, an undamaged *Pandokrátor* in the dome (which protrudes partially through the pitched roof). Below Christ, his eyes averted in the manner of Hellenistic portraits, Old Testament prophets, rather than the usual apostles, alternate with the twelve dome windows, each clutching a scroll with his prophecy anticipating the Saviour. Lower down, to the left above the *témblon*, the Archangel Gabriel, wings and robes swept back by the force of his rapid descent, approaches the Virgin opposite for the Annunciation.

Above the Virgin Enthroned in the apse, strangely averting her eyes to the right, Christ ascends to heaven in a bull's-eye mandorla, attended by four acrobatic angels. The *témblon* is intact, its Holy Gates (for the mysterious entries and exits of the priest during the liturgy) still in place. Instead of a true transept, there are two pairs of painted recesses on each of the side walls. Flanking the south door, Zozimadhon spoon-feeds Osia Maria (Mary the Beatified) of Egypt; Mary was an Alexandrian courtesan who, repenting of her ways, retired to the desert to perform austere penances for forty years and was found, a withered crone on the point of death, by Zozimadhon, abbot of St Paul's monastery near the Red Sea.

Over the door arch there's a fine Nativity, with, as ever, a preternaturally aged Infant being bathed, while on the right the angel gives the good news to the shepherds, one of whom plays a pipe. In the north recess nearest the apse, reflecting the episode described in Luke 2:28, Simeon lovingly holds Christ for his Presentation in the Temple, the child wearing a single earring in his left ear, as was the Byzantine custom for infant sons. Just above this is the Presentation of the Virgin as a small girl to Zakharias the high priest; between this and the north door is a rare *Áyion Keramídhi* – the head of Christ depicted on a tile. The *Panayía Arakiotissa*, in the opposite south-wall recess, is conceptually linked with the Presentation of Christ; having received back her son, the Virgin's expression is sorrowful in the knowledge of her son's eventual fate, as indicated by the two flanking angels proffering the instruments of the Passion.

Stavrós toú Ayiasmáti

In the next valley east of Lagoudherá, **Stavrós toú Ayiasmáti** (Stavros tou Agiasmati) is an attractive basilica-church, again once part of a monastery. You need to stop first in the village of **Platanistássa** (Platanistasa), where keykeeper Vassilis Hadjiyeoryiou lives – he is most easily found by enquiring at Makis' café, or ring in advance (he speaks some English) on ☎22652562. The church itself is located 7km to the north: 3km down-valley on the E906, the rest on a paved side road. The setting is even better than at Panayía toú Araká, in an almond grove at the margin of the forest, with a patch of the Mesaoría visible to the northeast. If it weren't for the fact that you have to shuttle Vassilis back to the village, you could explore the marked trail which links the church here with the one at Lagoudherá; this takes two-and-a-half hours each way.

The church itself is filled with late fifteenth-century **frescoes** by Philip Goul (cleaned in the 1980s); an inscription over the south door records both his artistry and the patronage of the priest Petros Peratis. The highlight is a **painted cross** in a niche on the north wall (the name *Stavrós* means "Holy Cross"), surrounded by small panels of episodes relating, however tenuously, to its power, sanctification and rediscovery, such as the Hebrews petitioning Pharaoh (top), or the vision of St Constantine in 312 AD (left).

Behind the *témblon*, and above an interesting Holy Table (for celebrating the Orthodox liturgy), the Virgin and Child both raise hands in blessing in the apse, flanked by archangels and the Old Testament prophets David, Daniel, Solomon and Isaiah; nearby the Communion of the Apostles has a single figure of Christ (usually there were two) offering the Eucharist to six with his right hand, and the Communion wine to the other half-dozen with his left. The four Evangelists are arranged in pairs to either side of the altar screen; the archangel Michael, in the arched recess to the right of the *témblon*, holds not the usual opaque orb but a transparent "crystal ball" containing the Christ child.

Elsewhere along the vaults and walls of the nave there's a complete gospel cycle, including such arcane details as apostles with their backs to the viewer in the Last Supper, Pilate washing his hands, trumpeters in the panel of the Mocking and Doubting Thomas probing Christ's lance wound. The crowing rooster in Peter's Denial is larger than any of the human figures. In the otherwise serene Assumption of the Virgin, a miniature angel strikes off the hands of an impious Jew who attempted to knock over the Virgin's bier. On the pediment of the west wall, the Ancient of Days presides over the descent of the Holy Spirit above the Crucifixion; Christ's blood drips down into Adam's skull below, the key-warden will tell you, in order to revivify it for the Redemption, shown outside in a niche of the uncleaned narthex.

This and other exterior frescoes are thought not to be by Goul, and were repainted in the 1800s to detrimental effect. Right of the Redemption unfolds the Last Judgement, while on the left stand the three patriarchs Abraham, Isaac and Jacob. The U-shaped narthex, extending around the north and south sides of the church, was used by local shepherds as a sheep pen before the monument's importance was recognized.

Madharí (Madari) ridge walking circuit

From either Lagoudherá or Platanistássa paved roads climb to the Tróödhos summit ridge, where the vine-draped villages of Álona and Polýstipos huddle just under 1100 metres. **POLÝSTIPOS** can offer a single agrotourism facility, *Evridiki's House* (☎ 22652216 or 99557643; two-bedroom unit ❸) on the through road, with balconied upstairs rooms and a coffee shop for snacks on the ground floor. The watershed is crossed a little higher, with a well-marked side road to the CYTA transmission station on the sides of 1613-metre **Mount Adhélfi** (Adelfi).

This is one possible starting point for the **circular nature trail** on Madharí ridge, but it's a long, shadeless slog from wherever you park up the Teisiá tís Madharís spur-path to the actual loop. Most hikers leave transport, and begin, from near **Kyperoúnda** (Kyperounta), 7km west via Khandhriá (Chandria). At the western edge of Kyperoúnda, just beyond the summit pass on the bypass road, a paved side road signposted for Spília and Kannávia heads north for 1800m to the saddle at 1335m elevation. Just to one side stands the familiar wooden paraphernalia marking the start of such trails, with a sign proclaiming "Glory be to God" in New Testament Greek (*Doxa Soi O Theos*) – plus a wooden plaque announcing the precise distance to be covered (a 13km loop). Up some steps from the Greek signage is a useful map-placard detailing all the walks in the region – the circuit in question, plus extensions to Lagoudherá, Spília, Koúrdhali and Ayía Iríni. Except for some clumps of midget golden oak (*Quercus alnifolia*) and a rare endemic juniper (*Juniperus excelsa*), there's little but low scrub en route, so the exposed ridge is best traversed early or late in the day during summer. Views of half the island, from the Kyrenia hills to the Akrotíri salt lake, are the thing: you gaze over nearer valleys and villages both north and south of the ridge, with the sea on three sides of Cyprus visible in favourable conditions.

Once clear of a more recent firebreak track, the **path** fluctuates to either side of the watershed (also the boundary between Limassol and Nicosia districts) until, some 45 minutes along, it reaches the 1500-metre saddle between **Madharí ridge** and Point 1613 (**Adhélfi peak**), with another half-hour's hiking bringing you to the fire tower up top – a bit more if you detour to the modestly described "Excellent Viewpoint" partway. Next, a little over an hour's descent drops you through more golden oak (*latziá* in dialect) to Point 1180 (**Selládhi toú Karamanlí**), before bearing due west for another hour-plus through the **Mávra Dhása**, a thick and so far unspoiled pine forest, to Point 1150 (Moútti tís Hóras), before climbing slightly for half an hour back to your start point. Allow well over four hours for the complete walk, not counting stops.

Minor churches: Tímios Stavrós and Kímisis tís Panayías

Immediately north of Madharí ridge, in the vicinity of Spília village (see next section), nestle two minor but enjoyable painted churches, both dating from the first quarter of the sixteenth century. The road to the western trailhead of the Madharí nature path continues 2km to a junction: left leads within 500m to Spília and thence Koúrdhali hamlet; straight descends 2km in tight curves to Ayía Iríni village.

Tímios Stavrós

The diminutive church of **Tímios Stavrós** at **AYÍA IRÍNI**, just north of and above the village on a hillock, had its frescoes cleaned and masonry consolidated throughout 1995; the key-custodian lives in the last village house on the right along the road, going downhill. Once inside, you'll see a rustic Nativity over the south door, with the Convention of the Archangels just east. The conch of the apse is devoted to the iconographic convention known as the Deisis, the only such depiction on Cyprus: the Virgin and John the Baptist flank a seated Christ, who proffers with his left hand a text proclaiming him to be the prophesied Christ and Judge of the Last Day. To the left of the apse, an angel lifts Christ from the sepulchre, an artistic convention combining the so-called "Utter Humiliation" variation of the Byzantine Deposition and the western *Pietà*. In the triangular pediment above the apsidal vault, there's an unusual, Westernized Holy Trinity, with the enthroned Father upholding the crucified Son, appropriately for a shrine of the Holy Cross (*Tímios Stavrós* in Greek).

Koúrdhali: Kímisis tís Panayías

The three-aisled basilica of **Kímisis tís Panayías** (Koimisis tis Panagias) in **KOÚRDHALI** (Kourdali), signposted as "Khrysokourdhaliótissa", lies just under 2km below the central junction in Spília, on the bank of a stream crossed by a tiny humpback bridge built entirely of roof-tiles. It was founded in the sixteenth century as the *katholikón* of a monastery by the deacon Kourdhalis, for whom the hamlet is named. The bulk of the surviving frescoes are on the west wall, surmounted by a naturalistic, Italo-Byzantine Crucifixion featuring, as to be expected from a sixteenth-century church, notables in Venetian apparel – including a rather scandalously attired Virgin in a low-cut dress, fainting into the arms of her friends. Subsequent episodes include a dramatic Doubting Thomas, at the far upper right of the panels here, with Christ all but daring the apostle to touch his wound. Right of the west door, in the Dormition of the Virgin above the donor portraits, a rather piratical-looking, long-fingered St Paul crouches at the foot of the bier. The eastern apse is taken up by a fine Virgin Orans, attended by archangels in Byzantine noble costume.

The guardian is a young nun, Sister Isidhora, who lives in the little monastic retreat-house on the terrace overlooking the church. As the *katholikón* of – in effect – a one-woman nunnery, the church is most reliably open daily for services at 5–7.30am and 4–5.30pm.

Spília

SPÍLIA village, like many of the more isolated Tróödhos settlements, was an EOKA stronghold; four statues in the plaza commemorate EOKA activists who managed to blow themselves up in a bomb-making safehouse nearby in Koúrdhali. Today, however, it's a resolutely peaceful place, with a small central **hotel** in the centre: the ✻ *Marjay Inn* (☎22922208, ⓦwww.marjay.com; ❸, internet discount). The rooms, of two to four beds with blonde-pine furniture and river-view balconies, are already comfortable and squeaky clean, though due for a refit in 2009. The inn is geared towards activity holidays – mountain biking and hiking – and reservations are required much of the year. At daughter Maria's excellent nearby **restaurant-bar**, ✻ *The Sama*, booking is essential (☎22316473 or 99571112) as the homestyle dishes are freshly cooked only for anticipated diner numbers, with hotel guests given priority and service limited (except peak season) to Friday supper through Sunday lunch. Downstairs from the rustic dining room is a stylish hubble-bubble bar, the only allowed smoking area.

Agrós

Besides the inns at Spília, Polýstipos and Askás, the only other feasible overnight option in Pitsyliá is **AGRÓS**, a large village more or less at the top (920m elevation) of Limassol district's commercial wine-grape region. Also known for its sausages, ham and rosewater, Agrós won't win many beauty contests but it's well placed for forays to nearby sights, as it lies roughly equidistant from several post-Byzantine frescoed churches. Being less frequented than the monuments of Marathássa and Soléa, these give more sense of personal discovery, and their surrounding villages deserve a brief stroll-through as well. In Agrós proper, there are no historic churches, despite its role as refuge for two venerable twelfth-century icons of Christ and the Virgin; the villagers themselves pulled down the 800-year-old, frescoed monastery housing them in 1894, during a protracted land-ownership dispute with the local bishop.

Agros' appearance on the tourism map is due almost entirely to its enormous, communally owned **hotel**, the three-star *Rodon*, 1km south of the village on the Potamítissa road (☎25521201, ⓦwww.rodonhotel.com; ❹). Refurbished in 2006 to four-star comfort, it offers some family units, a tennis court, pool, spa, gym and conference facilities, as well as a well-regarded restaurant – a reliable lunch venue in a region rather deprived of such. The Sunday lunch buffet (€17 plus drink) is good value despite the inevitable feed-trough atmosphere and thus heavily attended by Cypriots. Manager Lefkos Khristodoulou has been instrumental in rehabilitating local footpaths for various **walks around Agrós**; the best and most demanding of these is the traverse from Stavrós toú Ayiasmáti to Ágros via Lagoudherá and Madharí ridge, with transfers arranged for guests.

The only lodging alternative, uninspiringly set in the village itself, is the one-star *Vlachos Hotel* (☎25521330; ❷), with half board available. *Iy Kiladha*, just north of the *Vlachos* in a tree-shaded kink of the through road, is the main independent **taverna**. Agrós also has two **ATMs**, and a **post office**.

Peléndhri: Stavrós church

Of the villages with frescoed churches around Agrós, **PELÉNDHRI** (officially Pelendri, also sometimes rendered "Peléndhria") is the easiest to reach, on a paved road via Potamítissa. The main attraction here is the fourteenth-century painted **church of Stavrós** (repaired 2004), isolated at the south edge of Peléndhri, overlooking a reservoir; the key-keeping family lives in the last house on the right as you approach. A square ground plan divided into three aisles, unique in Cyprus, is capped by a very narrow, high dome supported by four columns; for once there is no narthex.

On your right as you enter, there's a Tree of Jesse, showing the genealogy of Jesus. Straight ahead on a pier, the two donors of the church are shown below Doubting Thomas; just to the left is a Lusignan coat-of-arms. At the rear of the central aisle, above the wooden lattice of the deacon's pulpit, are scenes from the life of the Virgin, some of the best-preserved frescoes in the entire building. Opposite this, the Nativity tells much about Lusignan domestic life, while Joachim and Anna present the infant Mary for blessing by the high priests, the most vivid of fourteen panels on the life of the Virgin. A multi-coloured *témblon* is in good condition, and to its left the enshrined cross for which the church is named stands encased in silver near a representation of the *Epitáfios* (the Dead Christ), next to a fresco of three *Ierárkhi* (Fathers of the Church) in the left-hand apse. In the vaulting of the main apse, an Ascension has two disciples pointing in amazement while two angels flank the Virgin, standing on a pedestal.

Peléndhri can also offer one of the best micro-wineries in the Tróödhos: Kostas and Marina Tsiakkas's **Pitsilia Winery**. They produce a full range of wines from both traditional native grapes like Xynisteri and imported varieties such as Mataro and Cabernet. Visits are generally by appointment (☎25991080), as they're a bit tricky to find; if you want to chance dropping by on spec, head about 2km southwest of Peléndhri on the Trimíklini road, then bear right 700m on a dirt track seemingly headed for the middle of nowhere; the winery buildings are perched right above the vineyards, a bit scorched after a March 2008 fire which did for much of the forest nearby.

Louvarás: the chapel of Áyios Mámas

The main Limassol-bound E110 road from Agrós via Káto Mýlos descends to Péfkos junction above **KALOKHORIÓ** (Kalo Chorio), where there's the only food (two **tavernas**, a *kléftiko* outfit near the police station) for quite some distance around. A four-kilometre side road takes off southeast from the westerly crossroads, ending at **LOUVARÁS**, whose dishearteningly modern outskirts give no hint of the traditional village core to the east, nor of the tiny but exquisitely painted **chapel of Áyios Mámas** (signposted as "Agios Mamantos"), hidden on the edge of the old quarter, at the very end of the paved road in. Don't confuse it with the bigger, newer church of Pródhromos nearby, just below which lives the current keeper, Mrs Penelope (no English spoken).

The little chapel, with frescoes dating from 1495, features Philip Goul at perhaps his most idiosyncratic. On the south wall, Christ heals the paralytic and the blind man, teaches, and meets the Samaritan woman at the well; the three sleeping guards at the Resurrection wear Lusignan armour. Also on the south wall, closer to the *témblon*, is an exceptionally expressive John the Baptist, clutching a staff which ends in a cross-and-anchor motif. Beside the west door, Christ casts out the demons from two visibly grateful lads, with one of the Gadarene swine lurking behind, ready to take the little devils over the brink; just below this, in the Last Supper, Christ does not (as in other local murals) attempt to prevent Judas from reaching for the fish. Over the door appear the donors of the church, two couples in late Lusignan dress, while above this soldiers in late medieval armour seize Christ in the Betrayal. At the very top of the apsidal pediment on the east side, the Ancient of Days hovers over the Annunciation – these images may be by a hand other than Goul's, since the episode is repeated on the south wall.

Saint Mamas and his lion

Prominent on the north wall of Louvarás church is a panel of the dedicatory saint, **Mamas**, cradling a lamb as he rides a rather bemused, anthropomorphized lion. The legend behind this peculiar iconography, found in many Cypriot churches, runs as follows: Mamas was a devout Byzantine hermit in the Paphlagonia district of Anatolia who refused to pay income tax since, as he logically pointed out, he had no income other than alms. The local governor ordered him arrested, but as he was being escorted into custody a lion – unknown in the region – leapt from a roadside bush onto a lamb grazing peacefully nearby. The saint commanded the lion to stop his attack, picked up the lamb and completed his journey into the capital riding on the chastened lion. Sufficiently impressed, the governor exempted Mamas from taxes thereafter, and ever since the saint has enjoyed fervent worship as the patron of tax-evaders (a massively popular cult in the Hellenic world) as well as herdsmen.

Palekhóri: Metamórfosis toú Sotírou

From Agrós (or Peléndhri), the quickest route to Palekhóri, 13km away, is eastward along the E903 ridge route; from Louvarás and Péfkos junction, you can link up with this via Áyios Theodhóros. **PALEKHÓRI** (Palaichori) is a sprawling, workaday place hidden in a gulch at the headwaters of the Peristeróna River – there are a few *kafeniá* down by the stream, and an **ATM**, but no other concessions to tourism. There is, however, an agrotourism **inn** 2km northeast at **ASKÁS** on the through road, *Evgenia's House*, comprising four large studios accommodating families (☎22642644 or 22642344; ❷), as well as a single **taverna**, Pernia, just east of Askás.

The small fifteenth- to sixteenth-century chapel of **Metamórfosis toú Sotírou**, signposted from the main bypass road, perches at the east edge of the old quarter, atop the slope up from the river. The engaging key-keeping priest lives in the apartment building two doors north, but in the evening (a likely arrival time if you've been touring all day) he may be conducting the liturgy down at undecorated Panayía Khrysopantánassa in the town centre.

The frescoes of Metamórfosis toú Sotírou rival those in Áyios Mámas at Louvarás for whimsy, with lions and rivers the main themes. Saint Mamas appears again, riding a particularly elongated feline; on the south wall, another lion approaches, as tradition holds, to bury Osia Maria (Mary the Beatified of Egypt) with his paw, while opposite her Daniel braves the lions in their den. To Daniel's left a miracle whereby the angelic diversion of a river saves a monastery is portrayed; in the Baptism of Christ, a crowned-and-sceptred water sprite – personification of the river, derived from pagan portrayals of river-gods – rides a fish in the Jordan. As befits a church dedicated to the Transfiguration (*Metamórfosis* in Greek), the panel of that episode on the south wall is particularly vivid, with two disciples cowering on the ground in awe. Scenes from the life of the Virgin are completely absent, though the apse features an elegant *Virgin as Mistress of Angels*. Below her to the left, a cow suckling her calf lends an engaging touch to the Hospitality of Abraham. In a nearby recess, Saint George lays a fraternal hand on the shoulder of Saint Demetrios with whom he rides; their equestrian pairing, common on Crete but unique here on Cyprus, shows these warrior saints' evolution from the ancient Dioscuri, Castor and Pollux, ever ready to rush to the aid of supplicants.

Mountain villages en route to Makherás

At Aplíki junction, you can turn up towards Farmakás onto a narrow but paved road around a large reservoir. **Farmakás** and its neighbour **Kambí** (Kampi) are spectacularly set overlooking the top of the valley draining to the dam. The two local showcase villages lie a few kilometres northeast along an improved road beyond Goúrri.

At **FIKÁRDHOU** (Fikardou) the vernacular architecture of stone, mud-straw bricks and tiled roofs is preserved – or rather embalmed – in the forty-plus houses of this **museum-village**; the permanent population has dwindled to three. Two of the dwellings are now a house museum (daily: Nov–March 8am–4pm; April–Oct 9am–5pm; €1.70), with plans, photos and text in the ticket office giving a full explanation of the project's aims. The house of Akhilleas Dhimitri, with its loom and period furnishings, is the occasional residence of the project's supervising archeologist and hosts a weaving workshop. The Katsinioros house has an olive press, *zivanía* stills and storage urns in its basement, and traditional women's implements in the peaked-roof upper storey.

It's a conscientious restoration job, but the result seems a bit lifeless without even the animation of a weekend population (though some of the buildings are reportedly for sale). The only tourist amenity thus far is a single café serving drinks and light meals. **LAZANIÁS**, 5km south on the way to Makherás monastery, is more of a going concern, and therefore less twee and perhaps more representative of such hill-villages.

Makherás monastery

The **monastery of Makherás** (Machairas), just east of Lazaniás, is distinguished by its setting on the north slope of Mount Kiónia, near the headwaters of the Pedhiéos River, and by its associations with **Grigorios Afxentiou**, second in command of EOKA after George "Dhiyenis" Grivas, and by all accounts a more sympathetic figure.

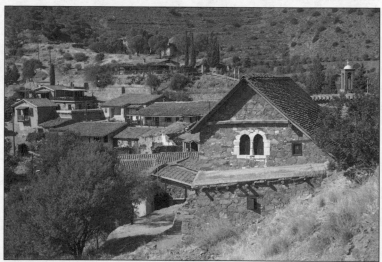

▲ The preserved village of Fikárdhou

The monastery was established by two hermits in 1148, who arrived from Palestine and, guided by the usual preternatural glow, found an icon of the Virgin attributed to the hand of Luke the Evangelist. Makherás ("The Cutler") is taken variously to mean the sharp-edged, thousand-metre ridge overhead, the biting wind swooping down from it in winter or the point in the foundation legend when a knife supernaturally materialized and a "voice not of earth" instructed the hermits to use it to free the icon from the underbrush. Soon the community had the support of the Byzantine emperor Manuel Komnenos, and it even enjoyed the subsequent patronage of Lusignan rulers – one of whom, Queen Alix d'Ibelin, was rendered mute for three years after sacrilegiously insisting on entering the *ierón* behind the altar screen. Makherás claims five martyrs (six, counting Afxentiou), commemorated on plaques in the courtyard.

It has also suffered two comprehensive fires (in 1530 and 1892), though the resulting bleak, echoing stone compound was admirably restored during 1997–98; the icon miraculously escaped the blazes and is the glory of the *katholikón*. There's also a one-room **museum** (Greek-only labelling), featuring photos of Afxentiou disguised as a monk – and of his charred remains after the British had finished with him (see below). As with several Cypriot monasteries, access to the non-Orthodox is restricted to **group visits** (Mon, Tues & Thurs only 9am–noon), and no photos are allowed.

Krysfíyeto toú Afxentíou

When he was not in monk's garb, the brothers of Makherás fed Afxentiou in his hideout, the **Krysfíyeto toú Afxentíou**, 1km below the monastery; a Greek flag, sign and memorial plaque point you down to the (much repaired) bunker in which he met his end on March 3, 1957. Tipped off by a shepherd, British forces surrounded the dugout and called on the occupants to surrender – EOKA members usually complied in hopeless situations. All of them did except Afxentiou, who, despite being wounded, held off a platoon of sixty for ten hours before being dispatched with a petrol bomb and high explosives.

Approaching the *krysfíyeto* (hideout), you pass a huge **statue**, erected just below the monastery at the expense of the diocese, showing a quadruple-life-size Afxentiou standing arms akimbo, guarded by an eagle (his *nom de guerre* was Stavraetos or "golden eagle"). The actual **hideout** is maintained as a shrine, with a photo of the man and regular floral offerings; if you visit soon after the death anniversary, you'll find dozens of laurel wreaths propped by the entrance, left by relatives, school groups and military organizations. The actual ceremony is held on the Sunday closest to 3 March, when native British subjects are explicitly not welcome.

Onward routes from Makherás

From Makherás your most obvious course is north down to **Nicosia**, 43km distant via the inviting, pine-shaded picnic grounds of Mándhra toú Kambioú and the adjacent sites of ancient Tamassos and Áyios Iraklídhios convent (see p.266). Towards **Larnaca district**, a somewhat rough dirt road heads due south through forest and past another picnic ground beside 1423-metre Kiónia peak, last outrider of the Tróodhos range. Áyii Vavatsiniás marks the start of the improved road surface down to **Khirokitia**, 33km distant from the monastery (see p.100). Alternatively, you can choose Vavatsiniá as your interim destination (16km), from where it's 10km more on paved road to **Páno Léfkara** (see p.102). Finally, heading east, you can brave about 8km of dirt track before emerging at **LYTHRODHÓNDA** (Lythrodontas), at the end of the E103,

with its historic *Avli Georgallidi* (☎99655100 or 22543236, ⓔavli@cytanet
.com.cy; ❸), three old houses joined together to make a five-room inn around
a courtyard, with airy and extensive common areas and meals available; reservations are suggested owing to its proximity to Nicosia.

Travel details

Buses

Agrós to: Limassol on Agros bus (Mon–Fri 1 daily,
at about 7.15am; 1hr 15min).
Kakopetriá to: Nicosia on Clarios bus (Mon–Fri
8 daily, Sat 4 daily, Sun 2 daily; 1hr).
Pedhoulás to: Nicosia via Kalopanayiótis on Clarios
bus (Mon–Sat at 6.45am; 2hr).

Plátres to: Limassol on PEAL bus (Mon–Fri at 8am,
Sat 6.15am, also Mon–Fri 3.45pm; 1hr).
Tróödhos to: Limassol on PEAL bus (Mon–Fri at
3.30pm; 1hr 15min); Nicosia on Clarios bus
(Mon–Sat at 7am; 2hr).

5

South Nicosia

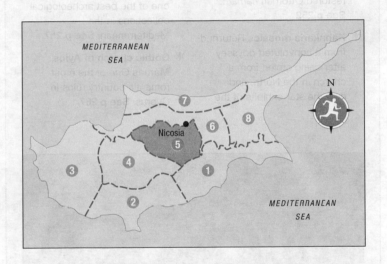

CHAPTER 5 # Highlights

＊ **Concert in the Kasteliótissa Hall** Attending an event in this Gothic architectural marvel with superb acoustics is also your best chance of gaining admission. See p.249

＊ **Ömeriye Hamam** Pamper yourself with a steam bath and all manner of alternative therapies in this exquisitely restored Ottoman *hamam*. See p.252

＊ **Kanakariá mosaics** Returned from a convoluted odyssey after being stolen from a church in the North, and now the star exhibits of the Makarios Cultural Centre. See p.255

＊ **Khrysaliniótissa district** Vernacular houses in this neighbourhood have been meticulously refurbished as part of the UN/EU-funded Nicosia Master Plan. See p.256

＊ **Cyprus Museum** Simply one of the best archeological collections in the Mediterranean. See p.257

＊ **Gothic church of Áyios Mámas** One of the most romantic country ruins in Cyprus. See p.267

▲ The Kasteliótissa Hall in action

5

South Nicosia and around

T he southern sector of divided Nicosia (*Lefkosía* in Greek, pronounced "Lefkosha" in dialect) is the capital and largest town of the internationally recognized Republic of Cyprus. Prosaically set and somewhat gritty, it's visited by few tourists apart from groups coached in to the Cyprus Museum, one of the best archeological collections in the Middle East, and required viewing. A relative lack of resort commercialism is refreshing, as is the surviving Gothic and Ottoman domestic and religious architecture of the medieval town. And if you're interested in learning what contemporary Cyprus is about, then crossing back and forth between the two sectors of the city (see Chapter 6) is an essential exercise, easily undertaken.

By comparison, there is little of note in the surrounding countryside under Greek-Cypriot control, part of the vast **Mesaoría** ("Between the Mountains"). Set between the Tróödhos range and Kyrenia hills, this is not so much a plain as undulating terrain, quilted with green or yellow grain according to season and dotted with large villages which have become dormitories for the capital. Here you become acutely aware of the island's division: roads close to the boundary – except for the permitted crossings shown on the map – are diverted or barred suddenly, and watchtowers dot the horizon. Amid this bleakness, just a few isolated spots really appeal, and then only if you have time (and a car) on your hands: the ruins of **Tamassos** and the nearby nunnery of **Áyios Iraklídhios**, a fine church-and-mosque duo at **Peristeróna,** another minor church at **Perakhorió**, paired with the scanty nearby remains (but good new museum) of ancient **Idalion**, and an exquisite Gothic ruin nearby at **Áyios Sozómenos**.

South Nicosia

SOUTH NICOSIA, depending on how many incorporated suburbs you include, today has between 200,000 and 280,000 inhabitants. Despite the relatively small population, it's a sprawling, amorphous, modern city that's far from immediately likeable. The dust and heat – on average 2°C higher than on the coast – are prostrating from April to October, grit coming in equal measure

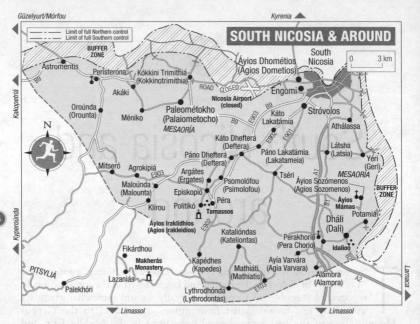

Güzelyurt/Mórfou · Kyrenia · South Nicosia

from the prevailing winds and nearby building sites, while its inland setting near the western edge of the Mesaoría is prone to earthquakes and flash-flooding from the river Pedhiéos (Pediaios). Since early Byzantine times every ruler has designated the place – nearly equidistant from every important coastal town – as capital by default, because the island's shore defences were poor, its harbours exposed to attack.

Medieval Nicosia's profile is due in varying proportions to the Lusignans, Ottomans and Venetians; the latter encircled the old town with five kilometres of walls, which largely survive. The map outline of the medieval quarter, still the city's core, has been variously compared to a star, a snowflake or a sectioned orange, but in the troubled circumstances prevailing since the 1950s a better analogy might be a floating mine, the knobbly silhouettes of its eleven bastions the detonators.

Old Nicosia began to outgrow its confines during the 1930s; the British solved this problem with post-war cantonment-style development just outside the walls, while the post-independence response was to throw up generic Middle-Eastern suburbs beyond, dotted with high-rises. The British as well as the Cypriots are to blame for the neglect and even desecration of the old city; many monuments, including a Lusignan palace, were senselessly pulled down at the end of the nineteenth century, and the Venetian ramparts first pierced by viaducts and later allowed to crumble at the edges. Most streets inside the walls are no longer architecturally homogeneous, defaced by thoughtless concrete construction of recent decades.

So the romantic orientalist's town, which the peripatetic Austrian Archduke Louis Salvator admired on the eve of British rule, has vanished forever. Especially around the Páfos Gate, the old town can be depressing and claustrophobic, qualities made worse by the presence of the Green Line, tensely palpable even when out of sight. Profuse wall graffiti in Hellenic blue is concerned exclusively with what is delicately termed the Cyprus Question, the search for a solution to the island's de facto partition. The Levantine ease of the coastal towns is absent: clusters of men stand or sit about Platía Eleftherías expectantly – at least until its pending refit (see p.249) – and by Cyprus standards there is considerable hustle from shop and restaurant proprietors in the one district gentrified for tourists. As in Limassol, an entire neighbourhood is given over to girlie bars and cabarets; the only other significant industries inside the Venetian fortifications appear to be cabinet-making, chair-making, metal-working and offset printing.

Lawrence Durrell bemoaned Nicosia's lack of sophistication and infrastructure in the mid-1950s; it's come a long way since then, with trendy boutiques showcasing the latest fashions, and excellent restaurants which only Limassol can rival. A small capital that might be expected to be provincial supports a cosmopolitan population which includes Lebanese, Iranians, Syrians, Africans, Bengalis, Sri Lankans and east Europeans, studying, working menial jobs or surviving as illegal refugees. Of late, much of the old town presents a collage of halal butchers, Russian/Georgian delis, Chinese takeaways, Indian knick-knack

The divided city

The **Green Line**, as the ceasefire line is known within the city limits, has existed in some form since the communal troubles of winter 1963–64: first as impromptu barricades of bed-frames, upturned cars and other domestic debris, later more sturdily fashioned out of oil drums, barbed wire, sandbags and sheet metal. Despite the recent thaw, and opening of various crossings, Nicosia is – as the authorities still remind you on wall signs and in tourist literature – Europe's last divided city. As such, the barrier exercises a morbid fascination on many visitors as well as locals. You find yourself drifting towards it repeatedly, trying to follow its length, peering through chinks when out of sight of the Greek, Turkish or UN watchtowers. Beyond the barricades stretches the "dead zone", here just a twenty- to fifty-metre-wide stretch of derelict, rat- and snake-infested houses – and a showroom full of dust-shrouded Toyotas and Datsuns, rushed in from the Famagusta docks on the day of the invasion to prevent their destruction, irretrievably trapped here ever since, as well as a small, now inaccessible Jewish cemetery for the city's tiny community.

Before **crossing points** opened in April 2003, the very existence of the **Attila Line** (the limit of Turkish army advance) constituted a provocation to which a steady trickle of Greek Cypriots responded. Periodically, refugee groups staged protest marches towards their home villages in the North, putting their own National Guard in the embarrassing role of trying to prevent them crossing (often they got several hundred metres, or even further, inside northern Cyprus); young men crashed the barriers on foot or in vehicles, only to be imprisoned by the Turks, with attempts every several months on average. A slogan overhead at one Greek sentry-tower – "Our frontiers are not these, but the shores of Kyrenia" – hardly argued for self-restraint.

All that is now (not very ancient) history, and despite what you may still be told at your coastal resort or your car-rental outlet, the Line is scarcely less porous than the average recognized border between an EU and contiguous non-EU country. The main catch concerning the Green Line within Nicosia (see p.259) is that only pedestrians are allowed across at the moment.

Nonetheless, the rift (while it endures) remains central to experiencing Nicosia and, by extension, of the island. The Greek area of the city is, indeed, mostly Greek in its monumental architecture, the Turkish zone largely Turkish and Gothic, but in the midst of each traces of the other element are marooned: mosques and houses emblazoned with a star and crescent in the south, belfried churches and dwellings with Greek Ottoman or Armenian inscriptions in the north, reminders of the pre-1974 heterogeneity of Cyprus.

shops and storefronts peddling cheap overseas calls to the phoneless; come to Nicosia on a national holiday and it is only immigrants – with no money to go anywhere else – who you'll see strolling about the parks. There are so many now, and so acutely racist is the reaction of most Cypriots to them, that two refugee NGO/counselling centres exist inside the Venetian walls.

Among the Europeans are, or have been, 1990s Serbian draft-dodgers, Russian businessmen laundering money and Romanian, Moldovan or Russian women swelling the ranks of the prostitutes – unforeseen legacies of non-aligned 1960s Cyprus's diligent cultivation of ties all round. You will also come across journalists monitoring the Middle East from a relatively safe haven, and delegates to the numerous conferences which punctuate Nicosia's winter calendar; less obvious will be the legions of spies and undercover agents which the city is famous for, another holdover of Cyprus's role as a pivotal point in the Cold War, though now they may just as likely be Syrian, Kurdish, Iranian, Israeli or even Turkish, each pursuing their own agenda.

Some history

Present-day Nicosia lies on or just north of the site of a Neolithic settlement, subsequently the Archaic town of Ledra. But the city only became prominent in Byzantine times, eclipsing Constantia (Salamis) after the seventh century AD, and embarking on a golden age with the arrival of the **Lusignan kings**. During the fourteenth century, they endowed the place with over eleven kilometres of fortifications, plus the palaces, churches and monasteries appropriate to a court of chivalry. Their surviving monuments constitute much of Nicosia's appeal; nowhere else on Cyprus except at Famagusta can you take in the spectacle of Latin-Gothic architecture transplanted to the subtropical Levant. The underpinnings of this hothouse fantasy were by their very nature transient: the Genoese raided Nicosia in 1373, and the Mamelukes sacked the city again in 1426. Following **Venetian** assumption of direct rule in 1489, Nicosia became more of a stronghold. With an eye to the growing Ottoman threat, the Lusignan circuit of walls shrank between 1567 and 1570, to a more compact, antiballistic rampart system designed by the era's best engineers. Monuments falling outside the new walls were demolished in the interest of a free field of fire. But it was all to no avail, as the Turks took the city on September 9, 1570, after a seven-week siege, swarming over the Podocataro and Constanza bastions. In a paroxysm of rape, plunder and slaughter graphically described by survivors, the victors dispatched nearly half the 50,000 inhabitants and defenders.

Under **Ottoman rule** the city stagnated, albeit picturesquely, not to regain a similar population level until the 1940s. Three centuries passed quietly, except for riots in 1764, in which a particularly unpleasant governor was killed, and mass executions of prominent Greek Cypriots (including the island's four bishops) in 1821, to discourage an imitation of the Greek peninsular uprising. The **British** raised the Union Jack here in 1878, but saw their Government House burnt down in the pro-*énosis* riots of 1931.

Colonial authorities moved the administrative apparatus outside the walls in 1946, paralleling the growth of the city. But during the 1950s and 1960s the capital was wracked, first by the EOKA struggle and later by violence between the Orthodox Christian and Muslim communities. After the events of December 1963 (see p.389), **factional polarization** proceeded apace: Greeks and Armenians were expelled or fled from mixed neighbourhoods in the north of the city, and any remaining Turks deserted the south, so that Nicosia was already de facto partitioned when the Turkish army reached the northwestern suburbs, and then penetrated the Turkish quarter of the old town, on July 22, 1974.

Since then, the growth of the new southern boroughs has been spurred by the necessity of quickly providing housing for tens of thousands of Greek refugees from North Cyprus. By contrast, old Nicosia has suffered even where not explicitly damaged by the conflict, as shopkeepers and residents close to the Line deserted their premises, leaving often exquisite buildings to decay. Only since the late 1980s has the neglect been reversed, under the aegis of the **Nicosia Master Plan**, funded by the United Nations Development Programme and the EU. Tentative co-operation between urban planners in the Greek and Turkish sectors, based on the assumption of a reunited city in the future, has resulted in co-ordinated restoration and pedestrianization of the most attractive neighbourhoods on both sides of the Green Line, and even (in 1979) the mundane but necessary completion of a joint sewage plant, left stranded in the Turkish zone after 1974. The population of "Nicosia within the walls" – increasingly foreign-born, as noted above – has stabilized, and given a final political settlement may have some future other than as a depressed, traumatized backwater. To date, historic residential neighbourhoods east of Sólonos have been fairly comprehensively refurbished, with particular concentrations of quite striking old houses near the Famagusta Gate.

Arrival, orientation, transport and information

Whether you approach along the motorway from Larnaca or Limassol, or in a more leisurely fashion from the Tróödhos foothills, arrival in Nicosia is not a thrilling prospect (the **airport** has languished in the dead zone, used as UNFICYP headquarters since 1974, its ultimate fate subject to a final peace settlement). You negotiate seemingly interminable suburbs indistinguishable from those of any other Mediterranean or Middle Eastern city, until suddenly thrust into the rotary system of thoroughfares paralleling the Venetian bulwarks. Most **bus terminals** are a short distance from the ramparts, or even on them, though some are set to move by 2010; see "Listings" on p.262, and our map on p.246, for current locations.

The municipality has turned parts of the Venetian walls and moat into **car parks** – the best areas are the moat between the D'Avila and Constanza bastions, with the top of the Tripoli bastion a runner-up. **Pay-and-display** tickets from the vending machine start at €1.25 for two hours; on nearby streets there are **meters** which cost €0.50–0.60 per hour, occasionally more in very high-use areas. Regulations are enforced Monday–Friday 7am–7pm, Sat 7am–2pm in theory – enforcement at off-peak times isn't consistent. Alternatively, you can use more remote, but cheaper, privately run car parks in the new city; for example, leaving the A1 motorway and entering the built-up area, keep an eye out, just past the Cyprus Airways headquarters, for a large car park on the right – offering a good set price for the whole day. The only fairly reliable fee-free street spaces in the old city are near the Archbishop's Palace, or outside the walls in a very few streets south of the Constanza bastion, or west of the Páfos Gate.

The longest street, the ring boulevard linking the Venetian bastions, changes names no fewer than four times; the ring road just outside the moat changes identity just as often. The busiest entrance to the old town is from **Platía Eleftherías** to pedestrianized and commercialized **Lídhras**, while in the opposite direction **Evagórou** leads out to the **new town**'s main commercial district beyond the walls, with a more orderly but by no means grid-regular street plan. **Leofóros Arkhiepiskópou Makaríou**, perpendicular to Evagórou, is the longest and glitziest boulevard, heading out towards the A1 motorway.

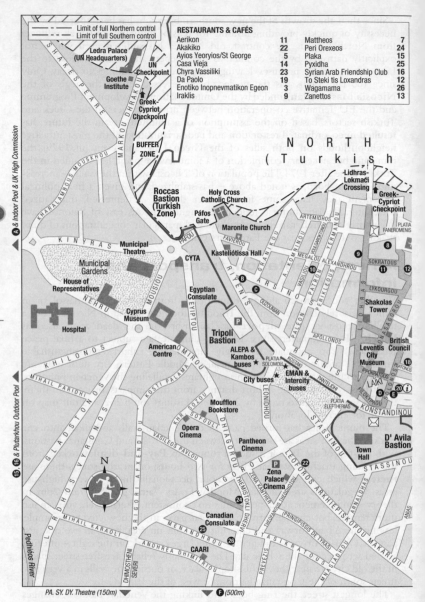

RESTAURANTS & CAFÉS		
Aerikon	11	
Akakiko	22	
Ayios Yeoryios/St George	5	
Casa Vieja	14	
Chyra Vassiliki	23	
Da Paolo	19	
Enotiko Inopnevmatikon Egeon	3	
Iraklis	9	
Mattheos		7
Peri Orexeos		24
Plaka		15
Pyxidha		25
Syrian Arab Friendship Club		16
To Steki tis Loxandras		12
Wagamama		26
Zanettos		13

Limit of full Northern control
Limit of full Southern control

Ledra Palace
(UN Headquarters)

UN
Checkpoint

Goethe
Institute

Greek-
Cypriot
Checkpoint

BUFFER
ZONE

SHAKESPEARE

MARKOU DHRAKOU

KHARALAMBOUS MOUSKHOU

Roccas
Bastion
(Turkish
Zone)

Holy Cross
Catholic Church

Páfos
Gate

Maronite Church

Kasteliótissa Hall

NORTH
(Turkish

Lidhras-
Lokmaci
Crossing

Greek-
Cypriot
Checkpoint

ARTEMIDHOS

PLATIA
FANEROMENIS

KINYRAS

Municipal
Theatre

CYTA

FAVIEROU

PAFOU

Egyptian
Consulate

EYIPTOU

Municipal
Gardens

House of
Representatives

NEHRU

MOUSIOU

Cyprus
Museum

Hospital

KHILONOS

MIHAIL PARIDHI

OMIROU

KOSTI PALAMA

GRANKOU

MEGALOU ALEXANDHROU

VASILIOU

PATRON

PERIKLEOUS

ARSINO

OUZOUNIAN

PALEON

APOLLONOS

RIYENIS

Tripoli
Bastion

ALEPA &
Kambos
buses

City buses

PLATIA
SOLOMOU

KOSTAKI PANTELIDHI

EMAN &
Intercity
buses

LEONIDHOU

PLATIA
ELEFTHERIAS

SOKRATOUS

LYKOURGOU

Shakolas
Tower

British
Council

Leventis
City
Museum

IPPOKRATOUS

LAIKI

FILOXENOU

KONSTANDINOU

STASINOU

Town
Hall

D' Avila
Bastion

STASINOU

GLADSTONOS

VYRONOS

LORDHOS

MIHAIL KARAOLI

VASILEOS PAVLOU

GRIGORI AFXENDIOU

DHIAGORA

DHIAGOROU

KNR SOZOU

SOFOULI

Moufflon
Bookstore

Opera
Cinema

Pantheon
Cinema

Zena
Palace
Cinema

EVAGOROU

THEMISTOKLI DHERVI

Canadian
Consulate

MENANDHROU

ANDHREA DHIMITRIOU

DHIMOSTHENI
SEVERI

CAARI

American
Centre

N

Pedhiéos River

LEOFOROS ARKHIEPISKOPOU MAKARIOU

THEODHOTOU

PRODHROMOU

THEOKRITOU

(PRINGIPISSIS DE TYRAS)

ARNALDHAS

PREVEZIS

STASIKRATOUS

MINA STAVROU

ANAS

ANIAS

PA. SY. DY. Theatre (150m) ▼   ▼ ⓕ (500m)

Nicosia has an **urban bus network** of about twenty lines, straggling off through the new town into further-flung suburbs; services run at half-hourly intervals between 5.30am and 7 or 8pm, twice as often at peak periods. They're cheap enough at about €0.70, but you probably won't use them unless you want to visit a distant embassy or cultural centre. No self-respecting Greek Cypriot will be caught dead on a bus or (worse) walking, and Nicosians more or less

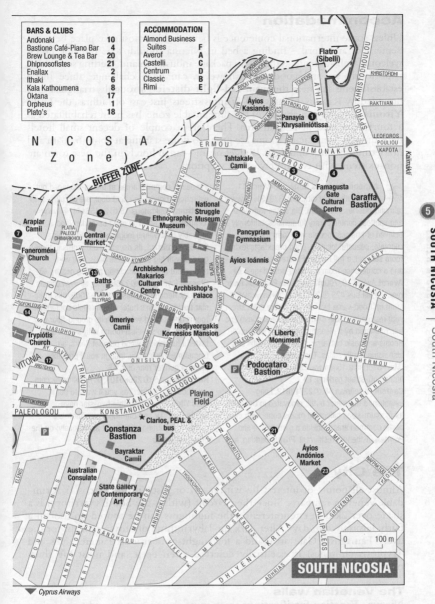

BARS & CLUBS

Andonaki	10
Bastione Café-Piano Bar	4
Brew Lounge & Tea Bar	20
Dhipnosofistes	21
Enallax	2
Ithaki	6
Kala Kathoumena	8
Oktana	17
Orpheus	1
Plato's	18

ACCOMMODATION

Almond Business Suites	F
Averof	A
Castelli	C
Centrum	D
Classic	B
Rimi	E

Cyprus Airways

obligatorily get a car for their eighteenth birthday. The **central terminal** for city buses is on Platía Solomoú, beside the Tripoli bastion. Full information is available here, and route and city maps are sporadically to be had from the **tourist office** at the courtyard in from Aristokýprou 11 (Mon–Fri 10am–1pm & 4–7pm, Sat 10am–1pm).

Accommodation

Unless some international conference is being held – most take place between September and April – finding a bed in Nicosia shouldn't be difficult; hotels welcome walk-in trade, as there's no package industry inland. Getting something salubriously set and good value, however, can be a challenge, since many establishments fall near the main **red-light district**, a roughly triangular area bounded by Riyénis, Lídhras and Arsinöis streets. Just east of Lídhras, the **Laïkí Yitoniá**, formerly an annexe of the disreputable zone, has been rehabilitated as a tourist-oriented pedestrian area. There are a couple of decent small hotels here, though front-facing rooms are prone to noise starting at about 6.30am and not letting up until midnight. Budget or mid-range hotels in the new town are non-existent, with two noteworthy exceptions.

Almond Business Suites 25-March 11, 1km south of old city. ☎22879131, ⓦwww .almond-businesshotel.com. Big suites with wi-fi and spotless contemporary furnishings, uniformly beloved of business people who form the main clientele; peaceful location, good breakfasts (extra, room service), a full range of secretarial services and a conference room are other advantages. ❺
Averof Avérof 19, 700m across the Pedhiéos River, reached via bus #23 ☎22773447, ⓦwww.averof .com.cy. Good-value two-star on a very quiet street, with restaurant (table d'hôte meals on request) and bar, managed by a pleasant Anglo-Cypriot couple. Rooms are basic but large, with full bathtubs and also some family suites. The public pool (May–Sept) is a 15min walk away on Ploutárkhou; limited off-street parking. ❸
Castelli Ouzoúnian 38 ☎22712812. Long-established three-star outfit, renovated in Oct 2000. Its medium-sized balconied rooms come with data ports; common areas include a gym, sauna and Polynesian-themed restaurant. Private parking, and

the use of common areas at the co-managed but overpriced Holiday Inn next door, are big pluses. ❻
Centrum Pasikrátous 15 ☎22456444, ⓦwww .centrumhotel.net. The most upmarket (and arguably best-value) lodgings in Laïkí Yitoniá, 2006-refurbished, its decent-sized rooms in three grades with big comfortable beds, free wi-fi throughout and free or cheap parking nearby. ❺
Classic Riyénis 94 ☎22664006, ⓦwww.classic .com.cy. Redone in phases 1999–2005, this three-star businessmen's hotel with multiple conference rooms offers good value with its ground-floor bar/ restaurant and smallish rooms with simple but tasteful furnishing, wood parquet floors, a/c, and (sometimes) balconies, though you'll probably prefer a quieter rear unit. ❹
Rimi Sólonos 5 ☎22680101, ⓔrimi@cylink.com .cy. About as "budget" as you'll want to get in Laïkí Yitoniá; rooms at this two-star have heating/a/c, TV and bathtubs, plus there's a restaurant (touting somewhat assiduously) on the ground floor. ❺

The City

Almost all points of interest lie within, on or just outside Nicosia's formidable Venetian ramparts. Since their circuit (within the South's territory) is a shade over 2km in circumference, the highlights can be toured on foot in a fairly leisurely two days. After dark the labyrinthine old town (except for the lively Famagusta Gate area, and a few nightspots around Faneroménis and Trypiótis churches) is essentially deserted, even eerie, and most life shifts outside the walls.

The Venetian walls

Nicosia's **Venetian fortifications** are its most obvious feature, and a good place to start your wanderings. Of the eleven bastions, named after Venetian personalities, five lie in the Greek zone and five, now confusingly renamed, in the Turkish zone; the Flatro bastion in the "dead zone" is under UN control. Three surviving gates, called Páfos, Kyrenia and Famagusta after the towns they face, breach the walls roughly 120 degrees apart. The Venetians engaged military engineers Ascanio Savorgnano and Francesco Barbaro to design the ramparts between 1567 and 1570. At the foot of the fortifications they scooped out a moat, which was never intended to carry water – though the Pedhiéos River, later diverted, managed to fill it sporadically. It was not the fault of the walls themselves that Nicosia failed to withstand the siege of 1570; the Turks took the city mainly because of the incompetence of the pusillanimous commander Nicolo Dandolo and the exhaustion of the defenders. The Ottomans maintained the ramparts, which were captured more or less intact; it is only since 1878 that substantial alterations have been made. Most of the following monuments are atop, or an integral part of, the bastions, the most obvious bits. Otherwise it's easy to tread the course of the walls without realizing it, a testimony to how domesticated they've become.

The Páfos Gate area

If you come from the Tróödhos by car, the **Páfos Gate** will probably be your somewhat grim introduction to the old city. Poised between the Greek and Turkish zones of the town, it's been a trouble spot since 1963. The flags of the South and the North, plus those of Greece and Turkey, oppose each other here across a ten-metre space, and signs on the Turkish-held Roccas bastion, warn off "trespassers". Originally this gate was called Porta San Domenico, after a Lusignan abbey just outside, which the Venetians demolished in 1567 when they contracted the circumference of the walls. The Ottomans had a large barracks and arsenal in and on it; the British made the chambers their police headquarters.

Just inside the gate stands one of the many anomalies of the post-1974 situation: the **Holy Cross Catholic church** and papal nuncio's residence, though squarely in the dead zone with its rear in Turkish-occupied territory, was allowed to reopen for business in 1976 on condition that the back door was sealed. The Maronites (see box, p.318) also have a church, school and clubhouse around the corner, though their main place of worship is now out in Lakatámia suburb. A few paces south of the Páfos Gate police station lies the barrel-vaulted **Kasteliótissa Medieval Hall**, all that remains of a thirteenth- to fourteenth-century Lusignan palace, whose superb acoustics make it a perfect venue for classical chamber concerts, many of them free, as well as exhibits – these are the only times the hall is open, so take advantage.

Moving anti-clockwise, the moats and next two bastions have been put to use as dusty parkland, playing fields, bus terminals or car parks, with the **D'Avila bastion** also supporting a small cluster of public buildings. Four viaducts now make up the walls and moat; the largest, **Platía Eleftherías**, is (beginning 2009) to be the focus of the most ambitious (and controversial) Master Plan project yet, a Zaha-Hadid-designed refit to make it a sweeping pedestrian link between old and new town (albeit in sterile concrete), rehabilitating the moat as parkland, and stripping the Venetian walls of all modern structures.

Bayraktar Camii and the Liberty Monument

The small **Bayraktar Camii** (Mosque of the Standard-Bearer), standing in a well-landscaped area on the **Constanza bastion**, marks the spot where the Ottoman flag-carrier first scaled the walls in the 1570 siege. Vulnerable as such individuals always were – it was essentially a suicide mission – he was cut down immediately by the defenders, and buried on the subsequently revered site. It was long believed that EOKA activists had bombed the mosque and tomb twice in 1962 and 1963, toppling the minaret the second time, but both incidents were actually the work of TMT provocateurs; the damage has been repaired and the mosque grounds are now kept locked to prevent recurrences.

A sign up front, in Turkish and Greek, informs passers-by that while the Greek Cypriots respect the remaining Islamic holy places in the South, the Turks have not reciprocated in the matter of churches in the North.

A haven of parkland also surrounds the **Liberty Monument** sculpture, on the **Podocataro bastion**, consisting of fourteen representative (Greek) Cypriot figures in bronze being released from a white marble jail by two soldiers, the whole scene presided over by a female personification of Liberty. Commissioned and opened to great hoo-hah in 1973 (ironically enough), the monument is now presumably such an embarrassing obstacle to communal reconciliation that it is unremarked on in most official tourist literature.

The Famagusta Gate

Tucked into an angle of the Caraffa bastion, the **Famagusta Gate** (Mon–Fri 9am–1pm & 4–7pm; free, plus special evening events) is the most elaborate and best preserved of Nicosia's three gates. Designed by Giulio Savorgnano (brother of Ascanio) as a copy of another such Venetian structure in Iráklion, Crete, and long known as the Porta Giuliana, the gate is essentially a tunnel through the walls; the inner facade, with its six coats of arms and original wooden doors, is far more aesthetic than the mean outer portal. After more than a century of neglect, the great domed chamber that opens out at the centre of the tunnel was refurbished in 1981 as an **exhibition and concert venue**; the heart of the latter is an acoustically marvellous, gently inclined tunnel surmounted by a dome like a miniature Parisian Pantheon. A side chamber, once either the Ottoman powder magazine or guard house, is now the exhibition hall. Beyond the outer portal stretches a small open-air amphitheatre used during an annual September festival.

The traditional centre

Using Platía Eleftherías as a gateway, you're set at the Y-junction of **Lídhras** and **Onasagórou** streets to explore the historical commercial district of Nicosia. An awkward architectural mix of British Raj, 1930s Rationalist, Greek Neoclassical and ugly 1950s and 1960s buildings lines these two main shopping streets, pedestrianized during the 1980s as part of the Master Plan. Sadly, for what was once a fairly glamourous shopping parade, Lídhras in particular is tacky with chain stores and fast-food cafés. At the corner with Arsinóis, on the eleventh floor of the **Shakolas Tower**, the air-conditioned **observatory** (daily 9.30am–5pm; €0.85) has sweeping views of both south and north Nicosia, plus a "museum" of poor reproductions from archival photos.

After years of skirmishes and negotiations, the Greek-Cypriot barricade at the **north end of Lídhras**, and the Turkish-Cypriot barricade at Lokmacı just sixty-odd paces north, were dismantled on April 3, 2008, to become the latest **legal crossing point** between the two sectors. Gone forever are proclamation battles by the opposing sides using loudhailers, and a Greek-Cypriot shrine to the lost homelands with "informative" displays on the Lídhras side. Still there, however, are a series of abandoned, bullet-pocked commercial premises, not only in the here-tided-up dead zone, but three or four doors to either side, where uncertainty of the future rather than warfare per se killed off commerce. It is not the first time the street has been embattled; during the late 1950s Lídhras was dubbed "Murder Mile" after EOKA's habit of gunning down its opponents here.

Platía Faneroménis

The north end of Onasagórou opens onto **Platía Faneroménis**, named after the huge **church** (daily 7.30am–1pm & 3–6pm) that dominates the square.

A hotchpotch of Neoclassical, Byzantine and Latin styles, this was erected during the final Ottoman years to replace a derelict medieval basilica. Inside the present structure are the remains of the four clerics murdered by the Ottoman governor in 1821. More compelling than the Faneroméni church, and effectively filling the adjacent tiny Platía Ikostiogdhóïs Oktovríou, the **Araplar Camii**, originally the sixteenth-century church of Stavrós toú Missirikoú, is a good example of the mixed Byzantine-Gothic style particular to Lusignan times. Inside (unfortunately usually locked), the octagonal-drummed dome rests on magnificent columned arches. Taking advantage of the setting with outdoor seating is the recommended *Mattheos* taverna (see p.260).

Laïkí Yitoniá and around

Just east of the Lídhras pedestrianization, the so-called **Laïkí Yitoniá** (Laïki Geitonia) or "Folk Neighbourhood" forms a showcase district reclaimed from the cabarets and girlie bars in the late 1980s, with restored premises made available to several indifferent restaurants or cafés (the very few exceptions are found on p.261) and souvenir shops. The municipality is also extremely proud of the nearby **Leventis City Museum** at Ippokrátous 17 (Tues–Sun 10am–4.30pm; donation requested), which won the European Museum of the Year award in 1991. This folk-cum-historical collection occupies three floors of a restored mansion, arranged thematically as well as chronologically from prehistoric to British eras. Exhibits include traditional dress, household implements, rare books and prints, with scattered precious metalware and archeological treasures. The best sections are those devoted to the Venetian and Ottoman periods, as well as postcard collections (mostly by Armenian photographers) on the first floor.

Around the corner on Sólonos, the **Trypiótis church** (open all day except for variable lunch hour), dedicated to the Archangel Michael, is the most beautiful of the old town's surviving medieval churches. On the south side, a conservatory protects two Gothic-arched windows. Over the door between, a fourteenth-century relief shows two lions being subdued by a being sprouting from leafy tracery, clutching hoops; to either side, mermaids and sea monsters gambol. Inside, the brown sandstone masonry has been left unpainted, as has the fine wooden *yinaikonítis* – indeed the whole interior is relatively restrained for a Cypriot church.

The Ömeriye Camii and Hamam

Variously spelled Omerieh, Omerye, Omergé (the phonetic, dialect pronunciation) and Omeriyeh, the **Ömeriye Camii** on Platía Tillyrías is the only Gothic house of worship converted into a mosque in Greek-Cypriot Nicosia. Originally it was the church of Saint Mary, part of a fourteenth-century Augustinian monastery largely destroyed by the 1570 Ottoman bombardment. Many Lusignan nobles were buried here, but as at Ayía Sofía cathedral in north Nicosia, the victors sacrilegiously "recycled" their tombstones to refloor the mosque during reconstruction. The Ottoman conqueror of Cyprus, Lala Mustafa Paşa, got it into his head that the caliph Omar had rested here during the seventh-century Arab raids on Cyprus – hence the name. Today it serves the needs of the city's multi-ethnic Muslim population; you are welcome to shed your shoes inside the ornate west portal and visit the simple, barn-like **interior** (Mon–Sat 10am–12.30pm & 1.30–3.30pm) with its shallow pitched roof and succession of rib vaults supporting this. You can also climb the minaret, but it's probably best to stash spare footwear in a daypack, as the top dozen or so steps are caked in a thick layer of pigeon shit. Be sure to follow the indicated walkway south around

▲ Relaxing in the Ömeriye Hamam

the apse for a flattering view of the church's flying buttresses. At dusk, the Arabic-speaking muezzin here vies with the Turkish tropes emanating from the minarets of the Selimiye Camii in north Nicosia, their unsynchronized calls to prayer stirring up formations of swallows.

The late sixteenth-century namesake **baths** across the square, long frequented mainly by prostitutes from three nearby bordellos, were restored beyond recognition as part of the Master Plan in 2002–04, and now offer – aside from steam baths – an assortment of massage, mudpack, essential oil and hot-stone therapies (€20–90). They're open 9am–9pm Tuesday, Thursday, Saturday for men, the same hours Monday, Wednesday, Friday for women, and Monday 10am–7pm for (straight) couples; they can also be hired for private functions.

The Hadjiyeorgakis Kornesios Mansion

A few steps down Patriárkhou Grigoríou from the Ömeriye mosque, the delightful fifteenth- to eighteenth-century **Hadjiyeorgakis Kornesios Mansion** (Tues, Wed, Fri 8.30am–3.30pm; Thurs 8.30am–5pm; Sat 9.30am–3.30pm; €1.70) is a unique Venetian-Ottoman hybrid – a wooden Turkish lattice balcony perches over a relief coat of arms – that easily overshadows most of the contents. Only the luxurious reception room, with its low divans and painted and carved ceiling, is an authentic reflection of the house in its heyday; most of the others serve as a contemporary antique gallery, though several rooms do exhibit assorted metal, glass and ceramic items from various eras.

The house is named for **Hadjiyeorgakis Kornesios**, a native of Krítou Térra in Páfos district, who served as the dragoman (multi-lingual liaison between the Ottoman authorities and the Orthodox Christians) of Cyprus from 1779 until 1809. With a fortune accumulated from vast estates and tax exemption, he was the most wealthy and powerful man on the island, but he met the usual end of Ottoman officials who became too prominent. A peasant revolt of 1804 was aimed at him and the Greek clerics, as much as at the Muslim ruling class; fleeing to İstanbul, he managed to stay alive and nominally keep office by seeking asylum in sympathetic foreign embassies, until he was beheaded in 1809 as part of the intrigues surrounding the consecutive depositions of the sultans Selim III and Mustafa IV.

Around the archbishop's palace

An alarming concentration of coffin-makers lines the street leading from the Hadjiyeorgakis Kornesios mansion to **Platía Arkhiepiskópou Kyprianoú**, flanked by a cluster of buildings including the city's diminutive cathedral and three museums. The **Archbishop's Palace** is the most immediately obvious monument, a grandiose pastiche built during the 1980s to replace its 1950s predecessor, shelled and gutted by EOKA-B in their July 15, 1974, attempt to kill Archbishop Makarios. Except for the "Cultural Centre" wing (see p.255), it is not open to the public. At the southeast corner of the palace precinct, a controversial, not to say downright hideous, **statue of Makarios** looks (below the waist especially) more like Lot's petrified wife than a cleric, as he stares down Koraï street towards the Liberty Monument. This was the first, and probably the worst, of a growing contingent of similar ones inflicted on the city.

Across the way sprawls the imposing Neoclassical façade of the **Pancyprian Gymnasium**, one of the more prestigious secondary academies for (male) Greek Cypriots since the 1880s. In *Bitter Lemons* Lawrence Durrell described his experiences teaching here in the mid-1950s, when it became a hotbed of pro-*énosis* sentiment.

The church of Áyios Ioánnis

Between the Gymnasium and the palace sits seventeenth-century **Áyios Ioánnis church** (Mon–Fri 8am–noon & 2–4pm, Sat 8am–noon), which gets top marks for the quantity (if not always the quality) of its eighteenth-century interior **frescoes** by Filaretos, whose work can also be seen at Monágri. Among recognizable scenes are the Last Judgement and the Creation over the south and north doors respectively, and on the south wall a sequence on the rediscovery of the Apostle Barnabas's relics. Despite its small size, Áyios Ioánnis is the official cathedral of the city; the archbishops of Nicosia are still consecrated here, standing on the floor medallion featuring a Byzantine double-headed eagle.

The Ethnographic and National Struggle museums

Just north, the **Ethnographic Museum** (Mon–Fri 9am–4pm, Sat 9am–1pm; €1.70) occupies the surviving wing of a fourteenth-century Benedictine monastery, handed over to the Orthodox to serve as the old archbishop's residence after Latin rule ended. There is, regrettably, no interpretation or discussion of the excellent collection of nineteenth- and twentieth-century ceramics, woodcarving and household implements. One, perhaps unintended, effect of a visit will be to make you *not* want to buy any contemporary craft souvenirs, as the quality of the small objects – *lefkarítika* (linen and silk work from Léfkara), *kolótzi* or engraved gourds, musical instruments, Nicosian silver filigree work – is so manifestly superior to modern work. Other exhibits are of carved and (usually) painted wood: magnificent chests, doors, cornices and chunks of wooden water-wheel in the exterior portico.

Just north of the Ethnographic Museum stands the purpose-built **National Struggle Museum** (*Mousío Agónos*; Mon–Fri 8am–2pm, also Sept–June Thurs 3–5.30pm; free), completed in 2001 to replace a far smaller facility, and representative of the then-prevalent trend to glorify EOKA and its works. Housed on several levels, it's an overwhelming accumulation of memorabilia, mostly

You can't help noticing that every large town in the South has a Gríva Dhiyení avenue, sometimes two. They honour a man as controversial as Makarios – and one who, particularly after independence, brought considerable misery to both Greek and Turkish Cypriots.

Born May 23, 1898, in Tríkomo (now renamed İskele), **George Grivas** attended Nicosia's Pancyprian Gymnasium before enrolling in the officers' academy in Athens, graduating just in time to see several years' duty in Greece's disastrous Asia Minor campaign. Grivas remained in Greece after the loss of Asia Minor, serving under General Papagos in the repulsion of the Italians on the Epirot front during winter 1940–41. Having idly sat out most of the German occupation of his adopted homeland, in 1944 he formed a guerrilla band of royalist officers known as **Khi** – "X" in the Greek alphabet – a collaborationist unit which devoted its time to exterminating left-wing bands. When full-scale civil war broke out in 1946, he re-enlisted as a lieutenant-colonel to help crush the communist-inspired rebellion.

A semblance of normal life, and elections, returned to Greece in 1951. Grivas ran with Papagos's party but failed to secure office – his forbidding, abstemious personality, appropriate to the battlefield, did not strike a chord with the Greek electorate. Disgusted, Grivas swore off electoral politics and returned to Cyprus the same year to foment an uprising there to throw off British rule. It was then that he met Makarios, whom he tried to convince of the necessity of some sort of rebellion. Neither Makarios nor Grivas's Greek sponsors were persuaded until an Athens meeting in early 1953, when Makarios, Grivas and ten others resolved to fight for *énosis* or union with Greece, founding **EOKA**, the *Ethnikí Orgánosis Kypríon Agonistón* or "National Organization of Cypriot Fighters".

At this point Makarios would only assent to violence against property, but during 1954 two caiques loaded with explosives and weapons made their clandestine way from Rhodes to Cyprus, landing on the then-deserted Páfos coast (see p.171). Most of the year was taken up establishing EOKA in Cyprus, with recruits taking oaths of secrecy, obedience and endurance till victory, similar to those of the IRA. Makarios gave his go-ahead for revolt in March 1955; EOKA made its spectacular public debut on April 1 with bomb explosions across the island. Self-introductory leaflets were signed "**Dhiyenis**", Grivas's chosen *nom de guerre,* after Dhiyenis Akritas, folk hero of a tenth-century Byzantine epic.

The insurrection gathered momentum throughout 1955 and early 1956, when Grivas halted a promising round of negotiations between Makarios and Governor Harding with timely explosions which also provoked Makarios's deportation. Thereafter Grivas

photo-archival, on EOKA's anti-colonial campaign of demonstrations, sabotage and murder. Exhibits include cartoons, graffiti (first prize to "When the English were living in huts, the Greeks were building Parthenons") and press comment of the time documenting British reprisals, searches, tortures and detention camps; the personal belongings of fighters (including Grivas); plus arrays of weapons and gruesomely ingenious bombs. The centrepiece of the displays is a memorial to EOKA's martyrs, plus a mock-up gallows commemorating the nine hanged at the city's Central Prison by the British in 1956 – along with their last letters from the death cells. Labelling, though now partly in English, remains minimal; the propaganda impact is visual, and primarily intended for Greek-Cypriot schoolchildren. Interestingly, the main emphasis is on opposition to (and from) the British, with little about adverse Turkish-Cypriot reaction (though there is a tally of victims of the TMT) – or the vast number of leftist Greek–Cypriots and British troops killed by EOKA.

and EOKA included murder in the scope of their operations, targeting British servicemen, leftist or pro-British Greeks and very occasionally Turkish Cypriots. From his movable headquarters in the Tróödhos – at or near Kýkko monastery – Grivas mocked the British with a barrage of communiqués and ultimatums. Numerous search and/or entrapment missions were mounted, and nearly caught the wily guerrilla leader in 1956 and again in 1959, the latter hunt aborted for political reasons.

When Makarios returned to Cyprus in 1959, Grivas – furious at the archbishop's acceptance of independence rather than *énosis* – stalked off to self-exile in Greece and a hero's welcome, including promotion to the rank of lieutenant-general. This went to Grivas's head, and his subsequent paranoid public utterances earned him denunciation by the Greek government.

By 1964, however, Greece, Makarios and Grivas had patched things up to the extent that the Athens government sent Grivas back to Cyprus, ostensibly to impose discipline on Greek irregulars who had infiltrated the island. This he did, but he also assumed command of Makarios's new **National Guard** and led several attacks on Turkish enclaves, most notably at Kókkina in 1964 and Kofínou in 1967, pushing Greece, Turkey and Cyprus to the brink of war each time. After the 1967 episode, American diplomacy secured what was hopefully his permanent removal from the island.

But the 1967–74 Greek junta, in its obsessive machinations to oust Makarios from office, found Grivas useful once again: in 1971 he returned to Cyprus disguised as a priest to organize **EOKA-B**, literally "The Second EOKA", whose express intent was the elimination of all enemies of Hellenism – and of the colonels – on the island. This meant anyone who stood in the junta's way: communists, socialists, centrists, and soon Makarios himself. Whether Grivas endorsed all of this, or as a royalist shared some of Makarios's disdain for the colonels and remained opposed to an "*énosis*" that would invite Turkey in for a chunk of the island, will never be known; he died in January 1974, still in hiding. Yet had he lived longer, Grivas would probably have led the July 1974 coup against his erstwhile comrade-in-arms – he had already approved at least one unsuccessful assassination attempt on Makarios. Those who knew him assert that his overriding qualities were impulsive chivalrousness (he was known to pay benefits to widows of his fighters out of his own pocket), murderousness (bands under his direct command killed nearly three hundred mostly leftist Greeks, far more than the British) and complete inability to consider the consequences of his actions. With hindsight, one can respect Grivas for his obvious dedication – but for little else.

The Makarios Cultural Centre and the Kanakariá mosaics

Within sight of both Áyios Ioánnis and the Ethnographic Museum is the entrance to the **Archbishop Makarios Cultural Centre** (Mon–Fri 9am–4.30pm, Sat 9am–1pm; €1.70), which owes its grandiose name to the presence of several research libraries and a very audible school of ecclesiastical music, where laymen learn to be chanters for Orthodox church services. On the upper floor, lit and opened only on request, resides Makarios's private collection of kitschy religious canvases with doubtful attributions, assembled for him by a French-educated Cypriot, Nikolaos Dikeos. The ground floor, however, is another matter, and for most visitors a tour of the **Byzantine galleries** here will be one of the highlights of a day in Nicosia.

Pride of place, and deservedly so, goes to the sixth-century **Kanakariá mosaics**, stolen from a church in North Cyprus in the late 1970s but returned to Nicosia in 1991 after a lengthy court battle (see p.357 for more details). Since late 1992 they have been displayed in the purpose-built, right-rear wing, though their layout here – an artificially flat surface – does not recreate their former position in Panayía Kanakariá church, in a curved apse, viewed from below. Originally, the Virgin Enthroned sat between the two archangels, with a band above containing the busts of the apostles. The most famous image is that of Christ clutching a scroll, looking like a young pagan god and – like all the figures here – adhering to Hellenistic, rather than later, iconographic conventions. Only one archangel, Gabriel, survived into modern times; his eyes, which look strangely averted in the mosaics' present position, would originally have been gazing at the Virgin. The apostles Matthew, James and Bartholomew were recovered more or less intact; all are distinguished by preternaturally large, asymmetrical eyes. In 1997 images of saints Thomas and Thaddeus were recovered, and subsequently joined their fellows at the exhibit here. It is hoped that soon the curved viewing perspective of the original church will also be recreated.

The mosaics are a hard act to follow, but the 150-plus **icons** in the adjacent gallery, retrieved from various Cypriot churches, along with a reconstructed apse full of fourteenth-century frescoes rescued from Áyios Nikólaos tís Stéyis in the High Tróödhos, acquit themselves commendably. Even when the exhibits are not of the highest artistic standard, they often prove unusual in some respect; under Lusignan influence, artists often made astonishingly free with the usual iconographic rules, especially in sixteenth-century variations of the Virgin and Child.

To the right, just inside the main door, stands a Prophet Elijah from the thirteenth century, being fed in the wilderness by the raven, symbol of God's providence; adjacent, an earlier, pensive Saint John the Baptist is rather more spruced up than his usual shaggy norm. Rarely seen topics include Saint Anne holding the Virgin and Child; the Burning Bush, as a herald of Christ; and a *Threnos*, similar to a Latinate *Pietà* with just the dead Christ and the Virgin, whereas Orthodox portrayals of the Deposition are usually group scenes. At the rear of the main gallery, a sixteenth-century icon of the Adoration of the Magi turns out to be a Renaissance-style family portrait; a *Virgin Orans* of the same period shows the donor family kneeling to either side. Costumes of the various figures were invaluable in dating these works, and offer an absorbing insight into medieval Cypriot life.

Tahtakale and Khrysaliniótissa districts

Heading north from Platía Kyprianoú along pedestrianized Ayíou Ioánnou, you shortly reach the small **Tahtakale (Taht-el-Kala) Camii**, the homely focus of the eponymous neighbourhood. Here the Master Plan has borne the most fruit, with dozens of old houses renovated for occupation by young families in an effort to revitalize the area. For a taste of the exotic, nineteenth-century Ottoman town accented with palm trees, arched mud-brick houses and domes, you need to continue across Ermoú into the **Khrysaliniótissa district**, strolling along Axiothéas, Ayíou Yeoryíou and Avtokratóras Theodhóras in particular.

This area is anchored by the namesake church of **Panayía Khrysaliniótissa** (Panagia Chrysaliniotissa), a rambling L-shaped building with fine relief carving on its exterior and arches under the two domes; most of its icon collection is now housed in the Makarios Cultural Centre. Construction was begun in 1450 by Helena Paleologina, the Greek wife of Lusignan King John II; the name, "Our Lady of the Golden Linen", is supposed to derive from its vanished original icon's having been found in a flax field.

Businesses and residences are used right up to the barriers here, in contrast to elsewhere in town; the dead zone also seems narrower, with North-Cypriot/

Turkish flags plainly visible over the housetops. But of the 23 types of exotic bazaars catalogued by Archduke Louis Salvator in 1873, effectively bisecting the town between the Famagusta and Páfos gates, only traces of the cabinet-making, tin-smithing, cloth and candle-dipping industries remain on the few commercial streets between Tahtakale and Khrysaliniótissa.

The Cyprus Museum

Founded early in the British tenure, the **Cyprus Museum** (Tues, Wed & Fri 8am–4pm, Thurs 8am–5pm, Sat 9am–4pm, Sun 10am–1pm; may open Mon high season; €3.50) is easily the best assemblage of archeological artefacts on the island. It stands between the Tripoli bastion and the pleasant **municipal gardens**, Nicosia's largest green space and, with its outdoor café, a worthwhile adjunct to any visit; on Sundays there's an outdoor market here, run primarily by and for the larger immigrant communities.

Tour the galleries anti-clockwise from the ticket booth for rough chronological order, but the museum is organized thematically as well. Typically for Cyprus, the pre-Classical displays are the most compelling, though every period from Stone Age to early Byzantine is represented. All told, it's an absorbing collection that requires at least two hours for a once-over. Individual labelling is often mercifully replaced with hall-by-hall or glass-case explanatory plaques placing the objects in context. The museum is frankly overstuffed, with many exhibit-worthy items in storage; ground is to be broken for an annexe following a final peace settlement.

Highlights of the collection

Room 1 is devoted to Neolithic items, in particular andesite ware and shell jewellery from Khirokitiá, and Chalcolithic fertility idols. **Room 2**, the Early Bronze Age gallery, features fantastically zoomorphic and beak-spouted composite red-clay pottery from the Kyrenia coast. The central exhibits illustrate aspects of a pervasive early Cypriot cult: two pairs of ploughing bulls, a rite conducted by priests (wearing bull masks) in a sacred enclosure, and a model sanctuary crowned with bulls' heads.

The pottery of **Room 3** presents the best pictorial evidence of Mycenaean influence in Late Bronze Age Cyprus. A gold inlaid bowl from Enkomi and a faience rhyton from Kition are the richest specimens here, though decorated *krater*s (wine-mixing bowls) are more revealing, portraying stylized humans in chariots drawn by equally fantastic horses. Recurrent left and right-handed swastikas obviously predate any Nazi associations, merely indicating Asian contacts.

Room 4 is dominated by its startling corner display of seventh- and sixth-century votive figurines from a **sanctuary at Ayía Iríni** near Cape Kormakíti, excavated in 1929. The shrine was active after 1200 BC as the focus of a fertility cult, yet few of the two thousand figurines discovered were female. Most of the variably-sized terracotta men are helmeted, prompting speculation that the deity was also one of war.

A limestone **Zeus Keraunios** ("Thunderer") from Kition, which adorned the now-retired C£10 note, hurls a missing lightning-bolt in **Room 5**. This and other Greek/Hellenistic statues show marked Assyrian influence in beard, hairdo and dress; Oriental voluptuousness in male or female facial expression decreases as the Hellenistic period is reached, but never entirely vanishes. Among several renderings of the goddess is a first-century AD Roman statuette of **Aphrodite of Soli** – an image reproduced ad infinitum across Cyprus in tourist literature proclaiming it "her" island, as well as on the defunct C£5 banknote.

A cast-bronze, large-than-life-size nude of the second-century Roman emperor **Septimius Severus**, unearthed at Kythrea in 1928, dominates **Room 6**. **Room 7A** showcases an intricate **wheeled stand** for a bowl, ranks of animal figures rampant on its four sides, with an account of its rescue by the Cyprus government from Turkish thieves (pre-1974) and German art dealers. Ancient Enkomi, near Famagusta, yielded this and other twelfth-century BC finds like the famous bronze "**Horned God**", one hand downturned in benediction.

Subterranean **Room 8** demonstrates the progression from simple pit-tombs under dwellings, as at Khirokitiá, to rock-cut chamber-tombs accessed by a *dromos* (passage). Other steps lead to **Room 11**, the royal Salamis tomb room. Trappings from a hearse, and chariot traces for the horses sacrificed in the *dromos* (see p.464), are overshadowed by the famous **bronze cauldron** on a tripod, with griffon and sphinx heads welded onto its edge. A metal throne was found together with an Egyptian-influenced, finely crafted bed and a throne or chair of wood and ivory.

Room 7B offers a miscellany of objects from around the island, including the original mosaic of Leda and the Swan from Palea Paphos. Gold specimens include the portion of the Byzantine Lambousa Treasure that escaped the attentions of plunderers in the nineteenth century (most of the hoard went to US museums, particularly the Metropolitan Museum in New York).

The exhibits are rounded off with **Room 14**'s terracotta figurines from all eras. Among the more whimsical are three humans and a dog in a boat, and a thirteenth-century BC side-saddle rider, recovered from thieves in the 1980s. *Ex votos* of expectant mothers depict midwives delivering babies, and strange bird-headed and earringed women fondling their own breasts. From the Meniko sanctuary dedicated to the Phoenician god Baal Hamman, an outsize, unsettling figure of a bull being led to sacrifice completes a spectrum of taurean worship begun in Room 2.

The art museums

Housed in a magnificent building just south of the Constanza bastion, the **State Gallery of Contemporary Art** (Mon–Fri 10am–5pm, Sat 10am–1pm; free) at Stassínou 24 is the only other significant museum in the new town. It highlights the best Cypriot painting and sculpture from the twentieth century; the sumptuous catalogue is yours to buy, either here or at Moufflon Books (see p.263). Rather tellingly, there are almost no Turkish-Cypriot artists.

Within the walls, about 150m west of the Makarios Centre along Apostólou Varnáva, the **Municipal Arts Centre** (Tues–Sat 10am–3pm & 5–11pm, Sun 10am–4pm; free), housed in a former Bauhaus-style generating plant, is the city's main venue for changing exhibits of avant-garde art (plus a permanent collection). There's a gift shop selling books, cards, posters and other souvenirs, as well as a posh attached restaurant/coffee bar, *Iy Palea Ilektriki*, serving Mediterranean-cum-Cypriot fare (☎22432559 for reservations).

Kaïmaklí

Nearly 2km northeast of the UN-controlled Flatro bastion, the suburb of **Kaïmaklí** – until 1968 a distinct village – shelters the finest domestic architecture outside the walls. Local Greek Orthodox architects and stonemasons first emerged during the Lusignan period, when the Latin rulers trained and used this workforce in the construction of the massive Gothic monuments of the city centre. Their skills persisted through subsequent changes of regime, and during the late Ottoman years master masons would often travel abroad for commissions.

Under British rule, there was no longer any need to conceal wealth from acquisitive authorities as there was under the Ottomans, and the former simple but functional mud-brick houses, with perhaps a pair of sandstone arches or a lintel, were joined by grandiose stone churches and dwellings sporting pillars, balcony grillwork, and other architectural follies. More recent Kaïmaklí history has not been happy. As a mixed district, it was the scene of bitter fighting and EOKA atrocities during December 1963, particularly in the Omórfita neighbourhood (Küçük Kaymaklı to the Turkish Cypriots); this, like much of Kaïmaklí proper, now lies in the Turkish zone.

Every Monday the south Nicosia municipality offers a walking **tour** of Kaïmaklí; just show up at 10am at the Laïkí Yitoniá CTO office. The three-hour outing, which involves a coach transfer in addition to the foot itinerary, is free, but patrons are "encouraged" to buy things at points of interest along the way. If you'd rather do it yourself, **bus** lines #46 and #48 serve Kaïmaklí. It's just about walkable from the Famagusta Gate anyway, and most of the interest is confined to the streets immediately around the main churches of Ayía Varvára and Arhángelos.

Pedestrian access to the North

From the Páfos Gate area, Márkou Dhrákou winds north towards the Green Line and the UN headquarters in the former Ledra Palace hotel. Opportunistic commerce makes itself felt here: souvenir stalls print commemorative T-shirts for UN forces (as well as archeological excavation teams), who hang their shirts out to dry from balconies of the **Ledra Palace**; estate-agents pitch abandoned or under-used properties in the area. Among these (though not for sale) is the former Greek embassy (now merely the chancery), which had to move to less precarious quarters beyond the Cyprus Museum – a fitting denouement for its pre-1974 intriguing. Cars must be left behind, either in one of the fee lots or kerbside spaces west of Márkou Dhrákou.

There are two separate halts at the Ledra Palace **pedestrian crossing**, at the Greek-Cypriot and Turkish-Cypriot posts respectively (the UN booth in between no longer vets anybody). The crossing is open 24 hours, and heading **from south to north** there are no formalities for EU nationals at the Greek-Cypriot booth, across from the Goethe Institute. Non-EU nationals should get themselves stamped out – read on for why. When you reach the Turkish-Cypriot booth, all nationalities present their passport and receive a free "visa" on a loose sheet of paper – make sure *not* to have your passport itself stamped, as this may cause difficulties re-entering southern Nicosia.

Beyond the Turkish-Cypriot checkpoint, the money-changers, souvenir stalls and taxi drivers of yore are much reduced, since the euro is widely used in the North and anybody who wishes can bring a vehicle through the Áyios Dhométios crossing-point further west. It's best, therefore, to regard this crossing as a way of visiting the monumental district of North Nicosia, for coverage of which see p.281. The same parameters and advice apply to the 2008-opened **Lídhras Street/Lokmacı** pedestrian crossing, which is bound to overtake Ledra Palace in popularity.

Returning **from north to south**, surrender your loose visa at the Turkish-Cypriot booth and then proceed to the Greek-Cypriot post, where in contrast to outbound trips one's passport will be scrutinized. EU nationals are automatically let in, but non-EU nationals will be quizzed and may have to prove that they did not enter the island via the North in the first instance (this is where the exit stamp noted above proves crucial). Noticeable quantities of shopping from the North, especially liquor or cigarettes, will be confiscated. The Cypriots themselves, however, assiduously practise cross-"border" retail therapy up to frequently changing limits.

Eating

Nicosia has numerous decent, authentic places to eat, but they are often well hidden – and emphatically not found in the much-touted Laïkí Yitoniá, a twee tourist trap whose nature will be familiar to anyone who's visited the Plaka in Athens or Paris's Quartier Latin. The better tavernas and less pretentious *ouzerís* are scattered fairly evenly across the old town, mostly within brisk walking distance of the walls. As everywhere in the South, metropolitan Greek chow, as well as exotic cuisines such as Japanese, Italian and Arabic, have grown meteorically in popularity since the millennium.

Within the walls

Aerikon Onasagóras 86–90, entrance (inconspicuous) on Sokrátous. On the second floor above the Bank of Cyprus HQ, this lives up to its name ("aerial") with a view terrace; the food's hybrid Greek/Cypriot, with plenty for vegetarians. Noon–6pm, not Sun.

Ayios Yeoryios Platía Paleoú Dhimarhíou 27. Old Nicosia's favourite taverna, especially at lunch (even ex-President Clerides has dined here). Punters come for excellent, mid-priced home-style fare, including wild asparagus with eggs, *óspria*, stews, artichokes and the like, washed down with choices from an excellent wine list. Sit inside or out on the little terrace, with its potted plants and latticework.

Casa Vieja Arkhangélou Mikhaïl 3. Though Cypriot-run, this Spanish tapas bar is fairly authentic. It's lodged in a lovely old house, with most platters in the €5–7 range. Dinner only, from 7.30pm.

Da Paolo Konstandínou Paleológou 52. Trattoria offering brick-oven pizzas and fresh pasta dishes; the summer seating outside overlooks the moat, while the interior is dimly lit and brick-clad. Dinner only until midnight.

Enotiko Inopnevmatikon Egeon Éktoros 40 ☎22433297 (no sign outside). Oddball multi-purpose centre, combining bookshop, "culture club" and taverna, run by a one-time anarchist, now belatedly (and fanatically) converted to the cause of *énosis*. His cuisine is more digestible than his politics, successfully combining metropolitan-Greek and island dishes – allow €23 each with house wine. Seating in the courtyard, or the revamped indoor *sála*; dinner only Mon–Sat. Credit cards accepted, reservations suggested.

Iraklis Lídhras 110. The best, locally produced, ice cream hereabouts; always has customers queuing for takeaway, whatever the hour, and there's a pleasant sit-down snack-café attached.

Mattheos Platía Ikostiogdhóïs Oktovríou, beside the Araplar mosque. One of the best spots for lunch inside the walls, with pleasant management, summer outdoor seating and a versatile, seasonally changing menu – quails, octopus, rabbit, *koupépia* with *kolokássia*, artichokes with *goutsiá*, lamb and spinach, or mixed vegetables, with puddings, *shamáli* and walnut cake to finish up. Closes 4pm, and all day Sun.

To Steki tis Loxandras Faneroménis 67 ☎22675757. Simple presentation, reasonable prices and high-quality ingredients for Asia Minor/metropolitan Greek *mezédhes* and grills make this a hit; reservations advised. Outdoor tables in summer. Dinner only; closed Sun.

Zanettos Trikoúpi 65 ☎22765501, ⊛www.zanettos.com. A deceptively tiny, shabby entrance gives way to a Tardis-like arcaded warren, founded in 1938, where the main décor is wall photos of past illustrious guests and the innermost salon unroofs as a summer patio. Despite its fame, not a tourist trap, and locally attended; the €18-a-head *mezé*, accompanied by Páfos bulk wine, encompasses snails, *pansétta krasáto*, liver slices, pourgoúri *mé fídes*, *ospriá* and a generous dessert comprising *mahallebí*, fruit and *halvás*. Noon–4pm Mon–Sat, 7pm–midnight daily; must book Fri/Sat pm.

The new town

Akakiko Arkhiepiskópou Makaríou 9A. Excellent, convenient and affordable Asian food, encompassing sushi, *teppanyaki* dishes and soups, plus Malaysian and Korean platters. Daily noon–late.

Chyra Vassiliki Arcade behind Áyios Andónios market ☎22349803. There are two *mayiría* or stewpot canteens at the edge of this covered market; this is the friendlier, cosier (all of six inside tables, parties should book) one for affordable *óspria*, salads and Cypriot casserole dishes. Mon–Sat, lunch only.

Peri Orexeos Themistoklí Dherví 4–6 ☎22680608. Superb mainland-Greek cuisine with lots of vegetarian *mezédhes* and savoury dips:

fáva, artichokes *àla políta*, courgettes with eggs, sausages, etc, as well as roasted main dishes. Portions are on the small side, and not bargain-basement at €17–24 for two to three platters per person, booze extra, but well worth it; booking recommended.

Plaka Stylianoú Léna 8, corner main square, Éngomi (Enkomi), 3.5km west of the old town ☎22352898. A good, moderately expensive *mezé* house out in the suburbs, where you're advised to fast before indulging in the purported 35 platters. Daily, dinner only; reservations advisable.

Pyxidha Menándhrou 5 ☎22445636. 2008-opened fish specialist that's already grabbed the top rating for such restaurants. Properly seasoned fish soup precedes fair-priced and wild fresh fish (eg sea bass), served in a converted 1930s house with white table nappery and a summer garden. Not surprisingly, booking mandatory. Open daily lunch and dinner.

Syrian Arab Friendship Club Vassilísis Amalías 17, Áyios Dhométios (Agios Dometios), 1.5km west of the Tripoli bastion ☎22776246. What started out as a four-table café for (allegedly) Syrian secret-services personnel to smoke their hubble-bubbles has grown into an ample garden restaurant, with seating under three parallel tents or marquees (kept well heated in winter). The €18-per-head *mezé* quantity will have you begging for mercy, and it's very good indeed – much the best Middle Eastern fare in town – though strict veggies should order à la carte. Wash it all down with a little bottle of *zivanía*, and you don't have to be a Syrian spy to enjoy the hubble-bubbles, still there in all their glory. Open 11am–midnight; large parties should book.

Wagamama Vassilíssis Themistoklí Dherví 16, corner Menándhrou. Same menu, format (and prices, in euro equivalent) as the UK Asian-fusion chain.

Drinking and nightlife

There's more nightlife in south Nicosia than the naff or dubious pubs in and around Laïkí Yitoniá would suggest, but much of it is out in the suburbs, and you'll need both a car and local contacts to find it. Exceptions, many at or near the trendy Famagusta Gate area, are listed below. The best mid-town strategy for Nicosia is to stroll by and see what's happening, as new openings and changes of format are frequent.

Andonakis Paleón Patrón Yermanoú 18. Ancient (1936-founded), rather commercial musical taverna, often importing top talent from Greece; events typically start 11pm. ☎22664697

Bastione Café-Piano Bar Athinás 6. Pretty much as described, sheltered under medieval vaulting; occasional live performances. Closed Thurs.

Brew Lounge & Tea Bar in old arcade between Ippokrátous (technically Ippokrátous 30B) and Aristokýprou. Founded by Frenchwoman Gabrielle Duval, this offers 24 kinds of quality tea, plus mixed drinks and a few snacks. Indoor/outdoor seating by season, contemporary but not overbearing soundtrack in background; a tasteful oasis in a desert of tourist tat. Open 11.30am–2/3am.

Dhipnosofistes Evyenias Theodhotou, corner Pindhárou. Musical *mezé* house that's currently home to five-member band Epea Pteroenda, sadly a bit more electrified and *bouzoúki*-fied than their intimate early days at *Kala Kathoumena*. Wed–Sat eve only.

Enallax Athinás 16–17. Long-running lodestar of the Famagusta Gate area, with live gigs (rock or Greek pop) Thurs–Sat.

Ithaki Nikifórou Foká 33. Large, indoor-outdoor music bar (Latin, live rock, theme nights), at its best in summer. Wed–Sat night only.

Kala Kathoumena Nikokléous 19, Stoá Papadhopoúlou. Also known as *Tou Simi* after the owner, this alternative café offers a nice contrast to the chain schlock on Lídhras, with herbal teas and backgammon on equal footing with inexpensive Middle Eastern coffees.

Oktana Aristídhou 6. Multi-functional, ever-popular coffeehouse that also does drinks and snacks, as well as stocking an impressive range of books in Greek and English; open 5pm–2am. In the basement of the same premises is a very quiet, chill-out hubble-bubble annexe, *Uq-Bar*.

Orpheus Athinás 24. Small musical bar with theme events most nights: live Italian or Spanish music on Fri, R&B on Tues, live jazz Thurs, DJs Fri–Sat, live piano other evenings.

Plato's Plátonos 8. Very congenial pub installed in an old arcaded house, with an improbably long list of drinks, good pub grub (especially chicken kebabs), and classic rock, jazz and blues out of the speakers. Nightly 8pm–2am (kitchen closes earlier).

Music and film

For **musical events**, south Nicosia has several medium-sized indoor venues, besides the Kasteliótissa Hall (see p.249): the **Famagusta Gate Centre**, with good acoustics for chamber concerts; the 1200-seat **Municipal Theatre** (T 22463028 or 22673218) across from the Cyprus Museum at the edge of the Municipal Gardens; and the **PA.SY.DY Theatre**, for orchestral works, at Dhimosthéni Sevéri 3, the continuation of Leofóros Evagórou. In the absence of a comprehensive, regular listings magazine, coming events in Nicosia (and indeed across the South) are best tracked on ⊛ www.cyprus-art.com.

Film hounds are catered to by numerous commercial cinemas, which include the Zena Palace at Theofánous Theodhótou 18 (T 22674128); the Opera on the corner of Sofoúlis and Khrístou Sózou (T 22665305); Pantheon just above Evagórou on Dhiagóra 29 (T 22675787); and last but by no means least the plush K-Cineplex at Makedhonitíssis 15 (T 22355824), with six screens and flawless sound system. For art-house fare, the British Council and French Cultural Centre host films (and other events) once or twice a month; for their addresses, see opposite. Other cinemas include *The Weaving Mill/To Ifandouryio* at Léfkonos 67–71 (T 22762275, ⊛ www.ifantourgio.org.cy; open all day for coffee or a glass of wine), with periodic film festivals, and the Friends of the Cinema Society, at Cine Studio in Makedhonitíssa (T 22420491).

Shopping

In general, **shopping** opportunities in south Nicosia are limited, although optical goods remain relatively inexpensive, and shoes are good quality and reasonably priced. In the new town, most department stores and fashionable boutiques are found along, or just off, the initial reaches of Arkhiepiskópou Makaríou, especially a block southwest on ultra-trendy Stasikrátous. For arts and crafts, and specifically tourist-orientated items, the following recommended shops are all within the walls unless otherwise specified.

Andhreas Haralambous Koräï 9, near Archbishop's Palace. This artist's paintings and models of his theatre sets fill several lofty rooms in a slightly dilapidated building. Open 11am–1pm & 6–11pm; T 22457280 to confirm days.
Chrysaliniotissa Multicraft Centre Dhimonáktos 2. Part of the revitalization of the eponymous district, this comprises eight traditional crafts shops arrayed around a courtyard – and with a handy coffeeshop included. Open 10am–1pm & 3–6pm.
Cyprus Handicraft Service Athálassas 186, in the new town. Textiles, lace, wall hangings, reed mats and other characteristic Cypriot crafts items. Open Mon–Fri 7.30am–2.30pm, plus Thurs 3–6pm.
Gallery Dhiakhroniki Arsinóis 84, ⊛ www .cyprusartgallerydiachroniki.com. Dwindling stock of antiquarian engravings and woodcuts from

Cyprus, the Middle East and Europe (more facsimiles now); icons by modern master Christos Christides; and often striking original art, sculpture and jewellery by top contemporary Cypriot artists and foreign painters. Engravings are partially mounted, and reasonably priced (discount on multiple purchases). If you don't find it here, there are two nearby annexe premises with more stock, as well as a reasonable in-house framing service.
Horis Synora/Sans Frontières Akhéon 6–8, about 600m west of the Cyprus Museum. Small gallery selling hand-made jewellery and other craft objects, as well as hosting art exhibitions. Hours generally 9.30am–12.30pm and 4.30–9.30pm, but ring T 22369435 to confirm.
Leventis City Museum Giftshop Ippokrátous 17. Specializes in reproduction Byzantine silverware.

Listings

Airlines Aegean, Themistoklí Dhervi 46, Suite 702 (T 22644000; British Airways, Esperídhon 15, 3rd Floor, Stróvolos (T 22799999; Cyprus Airways,

Arkhiepiskópou Makaríou 50 T 22751996 or toll-free 80000008; Egyptair, Themistoklí Dhervi 27, T 22559000; Emirates, Arkhiepiskópou

▲ Street barrow vendors, south Nicosia

Makaríou 66E ☎ 22817816; Gulf Air, Amfipóleos 20, Stróvolos ☎ 22588005; KLM, c/o Hollandia, Theofánous Theodhótou 24, ☎ 22671616; Lufthansa, Arkhiepiskópou Makaríou cnr Evagórou, Capital Centre, 6th Floor ☎ 22451777; Olympic Airways, c/o Amathus Navigation, Omírou 17 ☎ 22716500.

Bookshops 🕮 Moufflon, Sofoúli 1, opposite Chanteclair House, 150m southwest of Platía Solomoú, is the best bookshop in the Middle East, with a huge stock of new and used (displayed across the street) art, literature and archeology as well as material specific to Cyprus and the Middle East, and their own growing list of publications. They post material abroad and conduct searches for rare material ☎ 22665155, ⊛ www.moufflon .com.cy. It's unlikely you'd need to go elsewhere, but for the record there's Soloneion Book Centre, in Stróvolos suburb at Vyzandíou 24, plus Tillerman in the same district at Arkhiepiskópou Kyprianoú 77.

Bus terminals ALEPA, Platía Solomoú, for Páfos and Limassol; EMAN, Platía Solomoú, for Ayía Nápa; Intercity, Platía Solomoú, for Larnaca; Clarios, Constanza bastion, for Kakopetriá, Plátres and Tróödhos resort; Kambos, for Kýkko monastery, Trípoli bastion; Kapnos Airport Bus, from the Filoxenia Hotel training school.

Car rental Hertz, Salamínos 4, Éngomi (Enkomi) ☎ 22346010; Petsas, Kostáki Pantelídhi 24A ☎ 22662650; Sixt, Lemessoú 46D, Stróvolos ☎ 22333841.

Cultural centres American Centre, Omírou 33B ☎ 22677143; British Council, Aristotélous 1–3, off Onasagórou ☎ 22585000; French Cultural Centre, Jean Moreas 3–5 ☎ 22317771; Goethe Institute, Márkou Dhrákou, across from the Greek-Cypriot checkpoint ☎ 22674608; Russian Cultural Centre, Alassías 16, Áyii Omoloyíti (Agioi Omologitoi) ☎ 22761607 (15min walk from walls). Most have morning and late-afternoon split shifts, with evening special events.

Embassies/high commissions Australia, Ánnis Komnínis 4, corner Stassínou ☎ 22753001; UK, Alexándhrou Pálli, northwest of the old town by the Green Line ☎ 22861100; USA, corner Metokhíou and Ploutárkhou, Éngomi (Enkomi) ☎ 22393939.

Fruit and vegetable markets The old central market, best on Fri and Sat, is up on Platia Paleoú Dhimarkhíou, at the end of Trikoúpi by the Green Line; two others are the Wed-only street bazaar on the Constanza bastion, and the daily Áyios Andónios market at the corner of Dhiyení Akritá and Evyenías Theodhótou.

Post offices The main branch (open standard morning hrs, plus Mon, Tues, Thurs & Fri 3–6pm [4–7pm July–Aug], and Sat 8.30–10.30am), sits atop D'Avila bastion, entrance from Konstandínou Paleológou. A secondary branch, with standard morning-shift-only hrs, is at Lídhras 67.

Service taxis Travel and Express, Leofóros Salamínos, by the moat below Podocataro bastion ☎ 22730888.

Swimming pools The largest and most central indoor public one is on Loúki Akritá, just off our map, due west of the old city, across the Pedhiéos

Following the December 1963 communal disturbances, the British (as guarantors of the 1959 settlement) announced themselves unable to single-handedly maintain civil peace on Cyprus, referring the crisis to the United Nations. A March 1964 Security Council resolution mandated the dispatch of a 6000-strong UN peacekeeping force – comprising forces from the UK, Canada, Austria, Finland, Sweden, Denmark, Australia and Ireland – henceforth known as **UNFICYP**. The initially authorized period was six months, but this has been renewed more or less automatically ever since. What was intended as a stopgap measure pending a durable solution to Cyprus's ethnic problems showed signs over the years of becoming a permanent island institution.

UNFICYP's brief has always been narrowly defined: to keep hostile factions separate; to discourage atrocities by their mere presence; and, in their capacity as potential witnesses, to verify the facts of such incidents. However, UN troops have limited means of imposing calm; they cannot launch a pre-emptive strike to nip violence in the bud, but are only allowed to return fire if attacked – in which capacity they've sustained over 170 fatalities over the years. Nonetheless, UNFICYP arguably did prevent the death toll from 1964 to 1974 from being significantly greater. Detractors have, however, pointed out that by "stabilizing" newly formed Turkish Cypriot enclaves, UNFICYP accelerated the process of partition.

After the events of summer 1974 the deployment (if not the role) of UNFICYP changed radically. Instead of policing the boundaries of numerous scattered Turkish-Cypriot enclaves, troops now patrol the single, 180-kilometre-long ceasefire line and the buffer zone of varying width straddling it, where 150 watchtowers constitute landmarks. Duties include maintaining utility lines crossing the zone, and ensuring the safety of farmers wishing to cultivate their fields right up to the boundary. UNFICYP has been instrumental in defusing sensitive spots – especially in and around Nicosia where opposing Greek and Turkish troops are close enough to abuse each other verbally. Until the "borders" opened in April 2003, they also provided humanitarian aid to the remaining Maronites in the North (they still ship food to the Karpaz Greeks), as well as helping to settle disputes in the two remaining mixed villages of the South.

Amazingly the August 1974 **ceasefire** has substantially held, with only very occasional (sometimes fatal) potshots in or across the buffer zone. Northern officialdom and the Turkish army have repeatedly accused UN personnel of leaking strategic information to the Greek Cypriots, with resultant restrictions on UNFICYP movements in North Cyprus.

However tolerated UN personnel may be individually, many feel that their continued presence merely delays the day of reckoning – hopefully non-violent – between the two Cypriot communities, and that the islanders should be left to their own devices. Such sentiments are increasingly endorsed by the UN, no doubt enhanced by long-standing arrears in maintenance payments running to hundreds of millions of dollars. Troop-contributing countries themselves currently foot over half the annual bill of $48 million, with $22 million contributed by Greece and (southern) Cyprus. The Swedes left in 1988, saying they would not serve indefinitely without tangible progress towards a settlement. Denmark withdrew its troops in December 1992, and the Canadians followed in June 1993, leaving the UK with the burden of peacekeeping to either side of Nicosia – essentially a reversion to pre-1964 conditions, though forces west of town are now multinational. Somewhat ironically, Britain's Falklands adversaries, the Argentines, have (along with troops from Chile, Peru and Brazil) replaced the Danes and Canadians in the westernmost zone, while around Famagusta, Slovakian and Croatian troops predominate. UNFICYP will continue to be a Cyprus player until a definitive political settlement is reached, and for some time thereafter.

riverbed; the most convenient outdoor one is on Ploutárkhou, also west of the Pedhiéos in Éngomi (Enkomi). **Travel agencies** Elijela Travel, at Íonos 1, Éngomi ☏ 22664164, is the local booking rep for most of the agrotourism properties. Anthology Travel & Tours, Stassándhrou 7, Suite 101 ☏ 22757763, ⊛ www.anthologytravels.com.cy, organizes walking, cycling, birdwatching and archeological tours.

Around south Nicosia

The hummocky expanses around the capital hold little of compelling interest for a traveller, and access to many sites is complicated by the Attila Line. Still, certain highlights can be easily taken in while travelling between Nicosia and either the Tróödhos or the coast, and as such make worthwhile stops.

Peristeróna

Heading west from Nicosía towards the Soléa or Marathássa districts of the Tróödhos, you've a long diversion around the disused airport in UNFICYP territory; 34km along, the village of **PERISTERÓNA** straddles a usually dry stream. The five-domed, tenth-century **church of Áyii Varnávas and Hilárion** on the riverbank is very handsome even from the outside, but hang about purposefully and the café proprietor next door will appear with the key. The architecture inside is imposing, with two apsed side-aisles separated from the nave by arches, though there's not much else to see: a surviving sixteenth-century wall painting of King David, another twelfth-century one of the Virgin and Child, the huge restored *témblon* and an antique chest of uncertain date in the narthex depicting the siege of a castle.

The CTO makes much of the church's juxtaposition with a **mosque** a couple of hundred metres southwest, one of Cyprus's oldest and finest, as a token of the supposedly long, peaceful co-existence of the two main island communities, although the Turkish Cypriots accused vengeful Greek Cypriots of setting fire to it in 1976. Any damage seems to have since been patched up. The square groundplan with its high superstructure and arched, tracery-laden windows is decidedly Lusignan – prompting suspicions that this is in fact a converted church. The grounds are locked and fenced to prevent vandalism, but the front door may be ajar for peeks into the vaulted interior.

Tamassos and Áyios Iraklídhios

Ancient Tamassos and Áyios Iraklídhios convent, some 22km southwest of Nicosia, can easily be combined with a day-visit to the monastery of Makherás (see p.236), or longer forays into Pitsyliá (see p.229). From central Nicosia, the route out passes through the suburb of Stróvolos, and then Káto Dheftherá.

Tamassos

One of the oldest-known Cypriot settlements, **Tamassos** owed its existence to extensive local deposits of copper, first exploited in the Early Bronze Age. In Homer's *Odyssey*, Athena went to "Temese" to trade iron for copper; later the revenues from the local mines accrued to the Phoenicians, the kings of Salamis and the biblical Herod, though these beneficiaries fail to clarify who was actually living, working or ruling at Tamassos itself. Excavations since 1975 have revealed the foundations of a Classical temple of Aphrodite/Astarte with traces of copper on the floor, implying, as at Kition, that metallurgy was considered sacred and that the priests controlled the deposits. Continuing the metallic and mercenary theme, local farmers dug up a life-size bronze statue of Apollo in 1836 – and promptly hacked it apart, selling the bits to a scrap dealer. The head was salvaged and eventually found its way into the British Museum, though again it tells us little about Tamassan culture since it was made in Athens during the fifth century.

The **site** (daily: Nov–March 8.30am–4pm, April–Oct 9.30am–5pm; €1.70); exposed to date consists of about half an acre of jumbled foundations, on a slight slope overlooking grain fields at the northeast edge of the modern village of Politikó. The most interesting items are two sixth-century BC **subterranean tombs**, excavated in the 1890s but partially looted before then; the pitched roof of the larger, double-chambered tomb still has a hole made by the thieves. The sandstone masonry has been cleverly carved in places to imitate wood and bolts appropriate to wooden doors, a style reminiscent of the "house tombs" of Anatolian Lycia.

Áyios Iraklídhios convent

The **convent of Áyios Iraklídhios** (Agios Irakleidios), near Tamassos, honours Cyprus's first bishop-saint, a native of the region, who guided the apostles Paul and Barnabas from Larnaca to Tamassos during their missionary journey across Cyprus. They subsequently ordained Iraklidhios (Heracleidius) first bishop of Tamassos, and legend has him martyred on this spot at the age of sixty. By 400 AD a commemorative monastery of some sort had been established here, to be destroyed and rebuilt a number of times; the last reconstruction took place in 1773, though the present *katholikón* is three centuries older. After twice housing monks, it was taken over as a ruin in 1963 by an order of nuns, who transformed it as you see today; this was in fact Cyprus' only convent during Makarios's time.

To find the convent, drive through Politikó village until you see the obvious compound on a slight rise just south. Inside (**group visits** only Mon, Tues & Thurs 9am–noon), it's a peaceful, domestic, ship-shape world, alive with birdsong: canaries from the aviary are for sale, along with pickled capers. A dozen or so sisters read missals, water the flowerbeds or doze near sheets of newspaper laid down to catch droppings from the nesting swallows. In the *katholikón*, you'll be shown a smudged fresco of the two apostles baptizing Iraklidhios; **reliquaries** containing his purported forearm and skull; some icons; and the sole exposed portion of an old **mosaic floor** regrettably covered over by modern tiling. From the side chapel to the south, a narrow stairway descends to a small **catacomb** where it is said the saint lived his last years and was buried.

Perakhorió, Dháli and around

Heading south of the capital towards either Larnaca or Limassol, monuments near the two adjacent villages of Perakhorió and Dháli are worth a short halt if you've time.

Perakhorió

PERAKHORIÓ (Pera Chorio) is visited mainly for the sake of the twelfth-century church of **Áyii Apóstoli**, perched evocatively on a hill to the west, surrounded by the village churchyard (the key tends to be in the door). Inside, the contemporaneous **frescoes** are disappointing – surviving fragments appear to be of the same style as the work at Asínou, and if you've toured the Tróödhos you needn't feel guilty about missing them. Highlights include two from among a troupe of angels lining the drumless dome, just below a badly damaged *Pandokrátor*; two shepherds conversing, their shoulder bags hanging from a nearby tree, while the infant Jesus is bathed in a rather rustic *Nativity*; and a somewhat smudged Virgin in the conch of the apse, flanked by Peter and Paul. If you need a meal, the *Peristeri* taverna comes recommended.

Dháli and ancient Idalion
Four kilometres east, **DHÁLI** (Dali) is an altogether busier place, a formerly mixed village perilously close to the Attila Line. (Potamiá, 3km down the valley beside the buffer zone, remains bi-communal, though there are just a few dozen Turkish Cypriots left, among them Fatma Mehmet, a "star" of the recommended film *Our Wall* – see p.446.) On the main thoroughfare into the village the *Kendron Iy Myli* rates highly for dinner, especially at weekends.

The main local interest, however, is not in the village, but a few hundred metres outside, to the south. Here the fortified hillside site of **ancient Idalion** is fairly obvious, though the place is still under excavation, with portions periodically closed to the public. Deep pits and courses of masoned wall in various states of exposure are of essentially specialist interest, but 1990s digs uncovered several giant *pithária* (urns) which, after cleaning and repair, are to be reinstalled *in situ*, under protective canopies. Other local finds and explanatory diaoramas are featured in a small adjacent **museum** (Mon–Fri 8am–3pm, Thurs until 5pm; €1.71).

The small city here dated from the Bronze Age and survived almost until the Roman era. American consul-turned-antiquarian Luigi Palma di Cesnola spent several summers here, plundering (according to his boast) 10,000 tombs; yet such was the archeological richness of the area that local farmers subsequently ploughed up many painted votive figurines of Aphrodite, the most important local deity, and an American team continues digging. Legend places the killing of Aphrodite's lover Adonis by a wild boar in the area, and in early spring you can still see red anemones, which supposedly sprang from his blood, poking out among the rocks here.

Áyios Sozómenos: Áyios Mámas church
If you've come this far, it's eminently worthwhile detouring to one of the most evocative minor Gothic ruins in Cyprus, near Potamiá. Unless you're already at Dháli, leave the A1 motorway at Exit 6 (posted Potamiá) for some contrastingly unromantic Mesaória scenery during the approach from the northeast: a vast industrial estate east of the highway, then stinking cattle ranches. About 2km before Potamiá, bear north onto a minor but paved road, following a sign in the standard monument convention announcing "Áyios Sozómenos"; this immediately crosses the Yialiás stream, with hay fields and palm trees heralding your arrival at the ruined, mud-brick village of **Áyios Sozómenos**, sheltered under a low palisade.

The romantic, triple-apsed ruined church, apparently (despite the road sign) dedicated to **Áyios Mámas**, sits on high ground at the southwest edge of the village; dating from the early 1500s, it was built in a retrograde Lusignan style of a century or two earlier, and possibly never finished. The site is kept fenced and securely locked, but you can easily admire the delicate arcades dividing the nave from the two aisles, and the monumental west door flanked by colonnettes with elaborate capitals. The two south portals were unhappily bricked up at some later date.

Áyios Sozómenos itself has lain abandoned since some February 1964 inter-communal incidents, in which local cadres of TMT killed two Potamiá Greek Cypriots, while the next day Greek-Cypriot police took revenge by attacking the place, with more heavy casualties on both sides.

Travel details

Buses

Nicosia to: Ayía Nápa (Mon–Sat 1 daily, on EMAN; 1hr 15min); Kakopetriá (Mon–Fri 11 daily, Sat 4, Sun 2, on Clarios; 1hr); Kýkko monastery (Mon–Sat 1 daily at 11.30am, on Kambos Bus; 2hr); Larnaca (Mon–Fri 7 daily, Sat 2, Sun 4, on Intercity; 40min); Larnaca Airport (16–17 daily 5am–11pm on Kapnos; 45min); Limassol (Mon–Fri 19 daily, Sat & Sun 5, on LLL, plus Mon–Sat 1 daily on ALEPA; 1hr); Páfos (Mon–Sat 1 daily, via Limassol, on ALEPA; 2hr); Protarás (1 daily at 3pm on PEAL; 1hr 20min); Tróödhos (Mon–Sat 1 daily 10.20 or 11.30am, on Clarios; 2hr).

Introduction

The North

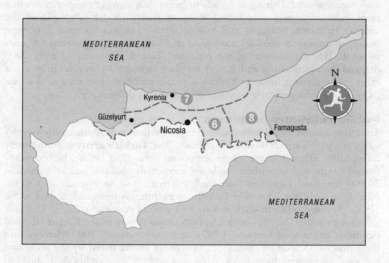

Introduction

The Turkish Republic of Northern Cyprus (TRNC) came violently into existence in August 1974 as a refuge for beleaguered Turkish Cypriots: first as the zone occupied by the Turkish army, later as the interim Turkish Federated State of Cyprus, and finally, by a unilateral declaration of independence in 1983, as the TRNC. Recognized by no state except Turkey, its creator and sponsor, North Cyprus was long condemned to isolation and underdevelopment. During the mid- to late-1990s signs of prosperity – often from dubious sources – appeared: fleets of recent-model cars replaced the antique Hillmans, Triumphs and Austins of yore, outlets for most European brands of consumer durables multiplied and cash dispensers attracted queues of locals. But the collapse of the mainland Turkish economy in early 2000 dragged the North along with it, and the place spent two-plus years in its worst crisis ever – serving, from the Turkish-Cypriot point of view anyway, as a spur to finding a final, equitable solution of the island's division.

Public relations problems

Travelling around, you'll notice several factors which contribute to the North's status as a pariah state. The ubiquitousness of the **Turkish army** is immediately off-putting: although there are fewer no-go areas than before, barbed-wire-fenced camps and unaesthetic military memorials abound, and an estimated 30,000 mainland conscripts still lend a barracks air to Kyrenia and north Nicosia in particular. The 1974 Turkish intervention is universally hailed as the "Peace Action" in North Cyprus, a nice Orwellian conceit.

Although nearly 20,000 Greek Cypriots chose to stay in the Karpaz (Kárpas) peninsula and around Kyrenia in 1974, and approximately 1000 Maronites on the Koruçam (Kormakíti) peninsula, systematic **harassment** by the army and the civil authorities have reduced those numbers to roughly 300 and 140 respectively. Since the "border" became porous in April 2003, their lot has improved, but there is still a long way to go.

The much-publicized **desecration** of Greek churches and graveyards is largely true, though Greek-Cypriot public relations artists occasionally overstate their case: the Byzantine monasteries of Akhiropiítos near Kyrenia and Khrysóstomos near Nicosia, both occupied by the Turkish army, had already been partly deconsecrated and used by the Cypriot National Guard before 1974. Greek Cypriots attribute the blame for desecration where it usually belongs – with the invading mainland army or settlers – since for many Turkish Cypriots, Orthodox shrines, monasteries and catacombs had also been sacred. A good example is Áyios Mámas in Güzelyurt (Mórfou), kept in good repair, unlooted, for three decades before resuming periodic Orthodox use from September 2004. But there have been cases of native Turkish Cypriots applying axes or sledgehammers to churches and cemeteries, and little evidence of repair or security.

Arrested development

Overall there's a feeling of grass growing between the cracks, often literally – this **dereliction** is due partly to the fact that the Turkish army in 1974 bit off rather more than the 120,000 Turkish Cypriots then resident on the island could chew. Most of the North is under-utilized, its villages half-empty: citrus orchards a couple of kilometres from Kyrenia or Güzelyurt die of neglect despite abundant water (admittedly now salt-tainted) to irrigate them. Ironically, *Yeşilada* (Green Isle) was the Ottoman epithet for Cyprus, a tribute to the groves and orchards which dotted the island until the eighteenth century. Public **infrastructure**, too, is starved of improvement funds, one result of keeping civil service rolls artificially swollen – the bill footed mostly by Turkey – to stem a brain drain. Major facilities, save for Ercan airport and Kyrenia harbour, are kept ticking over, but no more; improved highways are limited to a single strip either side of Kyrenia, another between Nicosia and Güzelyurt (Mórfou) and the vital Nicosia–Famagusta–Kyrenia highway. Except for some Saudi investment, most post-1974 international aid is shunted to the South; there's diminishing support from Turkey, which lately has had more pressing problems. Chronic **water shortages** are to be alleviated by a submarine pipeline from the abundant Manavgat waterfalls on Turkey's south coast, though it won't be completed before 2011 at the earliest. Meanwhile small dams (as in the South) have appeared everywhere, and giant balloons of fresh water have occasionally been floated across from Anatolia, despite losing most of their contents through leakage.

It was widely assumed that sufficient aid would materialize, and the place would really take off, following **international recognition**, so far withheld. At various times certain pro-Turkish and/or Muslim nations like South Korea, Azerbaijan, Bangladesh and Pakistan, with turbulent origins or ethnic conflicts similar to North Cyprus, considered extending recognition – but always backed down in the face of Greek or Greek-Cypriot threats in the international arena. In 1994 the Greek Cypriots convinced the European Court of Justice to ban any agricultural produce or clothing originating in the North, which then had to be sneaked into Europe under the Turkish quota. This throttled the Northern economy by limiting exports to about $60 million annually, forcing it to rely on other, less traditional foreign-currency earners. For much of the 1990s the TRNC was heavily dependent on **casino and sex tourism** from Turkey, but this inevitably entailed domination of the economy by mainland Turkish gangsters, with the acquiescence of the authorities. Of late the main customers are Greek-Cypriots, who eagerly patronize a cluster of a half-dozen brothels on the Lefkoşa–Güzelyurt road, plus another group north of Çamlıbel (Mýrtou).

The North also depends on fees at its various **universities**. There are nearly a dozen, attended by over 20,000 students (more than ten percent of the population); instruction is in English, a choice designed to attract students from the Gulf States and Africa. Most of these institutions, though, are little more than glorified crammers or miniature old-style UK polytechnics, with (often) fifth-rate instructors who wouldn't even get interviewed elsewhere, though the Eastern Mediterranean University in Famagusta has a solid reputation – and (tellingly) was once rated among the "top ten universities in Turkey".

Owing to the Greek-Cypriot-orchestrated embargo of the stigmatized North, and overpriced, artificially long air links from northern Europe, **conventional tourism** is relatively undeveloped. The trans-island freedom of movement since 2003 has inevitably brought changes, most obviously vast numbers of trippers (and overnighters) from the South, but off-season at least you can still enjoy the TRNC's sandy beaches, Crusader monuments and often excellent food in relative solitude, at a leisurely pace, in contrast to that of the busy South. Especially off the beaten track, people's helpfulness and hospitality is reminiscent of the Mediterranean of the 1960s and 1970s.

Native islanders vs Anatolians

The best lands and houses were allotted in 1975 to refugees from the South according to a complex point system; people were credited points for both commercial and residential property according to the value and type of such assets left behind. This government scheme was, not surprisingly, prone to abuse so that inequities in the distribution of real estate were widespread.

Poorer, isolated spots – fit mainly for goat-grazing – were assigned to **settlers** from Anatolia. Turkey, especially between 1975 and 1977, treated the North as a transportation colony (as indeed it had after the 1570 conquest), offloading families of 1974 campaign veterans, surplus urban underclass, landless peasants, and even low-grade criminals and psychiatric cases, until native Cypriots mobilized to oppose the process, and sent the worst elements packing. As no accurate census has been conducted since 1973, estimating current immigrant numbers is an inexact science, with guesses ranging from 50,000 to 100,000 (80,000 seems most probable). Their fate remains a big sticking point in any potential peace agreement, and their presence has caused chronic tension between native Turkish Cypriots and Turks, with the former considering themselves to have a higher standard of living and education. Relatively few of the settlers have participated in the recent conspicuous consumption, and their villages are unmistakably backward, dusty places living in a time-warp. The islanders pejoratively dub mainlanders *karasakal* or "black beard"; Turkey returns the compliment in a long-standing, patronizing quip characterizing Anatolia as *anavatan* (mother homeland) and North Cyprus as *yavru vatan* (baby homeland).

Starting in the early 1990s, a second wave of quasi-settlers came to the island, semi-legal migrant workers who have even lower status and less job/residence security than the original colonists; concentrated in Nicosia's old town, they are blamed for most northern Cypriot crime. The only other significant emigrant community is of Pakistanis, all from a handful of clans in the Punjab; as Muslims from a state generally supportive of the TRNC, with valuable English skills, they are easily granted residence/citizenship rights.

Since 1974 the Turkish army and nationalist ideologues in local government have diluted the British-ness and Cyprus-ness of the North, not only with settlement programmes, but also by erecting myriad busts of Atatürk and stark monuments commemorating the events of 1974. But a fair amount of *Kıbrıs Türktür* (Cyprus is Turkish) graffiti, scrawled by the TMT, the pre-1974 Turkish-nationalist action group, suggests that such sentiments are not completely new; indeed, the North has been subject to a campaign of **creeping annexation by Turkey**. First, the Cypriot pound was replaced by the unstable old Turkish lira; next, branches or affiliates of Turkish banks replaced most island ones; then, telephones were completely integrated into the Turkish system; and finally (as in the South), metric measurements were applied to motoring. Northerners have thus far resisted giving up left-hand driving, the most conspicuous remaining token of their separate identity. Those who oppose the process say all this is only to be expected, pointing out that "Mersin 10" – the special post code used to circumvent the International Postal Union's boycott of the North – just means the tenth county of Turkey's Mersin province.

Obstacles to reconciliation

Until the barriers came down in April 2003, many adults in the North, not having met a Greek Cypriot in three decades, found it hard to believe that *énosis* has almost no support in the South now. On a human level, they felt sorry for the local Greeks who were forced from their homes, but considered the Attila Line, guarded by mainland Turks, the best guarantee of personal safety. Those born since 1970 were indoctrinated in school to believe that EOKA activists would make kebab out of them should the existing barriers fall. When they did come down on April 23, 2003, the fear-mongers were proven wrong: since that date most people's behaviour has been exemplary.

But new, or renewed, friendships and general civility won't be a substitute for the hard graft of constructing a polity that functions. The position of more accommodating Turkish Cypriots has always been that the South must renounce the ideal of *énosis* and make the most of an independent, federal republic. Conciliatory Turkish Cypriots want to see veteran EOKA figures purged from positions of high responsibility in the South. What happened instead was (in 1992) the early release from prison of 1974 coup protagonist Nikos Sampson, and in 1995 the rehabilitation of 62 coup-supporting civil servants, actions causing enormous offence in the TRNC. Subsequent policies promulgated by the South, from the transliteration scheme that renamed many towns and streets to accelerated rearmament, plus continued adversarial actions in the international arena, compounded the damage. Such examples of continuing EOKA influence are reckoned further evidence of an underlying, unreconstructed Greek-Cypriot **attitude**: "You (Turkish Cypriots) are just 400-year squatters. Now get lost." At one point the Makarios government offered money and a one-way plane ticket to any Turkish Cypriot willing to resettle overseas, while the Orthodox Church encouraged Greek-Cypriot purchase of Turkish-Cypriot property at double its value, before the violent **coercion** of EOKA spawned open hatred and, ultimately, partition. Not that the North was slow to devise provocations of its own on an official or semi-official level. From 1999 through 2004, in response to growing unrest and opposition, the Denktaş regime or its extension, the UHH – essentially a resurrected TMT – stepped up **harassment of reconciliationists** in the North: hounding independent newspapers and websites, physically attacking demonstrators and journalists, prosecuting trade unionists and opposition politicans, and interfering with intercommunal meetings in the buffer zone.

This all acted to continually replenish the large **exile** community: while about 80,000 native Turkish Cypriots still reside on the island (North and South), easily three times that figure live overseas, mostly in Turkey, Britain, Australia and North America. (Proportionately, there is not such a diaspora from the Greek side.) After 1974, not enough Turkish Cypriots abroad responded to official pleas to return and "rebuild the homeland"; instead there was a slow leak outwards of those fed up with the settlers and political and economic stagnation – and of military-age lads fearful of two years' compulsory service under the harsh supervision of mainland Turkish officers. It seems certain that, in a population of about 200,000 (including 30,000 soldiers and 20,000 students at any time), the number of mainland settlers exceeds the level of native islanders. Among remaining Turkish Cypriots, rentier status – holding down a civil service post or being a landlord – seems to be the prime ambition, leaving the grunt work in hotels, kitchens and building sites to mainlanders, Pakistanis, eastern Europeans and even a few Brits. Failing that, many local and overseas Turkish Cypriots have opted to sell their post-1974 property titles to developers before any settlement renders them worthless – and thus creating more inconvenient "facts on the ground" for negotiators.

Underground Interdependence

Cyprus is simply too small to ever be hermetically divided: its regional economies, if not always its peoples, were too **interknit** under past regimes. Not many people know that the Turkish-Cypriot *Vakıf* adminstration has a substantial interest in Cyprus Airways, the Greek-Cypriot airline; the proportion's been reduced since shares were split, but the *Vakıf* is not about to sell up. Until the North's own dynamo came online in 1995, the South provided the North with electricity from its plant at Dhekélia, as a "humanitarian" gesture (but also to ensure that Nicosia's joint sewage system, based in the North, was not interfered with). Until the 1950s, **intermarriage** (or clandestine sexual affairs) between the two communities – and attendant religious apostasy in either direction – were far more common than generally admitted, and numbers of relationships have blossomed since the barriers came down.

Huge flocks of sheep graze the grain-stubble of the central plain, the Mesarya; even before the events of April 2003, a steady supply of them – along with market-garden produce – headed surreptitiously south across the supposedly impervious Attila Line, in exchange for tractors and other manufactured goods **smuggled** in the opposite direction. "Black" money from the South's large contingent of illegal immigrant workers heads North for wiring home to central Europe or Asia via the less regulated banking system of the TRNC. Cheap Turkish cigarettes, booze and pickled songbirds are exchanged across the Line for cash or the much-prized Greek-Cypriot brandy to an extent that both sides feel obliged to enforce customs limits. **"Legitimate" trade** is supposed to grow in accord with the so-called Green Line Agreements promulgated in August 2004 by the EU, though so far it hasn't. At present (2008), about 15,000 Turkish Cypriots work in the South, mostly commuting daily – a figure increased almost fourfold since April 2003.

Momentum towards a solution: a change of heart

Despite their overwhelming economic and diplomatic advantages, it was the Greek Cypriots who historically pressed hardest for a **resolution** of the island's division, whether prior to or part of EU membership. The Northerners always felt they had more to gain than lose from persistence of the status quo; their "enclave" was more comfortable than the besieged ones of 1963–74, with more ways out.

But with the northern economy in free-fall after 1999, and its ruling elite responding more harshly to dissent, the pendulum swung decisively to the North, even as pro-settlement sentiment cooled in the South. Beginning in late 2001 and continuing into early 2003, periodic, massive **street demonstrations** in Nicosia – occasionally comprising nearly half the civilian population of the North – put increasing pressure on the hardline regime. These gatherings, a new civilian government in Turkey and yet another UN censure of northern leader Rauf Denktaş for intransigence influenced the latter's decision to **open** several barriers on the **Green/Attila Line** to free movement in April 2003.

Opposition political parties and NGOs backing the demonstrations were also instrumental, despite continued threats and dire predictions by the northern government, in mobilizing the population in favour of both **EU membership** – whether or not Turkey ever joins – and a "yes" vote to the UN-promulgated **Annan Plan** for a solution to the island's partition. On the day (April 24, 2004), the two linked concepts carried in the North by a margin of 65:35, but this was not matched by approval in the South. Reunification advocates felt severely let down by their Greek-Cypriot counterparts, and to date few EU-related benefits have accrued to northerners (unless they have secured Republic of Cyprus passports). But the reconciliationists are in the ascendant, especially since the replacement of Denktae by more accommodating President Mehmet Ali Talat in 2005 and the victory of staunchly leftist Dimitris Christofias in February 2008 southern elections, and productive negotiations between the two continue as of writing.

6

North Nicosia and around

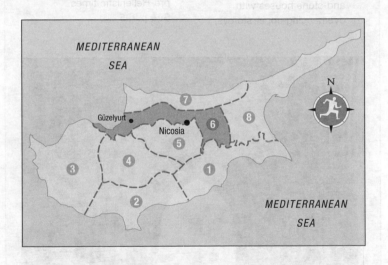

MEDITERRANEAN
SEA

Güzelyurt

Nicosia

N

MEDITERRANEAN
SEA

CHAPTER 6

Highlights

✱ **Büyük Han** This courtyarded inn, restored to its former glory, is the most impressive of Cyprus's purpose-built Ottoman Turkish monuments. See p.286

✱ **Selimiye Camii** Once the church of Ayía Sofía, sporting fine Gothic vaulting and relief carving. See p.286

✱ **Arabahmet district** Entire terraces of colourful, plaster-and-stone houses with overhanging upper storeys, skilfully restored like their less grand counterparts in the south of the city. See p.288

✱ **Ancient Soli** Excellent early-Christian basilica mosaics with animal, vegetable and geometric subjects. See p.294

✱ **Palace of Vouni** Perched high above the sea, this mysterious palace was used for less than a century in pre-Hellenistic times. See p.295

▲ Selimiye Camii (Ayia Sofía)

6

North Nicosia and around

While most visitors to North Cyprus are intent on reaching their chosen coastal resort as quickly as possible, it's worth remembering that **north Nicosia** and its suburb villages *are* to a great extent North Cyprus, with a third of its population. The events of 1974 and North Cyprus's UDI of 1983 made the city capital of a never-recognized (and now possibly provisional) state. What the relatively few day-visitors are after, though, is the town's concentration of Gothic and Ottoman monuments; there's little else available for the casual tourist, though dining opportunities have improved lately. Excursions elsewhere in North Cyprus's patch of Nicosia district head west past the agricultural centre of **Güzelyurt**, with a museum and lately reconsecrated monastic church, to intriguing ancient **Soli** and **Vouni** on the coast. Inland from these, the foothill oasis of **Lefke** is home to a controversial religious figure – though the town itself has few specific attractions other than its vernacular architecture.

North Nicosia

NORTH NICOSIA (*Lefkoşa* in Turkish, but actually an accurate rendition of the Greek-Cypriot dialect pronunciation of *Lefkosía*) is a much sleepier place than the southern portion of the city, with about 65,000 inhabitants, including satellite villages like Ortaköy, Haspolat and Gönyeli. The history of the two sectors, their medieval core enclosed by the same Venetian wall, was largely shared until 1974; the northern municipality's current orientation maps pointedly omit all walls and barriers, showing the old town as a unit, though the Turkish army deliberately ensured that all traditionally Turkish districts in the northwest of the city fell under their control.

The justification for north Nicosia's emergence as capital of the North, and continuance in that role, is epitomized by the story behind the huge Turkish-Cypriot flag picked out in nocturnally illuminated, white- and red-painted rocks on the foothills of the Kyrenia range, just north of town, placed for maximum provocative effect on south Nicosia. The current inhabitants of the nearest village, Tadkent (Vounó), all came from Tókhni in the South; on

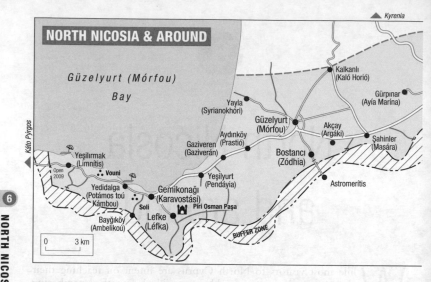

NORTH NICOSIA & AROUND

August 15, 1974, most of that village's Turkish-Cypriot men of military age were massacred there by an EOKA-B contingent. For the widows, orphans and very few survivors, responsible for the rock-flag with its flashing lights, the further existence of North Cyprus is insurance against a recurrence of such nightmares. Another grim reminder is Lefkoda's Küçük Kaymaklı district (Omórfita), a vast area of desolate houses, devastated December 22–25, 1963, by Nikos Sampson and his EOKA irregulars (see p.389). A cenotaph and modern mosque honour the many casualties, while the ruins have been left untouched as a memorial, shown (until 2003 at least) to schoolchildren to keep fear and hatred of the Greek Cypriots alive.

Far more than in south Nicosia, remoter corners in the old town lie desolate: especially in the northeastern district, dust-devils eddy along battered streets, windows are broken even on occupied buildings, and fine domestic and monumental architecture seems preserved more through inertia than any conscious effort. Outside the walls there is little of interest, with colonial-era brownstones being outstripped by the tatty modern constructions that increasingly disfigure the whole island. Within the walls live the most impoverished Anatolian settlers, principally ethnic Arabs and Kurds from Turkey's Hatay district, enhancing the Anatolian-village atmosphere; native Turkish Cypriots have almost without exception fled to the roomier, more desirable suburbs.

Arrival

Ercan airport lies around 20km southeast by road (off the dual carriageway towards Famagusta) and rather abruptly signposted – be alert. It was thoroughly overhauled in 2002–03, but still has few amenities: no bank ATMs, money-exchange bureaux or car rental booths, just a second baggage carousel and a tourist information post (open for arriving flights) to show for two years of work. There's also no public bus service for the airport; arriving as part of a package, you'll meet a courier who bundles you into a tour-agency **minibus** for transfer to your resort, or hands over your pre-reserved car. Otherwise, a **taxi** transfer to Kyrenia will cost at least £25/€33, to Famagusta £30/€40 and to north Nicosia about £8/€11 (sterling or euro accepted, change given in

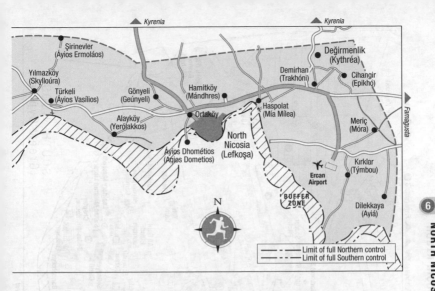

Kyrenia

Kyrenia

Şirinevler
(Áyios Ermoláos)

Değirmenlik
(Kythréa)

Yılmazköy
(Skylloúra)

Demirhan
(Trakhóni)

Cihangir
(Epikhó)

Türkeli
(Áyios Vasílios)

Gönyeli
(Geúnyeli)

Hamitköy
(Mándhres)

Ortaköy

Haspolat
(Mía Milea)

Meriç
(Móra)

Alayköy
(Yerólakkos)

North
Nicosia
(Lefkoşa)

Áyios Dhométios
(Aqios Dometios)

Ercan
Airport

Kırklar
(Týmbou)

N

BUFFER
ZONE

Dilekkaya
(Ayiá)

Famagusta

— · — · — Limit of full Northern control
— · · — · · Limit of full Southern control

NORTH NICOSIA AND AROUND | North Nicosia

YTL). Journey time to Kyrenia is about forty minutes. Given the lack of banking facilities here, come prepared with small-denomination sterling/euro notes handy for taxi-drivers.

North Cyprus' **second airport**, 3km south of **Geçitkale** (Lefkóniko, Lefkonuk), is currently disused. This is the "secret American base" of conspiratorial mythology, not actually very secret (you can drive right past it) and American only insomuch as Turkey used US-originated funds for its construction. In any future settlement, this facility may play an important role – either as a permanently staffed NATO, or Turkish, military base.

North Nicosia's compactness makes **overland arrival** relatively painless; junctions are fairly well signed, though **drivers** can easily get trapped in one-way systems, or leave roundabouts at the wrong exit. Approaching by road **from Famagusta**, you'll reach a roundabout north of town, currently at the edge of the built-up area, from which buses barrel south to the **bus terminal** on **Kemal Aşık Caddesi**, near the corner of **Atatürk Caddesi**. Coming **from Kyrenia**, you'll be pitched into another, even larger, round-about-with-monument at the northwest edge of the city, poised between Ortaköy (Orta Keuy) and Gönyeli (Geunyeli).

Parking usually presents few problems – as long as you don't try to leave your car in the congested, narrow, part-pedestrianized commercial streets of the old quarter. There are a few fee car parks in the old town – those near the Bandabulya and the Kumarcılar Hanı, marked on the map, are the most useful – but there are also two free, slightly remoter car parks in Arabahmet district, still a feasible walk from the sights. Unrestricted kerbside spaces are usually available along **İkinci Selim Caddesi**, just outside the old walls and again within walking distance. It is also sometimes possible to park near the Haydarpaşa Camii.

Entering north Nicosia **on foot from south Nicosia**, orientation couldn't be easier – once past the Turkish-Cypriot checkpoint at Ledra Palace, turn right at the first set of stoplights (Memduh Asaf Sokağı), turn right again and walk a few paces to begin a tour at the edge of the Arabahmet quarter. From the Lokmacı crossing, head straight on to meet Girne Caddesi.

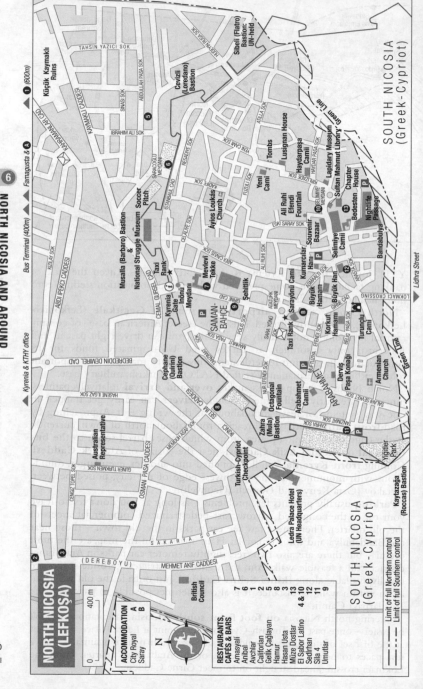

NORTH NICOSIA (LEFKOŞA)

N

0   400 m

ACCOMMODATION
City Royal   A
Saray   B

RESTAURANTS,
CAFES & BARS
Amasyali   7
Anibal   6
Avchlar   1
Califorian   5
Gelik Çağlayan   8
Hamur   3
Hasan Usta   13
Müze Dostlar   4 & 10
El Sabor Latino   12
Sedirhan   11
Sila 4   9
Umutlar

British Council

SOUTH NICOSIA
(Greek-Cypriot)

--- Limit of full Northern control
----- Limit of full Southern control

Küçük Kaymaklı Ruins

1 (600m)

Famagusta & A

Bus Terminal (400m)

Kyrenia & KTHY office

KARMANLAR ART CAD

KAYMAKLI CADDESI

TAHSIN YAZICI SOK

SİNASİ SOK

ABDULLAH PAŞA SOK

İBRAHİM ALİ SOK

Cevizli (Loredano) Bastion

Sibeli (Flatro) Bastion: UN-held

HASTANE PAŞA SOK

YENİ CAMİ SOK

ATİLLA SOK

RESADİYE SOK

SARAÇOĞLU MEYDANI

İSTANBUL CAD

GELİVİK SOK

MADFİYE SOK

KURP SOK

ABDİ ÇAVUŞ SOK

ALİ RUHİ SOK

Soccer Pitch

Musalla (Barbaro) Bastion & National Struggle Museum

Taxi Rank

KIZILAY SOK

ABDİ İPEKCİ CADDESI

CEMAL GÜRSEL CAD

Ayios Loukás Church

Yeni Cami

Tombs

Lusignan House

Haydarpaşa Camii

Lapidary Museum

Sultan Mahmut Library

Chapter House

Ali Ruhi Efendi Fountain

ESKİ SARAY SOK

Souvenir Bazaar

Kumarcilar Han

Selimiye Camii

SELIMIYE MEYDANI

Bedesten

Bandabulya

Nightlife Passage

P

HAYDAR PAŞA SOK

Green Line

Mevlevi Tekke

Kyrenia Gate

İnönü Meydanı

GİRNE CAD

Şehitlik

SAMAN-BAHÇE

ATATÜRK MEYDANI

Sarayönü Camii

Büyük Hamam

Büyük Han

Korkut Hamam

SELİMİYE SOK

ASMAALTI SOK

Turunçlu Camii

Lidhra Street

LOKMACI CROSSING

BEDREDDİN DEMİREL CAD

HASENE İLGAZ SOK

SELİM CADDESİ

MAHMUT PAŞA SOK

NUR EFENDİ SOK

POLIS SOK

SARA YOLU

Taxi Rank

MÜFTÜZADE EFENDİ SOK

BELIG PAŞA SOK

Derviş Paşa Konağı

Armenian Church

Green Line

Cephane (Quirini) Bastion

PINDAROU SOK

Australian Representative

Octagonal Fountain

Arabahmet Camii

Zahra (Mula) Bastion

KONCİ

NAZIMIYE SOK

ZAHRA SOK

SALAHİ ŞEVKET SOK

Yiğitler Park

Kaytazağa (Roccas) Bastion

SOUTH NICOSIA
(Greek-Cypriot)

GÜNER TÜRKMEN SOK

OSMAN PAŞA CADDESI

CENGİZ TOPEL SOK

Turkish-Cypriot Checkpoint

Ledra Palace Hotel (UN Headquarters)

MEDDAH SOK

(DEREBOYU)

SAKARYA SOK

MEHMET AKİF CADDESI

2

3

4

5

6

7

8

9

10

A

B

Orientation, information and accommodation

The northwestern roundabout shunts traffic southeast along the road that eventually splits into **Mehmet Akif Caddesi** (universally known as **Dereboyu** after the neighbourhood it threads through) and **Bedreddin Demirel Caddesi**. Bedreddin Demirel and Kemal Aşık's continuation Cemal Gürsel converge close to the **Kyrenia Gate**, the most historic entrance to north Nicosia's old town; just inside is the north end of **Girne Caddesi**, the main commercial thoroughfare and the continuation of Lídhras on the Greek side. Partway along its length is the swelling known as **Sarayuönü** (officially **Atatürk Meydanı**), effectively the city centre.

Like the rest of the town's tourist infrastructure, information provision can be haphazard. The way to individual attractions is not well marked, though once there, they do have bilingual identification placards. There are two **tourist information** booths (Mon–Fri 9am–5pm, Sat 9am–2pm), one just past the Turkish-Cypriot checkpoint near the Ledra Palace crossing, the other inside the Kyrenia Gate-house. The Kyrenia Gate branch organizes walking tours on Monday, Wednesday and Friday mornings, usually setting off around 9.30am.

Few foreigners overnight in north Nicosia, given the scarcity of "international-standard" **accommodation** and the abundant competition a short walk or drive away to the south. The existing two **hotels** are aimed at a business clientele, the better being four-star *City Royal* at Kemal Aşık Cad 19 (☎228 76 21, ⍇www.city-royal.com; ❸), with a spa, restaurant, indoor pool and inevitable casino. Its resolutely retro rival *Saray* at Sarayönü, the tallest and arguably ugliest building in the old quarter, is only really worth visiting for a drink at its rooftop-view bar.

The City

North Nicosia's sights can be seen in a single longish day; as on the other side of the Green Line, you won't need city buses but should rely on good shoes. Urban renewal, in accordance with the Master Plan (see p.245), has so far been limited to the pedestrianization of the **bazaar** and **Arabahmet district**, near the Green Line, the restoration of the **Büyük Han** and part of the **Bandabulya**, and ongoing (private) restoration of the **Kumarcılar Hanı** and some dwellings (plus a church) in Arabahmet; you will become painfully aware of what a larger influx of funding could accomplish.

The ramparts and the Mevlevī Dervish Tekke

The five bastions lying wholly within the Turkish zone are not, with one exception (see below), put to as much use as on the Greek side, though the moats are nominally parkland. What used to be the vice-presidential residence in unitary republican days, on the Cephane (Quirini) bastion, is now the North Cypriot presidential palace – with a new grandiose structure added beside the old in 2000. On the Musalla (Barbaro) bastion the army has erected a **National Struggle Museum** (variable hours), a predictable propaganda exercise in response to the one in south Nicosia.

Between these two ramparts stands the **Kyrenia Gate**, once the classic entry into the Turkish quarter, now stranded uselessly in the middle of Inönü Meydanı. In 1931 broad swathes were cut through the walls either side of the gate to allow the passage of motor traffic, isolating it as a sort of guard house. The Venetians knew it as the Porta de la Proveditore, or "Gate of the Military Governor", and fitted it with a portcullis and still-visible lion of Saint Mark;

6

The teachings of the Mevlevî order

A **tekke** is the ceremonial hall of any Islamic mystical **tarikat** or order; the Mevlevî *tarikat* is the outgrowth of the teachings of **Celaleddin Rumi**, later known as Mevlâna, whose life spanned most of the thirteenth century and took him from Balkh in Central Asia to Konya in Anatolia. He is most esteemed for the *Mathnawi*, a long devotional poem summarizing his teachings, which emphasized the individual soul's separation from God during earthly existence, and the power of Divine Love to draw it back to the Infinite. Quite scandalously to orthodox Muslims of his era, Rumi stressed **music** and **dance** as an expression of this mutual love and yearning, and the Mevlevî order became famous over time for its *sema* or "whirling" ceremony. Musical accompaniment always included at least one *ney* or reed flute, whose plaintive tones have approximately the same range as the human voice. As the *Mathnawi* explains in metaphor, the lonely reed of the instrument has been uprooted from its reedbed as the soul has been separated from the Godhead, and its voice is like the lament of the human soul for reunion with the Infinite.

after their victory, the Ottomans added an inscription lauding Allah as the "Opener of Gates".

Once inside Kyrenia Gate, almost the first thing on your left is the former **Mevlevî Dervish Tekke** (Mon–Fri: summer 9am–2pm, also Mon 3.30–5.45pm; winter 9am–12.30pm & 1.30–4.45pm; 5YTL). The Mevlevî order survived here as a vital *tarikat* until 1954, long after their proscription in Republican Turkey. As so often in Cyprus, the early seventeenth-century building matches or exceeds the exhibits for interest. Focus of the interior is a fine pine-wood turning floor, big enough for perhaps ten devotees; the former musicians' gallery is perched overhead. An archival photo shows one of the last ceremonies: the *şeyh* or head of the order watches over six dervishes revolving in the confined space, while above in the gallery sit players of a *ney* (reed flute), *oud* (Levantine lute) and *kudum* (paired drums), the instruments inextricably linked with Mevlevî observance. Today mannequins hold the same instruments inside glass cases; other displays include more archival photos, and – in a room to the side – a mock-up of the dervishes' refectory (communal meals and food preparation being an integral part of life in most dervish orders). In a multiple-domed side hall, its distinctive outline visible from the street, are serried tombs of sixteen *tekke* personalities, including founder Arab Ahmet and the last *şeyh* Selim Dede, who died in 1953.

Along Girne Caddesi to Sarayönü and the hamams

Tucked into a side street south of the *tekke* are more graves – this time arranged as a **Şehitlik** or Martyrs' Memorial from 1963, representative of many such in the North. A trilingual sign extolling the hundred-plus "unarmed and defence-less [civilian] victims of Greek thugs" is somewhat undercut by the presence of dozens of headstones for mainland Turkish soldiers who died in the opening days of the July 1974 campaign. In fact more than 1500 casualties were buried here in mass graves between July 24 and 28 (see p.421); the bones were exhumed three years later, and the current symbolic grave markers installed.

Immediately west of the Şehitlik, on the far side of Girne Caddesi, stands an altogether more cheerful sight, reflecting the benevolent side of Islam: the still-thriving **Samanbahçe** neighbourhood, a social housing project first funded in 1894 by the Cypriot *vakıf* or religious trust and finally finished in 1955. Its most striking feature is a round plaza, ringed by concave-fronted houses, with a round *sarnıç* or water cistern (still working) in the middle – an aesthetically pleasing ensemble, despite the evident humbleness of the dwellings, restored after 2004 and documented by an info-placard.

The commercial aspect of Girne Caddesi and the streets immediately around Sarayönü seems a faint echo of southern Nicosia, pitched primarily at soldiers and settlers from Turkey. **Sarayönü** itself has been the hub of Turkish life in Nicosia since the Ottoman conquest, and is still surrounded by the British-built post office, a rambling, colonial-standard-issue police station, law courts and numerous banks (ATMs). In Ottoman days it was called Konak Meydanı, after the governor's mansion (*konak*), more usually known as the *Saray* (palace), which stood to the southwest. Originally a Lusignan/Venetian palace, it was destroyed by the British early in the twentieth century; the popular term for the area (nobody actually says Atatürk Meydanı) is now reflected by the 1962-vintage *Saray Hotel* and the mock-Moorish pastiche of the little-used **Sarayönü Camii**. In the centre of the roundabout, a grey **granite column** from Salamis, stuck here by the Venetians after 1489 and so erroneously attributed to them, was once surmounted by their symbol, the lion of Saint Mark. The Ottomans did away with the lion and toppled the column in 1570, which remained prone until 1915 when the British re-erected it, capping it with a neutral metal globe.

From Sarayönü, Asmaaltı Sokağı leads southeast towards the bazaar and the main monumental zone. The **Büyük Hamam**, on a short street of the same name off Asmaaltı, was once part of a fourteenth-century church (St George of the Latins), of which only the ornate portal remains, slightly below ground level. Owing to structural and staffing problems, it's been closed since 2004 for "works". Another, less distinctive but well-managed steambath, the **Korkut Hamamı** (daily 8am–10pm), stands nearby on Beliğ Paşa Sokağı.

The hans and the bazaar

A *han* in medieval Turkey was an inn providing overnight lodging for travelling merchants and their horses. Such inns were once common across the island, but those in the South have been bulldozed or altered beyond recognition, and north Nicosia offers your best chance to see such buildings in Cyprus.

▲ The Bandabulya, north Nicosia's municipal market

President, until April 2005, of the Turkish Republic of Northern Cyprus (and its predecessor the Turkish Federated State of Cyprus), **Rauf Denktaş** was a classic example of a big fish in a small pond, long enjoying a role in the world spotlight that was far out of proportion to the size of his realm. His non-recognition as a head of state – Denktaş's official title at UN-sponsored negotiations from 1974 until 2004 was "representative of the Turkish-Cypriot community" – never prevented him from acting like one.

Pre-1974 career

Born in the Soléa valley village of Áyios Epifános, Denktaş trained as a barrister in London before serving as a protégé of Dr Fazil Küçük, later first vice-president of the unitary republic. Probably with the latter's knowledge, Denktaş in 1957 founded **Volkan**, a right-wing Turkish nationalist organization modelled on the lines of Sinn Fein to counter the Greek Cypriots' EOKA. This was succeeded by the even more militant and reactionary **TMT** (*Türk Mukavemet Teskilati* or "Turkish Resistance Organization"), analogous to the provisional IRA, banned (like EOKA) by the British but revived soon after independence. Officially, Denktaş had no connection with TMT after 1960, accepting instead the more respectable chairmanship of the Turkish Communal Chamber. But he was expelled from Cyprus for indirect involvement in the December 1963 disturbances, and sought refuge in Turkey (ex-President Glafkos Clerides later claimed he took Denktaş to the airport himself, at the latter's request). Denktaş was summarily deported to Anatolia upon being caught trying to land on the Karpaz (Kárpas) Peninsula in 1966, but returned under amnesty in 1968 to resume his leadership of the Communal Chamber. As the dominant personality in the Turkish community, soon elbowing aside even his mentor Dr Küçük, he acted as negotiator in the sporadic intercommunal negotiations which took place until the summer of 1974 – a strange role given his life-long conviction that living side by side with Greek Cypriots was undesirable if not impossible.

Modus operandi

Even before the 1974–75 establishment of a mono-ethnic North Cyprus, Denktaş was never squeamish about rough-and-tumble politics and pressure tactics. In 1963 he managed to get Emil Dirvana, the Turkish ambassador to Cyprus, recalled for condemning the TMT murder of two leftist barristers who favoured greater inter-communal co-operation. From 1970 onwards, outspoken domestic opponents were intimidated or placed under house arrest; Denktaş, through TMT, effectively pressurized Dr Küçük into early retirement in 1973, claiming that the latter displayed too much spine in his dealings with the mainland Turks. Denktaş spent most of 2000 to 2003 harassing the lively opposition newspaper *Avrupa* with criminal prosecutions, lawsuits and rent-a-thugs who firebombed or sequestered its offices (the paper, under courageous editor Şener Levent, is back in business, pointedly renamed *Afrika* as a comment on the North's Zimbabwe-like politics). Denktaş's chutzpah typically extends to his dealings with the Greek Cypriots. Early in the 1980s he demanded, and received, the exhumed bones of his mother from Páfos municipal cemetery for reburial in the hallowed North – the South's meek compliance was roundly criticized, especially by Orthodox refugees from the North denied the privilege of tending their ancestors' graves (assuming they hadn't been thoroughly desecrated).

Private party

Denktaş's political machine, the **UBP** (*Ulusal Birlik Partisi* or "National Union Party"), held civilian power uninterruptedly in North Cyprus from 1975 until late 1993, and while, as president, Denktaş was officially non-partisan, the UBP was still very much his creature. Little tolerance was exhibited within the party apparatus towards those who disagreed with him; his feud with Dervis Eroğlu, a former UBP prime minister even more hard-line than Denktaş on the question of a possible settlement, provoked the splitting-off of the Denktaş-loyalist **DP** (Democratic Party) in 1992. Government jobs were much easier to get with UBP or DP membership and, once employed, civil servants were "encouraged" in various ways to vote for these parties. Denktaş periodically (and tactically, as he always changed his mind) announced his impending resignation from all public offices, news greeted with relief by those fed up with his autocratic manner. The last instance was in 2004, when he promised to resign if the Annan Plan was approved by referendum; in the event he reneged on this by pointing out that, while the Turkish Cypriots may have voted yes to the plan, the Greek Cypriots hadn't. His 2000 to 2005 presidential term was in fact his last, with Denktaş in frail health since late 2002.

The master obstructionist sidelined

Despite (or because of) the UDI in 1983, more communally conciliatory elements in North-Cypriot public life always regarded him as a mere cat's paw of mainland Turkish policy, not acting (in contrast to Küçük) in the long-term interest of the Turkish-Cypriot community. Denkaş attracted some grudging admiration for a career as a wily, tenacious and even charming **negotiator**, but eventually most observers concluded that his consistent strategy of teasing the Greek Cypriots with proposals not really made in earnest, together with moving the goalposts when matters looked hopeful, was merely a cover for incorrigible intransigence. Thus, until the April 2004 referendum, he was long reckoned the chief obstacle to any federal settlement of the Cyprus issue – sentiments officially reflected in UN Security Council resolutions of November 1992 and April 2003, and by Richard Holbrooke's statement of May 1998.

In 2001, however, the international (and domestic) ground began to shift beneath his feet, and impending mortality – his own as well as that of long-time sparring partner Glafkos Clerides – began to tell. The **EU** made it clear that a decision on Cyprus's accession with the 2004 batch of new members would be made sometime in 2002, with or without the North's input, and with this concentrating minds – and possibly a mutual desire to make as statesman-like an exit from public life as possible – contacts between Denktaş and Clerides resumed in December 2001. Unfortunately, negotiations bore little fruit before Clerides left office in early 2003, replaced by the more hard line Таssos Papadopoulos.

Although the President's disrespectful nickname was (and remains) Kel ("Baldie" in Turkish), and he was increasingly dismissed as a Cold War relic for his knee-jerk right-wing politics, no successor of comparable (inter)national stature was ever allowed to emerge. His surviving son in particular, briefly head of the DP, was dismissed with the tag "Junior", doing his father's every bidding even in the latter's retirement. But as Denktaş the Elder's various defects became apparent even to former supporters, the northern public viewed the approaching end of the Denktaş era as an opportunity (perhaps the last) for improvements. The serious civil unrest and demonstrations of 2000 to 2004, and the consistently independent stance of the North's judiciary, had their effect. In contrast to prior style, where Denktaş circulated informally, confident that no one would bring forward the impending succession crisis by trying to assassinate him, the President of the North spent the twilight of his rule with a retinue of armed, frowning guards, just like any Third World caudillo.

Within sight of the Büyük Hamam is the seventeenth-century **Kumarcılar Hanı** or "Gamblers' Inn", whose pointed arches on the lower arcade enclosing the courtyard, and square-capitalled columns on the upper one, demonstrate Cypriot vernacular architectural influence. Sadly it's currently off-limits and half-demolished for a controversial refit by a businessman who has purchased it. The altogether grander **Büyük Han**, nearby at the corner of Asmaaltı and Kurtbaba, by contrast emerged from a decade-long (1992–2002) restoration as one of the island's finest buildings, and a signal commercial success. The "Great Inn" was among the earliest (1572) Ottoman public works following the conquest; it became the first city prison under British administration, but reverted in 1893 to a hostel for destitute families, something more like its original role. Each of the guest rooms in the upper arcade, now (like the lower ones) completely occupied by various artisans' shops, was originally heated by fireplaces. A little *mescit* (the Islamic equivalent of a chapel) balances on six columns over its own *şadırvan* or ablutions fountain, a design seen elsewhere only in Turkey at the Koza Hanı in Bursa, and the Sultanhanı near Aksaray. In the southwest corner a café-restaurant operates (see p.290).

Immediately south of the Büyük Han runs pedestrianized Arasta Sokağı, the heart of north Nicosia's **main shopping district**. Cloth and clothing, predominate, with machinists and junk metal depots in surrounding streets, but it's a far cry from the 26 different bazaars the city had towards the end of the nineteenth century. *Arasta* means a bazaar either physically built into the ground floor of a mosque or, if separate, one whose revenues go to the upkeep of a religious foundation. In this case the foundation concerned was probably the Selimiye Camii (see below), reached by following Arasta Sokağı east until you emerge in front of the Bedesten.

Immediately south stands the **Belediye Pazarı**, or covered municipal market (Mon–Fri 6am–5pm, Sat 6am–2pm), popularly known as the **Bandabulya** (a corruption of the Cypriot Greek *bandobolío* or "general store"). Like its counterpart in south Nicosia, this was erected in 1932; most of the stalls are devoted to fresh produce – most vivid in spring – and meat, though there are pair of luridly lit "Cyprus Delight" (*lokma*) outlets. Except for one by the entrance, antique and craft stalls of interest to tourists have moved to a designated row (see map, p.280 – "Souvenir Bazaar"), north of the Selimiye Camii, and inside the Büyük Han. The Bandabulya's eastern extension was refitted in 2006 as a nightlife and eating venue (see p.289).

The Selimiye Camii (Ayía Sofía) and Bedesten

The **Selimiye Camii**, originally the Roman Catholic cathedral of Ayía Sofía, is the oldest and among the finest examples of Gothic art in Cyprus, the work of French masons who accompanied the Crusades. Construction began in 1209 during the reign of Lusignan King Henry I and lasted 150 years; it was consecrated in 1326 while still incomplete, and the blunt-roofed bell-towers were never finished. The intricate west façade, with its triple, sculpted portal and giant window above, seems transplanted directly from the Île de France. Within, Lusignan princes were crowned kings of Cyprus before proceeding to Famagusta for a second honorary coronation as king of Jerusalem.

When the **Ottomans** took the city in 1570, they reserved their special fury for the cathedral, chopping up pulpit and pews for firewood and opening the tombs, scattering the bones within and using the tombstones as flooring; just a few stones escaped such treatment, and some can be seen stacked in a former side chapel. The pair of incongruous, fifty-metre-high minarets, unmissable landmarks almost at the exact centre of the old city, were added immediately, as was the ablutions courtyard fountain with trefoil-arched niches, but the building was only officially renamed the Selimiye Camii in 1954. You may be able to "tip" the custodian for the privilege of climbing a minaret for unrivalled views over the town.

Since the mosque still serves as a house of worship, there are no set visiting hours; try to coincide with the five prayer times, when you are allowed in shoeless, modestly attired and silent. The sense of internal space is as expected from such a soaring Gothic structure; abominating as good Muslims did all figurative representation, the Turks whitewashed the entire interior, so that the Selimiye presents a good example of clutter-free Gothic. But unhappily most of the original window tracery has disappeared over the centuries, replaced by tasteless modern concrete grilles. Other significant adaptations for Muslim worship include a *mihrab* (a niche indicating the direction of Mecca) and *mimber* (a pulpit from where the congregation leader may speak) set into the south transept, plus a women's gallery in the north transept. Outside, high up on the second, southeasterly flying buttress, hangs a small sundial; the *imam* resident in quarters at one corner of the Bedesten next door would consult it to determine the proper hours for prayer. Stroll a little further along this side of the building and you'll find a recommended café-restaurant working out of the former, fourteenth-century chapterhouse (see p.290), from whose outdoor seating you can contemplate the cathdral exterior at leisure.

Between the Selimiye Camii and the covered market hall, the **Bedesten**, was originally a sixth-century Byzantine church which eight hundred years later had the Roman Catholic Saint Nicholas of the English church grafted onto it, the whole becoming the Greek Orthodox cathedral during the Venetian period. Under the Ottomans it served for a while as a grain store and cloth market (though strictly speaking *bedesten* means a lockable bazaar for precious metals or jewellery), but was later allowed to deteriorate so that only the north vaulting remains intact. The magnificent north portal, with six coats of arms and concentric relief arches above, is the star attraction, though invisible for the moment, as the entire building, shrouded and scaffolded, is in the throes of a thorough, UN-sponsored restoration of uncertain completion date.

Other central monuments

Just north of the Selimiye Camii, on İdadi Sokağı, stands the **cistern-fountain** of **Ali Ruhi Efendi**, built in 1829 by the eponymous governor, with an Ottoman Turkish inscription inside a pointed-arch recess. This was one of nearly a dozen such built inside the walled town by the Ottomans to provide water for householders – and which functioned until quite recently.

Directly behind the apse of the Selimiye Camii, the diminutive **Sultan Mahmut Library** (closed for restoration) was founded by Ali Ruhi in the same year on behalf of the reforming Sultan Mahmut II. The appealing octagonal, domed building doubled as a *medrese* or religious academy; its resident collection of precious manuscripts and leather-bound books may or may not re-appear.

Directly across the Selimiye Meydanı stands the **Lapidary Museum** (Mon–Fri: summer 9am–2pm, also Mon 3.30–5.45pm; winter 9am–12.30pm & 1.30–4.45pm; 4YTL), occupying a Lusignan-era pilgrims' guesthouse. A jumble of unsorted stone relief-work in the building and the garden behind includes a Lusignan sarcophagus, a Venetian lion of Saint Mark, lintels with coats of arms, column capitals, Islamic headstones and gargoyles. But more compelling than any of these, and the first thing you see upon entering, is the delicate Gothic tracery window fitted into the north wall, all that was rescued from the Lusignan gatehouse that stood near Sarayönü until it was demolished under British rule.

Walking up Kırlızade Sokağı from Selimiye Meydanı, you can't miss the **Haydarpaşa Camii**. Once the late fourteenth-century Lusignan church of Saint Catherine, and restored in 1994 as an art gallery (open only for exhibits), this is the most substantial Gothic monument in Nicosia besides the Selimiye Camii. Great buttresses arc up to flank high, slender windows, the roofline rimmed with gargoyles. Over the south door sprouts an ornamental poppy or acanthus bud; the west façade with its carved portal is also adorned with (appropriately) a Catherine window, shaped like the wheel of the saint's martyrdom. A minaret was tacked awkwardly onto the southwest corner of the structure after the Ottoman conquest, rather than adapting the square, keep-like sacristy northeast of the apse. The glorious, airy interior, scarcely altered during the Ottoman centuries, features three ceiling bosses from which sprout fan vaulting, joining eight wall columns.

Continuing north along Kırlızade Sokağı, you pass the **Lüzinyan Evi/ Lusignan House** (summer Mon–Fri 9am–2pm, plus Mon 3.30–5.45pm; winter Mon–Fri 9am–1pm & 2–4.45pm; 4YTL), a restored fifteenth-century mansion which, while impressive enough – especially its carved ceilings – has no exhibits inside. Shortly after you reach the **Yeni Cami** or "New Mosque", the eighteenth-century replacement for a previous one destroyed by a rapacious pasha in his dream-inspired conviction that treasure was concealed underneath. The townspeople complained to the sultan, who executed the impious malefactor, presumably confiscating his assets to build the new mosque. Just the minaret and a Gothic arch of the original building, which must have once been a church, remain; the successor stands to one side, next to the tomb of the disgraced pasha. There are two more domed tombs across the narrow street.

The Arabahmet district

West of Girne Caddesi, the **Arabahmet district** is the counterpart to south Nicosia's Khrysaliniótissa neighbourhood, with imposing Ottoman houses on Zahra, Tanzimat and Salahi Şevket streets. As part of the Master Plan, many fine buildings on the narrow lanes between Tanzimat and Salahi Şevket have been renovated and let to various cultural and commercial organizations, though unlike near south Nicosia's Famagusta Gate, there are scarcely any restaurants or nightlife venues – the poor-Kurdish-village ethos here discourages entrepreneurs. The Green Line is less obtrusive here, so most other houses are still inhabited despite their semi-dereliction. Also forlorn is the elaborate, octagonal **Ottoman fountain** at the junction of Zahra and Tanzimat, allowed to run dry some years ago.

Arabahmet was, until the troubles, the **Armenian quarter**, and had been since the tenth century (though most of Cyprus's Armenians are much more recent arrivals from Anatolian Silicia). Salahi Şevket was, in British times and for a while after, Victoria Street, and plenty of ornate mansions still sport ironwork and Armenian (sometimes Greek) inscriptions over the doorways. The spire of the Roman Catholic church, straddling the Green Line, punctuates the south end of this street; east of it, now being restored from vandalisation and dereliction by an Italian firm, stands the fourteenth-century Armenian **church of the Virgin**, originally a Benedictine monastery but handed over to the Armenians as a reward for siding with the Ottoman invaders. Ironically, the Armenian community was expelled from this area at the end of 1963 by the TMT, for allegedly allying themselves with the Greek Cypriots.

Immediately west of the church sprawls the **Kaytazağa (Roccas) Bastion**, the point of closest contact to the South in all of North Cyprus – the buffer zone dwindles to nothing here. It was laid out as the Yiğitler Park in the late

1990s, to the consternation of the Greek Cypriots, who claimed it would make a perfect spying venue. From the edge of the landscaped area you can indeed take in the CYTA building, the municipal theatre and municipal gardens of South Nicosia, and (were you so inclined) easily converse with pedestrians on the sidewalk thirty feet below, at the base of the sloping fortification. With the opening of the Ledra Palace and Lokmacı crossings, the park's novelty value has waned, but the use of cameras here is still prohibited.

The attractive eighteenth-century **Arabahmet Camii**, named after one of the commanders of the 1570–71 expedition, serves as the fulcrum of the district; it was restored in 1845 and again, to good effect, during the 1990s. This mosque is only one of two examples of the Anatolian dome-on-square plan on Cyprus, a convention based partly on Byzantine prototypes. A hair of the Prophet's beard is kept inside and shown to the faithful once a year; in 1873 Archduke Louis Salvator of Austria saw instead an ostrich egg suspended before the *mihrab*. As at the Selimiye Camii, the floor is paved partly with Lusignan tombstones taken from a church formerly on this site; it also shelters the more venerated tomb of Kâmil Paşa, briefly grand vizier of the Ottoman empire towards the end of the nineteenth century and the only Cypriot ever so honoured.

The first main street north of the Line on which you can head east frm Salahi Şevket without obstruction is Beliğ Paşa Sokağı, with its **Derviş Paşa Konağı** (daily: summer 9am–2pm, plus Mon 3.30–5.45pm; winter 9am–1pm & 2–4.45pm; 5YTL), an ethnographic collection analagous to the Hadjiyeorgakis Kornesios house in south Nicosia. Once again, the well-restored nineteenth-century building proves at least as interesting as the embroidery, copperware and basketry adorning the recreated rooms. The original builder and owner **Derviş Paşa** was the publisher of Cyprus's first Turkish newspaper, archival copies of which are also displayed.

Eating and drinking

With the advent of "cross-border" tourism and more disposable income for many Turkish-Cypriots, the choice of **restaurants and cafés** in north Nicosia – including exotic cuisines – has improved greatly. The town centre still has preponderance of old-fashioned, continental-Turkish soup and kebab kitchens in keeping with the old quarter's population, though even here – especially in the plaza just west of the Büyük Han – more contemporary outlets are opening. The sole conventional **nightlife** venue in the old town is inside the Bandabulya's east annexe, where an entire gallery of contiguous bars and food counters have been arranged in imitation of İstanbul's Çiçeği Pasajı; it only really functions, however, on weekend evenings.

The Lefkoşa area specializes in after-dark **meyhanes**, the Turkish-Cypriot answer to the *mezé* houses of the South, and – it must be said – superior and more genuine in execution. There are claimed to be over half a dozen in the city and in nearby villages, none of the latter more than a twenty-minute drive away (if you don't get lost). The four most durable and reliable are listed below. Unlike in continental Turkey, they welcome women, though it's best to go in a mixed-gender group. We give phone numbers where known, as by their nature *meyhanes* are fairly informal affairs – check before setting off.

Restaurants and cafés
Amasyalı Girne Cad 174. Reliable and inexpensive *döner* and *iskender kebap*, plus soups and the casserole stews known as *sulu yemek*. Best (and busiest) at lunchtime.

Anibal Saraçoğlu Meydanı. Classic kebab-and-*meze* restaurant going since 1956, though regrettably it has sacrificed half its seating for a "sports bar", and gone up in price to about 30YTL a head. Erratic opening hours; always closed Sun.

Califorian Dereboyu Cad 74. This caused a sensation among trendier Lefkoshans when it opened in 2000, the first "American-style" diner in the North; the "misprint" name is in response to a trademark suit. The menu encompasses own-farmed chicken, Mexican snacks, burgers, fish and chips, all-American desserts and North American beers. Closed Sun lunchtime.

🏃 **Hamur** İkinci Selim Cad 46. *Hamur* means "dough" in Turkish, and that's the staple ingredient of the excellent, inexpensive *mantı*, *pirohu* and vegetarian *börek* purveyed at this lovely 1930s house where fireplaces blaze in the cooler months. Closed Sun.

Hasan Usta Cengiz Topel Sok, corner Dereboyu. Cypriot franchise of the famous İzmir milk-based pudding paradise: all the favourites like *sütlaç* (rice pudding), *keşkül* (custard) and *kazandibi*, as well as Asian ice cream (*dondurma*).

🏃 **Müze Dostlar (Bolkepçe)** Chapter House, Selimiye Meydanı 35. Friendly canteen run by the Friends of North Cyprus Museums, dishing out home-style platters (*molohiya* stew, chicken with *kolokasa*) for about 13YTL, plus beer, *ayran*, coffee or sodas to drink. It's a tough choice between tucking in outside by the Selimiye Camii's flying buttresses, or in the superb medieval interior; miraculously, not (yet) a tourist trap. Lunch only until 5pm.

🏃 **El Sabor Latino** Selimiye Meydanı. Indisputably the old town's sleekest premises – incongruously so given the slightly scruffy neighbourhood – though somewhat misnamed as the food is generic Mediterranean and Italian: Spanish tapas, Italian pasta, grills, fish, salads, some token Asian dishes. Between meal times, enjoy desserts and properly executed cappuccino or espresso. Allow 30–40YTL a head. Open all day, continuously. An equally successful branch (same menu) at Osmanpaşa Cad 28 occupies a fine 1930s Art Deco house with a conservatory.

Sedirhan Inside Büyük Han, ground level. The quality and portion size of the food – *helim böreği*, various kebabs – has improved of late, such that locals as well as tourists are seen here; in any case an unbeatable setting for just a drink.

Sila 4 Zahra Sok, corner Tanzimat Sok. The first – and still only – proper bar-with-taped-music to open in a fine old Arabahmet house, catering to both locals and foreigners.

Umutlar Girne Cad 51. Excels in the traditional Cypriot *şeftali kebap* (*sheftaliés* to Greek Cypriots

and London diners) as well as soups; pleasant seating indoors or outside in the pedestrianized lane.

Meyhanes

Avcılar Atatürk Cad 130 (may be no sign outside). As the name ("Hunters") implies, game and wild mushrooms are featured in season, but usual starters include wild *gömeç* (mallow) greens, *piyaz* (white beans), *eşeksiksin* humus, *çakistes* olives, grilled rabbit chunks and *bakla* beans. Home-made *makarna* (pasta) with grated cheese as a second course precedes kebab mains, with fruit as dessert. Ten tables are distributed across three rooms, packed out with political, trade-union and mafia personalities of every stripe – a measure of the traditional Cypriot social tolerance. The wall decor consists of ranks of bottles – some, disguised as Napoleon brandy, really Peristiany 31, the favourite Turkish-Cypriot tipple; beer, *raki* and wine are also on offer. Budget 30YTL a head, drink extra.

Dilekkaya Restaurant (Ahmet'in Yeri) Centre of Dilekkaya (Ayiá) ☎ 239 23 12 or 0542/851 77 72. To get here, go to the airport, then veer around it onto the old Famagusta road until you see signs to the village. Typical fare here includes *nor* cheese, chunky humus, eggs with *kaymak yağı* (extra-rich butter), seasonal wild vegetables, quails' eggs and stellar meat mains. Wine available, as well as the usual *raki*; prices similar to *Avcılar*. Roof terrace in summer, overlooking the little square.

🏃 **Gelik Cağlayan** Karaoğlanoğlu Cad 15 ☎ 227 33 63. A Nicosia classic, purpose-built as a nightclub-restaurant in 1948, now reopened after years of dereliction. Legend has it that the top four Greek- and Turkish-Cypriot honchos had a celebratory meal here on the eve of independence. A top-quality sixteen-platter *mezé* including pickled songbirds, veal tongue, quail eggs, capers, *samarélla* and *but pastırma* precedes full kebab and dessert; allow €50/95YTL for two with wine. Fri live Turksh, Sat live Greek (!) music; closed Sun.

Pilli Kebab Centre of Şirinevler village (Áyios Ermoláos, Ayaermola to Turkish Cypriots) ☎ 241 20 25 or 0533/860 90 12. As the name suggests, another popular meat-oriented *meyhane*, housed in an old double-arched building (summer seating outside on the *meydan*). Maybe not as cutting-edge as *Dilekkaya*, but a tad cheaper. Closed every fourth night when the proprietor moonlights at the airport, so ring to make sure it's open.

Listings

Airlines Cyprus Turkish Airlines, Bedreddin Demirel Cad ☎ 227 38 20; Turkish Airlines,

Dereboyu Cad 52 ☎ 227 10 61; AtlasJet, town agent ☎ 227 91 92 or airport, ☎ 231 41 88;

Pegasus, town agent ☏ 228 73 11 or airport ☏ 231 42 88.

Airport information Flight schedule confirmation: ☏ 231 48 06.

Banks and exchange Numerous banks near Sarayönü and on Girne Cad have ATMs. Otherwise, Sun Rent a Car at Abdi İpekçi Cad 10, also a *döviz* house, typically has the best rates for notes.

Books Kemal Rüstem, Girne Cad 22–26, opposite the *Saray Hotel*, has a decent stock of Turkish-English dictionaries, books on the North, and used English paperbacks.

Cultural centres/cultural interest offices Because of North Cyprus's international non-recognition, none of the institutions here officially has consulate or embassy status, despite depiction/description as such on tourist maps and literature. They exist primarily for cultural outreach to the Turkish Cypriots and provision of libraries and events for expatriates. They are: the American Centre & Liaison Office, Saran Sok 6, Küçük Kaymaklı, off map (☏ 227 82 95); the Australian Representation Division, Güner Türkmen Sok 20, in Köşklü Çiftlik district, northeast of the walled precinct (☏ 227 73 32); the British Council housed in the former embassy chancellery of the old unified republic, near the Green Line, at Dereboyu Cad 23 (☏ 227 49 38); and the German Cultural Centre, Yirmisekiz Kasım Sok 15 (☏ 227 51 61).

Post offices Central branch on Sarayönü Sok, just off Atatürk Meydanı (Mon–Fri 8am–1pm & 2–5pm, Sat 8.30am–12.30pm); parcels at the Yenİşehir branch, Atatürk Cad 6–9, corner Cevdet Yusuf Cad.

Travel agencies A very helpful one with fluent English-speaking management is Birinci Turizm (☏ 0542/851 03 90 or 0533/861 03 90), which can arrange hotels, air tickets, ferries to Turkey and competitive car rental, as well as currency exchange. They have proven useful for North Americans especially, who have few ways of making travel arrangements within North Cyprus.

Around north Nicosia

It is actually a bit easier to approach the western tip of North Cyprus from Kyrenia, but since the end of Ottoman rule the attractions below have always been part of Nicosia district. With an early start, all the following places can be toured in a single day from either Nicosia or Kyrenia. Given the course of the **Attila Line**, use of the pre-1974 main road from Nicosia through **Alaykoy** (Yerólakkos) is not possible; from the northwesterly roundabout between **Ortaköy** and **Gönyeli**, traffic heads west to Türkeli (Áyios Vassílios) and then to **Güzelyurt** on a fast road being further improved to motorway standard.

Güzelyurt (Mórfou)

Mention **GÜZELYURT** (Mórfou, Omorfo) to even the more conciliatory among the Greek- or Turkish-Cypriot communities, and you'll quickly learn how far apart are their respective acceptable minimum terms for an island-wide solution. Besides the loss of the tourist infrastructure and the Famagusta port, the abandonment of Mórfou plain, with its burgeoning citrus orchards, melon patches and strawberry fields irrigated by vast underground water reserves, was a crushing blow to Greek-Cypriot enterprise. Not surprisingly, the South has always insisted on the return of some – preferably all – of this region as part of any settlement; North Cyprus, with more than ten percent of its population now living here, has long balked at this. The unsuccessful Annan Plan indeed envisioned the return of the town, plus most of the surrounding villages, to Greek-Cypriot control; perhaps surprisingly, Turkish Cypriots locally resettled voted overwhelmingly in favour of consenting to move elsewhere.

Today, as in the past, Güzelyurt serves as the entrepot for the plain around, with little to detain casual tourists; it does, however, have an excellent **restaurant**. The *Niyazi Şah Aile Gazinosu* (daily; reserve ahead ☏ 714 30 64; live music Fri & Sat eves), just south of the northerly roundabout, on the west side

6

of the road, offers a fine six-platter *meze* including quail and a beer; it's possible to spend far more on the allegedly 42-platter seafood *meze*.

Approaching Güzelyurt from Kyrenia, railway buffs should keep an eye peeled for the Belediye Parkı east of the road, sheltering a **Baldwin locomotive** made in Philadelphia in 1924. This is one of two surviving relics (the other is in Famagusta) of the vanished railway across the Mesaoría, which ceased operating in 1951 after over half a century of transporting goods (and until the 1930s, passengers) between Famagusta and Gemikonağı (Karavostási).

The museum and church of Áyios Mámas

Towards the west end of town, past a nineteenth-century church with its belfry-top shot off, and the twin minarets of an enormous, Saudi-financed modern mosque, you'll find the local **Archeological and Natural History Museum** (daily: summer 9am–6.30pm, winter 9am–4.30pm; 6YTL), scarcely worth the admission fee for its bedraggled taxidermic collection (including two-headed, eight-legged lambs) and upstairs galleries of ceramic and metal artefacts from Toúmba toú Skoúrou and Soli that can't compare with any collection in the South. On the roundabout behind the museum, an exceptionally large **monument** honours Turkish Cypriots killed by EOKA in the South between 1950 and 1974 – plus a more recent casualty in 1980.

On September 1, 2004, after months (if not years) of discreet negotiations, and a thirty-year gap in observance, the progressive bishop of Morphou, Neophytos, celebrated a proper liturgy in the adjacent **church of Áyios Mámas**, long the cult focus of Cyprus's most beloved saint. This has now become an established major feast-day feature, and looks set to continue. The resident warden of the museum will admit you to the church.

Originally built in Byzantine times on the site of a pagan temple, the church acquired Gothic embellishments in the fifteenth century and had a dome added three hundred years later. The interior is in reasonable condition, considering the three decades of disuse, during which it functioned as a warehouse for icons rescued from around the district. A magnificent *témblon*, where lamps dangle from gargoyles, is matched by massive columns and imposing masonry.

However, the highlight is the purported **tomb of Mamas**, on the left as you enter the north door; above the undeniably ancient marble sarcophagus, a dangling curtain is festooned with votive offerings in the shape of ears – a strange image given that the saint principally warded off tax collectors. But the story runs that early during Ottoman rule, Turks, convinced that there was treasure hidden in the coffin, bored holes in its side, at which a sort of nectar oozed out, terrifying the desecrators into desisting. The stuff, which appeared thereafter at unpredictable intervals, was claimed sovereign against earache, and additionally could calm a stormy sea if poured on the waves. On the exterior west wall, there's a naive relief of Mamas on his lion (for the legend behind this iconography, see p.235).

Gemíkonağı

Soon after Güzelyurt you emerge on Mórfou bay, initially a shingled, windswept coast that's unlikely to tempt you in for a swim, but improving further along. **GEMİKONAĞI** (Karavostási), 17km west, was for decades the roisterous port for busy mines just inland; the 1974 war largely separated the two, but by then most of the open-cast pits were worked out anyway. Until the 1980s pyrites were still loaded for shipment to Turkey from one of two conveyor-belted jetties here, but even this has now ceased. The jetty could easily be adapted for loading such Güzelyurt citrus as are still harvested, but Famagusta-based civil servants have obstructed this strategy, so any fruit continues to be trucked at considerable extra cost to the latter port.

A strong local tradition of cabarets and girlie-bars continued on the watch of free-spending Danish UN troops stationed locally, but with the post-1992 arrival of penurious Argentines (UN troops are always paid at "home" rates), the local sin industry went the way of the mines. Now that Greek-Cypriots are permitted nocturnal forays hereabouts, there's been a modest revival, with two "night clubs" opening, plus a smattering of cafés and places to eat. The most conspicuous **restaurant** is the sea-view, white-nappery *Mardin,* where kebabs, simple fish dishes, *meze* platters priced à la carte and non-included service charge add up to a hefty bill; nearby *Hattuşas* is the more economical option for similar fare.

Lefke

LEFKE (Léfka), just 3km inland from Gemikonağı, sent three hundred Catholics to Nicosia in a futile attempt to help lift the Ottoman siege of 1570, but thereafter was always a staunchly Turkish–Muslim stronghold at the base of the Tróödhos foothills, and will stay that way under any comprehensive settlement. Formerly abundant water has fostered lush orchards, forming a stark contrast to surrounding bare hills and slag heaps. *Léfka* means "poplar" in Greek but it's predominantly a date-palm and citrus oasis, claiming to have the

Kıbrıslı Şeyh Nazim (1922)

Since the early 1980s, Lefke has acquired fame (or notoriety) as the home base of Naqshbandi Sufi leader **Kıbrıslı Şeyh Nazim** (or Nazem Rabban Haqqani Al-Kobrossi to his many Arabic-speaking followers). The Naqshbandi order of Sufism, originally active mainly in Turkey and Bulgaria, plus (formerly) Yugoslavia, emphasizes the personal authority of the *murshid* or spiritual leader, with teachings tending towards the reactionary. A trained engineer speaking smatterings of half-a-dozen languages (with a heavy, almost incomprehensible accent), Şeyh Nazim is a charismatic figure, considered by many to be dangerously so; Dr Küçük, the secularist vice-president under the old republic, saw fit to jail, then exile him to Lebanon. In 1974 he returned and set up the Turkish-Cypriot Islamic Society, ostensibly to promote greater piety in the notoriously lax religious environment of the North; this is one of several such local groups, whose membership does not much surpass a thousand. Both the late Turkish president Özal and North Cypriot leader Denktaş, who grew up in the same neighbourhood of Nicosia as the *şeyh* (and arranged his return to the island), have ranked among his adherents – as well as large numbers of Westerners, including pop singer Yusuf Islam (Cat Stevens), and more recently Bob (Mahmut) Geldof.

That said, Nazim is far from universally popular in the North itself, and local opinions on the man range from the dismissive to the unprintable. It is particularly galling to the *şeyh* – and a source of pride for the townspeople – that despite his long residence he has not made one firm convert from Lefke itself. Instead, he seems to have accrued all the requisite trappings – an admiring international coterie of groupies, shenanigans concerning financial "donations", a hash bust on the premises during the 1990s (though he himself was not present) – of a cut-price, Rajneesh-type guru.

Should you desire an audience with the great man, Şeyh Nazim is fairly accessible, provided he's not travelling abroad; just ask to be pointed towards the house near the Mahkeme Mescidi, at the northern edge of the town, though his followers will probably "vet" you. Şeyh Nazim spends considerable time in London, either at mosques in Peckham and Dalston or at the main Islamic priory on St Ann's Road in Haringey. See ®www.sheiknazim2.com/index.html for other centres worldwide.

best oranges on Cyprus, with apricots and plums for good measure. The Lefkans are traditionally proud farmers, known for not selling their land to any outsiders, but with the current water shortage, resistance to parting with real estate is crumbling. A single open-cast mine worked nearby until the late 1980s, but after the Attila Line severed links with the main mines further inland at Skouriótissa, the population fell from over five thousand to under three thousand. Of late there's been a modest influx of foreigners: instructors and exchange students (from the University of Sussex at Brighton) at the Lefke European University, and disciples of a charismatic religious leader (see box, p.293), who in their outlandish Muslim fancy dress stick out a mile on the streets of Lefke.

Drive through the town to catch a glimpse of the unremarkable but pleasing **Piri Osman Paşa mosque** at the edge of the oasis, flanked by palm trees and with the sere mountains as a backdrop. In the courtyard of the little mosque (usually locked) stands the ornate marble tomb of Osman Paşa, an Ottoman vizier supposedly poisoned as part of a political intrigue and buried here in 1820.

Back in Lefke proper, rambling old houses, many badly neglected, are scattered among the aqueduct-webbed greenery; up on the main road you'll see some British imperial architecture, the small university campus and a trilingual plaque marking the graves of the **Gaziveren incident** victims. In 1964 hundreds of EOKA activists attacked the enclave village of Gaziveren, near Yeşilyurt (Pendáyia), whose inhabitants held them off with a dozen hunting rifles, at the cost of these casualties, until Turkey threatened action and a ceasefire was negotiated. On the roundabout just below is an equestrian statue of Atatürk on a prancing, extremely well-endowed stallion.

For **accommodation**, there's the central *Lefke Gardens Hotel*, Fadil Nakipzade Sok 22 (☏728 82 23, ℻728 82 22; ❷), where your cultured hosts are Ergün and Gönül. In 2000 they renovated this former nineteenth-century inn, adding a new wing in traditional style to enclose a courtyard with a small pool; rooms – including some three- or four-bed family units – all have air con and satellite TV, and most have wooden balconies. The ground-floor **café–restaurant** is open to non-guests, and is the most reliable option in town; there's also a separate bar, popular with local students (who co-exist with green-turbaned or veiled devotees of the *şeyh*, sipping abstemious coffees out in the courtyard).

Soli

About 2km west of Gemikonağı, the partly enclosed ruins of ancient **Soli** (daily: summer 9am–6.45pm; winter 9am–4.45pm; 6YTL when warden present) are marked inconspicuously on the seaward side of the road – stay alert, as it's easy to miss the black-on-yellow "Soli" sign pointing inland, though nearly impossible to miss the huge protective roof.

Soli was one of the ten ancient city-kingdoms of Cyprus, legendarily founded early in the sixth century BC when the Athenian lawgiver Solon, supposedly resident for a while, persuaded King Philocyprus to move the city from a bluff overhead to its present site. But like Leonardo da Vinci's purported visit to Léfkara in the South, this probably never happened, and there has apparently been a town at this location since the Late Bronze Age, its name more likely a corruption of the Hittite *Siillu*. Whatever its origins, it became a hotbed of pro-Hellenic sentiment, and was the last holdout against the Persians in 498 BC. The name engendered that of Soléa, the Tróödhos foothill region inland, whose copper mines near present-day Skouriótissa spurred the growth of Soli, especially during Roman times, from which period most of the surviving ruins date. An expedition funded by the archeology-loving crown prince of Sweden excavated the theatre between 1928 and 1930, while the post-independence government restored it badly with modern materials in 1963 (the original masonry now lines the Suez Canal and the Port Said quays). A Canadian team uncovered the basilica and part of the agora after 1964.

An ugly concrete **theatre**, built over the original site from the second century AD, looks out over the narrow but lush, stream-watered coastal plain. Lower down by the car park and ticket booth are foundations of a large fourth- to sixth-century **basilica**, covered since the late 1990s by a hideous shed-roof; some sort of structure (but not this one) was arguably necessary to protect the fine fifth-century floor **mosaics** below, both geometric and animal. The most intact and famous of these, now difficult to make out except on bright days, show waterfowl flanked by dolphins, and a magnificent swan enclosed in a circular medallion surrounded by floral patterns. The five-aisled basilica was destroyed in the seventh century, and some of the mosaics were built over during construction of a smaller, later church closer to the apse, where a mosaic inscription asking Christ to protect the artisans has been partly obliterated. During the Lusignan period, Soli was apparently the see of the banished Orthodox bishop of Nicosia, who would have mulled over the vagaries of fate amid little but rubble.

Canadian excavations in the **agora**, west of the car park and below the amphi-theatre, were suspended after 1974 (as was all internationally recognized work in the North) and it is now fenced off, but before then a colonnaded paved street leading through the market to a nymphaeum had already been uncovered, as had the famous Aphrodite statuette and the bronze boy's head, both now in the Cyprus Museum in south Nicosia. The North's own 2005 digs unearthed various treasures from the necropolis.

Yedidalga and Yeşilırmak

Around 1500m northwest of Soli, at **YEDİDALGA** (Potamós toú Kámbou), acceptable **beaches** finally appear; the shore is pebbly but the warm sea shelves gently over a sand bottom, fine for pre- or post-ruin dips. At the roadside are two restaurants, better than anything in Gemikonaui, in particular *Aspava*, with an appealing environment and well-priced fish. It's debatable whether it's worth continuing the 6km past Soli to another cove at **Yeşlırmak** (Limnítis), coarse shingle on shore but with a sand base once you're in the water. Despite the bay's rather modest natural endowment, it's a popular place with no fewer than five **restaurants**, which however only operate during school holidays as their proprietors all live in the UK. The westernmost in line is the *Asmalı Plaj* with its "Guinness World Record" jumbo vine (*asma* in Turkish), planted in 1947. The easterly establishment is *Green River*, bounded on one side by the river draining this fertile valley with the taro (*kolokasa*) plantations for which it's famous. When the Pýrgos/Limnítis crossing opens – scheduled for early 2009 – the area will doubtless get busier.

Palace of Vouni

The mysterious hilltop **Palace of Vouni**, 3.5 twisty kilometres west of Soli, occupies a spectacular setting, with views both over the sea and inland to the Tillyrian ridges. Watch for a "Vuni Sarayı" sign pointing right a kilometre or so after the main road veers inland. Along the paved, 800-metre side road, you may notice a few charcoal burners' pyramids, vital since wood-burning bread ovens were banned in the interest of air quality and tree preservation. **Access to the site** is controlled by a lockable barrier near the road's start, so although the ruins (daily: summer 10am–5pm; winter 9am–1pm & 2–4.45pm; 6YTL charged at car-park hut) are only partially fenced, closed means closed here.

Vouni's history is controversial and obscure; even the original name is unknown, the modern one merely meaning "mountain" in Greek. It seems probable that the palace was first built around 480 BC by a pro-Persian king of Marion as an outpost to intimidate pro-Athenian Soli in the wake of a failed revolt; a few decades later another insurrection established a pro-Hellenic dynasty, which redesigned the premises. What is certain is that a decade or two after 400 BC the palace was destroyed by agents unknown upon re-establishment of Persian dominion.

The focus of the palace is a monumental seven-stepped stairway leading down into a courtyard, where a guitar-shaped *stele*, slotted at the top for a windlass, is propped on end before a deep cistern. This is one of several collection basins on the bluff top, as water supply was a problem – and a priority for a luxury-loving ruling caste, as suggested by the sophisticated bathing and drainage facilities in the northwest corner of the palace. At the centre of the *stele* is an unfinished carved face, possibly that of a goddess.

The original **Persian entry** to the royal apartments, along a natural stone ramp at the southwest corner of the precinct, was later closed off after the regime change and the entry moved to the north side of the central court, the residential quarters then arrayed around this in the Mycenaean style. After this remodelling, the palace supposedly grew to 137 rooms on two floors, the upper storey fashioned of mud bricks and thus long vanished.

Between the palace and the access road on its north flank is what's thought to be a temple with remains of an obvious **altar** at the centre. On the opposite side of the site, beyond the car park and just below the modern trigonometric point, are scarcely more articulate traces of a late fifth-century BC Athena temple, all but merging into the exposed rock strata here. Yet it must have been popular in its day, for a large cache of votive offerings (now in south Nicosia's Cyprus Museum) was found here.

Travel details

Buses

Güzelyurt to: Lefke (every 30min; 30min).

Nicosia to: Famagusta (every 20min; 1hr); Güzelyurt (every 30min; 45min); İskele (5–6 daily; 50min); Kyrenia (several hourly, departing when full; 30min).

Kyrenia and the
north coast

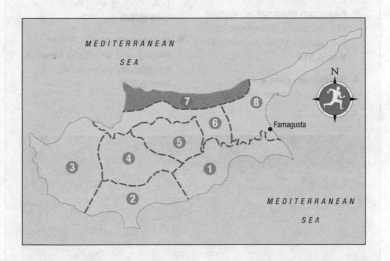

CHAPTER 7

Highlights

✳ **Kyrenia castle museum**
The best of various exhibits
is a Hellenistic shipwreck
recovered from a hundred feet
down. See p.306

✳ **Kyrenia harbour** Some
tourists never shake
themselves free from the
achingly picturesque old
harbour. See p.307

✳ **Lapta (Lápithos)** The most
attractive village in the
Kyrenia hills. See p.316

✳ **Koruçam (Kormakíti) village**
The ancestral stronghold of
the island's Maronite minority.
See p.319

✳ **St Hilarion castle** This
dilapidated castle, with its

bird's-eye view of Kyrenia,
was in military use until
recently – and it's easy to see
why. See p.322

✳ **Béllapais abbey** The last
surviving, postcard-perfect
Lusignan monastery.
See p.325

✳ **Monastery of Panayía
Absinthiótissa** Typical of
remote churches in the North
post-1974: grandly set, and
still imposing from outside,
but utterly gutted within.
See p.326

✳ **Buffavento castle** A wild
setting and sweeping views of
the Mesarya/Mesaoría.
See p.327

▲ Buffavento castle, Kyrenia district's highest castle

Kyrenia and the north coast

Kyrenia and its environs have long been considered the most beautiful landscape on Cyprus, thanks to the imposing line of high hills just south, which temper the climate and separate the area from the rest of the island. More than one writer has characterized the Kyrenia mountains as the quintessential Gothic range; the limestone crags seem to not only mimic the castles which stud them, but also suggest the delicate tracery of the Lusignan cathedrals in Nicosia and Famagusta, towns clearly visible from the heights, and the pointed arches of the medieval abbey at Béllapais, in the foothills. The ridge seems remarkably two-dimensional, rising to over a thousand metres from a very narrow coastal plain and running for some 70km roughly east to west, but plunging equally swiftly down to the Mesarya (Mesaoría) plain to form a veritable wall. In particular it acts as an efficient barrier to moisture-laden cloud, with rainfall on the north flank a good fifty percent higher than on the inland side. Springs erupt suddenly partway down the seaward slopes, keeping things relatively green and cool even in high summer and permitting the irrigation of various orchard and market-garden crops. Under exceptional conditions, Anatolia's Toros mountains are visible, 45 miles across the Karamanian Straits.

Sadly, the range has lost much of its original forest cover to fire, most notably in late June 1995, when an arsonist-set blaze consumed 180 square kilometres of forest and olive groves between Lapta village and Beşparmak peak. Reforestation was botched, relying extensively on exotic, quick-growing species like mimosa rather than the native pine and cypress; natural regeneration was hampered by a spate of dry winters, and the seemingly endless bare hillsides left by stripping the burnt trees for paper-pulp milling are now a feature of the landscape. Ironically, many olive groves that escaped the conflagration have since been assiduously grubbed out by developers.

Kyrenia, capital of the namesake district, is the linchpin of tourism here with its compact old quarter arrayed around a nearly circular harbour. When the distractions of the town have been sampled – within a day or two for most – **Karaman**, **Alsancak** and **Lapta**, spectacularly set foothill villages in what was once the most forested part of the barrier range, beckon to the west. A mixture of Turkish military facilities and hotels co-exist uneasily along the shore below, with the fishing anchorage of **Güzelyalı** marking the end of the strip developed for tourism and (most) real estate development. Beyond, the thinly populated

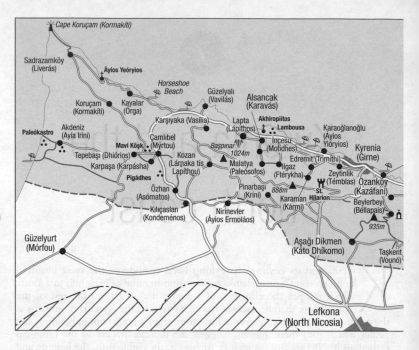

Koruçam (Kormakíti) peninsula, with its small Maronite population, makes a good destination for a day's drive, and you can return via the southwestern slopes of the Kyrenia hills on scenic, if little-travelled, back roads.

Southeast of Kyrenia, the Lusignan abbey of **Béllapais** very much tops the list of things to see, despite its relative commercialization; the surrounding village of **Beylerbeyi** and its neighbours **Ozanköy** and **Çatalköy** have always been sought-after dormitory annexes of Kyrenia, even before the current building boom. The **Kyrenia hills** themselves offer satisfying day-trip destinations: the celebrated castles of **St Hilarion** and **Buffavento** and the remote, abandoned monasteries of **Absinthiótissa** and **Antifonítis**. Down on the coast east of Kyrenia, a succession of excellent **beaches** – in particular Lara, Alagadi and Onüçüncü Mil – remain as yet almost undeveloped.

Kyrenia (Girne)

Despite unsightly expansion since 1974, **KYRENIA** (Girne, *Kerýnia* in Greek) – or more precisely its old quarter – can still claim to be Cyprus's most attractive coastal town, and the one with the most resonant reputation among foreigners – helped along by Lawrence Durrell, plus scores of other eulogizing and expatriate Brits. It's certainly the only resort on the island that has anything of the feel of the central Mediterranean, a fact which restaurateurs down at the ruthlessly picturesque harbour have no qualms about exploiting to the hilt.

Kyrenia's highlights – the harbour and its guardian castle, plus two minor museums – can easily be seen on foot in a day. Move away from the kernel of the old town, however, and you enter what's in effect a vast building site, outpacing

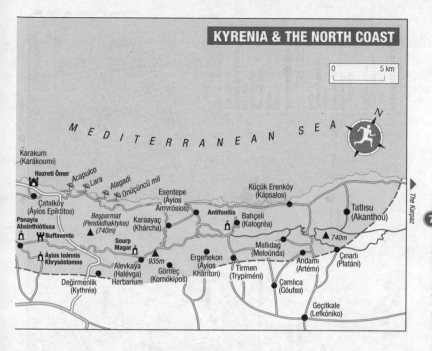

0   5 km

M E D I T E R R A N E A N   S E A

Karakum
(Karákoumi)

Hazreti Ömer   Acapulco
Lara   Alagadi
Onúçüncü mil
Esentepe
(Áyios   Küçük Erenköy
Çatalköy   Amvrósios)   (Kápsalos)
(Áyios Epíktitos)   Besparmat   Antifonítis   Tatlısu
Panayía   (Pendádhaktylos)   Karaayaç   Bahçeli   (Akanthoú)
Absinthiótissa   ▲ (740m)   (Khárcha)   (Kalogréa)
Buffavento   Sourp   Malhdağ   740m
Áyios Ioánnis   Magar   Ergenekon   (Meloúnda)   Çınarlı
Khrysóstomos   Alevkaya   935m   (Áyios   Arıdamı   (Platáni)
(Halévga)   Görneç   Kháriton)   Tirmen   (Artémı)
Değirmenlik   Herbarium   (Kornókipoş)   (Trypiméni)   Çamlıca
(Kythréa)   (Góufas)
Geçitkale
(Lefkóniko)

The Karpaz

7

KYRENIA AND THE NORTH COAST | Kyrenia (Girne)

almost anywhere in the Mediterranean. Construction of villas and apartments has increased twenty-fold since 2002, with scores of estate agents in town flogging them, and a specialized entourage – antique dealers, plant nurseries, Brit-style DIY shops and building supplies, outlets for Italian designer furniture and wrought iron, contractors' offices – to service them, largely displacing the former commerce serving local needs. Traffic is almost non-stop even in the off-season, and gridlock is guaranteed at peak hours. A new bypass road is nearing completion southwest of town, as the old one is now well inside the mess of four- to five-storey blocks, a skyline redeemed only by the magnificent backdrop of the Kyrenia range.

Some history

Kyrenia was founded by refugees from the Greek mainland in the tenth century BC, and counted among the ten city-kingdoms of Classical Cyprus. The chosen site, well east of the present castle, was conveniently near a source of suitable building stone at what's now called Khrysokava. The quarry doubled as a cemetery, and another necropolis soon appeared to the west. By the third century AD, Christians were living surreptitiously in the Khrysokava catacombs, prior to the establishment of Christianity as the official Roman religion. After Arab raids of the seventh century contemptuously swept through the town's rickety outer walls, the castle was built; thereafter the history of the place more or less parallels that of its castle (see p.305).

By 1300 the focus of Kyrenia had shifted northwest to within the present confines of the old town, though the eastern port was still in use, protected by a surviving Roman breakwater, and Khrysokava continued to supply building stone. The moat around the castle held water, and a chain across the medieval port's entrance permitted its closure in troubled times. The town surrendered to the Ottomans in 1570 and by 1600 was in relative decline, its moat now dry.

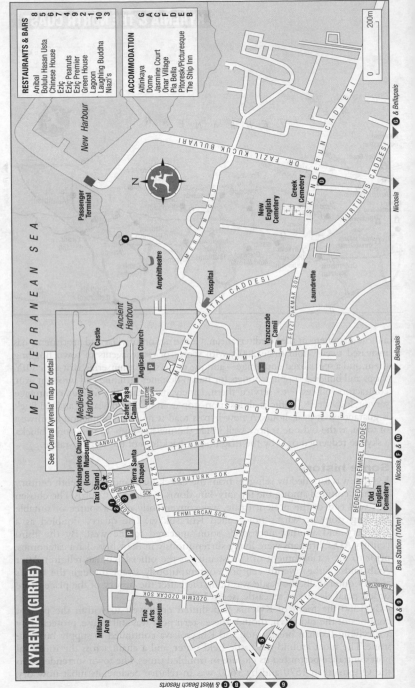

KYRENIA (GIRNE)

RESTAURANTS & BARS

Anibal	8
Bolulu Hasan Usta	5
Chinese House	6
Eziç	7
Eziç Peanuts	4
Eziç Premier	9
Green House	2
Lagoon	1
Laughing Buddha	10
Niazi's	3

ACCOMMODATION

Altinkaya	G
Dome	A
Jasmine Court	C
Onar Village	F
Pia Bella	D
Pitoresk/Picturesque	E
The Ship Inn	B

New Harbour

Passenger Terminal

N

M E D I T E R R A N E A N   S E A

Castle

Ancient Harbour

Medieval Harbour

Amphitheatre

Anglican Church

Archángelos Church (Icon Museum)

Cafer Paşa Camii

Terra Santa Chapel

Taxi Stand

See 'Central Kyrenia' map for detail

Fine Arts Museum

Military Area

Hospital

Yazıcızade Camii

New English Cemetery

Greek Cemetery

Laundrette

Old English Cemetery

MERSİN CAD

DR. FAZIL KÜÇÜK BULVARI

İSKENDERUN CADDESİ

KURTULUS CADDESİ

MUSTAFA ÇAĞATAY CADDESİ

NAMIK KEMAL CADDESI

FEVZI ÇAKMAK SOK

ECEVİT CADDESİ

ATATURK CAD

KORUTURK SOK

FEHMI ERCAN SOK

ZİYA RIZKI CADDESİ

CANBULAT SOK

KORDON BOYU

ERSIN AYDIN SOK

SOK

NERGIS CADDESI

BEDREDDIN DEMIREL CADDESI

SEDAT SIMAVI CAD

METE ADANIR CADDESI

ZİYA RIZKI CAD

OZDEMIR OZOCAK SOK

SEÇKIN SOKAK

SEHITLER CAD

K. ÖZÜRST SOK

BELEDİYE MEYDANI

▼ G & Bellapais

▼ Nicosia

▼ Bellapais

▼ Nicosia, F & 10

▼ Bus Station (100m)

▼ E & 9

▼ 8, C & West Beach Resorts

0   200m

302

7

KYRENIA AND THE NORTH COAST | Kyrenia (Girne)

Like the other ports on the island, Kyrenia only began to revive after the start of British administration, following the construction of roads to the interior and improvements to the harbour. Until the 1950s, the harbour economy relied on exporting carob pods, importing goods from Greece and Asia Minor and the construction of caiques.

As the British empire imploded after World War II, and redundant or retired colonial civil servants and army officers drifted homewards from less pleasant postings via Cyprus, many got no further than Kyrenia and its stage-set harbour. Foreign numbers plummeted after the events of 1974, as a result of confiscations by the early Turkish administration, and only during the late 1980s did they again attain three figures, against the town's current population of perhaps 20,000, many of whom are originally from Limassol. Since the millennium, however, expat numbers – even if only resident part-time – have soared.

Arrival, orientation and information

Visitors arriving **by plane** will be met by taxis and shuttle coaches, which take the main road from Ercan airport to Kyrenia (41km in total) via the northern edge of Nicosia; this (mostly dual carriageway up to here) becomes Ecevit Caddesi as it enters city limits from the south, ending at the mostly pedestrianized central plaza, Belediye Meydanı. Drivers can use the narrower but slightly shorter and less crowded bypass road over Beşparmak saddle, which enters Kyrenia on the east from Değirmenlik. A few **minibus** services still end within sight of Belediye Meydanı, but most **bus** services call at a newer station in the far southwest of town, just off our main Kyrenia map.

Ferry boats and catamarans from Turkey dock at the modern commercial harbour, about 1500m east of the town centre. The main west–east thoroughfare through town changes names a few times: one-way Ziya Rızkı Caddesi on the west side of Belediye Meydanı, Mustafa Çağatay Caddesi just east of Ecevit, and then finally İskenderun Caddesi between the turning for Béllapais and the access road to the port.

Parking is a problem year-round; besides the central fee lots (shown on our maps), a limited number of uncontrolled spaces lie along two narrow streets flanking the castle on its south and west. Except for the old harbour area, closed to wheeled traffic all day in summer and from 5pm to midnight off-season, cars are allowed to circulate along Kordon Boyu, the shore road.

The **tourist information bureau** (Mon–Fri 8am–5pm, Sat & Sun 10am–6pm) occupies the ground floor of the old customs building on the harbour, though it does little beyond dispensing glossy pamphlets in Turkish; when it's closed, the notice board outside may have some basic information, such as current museum opening hours and the like. There are numerous **internet cafés** in the centre, though few are long-lived enough to single out.

Accommodation

If you want to savour the atmosphere of the old quarter and aren't sold on the idea of basing yourself in a remote, self-contained holiday complex, you might consider one of the few small, en-suite **hotels** within a short distance of the harbour, sometimes with views of the water. If you can pay three-star rates, however, and are willing to rent a car, consider several small-scale **holiday complexes** with pools and other facilities towards or at the edge of town.

Altınkaya Béllapais Rd, 2km southwest of centre ☎815 50 01, ✆www.altinkaya-cyprus.com. Galleried one-bedroom units were redone in 2008,

complementing a nearly as recent wing of parquet-floored hotel rooms. They're all set in somewhat bleak grounds, but the location – suburban, but just

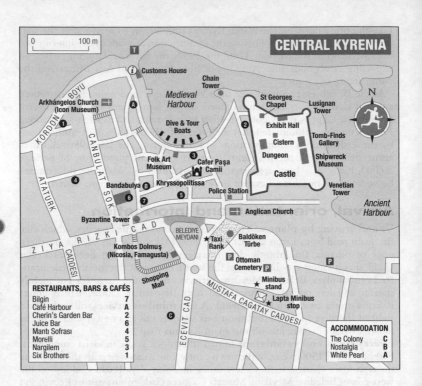

CENTRAL KYRENIA

0   100 m

Customs House

Chain Tower

Medieval Harbour

Arkhángelos Church (Icon Museum)

Dive & Tour Boats

St Georges Chapel

Lusignan Tower

Exhibit Hall

Tomb-Finds Gallery

Folk Art Museum

Cafer Paşa Camii

Cistern

Dungeon

Shipwreck Museum

Bandabulya

Khryssopolítissa

Castle

Police Station

Venetian Tower

Byzantine Tower

Anglican Church

Ancient Harbour

BELEDIYE MEYDANI

Baldöken Türbe

Taxi Rank

Kombos Dolmuş (Nicosia, Famagusta)

Ottoman Cemetery

Minibus stand

Shopping Mall

MUSTAFA CAGATAY CADDESI

Lapta Minibus stop

ECEVIT CAD

RESTAURANTS, BARS & CAFÉS

Bilgin	7
Café Harbour	A
Cherin's Garden Bar	2
Juice Bar	6
Mantı Sofrası	4
Morelli	5
Nargilem	3
Six Brothers	1

ACCOMMODATION

The Colony	C
Nostalgia	B
White Pearl	A

about walkable to the harbour – decent on-site restaurant, on-site car hire and friendly managing family are big pluses. ❸

The Colony Ecevit Cad ☎815 15 18, Ⓦwww.thecolonycyprus.com. Opened in 2003, this is the only real luxury hotel in Kyrenia. A less-than-brilliant location is compensated for by large, sumptuously appointed rooms with double glazing and internet access, the suites are worth the extra expense for superior baths. Common areas include the casino, several bars and restaurants, spa and fitness centre, plus the *pièce de résistance*, the rooftop pool terrace. Rooms ❼, suites ❾

Dome Hotel Kordon Boyu ☎815 24 53, Ⓦwww.dome-cyprus.com. Thanks to its colonial-institution status (since 1930) and Durrellian associations, this figures prominently in every package operator's brochure (though is easily booked direct). With all-year operation, a small fitness centre and a long-term, loyal staff, it is also a businessmen's favourite. Most rooms – and the imposing common areas, including the pleasant sea-view bar – were thoroughly renovated in 2006, going some way to justifying the price tag (though the lacklustre restaurant does not); a fresh-water pool now complements the famous sea-water pool carved into living rock. ❸

Jasmine Court Hotel Western edge of town ☎815 14 50, Ⓦwww.jasminecourthotel.com. The buildings look grim and dated from outside and the casino is diligently marketed, but the 14-acre site is a big plus, with a series of outdoor pool, lawns and lidos descending to the sea (there's no real beach). All units are suite format; there's a good children's programme, two on-site restaurants. Junior suite ❼, "king" ❾

Nostalgia Hotel Çafer Paşa Sok, near the round Byzantine Tower and Bandabulya ☎815 30 79, Ⓦwww.nostalgiahotel.com. A "boutique" hotel complex spread over two adjacent buildings, though it's for sale, so expect changes. The original, restored premises, with antique-furnished rooms, currently retains some of the feel of a French country inn, right down to the basic bathrooms; the superior *Nostalgia Court* annexe, purpose-built around a plunge-pool, is probably worth the extra for larger rooms and better baths. Both wings have their own attached restaurant, sharing a small spa and in-house car rental. ❷, superior annexe ❸

Onar Village Out of town on the main road to Nicosia ☎815 58 50, Ⓦwww.onarvillage.com. Not the most verdant setting since the 1995 fire – though the gardeners try valiantly – but offers good standards in its two wings of hotel rooms, and villas. All are enormous for their type, while the latter have full kitchens (with ovens), baths and individual water heaters – thus suitable for winter-long stays. The more recently built hotel wing, wrapped around an indoor pool, Turkish bath, gym and massage facilities, has better bathrooms but also much more road noise. On site restaurant, large outdoor pool and stunning views. Clientele tends to be mostly British, family and repeat. ❹

🏃 **Pia Bella** İskenderun Cad 14 ☎815 53 21, ⓦwww.piabella.com. Not the most inspired location, but once inside this three-wing resort (refurbished/enlarged in phases 2003–07) with its two pools and extensive gardens, impressions change. Superior standard rooms in the front building, with marble trim and parquet floors, face the original pool garden where the restaurant sets out summer tables. Of the two annexes, the middle structure (where the sauna, gym and spa is) is preferable, but both rear units are suite-format, plush and large with flat-screen TVs and ethernet hookups. Private rear parking area, friendly, attentive staff, wi-fi in common areas, consistently good reader feedback. ❹

Pitoresk/Picturesque Holiday Village Top of Orhan Durusoy Cad ☎815 62 22, ⓦwww.pitoresk .com. Nicely set complex with sea views in a former olive grove, alive with cats and caged birds. Choose between self-catering one-bedroom units, or B&B-basis standard rooms, both in split level cottages. There can, however, be noise from adjoining units – most interconnect. Medium-sized pool, appealing mock-traditional architecture designed by German architects, and full-service bar-restaurant. Self-catering ❷, B&B ❸

The Ship Inn 1.5km west of town, south side of the road ☎815 67 01, ⓦwww.theshipinn.com. Not a prime location, but once inside this is a pleasant development of one- and two-bedroom family villas arrayed around a pool and tennis/squash courts. A newer, larger conventional hotel-room wing contains a small fitness centre, indoor pool and sauna; the bright if bland-decor rooms themselves have tubs in the baths and a mix of inland and partial sea views. Returned Anglo-Cypriot management keeps a "pub" corner-bar and adjoining restaurant. Bookable direct by the week in the UK through T. Özdemir, ☎020/8947 9110, ✉taner @ozdemirt.freeserve.co.uk. Rooms ❷, villas ❸

White Pearl Eftal Akça Sok 23, Old Harbour ☎815 04 29, ⓦwww.whitepearlhotel.com. An old warhorse refurbished and relaunched in 2006–07, this has variable-sized rooms, most with balconies, a pleasant, wood-trimmed breakfast salon and an unbeatable roof bar (April–Oct). ❸

Kyrenia castle

An amalgam of different periods and thus irregularly shaped, **Kyrenia castle** (daily: summer 9am–7.15pm; winter 9am–4.15pm; 12YTL adult, 3YTL students) is only rivalled by the citadel of Famagusta for castellated interest on the island. The present Venetian structure is an adaptation of previous Byzantine and Lusignan fortresses: much of the walls' current thickness was achieved by simply filling the space between the compact Byzantine and overextended Lusignan fortifications with rubble. You can still see (and visit, see p.310) a now-superfluous Byzantine round tower near Belediye Meydanı, and another remnant, called the Koúla – possibly the base of a medieval lighthouse – out in the middle of the old port.

Some history

The Byzantines probably built the original castle atop the site of a Roman fort; Guy de Lusignan seized it in 1191, finding the Armenian wife and daughter of Isaac Komnenos hiding inside. It subsequently served as a bolthole during turbulent periods, as in 1426 when the Mamelukes overran the island, and again between 1460 and 1464 by Queen Charlotte, until she was deposed by half-brother James. Rebels and disgraced personalities were also incarcerated here throughout the Lusignan period, including the rebellious Ibelin lords during Henry II's rule, and Peter I's mistress Joanna d'Aleman, immured briefly by his wife before Joanna gave birth to the king's bastard and was then bundled off to a convent.

The castle was never taken by force, repelling a fierce Genoese attack in 1374; its defenders always starved under siege or surrendered, as in 1570 when the

Ottomans induced the defenders to capitulate by sending as a threat the severed heads of the Venetian commanders of fallen Nicosia. Thus the massive southeast, southwest and northwest towers – all constructed to slightly different specifications by the Venetians according to their military application – were not put to the test as at Famagusta. As elsewhere in the Ottoman empire, non-Muslims were forbidden access to the citadel after dark, when the ruling caste would retire there for the night. The British used it as a prison early in their administration, and again between 1954 and 1960 for EOKA captives.

A tour of the walls

Today you enter the castle from the northwest via a bridge over the former moat. The first passage on the left leads to the small but perfectly formed twelfth-century Byzantine **chapel of St George**, its four columns topped with Corinthian capitals; it stood outside the perimeter walls until the Venetians incorporated it into their circuit. A bit further along on the right, it's worth pausing in a vaulted chamber for "A Visual Introduction to Girne and its Castle", essentially a series of ink drawings by the late resident Kyreno-phile William Dreghorn, showing the evolution of the town and its fortifications from Roman times until the colonial era. Immediately opposite this, a ramp originally used for wheeling cannon heads up to the round northwest tower, and the start of a complete **circuit of the walls**. The expected views of the harbour are at your feet, and you can make out St Hilarion castle up on its peak; continuing towards the northeast tower, you pass over the usually locked exhibition/events hall.

The Lusignan **northeast bastion** is home to more Dreghorn drawings and a permanent display of military history; in both the lower and upper chambers, mannequins pose with the armour or uniforms, and arms, of each historical period in the castle's life. In the **southeastern Venetian tower**, a long gallery leads to its foundations where there's another mock-up of a Venetian cannon crew in action, plus Dreghorn watercolours.

A complete clockwise circuit finishes at the original Byzantine **west wall**, with its remains of Lusignan apartments (locked) and a chapel, but signs direct you to the Lusignan dungeon, a somewhat tasteless re-creation complete with nude, anatomically correct mannequins of torture victims and prisoners (including Joanna d'Aleman) languishing at the bottom of oubliettes. Between this and the tree-shaded **café** in the northeast corner of the broad courtyard is a subterranean, vaulted cistern, still with a fair bit of water inside.

The Tomb-Finds Gallery and Shipwreck Museum

Flanking the courtyard on its east are two superb archeological displays. The first is the **Tomb-Finds Gallery**, comprising three major exhibits spanning the Neolithic, Bronze Age and Hellenistic to Byzantine periods. In the main wing there's a reconstruction of a late Neolithic dwelling (c.4100 BC), one of seventeen such located at Vrysi-Áyios Epíktitos near Çatalköy, sunk slightly below ground level for protection. The diorama suggests a harsh, utilitarian life, with only a few bone-segment necklaces as a concession to luxury. In the adjacent hall an early Bronze Age (2075–1725 BC) tomb at Krini (modern Kırnı or Pınarbaşı) has been re-created with numerous clay funerary-gift vessels, many imported from overseas. The upstairs gallery is dedicated to finds from the ancient town at Akdeniz (Ayía Iríni); though the most spectacular, Archaic-age objects are at the Cyprus Museum, many Hellenistic and early Byzantine finds from the Paleokastro tomb complex are presented here, along with a mock-up of a catacomb. Glass and terracotta objects, large hoards of coins, oil lamps and a pyramidal display case of gold jewellery were recovered from nearby villagers or the result of internationally unrecognized excavations in 1986.

Next door, the **Shipwreck Museum** displays a cargo boat which sank just off Kyrenia some 2300 years ago, discovered over thirty metres down by a local diver in 1967. It is the oldest shipwreck known, and carbon-14 dating proved it had been in service for nearly eighty years and much repaired when it foundered. The boat had just plied the coast of Anatolia, judging by freight from Samos, Kos and Rhodes – most of it stone grain-grinders which could double as ballast, alongside nearly four hundred amphorae of wine. A four- to five-man crew subsisted mainly on almonds and such fish as they managed to catch.

The upper levels of the halls show photos of the archeological dive, and lead to the viewing platform over the preservative-soaked wreck itself, kept in a cool, dry, dimly lit environment now that it's out of protecting sea-bed mud. Curiously, the ship was built using the reverse of modern techniques: the lengthwise planks of Aleppo pine were laid down first, the cross-ribbing later.

Around the old harbour

Although the Cypriots closed off its former, exposed north entrance and constructed the long breakwater east past the castle after independence, Kyrenia's old **harbour** had ceased to be a working one well before 1974, despite being by far the safest anchorage on the north coast. Traces of its former importance remain in the medieval quay wall, where a pair of stone lugs pierced with holes were used as fastening points for mooring ropes. In 1916, the British were persuaded to preserve the derelict western chain tower by elaborating it into the sturdy customs house visible today, with some of the original fortification features still visible. The port is now devoted entirely to pleasure craft touting all-day tours along the coast, the rental of speedboats, scuba-dive operations and berths for a score or so of yachts. A day out on an **excursion boat**, leaving at 10.30am and returning at 5pm, will cost a minimum of 50YTL each in these fuel-fraught times, and should include *meze* barbecued on board, as well as several stops for snorkelling and swimming.

▲ Kyrenia harbour

Other museums

The former church of Arkhángelos (the Archangel Michael), whose belfry provides a prominent landmark on the rise west of the water, now houses the **Icon Museum** (daily: summer 9am–2pm, plus Mon 3.30–6pm; winter 9am–1pm & 2–4.45pm; 4YTL). The large collection on three levels (including the former women's gallery) offers an assortment of folksy seventeenth to nineteenth-century examples, rescued from unspecified churches in the district. The most unusual or artistically noteworthy include a Beheading of John the Baptist, with Herod's feast in full swing just above; Saint Luke with his emblematic ox; and three versions of the "Utter Humiliation", equivalent to a Western Deposition without spectators.

By contrast to the Icon Museum, the **Folk Art Museum** (summer Mon–Fri 9am–2pm; winter Mon–Fri 9am–1pm & 2–4.45pm; 3YTL), midway along the quay in a Venetian-era house, contains traditional rural implements and dress; the best single exhibit is the olive-wood olive press on the ground floor, made partly from unpruned trunks, but it's hardly a compelling display, with the house bidding to overshadow the collection.

Other monuments

More specifically Ottoman and Cypriot, the chunky **Cafer Paşa Camii** has stood one street back from the water since at least 1589, though some claim the building is a converted Lusignan warehouse. Just west stands the rather battered, early fourteenth-century Lusignan **church of Khryssopolítissa**, whose dilapidation has accelerated post-1974, though there are some interesting relief carvings on the exterior, especially around the blocked-up north portal.

A block inland from the *Dome Hotel*, on its own plot off quiet Ersin Aydın Sokağı, the **Terra Santa Catholic Chapel** is another undesecrated, late-medieval structure that still sees occasional use (Mass 1st & 3rd Sun of the month) in the tourist season. The only other functioning church in town is Anglican **St Andrew's**, just southwest of the castle, erected on English-owned land in 1913; immediately south and uphill is a remnant of the once-vast Ottoman cemetery, now edged by the town's main car park, with the **Baldöken (Fakizade) Türbe** (a free-standing tomb with a sheltering gazebo) as a focus.

Near the Byzantine Round Tower stands the 2006-revamped colonial **Bandabulya**, no longer home to produce sellers but rather a souvenir and pleasant, if predictably pricey juice bar (see opposite).

Eating and drinking

It's difficult to resist eating or just having a drink in the old port at least once, where a dozen restaurants and bars shamelessly exploit their position. Prices aren't always lower inland, or further west along Kordon Boyu, but food variety and quality – plus atmosphere – are usually superior. If you have your own transport, also consider driving out to remoter restaurants west of town (see p.312).

The seafront

Altı Kardeşler (Six Brothers) Kordon Boyu. If you want a sea view and unrivalled people-watching without the hustle of the old port, this is the place. The menu's limited to excellent, reasonably priced kebabs and *durum* (wraps), though mind the beer prices – that's how money is made here.
Eziç Peanuts Shore east of ancient harbour, near amphitheatre. One of three outlets of a local chain,

massively popular with locals, doing grills, pasta, salads and fish at moderate prices.
Green House Kordon Boyu. Popular youth hangout, with a menu divided between pizza, pasta, kebabs and Tex-Mex specialties. Pleasant seaside terrace seating during warmer months.

🏃 **Lagoon** Kordon Boyu. Currently *the* place to go in Kyrenia for reliably fresh fish, served in stylish surroundings. A seafood *meze* of about a dozen platters precedes the main course, which is followed by a sweet trolley. Allow about 40YTL each, plus drink. Large parties should reserve on ☎ 815 65 55.

Niazi's Kordon Boyu, opposite the west wing of the *Dome Hotel*. Long-established mecca for carnivores, featuring grills prepared on a central hooded fire. The full kebab at 25YTL (includes access to sweet trolley) represents excellent value, and quality is consistent – as attested by hordes of locals in here, especially at weekends.

Inland

Anibal Ecevit Cad 39. An offshoot of the Lefkoşa *Anibal*, this ultra-hygienic, airy outfit – its seating now sadly reduced to make way for an affiliated café – still does excellent full kebab with unusually salubrious *meze*-trimmings like mint leaves, spring onions, *sumac* and cabbage/celery *tursi* about 30YTL for the works.

Bilgin Simit ve Fırın Börek Stall and small café directly behind the Bandabulya, premises 6/6A. The best breakfast-on-the-hoof in Kyrenia: spinach, cheese or mince *börek* to take away only. They'll have run out, and closed up, by noon.

🏃 **Bolulu Hasan Usta** Mete Adanır Cad, under *Life Otel*. Main Cypriot outlet of an İzmir-based confectioner specializing in the mostly milk-based puddings which, rather than baklava and the like, are the true backbone of Turkish sweet-toothery. Humdrum location, assiduous service; open until late.

Chinese House 1.5km west of Kyrenia, diagonally opposite the *Ship Inn*. Reckoned tops on the island – North or South – for Cantonese, courtesy of Chinese chefs (but local management). The haunt of the great and good, with prices reflecting this – 37.50YTL per person (drink extra) for the set menu, which includes soup or spring roll plus three more courses, with few excluded items. Well-kept summer garden out front, ramps for the disabled. Dinner only; closed Sun.

Eziç Piliç Mete Adanır Cad, opposite Tempo Market. The original, flagship premises of this chain

has branched out from roast chicken (*piliç*) to pretty much the same menu as its two stablemates. There's indoor and garden seating at this very popular spot on the old bypass road, both eat-in and takeaway. Open noon to very late.

Eziç Premier Bahar Sok 16, well southwest of centre. North Cyprus' most imposing, if slightly snooty, "designer" restaurant complex, comprising a main hall with burgers, schnitzel, pizza, chicken and a few Chinese/Mexican platters, a "Café Espresso" wing (wi-fi signal) and a more exalted "Platinum" diner upstairs, with less fast food and more French/Italian dishes (allow 35–40YTL a head plus drink). There's a popular takeout service (☎ 444 88 88); get the whole picture at ⓦ www .eziconline.com

Juice Bar Bandabulya, east side. Nothing more or less – fresh-squeezed juices in a range of flavours encompassing mango, carrot, apple and kiwi rather than just orange. Seating indoors and out, though also incongruities like "Killing Me Softly" in Spanish over the sound system.

Laughing Buddha 1km up the main Nicosia road from the big roundabout, just below *Onar Village*. Kyrenia's other Chinese restaurant, installed in a characterful old house and purveying competent Cantonese food (MSG-free but a bit corn-starchy). Good set meals at 19YTL apiece for two, plus service charge and drink; going à la carte (allow 36YTL each) gives you access to duck and fancier seafood dishes. Sometimes closed Sun off-season. ☎ 815 87 15, ⓦ www.laughingbuddha-cyprus.com.

Mantı Sofrası Göksu Sok 3/4. Traditional, inexpensive Turkish snacks such as *mantı* (central Asian ravioli), *gözleme* and *çiğ böreği*, plus *ayran* to drink, served in the low-key interior or on the terrace. Serves all day continuously until early evening.

Morelli One block west of Anglican church. Upmarket continental food in an old house, with welcoming management; allow 40YTL each, though unlike at many such Kyrenia eateries the expense is worth it.

Nightlife and entertainment

Organized **nightlife** – or rather the lack of it – mostly conforms to the tenor of forty- to sixty-something tourism and part-time residence hereabouts. Even with a large student contingent, few music clubs or discos survive more than a year at a time. More sedentary, low-key **bars**, especially by the sea, have a longer shelf-life, and we list some of the more durable below. Out on the coast road well west of Kyrenia, a few "nightclubs" (*gece külübleri*) contain what remain of the area's hookers; most of those in the North have been moved either to brothels west of Guzelyalı or on the Lefkoşa–Güzelyurt road, sited for the maximum convenience of Greek-Cypriot customers.

Casinos have weathered the Turkish 2000–2002 economic slump and once again number more than a score, though most of the punters are now

Greek Cypriot. All of the larger seafront hotels and resorts in the Kyrenia area – plus many small inland resorts – have one, mostly equipped with fruit machines but also with a few hard-currency-only roulette tables. The casino at the *Jasmine Court*, open 24 hours, is claimed to be the largest in Europe. North Cypriots and resident students are theoretically banned from their premises, but in practice the restriction is a farce, with both seen playing by the hour on quieter weekday nights; alarm systems warn of impending Keystone-Koppish raids, giving the punters time to scarper.

In terms of more high-brow organized entertainment, a popular and well-regarded late May to late June **music festival** (Ⓦwww.bellapaisfestival.com) is held in the atmospheric surroundings of the Béllapais abbey refectory. It's been so successful that in 2008 a supplemental autumn festival was introduced. There are three **cinemas** in the Kyrenia area, much the best being the Lemar Cineplex 2, in the basement of the eponymous supermarket, just west of town. At least one of the two films will be foreign, first-run fare, in the original soundtrack.

Café Harbour Old Harbour. Probably the busiest and trendiest of the bars in the old harbour area, with live Turkish music some nights.
Cherin's Garden Bar Inland from Old Harbour. Taped sounds, seating with unbeatable castle views and three pool tables are the draw here.

Escape Beşüncü Mil/Pende Mili beach. Lovely, lawn-set "day-and-night club" just above the sand, attracting a youthful clientele despite relatively stiff admission fees; the more sophisticated, affiliated *Ice Lounge* is being built just overhead.
Nargilem Old Harbour, mid-front. Low-ceilinged student-and-youth boozer with taped music.

Listings

Airline Cyprus Turkish Airlines, Philecia Court, Suite 3, Kordon Boyu ☎815 25 13.
Banks and exchange Most central bank ATMs accept foreign plastic, with screen instructions in English. Otherwise, numerous *döviz buroları* (foreign exchange agencies) swap foreign currency notes instantly, traveller's cheques with a bit more bother (and a marginally lower rate). Rates vary noticeably between the bureaux, so comparison-shop first – Sun or Gesfi near the *Dome Hotel* are usually the most advantageous.
Bookshop The sole foreign-language outlet is The Round Tower opposite the Bandabulya, with a reasonable stock of new and used titles (including a few Rough Guides), along with upmarket crafts. The Byzantine structure itself is imposing, with an oculus (now glassed over) in the ceiling. Foreign newspapers can be found opposite the tower itself at Yaysat, on Ziya Rizki Caddesi.
Botanizing Local experts Maureen and Tony Hutchinson lead orchid and wildflower walks every Tues, Thurs and Sat during March and April; full details on ☎721 30 13, 0542 854 43 29, or Ⓦwww.walksnorchidsnorthcyprus.com.
Car rental Long-lived and reliable operators include Abant, İskenderun Cad 12, near the *Pia Bella Hotel* ☎815 45 24; Atlantic, in the *Dome Hotel* ☎815 30 53; Başpınar, Meyas Apt D-2,

☎815 71 06, Ⓦwww.baspinar-rentals.com; Oscar, Kordon Boyu opposite the *Dome*, also branch next to the *Pia Bella Hotel* ☎815 56 70; Pacific, Ecevit Cad 23 ☎815 25 08; Sun, Kordon Boyu ☎815 44 79, Ⓦwww.sunrentacar.com.
Ferry boat/catamaran agents Fergün, main office on the new harbour access road ☎815 17 70, or in the passenger terminal at the harbour ☎815 49 93; Akgünler, in the harbour passenger terminal ☎815 60 02.
Paragliding Operating from a small office at mid-quay on the harbour, the multinational staff at Highline Air Tours ☎0542/855 56 72, Ⓦwww .highlineparagliding.com, offer tandem flights up to four times daily in season (once in winter) from a launch point near St Hilarion castle. Conditions are generally excellent, with 45min soars the norm.
Post office Just off Belediye Meydanı (Mon–Fri 8am–1pm & 2–5pm, Sat 8.30am–12.30pm); parcel post in the basement (Mon, Wed & Fri 9–11.30am).
Scuba diving Blue Dolphin ☎0542/851 51 13, Ⓦwww.bluedolphin.4mg.com is about the best equipped school, with two "rib" boats; currently they operate out of the *Jasmine Court Hotel*. "Try dives" for novices or single dives for qualified persons both run at about £20, with all gear supplied; a PADI five-day Open Water or BSAC Ocean Diver certification course costs £200, Advanced Open Water certifica-tions £125. Longest running, based at "Escape"

Beach in Alsancak, is PADI/BSAC-certified Amphora ☎ 0542/851 49 24, 🌐 www.amphoradiving.com. They're a bit dearer at €30 per dive, €300 for a PADI Open Water certification, €180 for Advanced Open Water. Scuba Cyprus, essentially based on its wooden *gület* in the old harbour, can be contacted on ☎ 0533/865 2317, or 🌐 www.scubacyprus.com; prices are comparable to Amphora's. (See p.315 for general information on diving in North Cyprus.)

Taxis Most central ranks, 24hr, are Dome Taxi ☎ 815 23 76, by the eponymous hotel, and Güven, by the central car park ☎ 0533/866 06 51.
Traffic tickets Pay your "tolls" for speed-camera violations west and south of town at the police station shown on the central Kyrenia town plan – read the text on p.39 before binning tickets.

West of Kyrenia

The stretch of coast west of Kyrenia comprises the district's main hotel strip, with a good two-thirds of the North's tourism facilities either on the sea or just inland. Beaches are not brilliant, often merely functional – such as the "Halk Plajı" at **Kervansaray** district, with its snack bar and three unremarkable fish tavernas just above – but the character of the foothill villages with their eyrie-like situations compensates.

Karaoğlanoğlu (Áyios Yeóryios)

The first distinct community west of Kyrenia on the coast, **KARAO-ĞLANOĞLU** (Áyios Yeóryios) is remarkable only as the site of the Turkish landing at dawn on July 20, 1974; the village has been renamed in honour of a Turkish officer killed as he came ashore. A higher density than usual of grotesque monuments, including a cement abstract vaguely suggestive of an artillery piece (dubbed the "Turkish erection", complete with wedge-shaped testicles, by many local residents), marks the spot some 8km west of Kyrenia. There's also a "Peace and Freedom Museum" consisting mostly of disabled Greek-Cypriot military vehicles in an open-air display, a chronicle of EOKA atrocities against Turkish Cypriots and general glorification of the Turkish intervention.

The small (250m) **beach** itself, the first decent strand this side of Kyrenia and sheltered by a large offshore rock, was "Five-Mile Beach" in British times, but is now officially Yavuz Çıkartma ("Resolute Outbreak" in Turkish) or Altınkaya, after the rock and a namesake restaurant which overlooks it – though **Beşinci Mil** (or "Pénde Míli" in Greek) is still widely understood. The *Escape* beach-bar (see opposite) and Amphora Diving dominate much of the bay, the former charging a hefty fee for access and sunbeds.

Accommodation

The Karaoğlanoğlu area has a couple of modest **accommodation** options with beachfront settings, as well as one ostentatiously luxurious one. The *Topset/Emir Hotel* (☎ 822 22 04, 🌐 www.topsethotel.com; ❷), while probably overrated at three-star, has a well-kept, lush garden setting, with a large swimming pool (handy as there's some reef offshore), and two saunas. Off-season, the place tends to be taken over by German special-interest groups, who do yoga, Tibetan meditation, etc on the lawn. There are three wings of studio and galleried one-bedroom bungalows, as well as somewhat gloomy family quads; the "Emir" wings are of a higher standard.

The nearby *Riviera Beach Bungalows* (☎ 822 28 77, 🌐 www.rivierahotel-northcyprus.com; March–Nov) are more rustic and appealingly landscaped, with a large novelty pool, though again there's plenty of rock offshore, with only lido access to the sea. Choose from among three types of wood-trimmed units, including peculiar vaulted studio cottages (**②**) or galleried "superior" flats (**❸**), though direct-bookers must take a minimum of one week.

Finally, dominating the Kervansaray headland is the five-star, 2008-opened *Mercure* (☎650 25 00, Ⓦwww.mercurecyprus.com; **❽** rooms, **❾** suites), the plushest resort in the North, though clearly banking on business/conference trade. Several restaurants and cafés include a sushi bar; there's the obligatory casino and large spa. Standard rooms are large, with equally sizeable bathrooms; for once the "mountain view" rooms are as impressive as sea-view ones – you see the entire Kyrenia range. The highlight, perhaps, is the 75-metre-long seaside lap-swimming pool.

Eating

Karaoğlanoğlu has an ample choice of **restaurants**, from the most basic of Cypriot kebabs to affordable seafood in relatively elegant surroundings, often at a third less than the prices found at Kyrenia harbour.

The Address On the shore, well signposted from middle of village ☎822 35 37. Run by an ex-manager of *Niazi's* in Kyrenia, this restaurant matches it in quality. The menu stresses meat – allow 40YTL, including 5YTL for the sweet trolley but excluding drink – though there are also some fish or calamari plates for non-meat-eaters. Very tasteful environment, with a view of the breakers crashing just outside – but dress up in something better than beach wear, and book tables in peak season. May close at lunch part of winter.

The Ambiance Paraşut Sok ☎822 28 49. Opened in 2004, this quickly became the hottest see-and-be-seen restaurant in the North, though you're paying for the lovely sea/pool-side setting as much as for the food, which can be hit-or-miss. Lunch fare is snacky-Western, similar to Kyrenia's *Eziç* chain; the dinner menu is more ambitious with a meal of aubergine-mozzarella-tower starter, fish or steak and the inevitable sweet trolley setting you back 50YTL each before cracking into the wine list – and the service charge. Booking advised May–Oct.

Archways Centre of Zeytinlink (Temlos, Témblos) village, between Karaoğlanoğlu and Kyrenia ☎816 03 53. A revelation among local eateries, and thus equally popular with locals and expats: fair-priced, quality food served in tastefully rustique surroundings, though the menu's limited to full kebab (35YTL) and various à la carte meat or fish platters. Grilled orders include salad, yogurt, chips and coffee, but not (of course) a French wine

list. Be warned: extremely slow service almost nullifies its running-man symbol.

Jashan East edge of Karaoğlanoğlu on inland side of main road, near turning for *Riviera Beach Bungalows* ☎822 20 27. North Cyprus's best and longest-established Indian restaurant, with pretty authentic Indian/Pakistani dishes. Budget 35–40YTL a head including modest intake of drink.

Stonegrill Inland side of main highway, by Kervansaray turning ☎822 20 02. Local outlet of an Australian chain, where a fixed price is charged for three copious courses, comprising soup, *meze*-lite, and a choice of mains (meat, seafood, combos) which you grill yourself at the table on a hot stone. Drinks and the sweet trolley are extra, bumping up the likely bill to 33YTL minimum – retro (eg Sinatra) soundtrack included. Daily except Mon, lunch and dinner.

The Veranda East edge of Karaoğlanoğlu, north of the through road ☎822 20 53. Recommended for a nightcap in congenial surroundings, or a good, relaxed bistro-style meal, with an enclosed sun-porch overlooking the sea, outside seating in summer and an open fire in winter. Bar drinks are reasonably priced, and you can just snack on soup and grilled *hellim*, though a three-course meal – mostly continental dishes with added Cypriot flair and consistent quality, followed by good desserts – will set you back about 30YTL, drink extra (best avoid the fish). Reservations advisable in season. Closed Mon.

Karaman (Kármi)

With whitewashed houses scattered along a web of arcaded, cobbled lanes, **KARAMAN** is superficially the most attractive Kyrenia-hill village, though increasingly dwarfed by new villa projects at the outskirts. Still referred to, even by officialdom, by its Greek name Kármi, it has in recent decades acquired a reputation as an expats' Tunbridge-Wells-on-Med. After lying abandoned since

Traditional Cypriot food

Compared with the prefab fare of a typical Cypriot-resort taverna, the delicious food served up in locals' haunts will come as a pleasant surprise. After a long colonial hangover, in which traditional cooking was banished and "international cuisine" mandated by law, "slow food" has returned from internal exile. Cyprus has biomes ranging from subtropical to Alpine, fostering a plethora of native and exotic food plants. Field guides list over fifty edible species of what some disdain as "weeds", while seven wild mushroom species grow under pines or on fennel roots. Formerly, up to half the Orthodox calendar involved strict fasts from animal foodstuffs, which meant many imaginative vegetarian recipes.

South Nicosia's fruit stalls ▲

Bladder campion, mushrooms and wild leeks ▼

Favourite fruits

Cypriot fruit stalls spill out a cornucopia of seasonal produce, though luscious, large **strawberries** are available much of the year in the South. **Medlars** and **loquats** ripen in mid-spring, their large pips worth the bother for the orange flesh's delicate flavour. Ripe-to-touch **apricots** are next up, while **watermelons**, **dessert melons** and **plums** together are heralds of early summer. **Cherries**, solely from the Tróödhos villages and getting rarer owing to EU agricultural policy, are delicious in several varieties and hues.

Towards autumn, **prickly-pear** fruit – a sixteenth-century introduction from the New World, originally used as fencing – tastes like watermelon once you penetrate its defences. **Strawberry guavas** – supposedly the late President Makarios' favourite fruit – appear in October and November. **Oranges**, **mandarins** and **grapefruit** are ready in winter. The longest established eating **oranges** are called Jaffa, actually a misnomer as they're elongated rather than round like Jaffas elsewhere, juicy and almost seedless. The heirloom, non-acidic but seedy variety called *sherkérika* is good for sweet juice.

Wild traditional mezé

Mezé-houses or *meyhanes* are at their best from November to April, when rains nurture the wild greens, winter vegetables and mushrooms which enliven their winter menus. Sliced *kouloúmbra* or **kohlrabi root** is a refreshing, slightly sweet, palate-cleansing garnish found in many *mezé* arrays. **Caper** (*kappargá/kapa*) plants are pickled whole, thorns and all; **artichokes** are typically presented raw, with just the tips trimmed. Other wild late winter/spring greens, especially popular among Greek

Cypriots as Lenten delicacies, include **wild asparagus** (*agréllia/ayrellí*) in light and dark varieties and **bladder campion** (*strouthoúthkia*), all three typically sauteed with eggs or wild garlic. **Borage** (*óglossos*) and **dock** (*khristagáthí*) are also delicious fried alone in olive oil, served salted with lemon juice. Among the island's edible **mushroom** species, the fennel *plevrotus* can attain several kilos per specimen – equally good grilled, pickled or stewed. Particularly **Northern specialities** include *gömeç* (mallow greens), said to aid digestion, and *molohiya* (sometimes *mulihiya* or *melokhia*), another steamed, aromatic leaf distantly related to mallow, introduced from Egypt in the nineteenth century and an essential ingredient of meat stews.

▲ Traditional mezé

▼ Kebab on the grill

Ethnic meats

Kléftigo (Gr) or *küp kebap/fırın kebap* is arguably the national dish, a fatty slab of lamb or goat roasted with vegetables until tender in a domed oven with a small opening – you see these in almost every farmhouse. However, Greek Cypriots increasingly prefer less greasy **soúvla**, chunks of lamb or goat on a rotisserie spit. **Afélia** – pork in red wine and coriander seed sauce – is prepared only in the non-Muslim Greek community; *sheftália/deftalya, deftalı kebap* – small, savoury rissoles of mince, onion and spices wrapped in gut casing – are found all over the island. Also beloved of both communities is **tsamarélla/samarella**, lamb (or better, goat) salami made with tender flesh from just under the skin. **Sausages** in the South are apt to be seasoned with lentisc-tree berries, a bit like pepper, while lentisc leaves and branches are used to smoke *loúntza* and *hiroméri*, choice **cured pork snacks**.

▼ A kléftigo oven

Preserved baby fruits ▲

Soushoúkou ▼

"Cyprus" delight, south Nicosia ▼

Traditional sweets

Glyká/macun, assorted **preserved fruits** (and vegetables), are established village specialities occasionally offered to passers-by. The candying process renders unlikely items such as baby eggplants, Seville oranges and green walnuts, which are resolutely inedible raw, appetizing. More ubiquitous, and peddled assiduously to outsiders, is the island-wide **"Cyprus" delight** (*loukoúmi/lokma*), varying proportions of sugar, rosewater, pectin, nuts and fruit essences – there's no need for anything else (E-numbers, preservatives, etc), so scan ingredient lists carefully. **Soushoúkou** (sometimes *soudzoúki*), a confection of almonds strung together and then dipped like candle wicks in vats of grape molasses and rosewater, are sold widely in the South and make excellent trail-walk snacks; so does **pastelláki**, a sesame, peanut and syrup bar. *Palouzé*, purplish-brown **grape-must pudding**, is a slightly perfumed autumn speciality of the Limassol foothill wine villages. Last but not least, there is no more genuinely Cypriot culinary souvenir than *haroupómelo/harubu pekmezi*, chocolatey **carob syrup**, used in muffins and biscuits, or as an ice-cream/yogurt topping.

Naming a dish

In the North, *tahin* (sesame-seed purée) is served with lemon juice on top, a dish known as *eşeksiksin*; originally this was (*tahin*) *ekşisi* ("sour"), but in a story illustrative of the coarse Cypriot sense of humour, a Greek-Cypriot diner failed to get his tongue around the term and it came out as *eşeksiksin* ("may a donkey fuck it"). The *meyhane*-keeper and the customer came to blows over the perceived insult, but the name stuck, and nobody causes offence by ordering it as such today.

1974 (it was agriculturally too marginal to appeal to either Turkish Cypriots or Anatolians), the place was assigned a special development category in 1982. Only Europeans – except for two Turkish-Cypriot war heroes – were allowed to renovate the hundred or so derelict properties on renewable 25-year leases, and as a social experiment and architectural showcase it initially proved fairly successful. But subsequently the village has gotten rather twee and increasingly Little Englander, with the British-controlled residents' council excluding those they don't like the look of. Since the 1995 fire, Kármi's appeal has diminished, with many restaurants and shops operating fitfully and a number of cottages up for grabs – at startlingly high prices considering the short leases and general uncertainty surrounding titles in the North.

The "villagers" strongly support the North's position (settling here in the 1980s was a political statement), reckoning that their predecessors got their just desserts. Greek-Cypriot Kármi was an EOKA-B stronghold, heavily damaged in the 1974 fighting; for many years rainfall would leach the blue paint of "ENOSIS" slogans through the covering of new whitewash. The foreign community has always viewed any possible peace settlement with considerable ambivalence, and after April 2003, some leaseholders behaved appallingly towards Greek Cypriots coming to visit their former homes.

If you're here on a Sunday between 11am and 12.30pm, it's worth stopping in at the **old church** by the central car park to view the **icon screen** which residents have assembled (rather un-canonically) from other abandoned churches in the area, as well as a copy of the *firman* (concession) granted by the sultan in 1860 allowing the extension of the building.

Just before the *Hilarion Village* complex, a small sign ("Bronze Age Cemetery") points towards Bronze Age **chamber-tombs**, though they're hardly essential viewing. The most substantial of a dozen holes in the ground has a stone shelter built atop it, and incised slabs flanking the subterranean entry. One of these tombs was home to the so-called "Kármi Cup" (now in the Cyprus Museum in south Nicosia), a specimen of Minoan Kamares ware, important evidence of Middle Bronze Age contacts between Crete and Cyprus.

Practicalities

Whatever their attitudes towards each other, prospective leaseholders, the Greek Cypriots or the Northern authorities, the "villagers" welcome short-term visitors, who might stop in at the *Crow's Nest Pub* (Tues–Sat noon–3pm & 7pm onwards, Sun noon–8pm), or the *Spot Bar* down the lane. For full-on **meals**, combining western and Cypriot tastes, your most reliable option is *Treasure* (in the old school outside the village, closed Mon; ☎822 24 00), where you can get hearty *molehiya*-based stew with trimmings, dessert and a beer; Turkish Cypriots feel comfortable coming here, a good sign. At *Halfway House*, that distance down the road to Edremit village, a mother-and-son team provide a copious *meze* (dinner only; ☎822 33 14).

If you fancy **staying short-term** in the village, this needs to be arranged beforehand through the Karmi Service Center (ask for Binky or Anja, ☎822 25 68; often closed Nov–March), which manages 24 houses of various sizes (weekly rates typically £200–300). Otherwise, just east of and below Kármi is the small, well-vegetated *Hilarion Village* complex (☎822 27 72, ⓦwww.hilarion-cyprus.com) offering two types of bungalow: galleried studios (❷) with a small kitchen, bathtubs, water heaters, heating/air con, but no TV or phone, and two-bedroom villas (❸) suitable for a family of four. The management prefers to quote weekly rates of £270 for the studios, £400 for the four-person villas; there's a small pool, and a restaurant (half-board rates available) relying on organically grown produce.

Edremit (Trimíthi)

Going up to Kármi you'll pass through the much smaller village of **EDREMİT** (Trimíthi), 2km below, where you'll find an excellent **basketry-wares** specialist – the best in the North – across from the central church.

Just below, east off the through road, is ⚓ *The Hideaway Club* (☎ 822 26 20, ⓦ www.hideawayclub.com; closed Jan to late Feb), one of the more popular inland resorts. Choose between several grades of room: mixed sea/garden view standards (❸), or superior "VIP Suites" (❹), featuring exceptional decor – carpets, wrought-iron beds, fireplaces – and the ability to knock units together to form quads. English breakfast (included) is served by request on your own terrace during the warmer months, or at the decent poolside restaurant. The returned London-Cypriot hosts and their well-trained staff generally have a knack for knowing what clients (over-12s only) want – full bathtubs, CD players, complimentary robes, hammocks, book-swop library, internet access – and also quote advantageous weekly rates.

Alsancak and around

Some 5km west of Karaoğlanoğlu ⚓ *lu*, the main district of **ALSANCAK** (Karavás, Karava) fills a single ravine, with runnels and aqueducts everywhere irrigating the lemon orchards; olive groves and carobs are interspersed with abandoned houses higher up the slopes. It was founded after the first Turkish conquest as an overflow of Lapta and most of its present inhabitants are refugees from Páfos, who converted the huge church into a mosque; the carved *témblon* is still there, though the icons have vanished. Just north of here lie the remains of ancient Lambousa, while to the south Alsancak blends seamlessly with İncesu (Motídhes), the road out of the latter continuing uphill to **MALATYA** (Paleósofos), visited primarily for its waterfall. Go through the village, then continue along a narrow paved lane about 350 metres to just past a bridge. The dell in the rock cleft immediately upstream is watered by a ten-metre cascade surging from a lip of rock; it's most impressive in spring, assuming a wet winter.

Ancient Lambousa

Out on a promontory directly north of Alsancak, the twelfth-century **monastery of Akhiropiítos** (Acheiropoiitos) can only be glimpsed from a distance, as it falls squarely within a Turkish army camp, its buildings used as storage depots. The monastery takes its name ("Made Without Hands" in Greek) from a foundation legend asserting that the central church was teleported whole from Anatolia to save it from marauding infidels. Adjacent to seaward stands the emphatically made-with-hands chapel of **Áyios Evlámbios** (also off-limits), supposedly hewn from a single monolith. Both share the peninsula with the scant ruins of **ancient Lambousa**, of which the most famous relic is the so-called "Lambousa Treasure", quantities of sixth-century Byzantine silver and gold items dug up beside Áyios Evlámbios in 1905 and presently distributed among the Cyprus Museum in south Nicosia, the Medieval Museum in Limassol, the Metropolitan Museum in New York and the British Museum in London.

The only portions of ancient Lambousa now open to the public lie on the east side of the promontory. To reach them, take the turning for the *Mare Monte* hotel, bear left onto a dirt track when you reach the resort gate, and continue around the perimeter fence towards the shore; 4WDs can get within five minutes' walk of the site, other vehicles may have to stop the near side of deep ruts or mud-pots. The main things to see, just before the army-base barbed wire, are a series of **rectangular tanks** carved into the soft rock, the largest about the size of an Olympic swimming pool. These were fashioned by Roman-era fishermen to keep their catch alive prior to sale, and feature a pair of ingenious, diagonal sluices leading to the sea for water to flow in and out. Fairly obvious just inland is a complex of similarly rock-cut **cliff tombs**.

Practicalities

Most tourist facilities near Alsancak are on or north of the coast road, around the *Deniz Kızı Hotel*. A modest seaside alternative on the west side of Alsancak is *Citrus Tree Gardens* (℡821 28 72, 🔇www.citrus-tree.com; ❷), a small-scale complex of galleried units, with some quads appropriate for families; amenities are rather ordinary, but the place scores for the personal service, lending library, affiliated car hire and congenial proprietor.

Inland, the well-landscaped, four-star *Riverside Holiday Village*, at the east edge of town south of the main road, has indoor and outdoor pools, sauna, gym, kids' water-park and aviaries (℡821 89 06, 🔇www.riversideholidayvillage .com; ❷–❹); however, a casino has been installed by the indoor pool, and too many new "superior" units have been added, lending an air of impersonality. Their on-site **car-rental** outfit (same contacts, direct web bookings encouraged) is one of the busiest in the North, and still offers good service; otherwise use the resort's shuttle-bus service. Their local rival is Green, out at the eponymous filling station on the main highway (℡821 88 37, 🔇www .greenrentacar.com), honest and also with good-condition cars (most, unusually, with sound systems).

For **eating out** locally, the *St Tropez Restaurant*, roughly halfway between Karaoğlanoğlu and Alsancak (open Tues–Sat dinner, Mon too in summer, plus Sun lunch; ℡821 83 24, 🔇www.saint-tropez-cyprus.com), delivers three courses of very elegant Frenchified food (patés and terrines, then mains smothered under rich sauces) for about 60YTL a head, with exquisite desserts a highlight. Head chef and maître d' Hüseyin prides himself on his extensive Turkish, Italian and French wine list (budget extra for this); reservations are usually necessary.

In Alsancak village centre, *Cenap* occupies a pleasant old house, with outdoor seating in summer; despite an increasingly commercial vibe, and gaffes such as

---

Scuba diving in North Cyprus

Like the South, North Cyprus is an excellent place to learn to **dive** or just brush up on acquired skills. Dive sites comprise a mix of reefs, drop-offs and archeological relics, with plenty of marine life on view. The sea is at its warmest from May to November (21–28ºC), with just a long-john suit feasible in July and August for shallower dives. You should, however, use hoods and gloves from November to March – the latter are also necessary in any month for protection against the rather aggressive *lahoz/lágos* who have learned to mob divers for hand-feedings. Visibility is generally good, at times up to 25m.

There are nearly a score of dive sites around Kyrenia, ranging in depth from 10 to 45 metres. Even shallow day-divers should see huge groupers and enormous shoals of banded bream, with luckier sightings of scorpion fish, moray or even sea turtle. One popular outing near Kyrenia is to "Fred's Reef" near the new harbour, at about 21m depth, where fish appear for rations of Spam or boiled egg. More advanced sites include the recovery site of the Kyrenia castle's shipwreck, at 30m, or the 38-metre plunge at Zephyros reef well west of Kyrenia. All-day trips to a modern wreck site off the Karpaz (Kárpas) peninsula may be undertaken during high season. See p.310 for details of diving companies around Kyrenia.

KYRENIA AND THE NORTH COAST | West of Kyrenia

serving meat and fish together in their *meze*, it's popular with locals and reasonable value at about 70YTL for two with a bottle of *rakı*.

Lapta (Lápithos)

Draped over several canyon-split ridges, its dwellings scattered in spring-fed greenery or perched on bluffs, sprawling **LAPTA** (Lápithos) seems a more elaborate, shaggy version of nearby Alsancak. Left mostly unscathed by the 1995 fire, the village represents your best opportunity to see what the Kyrenia escarpment once looked like. Its abundant water supply has attracted settlers since the twelfth century BC, though most of them lived down at Lambousa until the Arab raids of the seventh century AD compelled them to retreat inland. Ancient Lapethos was one of the original city-kingdoms of Cyprus, and during the Roman era served as a regional capital.

Lapta was famous in former times for its silk, carved chests, potters and water-powered corn mills – and more recently for a strange snake-charmer who lived in a house full of serpents, some poisonous. He not only tamed them, but was apparently able to neutralize their venomous bites, and once appeared on Turkish TV to demonstrate his talents.

Lapta was originally a bicommunal village; the pair of mosques and seven churches and monasteries correspond to the nine separate historical districts, but the minaret of the seventeenth-century Mehmet Ağa Camii was severely damaged during the 1963–64 troubles and the Turkish Cypriots "persuaded" to leave. It's still mixed after a fashion: Turkish Cypriots, Anatolians and a burgeoning number of foreigners, who may soon be in the majority.

Practicalities

The developed coastline below Lapta supports several large resort **hotels**, but most of these are dominated by casinos, weekenders from the mainland or (in isolated cases) prostitution, and can no longer be unreservedly recommended for conventional tourism. The exception is the low-rise *LA Holiday Centre* (☏821 89 81, Ⓦwww.la-hotel-cyprus.com; ❸), where a pedestrian underpass gives access to a fair-sized natural beach with summer water sports. The complex, officially rated four-star, also has indoor and outdoor infinity pools, a

▲ The village of Lapta

tennis court and sauna/fitness centre. Rooms include galleried family quad units, or interconnecting standards.

Your most reliable full-service local **dining** options are the *Aphrodite*, down on the shore, or the well-signposted *Başpınar* ("Headspring") *Restaurant*, an appealing eyrie under plane trees at the very top of the village. Just adjacent, the fountain-water in question used to emerge from a tunnel after a long trip down the mountain, prior to entering a purportedly Roman aqueduct whose arcades partly support the restaurant; the massive growth in demand from the new villa projects has wrecked the water table and halted the flow. Despite this, the place remains a massively popular venue for weekend lunches especially, when goat or lamb stew, and *küp kebap*, are available only by advance arrangement (T821 86 61 or 821 89 42); on spec, fare will be rather more ordinary (chops with some *meze*) and a bit pricey for the locale.

Karşıyaka (Vasília) and Güzelyalı (Vavilás)

Some 18km west of Kyrenia, you reach an unmarked crossroads, though on the seaward side of the road there's an Atatürk bust at the middle of a plaza ringed with coffee houses. The inland turning leads shortly to **KARŞIYAKA** (Vasília, Vasilya), whose gushing fountain contrasts with its barren, sunbaked setting near the western end of the Kyrenia range. The abundant water allows for the irrigation of farmland and tomato hothouses in the plain below, but the village is about as far west as expats – and more casual tourists – are inclined to venture, with villa construction down on the plain clearly more profitable now than farming. Above Karşıyaka stand the shattered remains of the **monastery of Sinai**, which appears in no historical annals; the village itself has a Kármi-style church with an ornately carved, top-heavy belfry.

If you instead follow restaurant signs to seaward from the plaza with the Atatürk bust, **GÜZELYALI** (Vavilás, Vavilya) soon appears. Formerly a port for shipping carob pods, it still has three visible warehouses. Beautiful (*güzel* in Turkish) it ain't – nor are there any beaches worth mentioning – but it is an authentic outpost of Cypriot fishing culture, with a certain scruffy charm. The *Şirinyalı* restaurant (closed Thurs) here is an 1980s-style seafood place, basic in both decor and presentation of food, though the fish is fresh and won't break the bank at about 20YTL each; indoor and outdoor seating overlooks the water.

A bit past the crossroads, the road meets the sea again near the *Club Güzelyalı* hotel. Opposite this is a tempting-looking **beach**, which up close proves to be heavily striated with reef – though there is one sandy corridor to get into the water, in front of a seasonal beach-bar.

The Koruçam (Kormakíti) peninsula

The western reaches of Kyrenia district terminate in the **Kormakíti peninsula** (Koruçam Burnu), a rolling expanse of farmland and sparsely vegetated hills. Like the Akámas and the Karpaz, the other great promontories of Cyprus, it has a back-of-beyond feel and an interesting demographic history, in this case as the last redoubt of the island's thousand-year-old Maronite community.

Once past the turnings for Güzelyalı and Karşıyaka, and the reefy beach noted above (plus a cluster of brothels just beyond), the road bears inland on its long, indirect way towards Nicosia; the entire route is heavily militarized from here on, as it's the easiest way around the Kyrenia hills for potential invaders.

Kayalar to the cape

Less than a kilometre inland, by the clustered "nightclubs", a paved, narrow road heads west back towards the coast, and the village of **KAYALAR** (Órga), where mushrooming numbers of villas perch above crumbling dwellings occupied by settlers from Turkey. Just before reaching Kayalar, a few coves look appealing from afar, but up close prove to be reefy and (usually) filthy; the exception is so-called "**Horseshoe Beach**", also the only one with facilities, in the form of an eponymous seasonal café-restaurant at the top of the drop to the shore.

Beyond the modern, undesecrated Maronite chapel and bay of Áyios Yeóryios, the next settlement, **SADRAZAMKÖY** (Liverás), is too poorly sited to have attracted more than a handful of Anatolian settlers – but has attracted another unlikely, and sizeable, villa-village close to the shore. You can bump further along dirt tracks to the unmanned gantry-mounted beacon out on bleak **Cape Koruçam** (Kormakíti) itself; this is Cyprus's nearest point to Turkey, some forty nautical miles from Cape Anamur in Anatolia.

The Maronites of Kormakíti

The **Maronites** are an ancient Middle Eastern sect whose identity arose out of a seventh-century theological dispute between the Monophysites, who postulated a single, divine nature for Christ, and the mainstream Orthodox, who believed Christ was simultaneously God and Man. When asked their opinion by the Emperor Heraclius, the monks of the Monastery of St Maron in Syria proposed that Christ had a dual nature but a single divine will. For a time this was championed as an ideal compromise, but later the doctrine was deemed heretical and its adherents had to seek safety in the mountains of the Lebanon.

Supposedly, the Maronites first **came to Cyprus** in the twelfth century with the Crusaders, whom they had served in Palestine as archers and guides, settling primarily in the Karpaz and Kormakíti areas. A contending theory asserts that these merely supplemented an existing Maronite colony which had been on the island since the eighth century.

Although **Uniate Christians** – they acknowledge the supremacy of the pope, and still call themselves *Katholikí* (Catholics) – the Maronites have always been culturally similar to the Greek Orthodox majority, being historically bilingual in modern Greek as well as their own language (about which read on), and using Greek personal names. The Karpaz community assimilated ages ago through intermarriage, and like the island's Latin Catholics, the Maronites have for some years observed Easter on the same date as the Orthodox. Despite all this, the Maronites attempted to remain neutral in the struggle between the Greek Orthodox and Turkish Muslim communities, taking no part in EOKA excesses either before or after independence.

Accordingly, the Maronites of Kormakíti were among the enclaved Christians theoretically allowed to **remain in the North** after 1974, though in practice Turkish military and civil administration was until 2003 very nearly as hard on them as on the Greek Orthodox of the Karpaz peninsula (see p.361). Like them, Maronites were issued with identity cards by the Northern authorities, but not allowed to vote. Then there was the farce of the two *múkhtars* (headmen) for the village, one appointed by the North, one by the South – each considered a spy of the "sponsoring" regime, and amid a muddle of countermanded edicts, there was (and still is) no real authority in Koruçam. Most supplies and foodstuffs were brought in from the South, as the Maronites were, either by official choice or their own, not well integrated into the Northern economy.

Koruçam (Kormakíti)

The road hairpins on itself from Sadrazamköy to head back southeast, passing a tiny medieval chapel of the Virgin just before arriving at the once-prosperous Maronite "capital" of **KORUÇAM** (Kormakíti, the only northern village signposted with its pre-1974 name). Set amid gently inclined, pine-covered uplands, the little town gazes towards the Gulf of Mórfou and the great coastal bight to the west. Its permanent population, about 1100 in 1960, has dwindled to 130 mostly elderly residents; just a bare handful of children, taught by two nuns from a small, well-kept convent in the village centre, keep the primary school going. A priest is still resident, with mass celebrated regularly in the enormous modern church of Áyios Yeóryios; you can visit the interior at other times by applying to the convent or the nearby municipal coffee house, where Beirut football pennants hang near portraits of various Maronite patriarchs and civic leaders, while religious postcards and calendars flank mandatorily displayed images of northern leader Mehmet Ali Talat and Kemal Atatürk.

Although there are no Turkish-mainland settlers in Koruçam village proper, nearby houses, public buildings and productive farmland have been expropriated without compensation by the army, and secondary schools shut down, making the continued existence of a viable community impossible. By the mid-1990s, when the worst **harassment** eased (and telephones arrived), almost everyone between the ages of 12 and 45 in the four traditional Maronite villages had elected to emigrate, either to the South or abroad: rarely to ancestral but troubled Lebanon, more usually to Italy and England, where intermarriage with other Catholics is common.

What's left of the Kormakíti Maronite community now lives in the eponymous village, officially Koruçam. The three other traditional settlements, Karpaşa (Karpásha), Özhan (Aзómatoз) and Gürpınar (Ayía Marína), were completely (and forcibly) **abandoned** by 1996, Turkish Army officers occupying some houses, with the main Maronite monastery, Profítis Ilías near Gürpınar, long derelict. The remaining Maronites – average age 68 – were some of the few individuals allowed relatively free movement between the two sides of the island prior to 2003. This status made them useful business intermediaries – not least in the smuggling back and forth of title deeds for Greek-Cypriot properties whose refugee owners, despairing of a settlement providing for the right of return, elected to sell land or ruins to foreigners.

In 2003, living conditions for the Kormakíti Maronites **improved** markedly. With the Vatican discreetly fronting the money, airtight titles from both the northern and southern authorities for all their agricultural property were "ransomed", and the Turkish military induced to withdraw from them. Houses are now well kept, and there are even some confident new-builds, with the freedom to cross the barriers making full-time residence theoretically possible.

But even if Maronites' retention of their ancestral lands now seems more assured, connection with their **native language** – an elaboration of ancient Aramaic or Syriac called "Cypriot Maronite Arabic" or "Sanna" – remains threatened, even though ancient Syriac is still used in the church liturgy. Perhaps 120 fluent speakers – mostly in Kormakíti – remain out of an island-wide community of almost 5000, and the southern republic's public educational system is completely indifferent to the prospect of the tongue's disappearance within two decades. Help has come from an unforeseen source – a 2006 scholarly expedition from Malta took the first step in preserving the language by setting it down in Roman script – and there is now a school in Nicosia to teach it to the young.

Notwithstanding recent hopeful developments (see box, pp.318–319), the village only really comes to life at weekends, especially during hunting season when Maronites in the South come to visit. Their favourite target, opposite the church, is 🌴 *Yorgo Kasap Restaurant,* where some of the spirit of the multi-ethnic Cyprus of old can be recaptured. Before April 2003, Turkish Cypriots who came here for Sunday lunch were making something of a low-key political statement about the continued social segregation, and cocking a snook at the plainclothes policeman dining alone, keeping tabs on attendance. Yorgo's *meze* (including his own red wine) is not bargain-basement but it's great value and one of the most savoury on the island: *tashíni, talatoúra,* sheep's yogurt, pickled capers and cauliflower, succulent *kléftigo,* and to finish off, superb *köfter* – like the soushoúkou of the South, but without nuts.

The Mavi Köşk

Çamlıbel (Mýrtou), near the high point of the road to Nicosia, has become a major Turkish army strongpoint, though the direct road southeast from Koruçam to here is unrestricted. There's a tourist attraction of sorts just west, the so-called **Mavi Köşk** or "Blue Villa", better than a James Bond villain's hideout. To reach it, head southwest on the bypass road towards Güzelyurt, passing various army-camp entrances shut to the public, then turn right at a minor road with a fruit stall at the junction – if you pass a filling station you've gone too far. This is the narrow but more direct road to Koruçam. A few hundred metres along, there's an unmanned checkpoint; turn right here, and at the next gate you must leave a passport. Enter the military zone and park right in front of the **villa** (daily except Mon 9am–5pm; guided tours only; 0.50YTL); once inside you'll have to leave another piece of ID per group (a driving licence should do).

In unitary-Republic years the Mavi Köşk belonged to one **Byron** (or **Pavlos**, versions differ) **Pavlides**, a wealthy lawyer, auto-parts dealer, supposed gun-runner and associate of Archbishop Makarios, who stayed here on occasion. The villa and its past occupants are now firmly entrenched in the official demonology/mythology of the North, albeit in a slightly sanitized version as spieled by your (possibly English-speaking) guide. Tours visit most of the rooms and the gardens, including a breathtaking viewpoint above a bunker, from where Pavlides could supposedly watch for his gun-running ships in the Karamanian channel. One story goes that the decadent host would toss apples out of an upper-floor window to nubile young ladies bobbing in the courtyard pool; whoever caught the fruit would share his bed that night. The only slight problem with the anecdote is that Pavlides was decidedly gay, and the pool would have been full of hunky lads; the lucky winner could be smuggled into and out of Pavlides' bedroom by a secret tunnel (only a few yards long), which you're shown. Pavlides himself went into exile post-1974 and was shot dead by a Turk in 1986, in Italy.

This much is arguably fact; wilder speculation asserts, on the basis of a few zodiacal symbols in wrought iron outline on the walls, and a Bacchus-faced fountain-spout for wine (on the terrace by the refectory), that Pavlides and Makarios were satanists who conducted orgies here. In fact the villa is nothing more than a pastel-coloured kitsch 1960s period piece; some of the furnishings are original, though many have been looted since 1974.

Akedeniz: site and beach

From just south of Tepebaşı (Dhiórios), another road leads west towards **Akdeniz** (Ayía Iríni), near the important eponymous Late Bronze Age to Archaic site excavated in 1929; since the place yielded up its treasures, it's of strictly specialist interest, and anyway falls squarely within Turkish army territory, whose conscripts will insist on accompanying you around, if indeed they let you in at all.

Most visitors head this way for a patch of serviceable **beach** ceded by the military in 1994; indeed the turning just south of Tepebaşı towards Akdeniz is helpfully signposted "Beach/Plaj". At the Akdeniz village mosque, 5km along, bear left, and then again onto a dirt track, following more "Beach/Plaj" signs. It's just over 7km in total to the beach, trash-strewn like most public beaches in the North and equipped only with toilets, showers and a seasonal drinks stall. The shore itself is gravel on hard-packed sand, best for jogging on a calm day; dunes behind and sweeping views along the arc of the bay lend what beauty there is.

The Pigádhes sanctuary

Returning to the main road towards north Nicosia, you sense the beginnings of the Mesarya; corn and hay fields become increasingly common, and all open water disappears. Exactly 2km southeast of the junction at Çamlıbel, keep an eye out on the right for a narrow but paved track running between cypresses; the start is obliterated by a ditch, though a helpful sign has been erected. After about 250m, you reach the fenced enclosure (unlocked gate) containing the Bronze Age shrine known as **Pigádhes**. The most prominent structure is a restored stepped altar of rough ashlar masonry, carved with geometrical reliefs and crowned by a pair of stone "horns of consecration" reminiscent of Creto-Minoan sacred art of the same period. Around this sprawl the foundations of the courtyard sanctuary, plus more trees which make the site fairly easy to spot from the road. Though not dazzling in impact, it's an intriguing antiquity, worth the short detour and the slight risk to your undercarriage involved in crossing the roadside ditch.

Alternative return to Kyrenia

For an interesting return route to the Kyrenia coast, bear north at Kılıçaslan (Kondeménos) towards **Kozan** (Lárnaka tís Lapíthou), beautifully set on the southern slopes of Selvili Dağ (Kyparissóvouno), at 1024m the summit of the Kyrenia range. A few grapevines are coaxed from sunny terraces, but nothing like the profusion south of the Tróodhos. The main church here is now a mosque, though Panayía tón Katháron monastery visible just west was thoroughly sacked after 1974.

The onward road over a 500-metre-high saddle in the ridge ahead is steep and single-lane, but also paved and scenic, descending to Karşıyaka to pick up the coastal highway; at the pass, just west, there's a seasonal **restaurant** in the forest, and almost immediately opposite this the start of the **colonial-era road** running along the ridge. Blasted through in the early 1950s at a purported cost of £300 per mile, this is now paved (if one-lane) and can be followed east past the highest summits all the way to St Hilarion castle (see p.322). It's a scenic run, with man-high pines recovering from the 1995 blaze, which fortunately didn't entirely devastate the highest ridges. About 5km along, well commemorated with flags and a plaque, a **Turkish tank** lies where it foundered while attempting a flanking manoeuvre on August 2, 1974, miraculously halting several metres down a steep slope; the four-man crew escaped.

Inland from Kyrenia

Immediately **southeast of Kyrenia** cluster several inland villages which, even more than those to the west of town, have been particularly favoured by foreigners since the start of British administration. The coastal plain seems wider and more gently pitched, and the hills are further in the background, permitting more winter sun than at Kármi or Lapta. Even the laziest visitor manages to make it up here, if only to see one of the crown jewels of North-Cypriot tourism, the romantically half-ruined **Béllapais abbey**.

Further inland along the watershed of the Kyrenia hills are scattered a handful of castles and monasteries, evocatively set on rock spires or down in wooded valleys, and justifiably some of the biggest tourist attractions in the North. Sited to be in visual communication with each other, Kyrenia and Nicosia, the castles of **St Hilarion**, **Buffavento** and **Kantara** served as an early-warning system for pirate raids on the north coast. At the start of the Venetian era, they were all partially dismantled to prevent further mischievous use, though the development of artillery had effectively made them obsolete already. All of these sights are served by roads of decent standard taking off from the two main Kyrenia–Nicosia routes.

St Hilarion castle

Just west of the main Kyrenia–Nicosia highway, in the Kyrenia hills, **St Hilarion castle** (daily: summer 8am–6pm, last admission 5pm; winter 9am–4.30pm, last ticket 3.30pm; 7YTL) – *Aï-Lárko* in Cypriot dialect – is the westernmost and best preserved of the three redoubts built by the Byzantines and Crusaders. With (nocturnally illuminated) walls and towers seeming to sprout out of the rocks almost at random, it's a fairy-tale sight living up to Rose Macaulay's much-quoted description – "a picture-book castle for elf-kings" – and the rumour that Walt Disney used it as a model for the castle in *Snow White and the Seven Dwarfs*. Local legend once credited St Hilarion with 101 rooms, of which 100 could easily be found; the last, an enchanted garden, contained a fabulous treasure belonging to an elusive "queen" of Cypriot folklore, probably a holdover of Aphrodite worship. Shepherds or hunters stumbling through the magic doorway of the treasury had a tendency to awaken years later, Rip Van Winkle-like, empty-handed among the bare rocks.

Some history

The castle's history is almost as intricate as its battlements, with occasional valiant or grisly episodes belying its ethereal appearance. The saint of the name was a little-known hermit who fled Palestine during the seventh century to live and die up here, purging the mountain of still-lurking pagan demons; a Byzantine monastery, and later a fort, sprang up around his tomb.

Owing to its near-impregnability, it was one of the last castles taken by the Crusaders in 1191. The Lusignans improved its fortifications throughout the early thirteenth century and knew Didhymi, the Greek name for the twin peaks overhead, as Dieu d'Amour. St Hilarion was the focus of a four-year struggle between Holy Roman Emperor Frederick II and regent John d'Ibelin for control of the island, won by John's forces at the battle of nearby Agírda (today Ağırdağ) in 1232. During the subsequent 140 years of peace, sumptuous royal apartments were added, so that the castle doubled as a summer palace and, during 1349–50, as a refuge from the plague.

In 1373, during the Genoese invasion, the castle again acquired military importance as the retreat of the under-age King Peter II. His uncle and regent John of Antioch, misled by his hostile sister-in-law Eleanor of Aragon into believing his bodyguard of Bulgarian mercenaries treasonous, had them thrown one at a time from the highest tower of the castle. The tale sounds apocryphal, and it is likely many of the men were simply sent on their way, but whatever the case, without his loyal retinue John – implicated in the murder of Eleanor's late husband, Peter I – was easy prey for the vengeful queen and her courtiers, who lured him to supper in Nicosia, where they stabbed him.

The Venetians rendered the castle useless, they thought, for modern warfare. But in 1964 beleaguered Turkish Cypriots found the castle not so militarily obsolete after all, using it as headquarters of a large enclave which included several Turkish communities straddling the main Kyrenia–Nicosia road. A small garrison of teenage TMT activists was able to fend off EOKA attacks on the castle, and the Turks remained in control of the place thereafter. With passage on the traditional main highway prohibited to solo Greek vehicles, and possible only in slow, UN-escorted convoy, the central government was forced to construct a bypass via Beşparmak (Pendadháktylos). In 1974 St Hilarion and its surrounding enclave were a primary goal of Turkish paratroop landings early on July 20.

The site

Although St Hilarion itself is now very much open for visits, the twisty but well-marked approach road from the highway still passes through two Turkish army bases, with signs forbidding stopping or walking, let alone photography. It's also closed to civilian traffic just before sunset, so if you tarry too long you'll be obliged to leave the area via the single-lane ridge road west to Karşıyaka. Partway along, the restricted zone ends just past a clearing where the Crusaders held their jousting tournaments, and suddenly the castle appears, draped over the bristling pinnacles before you. You'll spend a good hour scrambling over the crags to see it all. It's hot work in summer: come early in the day, and bring stout shoes – beach- or pool-wear won't do on the often uneven ground.

First you cross the vast lower bailey beyond the ticket booth, where medieval garrisons kept their horses; stables house an eminently missable "Introduction" display, but the wildflowers here (and higher up) are spectacular in March. Once through the hulking **gatehouse** and tunnel into the middle enceinte (the defended area enclosed by the castle walls), your first detour is to the roofless but otherwise intact **Byzantine chapel**, the earliest structure in the castle. You continue through a myriad rooms on a variety of levels; these include the the handsome vaulted **belvedere** just beyond it, and the monastic refectory, later the royal **banqueting hall** and now a balconied drinks café and postcard shop, up some stairs north of the chapel. Just west of this, the old buttery, kitchen and castellan's room have been mocked up with **mannequins** illustrating aspects of Lusignan domestic life.

An **arched gate** and serpentining, stony stair-paths beyond allow entry to the upper enceinte; you can scramble immediately up south to the highest towers. The more outrageously perched, **"Prince John's"**, is the purported venue for the massacre of his Bulgarian auxiliaries. Alternatively, climbing towards the west end of the complex, you'll pass the aqueduct and largest cistern (now just a dangerously deep mud-puddle), which supplied the otherwise waterless garrisons here. The ascent of the western tower and "*zirve*" (summit, elevation 732m) is well hand-railed. Excursions end at the **royal apartments**, whose Gothic-tracery **windows** afforded the TMT garrison a good view of their mortal enemies in Kármi before 1974.

Ozanköy and Çatalköy

East of Kyrenia, and reachable from the coastal highway by a secondary road, are two attractive settlements. **OZANKÖY** (Kazáfani, Kazafana) was, before the troubles began, a mixed village famous for its carob syrup and olive oil; at the central Zorlu Market you can still buy a bottle of *harup pekmezi* (carob syrup) for about 10YTL – excellent over oatmeal or baked into muffins, and perhaps the most authentic Cypriot souvenir (see *Traditional Cypriot food* colour section). In the faded-frescoed medieval church of Panayía Potamítissa, now the village mosque, a fourteenth-century tomb in one corner sports a bas-relief of the occupant in period dress. Ozanköy also supports one of the more long-running village **restaurants** in the area. *Erol's* (dinner only; closed Sun; ☎815 91 36 or 0533/864 63 72), well signposted at the southeastern edge of Ozanköy, is slightly pricey for local cuisine, but the quality, especially of the meat, is high. For that amount you'll get home-made soup, chops, garnish and nibbles, plus a beer in winter, but their famous hot/cold *meze* in high season, when more customers are about (and reservations are suggested).

ÇATALKÖY (Áyios Epíktitos) is built atop a peculiar low escarpment riddled with caves; the hermit Epiktitos lived in one of these during the twelfth century. Above the village lies the *Dedeman Olive Tree* (☎824 42 00, ⓦwww.dedeman.com; ❺), one of the more luxurious yet good-value **suite-hotel** complexes in the North and represented by most package companies. Arrayed around an enormous pool are three types of accommodation: a wing of very large hotel rooms with high-quality furnishings, a few three-bedroom bungalows sleeping five and (closest to the pool and thus popular) one-bedroom suites. Double-occupancy prices are the same throughout, and there's no true self-catering. With massive common areas, a casino and on-site restaurants, the management has set its cap for "conference and business tourism" (for which read Turkish mainlanders).

On the east side of the village stands ✻ *Anı* (☎824 43 55), one of the best and fairest-priced fish **restaurants** in the North. About 40YTL each (in a party of four) will get you *meze* with cold and hot starters, including *barbunya* fish, plus their speciality, succulent whole *lahoz* baked in salt (must be pre-ordered); all their vegetables are own-grown – and they're able to find fresh fish even in midsummer. The interior has a woodstove and central hearth going in winter.

Çatalköy is also home to the English-run **Çatalköy Riding Club** (☎0533/845 47 41, Di, or 0533/845 47 42, Bev; ⓦwww.catalkoyridingclub .com; closed Mon), with lessons from £20 per hour and trail rides ranging from ninety minutes to a full day, though they're mostly geared for one-week packages inclusive of locally arranged accommodation.

Beylerbeyi (Béllapais): village and abbey

A couple of kilometres inland and uphill from Ozanköy on a secondary road, the village of **BEYLERBEYİ** (Béllapais, Bellabayıs) occupies a sloping natural terrace overlooking the sea, a ravine to the east providing definition. **Lawrence Durrell**'s sojourn here during the 1950s put it on the literary and touristic map, and his former house – near the top of the village at Acı Limon Sokağı 15 – sports an ornamental ceramic plate over the door. Here he finished *Justine*, the first volume of the Alexandria Quartet, and entertained a succession of British literati who had already made – or subsequently went on to make – their mark as travel writers or chroniclers of the eastern Mediterranean. His large house has been somewhat tastelessly revamped by several successive owners, but the mains-water standpipe which figured so prominently in the drama of Durrell's purchase of the property still protrudes from the wall opposite, emblazoned 'ER 1953'. Indeed the village is supplied with some of the best **water** in the Kyrenia range – there's a popular kerbside fountain on the approach road.

Frankly there are more attractive villages in the Kyrenia hills than Beylerbeyi: there's little greenery and open space and cobbles have long since vanished from the lanes. The glory of the place resides definitively in the nocturnally illuminated Lusignan **abbey of Béllapais**, at the northern edge of the village.

The history of the abbey

Béllapais abbey was originally founded as St Mary of the Mountain just after 1200 by Augustinian canons fleeing Palestine. Almost immediately the brethren changed their affiliation to the Premonstratensian order under Thierry, the man behind the construction of Ayía Sofía cathedral in Nicosia, and adopted the white habits which gave the place its nickname of the "White Abbey". Lusignan King Hugh III richly endowed it later the same century; he also conferred on the abbot the right to wear a mitre, sword and golden spurs, which only puffed up the abbey's pretensions in its frequent squabbles with the archbishopric of Nicosia – as did a gift of a supposed fragment of the True Cross in 1246.

Subsequent Lusignan kings were benefactors, some even living in the abbey, but it proved a tempting target for the Genoese plunderings of 1373, after which it spun into both moral and physical decline; the friars' scandalous reputation was owed to their concubines, and the practice of only accepting their offspring as novices. The Venetians shortened the long-standing name, Abbaye de la Pais (Abbey of Peace), to De la Pais, from which it was an easy elision to Béllapais.

The Turks dispersed the community in 1570 and handed the abbey over to the Orthodox Church, while a village – apparently populated by descendants of the monks – grew up around the monastery. The site subsequently suffered from being used as a quarry by villagers and even the British, who despoiled the buildings in various ways before their embryonic antiquities department began repairs early last century.

Visits to the abbey

You approach through a promenade of palm trees that lend an exotic touch to the Gothic ambience, though the cloister's courtyard is still garnished with the robust cypresses planted by Durrell's Mr Kollis in the 1940s. **Admission** policies are somewhat flexible (nominally daily: summer 9am–8pm; winter 9am–4.45pm; 7YTL), since the (not especially recommended) *Kybele* restaurant operates within the grounds until 11pm, so in practice you can see much of the complex (at a slight distance) from the restaurant's access path.

Except for its western arcade, where the vaulting has vanished, the graceful fourteenth-century **cloister** is intact (though the tracery is gone) and enlivened by carvings of human and monster heads on the corbels. Just south of this, the thirteenth-century **church**, used by the Greek Orthodox community here until its last members were forced out in 1976, is open for visits. The interior is much as the Greeks left it, with intricately carved pulpit, *témblon* and bishop's throne still visible in the dim glow of five fairly restrained chandeliers. Over the entrance, a horseshoe-shaped wooden *yinaikonítis* seems to defy gravity; the rib-vaulted ceiling is rather more substantially supported by four massive columns. Underfoot, several Lusignan kings are thought to be entombed beneath the floor pavement. A stairway outside climbs to a rooftop **parapet** that's the best vantage point for the ruined chapterhouse to the east of the cloister, and also leads to a small treasury, atop the church's north aisle, and the upper-storey dormitory, of which only one wall survives.

On the north side of the cloister, a Roman sarcophagus once served the monks as a washbasin before they trooped into the magnificent **refectory** (which today hosts the local music festival; see p.310). Six bay windows frame the sea, with a thirty-metre drop below them along the edge of the escarpment on which Béllapais was built. A raised pulpit in the north wall, from where scriptural selections would be read during meals, is accessible by a narrow spiral stairway. During the late 1800s, British forces barbarically used the refectory as a shooting range – hence the bullet holes in the east wall, where a higher rose window admits more light. A stairway leads from the ruins of the kitchen at the refectory's west end down to an **undercroft** with magnificent "palm" vaulting sprouting off low columns; it's currently used as an exhibition venue.

Practicalities

Parking in the village is a non-starter in season – you must use the small designated car park behind the monastery, or (more likely) two areas about 500m west. There's a recommended **car hire** outlet in the very centre: Bellapais Rent a Car (☎815 75 10, ⓦwww.bellapaisrentacar.com), with free (Ercan) airport pickup service. Failing that, the bus service from Kyrenia is reasonably frequent.

Lest he accomplish nothing all day, Durrell was warned away from the "Tree of Idleness" (a now-sickly mulberry) shading its attendant *Ulusoglu* **café** on the square southwest of the abbey. Across the street, the *Huzur Ağaç* ("Tree of Repose" in Turkish) **restaurant** is a modern full-service outfit with indifferent food, tackily souvenir-festooned and coach-tour-oriented. For better eating, head west down the main street to unpretentious but wholesome *Paşa* (dinner only; closed Sun), where under 15YTL will see you to *ayran*, soup and either *pirohu* (vegetarian ravioli) or a *pide*. Alternatively, try either of the restaurants attached to our accommodation recommendations.

The best two among several **accommodation** options in and around Beyler-beyi are quite close to the abbey. The excellent ⚵ *Bellapais Gardens* (☎815 60 66, ⓦwww.bellapaisgardens.com; ❻), just below the abbey refectory and north wall, is a well-laid-out, human-scale bungalow cluster with its own, very competent restaurant featuring nouvelle Cypriot and continental specialities (allow 35YTL) and North Cypriot microwinery products. The quite plush, galleried one-bedroom cottages, redone in 2006, dot the slope leading down to an idyllic spring-fed pool built at the base of the abbey. The level of service from Sabri ("Steve") Abit and colleagues, breakfast quality and easy (for Bellapais anyway) parking guarantee a loyal repeat clientele.

A bit southeast of the abbey grounds, overlooking the ravine, is ⚵ *The Gardens of Irini* (☎815 21 20, ⓦwww.gardensofirini.com). Rather miraculously, the property has been in the hands of the same British-bohemian family (who knew Durrell well) since 1952, and today daughter Deidre Guthrie offers two tastefully restored self-catering cottages (studio & 1-bed) at weekly rates of £245 for two (1 child possible also in larger cottage). Breakfast is available for an extra £5 charge, as are evening meals, drinks and light lunches by arrangement at the *Guthrie Bistro*.

Panayía Absinthiótissa monastery

The **monastery of Panayía Absinthiótissa** enjoys a grand setting amid juniper forest on the south flank of the range, gazing out across the Mesarya. Founded in late Byzantine times, it was taken over by Latin monks in the fifteenth century, and well restored during the 1960s – only to suffer comprehensive vandalization since 1974.

Despite its condition, Absinthiótissa still merits a visit, perhaps as a detour on the way between Kyrenia and north Nicosia. **Getting there** is fairly easy: from the divided highway linking those towns, turn east towards Aşağı Dikmen (Káto Dhíkomo) and Taşkent (Vounó); after about twenty minutes of mostly single-lane driving, you'll reach the latter village, just after the giant Turkish-Cypriot flag and Atatürk slogan painted on the hillside. At the junction opposite the central shop, head north uphill along an initially paved lane, which forks after 500m; take a right, away from the gravel pit, and another right at a water tank. The monastery is in sight most of the way, so there's little chance of getting badly lost, but a 4WD vehicle is useful to skirt the yawning quarry pits.

The outsized, twelve-windowed drum and dome of the **church** are visible from afar, but approaching you'll notice the peculiar narthex which the Catholic monks added, with apses at each end; inside, there's marvellous Gothic rib-vaulting. Any frescoes have been defaced or stolen since 1974; the only other thing to admire is the **refectory**, north across the courtyard, with shallow ceiling vaulting and lancet windows outlined in 1960s brickwork.

Buffavento castle

Buffavento, the least well preserved but most dramatically sited – and at 940m the highest – of the Kyrenia hill-castles, requires some effort to reach, but will appeal to those who like their ruins wild and slightly sinister. There is no guard, admission fee or any restriction on access since the Turkish Army abolished its no-entry days some years back.

Getting there

The usual method of **getting there** involves taking the inland turning off the coast road east of Kyrenia, following the signs for Famagusta (not Esentepe), just

▲ Panayia Absinthiótissa

past Çatalköy. The only local village, reached by a slip road partway along, is scruffy **Arapköy** (Klepíni, Klebini). A curious legend once held that no more than forty families could reside in the place, or the Angel of Death would cull the surplus within the year; there are still only about 150 people here, a mix of native Turkish Cypriots, Anatolian settlers and a few foreigners attracted by the views.

At the very top of the grade, when the Mesarya comes into view, sits the *Bufavento Beşparmak* **restaurant**, the area's only amenity, with rustic decor, kebab-dominated fare and a fireplace for winter. Just opposite this, take the paved road heading west, marked "Bufavento Kalesi", for 6km through unscathed forest and scrub to the principal castle car park. A jeep track continues 250m in zigzags right (north) further up to the start of a stair-path, where an olive tree grows in a stone planter ring across from a trilingual marble memorial to victims of a 1988 air crash: a small aircraft, approaching Ercan in misty conditions, failed to clear the ridge above and disintegrated nearby.

From the lower parking area, it's a 25-minute walk up through junipers alive with birds to the castle, which blends well into the rock on which it's built; though the stair-path is in good condition, there's a consistent southern exposure, so you'll bake in summer unless you go early or late in the day.

Incidentally, don't believe maps – either internationally published ones, or those issued by the North Cyprus tourist office – which imply that the easiest approach is from the south, via Güngör (Koutsovéndis) and the tempting-looking monastery of **Áyios Ioánnis Khrysóstomos**. Beyond Güngör all tracks are unmarked, and a giant army camp blocks the way, placing the deconsecrated monastery off-limits as well.

Conversely, the paved road west from the car-park emerges at Taşkent after about 10km, making it possible to visit Buffavento in tandem with Panayía Absinthiótissa (see p.326).

The site

Buffavento probably began life as a Byzantine watchtower in the tenth century and was surrendered to Guy de Lusignan in 1191. The Lusignan kings used it mostly as a political prison, in particular Peter I who – warned reluctantly by his friend John Visconti of Queen Eleanor's infidelity – repaid the favour by locking Visconti up here to starve to death.

Decommissioned by the Venetians, the vaulted buildings, almost all fitted with cisterns, are in poor-to-fair condition, and home now only to bats; they're a pretext, really, for a nice walk in the hills. You can follow the stair-path (fitted with handrails) from the graffitied **gatehouse** up through a jumble of walls to the highest tower, where a natural terrace affords superb views, and where signal fires were lit to communicate with St Hilarion and Kantara castles.

Up top here, you'll usually learn how the place got its name (Buffavento means "wind gust"), and enjoy perhaps the best views on Cyprus: Kyrenia, Nicosia and Famagusta are all visible in the right conditions, as are the Tróödhos mountains and indeed half the island. Visiting at dusk, there's the spectacle of Nicosia's lights blazing to life.

Around Beşparmak (Pendadháktylos)

Coming up from the north coast, you can't help noticing the sculpted bulk of **Beşparmak** (Pendadháktylos), the "Five-Finger Mountain", just to the east of the Kyrenia–Nicosia bypass road. Although of modest elevation at 740m, its suggestive shape has engendered legend: the Greeks say the Byzantine hero Dhiyenís Akrítas left the imprint of his hand here after leaping across the sea from Anatolia.

Sourp Magar monastery

You can get a good view of the peak's south flank by turning left at the watershed along the signposted Alevkaya (Halévga) forest road (away from the marked Buffavento turning and restaurant): paved and scenic, but one-lane with occasional turn-outs and thus slow going. Downhill to the north after 7km, you'll glimpse the roofless, thoroughly vandalized remains of the Armenian monastery of **Sourp Magar**, or St Makarios of Egypt. Founded by Copts in the eleventh century, it became the property of the island's Armenian community four hundred years later; the monastery sheltered Armenian refugees during the 1920s, was the venue for an important festival every May 1 until 1974, and also served as a children's summer camp.

Heading east, take a hairpin left from a shady clearing with two round picnic tables, a water spout and rudimentary signage. Just under a kilometre's bumpy, rutted driving brings you to the gate of the irregularly shaped monastery enclosure. Beside a withered orchard stands the tiny church, with pilgrims' cells lining the east and south perimeter walls. Absolutely nothing has been left intact by the Turkish army, venting its fury on a shrine of its historic enemies, and it's only worth visiting for the setting amid dense, unscathed forest. In summer only a small **café/snack bar** run by a father-and-son team operates out of one of cells, repaired for the purpose.

The North Cyprus Herbarium

Just 100m east of the turning for Sourp Magar, the ridge road emerges onto a secondary paved road up from the Nicosia–Ercan airport expressway; turn right to reach, after 300m, the vast picnic grounds around the forestry station at **Alevkaya (Halévga)**. In 1989 the main building here was refurbished and opened as the **North Cyprus Herbarium** (daily 9am–4pm; free) under the direction of Dr Deryck Viney of Kármi. With over a thousand preserved specimens of plants endemic to the island, pressed in folders or pickled in spirit, this is really more of a library and research facility than tourist attraction; however, it is a handy place to pick up a number of flora guides offered for sale, including Dr Viney's two-volume manual of Cypriot plant life.

Antifonítis monastery

The twelfth-century **monastic church of Antifonítis** (Antifonidis), tucked into a pine-covered valley northeast of Alevkaya, was once the premier Byzantine monument of the Kyrenia hills. It takes its name – "He Who Answers" – from the foundation legend, in which a rich man and a poor man met at the place. The pauper asked for a loan from the grandee, who retorted, "Who will act as witness that I have loaned you the money?", to which the penniless one replied, "God". At once a celestial voice was heard sanctifying the transaction, and the monastery grew up around the miracle.

Getting there

There are two usual approaches, from either the ridge road or the coast road. From the herbarium and recreation area, proceed northeast on the paved road, shunning the turn down to Karaağaç (Khárcha) but turning down towards Esentepe (Áyios Amvrósios). Some 2km along this, bear right and uphill, following signage to "Antifonidis" for about 4km until you reach the short, steep, final side track down again towards the monastery, its dome peeking above dense foliage near the base of a valley.

From the coast road east of Kyrenia, turn off at the large village of **Esentepe** (Áyios Amvrósios, Aykuruş), once known for its apricots and crafts, now resettled partly by natives of Áyios Nikólaos in the Páfos hills. Traverse to the high end of the village, following signposting to Alevkaya and Lefkoşa, but at the next junction, bear left following the "Antifonidis" sign rather than continuing straight towards the watershed.

The site

You can drive right up to the walled compound enclosing the church, which is wardened and **open for visits** daily except Thursday; nominal hours are 9am–4.45pm, but you'd be pushing your luck to show up after 2pm. The courtyard surrounds the twelfth-century *katholikón* which, while appealing, doesn't rate for architectural purity: the vaulted Lusignan narthex on the west side dates from the fourteenth century, and the Venetians added an arched loggia to the south in the following century.

Although Greek graffiti goes back two centuries, most of the heartbreaking vandalization of the church's interior has occurred since 1974. Of its once-vivid and notable frescoes, only the magnificent *Pandokrátor* survives undamaged in the huge irregularly shaped dome – supported by eight columns and covering the entire nave – plus the occasional saint or apostle out of reach on arches and columns. Although the building is now locked at dusk, the dome re-tiled and its windows secured against birds or bats, it's very much a case of too little, too late.

Leaving Antifonítis heading eastwards, within a minute or two there's another major junction at a pass with an abandoned building. Heading down to the south leads towards Tirmen (Trypiméni) and Gönendere (Knodhára), a straight course along a dirt forestry track follows the Kyrenia range crest, while down and left on paved surface threads through the rather poor village of Bahçeli (Kalogréa) to the coast road.

East of Kyrenia: the coast

In contrast to the shoreline west of Kyrenia, the coast to the east was historically undeveloped, any villages being built some way inland, out of reach of pirates. All that changed with the 2004–2008 opening of a wide, well-graded road to the district boundary (and beyond), now just over thirty minutes distant. Villas are sprouting in vast numbers all the way to Tatlısu (Akanthoú), formerly one of the few areas where carob orchards were still lovingly pruned and ploughed. Tucked between rocky headlands beyond the *Acapulco Beach Club* are the best (if somewhat exposed) beaches in the district, lonely except on summer weekends.

Karakum (Karákoumi)

The first beach of any significance east of town is at **KARAKUM** (Karákoumi), accessible by a side road opposite the inland turning for the *Courtyard Inn* and then left at the first T-junction: two tiny, dark-sand coves either side of a promontory, the last few hundred yards for jeeps only. The *Courtyard Inn* itself, one of the longest established of Kyrenia's international-cuisine restaurants, is Pakistani-managed, so the pub-style menu is now complemented by good curries and other subcontinent specialities, though English-style Sunday off-season lunch is still a big draw.

A bit further east, about halfway to the turning for Çatalköy, a seaward driveway leads a few hundred metres to the *Paradise* poolside **restaurant** (☏ 824 43 97 or 0542/851 76 66 for reservations; closed Nov–March) run by the Derviş family. The mixed *meze* is strong on vegetarian items like *molehiya*, braised spinach,

You may find, if you're not staying at shorefront hotels, that you will be charged a fee (8–12YTL per person) for use of many beaches either side of Kyrenia. In 1991 the government, in an effort to keep "riff-raff" off beaches frequented by tourists, instituted the charges along with a ban on bringing one's own food and drink onto the sand. While the fees may not seem excessive to a foreigner, they are well beyond the means of the miserably paid Turkish soldiers, and represent a considerable hardship for a typically large family of mainland settlers.

The local uproar was so great that the tourism ministry was forced to set aside various sandy but undeveloped bays, mostly east of Lara, as *halk plajlari* or "public beaches". They are accordingly very popular on weekends in season when large groups of Cypriots descend on them, though you should have the water almost to yourself as they're not especially keen swimmers. The main advantages of patronizing a fee beach will be guaranteed presence of certain amenities (umbrellas, snack bar) and a far higher degree of cleanliness owing to regular raking and rubbish collection.

succulent *hellim*, beans with courgettes or stuffed aubergine, and may also include *bumbar* (skinny sausages), calamari rings, plus a portion of fish. Son Mustafa is responsible for twelve adjacent self-catering **bungalows** (phone as above, ⓦ www.paradisebungalows.50megs.com; £125 per week for two; wi-fi zone).

The main eastern beaches

Unless you're staying here, it's best to skip **Acapulco Beach** and its resort complex (characterized by some as "Butlins without the redcoats"), surrounded by barbed-wire-fringed army installations and incorporating the Neolithic site of Vrysi (finds from which are featured in a Kyrenia castle exhibition). **Lara Beach**, 3km east, is reached by a paved drive just before the power plant leading to a sandy *halk plaj* (pay beach) some 200m long with rock outcrops, and a seasonal snack bar under a palm tree. The closest local full-service **restaurant**, up on the main road back towards "Acapulco", is *Valley View*, with seating overlooking the pine-covered ravine of the name, and a good following among both locals and tourists for the sake of its *meze*, seafood and fruit for dessert.

Beyond Lara the coast road has been improved as noted, though exits to some choice bays were not provided. A Siemens-designed power plant, its obsolete and polluting technology the source of considerable controversy, was completed just east of Lara at **Teknecik** in 1993 to eliminate the North's dependency on the Dhekélia generator in the South.

Alagadi ("Turtle Bay")

Four **restaurants** – *Hoca, Benöz, Esenyalı* and *St Kathleen's* – plus a mushrooming quota of villas – signal your arrival at the sand-and-shingle "Esenyalı Halk Plajı". Of these, *St Kathleen's* and *Hoca* have the largest local following and the most durable operating record; food at the former is good, but the management can be tricky – confirm prices by the menu first. *Hoca* often has fresh fish, courtesy of owner Ahmet's early-morning fishing trips.

For beaches, it's better to continue on the new inland road (the coast-hugging track is blocked shortly) just over a kilometre to **Alagadi** (Alakáti), reached by a 500-metre-long dirt side track from a sharp curve. This ends at two separate car parks serving a vast sandy bay over a kilometre long, with no facilities aside from toilets, the *Alagadi Turtle Beach* snack bar and Cengiz Bergun's mobile **scuba school** (ⓣ 0533/868 31 65 or 223 62 35). As it's a *halk plaji*, there's no clean-up

Sea turtles in North Cyprus

In North Cyprus, **sea turtles** – predominantly green but also a few loggerhead – lay their eggs at several beaches, but especially at Alagadi and "Golden Beach" on the Karpaz peninsula. In 1990, through the combined efforts of Kutlay "Jimmy" Ketço and an expat couple, the Society for the Protection of Turtles (SPOT) was founded locally. Together with researchers from Glasgow University, they formed a new umbrella group, the Marine Turtle Research Group (see ⓦwww.seaturtle.org/mtrg /projects/cyprus/ for more information). Their most signal accomplishments to date have included persuading builders not to remove sand from nesting beaches, tagging turtles so that their movements can be followed, and placing mesh over fresh nests to discourage predators.

During the height of the nesting season (July–Aug), SPOT maintains a **visitors' centre** behind Alagadi Beach, dispensing information all day and conducting occasional tours to watch turtles hatching from 6pm onwards. In theory, locking gates bar access to both Alagadi and Onüçüncü Mil beaches from 8pm to 8am to reduce any interference with nesting turtles. For a full description of the sea-turtle life cycle, see the box on p.175.

of rubbish – predominantly from the permanent "island" of Arab rubbish reported by yachtsmen off Syria, judging from product labels – that washes up here; the western half is more protected and thus apt to be cleaner. The cove here is known to expats as "Turtle Bay", after its status as a sea turtle egg-laying site, but between the rubbish, the weekend barbecues and the manoeuvring jeeps (despite signs prohibiting the practice), the hatchlings' life expectancy was historically rated as low. This has improved in recent years (see box above).

Onüçüncü Mil

The headland to the east of "Turtle Bay" is possibly the site of ancient Alakadi; beyond this promontory is yet another bay, **Onüçüncü Mil** ("Thirteenth Mile" after its distance from Kyrenia), tricky to reach from the main road since its improvement. To get there, turn off the main highway through an unmarked gap in the guardrail, which immediately gives onto a paved access drive through an unfinished holiday village and then through olives, descending to a dirt-surface car park just behind the beach, much the best on the Kyrenia coast (though devoid of facilities). At either end of Onüçüncü Mil's sandy crescent, eerie jumbles of eroded limestone rear up like ruined fortifications, making it difficult to distinguish between them and man-made ancient masonry.

Travel details

Buses

Kyrenia to: Famagusta (hourly; 1hr 30min); Güzelyurt (several daily; 1hr); Nicosia (every 15min; 30min). Daily out-and-back minibus services exist for most villages between Bahçeli in the east and Tepebaşı on the Kormakíti peninsula, but there are usefully frequent schedules only for Çatalköy, Ozanköy, Beylerbeyi and Lapta.

Ferries and catamarans

Kyrenia to the following Turkish ports: Alanya, 2 weekly catamarans (Wed & Sun; 3–5hr); Taşucu, 1 car ferry daily Mon–Fri around noon (4–5hr); plus 1 daily passenger-only catamaran, weather permitting, at around 9.30 (2–3hr). See pp.33–35 for a complete discussion of companies and fares.

Famagusta and the Karpaz peninsula

CHAPTER 8

Highlights

✳ **Venetian walls of Famagusta**
Among the strongest and most complete medieval fortifications in the Mediterranean. See p.333

✳ **Lala Mustafa Paşa Camii**
Formerly the cathedral of St Nicholas, this church-mosque is the most sumptuous Gothic monument on Cyprus. See p.340

✳ **Ancient Salamis** Ancient frescoes and mosaics, Mycenean-style tombs plus an excellent beach alongside. See p.345

✳ **Monastery-museum of Apóstolos Varnávas** A former monastery now serves as the

North's de facto archeological museum. See p.350

✳ **Panayía Theotókos** Contains exquisite Byzantine frescoes, the only intact ones surviving in the North. See p.353

✳ **Kantara castle** At the base of the Karpaz peninsula, Kantara castle completes a satisfying trio begun by St Hilarion and Buffavento. See p.354

✳ **Karpaz peninsula** This remote area has numerous ancient churches, best of these the basilicas at Ayía Triás and Áyios Fílon. See p.357 & p.361

✳ **Nangomí ("Golden Beach")**
Superb turtle-nesting beach beyond Dipkarpaz. See p.362

▲ Kantara Castle

8

Famagusta and the Karpaz peninsula

T he **Mesarya** (Turkish for Mesaoría) plain, hummocky and relatively confined around Nicosia, opens out to steppe-like dimensions as it approaches the long arc of Famagusta Bay. This coast has been advancing slowly east over millennia, thanks to silt brought down by the Kanlıdere River (the Pedhiéos in Greek), in recent centuries flowing intermittently at best – though after winter rains it becomes a deep, raging torrent near Nicosia. Amazingly, the Mesarya was densely wooded, and a favourite Lusignan hunting ground, until the sixteenth century; climate change and Ottoman neglect are together responsible for the landscape's current appearance.

At the southeast corner of the Mesarya, just as the terrain begins to rise to bluffs beyond the Attila Line, looms the town of **Famagusta**, a Turko-Gothic chimera with no equal on Cyprus. Before the Ottoman era, the de facto capital of Cyprus had always been in the immediate environs of Famagusta, with a combination of geology and military history determining its precise location in each era. The present-day city is the successor to ancient **Salamis**, a few miles north on the far side of wetlands fed by the here-sluggish Kanlıdere and fringed by beaches. Salamis in turn replaced older **Enkomi-Alasia** as the main port of the region; the narrow strip of plain between the two is peppered with **tombs** of various eras, one – supposedly that of the Apostle Barnabas – Christianized and still venerated. A **monastery** which honoured him now serves as the North's archeological museum. Famagusta town contrasts with its featureless surroundings, which at twilight take on a sinister aspect, perhaps from the numerous ancient dead in the graves of Bronze Age and Roman cities.

The sandy shoreline of Famagusta Bay and the hotel-riviera at Varósha, south of Famagusta, saw the first mass tourism in Cyprus after independence, but now that Varósha is off-limits, the little fishing port of Boğaz marks the end of the resort strip extending north of Salamis. It's also one gateway to the long, narrow **Karpaz peninsula**, the island's panhandle and likened by Winston Churchill, and various demagogic Turkish politicians, to a "dagger aimed at the underbelly of Anatolia". Today it is in fact almost insignificant militarily – depopulated, remote, and sprinkled with traces of past importance, especially the early Christian sites of **Ayía Triás** and **Áyios Fílon**. The **castle of Kantara** effectively marks the base of the peninsula; the **monastery of**

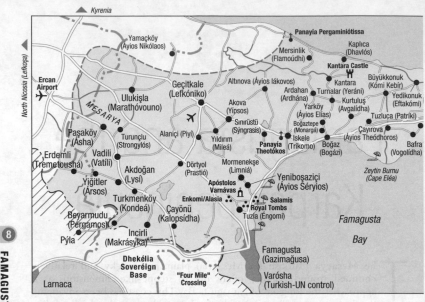

Apóstolos Andhréas sits near the far end, between one of the finest beaches on Cyprus and the desolate cape itself.

Famagusta (Gazimağusa)

Its Venetian walls now enclosing almost nothing, the silhouettes of its exotic Gothic churches colliding in your field of vision with palm trees and upturned fishing boats, **FAMAGUSTA** (Gazimağusa, Mağosa – pronounced, approximately, "[gazi] mouse-uhh") is the architectural equivalent of a well-behaved houseplant gone to seed in its native jungle. The official Greek-Cypriot name, *Ammókhostos*, means "sunken in sand"; its ramparts and deep harbour protect the old town from such a fate, but to the north sand piles up in dunes, while offshore Maymun Adası (Monkey Island) is essentially a shifting spit. The climate is nearly subtropical, the sea air eating away metal and stone alike; in the era before swamp drainage, malarial mosquitoes had a similar effect on the people. All told, not much of a prospect for greatness.

Yet this was, during the fourteenth century, the wealthiest city on earth, of sufficient romance for Shakespeare to supposedly make it the partial setting for *Othello*, a theory based on the brief stage instruction "a seaport in Cyprus". Today Famagusta is a double city: the compact walled town, a crumbling Lusignan-Venetian legacy, and the sprawling, amorphous new town, partly derelict since 1974. If conditions do not change on Cyprus, some or all of it could embody the epithet "sunken in sand" within decades.

The character of Othello appears to be based on a historical Venetian solder serving in Cyprus, Franceso de Sessa, known as Il Moro for his dark complexion and banished in 1544 for an unknown offence – along with two subordinates, possibly the models for Iago and Cassio.

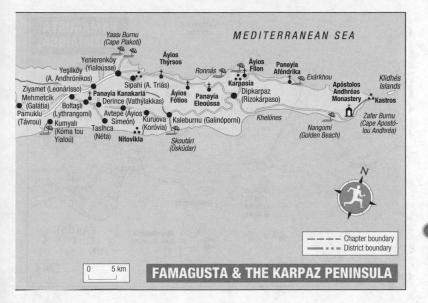

Chapter boundary
District boundary

0   5 km

FAMAGUSTA & THE KARPAZ PENINSULA

Some history

By Cypriot standards Famagusta is a young settlement, though not quite so new as Limassol. Some spuriously derive the name from "Fama Augusta" after the Emperor Augustus, implying an imperial Roman foundation, but the place is first heard of only after the seventh century, when the survivors of Arab-sacked Salamis drifted here. It pottered along as a **Byzantine** fishing port and only natural deep-water harbour on the island.

All that changed suddenly in 1291, after Palestinian Acre fell to the Saracens; **Christian merchants** poured in as refugees from a dozen entrepots on the Middle Eastern mainland. The pope forbade any trafficking with the infidel on pain of excommunication, thus guaranteeing Famagusta's **monopoly** as a trans-shipment point – and its spectacular growth. Every commodity of East and West changed hands here; the city became a babel of creeds, tongues and nationalities, reducing the native residents to a minority. Fortunes were made overnight, engendering spectacular nouveau-riche vulgarity: merchants' daughters wore more nuptial jewellery than certain European monarchs, and the prostitutes were as wealthy as the merchants, one of whom, purportedly ground up a diamond to season a dish at table in full view of his guests.

Foreigners were fascinated and horrified in equal measure; St Bridget of Sweden, preaching in front of the cathedral in 1371 on her way back from the Holy Land, railed against the immorality of the city. The multiplicity of sects (and perhaps guilty consciences) resulted in scores of churches being built, supposedly one for every day of the year – many of them still standing.

But Famagusta's heyday lasted less than a century, for in 1372 a diplomatic contretemps triggered its decline. At the coronation of the Lusignan boy-king **Peter II**, a tussle between the Genoese and Venetian envoys over the protocol of leading the royal horse degenerated into a brawl with massive loss of Genoese life and property. In revenge a Genoese expedition ravaged Cyprus over the next year, occupying Famagusta and displacing its traders to Nicosia. James II expelled the Genoese in 1464, but it was already too late, and his Venetian

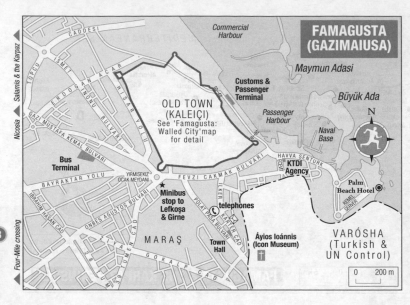

FAMAGUSTA (GAZIMAIUSA)

Commercial Harbour

Maymun Adasi

Customs & Passenger Terminal

Büyük Ada

N

OLD TOWN (KALEİÇI)
See 'Famagusta: Walled City' map for detail

Passenger Harbour

Naval Base

Bus Terminal

KTDI Agency

Palm Beach Hotel

Minibus stop to Lefkoşa & Girne

telephones

MARAŞ

Town Hall

Áyios Ioánnis (Icon Museum)

VARÓSHA (Turkish & UN Control)

0   200 m

widow **Queen Caterina Cornaro** presided over a diminished town before abdicating at the behest of her Venetian minders in 1489.

Anticipating the growing Ottoman threat, **Venetian** military governors improved Famagusta's **fortifications** just as they had at Nicosia and Kyrenia. So when the Turks appeared in October 1570, having taken the rest of Cyprus with relatively little resistance, it required a ten-month siege to reduce the city, where the heavily outnumbered Venetian garrison put up a heroic defence.

Under **Ottoman rule**, walled Famagusta became an emblem of decay; with almost every building levelled or severely damaged, for centuries the space within the walls lay desolate, inhabited only by garrisons commanded by soldiers disgraced elsewhere. Ottoman sultans favoured it as a **place of exile** for political prisoners, most famously (during the nineteenth century) the Turkish nationalist poet Namik Kemal and Suphi Ezel, founder of the Ezeli sect (a rival of the Bahai faith). Christians were forbidden entry to, let alone residence in, **Kaleİçi** (the area within the ramparts), so that the predominantly Greek Orthodox town of **Varósha** (Maraş in Turkish) sprang up just south.

With independence and the subsequent **communal troubles**, old Famagusta again served as a Turkish stronghold. Greek Cypriots who had early in the twentieth century ventured into Kaleİçi to live were expelled in 1964, while **Turkish–Cypriot refugees** streamed into town from vulnerable villages on the Mesarya. This trend accelerated during the tense weeks between July 20 and August 15, 1974, when the EOKA-B-dominated National Guard attacked any Turkish Cypriot they found outside the walls; the luckier ones entered Kaleİçi via a network of pre-dug tunnels, joining both besieged civilians and the TMT garrison holding down the port and walled town. Old Famagusta was relieved by the advancing Turkish army on August 15, after the Greek Cypriots **abandoned Varósha** in the face of air raids. After the ceasefire took effect the next day, the Turkish army pushed forward into Varósha, which, except for a few UN observation posts, they have controlled ever since (see box, p.344).

The City

Famagusta is usually visited as a full day-trip or shorter outing from a beachfront base just north. Interest is confined almost entirely to the Kaleiçi (town within the walls), but don't raise your expectations too high. What you mainly get are the walls, built to last by the Venetians, and such churches as escaped Turkish ordnance and British vandalism. It's claimed that the Ottomans fired more than 100,000 cannonballs into the town during their siege, many of which are still seen lying about. Devastated neighbourhoods were mostly never rebuilt, leaving vast expanses of empty ground that can have changed little since the day the Ottomans entered the city. Since 1996 the historic centre has been partly and attractively pedestrianized, especially around the Lala Mustafa Paşa mosque, and some medieval buildings given a new role.

The city walls

More complete than İstanbul or Antioch, stronger than Fez,
Jerusalem and even Avila, [a] prince of walled cities...

So enthused Colin Thubron in 1972 – as well he might, given the **walls**' average height of fifteen metres, thickness of eight metres, their fifteen bastions and five gates. The Venetians gradually raised them atop existing Lusignan fortifications between 1489 and 1540, according to the latest precepts of engineering and ballistics. Yet they were ultimately an exercise in futility, considering the Ottoman victory, though structurally they mostly withstood the siege.

The ramparts are still dry-moated on their three landward sides, overgrown with weeds on top, and impossible to circumambulate owing to partial occupation by the Turkish army. Content yourself instead with a stroll up the ramp near the southwestern **Land Gate** to the most spectacular bit, the **Ravelin** or **Rivettina Bastion** (open Mon–Fri only; 5YTL). This complex of galleries was protected by a double moat, the main one now crossed by a wooden bridge. The Ottomans dubbed it the *Akkule* or "White Tower", from the Venetians' waving of the white surrender flag from this point.

At the southeast corner of the perimeter, the **Canbulat Bastion** (sometimes Canpolat or Cambulat) takes its name from an Anatolian bey who, confronted by a spinning, knife-studded wheel which the Venetians had mounted in the gate here, charged it with his horse. Both were cut to ribbons, but the infernal machine was also destroyed. Turkish women used to come to his tomb in the bastion, from which a fig tree grew, to pray for sons as valiant as Canbulat, and then eat the fruit to ensure conception.

Today the interior is home to a small **museum** (daily: summer 9am–7pm; winter 9am–12.30pm & 1.30–4.45pm; 5YTL). The admission fee isn't really warranted by the mediocre pottery, traditional dress, Ottoman weaponry, amphorae and Iznik tiles on show. On the wall, a famous engraving by Stephano Givellino of the siege, its text translated into English, somewhat redeems the collection.

The harbour lies just beyond the ramparts, formerly accessible by the now-closed **Sea Gate**, which along with the Citadel (see p.342) was one of the earliest Venetian improvements. Beside it squats a highly naturalistic **Venetian lion**: according to legend, once a year the mouth opens, and anyone lucky enough to be there at the unpredictable moment can stick their hand down its throat and extract a treasure.

Around Namik Kemal Meydanı

Entering Kaleiçi through the **Land Gate** and along pedestrianized İstiklal Caddesi, you pass a concentration of basic restaurants and jewellery shops before

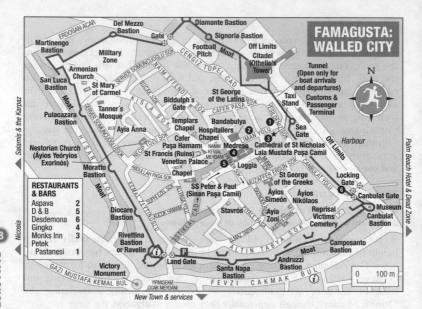

reaching mid-fourteenth-century **SS Peter and Paul** (later the Sinan Paşa Camii) on the left. Supposedly built by a merchant from the profits of a single transaction, it's a rather inelegant, workaday church, its good condition assured by later roles as a mosque, public library and theatre (though currently disused).

Just north across the street, the Venetian governor's palace is little more than a shell, though the remaining east façade is admittedly impressive. It faces **Namık Kemal Meydanı**, the town's central square, named after the dissident Ottoman writer; a bust of the man stands outside, near the *medrese* (Koranic academy). His **dungeon** (daily 7.30am–2pm plus Mon 3.30–6pm; 5YTL), where he spent 38 months during the 1870s at the sultan's pleasure for writing a seditious play, incorporates a surviving corner of palace. North of the palace precinct, the equally ruined church of **St Francis** abuts a set of disused Turkish baths, the Cafer Paşa Hamamı.

Lala Mustafa Paşa Camii (St Nicholas Cathedral)

Dominating the eastern side of the square, the **Lala Mustafa Paşa Camii** (4YTL "donation" required when warden present) is the most magnificent and best-preserved Lusignan monument in town, and arguably in all Cyprus. Completed between 1298 and 1326 in imitation of Rheims cathedral, it outshines its sister church in Nicosia; here the Lusignan royalty received the honorary crown of lost Jerusalem after their coronation in the official capital, and here too Queen Caterina Cornaro formally abdicated in 1489.

Regrettably, the twin towers were decapitated during the 1571 bombardment; after seizing Famagusta, the Ottomans engaged in more deliberate alterations. As in Nicosia they emptied the floor-tombs, including those of James II and his infant son, last of the Lusignan dynasty; destroyed all accoutrements of Christian worship; and added the minaret which – lower than the pair on Nicosia's Selimiye Camii – happily detracts little from the building's appeal.

The church-mosque reveals itself to best advantage from the **west**, where the gables of three magnificent porticoes point up to the fine six-paned window

The **1570–71 siege of Famagusta** was one of the great medieval battles: for ten months a force of 8000 Greeks and Venetians held off an Ottoman army of almost 200,000, and the outcome might have been different had promised relief from Venice and Crete arrived. The brilliant Venetian commander **Marcantonio Bragadino** was as resourceful with the limited means at hand as could be expected; Lala – "The Mentor" – Mustafa Paşa, his Ottoman counterpart, was a veteran if unimaginative campaigner with an explosive temper.

The entrance of Famagusta harbour could be chained shut, starting from a salient of the Othello Tower; the opening at the south end of Maymun Adası (Monkey Island) didn't then exist. So the Turks concentrated on assaults of the south and west land walls, avoiding the north wall with its formidable Martinengo Bastion. Armenian sappers dug coils of trenches towards the ramparts deep enough to completely conceal the Turkish soldiery except for their turban-tops; the main evidence of their presence around the city was a forest of campaign tents five kilometres wide. The sappers also burrowed under the fortifications, setting off mines, while the Ottoman artillery of 150 guns (as opposed to the 90 small-bore weapons of their adversaries) reduced the walls from afar.

Despite this pounding, the attackers made little progress over the initial winter of siege, with Bragadino organizing bold sorties to create the impression that he had manpower to spare – and also to raid for necessary food. On July 7, 1571, the Turks gained a foothold on the Rivettina Bastion, and started to scale the walls. Realizing the structure was useless for its intended purpose, the Venetians detonated a mine of their own prepared for such a moment, burying a thousand Turks (and a hundred of their own men) in the resulting rubble, which partly blocked further enemy advance. The defenders fell back behind improvised barricades of earth-filled carts and sandbags; any relief fleet had failed to materialize, and the situation inside the city became increasingly desperate, with plague spreading and rats or cats figuring in the diet. On August 1, having lost nearly three-quarters of his forces, Bragadino ran up the white flag, and negotiated a **surrender** whereby civilians were to be unmolested while he and his men would be given safe conduct to Crete in Turkish ships.

When the remnant of the garrison emerged from the smoking ruins and staggered over to the Turkish lines, the besiegers were amazed that so few men had been able to resist so courageously against hopeless odds, and were moved to pity by their woebegone appearance. At first the defeated were received with kindness and courtesy, even by the volatile Lala Mustafa himself, but the flouting of Turkish might for so long – and his own casualties of over 50,000 – must have preyed on the general's mind, for Bragadino's audience with him suddenly turned sour. Lala Mustafa abruptly demanded the Venetian officer Quirini as a hostage against the safe return of the Turkish fleet from Crete; when Bragadino protested that this hadn't been part of the agreed surrender, Lala Mustafa accused him of murdering fifty civilian prisoners in the last weeks of the siege. Working himself up into one of the towering rages he was known for, the Turk summoned his executioner and before Bragadino's horrified eyes Quirini and two other subordinates were hacked to bits. Then came Bragadino's turn: his nose and ears were sliced off, and he was thrown into a dungeon for ten days before being retrieved, publicly humiliated in and finally chained between two pillars in front of the cathedral and flayed alive.

Though many subordinates disapproved of all this. Lala Mustafa Paşa was not to be mollified: he gutted the body, stuffed Bragadino's skin with straw, and paraded it around town on a cow, under the red parasol which the Venetian had jauntily used when marching out to give himself up. The stuffed skin was later ransomed from İstanbul at considerable cost by Bragadino's descendants; it now rests in an urn at the Venetian church of SS Giovanni e Paolo.

with its circular rose. Two series of six columns stalk the **interior** of the nave, supporting superb vaulting; the austere, whitewashed decor allows an appreciation of the cathedral's elegance, undistracted by the late-medieval clutter which would have accumulated had the building remained a church. In the **courtyard** out front, a giant sycamore fig is supposedly as old as the building; to one side, a small Venetian **loggia** has been converted to an Islamic ablutions fountain. Across the courtyard from the loggia, a *medrese* is now a recommended bistro, in front of which (moved from their original location by the loggia) stand two granite columns from Salamis, between which the hapless Bragadino was flayed (see box, p.341). Across Liman Yolu, the **Bandabulya** or old covered market has been restored and tenanted by cafés, a restaurant and souvenir stalls.

The Citadel (Othello's Tower)

The treasure-lion in front of the Sea Gate is complemented by a larger relief Lion of St Mark above the entry to the **Citadel** (daily: same hours as Canbulat Bastion; 7YTL), north across the oval roundabout. A Lusignan fort extensively remodelled by the Venetians between 1489 and 1492, this strongpoint is popularly known as "**Othello's Tower**", after Famagusta's Shakespearean connections. On the far side of the courtyard, partly taken up by a stage used for folkloric performances, the pigeon-infested **Great Hall**, 28m long, has fine limestone rib vaulting mostly, however, eaten away by the all-corroding sea air.

From the **northeast tower**, you can peer over the industrial harbour; you'll get no closer, as the protruding citadel mole is as militarily important today as in medieval times. Up on the perimeter parapet, **ventilation shafts** or cistern mouths alternate with rooms whose roofs were stove in by the bombardment. A few shafts lead down to Lusignan passages and chambers which the Venetians either filled up or simply sealed at one end, giving rise to the theory that somewhere in this citadel is hidden the fortune of the Venetian merchants, forced to leave the city empty-handed by the victorious Ottomans. This legend has exercised the Turkish imagination ever since, with investigations conducted periodically; similar hollows in the Martinengo Bastion served as bomb shelters for two thousand civilians during August 1974.

Minor churches

Just south of Othello's Tower, **St George of the Latins** is one of the oldest Famagustan churches, originally part of a fortified monastery which may predate the Lusignan ramparts. Today it's merely a shell, but a romantic one; on the surviving apse and north wall, a group of carved bats peer out of a column capital. Nearby on Naim Effendi Sokağı, **Biddulph's Gate** is a remnant doorway of a vanished mansion, named in honour of an early British high commissioner with conservationist instincts.

Naim Effendi leads towards the northwest corner of Kaleiçi, a military zone since 1974; the Martinengo Bastion here was never stormed by the Turks in 1570–71, and the returning modern Turkish army seems to have taken the hint of impregnability. Access to **Ayía Ánna**, **St Mary of Carmel**, the **Armenian Church** or the (converted) **Tanners Mosque** is therefore restricted, with photography out of the question, though they are no longer fenced off and you can at least drive by them.

Outside the military zone stands fourteenth-century Nestorian **Áyios Yeóryios Exorinós**, usually locked except for special events, or Sunday religious services by the local expatriate community. Built by one of the fabulously wealthy Lakhas brothers, he of the jewel-grinding incident (see p.337), it was the pre-1964 parish church of the small Greek Cypriot community. The epithet *exorinós* means "the exiler", after a strange legend, reminiscent of that accruing to Áyios Misitikós in Páfos (see p.158): dust gathered from the floor and tossed in an enemy's house would cause them to die or leave the island within a year.

Nearby on Kışla Sokağı, back towards Namik Kemal Meydanı, the adjacent box-like chapels of the **Knights Templar** and **Knights Hospitaller**, both fourteenth-century, enjoy a proximity which those rival orders never had in their day. The Templars' chapel is distinguished by a small rose window out front, and is now used as a theatre and art gallery; the Hospitallers' chapel is currently a bar. Inside (a modern passage interconnects them) they're bare in the extreme, enlivened only by fine ceiling vaulting. The otherwise unremarkable Lusignan church of **Stavrós**, two blocks south of Namik Kemal Meydanı, marks a small concentration of **arched lanes** and **medieval houses** on Lala Mustafa Paşa Sokağı and perpendicular Erenler Sokağı. A few steps east, half-demolished **St George of the Greeks**, an uneasy Byzantine–Gothic hybrid whose three rounded apses clash with two rows of column stumps, stands cheek by jowl with the purer Byzantine but equally dilapidated **Áyios Simeón**, tacked onto its south wall. Two more tiny but exquisite late-Byzantine chapels stand just south amid palm-tree greenery: battered **Áyios Nikólaos**, and intact **Ayía Zoní**.

Maraş (Varósha)

Polat Paşa, the commercial main street of the inhabited portion of **Maraş**, currently parades grandiosely to nowhere; behind the oil-drum-and-sand-bag barricades at its south end, where it detours abruptly, rusty street and shop signs in Greek and the dome of a church (see below) are visible. About halfway down, in front of the courthouse, a parked locomotive, built in 1904 by a Leeds company, plied the now-vanished Lefke–Famagusta railway from 1907 until 1951: the tracks were to have been extended to Larnaca, but the mayor vetoed the plan to protect local camel-drivers from competition. He was roundly jeered for the decision, but in the event the camel caravans outlasted the trains by over a decade.

The only part of Varósha ever open to foreign civilians is the modern **Áyios Ioánnis church** (theoretically open Mon–Fri 9am–1.30pm; 3YTL), clearly visible about 150m into the restricted zone, accessed off İlker Karter Caddesi. A sentry here will allow you to drive up to the church, which now shelters a collection of icons, few of significant artistic merit.

Out on the shore, the Palm Beach Hotel is virtually the last occupied building in Maraş before the dead zone; beyond sheet-metal barricades, emblazoned with no-photography signs, begins the Benidorm like row of abandoned 1960s hotels, many bearing marks of shelling.

Practicalities

Coming **by boat** from Mersin, Turkey, you'll dock at the passenger terminal, just east of the Sea Gate, though arriving vehicles are sent out via the gate by the Canbulat Bastion. **By land**, the road from Salamis (İsmet İnönü Caddesi) and the Nicosia highway (Gazi Mustafa Kemal Bulvarı, where the **bus terminal** is) converge on Yirmisekiz Ocak Meydanı, the victory-monument roundabout directly opposite the old city's Land Gate. So too does the way in from the Four-Mile (Strovília) Crossing, along Onbeş Ağustos Bulvarı. **Parking** within the old town presents few problems, though pedestrianization, traffic-control barriers and a one-way system complicate matters to either side of İstiklal Caddesi. If necessary, drive to the thinly populated areas around St George of the Greeks, the Canbulat Gate or Othello's Tower.

Only a fraction of Varósha (Maraş) is currently inhabited; the rest, by the terms of the 1974 ceasefire, is technically UN territory but effectively under Turkish army control, a ghost town entered only occasionally by UNFICYP forces since then. Their patrols, and specially escorted journalists, reported light bulbs burning for years, washing in tatters on the line and uncleared breakfast dishes, so precipitous was the Greek Cypriots' departure. Behind the barbed wire and oil-drum barricades, weeds have attained tree-like dimensions on the streets and inside buildings, while cats, rats and snakes prowl as in Nicosia's dead zone. The fate of the Famagusta Archeological Museum's contents is unknown, but unlikely to be happy in light of how the magnificent, private Hadjiprodhromou archeological collection was looted and dispersed for sale quite openly on the international market. In contrast to the automotive "time capsule" in Nicosia, the Turks here helped themselves to the contents of an automobile showroom, with the exception of a single Alfa Romeo still inside.

Varósha has figured high on the agenda of every intercommunal negotiating session since 1974. Greek Cypriots see its return to use as an initial gesture of good faith for progress on any other issue: the town has practical as well as symbolic significance, since with nearly 40,000 former Greek inhabitants its **resettlement** would solve a good chunk of the South's refugee problem. Bed capacity across the North usually outstrips demand, so the Turkish Cypriots have never much coveted the 33 decaying, far-from-state-of-the-art **hotels** lining Varósha's six-kilometre-long Glóssa beach, but they have periodically proposed that a limited number of Greek Cypriots return to renovate and manage the 4000-bed resort – which is built on land leased from the island's *vakıf* or Islamic trust. The South has always refused, deeming these offers as rigged so that the hotels would be run largely for the North's financial benefit. Meanwhile, most of Varósha has attained write-off condition, and it's hard to avoid the suspicion that the Turkish side has always retained it as a **bargaining chip** to use at some crucial stage of negotiations.

The **tourist information** bureau (Mon–Fri 8am–5pm, Sat–Sun 9am–6pm) is inside the Rivettina Bastion and is better stocked than Kyrenia's. Since nearly all of the pre-1974 hotels were in now-inaccessible Varósha, there is next to no palatable **accommodation** in or immediately around Kaleiçi – almost all visitors stay out on the beaches near Salamis. On the shoreline next to the dead zone, nominally five-star *Palm Beach Hotel* (☎366 20 00; ⑨) is offered by most UK package operators, but is overpriced for walk-in guests, relying on business and casino trade. The rooms are also small, though the grounds do offer several (exorbitant) bars, beachfront water sports, tennis courts and a gym.

Eating, drinking and nightlife

Paralleling the dearth of in-town accommodation, eating and drinking options are similarly limited – you can count **restaurants** of distinction on one hand with fingers to spare, simple affairs for local tradesmen and shoppers on the other. However, there's enough choice for a midday meal, though off-season pickings can be slim. As for consistent **nightlife**, you're pretty much restricted to the nightclub and casino at the *Palm Beach Hotel*, one of the few bars operating in restored medieval buildings, or (in summer) the day-and-night disco-café 4km north upcoast at **Glapsídhes beach**, also the closest decent swimming to town.

8

Aspava Liman Yolu, opposite apse of Lala Mustafa Paşa Camii. Carniverous plates and salads with garden seating in summer and an eyeful of Lala Mustafa Paşa Camii.

D&B Café Namik Kemal Meydanı. Popular student hangout, placed unimprovably opposite the west façade of Lala Mustafa Paşa Camii, with outdoor tables in season. Strictly European grub (pizzas, grills, salads).

Desdemona Restaurant & Bar Canbulat Yolu 3. Built into a vaulted bastion with no windows, this drippingly atmospheric outfit purveys high-quality, 15-platter meze, more Turkish-style than Cypriot; their mixed grill is by contrast worth avoiding. Especially out of season, it doubles as a locals' bar, with piped mainland-Turkish music.

Gingko Namik Kemal Meydanı, inside the medrese. The setting alone – under medieval domes and arches, classical music playing – would repay a visit, but the food quality (as do prices) very nearly match that of Nicosia's Sabor. It's OK to have just a coffee and dessert. Daily 10.30am–midnight.

Monks Inn Pub Bistro Lane behind the apse of Lala Mustafa Paşa Camii. Classy bar inside arcaded medieval premises; light snacks too. Mon–Thurs eve, Fri–Sat from noon; closed Sun.

Petek Pastanesi Liman Yolu, corner Yeşildeniz Sokağı. Cavernous, two-level oasis of glitz in the often down-at-heel old town. Enjoy a slightly pricey pudding, sticky cake or ice cream at seating around an indoor fountain, or (in winter) near the fireplace beyond the tempting sweet counters.

Listings

Airline agents AtlasJet ☏365 02 51; Cyprus Turkish Airlines ☏366 77 99; Pegasus ☏630 15 88.
Car rental Benzincioğlu, Gazi Mustafa Kemal Bulvari ☏366 54 79; Sur, İsmet İnönü Cad 7 ☏366 47 96; Tab, İsmet İnönü Cad 7 ☏366 13 23.
Ferry agency The unhelpful KTDI sales office is on Ecevit Cad (☏366 45 57), southeast of the Venetian walls near the naval base; best try in the passenger terminal itself 90min before sailing.

Internet cafés Highly changeable, but at least one will be operating opposite the university's main gate.
Post offices Main branch on İlker Karter Cad, Maraş (Mon–Fri 8am–1pm & 2–5pm).
Telephones The Telekomünikasyon Dairesi in Maraş (daily 8am–1pm & 2–6pm) sells telecards; the most convenient pay phones are on Liman Yolu near the medrese.

Salamis

Cyprus' most famous and important ancient city, **Salamis** remains the island's most prominent archeological site, for once living up to the tourist-brochure hype. Even if your interest is casual, you'll need a couple of hours to see the best-preserved highlights; a half-day can easily be spent here, especially if you retire to the wonderful beach that fringes Salamis to the east. The monuments, mostly Roman and Byzantine, are widely scattered – it's well over a kilometre from the entrance to the ancient harbour, for example – and vehicles are no longer allowed past the amphitheatre, so you'll need stout footwear, sun protection and drinking water. Furthermore, leave nothing valuable in sight in your **car**, as Salamis has a consistent pattern of car break-ins. Otherwise, any **bus** from Famagusta towards Boğaz or beyond to the Karpaz peninsula runs past the site entrance.

Some history

To Salamis is ascribed quasi-mythical foundation in the twelfth century BC by Trojan war hero **Teucer** (Tefkros), exiled by his father King Telamon from the **Greek isle of Salamis**. The young city shared not only the name but the Mycenaean culture of its parent – borne out by the finds in the nearby royal tombs (p.349) – and quickly replaced nearby Enkomi-Alasia as the chief settlement on the coastal bight here. By the eighth century it was already the greatest of the ten Cypriot city-kingdoms, and within two hundred years Salamis was the first place on the island to mint coinage.

The city was the leader in the first fifth-century revolt against the Persians; **Onesilos** temporarily deposed his brother King Gorgos, a Persian collaborator, and commanded a hastily thrown-together Hellenic confederacy at the Battle of Salamis – lost mostly because of treachery on the part of Kourion. Later that same century, native son **Evagoras** – a remarkable man for whom numerous streets in the South are named – shrewdly united the Cypriot city-kingdoms in another, more durable, pro-Hellenic federation, with culture as well as politics oriented towards peninsular Greece. Despite political and military ingenuity Evagoras could not actually prevail against Persia, but over a decade fought the oriental empire to a standstill, finally negotiating a vassalage relationship.

Salamis actively assisted Alexander the Great and was subsequently rewarded with the copper revenues of Tamassos. But under the Ptolemaic kings, the city briefly fell on evil times. Its last king, **Nicocreon**, rather than surrender to the besieging Ptolemy I, committed suicide in 295 BC, as did all his surviving relatives, who set the royal palace alight before doing so.

During the **Roman** era, when Paphos ranked as the official capital of Cyprus, Salamis remained the island's main commercial centre and figured prominently in early Christianity: another native son, the Apostle Barnabas, lived and died here (see box, p.351). In the Jewish revolt of 116 AD, the city's entire gentile population was apparently slaughtered; after the Romans had quelled the rebellion, Jewish residence on the island was forbidden, an edict not countermanded until a small colony of European Jews settled nearby at the Mesaorian village of Koúklia (today Köprülü) late in the nineteenth century.

The **Byzantines** renamed Salamis **Constantia** and designated it an archbishopric and capital of the island again, but mid-fourth-century earth-quakes and tidal waves badly hurt the city, and the Arab invasions of the seventh century, along with the silting-up of its harbour, administered the final blow, after which neighbouring Famagusta began its ascendancy. Bits of ancient Salamis, used as a convenient quarry throughout medieval times, are scattered across contemporary villages and towns of the Kanlıdere (Pedhiéos) River's flood plain adjacent.

Salamis had only been partially **excavated** by a Franco-Cypriot team before 1974, and assuming a political settlement which permits further authorized research, more archeological treasures can be anticipated under the dunes that have largely covered the city since its abandonment.

The main site

The ruins lie eight to nine kilometres north of Famagusta between the main highway and the beach. More effectively than the small official "Salamis" signs, a placard for the *Bedi Restaurant* marks the one-kilometre side turning off the coast road to the **site entrance** (daily: summer 9am–7pm; spring/autumn 9am–6pm; winter 9am–1pm & 2–5pm; last ticket sold 1hr before closing; 9YTL), flanked by an "improved" beach and said restaurant.

The gymnasium and the baths

A sign directs you towards the walkway of the **gymnasium's east portico**, once covered over and still mosaic-paved in variegated Byzantine marble, with two rectangular plunge-pools at either end. The northerly one is ringed by a gallery of headless statues, decapitated by Christian zealots in a fury against pagan idolatry; some are now in the Cyprus Museum in south Nicosia, others have disappeared since 1974.

To the west, an impressive **colonnade**, re-erected during the 1950s, stakes out the quad of the gymnasium's palaestra. The eastern series is taller, and the whole

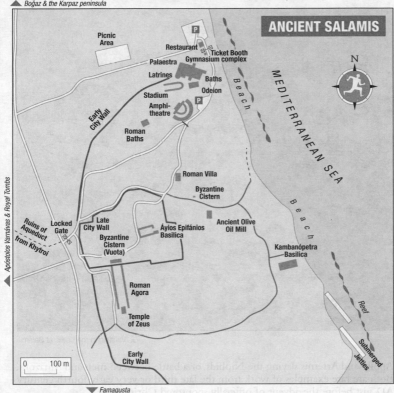

mismatched, because the Byzantines recycled Hellenistic and Roman columns from the theatre and another building without too much regard for symmetry or which capitals belonged where. The semicircular structure at the palaestra's southwest corner is a latrine, capacity 44; the flush pipe and tank are still visible at the rear, as are armrests to one side. Privacy was not a concern, elimination being considered by the Romans as another social event.

East of the palaestra and portico loom the **baths**, like the gymnasium a Byzantine reworking of Hellenistic and Roman predecessors. Just off the portico another set of cool-water pools – one nearly circular, one octagonal – sandwich the giant **west-central hall** (reckoned the *tepidarium* or mildly steamy anteroom) whose underfloor heating cavity is exposed. Over the south entry, a Christian **fresco fragment** shows two faces, one angelic, executed in a naturalistic, almost Buddhist style. At the seaward end of the **east-central hall** (probably the *caldarium* or hot-plunge room) another, elevated, pool has been partially restored, and a dank, crypt-like cavity can be entered. This hall contains more mosaics: a patch of abstract and floral motifs in a niche of the north wall, and another one of three pomegranates on a branch in the northerly semi-dome of the **north hall**, probably a hot-steam "sauna" chamber.

The best, most complete **mosaics** in the entire complex, however, are found in the south bays of the **south hall**. The smaller one shows the river god Evrotas – part of a damaged version of Leda and the swan – while the other displays the shield and quiver of a warrior, part of a scene whose identity is disputed: either

▲ Vaulting in the baths at Salamis

Apollo and Artemis slaying the Niobids, or a battle between men and Amazons. Both are rare examples of work from the late third or very early fourth century AD, just before the advent of officially sponsored Christianity.

The amphitheatre and Áyios Epifánios basilica

Another paved, partly colonnaded way leads south from the palaestra, between a vaulted structure with banks of seats – probably an **odeion** – and an unexcavated area to the west, thought to be a small **stadium**. Both are overshadowed by the fine Roman **amphitheatre**, dating from the reign of Augustus and not over-restored as these things go. From the top eighteen surviving rows of seats you have excellent views over the site. Occasional performances still take place during the tourist season, though not attracting anything like the original capacity of 15,000.

As you continue southwest of the amphitheatre along the paved drive, there initially seems little left of the six-aisled **Áyios Epifánios basilica** other than four rows of fourteen column stumps, but at the rear (east) of the southernmost naves, mosaic flooring covers a **crypt**, the presumed tomb of the patron saint, emptied by Byzantine Emperor Leo of its holy relics. In the manner of so many post-Arab-raid churches on Cyprus, this shrunken area around the crypt was refurbished for use after the rest of the basilica was destroyed.

Nearby, an **aqueduct** bringing water from ancient Khytroi (today Değirmenlik/Kythréa) ended at the giant Byzantine cistern or Vuota beside the Roman agora, at the far end of which are the negligible remains of a **Zeus temple**. In the opposite direction, a Roman street has recently been uncovered, leading to the **Roman villa**.

Kambanópetra basilica and the beach

Most recently excavated, the romantically set fourth-century **Kambanópetra basilica** overlooks the sea from one curve of a dirt track leading towards the southeast corner of the archeological zone. Its western forecourt, with small rooms giving onto it, may have been a colonnaded agora or an early monastic cloister. The central apse of the three-aisled nave was provided with a synthronon or seats for church dignitaries, while a fourth aisle to the south contains half-a-dozen marble sarcophagi.

A handful of standing columns to the east belong to yet another set of **baths**, as suggested by some tumbled-over hypocaust bricks and a tank with a fill-hole. The highlight here is a magnificent *opus sectile* floor, comprising concentric rings of alternating light and dark triangles, the most elaborate mosaic at Salamis.

The **beach** fringing the entire site is particularly accessible just below Kambanópetra. A reef encloses a small lagoon, extending all the way south past a cape before subsiding, and north towards the car-park (limited gaps through it); snorkelling in the metre-deep water, you see not only fish but long courses of man-made stone – the jetty or breakwater of the ancient port – on the sea floor. The wind is often brisk here, and ancient harbour facilities were distributed to either side of the point, for use according to the weather.

The Royal Tombs

Just 100m south of the disused, locked Salamis west gate, a side road heads off west for 500m to the access lane for the **Royal Tombs** (partially fenced; same timings as Salamis site; 7YTL). Two of the nearly 150 eighth- and seventh-century burial sites here caused a sensation when discovered in 1957, because they confirmed Homer's descriptions of Late Bronze Age funerary rites, still being observed here five centuries after the original Mycenaean homeland on the Greek Peloponnese had passed its zenith.

Most of the tombs had been looted in antiquity, but others, in particular **Tombs 47 and 79** east of the access drive, yielded the elaborate remains of several royal funerals. Precious metal or ivory objects, pottery, weapons and food containers were all intended to serve the dead in the underworld, and included the famous ivory-inlaid throne and bed – showing profound Phoenician/Egyptian influence – now in the Cyprus Museum.

All the tombs save one opened east, and were approached by gently slanting *dromoi* or ramps – on which the most telling artefacts were unearthed. Over the years at least four ceremonial chariots bearing a king's bier had been drawn by two pony-like horses to a certain point on the ramps, where the deceased was cremated after the horses (and frequently favourite human servants) were ritually sacrificed. East of three of the tombs the preserved skeletons of the slaughtered horses have been left rather gruesomely *in situ*, protected by glass plates. A few of the terrified horses broke their own necks at the deadly moment by lunging in their tackle, and at least some of the attendants did not willingly follow their masters in death, as can be gathered by human remains in the *dromoi* discovered bound hand and foot.

Officially **Tomb 50**, "St Catherine's prison" became associated with that Alexandrian saint through a Cypriot legend making her as a native of Salamis, imprisoned here by her father the Roman governor for refusing an arranged marriage. That this tomb didn't start life as a Christian place of worship was proven by the well-preserved pair of fossilized horses found adjacent; the T-shaped subterranean interior, with a vaulted antechamber and tiny burial recess, still bears some ecclesiastical trappings.

Tombs west of the access drive include a prominent tumulus concealing a mud-brick **"beehive" chamber** nearly identical in design to those at Greek Mycenae. The small site **museum** (same timings and ticket) displays plans and photographs of the tombs and excavations, plus a reconstruction of one chariot used to transport the dead kings: the brass fittings and horse ornamentations are original, remounted on facsimiles of the long-decayed wooden structures.

Salamis area practicalities

The shoreline north of Salamis towards Boğaz features intermittent sandy patches, occasionally ballooning out into wide **beaches**; eucalyptus, planted by the British to drain the local marshes, thrive just inland, though mosquitoes still abound on summer nights. All international-standard **accommodation** on this stretch enjoys a beachfront location, though patronage is down given a slump in casino tourism and the fitful marketing of the area by UK package operators. Affordable choices are a bit limited since the Park Hotel, just north of Salamis, was gutted in 2008 prior to becoming another luxury resort. Choose between the smallish, casino-less, notionally three-star *Mimoza* (℡378 82 19, ⓦ www.mimozabeachhotel.com; ❷), adjacent to the mammoth *Salamis Bay Conti*, whose pool abuts the excellent beach. The tile-floor rooms, however, are basic, with tiny bathrooms, and for a similar amount the next-door, self-catering *Kocareis Bungalows* (℡378 82 29, ⓦ www.kocareisresort.com; small apt ❷, large ❸) is preferable. Galleried family units sleep four, plus there are proper stoves and fridges, and free airport pick-up. On site also is a respected **restaurant** stressing fish, salad and chips as well as more snacky fare.

Monastery-museum of Apóstolos Varnávas

Continuing 500m further on the same road serving the Royal Tombs, you soon approach the former **monastery of Apóstolos Varnávas** (daily: summer 9am–7pm; winter 9am–1pm & 2–4.45pm; 9YTL), refurbished during the 1980s as a museum. A monastic community first arose on this low hill in the fifth century following the discovery of the purported tomb of the Apostle Barnabas, with the Byzantine emperor himself funding construction. The Arab raiders destroyed this foundation during their seventh-century pillagings; the present church and cloister date from 1756, though some ancient columns from Salamis are incorporated.

Until 1974 Apóstolos Varnávas was a favourite pilgrimage goal among Famagustans, with sequential baptisms conducted by one of three look-alike, Santa-Claus-bearded monks: Barnabas, Stephanos and Khariton. Since 1917 these three (biological) brothers had presided over the monastery, supporting it through sales of honey and mass-produced icons popular with nearby villagers, but of limited artistic merit. Somehow they contrived to stay after August 1974, but finally, too weak and old to combat Turkish harassment, gave up and moved south in 1976, living out their days at Stavrovoúni monastery near Larnaca.

The museum and tomb of Barnabas

It's certainly not the **icon collection**, housed in the *katholikón*, that justifies the entrance fee; the oldest and most artistically worthy is an unusual *Herod's Banquet*

Barnabas (Varnávas in Greek) of Salamis was the companion of the Apostle Paul on missionary voyages around Cyprus and Asia Minor before their falling-out over whether or not Barnabas's cousin Mark was to accompany them. He is generally regarded as the apostle most influential in introducing Christianity to the island, and – long after his demise – with perpetuating its independent status through miraculous intervention.

His activities having aroused the ire of the Salamis Jewish community into which he had been born, Barnabas was martyred by stoning in about 75 AD; thereafter matters become apocryphal, with most accounts having Mark interring the corpse at an undisclosed location. There things would have rested (in all senses) had it not been for an ecclesiastical squabble four hundred years later.

Late in the fifth century the Church of Antioch, having been founded by Peter and thus an **apostolic see**, claimed precedence over that of Cyprus, which retorted (initially unsuccessfully) that as a foundation of the Apostle Barnabas the island's Church was also apostolic and of equal rank. Subordination to the Syrian archbishopric was only avoided through the supernatural assistance of Barnabas himself, who appeared in a dream to Anthemios, Archbishop of Salamis, and bade him unearth the apostle's remains from a lonely spot on the Mesaoría marked by a carob tree. Following these instructions, the cleric indeed found a catacomb matching the description and containing what could have been the bones of Barnabas, clasping a mildewed copy (in Hebrew) of the Gospel of St Matthew. Armed with these incontrovertible relics, the Cypriots went to Constantinople, where a synod convened by Emperor Zeno was sufficiently impressed to grant special privileges to the island's Church.

Most importantly it was to remain autocephalous (autonomous), deferring only to the sees of Constantinople, Alexandria, Antioch and Jerusalem in importance, and in later centuries pre-eminent over larger autocephalous churches, such as those in Russia. Cypriot bishops elected their own archbishop, who was permitted to sign his name in red ink in imitation of the Byzantine emperor, wear imperial purple and wield a sceptre instead of a pastoral staff. When Cyprus fell to the Ottomans, these hitherto symbolic privileges acquired practical import inasmuch as the clergy were charged with the civil as well as the spiritual administration of their Orthodox flock. Following independence, Archbishop Makarios revived the medieval term "ethnarch", further blurring the lines between secular and ecclesiastical power, with ultimately catastrophic consequences.

(1858), with John the Baptist being beheaded. Most seem scrabbled-together replacements for 35 more valuable ones, which mysteriously went missing from the lightly guarded premises in 1982, with more disappearing in 1997.

The former cells around the landscaped courtyard have been converted into what is at present the North's best **archeological museum**; how much, if any of it, is based on the looted Hadjiprodhromou collection or the holdings of the inaccessible Famagusta Archeological Museum (see box, p.344) is uncertain. Eras are presented slightly out of order, proceeding clockwise from the Bronze Age to the Venetian period, with a mixed Ottoman/Classical Greek wing at the end. Labelling gives only dates, with few indications of provenance.

The Bronze Age room features incised red polished and white slip pottery, as well as bronze items. A model house and set of miniature plates appear in the Geometric room; Archaic jugs exhibit Mycenaean influence in their depiction of an archer and birds. Among terracotta votive figurines and chariots stands an unusual wheel-footed horse – definitely not a chariot – on which a lyre-player entertains two other riders.

Star of the Classical section is a woman in a headdress – possibly the goddess Demeter – holding a poppy; Cyprus was one of the earliest centres of opium production. Two stone lions squat, haunch to haunch, with their tongues out, near a perfectly formed sphinx; continuing the animal theme, some Hellenistic child's rattles are in the shape of wild boars. An access path from the monastery car park leads – past a partly uncovered necropolis – to a little mausoleum-chapel, shaded by a carob tree and erected during the 1950s over a catacomb that is the presumed **tomb of Barnabas**. Stairs (flick the light switch) lead down to two rock-cut chambers with room for half-a-dozen dead, similar to the crypt of Áyios Lázaros in Larnaca – and far older than Christianity. Since the barriers came down in April 2003, both monastery and catacomb are popular targets for weekend pilgrims from the South, who have thoroughly re-Christianized the premises with an assortment of inexpensive icons and offertory candles in the tomb. But even before then, candle drippings and floral offerings proved that local Muslims continued to revere the cave regardless of the departure of its Orthodox custodians. The stratum of simple, fervent belief runs deep in Cyprus, predating the monotheistic religions and not respecting their fine distinctions.

Enkomi-Alasia

From the monastery-museum it's a short drive southwest to a T-junction. Turn right – just beyond the junction is the inconspicuously signed entry to the Bronze Age town of **Enkomi-Alasia** (daily: summer 9am–7pm; winter 9am–1pm & 2–4.45pm; 5YTL), opposite a water tank. Founded around 2000 BC, it was first referred to four centuries later on some Pharaonic tablets as "Alashya" (Éngomi is the modern Greek name of the nearest village), because from the sixteenth century BC onwards it acted as a thriving copper-exporting harbour, in an age when the coast was much closer and the river Pedhiéos more navigable than today. Mycenaean immigration swelled the population to 15,000 by the twelfth century, but fire and earthquake mortally weakened the city during the eleventh century, after which it was abandoned in favour of Salamis.

The site

Excavations sponsored by the British Museum began in 1896, revealing the most complete Late Bronze Age town on Cyprus, and were continued by periodic French, Swedish and Cypriot missions until 1974. The town plan was a grid of narrow, perpendicular streets and low houses, surrounded by a wall; Alasia was initially thought to be a necropolis for Salamis, since human skeletons were discovered under each dwelling.

Also found here was an as-yet-undeciphered tablet in Cypro-Minoan script; the famous "**Horned God**", possibly an avatar of Apollo whose worship was imported from Arcadia in the Peloponnese; and an exquisite silver bowl inlaid with ox-head and floral designs, whose only known equal also came from Arcadia. These and other treasures are distributed between the British Museum and the Cyprus Museum.

Notwithstanding these glories, the site is today of essentially specialist interest. Little remains above waist level, and there's absolutely no labelling (though the ticket office issues a helpful leaflet); problems of interpretation are complicated by survivors of the eleventh-century earthquakes having divided up damaged open-plan houses with crude rubble barriers. The town was originally entered via a north gate; west of the main longitudinal street, the "Horned God" was found in a sanctuary marked by stone horns similar to those at Pigádhes, surrounded by the skulls of animals worn as masks during the celebration of his cult. At the south edge of the exposed grid stands the so-called **House of Bronzes**, where many such objects were discovered in 1934.

Boğaz

BOĞAZ (Bogázi) could make a fairly pleasant base with its fishing anchorage and small beach, though oil-storage tanks and a cement plant across the bay are a bit disconcerting. Better value of two local **hotels** is smallish *Exotic* (☎371 28 81, Ⓦ www.cyprusexotic.com; ❸), near the south end of the strip on the inland side of the road, slightly set back from the noisy cement trucks which rumble through here in the morning.

More numerous seafood **restaurants** flank the road here; their fish is fresh enough, but they've become fairly touristy, expensive and much of a muchness, even more so since trippers from the South began arriving. *Kıyı*, opposite the *Exotic*, is probably the best-priced of the bunch. The only alternative, 2km south among sprouting villas, is *Moon Over the Water* (reserve on ☎371 32 97; Fri–Sat lunch, plus Sun all day; closed Jan; also Mon–Thurs high season), run by and for expats with a good line in pub-style grub.

İskele (Tríkomo)

Approaching Boğaz from Nicosia or Kyrenia, you'll almost certainly pass through **İSKELE** (Tríkomo), notable as the birthplace of notorious EOKA leader George Grivas and, less controversially, of Vassos Karageorghis, Cyprus's foremost archeologist. In the central square and roundabout, the diminutive fifteenth-century Dominican chapel of **Áyios Iákovos** (locked, signed as "St James") is plunked down like a jewel-box; supposedly the early twentieth-century Queen Marie of Romania was so taken with it that she had an exact replica built on the Black Sea coast as a royal chapel.

Some 300m west on the way to Geçitkale (Lefkóniko) stands the double-aisled Byzantine church of **Panayía Theotókos**, constructed from the twelfth to fifteenth centuries. It is now a so-called "**Icon Museum**" (daily: summer 9am–6pm; winter 9am–4pm; 5YTL) of collected modern icons of negligible artistic merit; what justifies the admission charge are the best surviving **frescoes** in the North, stylistically related to those at Asínou in the Tróödhos.

The oldest are in the south aisle, where scenes from the life of Joachim and Anna, the Virgin's parents, predominate, appropriately for a church dedicated to the Virgin. In the arch of the south recess, below the dome, *Prayer of Joachim in the Wilderness* faces *Meeting of Joachim and Anna*, where the couple embrace while a maidservant looks on; the north recess arch is *Prayer of Anna* (for offspring; the couple had been childless) and *Presentation of Gifts to the Temple*. In the apse, over the altar, a Virgin Orans presides below a fine Ascension, with Christ borne heavenward by four angels, while an archangel and six awed disciples look up from either side.

But the most arresting image is a severe Pandokrátor in the dome, where the frowning Christ averts his gaze towards a surrounding inscription, identifying him as "Overseer of All", who searches hearts and souls, concluding with the injunction: "Mortals, Fear the Judge!" Angels on bended knee worship all around while, below, a bust of Christ flanked by the Virgin and John the Baptist awaits the Throne of Judgement, with the instruments of the Passion.

The Karpaz (Kárpas) peninsula

The remote "panhandle" of Cyprus, known variously as the **Karpaz, Kárpas**, **Kırpaşa** or **Karpásia peninsula**, presents a landscape of rolling hills and grain fields, partly domesticated with vineyards or olive and carob trees – plus an ever-growing number of villa projects – but still fringed by some of the loneliest beaches on the island. In ancient times it was fairly densely inhabited, this history leaving a concentration of small **archeological sites** and **early Christian churches** more interesting than the celebrated **monastery of Apóstolos Andhréas** near the far cape. The inhabitants were once noted for relict traditions which had died out elsewhere, for their craftwork and for a smattering of blue or green eyes – and more finely chiselled features – that hinted at Frankish or Arab settlement.

Until 1974 the peninsula was an ethnic mosaic, Turkish villages such as Áyios Simeón, Koróvia and Galinóporni alternating with Greek ones like Rizokárpaso, Ayía Triás and Yialoússa. However only a handful, like Kómi Kebír and Áyios Andhrónikos, were actually mixed; Denktaş reportedly came through in 1964 to urge such Turks to segregate themselves. They refused then, though a fortified enclave eventually formed around the kernel of Áyios Simeón, Koróvia and Galinóporni. The Republican government aggravated the problem, it is claimed, by routeing and paving the main road through the Orthodox villages, leaving the Muslim settlements to fend for themselves. Today the crumbling villages – certainly the smaller ones – seem at least fifty percent resettled by mainland Turks. But the peninsula, superfluous to the argument of who controls the North, is no longer heavily garrisoned by the Turkish army.

In 1998 the Northern authorities improved and re-routed the road up to **Yenierenköy** (Yialoússa), greatly easing travel in the peninsula. This road and its continuation – of nearly as good standard, up to Dipkarpaz (Rizokárpaso) – bypass most of the villages discussed below, so slight detours are required to visit them and nearby attractions. Infrequent **buses** run from Famagusta only to Yenierenköy, so you will need a **car**. You can see the most interesting sights in a single, long day (beginning from a base near Salamis), but to really savour the area you'd want two, especially starting from Kyrenia – a fairly brutal, 250-kilometre round-trip drive by the shortest routes; thus two overnights on the peninsula are highly recommended. There are now several **petrol stations** along the main trunk route.

Since the advent of all but unrestricted movement for Cypriots in April 2003, Karpaz has become a firm favourite with **Greek–Cypriot trippers**, who revel in empty beaches, fresh seafood and Orthodox monuments the likes of all of which are getting progressively harder to enjoy in the South. In response, tourist facilities are multiplying – as are establishment signs in slightly wonky Greek, proudly proclaiming the proprietors' Cypriot origins – although, human nature being what it is, prices have climbed and quality dropped at certain outfits.

Kantara castle

Poised where the Kyrenia range subsides into rolling hills, **Kantara castle**, the easternmost and lowest of the Byzantine/Crusader trio, is as good a spot as any to call the base of the peninsula. Even here the Karpaz is so narrow that the castle simultaneously surveys shoreline along both the north coast and the Bay of Famagusta. The name is thought to derive from the Arabic *qantara*, "arch" or "bridge", though it's difficult to pinpoint such a structure in either this citadel or the surrounding landscape.

Traditionally the castle is reckoned to be where Isaac Komnenos surrendered to Richard the Lionheart in 1191. Like St Hilarion, it figured prominently in the 1229–30 war between the supporters of the Holy Roman Emperor Frederick II and the Lusignan–Ibelin cartel, and again during the Genoese invasion, when regent John of Antioch was smuggled out of prison in Famagusta to this hideout disguised as a pot-tinner. Like the other two Kyrenia hill-castles, Kantara was part-demolished by the Venetians early in the sixteenth century, but it is still the best preserved of the three. From Boğaz it's at least a thirty minute drive to the castle, via dilapidated Yarköy (Áyios Elías), finally reaching, after a paved but narrow, curvy one-lane section, pine-swathed **Kantára village**, the closest thing to a hill-station in the Kyrenia range. Among the boarded-up Greek summer villas and dried-up fountains, there's a single **restaurant** with energetic, English-speaking management who make it a going concern in summer at least. From the central junction by the restaurant, turn right to follow the ridgeline, and signs for the castle and picnic grounds; the tarmac gives out just before the car park, 4km east of the village.

The site

Just over 700m above sea level, most of the complex (unenclosed but 6YTL if warden present, typically summer 9am–6pm, winter 9am–4.45pm) faces east, the only direction with easy access. You enter the outer enceinte through a **barbican** flanked by a pair of towers, then climb steps to the inner ward. First stop will probably be the massive **southeast tower**, its lower part a cistern which occasionally doubled as a dungeon. Further along the southeast wall are the **barracks**, a trio of rooms fitted with loopholes; adjacent, an obvious latrine was flushed by the castle's sophisticated plumbing system. Up to here the buildings are in good condition, down to the woodwork and rib-vaulted ceilings, and could be used tomorrow. Beyond this point, however, Kantara is quite ruinous until the southwest corner of the battlements, where one chamber contains a hidden **postern gate** for surprising besiegers.

Crossing the rubble of the inner bailey, or returning to the southeast tower, you attain the **northern towers**; their design – two long galleries equipped with arrow slits and joined by a square chamber – is a remarkable piece of military engineering. Of the highest watchtower, once used to communicate with Buffavento to the west, just one wall and a Gothic window survive; the northeast bastion, by contrast, is impressively complete.

Kaplica (Dhavlós)

From either the castle or village of Kantára, you can plainly see **KAPLICA** (Dhavlós) and its bays just below on the north coast. To get here, return to the four-way junction in Kantára village for the sharp but brief descent. Kaplıca village, resettled by mainlanders, is actually 1km inland from the main beach, a 400-metre stretch of sand that's the first really good beach east from Onüçüncü Mil (see p.332). Dominating this cove is the *Kaplıca Restaurant*, popular at weekends (reserve then), with *woppa* and *şiş kebap* prominent on the menu. The management keeps equally busy **rooms** (☎387 20 32, ⊛ www.kaplicabeach.8m .com; ❶) downstairs: basic but en suite, with fans and TV, opening right onto the sand. Just to the east matters have been rather spoiled with an enormous caravan park; another unsullied sandy patch (with a fish-fry shack) lies about 5km to the west.

Zeytin Burnu to Kumyalı

A few secluded, sandy beaches relatively near Boğaz can still be found to either side of **Zeytin Burnu** (Cape Eléa). For the first one, head southeast out of the central crossroads in the village of **Çayırova** (Áyios Theodhóros) on the most prominent dirt track, always turning towards the sea when given the choice. Soon you emerge at an impromptu car park/turnaround area near Zeytin Burnu; the shore below can be debris- and seaweed-strewn, but walk to the far end of the 400-metre beach and the litter thins out. Up on the headland closing off the cove are the sparse remains of ancient **Knidos**.

East of Çayırova, a paved side road leads to a vast area designated as an official tourism development zone, borne out by mushrooming villas and the monstrously kitsch *Kaya Artemis* resort, its main building in the form of an ancient temple. Your next real opportunity for a quiet swim is the small, reefy beach below **Kumyalı** (Kóma toúYialoú), encroached on by a fishing port. The village itself, sturdily built from local stone (nearby quarries supplied material for the walls of Famagusta), has two notable churches: a sixteenth-century one about 1.5km west, and a slightly older one on a knoll close to Kumyalı.

Panayía Kanakariá church and beyond

The intriguing fifth- to twelfth-century monastic church of **Panayía Kanakariá** stands at the western edge of Boltaşlİ (Lythrangomí), reached via a side road east from the main trunk route at Ziyamet (Leonárisso). Today it is firmly locked – rather a case of bolting the stable door after the horse has fled (see box opposite), but enough can be seen from outside to convince you of the building's merit. Nave and aisles represent an eleventh-century revamping of the original fifth-century structure, of which only the apse (former home of the mosaics) remains. The domed narthex was added shortly afterwards, while the high, drummed central cupola followed in the 1700s.

The wide, improved road beyond the village threads through the eminently scenic territory of this former Turkish-Cypriot enclave, an excellent alternative approach to or return from Dipkarpaz, 26km distant, though commercial maps still show this as dirt track. (You emerge just west of the Dipkarpaz police station; in the other direction the way's not marked.) En route the dedicated can seek out (with local directions, they're unsigned) the enormous cliff-tomb at **Derince** (Vathýlakkas), the free-standing one at **Avtepe** (Áyios Symeón) hamlet and the seaside, Bronze Age fortress at **Nitovikla**, 3km south by jeep track from **Kuruova** (Koróvia). Just before **Kaleburnu** (Galinóporni), the largest of these villages, another seaward track leads to **Üsküdar** (Skoutári) beach, not superlative but acceptable for a dip.

Yenierenköy and Ayías Triás basilica

YENIERENKÖY (Yialoússa, Yalusa), the second-largest village on the peninsula, has been mostly resettled by inhabitants of Tillyría's Kókkina (Erenköy) enclave since 1975. It offers the last reliable **fuel** before the end of the peninsula, a **bank** which (theoretically) will handle foreign exchange, and a friendly **tourist information office** (daily June–Sept 9am–5pm; sporadically Oct–May). Just northeast, to one side of **Yassi Burnu** (Cape Plakotí), stands *Club Malibu Hotel* (☎374 42 64, ⓦwww.clubmalibucy.com; ❷), with some

The sixth-century **mosaics** which formerly graced the apse of **Panayía Kanakariá** are contemporary with those at Ravenna; *in situ*, they consisted of a Virgin and precociously aged Child flanked by the archangels, while above the Virgin busts of various evangelists and apostles, particularly Matthew, Andrew, Bartholomew, Luke, James, Thaddeus and Thomas, ran in a curved band. Art historians disagree on their merit, but the expressiveness of the figures compensates for the crudeness of their tesserae (the pigmented or gilded glass cubes used to compose a mosaic).

Even before independence, the mosaics had suffered at the hands of superstitious villagers who considered the tesserae effective against skin disease. Worse was to follow; at some point between 1974 and 1979, thieves broke in through the windows of the drum and hacked off four sections of mosaic. Their whereabouts were unknown until the late 1980s, when American art dealer Peg Goldberg purchased them for just over $1 million from a Turkish-Dutch duo, **Aydın Dikmen** and **Michel van Rijn**, brandishing a dubious export permit from the North Cyprus government. The mosaics were offered for sale to California's Getty Museum for twenty times that amount, but the museum management contacted the Los Angeles police, and by now Cyprus's Autocephalous Orthodox Church and Department of Antiquities were also aware of matters.

The Church and government of the Republic sued jointly for the return of the mosaics in the US District Court of Indianapolis, winning their case in August 1989; the presiding judge essentially agreed with the Greek-Cypriot contention that an export licence granted by an internationally unrecognized state was invalid, and that the artwork remained the property of the Cypriot Church. Following a failed appeal by the dealers, the mosaics returned to the South in the summer of 1991, and are now displayed in a special wing of the Archbishop Makarios Cultural Centre (see p.255). Shortly after, a judgment in Texas concerning frescoes removed from the fourteenth-century church of Áyios Efimianós on the Mesarya also found in favour of their eventual return to the South (they are still in Texas pending a political settlement).

By the mid-1990s, Van Rijn had fallen out with his partner Dikmen and, ostensibly tired of a life of art crime, approached the Greek-Cypriot authorities and offered to co-operate in retrieving more stolen mosaics and frescoes – for a small commission to cover "expenses" only. With money fronted by wealthy Cypriot businessmen, and the Greek-Cypriot consul in The Hague as his contact and paymaster, in September 1997 Van Rijn negotiated with Dikmen through intermediaries to buy the mosaics of Thaddeus and Thomas, plus considerable quantities of other religious art from the North, including several important frescoes lifted from the walls of Antifonítis monastery (see p.329). Under threat of arrest and prosecution, Van Rijn agreed to organize a sting operation to catch Dikmen, now in Germany; the trap was sprung at the Munich Hilton in October 1997, and Dikmen's basement was searched and found to contain several rooms full of treasures from the North, now all in South Nicosia.

With court orders of limited efficacy in other cases of antiquities theft, the Southern authorities have had to resort to such James-Bond-ish doings to obtain satisfaction – at a price of about half a million pounds, all of which (excluding Van Rijn's fee) was presumably also recovered in the sting operation.

---

beachside bungalows and an on-site **scuba outfitter**, Mephisto (☎0533 867 37 74, ⓦ www.mephisto-diving.com), small and well priced, with fourteen of the less frequented Cypriot dive-sites around the peninsula.

The inland turning from the southern edge of Yenierenköy leads to **SİPAHİ** (Ayía Triás), with lots of fair-complexion Bulgarian Turks, and its **early Christian basilica of Ayías Triás**. The site (fenced but gate always unlocked; 5YTL) lies at the northerly exit of the village going downhill towards the sea,

▲ Ayias Trias basilica, Karpaz peninsula

just west of the road. The fifth-century, three-aisled basilica seems far too large for the modest early village partly excavated here. Given their similar style, it's likely that the same craftsmen who decorated the Eustolios annexe at Kourion are responsible for the vivid **nave mosaics** here, which are entirely but engagingly geometric. An inscription at the west entry relates that three men sponsored the decoration in honour of a vow, while up by the apse another inscription informs that Iraklios the deacon paid for that section of the floor.

In the **north aisle mosaics** there are several exceptions to the pattern of abstract imagery, including a cluster of pomegranates, diagonally opposite one of two pairs of sandals. This curious symbol, common in the early Christian Middle East but found nowhere else in Cyprus, may represent the pilgrimage through this world to the next. The baptistry, just southeast of the basilica, has a deep, marble-lined cruciform font, largest on the island.

The coast east of Yenierenköy

The inland detour to Sipahi and the coastal route join up again before **Áyios Thýrsos** (Ayterisos, Aytherisso), a tiny anchorage with two eponymous churches: an eighteenth-century one with fine rib vaulting and a carved altar, next to *Deks* restaurant, and an older, very sea-weathered shrine down by the water, with wish-rags at the door and an interior crypt in which a healing spring once trickled – bring a torch for the steps down.

The broad trunk road, and villa projects, cease for now at Áyios Thýrsos. Less than 1km east is one of the peninsula's best seafood **restaurants**: ☙ *Alevkayalı* (☎0533/876 09 11), where for about €20/34YTL you'll get a huge fresh-fish platter, salad, a mini-meze and a beer; in spring they've *ayrelli* (wild asparagus). It's bidding to eclipse the adjacent *Theresa Restaurant*, fallen on hard times with a management change; the affiliated hotel across the way (☎374 42 66, ❻www .theresahotel.com; ❶) has en-suite rooms but is extremely spartan, and you might consider the 2005-opened, seafront *Balcı Plaza* (☎0533/862 93 03, ❻www.balciplaza.com; ❷) 2km east, a comfortable apart-hotel in landscaped grounds. Between these two, winter-weekend hunters pack out another restaurant, *Çira'nin Yeri (Yiannagis)*. The "*Çira*" (Cypriot dialect for "the Mrs") is a Yialoússa Greek-Cypriot who elected to stay after 1974, was ill-treated by the Turkish Army for her doggedness and lost various family members. Her endurance was rewarded, as she (and surviving son Yiannagis) can barely cope with the crowds, and the food is excellent.

Minuscule, tenth-century **Áyios Fótios**, the next church passed, is accessible by a non-motorable, 300-metre track some 5km past Áyios Thýrsos; after 3km more, a paved side-turning leads up through pines to sixteenth-century **Panayía Eleoússa (Panaghia Elusa, Sína)**, unusual and worth the slight detour. It's an asymmetrical two-apsed (rather than usual three) church, with the smaller, narrower north aisle divided from the main one by a double archway similar to Panayía Iamatikí's (see p.132). Such lopsided double churches are also found in the Greek islands where a Latin Catholic medieval ruling class conceded some space of worship to the Orthodox peasantry, and something similar probably occurred here. The carved south portal (always open) shows marked Lusignan influence, while a large ruined outbuilding adjacent suggests the church may have had monastic status.

Panayía Eleoússa romantically overlooks the broad sweep of **Ronnás** bay. Here dunes lap a fine beach favoured by egg-laying turtles, but the prevailing wind brings a lot of garbage, and even 4WD vehicles may founder in the sand-tracks towards the water.

Dipkarpaz and around

From Ronnás the road turns inland to straggly **DIPKARPAZ** (Rizokárpaso), the remotest yet largest village on the peninsula, with a population of around three thousand, and a huge modern mosque overshadowing the main triple-aisled

The 1974 war effectively bypassed the peninsula, so there was no panicky exodus of civilians in the path of the oncoming Turkish army. Thus of the nearly 20,000 **Greek Cypriots** who tried to stay in the North, most of them lived in the Karpaz. But since then, systematic harassment by the Turkish army and the North Cypriot government has reduced this population to a handful of middle-aged and older individuals. Secondary education was no longer allowed after 1975, with only two Greek primary schools functioning thereafter, so any children aged over 11 had to go south for continued education, without any right of return. Only if youths stay continuously are they able to inherit property, as houses can only be left to relatives still living in the North; the (desired) result is that as the Greeks die out, the North's government seizes their property and hands it to settlers – sometimes even expelling a living Greek-Cypriot occupant to the South if a building or fields are coveted. Similarly, no Greek-Cypriot doctor practises anywhere on this side of the Line, and while the right to private land lines was conceded in 1996 after UN pressure on the North, in practice few phones have been installed. Nor are the local Orthodox allowed to vote in local elections, and they need permits to travel outside their village.

Not surprisingly, then, fewer than 300 stubborn Greeks continue to eke out a subsistence livelihood on the peninsula: about 230 in Dipkarpaz (Rizokárpaso), fewer than 50 in Sipahi (Ayía Triás), plus a few scattered others. UN lorries make a weekly run to drop off basic food staples for the Greek Cypriots, as their poor Turkish and restricted participation in the local economy mean most of them can't or won't shop locally. Before 2003 the Orthodox were allowed to visit doctors and relatives in the South on one-week visas, shuttled to the Ledra Palace crossing in Nicosia by Turkish-Cypriot authorities for a fee; relatives from the South could not make reciprocal visits.

Relations between the Greek Cypriots and goat-grazing **Anatolian settlers** are habitually strained, somewhat better with Turkish Cypriots or Bulgarian-Turkish immigrants used to farming, though coffeehouses in Sipahi and Dipkarpaz remain ethnically segregated. Greek-Cypriot living conditions here are undeniably humiliating, as per an official 2001 judgment by the European Court of Human Rights; "We live like animals" can be an unsolicited local comment on the situation. This is often voiced in tandem with the fatalistic belief that the invasion and its aftermath were God's punishment for their sins – sentiments expressed regularly by Greeks since the Turks first appeared in Anatolia during the tenth century.

Under the circumstances, the **opening of the "border"** on April 23, 2003, was a godsend for the enclaved Karpaz Greeks. The secret police who used to dog every public conversation with outsiders could no longer cope with the flood of Greek-Cypriot company; freedom of mobility and vastly increased access to euros have improved living standards, at least for a handful of restaurateurs and café-owners. A hopeful development, in September 2004, was the reopening of the secondary school in Dipkarpaz, though it has only 27 students and textbooks are censored for "Greek propaganda". Another small but positive sign: Muslim children are learning Greek, either from elderly Orthodox neighbours or visitors from the South. As with the Maronites of Kormakiti, the patience of the holdouts may eventually be rewarded.

church of the remaining Greek Orthodox inhabitants on the modern main square. Once a prosperous place, Dipkarpaz has been effectively reduced to an Anatolian-Kurdish village, with added poignancy in formerly imposing arcaded houses used as poultry pens and hay barns. Besides its central coffee houses – the Greeks' *Ayios Synesios* now prominently signposted, and assiduously attended by Greek-Cypriot trippers and Turkish-Cypriot hunters alike – the main tourist amenity is a worthwhile **accommodation** scheme, 🏕 *Karpaz Arch Houses*

(☎372 20 09, ⓦwww.karpazarchhouses.com; B&B ❶), 500m from the mosque, just off the Áyios Fílon road. Part restoration, part new-build (and expanding across the way in 2009), this is arrayed around a pedestrianized former village street and garden areas; the closer you are to the original arcaded building with its over-arch "penthouse", the better the studio units, some interconnecting for families. Breakfast is taken in the old coffee house, now the scheme's office. Immediately adjacent is the excellent ⅍ *Manolyam Restaurant*, where both locals and visitors are made to feel at home and five mini-meze platters are provided free with mains and drink.

Áyios Fílon and Aféndrika

The early Christian sites of Áyios Fílon and Aféndrika both entail a slight but eminently worthwhile detour north from Dipkarpaz over the northerly of the two ridges enclosing the village (follow signs for *Karpaz Arch Houses* and *Oasis*).

The basilicas of **Áyios Fílon** (Ayfilon), 3km along, are the most obvious remains of ancient Karpasia – even from the ridge you can easily spot the cluster of washingtonia palms and the resort buildings flanking them. Typically, the half-ruined tenth-century chapel, of which only the apse and south wall are intact, sits amid foundations of a far larger, earlier basilica and baptistry, perhaps the seat of the saintly Philon, first bishop of Christian Karpasia. The bapistry's extensive *opus sectile* flooring includes an abstract ring design similar to that of Kambanópetra at Salamis. Just to the north, the ancient jetty sticks 100m out to sea, its masonry furrowed where long-vanished iron pins held the stones together. The rest of Hellenistic and Roman **Karpasia**, which supplied building stone for both church and baptistry, lies scattered west of the road in, but it's a long slog through thorn-bushes to never-excavated walls and a necropolis.

Immediately beyond the palm trees stands *Oasis at Ayfilon*, a combination **restaurant-inn** spread over several buildings (☎0542/856 50 82 or 0533/868 55 91, ⓦwww.oasishotelkarpas.com; B&B ❶). A 2006 management change improved the restaurant's fare (grilled fish and meat), though the pastel-decor rooms remain basic (not en suite) but cheerful, with solar showers in a separate building. Everything overlooks a "private" 30-metre beach lapped by a bay where turtles can often be seen in the water, but much the best swimming hereabouts is at so-called **Dipkarpaz Halk Plajı**, a 700-metre fine-sand bay just 400m west, along a dirt track 200m before the church.

Beyond Áyios Fílon, the narrow, mostly paved main road swings east 5km more along the coast to **Aféndrika**, another important ancient town, originally larger than Karpasia. All that remains today are three contiguous ruined churches: Panayía Khrysiótissa, a twelfth-century ruin inside which huddles a smaller chapel two hundred years younger; formerly domed, double-apsed Áyios Yeóryios, its west end missing; and three-aisled Panayía Asómatos, mostly roofless but still impressive. West of the churches is a necropolis, while in the opposite direction the chambers of the citadel were partly cut into the outcrop on which it was built. The now-dirt road continues 1km to where a distinct path leads 600m north across fields to sandy **Exárkhou** cove. Given the excellence (if variable cleanliness) of Dipkarpaz Halk Plajı though, the trip isn't always worth the effort.

Southeast of Dipkarpaz: Khelónes and Tuzlukuyu

Dipkarpaz is the peninsula's last village; beyond supposedly stretches a "national reserve", posted as off-limits to hunters, though this doesn't deter crowds of Sunday shooters who come here from all over the North to bag partridge from November to March. Other conspicuous "wild" life consists of about five hundred skittish donkeys, descendants of domestic ones who escaped in 1974 when their Orthodox owners had to abandon them. They have since multiplied and become a nuisance, trampling seeded fields and eating crops, though plans to capture or if necessary cull them have been dropped.

Some 5km east of Dipkarpaz, the road passes the *Blue Sea* restaurant at the promontory (and rock-studded beach) called **Khelónes**, offering fresh if unadorned fish from the adjacent anchorage. Fisherman-proprietor İrfan also keeps a small, one-star hotel upstairs (℡372 23 93, Ⓦwww.blueseahotel.org; B&B ❶), its formerly cell-like sea-view rooms improved in 2006.

The closest alternative lunch stop is about 6km further at **Tuzlukuyu** (Almyrólakkos), where Greek-Cypriot-run *O Almyrolakkos* (℡0533/844 13 92) makes a good fist of fish or meat mains, chips, a mini-meze and a beer for about €14/24YTL a head; it gets groups of pilgrims, which can slow down service, but quality seems unaffected.

Nangomí ("Golden Beach")

Continuing northeast, the road bears inland again for a while, passing through fields and pastures surprisingly well tended for such a depopulated region. Some 13km beyond the *Blue Sea* begins the best beach in the North, if not the entire island, initially hidden behind a line of scrub-covered knolls halting the advance of vast dunes. Known officially pre-1974 as **Nangomí**, it has lately been dubbed "**Golden Beach**", though the strand can be a distinctly orange tint in full daylight.

Westerly access is provided by a dirt track, flanked by multiple signage for **rustic beachfront bungalows** – including *Burhan's* (℡0533/864 10 51; ❶) – threading a conspicuous gap in the barrier hillocks, leaving you with a five-minute walk to the water. Some 2km further is the easier access lane to the biggest **parking area** and rustic bungalows at *Hasan's Turtle Beach* (℡0533/864 10 63; ❶), where Hasan offers simple grills. Alternatively, follow the rising main road skirting the edge of the dunes, and the wild, spectacular beach extends obviously southwest, though the walk down from several lay-bys is no shorter. At the highest curve there's another simple restaurant/bungalow outfit, *Big Sand* (℡0533/865 34 88; ❶), with sweeping views.

The five-plus kilometres of sand – gently shelving, not much surf, so good for kids – could easily accommodate most of the North's population on a summer weekend, and probably does on occasion. Given the rather impermanent nature of development so far, there's some hope for its preservation, as the tip of the peninsula has been declared a protected area: good news for the quail and other birds living in the dunes, and the **sea turtles** who lay eggs here.

Apóstolos Andhréas monastery

The peninsula phone lines end at the sprawling, barracks-like **monastery of Apóstolos Andhréas**, long a lodestone for Cypriot pilgrims. The spot has been revered since legend credited the Apostle Andrew with summoning forth a spring on the shore during a journey from Palestine, using the water to effect cures. By Byzantine times there was a fortified abbey here, long since disappeared but a plausible alternative to Kantara as the site of Isaac Komnenos's capture by Richard the Lionheart.

The tradition of mass popular pilgrimage, however, only dates from the well-documented experience of **Maria Georgiou**, an Anatolian Greek whose small son was kidnapped by brigands in 1895; seventeen years later the apostle appeared in a dream and commanded her to pray for the boy's return at the monastery. Crossing the straits from Turkey in a crowded boat, Georgiou happened to tell the story to a young dervish passenger, who grew more and more agitated as the narrative progressed. He asked the woman if her lost son had any distinguishing signs, and upon hearing a pair of birthmarks described, cast off his robes to reveal them and embraced her. The son – for he it was – had been raised a Muslim in İstanbul, but upon docking on Cyprus was rebaptized, to general acclaim. Subsequent **miracles** – mostly cures of epilepsy, paralysis and blindness – at the monastery enhanced its prestige and made it enormously wealthy through votive donations. But the faithful never missed the opportunity for a fun day out as well, eventually scandalizing the church into censuring the carnival atmosphere.

All that came to an abrupt end **after 1974**, when the pilgrims' hostel was occupied by the Turkish army, and the monastery shrunk to a pathetic ghost of its former self. For years the place was entirely off-limits to outsiders, but after 1988 it was signposted by yellow-and-black placards ("Manastır") as a tourist attraction, run as a sort of zoo to prove North Cyprus's religious tolerance. "Zoo" is not such an arbitrary characterization, with over fifty cats (still) far outnumbering the population of elderly caretakers, plus (until 1999) several enormous pigs at any given time, raised for sale in the South, and incidentally (one assumes) to annoy the local Muslim population.

Visiting the monastery

From 1996, among "confidence-building" measures instituted jointly by North and South, Greek-Cypriot pilgrims from the South were allowed day-trips to the monastery twice yearly (Aug 15 & Nov 30), coached in under Turkish-Cypriot and UN escort from Ledra Palace as a quid pro quo for Turkish Cypriots making occasional trips to the Hala Sultan Tekke near Larnaca. Unsurprisingly, the complex deteriorated over the decades when the northern regime refused to permit any maintenance; in 2001 repairs supposedly began, under the presumably neutral aegis of the US and UN, though there's little to show for it as yet.

Since April 2003 things have changed at Apóstolos Andhréas, though not as radically as you'd think. Despite almost daily minibus-loads of pilgrims, and well-attended Sunday services (there's a priest now), facilities on the grounds are still limited to a drinks café and a *panayır* (a forest of trinket stalls). You'll always get into the nineteenth-century *katholikón* (donation box), of little intrinsic interest since being fairly comprehensively stripped of its more valuable icons, though lately it's a bit sprucer inside, and full of *támmata* or tin votaries in the shape of the body part or object needing curing or acquisition. But you're unlikely to enter the fifteenth-century **crypt-chapel** below the main church, where the **holy well** of the apostle flows audibly below a heavy stone cover; both Turkish and Greek Cypriots still esteem this water for its therapeutic properties, collecting it from sea-level taps outside.

Zafer Burnu (Cape Apostólou Andhréa)

From the monastery, 5km of rough track brings you to Cyprus's John o' Groats, **Zafer Burnu**, the definitive northeastern tip. A flag-topped, cave-riddled rock, the Neolithic Kastros settlement, was later site of an ancient Aphrodite temple, of which nothing remains; the goddess was by most accounts in a savage aspect here, a siren-like devourer of men in the sea below. Beyond an abandoned guard house and around the offshore **Klidhés (Klides) Islets** (the "Keys"), nested by sea birds, many a ship has been wrecked. Even modern shipping, often evident on the horizon, gives the cape a wide berth.

Travel details

Buses

Famagusta to: Kyrenia (every 30min; 1hr 10min); Nicosia (every 30min; 1hr); Yenierenköy (several daily; 1hr).

Ferries

Famagusta to: Mersin, Turkey (3 weekly, typically Tues, Thurs, Sun at 8.30pm; boat condition poor; 10hr).

Contexts

Contexts

History

The history of Cyprus, strategically located just offshore from the Middle East, can't help but be long and chequered. The following summary is slanted towards antiquity and events of recent decades, enabling a reader to grasp what they are most likely to see in a museum – and on the street.

Beginnings

Settlements of **round stone dwellings** along the north coast and at Khirokitia and Tenta near Larnaca, as well as graves near Parekklishá, indicate habitation as early as 8000 BC; the origins of these first **Neolithic** settlers are uncertain, but items in obsidian, a material unknown on Cyprus, suggest the Middle Eastern mainland opposite. The first Cypriots hunted, farmed and fished, but were ignorant of pottery, fashioning instead rough vessels, idols and jewellery from stone. Religious observance seems to have been limited to **burial practices** – the dead were interred under or near dwellings in a fetal position, with their chests crushed by boulders to prevent them from haunting the living.

Following this initial colonization, a three-millennia-long hiatus in archeo-logical evidence, so far unexplained, ensued until the so-called **Neolithic II** culture appeared after 4500 BC. Sites at Vrysí-Áyios Epíktitos (Çatalköy) near Kyrenia and Sotíra in the south yielded quantities of "red combed" and abstractly painted ware, the first indigenous **ceramics**.

The **Chalcolithic** period, whose cultures emerged after 4000 BC in a gradual transition from the late Neolithic, saw settlement of the previously neglected western portion of Cyprus. The era takes its name from the discovery of copper (*chalkos* in ancient Greek) implements, but more important – as indications of developing **fertility cults** – are limestone female idols at Lémba and Kissónerga, and cruciform grey-green picrolite pendants at Yialiá, reminis-cent of similar work in the west Aegean.

With the dawn of the **Early Bronze Age** (reckoned from 2500 BC onwards), the focus of Cypriot life shifted to the Mesaoría and its perimeter, conveniently near the first **copper mines**, with imported tin permitting the smelting of bronze. Curiously, no confirmed habitation has yet been excavated, but settle-ments have been inferred from the distribution of elaborate subterranean chamber **tombs or shrines** and their contents, especially at Vounous near Kyrenia. Ceramics executed in red clay apparently spread across the island from north to south; deeply incised, whimsical zoomorphic or composite ware, imaginatively combining humorous aesthetics with function, appeared along with cruder models of figures engaged in elaborate religious ceremonies pertaining to a bull-centred fertility cult. The **bull**, brought from Asia, permitted the ploughing of hitherto unusable land, and models show this also.

Well into the second millennium BC, during the so-called **Middle Bronze Age**, settlements appear on the south and east coasts of Cyprus, facing probable **overseas trading** partners; commerce with immediate neighbours, fuelled by the copper deposits, was by now well developed. The most important eastern port was Enkomi-Alasia, the second name soon to be synonymous with the island. Rectangular or L-shaped **dwellings** with flat roofs completely supplanted round ones, and, ominously, **forts** – their inland positioning indicative of civil conflict over the copper trade, rather than of threats from outside – sprang up at various sites around the Mesaoría. Both transport and warfare were facilitated by the recent importation of **horses**. In religious life, female **plank idols**, alone or nursing infants, and bird-headed, earringed figurines were important – the latter probably intended as symbolic companions for interred men, or manifestations of an earth goddess reclaiming one of her children.

The Late Bronze Age

As Cypriot political and commercial transactions got more complicated, a **writing script** became necessary: the earliest known Cypriot document, from the **Late Bronze Age**, is an incised clay sixteenth-century BC tablet unearthed at Enkomi-Alasia. Although the eighty still-undeciphered characters are called **Cypro-Minoan** after their supposed derivation from Cretan Linear A, their origins or language have not been proved. Pottery finds, however, at Toúmba toú Skoúrou and Ayía Iríni on the bay of Mórfou indicate the necessary contacts with Minoan culture. Fragmentary passages were often inscribed on cups, cylinder seals and loomweights, implying common use of the language across Cyprus, though the Enkomi-Alasia tablet remains the only known complete text.

Foreign records, especially Egyptian, suggest that the island was consistently referred to as **Alashiya** (or Asy, or Alasia) by the fifteenth and fourteenth centuries BC and also imply that for the first time Cyprus had a loosely united **confederation** of towns. Of these, **Kition** (modern Larnaca) and **Enkomi-Alasia** came to the fore, their high standard of living reflected in elaborate **sanitary facilities**, including bathtubs and sewers. Two new ceramic styles emerged: so-called "base ring", shiny and thin-walled in imitation of metal, usually with a basal ring; and "white slip", with brown or black patterns executed on a primer coat of white slurry.

Arrival of the Myceneans

The most dramatic change in island culture was prompted by the **arrival of the Myceneans** from Peloponnesian Greece, replacing the Minoans as the main Hellenic influence in the east Mediterranean after 1400 BC. Their immediate influence was most obvious in contemporary **pottery** – "rude style" pictorial *krater*s, showing mythological scenes and bestiaries (including the octopus, a Minoan favourite) – though it's still uncertain whether such items were brought by the Myceneans to trade for copper, or whether their production techniques were adopted by local potters using wheels for the first time. From the same period date the notable enamelled *rhyton* (a horn-shaped drinking vessel – now in the Cyprus Museum) from Kition, with three series of hunters and animals, and the famous silver bowl of Enkomi-Alasia, inlaid with a floral and bull's-head design.

Around 1200 BC, Mycenean civilization in peninsular Greece collapsed, overwhelmed by invading tribes from north of the Black Sea, an event which had a profound knock-on effect in Cyprus. Rogue Mycenean survivors fled Greece via Anatolia, where others joined them to become the raiding "sea peoples" mentioned in Egyptian chronicles of the time. They established an initial foothold on Cyprus at **Maa** (Paleókastro) in the west of the island, choosing a headland easily defensible from both land and sea, and proceeded to destroy Enkomi-Alasia and Kition. Both were soon rebuilt with fortification walls reminiscent of the Mycenean Argolid, with ashlar blocks used for these and individual buildings.

Religious shrines were closely associated with the **copper industry**; in separate temple niches at Enkomi-Alasia were discovered the famous "Horned God", possibly a version of Apollo syncretized with aspects of the indigenous bull-cult, and the so-called "Ingot God", a spear-wielding figure poised atop an ingot shaped like a stretched oxhide, then the standard form of copper export. While Kition was not so spectacularly rewarding in artefacts, the sanctuaries here formed a huge complex of multiple temples with more Middle Eastern characteristics, though again in intimate association with copper forges. Large numbers of **bull skulls** have been found on the floors of all these shrines, implying their use as ceremonial masks – and the retention of bull worship and sacrifice.

At this time the Paleo Paphos **Aphrodite** shrine first attained prominence. Her cult and that of the smithing deity were not so disparate as it might seem: in mainstream Hellenic culture, Aphrodite was married to Hephaestos, the god of fire and metal-working. A voluptuous female bronze statuette found at Enkomi-Alasia is thought to be the consort of the martial ingot deity, and terracotta figurines of the Great Goddess with uplifted arms were among finds at the Kition temples.

In general, Mycenean influence was on the rise in Cyprus even as the same culture died out in its Aegean birthplace. But the immigrants introduced few of their religious practices and conventions wholesale, instead adapting their beliefs to local usage. Mycenean technology did, however, invigorate local **metallurgy**, permitting the fashioning of such exquisite objects as the square, often wheeled stands for libation bowls found at Enkomi and Kourion, their sides intricately decorated in relief figures. The concept of kingship and **city-states** with Hellenic foundation-legends became institutionalized after Mycenean-Anatolian settlement at the seven "capitals" of Salamis, Lapethos, Marion, Soli, Palea Paphos, Kourion and Tamassos; pure or "Eteo-Cypriot" culture retreated to Amathus.

A violent earthquake finished off Mycenean Enkomi-Alasia and Kition around 1050 BC; Palea Paphos continued to be inhabited, but effectively the Bronze Age was over. Not, however, before the Mycenean-tutored island smelters had apparently mastered the working of **iron**, as borne out by large numbers of iron weapons appearing in excavated sites of the early eleventh century.

The Geometric era

The beginning of the **Geometric era** in Cyprus was an echo of the "Dark Ages" in surrounding realms: the Mycenean homeland was now thoroughly overrun by invaders, the Hittite empire of Anatolia had collapsed, and Egypt was stagnant, leaving Cyprus essentially **isolated** for around two centuries. Most Cypriots gravitated towards the Mycenean-founded city-kingdoms, such as Salamis; nearby Enkomi-Alasia was gradually abandoned after the mid-eleventh-century earthquake, which rendered its harbour unusable.

Despite the cultural doldrums, early Geometric **pottery** is quite startling; cups and shallow dishes were popular, painted boldly in black rings, very occasionally with human or animal figures. **Funerary customs** show Mycenean habits, especially among the population descended from immigrants: chamber tombs were approached by long *dromoi* or passages, and slaves were occasionally sacrificed to serve their deceased master. Cremations took place at Kourion, while ossuary urns were filled with old bones when reusing a tomb – an increasingly common strategy. In one grave at Palea Paphos, **syllabic Greek script** was found for the first time on a meat skewer, spelling the name of the deceased in Arcadian dialect – partial confirmation of the foundation myth of Palea Paphos by Agapinor, leader of the Arcadian contingent in the Trojan war.

Following stabilization in the west Aegean around 800 BC, trade and other **contacts resumed** between Greece – particularly Euboea – and the indigenous or Eteo-Cypriot centre of Amathus, more extroverted than the Myceno-Cypriot centres. Further fresh input was provided by the peaceful **Phoenician** resettlement of Kition, whose temples had never been completely abandoned even after the natural disaster of the eleventh century. The Phoenicians, an up-and-coming mercantile empire of the Middle East, rededicated these shrines to Astarte, the oriental version of Aphrodite; the **multiple sanctuary**, rebuilt after a fire in 800, was the fulcrum of Phoenician culture on Cyprus, with worship continuing until 312 BC. Not surprisingly, bichrome pottery of the eighth century BC throughout the island shows Phoenician characteristics of dress style and activities.

These exceptions aside, Geometric culture on Cyprus was **deeply conservative** – Mycenean observances, even when melded with Eteo-Cypriot expression, maintained static or even retrospective forms, a trend accentuated by the two-century gap in communication with the outside world. The seven city-states were ruled by despotic monarchies, unmindful of the recent experiments in representative government in Greece; the Arcadian dialect continued to be written in syllabic script, rather than a true alphabet, until the fourth century BC.

No better demonstration of this traditionalism can be found than the Salamis **royal tombs** of just before 700 BC, where the details of several burials seem to have been taken from public readings of Homer. The grave artefacts themselves are manifestly Oriental, in a blend of Phoenician and Egyptian styles, reflecting the royal taste of the time; but the numerous roasting spits (similar to the inscribed one at Palea Paphos), the skeletons of sacrificed chariot-horses at the entrance to tombs, and great bronze cauldrons containing the ashes of cremated royalty can only be accounted for in the light of the Homeric epics. Here was a perhaps politically motivated revival of the presumed funerary customs of the Trojan War character Teukros, the reputed Mycenaean founder of Salamis.

Ancient zenith: the Archaic era

The start (750 BC) of the **Archaic era** on Cyprus arguably overlapped the end of Geometric by half a century, but the signal event was the island's domination by the **Assyrians** between 708 and 669 BC; however, Cypriot kings were merely required to forward tribute regularly, and this episode left little trace on island life other than some suggestive beards and hairstyles in later sculpture. Upon the departure of the Assyrians, a century of **flourishing independence** followed, producing some of the finest ancient Cypriot art, combining innate inventiveness with a receptivity to surrounding influences.

Art and religion

Archaic Cyprus excelled for the first time in large-scale limestone **sculpture**, which exhibited strong similarities to that of Ionia in Asia Minor. Figures were nearly always robed in the Ionian manner, rarely nude, with great attention paid to facial expression – contrasting with an often cursory rendering of body anatomy. Large almond-shaped eyes, prominent eyebrows and more than a trace of the celebrated "Archaic smile" were often conjoined with Asiatic hair- and beard-styles, bound by head bands or, later, elaborate head-dresses. A famous example is the **statue of Zeus Keraunios** (Thunderbolt-Hurler) from Kition. Female statue-heads were adorned with suggestions of **jewellery** matching in all respects exquisitely worked gold and precious-stone originals which have been found. **Pottery** advanced from the abstract to bichrome figurative ware, especially the so-called "free-field" style, where single, well-detailed animal or human figures are rampant on a bare background.

Religious observance in Archaic Cyprus varied considerably, a function of the increasing number of foreigners visiting or living on the island. In contrast to cosmopolitan ports where the Greek Olympian deities and exotic foreign gods like the Egyptian Bes or Phoenician Astarte competed for devotees, the important **rural shrines** of the seventh and sixth centuries were more conservative in their adoration of old chthonic gods, or localized variants of imported divinities. The Phoenicians had their own rural cult, in addition to the Kition temples: that of Baal Hamman at Méniko, in the middle of the island near the copper mines they controlled, though it displayed many elements – such as bull sacrifice – of native Cypriot religion. The other most important sanctuaries were that of Apollo Hylates near Kourion and the long-venerated shrine at Ayía Iríni (Akdeniz), where two thousand terracotta figurines were discovered.

Such **figurines** were typically arranged as ex votos around the altar of the usually simple courtyard shrines; in accord with Cypriot belief that the deity often resided in the temple, these clay figures served as permanent worshippers, ready for the divine presence. Some of the terracottas were realistically modelled for individual detail, and so have been taken to be gifts of a particular worshipper, made to order at workshops adjacent to the shrines. Figurines of musicians and women in various attitudes (including childbirth) accumulated logically enough at Aphrodite or mother-goddess shrines, while the preferred offerings to male deities – and the bulk of the finds at Ayía Iríni – were bulls, horse-drawn chariots or helmeted warriors.

Persian influence

The sixth century BC saw a brief interval of direct Egyptian rule which, while stricter than the Assyrian era, left a similarly subtle legacy in the form of more outlandish beards or head-dresses on statues. Monumentally, this period is characterized by the strange subterranean "house" tombs at Tamassos, possibly built by Anatolian masons. The newest Asian power on the horizon, the **Persians**, assumed control over Egypt in 545 BC; with their existing ties to the Middle East through the Phoenicians, and relatively weak military resources, it was easy (and prudent) for the Cypriot kingdoms to reach a vassalage arrangement with King Cyrus in 545 BC. Yet a measure of autonomy was preserved, and Evelthon, the late sixth-century king of Salamis, even minted his own coinage.

In 499 BC, however, this *modus vivendi* dissolved as Persian rule under Darius became harsher and the non-Phoenician Cypriots joined the **revolt** of the Ionian cities. **Onesilos of Salamis** mutinied against his brother the Persian puppet-king and rallied the other Myceno-Cypriot city-kingdoms, but this hastily patched-together confederation, despite land and sea reinforcements from the Ionians, was defeated in a major battle at Salamis, largely due to the treachery of the Kourion contingent. Onesilos' head was stuck on the city gate of pro-Persian Amathus as a warning to other would-be rebels, though after it filled with honeycomb an oracle advised the townspeople to bury it and revere his memory. After this battle, each remaining Cypriot city-kingdom except Kition was besieged one by one, Soli and Palea Paphos being the last to capitulate in 498; a prolonged resistance against the mighty Persian empire made possible by vastly improved stone and mud-brick fortifications. **Pro-Persian Phoenicians** took the opportunity to extend their influence northward, installing kings on the thrones of Marion and Lapethos; in the aftermath of the revolt, the hilltop palace of Vouni was also built by the king of Marion to intimidate nearby pro-Hellenic Soli. Cyprus would not be independent and united again until the twentieth century.

Decline: Classical Cyprus

By the start of the fifth century BC, Cyprus had ten **city-kingdoms**: Kyrenia, Idalion, Amathus and Kition were added to the Myceno-Cypriot seven, with Soli subsumed into Marion. The island now became thoroughly embroiled in the struggle between Greece and Persia; **Athens** repeatedly sent forces to "liberate" Cyprus, but the distance involved, plus pro-Persian factions on the island, made any victories transient. The Athenian general **Kimon** led three expeditions against the pro-Persian strongholds of Marion, Salamis and Kition, dying at the hour of victory on his last attempt in 449 BC, outside the walls of Kition. Deprived of leadership, the Greeks sailed home, and the next year the Athenians signed a treaty with the Persians agreeing to drop the matter.

But if the political results of these campaigns were minuscule – the palace at Vouni was rebuilt to a nostalgic Mycenean plan, though oligarchic, dynastic rule continued at most city-kingdoms whether pro-Greek or not – profound **cultural effects** attended the five decades of contact with Greece. A craze for Attic art swept the island in everything from pottery – imported via Marion and Salamis – to coinage, to the marked detriment of local creativity. Sarcophagi and Attic-style memorial *stelae* began to rival rock-cut tombs in popularity; the worship of Herakles and Athena as deities came into vogue, and many Phoenician divinities acquired a Hellenic veneer.

Before the truce, however, the Phoenician regime at Kition, perennial allies of the Persians, had again struck northwards, taking Idalion in 470 BC. The Persians took the peace itself as a cue to again tighten their control on the island, and the stage was set for the emergence of a great Cypriot patriot and political genius, **Evagoras I of Salamis**. Born in 435, at the age of 24 he overthrew the Phoenician puppet-king of that city, but skilful diplomatic spadework and judicious payment of tribute to the Persians ensured no repercussions then or for a long time after, giving him the necessary breathing space to build up his defences and elaborate sophisticated intrigues. Though fiercely pro-Hellenic, he was able to act simultaneously as a mediator between the Athenians and the Persians, even convincing the latter to lend him a fleet for use against the Spartans on behalf of Athens, which duly honoured him after victory was accomplished. Evagoras' court became a haven for Attic artists and soldiers in exile, voluntary or otherwise, and he vigorously promoted Greek culture throughout his expanding dominions, including the introduction of the **Greek alphabet**, which slowly replaced the Cypriot syllabic script over the next century.

His conduct of domestic statecraft, however, tended towards the megalo-maniac; in attempting to forcibly **unite** all the Cypriot city-kingdoms, Evagoras alienated Kition, Amathus and Soli sufficiently that they appealed for help to the Persians. Evagoras had finally overreached himself; despite some aid from the Athenians, he failed to depose the king of Kition, and another treaty in 386 between Greeks and Persians, acknowledging the latter's hegemony over the island, left him to confront the eastern empire effectively alone. But with some support from Anatolian Greek city-states he managed to carry the fight to the enemy's home court by landing on the Syrian coast. Though the Persians returned to Cyprus in force in 381, sacking Salamis, Evagoras battled them to a stalemate and negotiated relatively favourable surrender terms, keeping his throne. He and his eldest son were apparently murdered in a domestic plot at Salamis in 374 BC; he was a hard act to follow, and Evagoras' descendants were comparatively insignificant, not having his touch in handling the Persians – least of all in another abortive revolt of 351. Of his **successors** only Pytagoras salvaged a shred of dignity as a culturally pro-Hellenic vassal king of the Persians, ushering in the Hellenistic era.

Recovery: Hellenistic-Roman Cyprus

When **Alexander the Great** appeared on the scene in 333, the Cypriot city-kingdoms responded unequivocally, furnishing 120 ships for his successful siege of Persian Tyre. But following his general victory in the east Mediterranean it soon became clear that, while finally rid of the Persians, Cyprus was now a subordinated part of the Hellenistic empire, without even the minimal freedoms which had been conceded under their old masters.

When Alexander died in 323, the island became a battleground for his successors **Ptolemy** and **Antigonos**; the city-kingdoms divided their support, and **civil war** was the result. Ptolemy's forces initially prevailed, and losing-side cities – Kition, Marion, Lapethos and Kyrenia – were razed or severely punished. **Nicocreon**, the pro-Hellenic king of Salamis, was promoted for his loyalty, but in 311 he was denounced for plotting with Antigonos, and Ptolemy sent an army under his deputy Menelaos to besiege Salamis. Rather than surrender, Nicocreon and his family set their palace alight and committed suicide, so the truth of the accusations remains uncertain; in any event the dynasty founded by Teukros died with them.

Antigonos's adherents were still very much in the picture, though, and the dynastic war continued in the person of his son Demetrios Polyorketes, who defeated both Ptolemy and Menelaos and single-handedly ruled the island from 306 to 294. The pendulum swung back one final time, however, for when Antigonid forces let their guard down momentarily, Ptolemy I Soter of Egypt – as he now styled himself – retook Cyprus, commencing two and a half centuries of relatively peaceful and prosperous Ptolemaic, **Egyptian-based rule**.

Cyprus became essentially a province of the Alexandria-based kingdom, exploited for its copper, timber, corn and wine, and administered by a military governor based first at Salamis, later at Nea Paphos. All city-kingdoms were now defunct, replaced by four **administrative districts** and uniform coinage for the whole island; its cultural life was now thoroughly Hellenized, with the usual range of athletic, dramatic and musical events. To existing religious life were added the cult of deified Ptolemaic royalty and a fresh infusion of Egyptian gods. Art was largely derived from Alexandrian models, with little originality evident. Portraits in the soft local limestone or terracotta made up the majority of statuary, with the marble work common elsewhere in the Hellenistic world relatively rare. The only idiosyncratic expressions were in funerary architecture, especially at Nea Paphos, where the subterranean "Tombs of the Kings" were a blend of Macedonian and Middle Eastern styles.

During the first century BC, the decline of the Ptolemies was matched by the growing power of republican **Rome**, which annexed Cyprus in 58 BC; in a see-saw of fortunes the island reverted to Egyptian control twice, but Roman rule was consolidated in the imperial period after 31 BC. The *Koinon Kyprion* or civic league of the Ptolemies continued functioning, charged with co-ordinating religious festivals, including emperor-worship. The four Ptolemaic districts were also retained, but Cyprus as a whole was administered as a senatorial province through a proconsul (among them the orator Cicero), still based at Nea Paphos. Salamis, however, remained the most important commercial centre on the island, with a population of over a quarter of a million.

Hellenistic **stability and prosperity** continued, permitting massive public works, some redone several times in the wake of earthquakes; Roman roads (except for traces), bridges and aqueducts have long since vanished, but their gymnasia, theatres and baths constitute most of the archeological heritage visible on Cyprus today. Wealthier private citizens also commissioned major projects, like the sophisticated villa-floor **mosaics** at Nea Paphos. Otherwise, however, not much effort was expended to Latinize the island – Greek continued to be used as the official language – and as a largely self-sufficient backwater, Cyprus took little part in the larger affairs of the Roman empire.

Christianity and the Byzantine era

Christianity came early (45 AD) to Cyprus, which was evangelized by the apostles Paul and Barnabas, the latter a native of Salamis. The pair ordained Iraklidhios of Tamassos as the island's first bishop, and supposedly converted Sergius Paulus, proconsul at Nea Paphos. Barnabas was subsequently martyred by the Jews of Salamis, who participated in the major **Jewish rebellion** which swept across the entire Middle East in 116 AD. Cyprus was particularly hard hit since, being politically and militarily insignificant, it was lightly garrisoned; some accounts report Salamis' entire gentile population slaughtered by the rebels. The insurrection was finally put down by Hadrian, and a decree promulgated expelling all Jews from Cyprus. Yet Christianity spread slowly on the island, as suggested by the enthusiastically pagan Paphos mosaics – executed on the eve of Emperor Constantine's designation of Christianity as the preferred religion of the eastern empire in 323.

The Roman empire had been divided into **western and eastern portions** in 284, and local Cypriot administration transferred to Antioch in Syria – a situation which would last until the fifth century, when the opportune discovery of the relics of Barnabas (see p.351) provided justification for Cyprus's **ecclesiastic and civic autonomy**, answerable only to the capital of the eastern empire, Constantinople. Cyprus's prestige was further enhanced by the visit in 324 of Helena, Constantine's mother, who as legend has it left fragments of the True Cross and the cross of the penitent thief.

The break with antiquity was punctuated not only by a new faith and governmental order, but by two cataclysmic **earthquakes** – in 332 and 365 – which destroyed most Cypriot towns. Rebuilt Salamis was renamed Constantia, and again designated capital of the island. As elsewhere in **Byzantium** – that portion of the empire centred on Constantinople – some of the more inhumane pagan-Roman laws were repealed, and mass conversion to Christianity proceeded apace, as evidenced by the huge fifth- and sixth-century basilica-type cathedrals erected in all towns. Foundations and **mosaic floors** for many of these are the most attractive early Byzantine remains on Cyprus; little else survives, however, owing to the repeated, devastating **raids** of the **Arab caliphate**, beginning in the seventh century AD. Their intent was not to conquer outright but to pillage, and to neutralize Cyprus as a Byzantine strong-point; the Arabs' only significant legacy is the Hala Sultan Tekke near Larnaca.

An immediate result of the raids was the **abandonment** of most coastal cities, which were far too vulnerable, as well as plague- and drought-ridden. By the terms of an **Arab-Byzantine treaty**, the island was to accept Muslim settlers, remain demilitarized except for naval bases of each side and pay taxes equally to both the caliphate and the Byzantine empire. Except for occasional skirmishes, this strange condominium agreement endured for three centuries, while Cyprus thrived on its silk trade and food exports, and served as a convenient place to exile dissidents from both Constantinople and the caliphate.

Only in 963 did Byzantine Emperor **Nikiphoros Phokas** permanently end Arab co-rule on Cyprus, and the Muslim colonists left or converted to Christianity. For another two centuries Cyprus had a peaceful, if heavily taxed, respite as a fully-fledged province of Byzantium, during which most of its **existing towns** – Kyrenia, Famagusta, Nicosia, Limassol – were founded or grew suddenly, with formidable **castles** raised against the threat of further attacks. At the same time, in the Tróödhos mountains, the first **frescoed chapels** were endowed by wealthy private donors.

Western Latin rule

Trouble loomed again in the eleventh century, however; the 1054 **schism** between the Catholic and Orthodox churches fostered political antagonism between the Byzantine empire and most Latin principalities, and after their defeat of the Byzantines at the Battle of Manzikert in 1073, the **Seljuk Turks** were able to spread south and occupy the Holy Land. In response, the **First Crusade** was organized in western Europe during 1095, and Cyprus lay near or astride the Latin knights' path towards the infidels. Although the first two Crusades bypassed the island, the knights soon established mini-kingdoms in Palestine, and the Seljuks also occupied most of Anatolia, allowing a capricious Byzantine prince, **Isaac Komnenos**, to declare Cypriot independence from a fatally weakened Constantinople in 1184 and reign for seven years. Greedy, cruel and unpopular, he was hardly an improvement on the succession of incompetent and unstable emperors in the capital; this misrule made Cyprus a ripe plum for the Crusaders.

In April 1191 a small fleet bearing the sister and fiancée of **Richard the Lionheart** of England hove to off Limassol. Isaac, realizing their value as hostages, tried to inveigle the two women ashore, but they wisely declined; he then refused them provisions. When the English king himself appeared, he landed in some force, considering his kinswomen to have been gravely insulted. After unsuccessfully attempting to secure Isaac's co-operation in the Third Crusade, Richard and friends pursued the Byzantine forces across the island, defeating them at the battle of Tremetoushá on the Mesaoría; Isaac surrendered at the end of May, sent away in silver chains on his insistence that he not be put in irons. Richard had never intended to acquire Cyprus, and was still keen to resume crusading; having plundered the island, he flogged it to the **Knights Templar** to raise funds for his army. The Templars put forty percent of the purchase price down and had to raise the balance by confiscatory taxation; the Cypriots not unnaturally rebelled, with the knights quelling the revolt brutally to save their skins.

Having received rather more than they'd bargained for, the Templars returned Cyprus to Richard, who quickly resold it to **Guy de Lusignan**, a minor French noble who had been Jerusalem's last Crusader king before losing the city to Saladin in 1187. Cyprus was essentially his consolation prize; Guy recreated the feudal system of his lost realm, parcelling out fiefs to more than five hundred supporters – principally landless allies without future prospects in what remained of Crusader Syria – and the **Knights Hospitallers of St John**, who soon displaced the Templars. Guy's brother and successor **Aimery** styled himself **king of Cyprus and Jerusalem**, the latter an honorary title used by all subsequent Lusignan rulers, though the Holy City went permanently back to Muslim control after 1244.

The Lusignans

Under the **Lusignans**, Cyprus acquired a **significance** far out of proportion to its size. European sovereigns, including **Holy Roman Emperor Frederick II Hohenstaufen**, stopped off obligatorily during subsequent Crusades, and the Lusignans – and their deputies the **Ibelins** – married into all the royal houses of Europe. **Regencies** for under-age princes were common, owing to the short life-expectancy of Crusader kings; an unusually long regency for Henry I in the early thirteenth century caused complications, obliging the Ibelin regents to defend Henry's title to the throne in a prolonged war against counter-claimant Frederick II Hohenstaufen.

Monumentally, the Byzantine **castles** of the Kyrenia range were refurbished, and new ones built around the capital Nicosia and the eastern port of Famagusta, which after the **1291 loss** of Acre, Sidon and Tyre, the last Crusader toeholds in the Holy Land, saw an influx of Christian refugees from across the Near East. For barely a century **Famagusta** served as the easternmost outpost of Christendom, and became one of the world's wealthiest cities owing to a papal prohibition on direct European trade with the nearby infidel. No longer having to siphon off resources to defend a slender Syrian coastal strip also improved the military and financial health of the Cypriot kingdom. The Lusignan royalty were crowned in two massive Gothic **cathedrals** at Nicosia and Famagusta: coronations for the Kingdom of Cyprus were conducted at Nicosia; at Famagusta, opposite the Holy Land, the honorary ceremony for Jerusalem took place. All major **monastic orders** were represented, though the sole surviving foundation is Béllapais abbey.

The nobility's **everyday life** was notorious for its luxury and ostentation, privileges definitely not shared by the common people. The Greek Orthodox population, which had initially welcomed the Crusaders, soon found itself effectively excluded from power or material security. Most lived as **serfs** of the Catholic overlords, and by a papal edict of 1260 the Orthodox archbishops were **subordinated** to a Catholic metropolitan and furthermore exiled to rural sees. Orthodoxy was limited to a rearguard holding action, awaiting a change in its fortunes; yet during this time many of the finest frescoes were painted in rural chapels of the Tróödhos Mountains.

▲ Famagusta's St Nicolas cathedral, converted for Muslim use as Lala Mustafa Paşa Camii

In general, the Lusignan **kings** were a visibly overweight, mediocre bunch, traits probably resulting from a combination of hereditary thyroid problems with "riotous and unclean living", as one historian of the time put it. The most extravagant sovereign was **Peter I** (reigned 1358–69) who, in contrast to the live-and-let-live attitude of his lethargic predecessors, canvassed Europe for support for his mini-Crusades along the neighbouring Muslim coasts, culminating in a thorough sacking of Alexandria in 1365. An inveterate womanizer, he was in the arms of one of his two mistresses when certain nobles, tired of his increasingly erratic behaviour and disregard for feudal law, burst into the bedchamber and murdered him.

Decline followed Peter's murder, though that was more the last straw than the root cause. If the Lusignans governed the Cypriot kingdom, the Venetians and Genoese were rivals for supremacy in its commercial life; at the 1373 Famagusta coronation of Peter II, a dispute between the two factions over who would have the honour of leading the young king's horse escalated into destructive anti-Genoese riots. Incensed, **Genoa** sent a punitive expedition to ravage the island. For a year de facto civil war raged, ending with the return of the throne to the Lusignans only on payment of a huge indemnity – though the royal family was actually held prisoner in Genoa for eighteen years – and the retention of Famagusta by the Genoese. But the damage had been done; both Cyprus and the Lusignans were disastrously weakened economically and politically.

A harbinger of worse "infidel" attacks to come occurred in 1425–26, when the **Mamelukes** of Egypt, still smarting from Peter I's attack on Alexandria, landed on the south coast to plunder Limassol and Larnaca. **King Janus** confronted them near Stavrovoúni monastery, but was defeated and taken prisoner; the Mamelukes continued inland to sack Nicosia before returning with their treasure to Egypt. Janus was only released three years later after payment of a huge ransom and a humiliating promise of perpetual tribute to the Mamelukes.

With Janus's dissolute successor **John II**, the Lusignan saga entered its last chapters. He complicated matters by favouring his bastard son, **James II**, over his legitimate daughter **Charlotte**, and after John died in 1458 his strong-willed offspring spent six years disputing the succession. Securing Mameluke aid – which in effect meant an extension of the onerous tribute – James returned from Egypt and deposed his sister; he followed this by finally evicting the Genoese from Famagusta, though it was far too late to restore that town to its former importance. A roistering, athletic man, James was relatively popular with his subjects for both his daring exploits and his fluency in **Greek**; indeed the language had recently begun to replace French in public use.

James did not run true to family form in his own choice of consort, marrying a Venetian noblewoman, **Caterina Cornaro**. Both the king and his infant son died mysteriously within a year of each other (1473 & 1474) – Venetian poisoning has been suggested – leaving Queen Caterina to reign precariously in her own right. Charlotte, in exile, intrigued ceaselessly against Caterina until Charlotte died in 1485. Besides her foiled plot to assassinate Caterina, there was a Catalan-fomented rebellion in 1473. All this, and the growing **Ottoman threat**, convinced the Venetians that Caterina was better out of the way, and she was persuaded to **abdicate** in 1489, being given as a sop the town and hinterland of Asolo in the Veneto, where she continued to keep a court of some splendour.

The Venetians

Three centuries of Lusignan rule were over and the **Venetians** now governed the island directly through a *proveditore* or **military governor**. Their tenure was even more oppressive than the Lusignan one from the point of view of ordinary people; Cyprus was seen simply as a frontier fortress and money-spinner, the island otherwise being neglected and inefficiently administered. The Lusignan nobility retained their estates but were excluded from political power. The Venetians devoted most of their energy to overhauling the fortifications of Kyrenia, Nicosia and Famagusta in anticipation of the inevitable Ottoman attack. In the end, however, the undermanned Venetian forces were no match for the Turkish hordes, especially when relief failed to arrive from Venice: Nicosia fell after a seven-week **siege** in 1570, with almost half its population subsequently massacred, while Famagusta held out for ten months until July 1571 in one of the celebrated battles of the age (see box, p.341). The victor, **Lala Mustafa Paşa**, perhaps irked at having been so valiantly defied by the tiny garrison, reneged on his promises of clemency, flaying commander **Marcantonio Bragadino** alive after butchering his lieutenants.

Surrounded on three sides by Ottoman territory, it was almost certain that Cyprus would eventually fall to the Muslim power, but the specific impetus for the 1570–71 campaign is interesting. The incumbent sultan, **Selim the Sot**, had a particular fondness for Cypriot Commandaria wine; his chief adviser, **Joseph Nasi**, was a Spanish Jew whose family had suffered at the hands of the Venetians during their long exile after the 1492 expulsion, and who longed to take revenge – and perhaps secure a haven for Jewry. The invasion plan was hatched over the objections of the grand vizier and others, who considered it unfeasible, and feared the wrath of the European powers. Selim died just three years later, fracturing his skull by slipping in his bath – while drunk on Commandaria.

Stagnation: Ottoman rule

Because the Lusignans had never made any attempt to bridge the gap between ruler and ruled, they remained an unassimilated upper crust, all trace of which was swept away by the Turkish conquest. By 1573 most of the monasteries and Latin churches had been destroyed, and most surviving **Catholics** had departed or converted to Islam; the tiny "Latin" minority in today's Cyprus is all that survives from this era. Other ancestors of the present **Turkish population** date from the year of the conquest, when Ottoman soldiers and their families formed the nucleus, some twenty thousand strong, of initial settlement, later supplemented by civilians from Anatolia (see box, p.380). Their relations with the native Greek population were, if not always close, usually cordial.

The Greek Orthodox peasantry, perhaps surprisingly in the light of later events, actually **welcomed** the Ottomans at first; both shared a hatred of the Franks, whose feudal system was abolished and lands distributed to the freed serfs. The Greeks also appreciated Ottoman **recognition of their Church:** not only were certain Catholic ecclesiastical properties made over to Orthodoxy, but in 1660 the archbishop was officially acknowledged as the head of the Greek community in accord with prevailing Ottoman administrative practice, with the right of direct petition to the sultan. This was followed in 1754 by the revival of the role of **ethnarch**, with comprehensive civil powers, and in 1779 by the stipulation for a **dragoman**, a Greek appointed by the ethnarch to liaise with the island's Turkish governor. The most powerful and famous dragoman was **Hadjiyeorgakis Kornesios** (see p.252).

None of this, however, was done in a spirit of disinterested religious tolerance; the Ottomans used the ecclesiastical apparatus principally to collect onerous **taxes**, and the clerics, who eventually all but ran the island together with the dragoman, made themselves every bit as unpopular as the Muslim governors. In fairness, the clergy often attempted to protect their flock from the more rapacious exactions of the various governors, who – minimally salaried and having paid huge bribes to secure their short-term appointments – were expected to recoup their expenses with exactions from the populace. People unable to meet assessments forfeited **land** in lieu of payment, the original source of the Orthodox Church's still-extensive real-estate holdings.

If the Greeks had hoped for a definitive improvement in their lot with the end of Frankish rule, they were thoroughly disillusioned, as Cyprus became one of the **worst-governed and neglected** Ottoman provinces. Almost all tax revenues went to İstanbul, with next to nothing spent to abate the drought, plagues and locusts which lashed the island, or on other local improvements; Turkish medieval monuments are rare on Cyprus, reflecting the island's low prestige. Between 1571 and the late 1700s the population dropped sharply, with many Greeks **emigrating** to Anatolia or the Balkans despite administrative reshuffles aimed at staunching the outflow.

These conditions ensured that the three Ottoman centuries were punctuated by regular **rebellions**, which often united Muslim and Christian peasantry against their overlords. The first occurred in 1680; in 1764 the excesses of the worst governor, **Çil Osman**, precipitated a longer and bloodier revolt in which he was killed, the Turkish commander of Kyrenia mutinied, and the Greek bishops appealed to İstanbul for the restoration of order. With the rise of Balkan nationalism later that century, the *Filikí Etería* (Friendly Society), the Greek revolutionary fifth column, was active on Cyprus after 1810. To forestall any echo of the

Who are the Turkish Cypriots?

The number of **Muslims** on Cyprus, even during the most vigorous periods of Ottoman rule, never exceeded about one-third of the population, and had already declined to about one-quarter when the British arrived in 1878. The word "Muslim" is used deliberately, since religious affiliation, not race or ethnicity, was the determining civic factor in the Ottoman empire; the present-day Turkish Cypriots are in fact descended from various sources.

At the time of the 1571 conquest, Ottoman **civil servants** arrived with their families, whose descendants tend to preserve their aristocratic consciousness to this day. Some twenty thousand **janissaries**, by definition of Anatolian or Balkan Christian origins and adherents of the Bektashi dervish order, took as wives the widows of the defeated Venetians, as well as a number of Orthodox Christian virgins. Roughly another ten thousand civilian transportees from Anatolia consisted of skilled, town-dwelling craftsmen, landless farmers, **Turkmen** nomads brought over for the sake of their reed- and textile-weaving skills, **Alevî** mountaineers, and various prison convicts transported to a more comfortable exile on Cyprus. **Africans** from Sudan also arrived, mostly working as porters in and around Larnaca and Limassol, and obliged by local colour consciousness to marry less desirable, "low-class" women. Muslim **Gypsies** tagged along from Anatolia, and while allowed to settle, they were (and are) discriminated against as much as anywhere else in the Balkans – despite taking the Turkish-Cypriot side in the battles of recent decades.

The so-called **Linovamváki** (Cotton-Linen) sect, which practised Islam outwardly but maintained Christian beliefs (including baptism) in private, arose mainly among Venetian civilians (names like Mehmet Valentino occur in old archives); curiously, they spoke Greek in preference to Turkish, and many villages such as Áyios Ioánnis, Monágri, Louroujína (today Akıncılar in the North), Vrécha and most of the Tillyría region were once almost exclusively inhabited by Linovamváki. After 1878, evangelization of this group by both Muslim and Christian clerics, and the resulting assimilative marriages, resulted in a hitherto unknown polarization in island society; in the North today, many of the more fanatical nationalists are in fact of Linovamváki background, eager to deny a practice – propitiation of all local deities without prejudice – which was once common in the Ottoman empire.

A more recent development is proselytization by the **Bahai** faith, with approximately five hundred adherents in the North. It was founded by the adoptive son of the holy man Mirza Ali Mohammed (Al-Bab), hanged as a troublemaker by the Iranian shah in 1850. Al-Bab's biological son, Süphi Ezel, was exiled first to Edirne, then to Famagusta, and while the **Ezeli** rite is no longer a vital religion in the North, his tomb remains a focus of pilgrimage for Iranian believers.

There are also a number of "**Palestinian**" – or rather part-Palestinian – northerners, descendants of Turkish-Cypriot women who, during the 1930s Depression, amid dire conditions on the island, were married off to Arab Muslims in Palestine; after its partition in 1948, many returned with their husbands and families.

Given these motley, often "heretical" origins of the Turkish Cypriots (the janissaries and Alevîs being particularly tolerant of alcohol consumption), it's hardly surprising that observance of orthodox Islam on Cyprus has always been lax – despite recent Saudi agitation – and that fervent Turkish nationalism had to be whipped up by outsiders after World War II.

mainland Greek rebellion, Governor **Küçük Mehmet** got permission from the sultan in 1821 to execute the unusually popular **Archbishop Kyprianos**, his three bishops and hundreds of leading Greek Orthodox islanders in Nicosia, not so coincidentally confiscating their considerable property and inaugurating another spell of unrest on the island, which ended in the revolt of 1833.

Such incidents were not repeated after European powers established more trading posts and watchful consulates at Larnaca, and the Church's power **waned slightly** with the suspension of its right to collect taxes and the emergence of an educated, westernized class of Greek Cypriot. As the nineteenth century wore on, **Britain** found itself repeatedly guaranteeing the Ottoman empire's territorial integrity in the path of Russian expansionism; in 1878, this relationship was formalized by the **Anglo-Turkish Convention**, whereby the Ottomans ceded occupation and administrative rights of Cyprus – though technically not sovereignty – to Britain in return for having halted the Russian advance outside Bstanbul during the 1877–78 Russo-Turkish war, and for a continued undertaking to help defend what was left of Turkish domains. Curiously, Britain's retention of Cyprus was **linked** to Russia's occupation of Ardahan, Kars and Batumi, three strongpoints on Turkey's Caucasian frontier; Kars and Ardahan were returned to republican Turkey in 1921, but in the NATO era Turkey's and Britain's continued alliance against the Russian threat still served as ostensible justification for the latter's occupation of Cyprus.

British rule

British forces landed peacefully at Larnaca in July 1878, assuming control of the island without incident; ironically, the British acquisition of Egypt and the Suez Canal in 1882 made Cyprus of secondary importance as a **military base**, with civilian high commissioners soon replacing military ones. The Greek Orthodox population, appreciating Britain's cession of the Ionian islands to Greece in 1864, hoped for the same largesse here, and the Bishop of Kition's greeting speech to the landing party alluded directly to this. Free of the threat of Ottoman repression, demands for **énosis** (union) with Greece were reiterated regularly by Greek Cypriots until 1960 – and beyond. By contrast, from the very outset of the colonial period Turkish Cypriots expressed their satisfaction with the status quo and horror at the prospect of being Greek citizens.

What the Cypriots got instead, aside from separate Greek- and Turkish-language education, was a modicum of **better government** – reafforestation, an end to banditry and extralegal extortion, an English legal system, water supplies, roads and quelling of disease and locusts – combined with a continuance of **crushing taxes**, which precluded any striking economic growth. An obscure clause of the Anglo-Turkish Convention mandated that the excess of tax revenues (appreciable) over local expenditures (almost nil) during the last five years of Ottoman rule was theoretically to be paid to the sultan's government, a rule which pressured colonial administrators to keep programmes modest so as to have some sum to forward – or to squeeze the Cypriots for more taxes. The practice was widely condemned by Cypriophiles and Turkophobes in England, including Gladstone and Churchill, but amazingly continued until 1927. Worse still, the monies went not to İstanbul, but to bondholders of an 1855 loan to Turkey on which the Ottoman regime had defaulted. So while Cyprus regained its former population level, the British-promised prosperity never appeared, the islanders in effect being required to **service an Ottoman debt**. The only apparatus of self-government was a rudimentary **legislative council**, numerically weighted towards colonial civil servants and with very limited powers.

Following Ottoman Turkey's 1914 entry into World War I as one of the Central Powers, Britain declared most provisions of the Anglo-Turkish Convention void, and formally **annexed** Cyprus. The next year she secretly offered it to Greece as an inducement to join the war on the Allied side, but Greece, then ruled by pro-German King Constantine I, declined, to the Greek Cypriots' infinite later regret. In the 1923 Treaty of Lausanne, republican Turkey renounced all claims to Cyprus, but the island did not officially become a colony until 1925, by which time calls for *énosis* were again being heard. These increased in stridency, leading in **1931** to the first serious **civil disturbances**: the Greek-Cypriot members of the legislative council resigned, and rioters burned down the Government House, a rambling bungalow diverted from use in Ceylon. The Cypriots' anger was not only sparked by the *énosis* issue, but also from disappointment at the modest level of material progress under British rule, especially the woebegone state of agriculture.

Advent of the Left

The British **response** to the mini-rebellion was predictably harsh: reparations levies for damages, bans on publications and flying the Greek flag, proscriptions of existing political parties (especially the KKK or Communists, who had organized strikes in 1929 at the Tróödhos asbestos mines), and imprisonment or deportation of activists – including two bishops. The legislative council was abolished, and Cyprus came under the nearest thing to martial law; only the **PEO** or Pancyprian Federation of Labour, though driven underground until 1936, remained as a pole of opposition to the colonial regime, and a haven for left-wing Turkish and Greek Cypriot alike. **AKEL**, the new **communist party**, grew out of it in 1941, and has remained an important faction in the Greek-Cypriot community to this day. Municipal elections were finally held in 1943, and served as a barometer of public sentiment through the balance of the colonial period; the British could not very well profess to be fighting fascism while simultaneously withholding basic political freedoms.

During **World War II**, Cyprus belied its supposed strategic value by escaping much involvement other than as an important supply depot and staging post. The island suffered just a few stray Italian raids from Rhodes, and German ones from Crete; after the German difficulties on Crete, Hitler had forbidden another paratroop action to seize Cyprus. About 28,000 Cypriots, both Greek and Turkish (plus hundreds of Cypriot donkeys), fought as volunteers with British forces in Europe, the Middle East and North Africa, and the Greeks at least expected some political reward for this at the war's end.

The extent of this was the 1947 offer by Governor Lord Winster of a **limited constitution** of self-rule, similar to that tendered in other colonies at the time. It was summarily rejected by the enosist elements, principally the Orthodox Church, who proclaimed that anything less than *énosis* or at least provision for its eventual implementation was unacceptable – a stance which guaranteed later bloodshed. AKEL was lukewarm on the idea; they were busy mounting the inconclusive but heroic 1947–48 **strike** in the American-run copper mines of Soléa district. The Americans had at least one other toehold on the island: an electronic listening post at Karavás (now Alsancak) on the north coast near Kyrenia, opened in 1949 to monitor all radio broadcasts from behind the Iron Curtain, and the first of several local facilities designed to keep tabs on Soviet doings in the incipient Cold War.

The postwar years

By 1950, demands for *énosis* had returned to the fore; in a **referendum** campaign organized by newly elected Archbishop and Ethnarch **Makarios III**, results showed 96 percent support for *énosis* among Greek Cypriots. They seemed to ignore the fact that Greece, dominated by far-right-wing governments and still a stretcher case after the rigours of German occupation and a civil war, was a poor candidate as a partner for association; yet so great was the groundswell for union that even the PEO and AKEL subscribed to it after 1950, though they could both expect a fairly unpleasant fate in a rightist "Greater Greece". In general outsiders have had trouble understanding the enormous emotional and historical appeal of *énosis*, whose advocates readily admitted that Cypriot living standards would drop sharply once the island was out of the sterling zone and yoked to chaotic, impoverished Greece.

Soon the theoretical possibility of *énosis* dawned on the island's **Turkish minority** – some eighteen percent of the population – who began agitation in opposition, advocating either the status quo or some sort of affiliation with Turkey rather than becoming a truly insignificant minority in a greater Greece. As the Turkish Cypriots were scattered almost uniformly throughout the island, the option of a separate Turkish-Cypriot province or canton was not available without painful population transfers.

Many Greek Cypriots subsequently accused the British (and to a lesser extent the Americans) of **stirring up** Turkey and the Turkish Cypriots against them, and while there is ample truth to this – divide-and-rule was very much a colonial strategy – mainland Turkey itself would probably have eventually become involved without cues from Britain, and the Turkish Cypriots were certainly not quiescent. Greek Cypriots saw the situation as a non-colonial problem of the island's wishing to transfer its allegiance to the "mother country"; Britain, in their view, transformed matters into a general Greco-Turkish dispute under the guise of "harmony in the southeast flank of NATO", ensuring that Turkey would forcefully block any move towards *énosis*.

After Egyptian independence in 1954, **British Mid-East Military HQ** was moved to Cyprus over a period of twenty months, making self-determination far less likely, and the British position increasingly inflexible – thanks to such intemperate Tory personalities as Anthony Eden, and increasing support for this policy by the Americans. In July of that year, the minister of state for the colonies declared that "certain Commonwealth territories, owing to their particular circumstances, can never expect to be fully independent" – and went on to express fears of a pro-Soviet AKEL dominating an independent Cyprus. To Greek Cypriots this utterance seemed ludicrous in the light of independence being granted to far less developed parts of Asia and Africa. That "never" closed off all avenues of communication with more moderate Greek Cypriots, and came back to repeatedly haunt the British over the next five years.

In **Greece** the government encouraged a shrill, anti-British media barrage in support of *énosis*, available to any radio set on Cyprus. For the first time Greece also tried to internationalize the Cyprus issue at the **UN**, where it failed to get a full hearing, though Turkey bared its teeth in preliminary discussions, a promise of trouble in the future. Only the Greek ambassador to London astutely saw that the mainland Turks were now an interested party and would have to be included, or at least mollified, in any solution.

Together with **General George Grivas** (see box, p.254), alias"Dhiyenis" after the hero of a Byzantine epic, Archbishop Makarios in 1954 secretly founded **EOKA**, *Ethnikí Orgánosis Kypríon Agonistón* or "National Organization of Cypriot Fighters", as an IRA-type movement to throw off British rule. Late that year several clandestine shipments of arms and explosives were transferred from Rhodes to the Páfos coast, though the archbishop initially shrank back from advocating lethal force against persons, restricting Grivas to sabotage of property. EOKA's campaign of violence on Cyprus began spectacularly on April 1, 1955 with the destruction of the Government radio transmitter, among other targets.

Overseas, a hastily scheduled **trilateral conference** in July 1955, convening representatives of Greece, Turkey and Britain, flopped miserably; Makarios remarked that Greece's attendance had merely legitimized Turkish involvement in the Cyprus issue. Two months later, massive, Turkish-government-inspired **rioting** in İstanbul caused staggering loss to Greek property and effectively dashed any hope of a reasonable future for the Orthodox community there.

Newly appointed **High Commissioner John Harding**, a former field marshal, pursued a hard line against EOKA; ongoing negotiations with Makarios, who distanced himself at least publicly from the armed struggle, were approaching a breakthrough when Grivas set off more strategically timed bombs. Talks were broken off and the archbishop and two associates **deported** in March 1956 to comfortable house arrest in the Seychelles. Deprived of its ablest spokesman, EOKA now graduated to murderous **attacks** on Greek Cypriots who disagreed with them, as well as on British soldiers and civilians. The island terrain was ideal for guerrilla insurgency; despite searches, internments, collective punishments for aiding EOKA and other now-familiar curtailments of civil liberties in such emergencies, the uprising couldn't be quelled. An estimated 1200 guerrillas, based primarily in the Tróödhos, tied up 25,000 regular British Army troops and 4500 special constables. The latter were overwhelmingly composed of Turkish-Cypriot auxiliaries – who often **tortured** captured EOKA suspects under the supervision of British officers, an assigned task which perceptibly increased intercommunal tensions. These auxiliaries were attracted by pay rates of £30 a month, then a small fortune on the island; no Greek Cypriot could expect to last long in such a post without being done away with as a traitor by EOKA. Spring and summer of 1956 also saw the **hangings** of nine convicted EOKA men, touching off violent protests in Greece and plunging British-Greek relations to an all-time low. When Harding issued an ultimatum for the surrender of insurrectionist weapons, EOKA responded contemptuously by parading a riderless donkey through downtown Nicosia, emblazoned with banners reading (in Greek and English) "I surrender" (see p.407 for the role of the donkey in Cypriot society).

International pressure in **1957** – and Britain's realization that no other Greek-Cypriot negotiating partner existed – secured Makarios's release, just after Greece finally managed to get Cyprus on the UN agenda, resulting in a resolution accepting independence "in principle". Harding was replaced with more conciliatory civilian **Governor Hugh Foot**, and a constitutional commissioner, Lord Radcliffe, was dispatched to make more generous proposals for limited self-government than those of 1947. These were again rejected by the Greek Cypriots, because they didn't envision *énosis*, and by the Turkish Cypriots – represented by the **Turkish National Party**, headed by future vice-president **Fazil Küçük** – since it didn't specifically exclude that possibility.

After isolated intercommunal incidents, the **TMT** or *Türk Mukavemet Teskilati* (Turkish Resistance Organization) was founded early in **1958** to counter EOKA by working for *taksim* (partition) of the island between Greece and Turkey. But TMT's cell structure was modelled on EOKA, and it also duplicated EOKA's rabid **anti-communism**, killing various left-wing Turkish personalities and pressurizing Turkish Cypriots to leave PEO and AKEL, the last unsegregated institutions on the island. TMT also organized a boycott of Greek-Cypriot products and shops, just as EOKA was presiding over a Greek-Cypriot boycott of British goods.

Intercommunal clashes – and resumed rebellion

A June 1958 bomb explosion outside the Turkish press office in Nicosia – later shown to have been planted by TMT provocateurs – set off the first serious **intercommunal clashes** on the island. In Nicosia, Turkish gangs expelled Greeks from some mixed neighbourhoods, and induced some Turks to abandon villages in the south of the island in favour of the north – a forerunner of 1974 events. Shortly after, in what became known as the **Gönyeli incident**, seven EOKA suspects were released from British custody to walk home through a Turkish-Cypriot area, where they were duly stabbed to death. EOKA retaliated by targeting Turkish-Cypriot policemen, and stepping up assaults on the British after a year's lull. The resumed war of attrition between EOKA and British forces became increasingly dirty and no-holds-barred, with the latter nursing a racial loathing for their adversaries; the **death toll** for the whole insurrection climbed to nearly six hundred. Of these almost half were left-wing or pro-British Greek Cypriots killed by EOKA, while eventually 346 UK squaddies were interred in a special military cemetery, today found in the buffer zone. **Truces** were declared in late summer by both TMT and EOKA, with many displaced Cypriots returning to their homes in mixed areas. The EOKA truce did not, however, extend to AKEL members, who now favoured independence again – and continued to suffer fatal consequences.

One final Greece-sponsored UN resolution for Cypriot "self-determination" (by now code for *énosis*) in 1958 fell short of the required two-thirds majority in the General Assembly, so Makarios began to accept the wisdom of independence, especially as both the British, particularly Prime Minister Harold Macmillan, and the Turkish Cypriots were threatening to revive the option of partition and massive population movements. The bloody July 1958 anti-royalist coup in Iraq, hitherto one of Britain's staunchest Middle East allies, and the subsequent loss of unrestricted use of its two airfields, had also reinforced British and American resolve not to let Cyprus' valuable military facilities fall into "unreliable" hands.

Throughout the later 1950s, EOKA, Greece and most Greek Cypriots had failed to take seriously the **mainland Turkish position**: that Turkey would act to prevent strategically vital Cyprus becoming Greek territory, as Crete had after a fifteen-year period of supposed independence at the start of the century. Less genuine, perhaps, was Turkey's new-found concern for its "brothers" on the island; programmes broadcast regularly over Radio Ankara agitated feelings in its communal audience just as mainland Greek programmes did in theirs. The British, now faced with hostility from Turkish Cypriots as well as from the Greeks, and contemplating the soaring costs of containing the rebellion, desperately sought a way out. Various proposals were briefly mooted by the UK and the US, including NATO administering Cyprus, a joint Greek-Turkish-British tridominium over the entire island, or an "orderly" partition into mainland-Greek- and Turkish-administered cantonments, all with the express intent of preventing any military use of the island by the Communist bloc.

The granting of independence

In February 1959, the foreign ministers of Greece and Turkey met in **Zurich** to hammer out some compromise settlement, with a supplementary meeting including the British and Cypriots in **London** a few days later. The participants agreed on the establishment of an independent Cypriot republic, its **constitution** to be prepared by an impartial Swiss expert. Of its 199 clauses, 48 were unalterable, with *énosis* or *taksim* expressly forbidden. The two ethnic communities were essentially to be co-founders, running the republic on a 70:30 Greek:Turk **proportional basis** that slightly favoured the Turkish minority. A single fifty-seat House of Representatives – with fifteen seats reserved for the Turks, two separate communal chambers funded partly by Greece and Turkey, and a Greek-Cypriot president plus a Turkish-Cypriot vice-president elected by their respective communities was also envisioned. The high court would be headed by a tie-breaking foreign justice. After considerable hesitation and misgivings – and, allegedly, blackmail by the British secret services with compromising material of a sexual nature – Makarios assented to the constitution.

The meetings also produced three interrelated **treaties**, incorporated as articles of the constitution. Britain, Turkey and Greece simultaneously entered into a **Treaty of Guarantee**, by which they acted as guarantors to safeguard Cypriot independence. A **Treaty of Establishment** stipulated the existence of two main British military bases, their extent to be determined, and other training areas. The **Treaty of Alliance** provided for the stationing of Greek and Turkish military forces, at Yerólakkos (Alaykoy) and Gönyeli respectively, and the training of a Cypriot army, presumably as an arm of NATO; this provision was roundly denounced by AKEL, and indeed in the long run this treaty was to prove the most destabilizing element of the package.

Makarios, who had been in Greece since 1957, was finally permitted to **return to Cyprus**, where an amnesty was declared for most EOKA offenders. Grivas and the more hard-line enosists, excoriating Makarios for his supposed betrayal of the cause, flew off to self-imposed exile in Greece, while certain supporters

Dr Fazil Küçük (1906–1984)

The first official leader of the **Turkish-Cypriot community**, Dr Fazil Küçük was a man of many parts – prodigious drinker, foul-mouthed frequenter of *meyhanes* with large groups of friends, and a journalist, in addition to being a politician and medico. He founded the still-existing *Halkın Sesi*, long the main Turkish-Cypriot newspaper, and often used it as a platform to indulge his bent for elaborate practical jokes. Although Küçük started his political career as an instrument of Turkish mainland policy on the island, he increasingly stood up for long-term Turkish-Cypriot interests, and was forced into early retirement in 1973 by TMT for not being malleable enough in the eyes of his "handlers". When Ahmet Berberoğlu was similarly given a non-refusable offer, Rauf Denktaş was appointed unopposed as leader of the community. Unlike Denktaş, however, "Doktor" – as he was universally known – was also universally loved; about 100,000 people, virtually the entire Turkish-Cypriot population then in the North, attended his funeral in 1984. Küçük's last oral "will" to his lawyer was for regular libations of Peristiany 31 brandy, "Doktor"'s favourite tipple, to be poured over his grave in Hamitköy (Mándhres). This was done just once, with such alarming results for the Turkish-army guard of honour posted there that the grave was cemented over to prevent recurrences.

▲ Fazil Küçük (speaking) and Archbishop Makarios (centre) at a ceremony to mark Cypriot Independence, 1960

stayed behind, punctuating most of 1959 with fulminations against the independence deal. They and others induced the bigotedly anti-Turkish-Cypriot **Mayor Themistoklis Dhervis of Nicosia** to form the first opposition party, the **Democratic Union**, which contested the presidential elections of December 1959 against the archbishop's **Popular Front**. Makarios won handily with two-thirds of the vote, while Fazil Küçük ran unopposed for vice-president.

Elections for the **House of Representatives** in February 1960 were poorly attended, with absenteeism and abstention rates of up to sixty percent in some districts reflecting popular disgust at the civic arrangements – and a poor omen for the future. The Popular Front took thirty seats, its coalition partners AKEL five, while Küçük's National Party got all fifteen Turkish seats. Polling for the powerful **communal chambers**, charged with overseeing education, religion, culture and consumer credit co-ops, showed a similar profile, though in the Greek chamber one seat each was reserved for the Armenian, Maronite and "Latin" communities.

Final independence, which had been set for no later than February 1960, was postponed until **August 16, 1960**, as the Cypriots and the British haggled over the exact size of the two sovereign bases. By coincidence, Venetian and British rule lasted exactly the same duration: 82 years.

The unitary republic: 1960–64

The Republic of Cyprus seemed doomed from the start, with EOKA and TMT **ideologues** appointed to key cabinet positions. Neither organization completely disbanded, but maintained shadowy existences, waiting for the right moment to re-emerge. They and others made Makarios's life difficult: the enosists considered that he'd sold them out, the Turks and Turkish Cypriots were convinced that he was biding his time for an opportunity to impose *énosis*, and many Communists felt he was too accommodating to the West.

On a **symbolic** level, communal iconography, street names and so on all continued referring to persons and events in the "mother" countries; the respective national flags and national days were celebrated by each community, and while there is a Cypriot flag, there never was a national anthem. Such institutionalized separatism was inimical to fostering a national consciousness. The **constitution**, an improbably intricate one for a population of just over half a million, proved unworkable in practice. Greek Cypriots chafed at it because it had been imposed from outside, while Turkish Cypriots took every opportunity to exploit numerous clauses benefiting them. It was, as several outside observers remarked, the only democracy where majority rule was explicitly denied by its founding charter. It did not seem to have occurred to the constitution's drafters that, by not providing for cross-communal voting (whereby, for example, presidential and vice-presidential candidates had to secure a majority of votes in *both* communities), Cyprus was condemned to rampant tribalism.

The **70:30 ratio**, applicable in all civil service institutions, could not be reached within the five months prescribed, and the **army**, to be set up on a 60:40 ratio with ethnic mix at all levels, never materialized, since the Turks insisted on segregated companies; instead Makarios eventually authorized the establishment of an all-Greek-Cypriot **National Guard**. Both the president and the vice-president had **veto power** over foreign affairs, defence and internal matters, exercised frequently by Küçük. Laws had to clear the House of Representatives by majority votes from **both communal factions**: thus eight of the fifteen Turkish MPs could defeat any bill. When agreement could not be reached in the first two years of the republic's life, colonial rules were often extended as **stopgaps**.

For much of 1962, Cyprus had no uniform income tax or customs excise laws, the Turks having blocked them in retaliation for Greek foot-dragging on implementation of separate municipalities for the five largest towns. Another concession to the Turkish Cypriots was the maintenance of **separate municipalities**, first set up in the 1950s, for each community in those towns – something the Greek Cypriots considered an incredibly wasteful and time-consuming duplication of services, as well as (correctly in light of later events) stalking horses for island-wide partition. Yet the Greeks did not hesitate to pass **revenue** laws through their own chamber when frustrated in the parliament, thus perpetuating the apartheid by providing services only to the Greek-Cypriot community and those Turks choosing to acknowledge its jurisdiction.

Among the hardline elements, the TMT struck first, against its own community: on April 23, 1962 gunmen murdered **Ahmet Gurkan** and **Ayhan Hikmet**, leaders of the only Turkish-Cypriot political party to oppose Küçük's National Party, promoting closer co-operation between two communities. It was a reprise of numerous such attacks in 1958, and, now as then, no action was taken against TMT or its backers; **Rauf Denktaş**, protégé of Küçük, even managed to get Emil Dirvana, Turkish ambassador to Nicosia and one of many to condemn the murders, recalled. There would be no other significant Turkish-Cypriot opposition group until the 1970s.

In late November 1963, Makarios proposed to Küçük **thirteen constitutional amendments** to make bicommunal public life possible. These included the abolition of both the presidential and vice-presidential right of veto, the introduction of simple majority rule in the legislature, the unification of the municipalities and justice system, and an adjustment of communal ratios in civil service and the still-theoretical army. Apparently, this proposal had been drafted with the advice of the British high commissioner; Greece subsequently deemed the bundle incredibly tactless, even if such reforms were worth introducing gradually. Turkey was sent the suggestions and denounced them, threatening military action if they were introduced unilaterally, even before Küçük had finished reading them, leaving him little room to manoeuvre. These infamous proposals are claimed to be part of a secret Greek-Cypriot strategy known as the **Akritas Plan**, whereby political obstacles to *énosis* were to be eliminated incrementally and discretely – and Turkish-Cypriot objectors eliminated physically if necessary. It was, and remains, a Turkish codeword for enosist perfidy, and widely distributed printouts of the supposed plan have never been convincingly demonstrated to be a hoax.

Further intercommunal fighting

Reaction to the Turkish refusal was swift: on **December 21, 1963** shots were exchanged between a Greek-Cypriot police patrol and a car full of Turkish Cypriots – the precipitating factor, as so often in Cypriot violence, was prostitution – and within hours EOKA and TMT were at it again. EOKA struck at Turkish neighbourhoods in Larnaca, and also in the mixed Nicosia district of Omórfita (Küçük Kaymaklı), where an EOKA detachment under one **Nikos Sampson** rampaged through, seizing seven hundred hostages. In retaliation the Armenian community, accused of siding with the Greek Cypriots, was expelled by TMT from North Nicosia on 23 December, and mainland Turkish troops left their Gönyeli barracks next day to take up positions along the Nicosia–Kyrenia road, with more forces concentrated on the Turkish mainland opposite; the mainland Greek force at Yerólakkos also deployed itself. Barriers, known as the **Green Line** after an English officer's crayon mark on a map, were set up between Greek and Turkish quarters in Nicosia after a UK-brokered ceasefire took effect on Christmas Day.

Already, all Turkish Cypriots had **resigned** from the government and police forces, to begin setting up a parallel administration in north Nicosia and in the rapidly growing number of **enclaves**. Denktaş and the TMT promulgated a communal law making it "treasonous" for any Turkish Cypriot to have commercial or administrative dealings with Greek Cypriots, a ban enforced by ostracization, beatings or worse. Any Turkish Cypriot who might have thought to continue at his post in south Nicosia would have to run a gauntlet of both his own co-religionists, enforcing the sequestration, and Greeks who might shoot first and ask questions later. The enclaves in fact constituted a deliberate policy of laying the basis for later partition. Most Turkish-Cypriots from now on asserted that the 1960 constitution was **defunct**; there were merely two provisional regimes on the island pending the establishment of a new arrangement. Makarios agreed that the 1960 constitution was hopeless – but differed in his conclusions: namely that majority rule would prevail as per his suggested amendments, with minority guarantees, whether the Turks liked it or not.

International repercussions

Because of the superpower interests involved, Cypriot intercommunal disputes again took on **international** dimensions. The Greek Cypriots preferred, as they always had done, the UN as a forum; the US, UK, mainland Turkey and the Turkish Cypriots pressed for **NATO intervention**. Turkish opinion, expressed through Küçük's and Denktaş's rightist Turkish National Party, helped plant the seeds of implacable American hostility to Makarios by successfully painting him with a pink (if not red) brush, calling attention to his forthright espousal of the **Non-Aligned Movement** and purchase of arms from the USSR and Czechoslovakia. In the end, the Cypriot government, with the support of the Soviets and Greek Premier George Papandreou, had its way: in February 1964, a UN resolution dispatched **UNFICYP** (UN Forces in Cyprus) for an initial three-month peace-keeping assignment – extended later to six months and renewed since then without a break. In addition, a **tripartite truce force**, composed of Greek, Turkish and British (from the sovereign bases) soldiers, was formed, under the partial leadership of Lieutenant Commander Martin Packard, and a UN civilian mediator was also appointed. George Ball, who as US under-secretary of state had unsuccessfully tried to persuade Makarios to accept occupation by a NATO landing force, was later overheard to say "that son of a bitch [ie Makarios] will have to be killed before anything happens in Cyprus".

Little was accomplished immediately by UNFICYP; the death toll from communal disturbances in the six months after December 1963 reached nearly six hundred, with Turkish Cypriots suffering disproportionately. The presence of ten thousand **mainland Greek troops**, now also on the island, gave EOKA and Greek Cypriots a false sense of being able to act with impunity. After TMT occupied St Hilarion castle and the Kyrenia–Nicosia road to form a core enclave, US President Lyndon Johnson sent Turkish Premier İnönü a letter, in his inimitably blunt style, warning him of plans to invade. At the same time the US administration pressurized Greece to follow its prescription or possibly face Turkey alone on the battlefield; heads were to be knocked together, if necessary, to preserve NATO's southeast flank.

The UN mediator having reached a dead end (and himself soon dying anyway), the **Acheson Plan** – named after the incumbent US secretary of state – was unveiled in mid-1964. It amounted to double *énosis*: the bulk of the island to Greece, the rest (plus the cession of the tiny but strategic Greek isle of Kastellórizo) to Turkey – effectively partition and the disappearance of Cyprus as an independent entity. After initial consideration by both Greece and Turkey, the Greeks rejected the idea because of vociferous objections from Nicosia.

The Turkish-Cypriot enclaves

The **Kókkina incident** (see p.185) made world headlines in August 1964, when the newly formed National Guard, commanded by a returned Grivas, attacked this coastal enclave in an effort to halt the landing of supplies and weapons from Turkey. Guarantors Greece and Turkey were again brought to the brink of war as Turkey extensively bombed and strafed the Pólis area, causing numerous casualties, and Makarios threatened to sanction attacks on Turkish Cypriots throughout the island unless Turkey ceased its air strikes. It was the first, but not the last, time that US-supplied NATO weapons were used in contravention of their ostensible purpose.

Since January 1964, **Martin Packard** – one of the few British military personnel to emerge with much credit from the post-independence period – had been conducting an all-but-one-man, increasingly successful campaign to rebuild trust between the two communities, persuading combatants to disarm, and proposing to dissolve the newly formed enclaves and escort the inhabitants back to formerly mixed villages, with UN protection where necessary. But his reintegrationist campaign was opposed by interested parties, who succeeded in securing Packard's removal from the island in June despite objections from both

Greek- and Turkish-Cypriot community leaders with whom he was uniformly popular (see p.443, "Books", for more).

Any residual trust between the two island communities was destroyed by the end of 1964, with the Turkish Cypriots well **barricaded** in their enclaves, the central government responding by placing a ban on their acquisition of a wide range of essential materials deemed militarily strategic. The enclave inmates, numbers swelled by Turkish army personnel, retaliated by keeping all Greeks out, setting up a TMT-run state-within-a-state with its own police, radio station and other services, which provocation EOKA could not resist on numerous occasions.

Despite all this, Cypriot **economic progress** post-independence was considerable – though heavily biased towards the Greek Cypriot community, whose attitude towards the Turkish Cypriots at best resembled sending naughty children to bed without supper. The first of many **irrigation dams** to ease chronic water problems began to appear on the slopes of the Tróödhos range and Kyrenia hills. Tourism became important for the first time, primarily on the sandy coast to either side of Famagusta and to a lesser extent around Kyrenia.

A twilight zone: 1965–74

The new UN mediator **Galo Plaza**, in his March 1965 report, astutely diagnosed the shortcomings of the 1960 constitution and made forthright suggestions for a new one – principally that the Greek Cypriots must decisively renounce *énosis* and that the Turkish Cypriots must acquiesce to majority rule, with guarantees for certain rights. This did not go over well with them or with the mainland Turks, who arranged to send Plaza packing.

After April 1967 Greece had been taken over by a **military junta**, anxious – with American approval – to remove the "Cyprus problem" from the global agenda. However, secret summer meetings with Turkey, exploring variations of the Acheson Plan, came to nothing. In November, Grivas's National Guard attacked **Kofínou**, another enclave between Limassol and Larnaca, with considerable loss of Turkish life; Greece and Turkey both mobilized, Ankara again tendered an ultimatum to Athens and American diplomats got little sleep as they shuttled between the two capitals. Despite its soldierly composition, the Greek regime meekly complied with Turkish demands; **Grivas** and most of the ten thousand smuggled-in mainland soldiers were shipped back to Greece. The National Guard, however, remained – a Trojan horse for future plots.

In 1968 the UN sponsored direct **intercommunal negotiations**, which sputtered along until 1974, with **Glafkos Clerides**, president of the House of Representatives, and Rauf Denktaş as interlocutors. Substantial agreement on many points was actually reached, despite the Turks pressing for implementation of a high degree of local communal power in place of a spoiler role at the national level, and the Greek side holding out for more comprehensive central control. But Makarios never made the necessarily dramatic, generous concessions, and Clerides repeatedly threatened to resign in the absence of what he saw as a lack of consistent support from Makarios.

The enclaves were, though, finally **opened** to the extent of supplies going in and people coming out; with UN mediation, local arrangements – such as joint police patrols – were reached for a semblance of normal life in less tense areas of island. But in most respects Turkish-Cypriot community leaders still enforced a policy of **self-segregation** as a basis for a federal state. But whether they meant a federation as most outsiders understood it, or merely federation masquerading as partition, was debatable. The Turkish Cypriots, biding their time in cramped and impoverished quarters, perhaps knew something that the Greek Orthodox islanders didn't or wouldn't realize: that Turkey was in earnest about **supporting** their cause materially and militarily as well as morally.

Both Makarios and Küçük were overwhelmingly re-elected early in 1968, though Makarios's three bishops had repudiated him for dropping *énosis* as a realistic option. This was just one aspect of his **deteriorating relations** with the Greek colonels, who – with CIA approval – instigated repeated **plots** to eliminate him using Greek regular army officers, who by now controlled most of the National Guard. A bizarre **counterplot** of the same year deserves mention: **Polycarpos Georgadjis**, a former EOKA operative and minister of interior, provided one Alekos Panagoulis in Greece with the explosives for an abortive attempt to kill junta chief Papadopoulos. Exactly why Yiorgadjis would do this – considering that EOKA and junta aims were now identical – remains a mystery; he was also implicated in a March 1970 attempt on Makarios's life, and was himself assassinated by two unknown persons a week later (his widow, interestingly, soon married Tassos Papadopoulos, the 2003–08 president of Cyprus).

Grivas slipped back into Cyprus during 1971 and founded **EOKA-B** for the purpose of resuming the struggle for *énosis*, but the old trouble-maker, in his 70s, died in January 1974, still in hiding. EOKA-B and its allies set in motion various devices to destabilize the elected government of Cyprus, reserving – as had its predecessor – special malice for AKEL. Publicly, the Greek junta demanded, and eventually got, the resignation of **Spyros Kyprianou**, long-time foreign minister and future president. The three dissident bishops of 1968, still acting as junta placemen, proclaimed Makarios defrocked, reducing him to lay status. Makarios retaliated by **dismissing the three bishops** with the help of other Middle Eastern prelates and creating three new, subordinate bishoprics – those of Mórfou, Nicosia and Limassol – to reduce the future chances of such a ploy. He was re-elected as president in 1973 unopposed; in the same year Küçük was replaced as nominal vice-president by Rauf Denktaş.

1974: coup and invasion

The Greek junta, by early 1974 tottering and devoid of any popular support at home, now tried a Falklands-type diversion, with the encouragement – if not outright connivance – of CIA agents in Athens. Makarios, well aware of the intrigues of the junta's cadres in his National Guard, had proscribed EOKA-B in April 1974, and wrote to the Greek president on July 2 demanding that these officers be withdrawn. The junta's response was to give the go-ahead for the **archbishop's overthrow**, which, despite advance knowledge, Makarios's primarily left-wing and poorly armed supporters proved powerless to prevent.

Early on **July 15**, National Guard troops attacked the archiepiscopal palace, gutted it and announced the archbishop's demise. But Makarios, in the nearby presidential residence, escaped to loyalist strongholds in Páfos district; on learning this, a Washington diplomat was overheard to remark, "How inconvenient". With British help, the archbishop left the island for the UK, which offered lukewarm support, and then the US, where he was refused recognition as head of state by Henry Kissinger, a man who had done as much as anyone to oppose – and possibly depose – him.

Unfazed, the coup protagonists proclaimed as president **Nikos Sampson**, long-time EOKA activist, Turkophobe warlord and head of the (anything but) Progressive Party. A contemporary foreign correspondent characterized him as "an absolute idiot, though not quite illiterate – a playboy gunman. He spends every night in cabarets getting drunk, dancing on tables, pulling off his shirt to show his scars." A notorious photo showed him in battle regalia, one foot atop a dead Turkish Cypriot he'd killed as a "hunting trophy". Small wonder, then, that his term of office and EOKA-B's direct rule would last exactly eight days.

On reflection (not their strong point), the EOKA-B people might have realized that their coup would give Turkey a perfect **pretext** to do what it had long contemplated: partition Cyprus, claiming as guarantor to be acting as protectors of the threatened minority. Indeed many Turkish-Cypriot fighters in the North pre-1974 recall receiving coded messages weeks before the coup, telling them to prepare for action. Post-coup international opinion initially favoured Turkey, whose prime minister **Bülent Ecevit** went through the proper legalistic motions on July 16–17 of flying to Britain to propose joint action for protecting the Turkish minority, restoring Cypriot independence and demanding that Athens withdraw its officers. While Sampson did indeed say "Now that we've finished with Makarios's people, let's start on the Turks," EOKA-B finally killed more Greek Cypriot opponents – an estimated five hundred interred in mass, unmarked graves, including many wounded buried alive – than the almost three hundred Turkish Cypriots slaughtered at Tókhni and three villages around Famagusta.

"Phase I"

Just before dawn on July 20, Ecevit authorized the **Turkish invasion** of Cyprus, entailing amphibious armoured landings, napalm strikes, bombing raids on many towns and paratroop drops around Kyrenia and Nicosia. "**Phase I**" of the campaign lasted from **July 20 to July 30**: despite the demoralizing coup, and being outnumbered four to one, the Greek Cypriots managed to confine Turkish forces to a lozenge-shaped bridgehead straddling the Nicosia–Kyrenia road. The initial Turkish landing west of Kyrenia, the first time its forces had fought since the Korean War, was a near-fiasco, as were many supporting naval and air force operations. For starters, Turkey was expecting little resistance from the Greek Cypriots, and threw poorly equipped, trained and disciplined conscripts into the opening battles. Soldiers disembarked without water bottles in the July heat, and tanks rolled ashore with no ammunition and insufficient fuel. Turkish air-force jets managed to sink two of their own landing craft, while completely missing the contents of a Cypriot National Guard tank camp (though the Greek Cypriots also mistakenly shot down two Hercules transports bringing reinforcements from Greece). A Greek naval fleet, a radar phantom as it turned out, was reported southwest of Cyprus; three Turkish destroyers sailed to meet it, but Turkish jets attacked and sank one of these when the captain failed to give the right password (the US had supplied Greece and Turkey with identical vessels). The brigadier general in charge of operations was killed as he came ashore, with the next-highest-ranking officer, for some days, being a captain. UN observers subsequently estimated a ratio of seven Turkish to every Greek casualty over the war; much of this can be attributed to pre-landing lectures by Turkish religious leaders, who assured the raw recruits that death in battle with the infidels ensured a direct path to Paradise. To such pep talks – and not (as often alleged) the ingestion of drugs – was owed the repeated and oft-corroborated spectacle of human wave attacks by wild-eyed Turkish cannon fodder, marching zombie-like into Greek-Cypriot machine-gun fire, until the latter ran out of ammunition and had to retreat.

In Greece, the junta chiefs ordered their army to attack Turkey across the Thracian frontier; its officers refused, precipitating the junta's collapse on **July 23**, the same day Sampson fell from power. Glafkos Clerides replaced him as acting head of state in Makarios's absence, as a civilian government took power in Athens. The first round of hastily arranged **negotiations** between the Greek, Turkish and British foreign ministers convened in **Geneva**, resulting in the ceasefire of July 30. On August 8, talks resumed, with Clerides and Denktaş additionally present. The Turkish military, with little to show for the heavy casualties sustained during Phase I, and their forces increasingly vulnerable as the Greek Cypriots comprehensively mined the perimeter of their toehold, began to pressurize their civilian leaders to be given a freer hand. Accordingly, on the night of August 13–14, the Turkish foreign minister gave Clerides an **ultimatum** demanding approval of one or the other Turkish plans for "federation": either six dispersed cantons or a single amalgamated one under Turkish-Cypriot control, adding up to 34 percent of Cyprus. Clerides asked for 36 hours to consult his government, which was refused at 3am on August 14; ninety minutes later, the Turkish army resumed its offensive.

"Phase II"

"Phase II" was a two-day rout of the Greek Cypriots, who had insufficient armour and no air support to stop the Turkish juggernaut, this time manned by crack troops. The Greek Cypriots – as opposed to the Greek officers, whom the Turks always regarded with contempt – had acquitted themselves splendidly during "Phase I", far exceeding their brief to hold the line for 36 hours until massive aid arrived from Greece, which never did; come "Phase II", they were completely exhausted, demoralized and literally out of fuel and ammunition.

The behaviour of the Turkish infantry in both phases of the war featured sporadic, **gratuitous violence** against Greek-Cypriot civilians unlucky enough to lie in their path; word of the rapes, murders and widespread looting which marked their advance was enough to convince approximately 165,000 Greek Cypriots to flee for their safety. Had they in fact not done so, the entire purpose of the campaign – to create an ethnically cleansed sanctuary for the Turkish Cypriots – would have been confounded.

At a second ceasefire on August 16, the areas occupied by the Turkish army totalled 38 percent of the island's area – slightly more than Turkey had demanded at Geneva – abutting a scalloped boundary, henceforth the **Attila Line**, extending from Káto Pýrgos in Tillyría to Famagusta. The Greek-Cypriot **death toll**, combatants and civilians together, rose to 3850. The **missing** supposedly numbered 1619, though it now seems likely that several hundred of these were leftists killed by EOKA-B activists and Greek junta officers, as noted on p.393, or – as Turkish army units often found them – chained to their gun emplacements or shot in the back. Others – over two hundred National Guardsmen – were shown by Greek-Cypriot journalists in spring 1998 to have been killed by the Turkish army and buried in unmarked graves by the Southern government, to be exploited for propaganda purposes. Turkish Cypriots living in the South were put in an untenable position by the Turkish "peace action", as it was termed; EOKA-B units occupied or cleared out most of their enclaves, with reprisal killings at several points.

Since July 15, a flurry of **UN Security Council resolutions**, calling on all concerned to desist from warlike actions and respect Cypriot independence, had been piling up, blithely disregarded then and ever since. With the benefit of hindsight, UK parliamentary and US congressional committees duly condemned the timidity, lack of imagination and simple shamefulness of their governments' respective past policies towards Cyprus, specifically the absence of any meaningful initiative to stop the Turkish war machine. The **British** pleaded that with just over five thousand men on the sovereign bases, there was (despite their role as guarantor) little they could have done – other than what they actually did: half-heartedly interpose a small fleet between Cyprus and Anatolia as a deterrent in the four days before July 20, ferry tourists to safety out of the North, and shelter in Sovereign Base territory Turkish Cypriots fleeing EOKA-B gunmen in the South. In retrospect, it seems the UK had been content to follow American dictates rather than pursue an independent course.

On the part of the **US**, there was more of a failure of will than inability to do something. President Nixon, on the point of resigning over Watergate, had deferred to the archpriest of *realpolitik*, **Henry Kissinger**, who made no secret of his "tilt" towards Turkey rather than Greece as the more valuable ally in the Aegean – once the colonels' junta had served its purpose – or of his distaste for Makarios. Thus was the integrity of Cyprus sacrificed to NATO power politics. The only substantive American congressional action, over Kissinger's objections, was the temporary **suspension of military aid** to Turkey.

During anti-American riots in Nicosia on **August 19**, **US Ambassador Rodger Davies** and a Cypriot embassy employee were gunned down by EOKA-B hitmen aiming deliberately from an unfinished building opposite. Assertions that Davies was the CIA paymaster and handler for the EOKA-B coup do not hold water, as he was an Arabist by training and had been in the job for less than two months – though this does not rule out "conduct incompatible with diplomatic status" by his predecessor, for whom the gunmen may have mistaken him. Eleven days later, **Vassos Lyssarides**, head of the socialist **EDEK** party supporting Makarios, narrowly escaped death at the hands of the same bunch. These lurid events demonstrated that clapping Sampson in jail – where he remained until 1992 – wouldn't cause his associates to simply disappear.

1974–91: de facto partition

While still acting head of state, Clerides acknowledged that the Greeks and Greek Cypriots had been acting for years as if Turkey did not exist, and that some sort of **federal republic** was the best Cyprus could hope for. Makarios returned on December 7, 1974 to a diminished realm, and contradicted Clerides: the Greek Cypriots should embark on a "long-term struggle", using their favourite method of **internationalization**, to induce the Turkish army to leave and get optimum terms from the Turkish Cypriots. This prefigured a final break between the two men the following year. In his homecoming speech in Nicosia, with half the South turned out to welcome him, Makarios also forgave his opponents – not that he had much choice, with EOKA-B operatives still swaggering about in full battledress. But others, especially those who had lost relatives at the hands of either EOKA-B or the Turks, were not in such an accommodating mood; three-plus decades on, assessing blame for the 1974 fiasco still occupies a certain amount of the South's agenda, and few people are willing to discuss it publicly (the main reason it took three editions of this guide to recruit a Greek-Cypriot viewpoint for "The events of summer 1974", p.414).

Top priority was given to **rehousing refugees** from both communities: the Turkish Cypriots simply occupied abundant abandoned Greek property in the North, but it took the South more than a decade to adequately shelter those who had fled the North. The international community, so disgracefully sluggish

Politics and elections in the South

Coalitions are a fact of life among the Greek Cypriots, since no one party is strong enough to govern alone. And in such a small society horse-trading and flexibility are vital; stances or declarations of one campaign are cheerfully eaten in the presence of new coalition partners at the next elections. Even very small parties – the threshold for entry into the parliament is 1.8 percent of the vote nationwide – are assiduously courted as partners, while shifts of party share of even a percentage point or two are hailed as major victories, or catastrophes. The South's **president** exercises considerable power, appointing all ministers. Both presidential and **parliamentary** elections occur every five years, but are at present out of sync: the former in years ending in 3 and 8, the latter in years ending in 1 and 6.

Tó Kypriakó or the **"Cyprus Question"** is theoretically the paramount electoral issue. In general, centre-right **DIKO** has stood for an idealistic solution, relying on cumulative international pressures to get the Turkish army to depart and the Turkish Cypriots to come to terms. Centrist **DISY**, preferring a pro-NATO/EU alignment, has advocated pragmatic deal-cutting directly with the Turkish Cypriots to get as many refugees home as quickly as possible. **AKEL** and **EDEK** point to their record of never having systematically harassed the Turkish-Cypriot community as a valuable asset for bridge-building in a theoretical federal republic. Left unarticulated are the massive concessions required, with some politician(s) allotted the unenviable task of announcing which refugee constituents could go home to the North, and who would have to stay in the South. After 1974, leftist parties were in a position to exert additional pressure, with many **social-welfare measures** introduced for the first time to alleviate some of the misery caused by the refugee influx.

In the House of Representatives elections of **1976**, AKEL, EDEK and Makarios's Popular Front combined to shut out Clerides' DISY party, thanks to a first-past-the-post system. After Makarios's death in 1977, his groomed successor Kyprianou served out the remainder of the archbishop's presidential term, then re-elected unopposed in **1978** as head of DIKO, an ostensibly new party, but still widely seen as Makarios's creature.

By **1981**, the system had changed to proportional representation; AKEL and DISY finished in a dead heat, with DIKO and EDEK holding the balance of power in the last 35-seat parliament; the **1983** presidential voting returned Kyprianou to office with AKEL backing, again excluding Clerides.

In the **1988** presidential contest **George Vassiliou**, a professional businessman and political outsider, was elected, backed by AKEL and DISY who, despite their wide differences on domestic issues, agreed that the timely resolution of the "Cyprus Question" was imperative. The **1991** parliamentary polls showed a slight rightward swing in the House, now enlarged to 56 seats.

On his fourth try for the presidency in February **1993**, DISY candidate **Clerides** upset AKEL-supported incumbent Vassiliou by less than two thousand votes in run-off polling. The result was regarded as a rejection of the UN-sponsored negotiations to date and an endorsement of Clerides' intent to pursue EU membership more strongly. The parliamentary elections of **1996** saw DISY and AKEL representation enhanced at the expense of DIKO and EDEK, though DISY entered into a coalition with EDEK (dissolved in January 1999). Clerides was re-elected president in **1998** by another razor-thin margin, polling second in a crowded first-round field but besting independent George Iakovou in the run-off.

while the problem was being created, was reasonably generous and prompt with reconstruction **aid** – aid which, however, went primarily to the South.

Strangely, **intercommunal negotiations resumed** almost immediately, though at first they centred almost entirely on the fate of Cypriots caught on

The House elections of May **2001** were on one level a reprise of 1981's, with AKEL and DISY again neck-and-neck, but with some startling differences. An unprecedented eight parties got parliamentary representation, 23 new deputies included six women among them, but the biggest surprise was the selection, with support from DIKO and EDEK (briefly renamed KISOS), of AKEL head Dimitris Christofias as president of the House, succeeding Kyprianou. This was an historic first occupation of high office by Cyprus Communists, defying DISY warnings that this would send the "wrong" message to the EU, and seen as a quid pro quo for AKEL's support of a DIKO or KISOS presidential candidate in 2003.

In the presidential contest of February **2003**, Clerides – despite a constitutional ban on a third run – announced in January that he would stand for a limited term. His opponent, DIKO's Tassos Papadopoulos, gained the support of AKEL as promised, plus EDEK and the Greens, scoring a decisive first-round victory over Clerides.

The first **Euro elections** with Cypriot participation, in June 2004, saw the four seats at stake taken by DISY and AKEL. In theory two more seats are reserved for Turkish Cypriots, should a settlement materialize before the next Euro elections in 2009.

The May **2006** House poll saw DIKO and EDEK improve their standing at the expense of AKEL and DISY. This made a repeat Papadopoulos victory in the February **2008** presidential contest more likely – until AKEL House chief Dimitris Christofias threw his hat in the ring. In a three-way contest with DISY figure Ioannis Kasoulides, with ballot numbers swelled by special DISY- and AKEL-chartered aircraft bringing home overseas Cypriots to vote, "Tassos" was shockingly eliminated in the first round, with Christofias besting Kasoulides in the run-off, then forming a "unity" government of AKEL, EDEK and DIKO ministers.

Greek-Cypriot political parties

AKEL *Anorthotikón Kómma tou Ergazoménou Laoú* or "Regenerative Party of the Working People" – in plain English, the Communist Party of Cyprus; historical enemies of EOKA and conciliatory towards the Turkish Cypriots. Until the early 1990s unreconstructed rather than Euro-communist, but now bourgeois and "social-democratic". Chaired by President Dimitris Christofias.

DIKO *Dhimokratikó Kómma* or "Democratic Party", centre-right party that's an outgrowth of Makarios's Popular Front; pursues a relatively tough line in negotiations with the North. Marios Karoyian has been party chief since 2006.

DISY *Dhimokratikós Synayermós* or the "Democratic Rally", formerly chaired by Glafkos Clerides, now headed by Nicos Anastasiades; despite a right-wing domestic and foreign policy, was the only party to back the Annan Plan.

EDEK *Eniéa Dhimokratikí Énosis Kéndrou* or "United Democratic Union of the Centre" – despite the name, a socialist party led since the 1960s by Vassos Lyssarides, perennial also-rans and coalition partners; after the 2001 elections, Lyssarides finally bowed out in favour of new chief Yiannakis Omirou.

Kínima Ikológi Perivallontistí (Cyprus Green Party) The ecologists, who managed to get a parliamentary seat in both the 2001 and 2006 elections.

New Horizons/European Party Irredentist, anti-federation party, opposed to UN-brokered negotiations; got a seat in the 2001 election, increased to three in 2006 by merger with European Party.

the "wrong" side. Greeks in the South separated from relatives and homes in the North were at first allowed to rejoin them; the government initially attempted to prevent Southern Turks from **trekking north**, but by early 1975 this too had happened. This departure was not entirely voluntary, especially in the case of Turkish Cypriots with extensive properties or businesses in the South, or with Orthodox Christian spouses; accounts abound, especially in the Páfos area, of Turkish and British army trucks virtually rounding up Turkish Cypriots, with their neighbours compelled to rescue those – usually non-observant Muslims or converts to Orthodoxy – who wished to stay behind. Once these Turks were safely on the "right" side of the Attila Line, most remaining northern Greeks were expelled and the North pronounced, over the South's protests, that an equitable exchange of populations had been carried out.

The North declared itself the **Turkish Federated State of Cyprus** (TFSC) in February 1975, though as always what the Turkish Cypriots meant by federation, and with whom, was quite different from what the South had in mind. Clerides and Denktaş, brought together again by UN Secretary-General **Kurt Waldheim**, made hopeful noises through much of 1975, but no substantive progress was registered. In 1977, Makarios and Denktaş met for the first time in fourteen years at the latter's request, agreeing on various **general guidelines** for a bicommunal, federal republic, the details of territorial jurisdiction to be determined later but envisioning a reduction in the amount Turkish-Cypriot-held territory.

After **Makarios died** in August 1977, **Spyros Kyprianou** replaced him as president and Greek-Cypriot representative at the on-again, off-again talks. As an initial goodwill measure, it was first suggested in 1978 that the empty **ghost town of Varósha** be resettled by its former Greek-Cypriot inhabitants: the Greeks wanted this to precede any other steps, while the Turks would only countenance it under limited conditions and as part of an overall settlement. The reopening of Nicosia international airport was also periodically proposed, though it is now obsolete and virtually unusable owing to urban growth (and summer temperatures in the Mesaoría, which limit modern jets). In 1981, Waldheim seized the initiative by presenting an "evaluation" of the talks thus far, and generating for the first time **detailed proposals** for the mechanics of a federal republic, which came to nothing.

In the international arena, the South increasingly protested against Turkish and Turkish-Cypriot practices in the North – specifically the **expulsion** of most Greek Cypriots and the denial of human rights to those remaining, the **settlement** of numerous Anatolian Turks to alter the demographic balance of the island and vandalism against Greek religious property. In short order a comprehensive and well-orchestrated embargo of the North was imposed with the assistance of most international agencies, which extended from declarations of its postal service and ports of entry as invalid, to consistent referral to the North's officeholders, civil servants and government as "so-called" or within inverted commas. Such boycotts of the North have ensured – among other things – that **archeological sites** are mostly neglected, since no archeologists would be permitted to work in a Greek-speaking country again if they were known to have visited the North, even just to inspect their old digs.

The North put another spanner in the works by unilaterally declaring full independence on November 15, 1983 as the **Turkish Republic of Northern Cyprus** (TRNC), generating the usual storm of pious UN resolutions of condemnation and widespread overseas support for the Greek-Cypriot position. To date no other state besides Turkey has recognized the TRNC. Yet talks towards a peaceful island-wide solution continued: early 1984 saw more proposals by Kyprianou to the UN, not significantly different from those before or since. **Javier Perez de Cuellar**, the new Secretary-General, presented successively refined draft frameworks for a federal settlement between 1985 and 1986; first the South said yes, but the North no; then the Turks agreed, but Kyprianou wavered until the **opportunity was lost** – behaviour for which he was roundly pilloried, and which contributed to his loss of office in 1988. He returned from the political dead in 1996, serving as president of the House of Representatives until shortly before his death in 2002.

1991–95: more fruitless talk

Late in 1991, Cyprus returned to the world stage; President George Bush, needing another foreign-policy feather in his cap prior to the 1992 US elections, called for **new peace conferences**, and visited both Turkey and Greece enlisting support – the first American presidential junket to either country in decades. Intercommunal meetings did not actually materialize until mid-1992, with **Boutros Boutros-Ghali** now UN Secretary-General. His "Set of Ideas" was broadly similar to all previous proposals: Varósha and some or all of the Mórfou plain would revert to Greek-Cypriot control, and Turkish-Cypriot-administered territory would shrink to 28 percent of the island's surface area. Left discussable was the degree of Greek refugees' return to the North; by gerrymandering the boundaries of the Turkish-Cypriot zone, most Greek Cypriots could go home without complications – Varósha and Mórfou taking most of the total – and even if all Greeks formerly resident in the agreed Turkish zone decided to go back, they would still be in a minority there.

Politically, a joint foreign ministry and finance ministry was foreseen, with the Cyprus pound reintroduced throughout the island. Either a rotating or an ethnically stipulated presidency was suggested, plus a two-house legislature, with the upper house biased towards the Turkish Cypriots in the sense that each federal unit would be represented equally, as the states are in the US Senate, rather than proportionately. Boutros-Ghali circulated a **tentative map** showing proposed adjustments of territory in a bizonal federation, to which many in the North reacted strongly. "We won't be refugees a third time" was a typical headline, referring to the previous compulsory shifts of 1964 and 1974.

July and October sessions between Vassiliou and Denktaş at the UN were unproductive; the Security Council passed yet another **resolution** in November 1992, the most strongly worded in years, mostly blaming failed negotiations on Denktaş for refusing to accept the Boutros-Ghali settlement guidelines. Denktaş's reaction was to threaten immediate resignation. Many began to suspect that Denktaş was content with the status quo, and had merely been humouring world opinion by his attendance at successive conferences.

Cyprus virtually disappeared from the international agenda during 1993 and 1994, except for the UN's recycling of the "Set of Ideas" as the so-called "**Confidence Building Measures**" (CBMs), in particular the rehabilitation of Nicosia airport and Varósha, and UN-mediated "informal talks" between Denktaş and new Greek-Cypriot president Clerides during October 1994. The UN announced that all essential elements for a solution were on the table, with only the political will lacking on each side to implement one.

Since his election in 1993, President Clerides had presided over a progressively **rightward tilt** in Southern politics. One conspicuous instance of this, early in 1995, was the reinstatement with back pay of 62 coup supporters – educators, civil servants and police officers who'd been cashiered years before – and the

Given the record of murderous suppression by TMT of its opponents, multiple parties or even factions were not actively encouraged among Turkish Cypriots until well after the founding of the Turkish Federated State of Cyprus in 1975. Even since, dubious tactics have often been used to nip budding opposition, though since the late 1990s conditions have more resembled genuine **pluralism.**

In **North Cyprus**, the political designations "Left" and "Right" do not equate to their meanings elsewhere: leftist parties advocate economic liberalism, free trade and a positive attitude towards the EU, along with an unfettered press and a more flexible position on the "Cyprus Question", while conservative parties stand for heavy state intervention in commerce, protectionism for select industries, complete deferral to Turkey rather than the EU, a swollen civil service and a hardline stance in negotiations with the South.

North Cyprus has a tiny electorate of about 125,000, with a high degree of **overlap** between government figures, business bigwigs and the habitual ruling parties, with politicking inevitably personalized. Though both a **president and a prime minister** are stipulated, President Denktaş was always the dominant figure until his 2005 retirement. Presidential and parliamentary elections have been held more or less together every five years, recently in years ending 5 and 0.

The first northern elections were in **1976**: Denktaş won easily with three-fourths of the vote and a like percentage of seats for his **UBP** in a forty-seat Assembly. In **1981** the UBP no longer enjoyed an absolute majority, sharing a hung parliament with the **TKP** and the **CTP**. Following an unstable period, the assembly was expanded to fifty seats, allowing Denktaş to fill ten vacancies with compliant appointees. In **1985**, only parties polling over eight percent were awarded seats, forcing splinter factions to disappear or amalgamate. A prohibition against more than two consecutive presidential terms was eliminated, and Denktaş ran as an **independent**. Although he retained office, the UBP's share of votes declined to just over a third, reflecting widespread disillusionment. Yet because of the various "reforms", its proportion of Assembly seats remained about half.

Denktaş was re-elected again in early **1990**, and prior to the May Assembly elections, more **changes in election laws** were introduced. These included a bonus-seat system for high-vote parties and a prohibition against coalition governments. The opposition's response to this last condition was to combine three smaller parties into the **DMP** (Democratic Struggle Party), running on a platform of less corruption, better economic management and liberalization of the official electronic media. But with just under half the vote, the DMP received less than one-third of Assembly seats, because of the bonus rule. Despite voter intimidation and the biased media, the UBP might well have still won fair elections.

In late 1992 Denktaş fell out with his prime minister **Derviş Eroğlu**, who accused the president of being (of all things) too "flexible" in dealings with the South. Ten MPs loyal to Denktaş defected, forming the *Demokrat Partisi* (**DP**), led by Hakki Atun and Serdar Denktaş. **December 1993** elections resulted in a near-tie between Eroğlu's UBP and the DP, a deadlock broken by DP's entry into an unprecedented

exiling of their opponents to minor posts. This was done unilaterally by the Clerides administration, over the objections of his parliament.

Spates of **terror attacks** and **gangland crimes** convulsed the South throughout 1995. The campaign of terrorist group EKAS, the "Greek-Cypriot Liberation Army", to extort donations from wealthy businessmen for ostensibly patriotic purposes was suppressed, but their activities were overshadowed by a series of car bombings, arson attacks and fatal shootings, all part of a battle to control the lucrative trade in cabaret girls, gambling dens and drugs. None of coalition with Özker Özgür's CTP. In **March 1995**, this coalition crumbled, which doubtless contributed to Denktaş's decision to stand yet again in April presidential elections, despite his announced intention to resign during 1995. Denktaş suffered the minor humiliation of a runoff against rival Eroğlu, which he won through the support of TKP and CTP members convinced Denktaş was the lesser of two evils. Shortly thereafter, the CTP–DP coalition revived under PM Hakki Atun; but in January 1996, Deputy PM Özker Özgür threw in the towel, exasperated by Denktaş's continued obstructionism in negotiations with the South, and was replaced at the CTP helm by Mehmet Ali Talat.

In **December 1998** parliamentary elections, the DP and TKP seat share remained stable, but the UBP increased its strength, mostly at the CTP's expense – with which, curiously, it entered into yet another coalition until June 2001, when the TKP bowed out and was promptly replaced by the UBP.

Presidential elections of **April 2000** saw a reprise of Denktaş vs. Eroğlu, and proved the most bizarre yet. Again Denktaş would have been forced into a runoff against his perennial rival, except that Eroğlu mysteriously conceded before the second round took place. No cogent explanation was given, though almost certainly mainland Turkish pressure secured the desired result.

Prior to parliamentary polls of **December 2003**, the authorities attempted to pad the registration rolls by hastily granting North citizenship to settlers, who were expected to vote for anti-settlement parties. The desired result was the CTP forced into a coalition with the DP; this duly collapsed in October 2004, with fresh elections in **February 2005** (after Turkey had received a green light from the EU to begin accession negotiations) rewarding **Mehmet Ali Talat's** CTP with exactly half the seats, but again locked in coalition with the DP. But in **April 2005**, Talat won the presidential contest against Eroğlu, and the DP was replaced in the coalition in September 2006 by an independent assemblyman and Mustafa Akıncı's pro-settlement **BDH**.

Turkish-Cypriot political parties

CTP *Cumhuriyetçi Türk Partisi* or "Republican Turkish Party", headed by Prime Minister Ferdi Sabit Soyer; analogous to the namesake centre-left-secularist Anatolian party. Theoretically conciliatory towards the South, though has only been effective in this respect since 2007.

DP *Demokrat Partisi*, a personality-centred hiving-off from the UBP and component of recent coalition governments, run by Serdar Denktaş, son of Rauf Denktaş.

TKP *Toplumcu Kurtuluş Partisi* or "Communal Liberation Party", headed by Mustafa Akıncı, a centre-left grouping strongly favouring rapprochement with the South. Combined in 2003 with pro-settlement United Cyprus Party to form the **BDH** (*Bariş ve Demokrasi Hareketi*) or "Peace and Democracy Movement".

UBP *Ulusal Birlik Partisi* or "National Unity Party", established by Rauf Denktaş in 1974 and governing the North alone until 1993; now headed by Tahsin Ertuğruloğlu.

the crimes was solved, and in December President Clerides made the sensational announcement that this was hardly surprising, given the **police** force's involvement in the underworld, and demanded the resignations of the national police chief and his deputy. All this severely dented the South's overseas image of savouriness and safety, and provided a propaganda windfall to the North, which was not slow to exploit it after years of being on the receiving end of a Southern slander campaign implying that North Cyprus was a dark and dangerous place heaving with Anatolian barbarians.

1996–99: resurgent tensions

Cynics reckon Cyprus only gets international attention when UNFICYP, balking at the cost of operations, threatens to leave; when it's a US presidential election year; or when the Cypriots themselves do something drastic to concentrate overseas minds. Before Bill Clinton, with Haitian, Bosnian and Israeli "successes" notched on his belt, could dispatch special envoy Richard Holbrooke to the island in 1996, events overtook such a turn.

Since a 1992 decision to scale down the UNFICYP presence, a regular pattern of **border incidents** had involved demonstrations by Southern refugee groups attempting to march to their old homes, counter-representations by Northerners and pitched battles on each side with their own police. Usually these were on or near the anniversary of the 1974 events, but every few weeks year-round a young male Greek-Cypriot motorist rammed barriers at a checkpoint and led Turkish soldiers on a merry chase before capture and a long prison term. The northern regime also began abducting or even killing Greek-Cypriot fishermen off Famagusta whom it claimed drifted into its territorial waters, as well as apprehending unarmed Greek Cypriots who strayed too far into the buffer zone.

But the worst such episode was in **August 1996**. Nationalist Greek-Cypriot motorcyclists announced a "rally", beginning in no-longer-divided Berlin and finishing in Kyrenia, to "end" the partition of Cyprus. The Orthodox Church of Cyprus provided material and moral support to the bikers who, though prevented from crossing the Attila Line, caused considerable provocation by riding through the buffer zone near Dherínia, accompanied by hundreds of stone-throwing, shouting **demonstrators**, unrestrained by southern police. The Turkish Cypriots had learned of the rally plans and invited a rent-a-mob of their own: ultra-nationalist, paramilitary Grey Wolves from the Turkish mainland, armed with batons and iron staves. Allowed into the buffer zone by the Turkish army, the Grey Wolves and similarly equipped Turkish-Cypriot policemen administered savage beatings to the Greek Cypriots, killing one – all action broadcast live on international television. Three days later, after the victim's funeral at nearby Paralímni, another riot erupted near Dherínia when the deceased's cousin attempted to scale a flagpole on the Turkish-Cypriot side of the buffer zone and pull down the Turkish flag; he was immediately shot dead by the Turkish Cypriots rather than arrested, and numerous UN peacekeepers were wounded by more Turkish gunfire as the crowds went berserk. The Greek-Cypriot ultra-nationalists had two **martyrs** (as perhaps was intended); belligerent soundbites were heard in Ankara, Athens and Nicosia South and North; and the Southern government – despite never officially endorsing the motorcylists' rally – laid on a second, de facto state funeral at Paralímni cathedral, attended by major dignitaries in both cases. It took weeks for cooler heads to prevail (the violence badly hurt tourism) and the threat of further skirmishes to recede – but not before two Turkish-Cypriot soldiers had been shot in revenge, by persons unknown firing from the "Five Mile Crossing" of the Dhekélia SBA.

Denktaş broke off further contact with Clerides in 1997, while Clinton's would-be envoy Robert Holbrooke opined that "this island is capable of exploding at any moment". In May 1998, the TRNC position **hardened** still further; Denktaş declared dead the notion of two federated zones under one government and demanded international recognition of the North as a separate and equal state prior to any further negotiations.

Alarmist scenarios of renewed, large-scale fighting on Cyprus were aired, given how each side was **stockpiling heavy weapons**: the Greek Cypriots supplied by

France, Greece, the Czech Republic and Russia, the Turkish Cypriots (of course) by Turkey. Although the South still commanded appreciable international sympathy and an impressive number of UN resolutions in its favour, they would still have come off worse in world opinion – not to mention militarily, outnumbered three to one in manpower – if they used this arms build-up to force the Turkish army off the island. The absence (except for August 1996) of overt clashes since 1974 should not, as the North's backers did, have been mistaken for true peace. Cyprus was still (and remains) one of the most **militarized** territories on earth: nearly 90,000 men under arms on all sides (including UN and British personnel), versus about 250,000 civilian males of fighting age.

Amid the South's resurgent jingoism, a hard-learned lesson of 1974 was in danger of being forgotten: that Cyprus is essentially indefensible from Greece, despite a much-vaunted 1993 defence pact with Greece, involving regular joint exercises with the Greek navy and air force. Without a significant air force of its own, offensive strategy for the South means having permanent, Greek-equipped **air bases** on its territory – an option which continues to preoccupy the Turks as it did during the 1960s. Accordingly, a Greek air-force base for F-16 fighters was built right next to the Páfos civilian airport – far from impregnable and considered locally as something of a joke.

If the Páfos air base concentrated Turkish minds, it was nothing compared to the disquiet provoked by the South's proposed 1997 purchase of sophisticated **Russian SS-300 surface-to-air missiles**. This highly mobile, truck-loaded defensive weapon, together with its state-of-the-art "Tombstone" radar guidance system, was publicly pooh-poohed by NATO members but privately admitted to be more effective than the Patriots used during the Gulf War. The integrated **radar system**, part-staffed by Russians and to be installed on Mount Olympus near the British site, would also be able to monitor NATO aircraft movements throughout the Middle East. From the moment the scheme was announced, Turkey threatened to use any means necessary – including intercepting the missiles while they sailed through the Bosporus Straits, or bombing them once delivered – to prevent installation. Apparently they had a healthier respect for the SS-300's potential to upset the local strategic balance than other NATO countries; the missiles were primarily meant to target not fighters but C-series transport planes full of Turkish paratroopers to be dropped on the South, a nightmare scenario for the Greek-Cypriot command.

Throughout 1997 and 1998 diplomatic pressure was brought to bear on President Clerides by the US, UK and others to **cancel** their deployment, while the cash-strapped Russians insisted that the deal was done and that somebody was going to have to cough up the purchase price. Finally, in late December 1998, Clerides caved in and announced that the missiles would be stationed on Crete instead, which only partly mollified the Turks. In retrospect the threatened missile purchase was a clumsily handled bargaining chip, to be abandoned as a "concession" once international attention was again focused on the island; if the Greek Cypriots had really been serious about acquiring both a defence system and a negotiating tactic, they would have installed missiles secretly with no fanfare, presenting it to the world as an accomplished fact.

2000–03: Northern meltdown

Matters might have continued deadlocked indefinitely if domestic unrest in the North, coupled with the collapse of the Turkish economy, hadn't

The Orthodox Church in Cyprus

Both Greek and Turkish Cypriots concede that the former are among the most religiously observant in the Orthodox Christian world, and much more devout than Muslim islanders; in no other eastern-rite country will you find, for example, *nistísima* or special vegetarian fare offered during Lent at local franchises of *McDonald's*. But the faithful have been poorly served in recent years, to put it mildly, by the Autocephalous Church of Cyprus, as ungodly an institution – once up the hierarchy from often conscientious parish priests – as you would never hope to see. It is a (if not the) major obstacle to communal reconciliation, xenophobic, anti-semitic, homophobic, thoroughly corrupt, and often involved in enterprises (especially real estate) that would be the province of lay mafias in other countries.

Church scandals

Much of the period from 1998 to 2008 was occupied by **scandals** which were trumpeted by the media and forfeited the Church much of its previous authority. First there was the 1998 case of the **deacon in Mórfou diocese**, a candidate for bishop, who took the precepts of the New Testament at face value: succouring the poor and conducting baptisms and weddings free of charge. Archbishop Chrysostomos I of All Cyprus, fearing depletion of the church's coffers, presided over a framing campaign whereby provocateurs tried to implicate the deacon in acts of buggery by throwing condoms into his cesspit, to be conveniently produced as evidence later (unfortunately they neglected to open the packets). When two essential "witnesses" fled abroad, the case was dropped, but the candidacy was already retracted.

The former, mid-1990s **Bishop of Limassol, Chrysanthos**, was among the most compromised in the church's upper echelons. He kept an American mistress and borrowed money to play the Nicosia stock market, losing it all. His creditors blew the whistle, the fraud squad flew out from Britain to interview him, and criminal proceedings were considered; he was defrocked, briefly banned from officiating at any service and made to do austere penances before leaving for America.

Chrysanthos had been instrumental in establishing two **convents** around Limassol; there are ten functioning on Cyprus at present, up from just one in Makarios's time. In the current climate, formerly murmured cynical sentiments are now openly voiced, namely that the convents exist partly to satisfy the "urges" of ecclesiastical higher-ups, who can't be seen visiting the traditional red-light districts or the modern "night clubs" which have replaced them. Assuming, of course, that the majority of the nominally celibate clergy are straight, which seems to be a moot point.

The **Limassol bishop** after 1999, **Athanasios**, proved a completely different sort from his predecessor, taking his pastoral mission seriously – and promised to be a strong candidate in any uninfluenced election to succeed the ailing archbishop of Cyprus. Bishop Chrysostomos of Páfos, sensing his pre-eminent position threatened, attempted during 2000 to repeat the dispatch of the unfortunate Mórfou deacon by accusing the new bishop of homosexual acts. Two archimandrites (senior priests) and two lay witnesses duly came forward to give evidence; a three-member **ecclesiastical tribunal**, split between the old guard and a reformer, failed to reach the necessary unanimous verdict, but the two veterans refused thereafter to co-officiate with Athanasios. The Church was forced to call in bishops from abroad for a full, thirteen-member **synod** (the island then only had nine), which found the Bishop of Limassol

reignited interest in an equitable settlement, not least among the Northern population.

On July 8, 2000, **Şener Levent**, editor of **Avrupa** (Europe), one of the few opposition newspapers in the North, was detained, along with three of his staff, on charges of spying for the South and "instigating hatred against the Turkish Republic of North Cyprus and the Turkish army", potentially facing five years in innocent within a day. A resourceful journalist then obtained phone records showing the two lay witnesses to have been coached by the Bishop of Páfos and his crony, the Bishop of Arsinoë (Pólis), and the two civilians were prosecuted and jailed for conspiracy for three months in early 2001. Chrysostomos's reputation, already poor – his nickname in some quarters is "The Goat" – lay in tatters; briefly it looked like he too would face **criminal prosecution**, but in the end only the two archimandrites were charged with conspiracy to defame and went to trial – mysteriously suspended in April 2001 by Attorney General Alekos Markides after Athanasios, acting as a prosecution witness, forgave the two conspirators in court. Cyprus at large was less indulgent; the Church, despite the mysterious halt in proceedings, had had its dirty linen thoroughly washed in public, and its credibility was at rock-bottom.

The main response since has been a massive **recruitment** drive for monks and nuns in schools, an acceleration in the **reoccupation** of empty or derelict monasteries, and their ostentatious signposting despite a resounding lack of intrinsic interest. Monastic premises are just a fraction of the huge amount of **property** owned by the Church, which it collects rents on, or sells outright as building sites, for everything from most foreign embassies to many coastal hotels. Increasingly murmurs are heard that taxes ought to be paid, and that the Autocephalous Church is hardly a "charitable", institution any longer. But AKEL, the Church's old enemy, was unable or unwilling to obtain any satisfaction on this in the House of Representatives after 2001.

Elections for archbishop
Since 2002, Archbishop Chrysostomos I had become senile, wheelchair-bound and (after 2005) comatose; his staff and family members set to work forging his signature and thus managed to embezzle huge quantities of church funds before being detected. It became clear that a **successor** would have to be chosen while the incumbent was still alive (a Cypriot first), and so Chrysostomos was forcibly retired in autumn 2006. By tradition, the new archbishop ought to be the most senior from among the bishops of Kyrenia, Salamis, Mórfou, Arsinoë, Trimithi, Kýkkou, Limassol, Kition and Páfos – in 2006, the Bishop of Páfos, aka "The Goat". But in Cyprus bishops and archbishops are elected by a complex system of successive polls: first parishioners choose 1400 delegates, who in turn elect 100 delegates, who then choose the winner together with a tribune of 33 clerics; the support of a civilian political party is also essential. The main candidates were Athanasios of Limassol, the popular Bishop Nikiphoros of Kýkkou, and "The Goat". To widespread disgust, Athanasios and Chrysostomos cut an under-the-table deal; for reasons unknown, Nikiphoros then quit the race, swinging decisive support to "The Goat", who hadn't been expected to reach the second round of polling, with only about twenty percent initial support.

Political parties emerged with hardly more credit – AKEL openly backed Nikiphoros, but then waxed indignant when Chrysostomos II of All Cyprus – the ex-Goat – endorsed first incumbent Papadopoulos and then DISY figure Ioannis Kasoulides in the 2008 presidential race. The result of all this is that the church's **prestige** is at an all-time low, unlikely ever to recover until or unless a progressive bishop like Neophytos of Mórfou, who has distinguished himself from his fellows through his support for communal reconciliation and by remaining free from scandal, attains the top office.

jail. Their release ten days later, following local and international pressure, was the cue for opposition demonstrations 10,000 strong; on July 24, more street rallies protesting against the ongoing economic stagnation and the first in a wave of bank failures turned violent, with organizers arrested. Judicial harassment of *Avrupa* continued through the year, with contributing journalists (and politicians) Özker Özgür and İzzet Izcan hauled into court for sedition, and lawsuits by the

Denktaş family for libel. On November 27 the *Avrupa* premises were set alight (an "electrical fault" was officially announced), on May 24, 2001, the printworks used by *Avrupa* were bombed, and by mid-December 2001 *Avrupa* had been closed down and its plant confiscated in lieu of civil damages to the victorious Denktaş. Levent managed to reopen the paper in early 2002, rechristened *Afrika* in line with the Zimbabwe-type public culture prevailing in the North, but ended up serving some months in jail after a fresh prosecution in August 2002. By late 2003, journalists at normally tame *Ortam* and *Kıbns* were also being prosecuted for stories deemed insulting to the powers that were.

Meanwhile, a free press was not always foremost in Turkish-Cypriot minds. The implosion of the mainland Turkish banking system early in 2001 took with it most North Cypriot **banks**; by the end of the year seven island-based financial institutions had collapsed, to the tune of $200 million worth of uninsured deposits. Unlike in Turkey, there were no bailouts whatsoever, and most other banks continued on artificial life-support, acting primarily to launder money and hand out unsecured loans. Only those existing prior to 1974, and insured mainland-based banks, survived. Observers were treated to the unedifying spectacle of increasing destitution juxtaposed with a growing range of consumer durables on sale to an elite of regime-connected apparatchiks that could still afford them.

The mainland Turkish intervention, and its three-decade aftermath, was increasingly seen as a classic example of "Be careful what you wish for". Though unanimously acclaimed by Turkish Cypriots at the time, a growing proportion of them deemed the mainlanders to have long outstayed their welcome, and to have become new, onerous masters replacing the Greek Cypriots. By paying to keep the North afloat, including directly employing an estimated 36,000, Turkey expected to call the shots locally, down to the last detail. Long-simmering resentment of Turkish tutelage finally boiled over early in 2001, when, in response to an announced $350 million "aid" package from the mainland, the teachers' union took out a newspaper advert suggesting what they could do with the money. For their troubles the union offices were raided, a court case instituted, and over the next year various individual instructors sacked from their jobs. Despite this intimidation, they and several other unions, NGOs and opposition parties went on to form the Group of 41 by mid-summer, under the slogan "This Country is Ours", which would within a year become the 92-member "**Common Vision**", coordinating street demonstrations over the next twenty months.

The ruling elite was not slow in reacting; the **UHH** (*Ulusal Halk Hareket* or National Patriotic Movement), seen as the reincarnation of TMT, was formed in May, and promptly stepped up intimidation of anyone wishing to cross into the South, especially to attend communal reconciliation events in the buffer zone, at Pýla village or the Ledra Palace.

Most ominously from the Turkish nationalists' point of view, during 2001 there was a sharp rise in Turkish-Cypriot applications for **passports** issued by the South. Already, since the early 1990s, there had been an estimated four thousand northerners holding Republic of Cyprus passports, these individuals periodically threatened with prosecution from the TRNC authorities. By late 2005, the figure had reached 35,000 RoC passport-holders in the North. Obtaining such a document was a hedge against there being no settlement in the near future; should the South alone join the EU (as eventually happened), Turkish Cypriots counted among its citizens would be free to seek better lives either in the South or in western Europe. As the GDR's experience of its citizens fleeing to the West via Hungary in 1989 demonstrated, when a regime starts haemorrhaging its most intrepid folk, its days are numbered.

To all this agitation, Rauf Denktaş had only the following retort: "Those who are against Turkey are wrong. There is no Cypriot culture, apart from our national custom of drinking brandy. There are Turks of Cyprus and Greeks of Cyprus. The only true Cypriots are its donkeys." The last sentence, unrecorded in the international media, was a calculated jibe at anyone advocating an island-based patriotism; in both Greek and Turkish, "donkey" (and additionally in Turkish, "son of a donkey") are exceptionally abusive insults – Cypriot farm boys traditionally had their first sexual experience with the back end of a donkey-mare.

Perhaps it was Denktaş's desire to go down in history as a great statesman; or pressure from Turkish businessmen feeling that the Cypriot tail had wagged the Anatolian dog long enough; or maybe the IMF implying that bail-out aid to the prostrate Turkish economy would be more generous if Cyprus was sorted; or perhaps the looming June 2002 EU decision on Cypriot membership. In any event something – probably not Northern public opinion – prompted Denktaş to **renew communication** with Clerides after a four-year gap, under the aegis of new UN Special Cyprus Adviser Alvaro de Soto. On December 6, 2001, Clerides responded to an invitation from Denktaş to attend dinner in North Nicosia, the first visit by a Greek-Cypriot leader to the Turkish-Cypriot zone since 1974. After a reciprocal visit by Denktaş to the South on December 29, the two men – who had known each other since acting as prosecutor and defence respectively for EOKA suspects being tried in a colonial Crown Court during the 1950s – agreed to meet regularly from mid-January onwards to hammer out a solution.

Against a backdrop of continued harassment and prosecution of opposition figures in the North, **six rounds** of high-level talks occurred in Nicosia between January and September, but by October Denktaş was too ill with heart disease to continue. Based on the talks to date, UN Secretary-General Kofi Annan presented what became known as the first **Annan Plan** for a federal solution in mid-November. Turkish Cypriot opposition groups organized **massive rallies**, sometimes comprising over half the adult population of the North, in central Nicosia every month from November until February 2003, demanding a federal settlement and EU membership for the entire island. In February, Clerides unexpectedly lost the southern **presidential elections** to more hard-line DIKO chief Tassos Papadopoulos, and the prospects of success in negotiations seemed slimmer than ever. In March 2003 Denktaş rejected the Annan Plan's third version, earning himself yet another censure from the Security Council.

Good Wednesday: barriers down

Denktaş's (indirect) response was another bolt from the blue – the announcement, on April 23 during Orthodox Holy Week, a date subsequently dubbed **"Good Wednesday"**, of the **lifting of most restrictions on crossing the Green/Attila Line** in either direction. Some speculated that Turkey had had a word in his ear; others that it was a safety valve for accumulated popular misery in the North, permitting routine shopping and employment in the South which had hitherto been done clandestinely – and a bonanza for northern tourist enterprises who suddenly found themselves with new, Greek-Cypriot customers. Four official "border" points opened immediately, and thousands of islanders began crossing back and forth, with moving reunions a-plenty, visits to home villages, churches and mosques, and a general euphoria and conviction that "people power" had left the politicians far behind. By late 2003, well over half of each community had been to the "other" side at least once, with almost none of the violence promised by ultra-nationalists in each camp.

The South, initially caught on the hop, eventually reciprocated with measures designed to facilitate trade and communications between the two parts of the island, and made it much easier for Turkish Cypriots to join professional organizations and get official paperwork done in the South. Turkey responded by allowing Greek Cypriots to visit that country for the first time in 29 years, though official Turkish recognition of the South was (and still is) not yet on the table.

Closer to home, Greek-Cypriots resented the necessity of showing passports (later just ID cards) at the barriers to travel as tourists into what they felt was their own country. Among visitors, some refused to spend a cent in the North, picnicking instead at the roadside; others ostentatiously patronized only Turkish-, Maronite- or Greek-Cypriot businesses, while snubbing settler-run enterprises. During 2003–2005, the North became established as a "**dirty weekend**" **venue** for some Greek Cypriots, where they go in their off-hours for anything – hookers, casinos, wild mushrooms or asparagus, pickled songbirds, oriental sweetmeats – that's cheaper, better or more legal than at "home". Since then, numbers of crossings from South to North have fallen sharply, as the novelty wore off and disillusionment set in.

Less frivolously, the breaching of the divide awoke the North from its long developmental slumber. Sensing that a definitive settlement might come sooner than later, and resolved to create facts on the ground, contractors commenced a **building boom** (see p.44) which shows little sign of abating, disfiguring much of the north coast and promising to reduce the aesthetic and ecological differences between North and South to nil.

2003–04: the end of Annan, the start of EU membership

Negotiations for the **accession of Cyprus to the European Union** (EU) proceeded in parallel with the UN-sponsored peace talks throughout 2002 and the first third of 2003. As part of the South's decreased reliance on an UN-brokered settlement, membership of the EU had been vigorously pursued since the early 1990s as a way of forcing the issue: Europeanization versus Makarios's old strategy of internationalization. Turkey would thus be occupying the territory of an EU member state, and denying universally accepted, pan-European rights of residence and commerce to its former Greek-Cypriot inhabitants. After considerable misgivings about inheriting an unsolved communal conflict, and the penetration of both economies by organized crime and money-laundering, the EU gave "Cyprus" a clean bill of health – and made it clear that, were there no final solution by May 1, 2004, the South alone would join along with nine other new candiates. Although this was intended as a warning to the Euro-phobe TRNC (who declined to send any official delegation to Brussels for negotiations, leaving it to opposition politicians and NGOs to talk to EU and mainland Greek officials), it had the effect of removing most incentives for the South to progress meaningfully towards reunification.

EU membership, confirmed by an accession treaty of April 16, 2003, had profound, perhaps unintended, consequences. As elsewhere, thousands of resident foreigners got voting rights in municipal and Euro-MP elections, conceivably in numbers sufficient to decide habitually close polls, a tricky possibility on an island with a history of being bullied by powerful outsiders. This supposed catalyst to a federal solution still risks backfiring, as membership for the South alone may just consolidate the island's partition, with or without Turkey actually acting on its periodic threat to **annex the North** outright if Cyprus got into the EU, and Turkey didn't. This is less likely to happen since Turkey itself got a date to begin accession negotiations in December 2004; besides the tremendous international outcry which would follow formal annexation, Turkey would find its own entry negotiations abruptly halted. Before December 2004, the Turks viewed EU membership, for either the South alone or the entire island, as back-door *énosis*, since Greece is a member and Turkey – for the immediate future – is not. By March 31, 2004, the **Annan Plan** had gone through five versions, most of the successive changes answering Turkey's (and Denktaş's) objections. Versions three and above contained the interesting provision, never before featured in UN plans, for Britain to cede half its SBA territory to any future federal republic (ninety percent of this, however, to the Greek-Cypriot entity). Other territorial adjustments (amounting to eight percent of the island's area) were as expected, with land – including Varósha, most of the Mórfou plain and large numbers of formerly Greek Cypriot villages on the Mesaória – returned to the South over a three-year period along a curiously shaped border allowing up to 100,000 refugees to go home. However the rest of the convoluted document, running to over a thousand pages, merely repeated many of the mistakes of the ill-fated 1960 Constitution and added some new ones (see p.410) manifestly contrary to the principles of both the UN and EU.

The UN compounded its errors by scheduling the **referendum on April 24, 2004**, just a week before EU accession, in the hope that a unified island would join. Even given that various versions had been under discussion since October 2003, it was a hopelessly abbreviated time to explain such a complex settlement, and neither government on the island displayed much interest in doing so. "NO" forces in the South quickly mobilized, while President Papadopoulos made an impassioned three-hour address on April 7 condemning the plan. "YES" advocates, including UN envoy Alvaro de Soto, were intimidated, accused of being *Tourkófili* (Turk-lovers) and denied access to government media and private advertising, which were both put at the full disposal of the anti-Plan forces. Bishop Pavlos of Kyrenia threatened parishioners who voted "yes" with eternal damnation, while a fellow bishop stocked his fridge with champagne for a bash with his old EOKA mates in the likely event of the Plan's defeat. The only notable politicians to defend Annan were DISY cadres and ex-presidents Clerides and Vassiliou, and the only major newspaper to do so was *Politis*. International figures were resigned to defeat in the South, but hoped that the margin would be narrow enough so that the referendum could be soon resubmitted to the electorate, after minor tinkering. When AKEL – commanding nearly one-third of voters – joined the "no" camp on April 21, having failed to get the poll delayed, the Annan Plan was doomed to a **crushing defeat**. On the day, Greek Cypriots voted against it by a margin of 3:1, while Turkish Cypriots defied Denktaş and Turkish nationalist rent-a-mobs by favouring it by 2:1, but to no avail as both communities had to vote "yes". Turnout was nearly identical on both sides (87–88 percent), so nobody could say the poll was unrepresentative.

Recriminations and post-mortems began at once. EU Enlargement Commissioner Günter Verheugen accused President Papadopoulos of betrayal by pretending to accept the Annan Plan in principle but actively campaigning against it. The EU warned that the North would be rewarded for its "yes" stance by direct "convergence" aid (259 million euros) – never actually delivered – and a possible end to its international embargo, leading to a Taiwan-ish status. South Cyprus alone entered the EU and went straight to the doghouse, while Turkey basked in the unaccustomed role of UN poster-child for its support of the plan. UN Secretary-General Annan expressed his regrets for the missed opportunity, reiterated that no "alternative" plan was available, and essentially washed his hands of the island until the Greek Cypriots had a change of heart.

Despite the conduct of the "NO" camp, it's undisputable that there were fatal problems with the plan, and southern voters would likely have rejected it even if Papadopoulos and/or AKEL had backed it. **Reasons for a negative vote** were almost as numerous as Greek-Cypriot voters, but fell under the general categories of inadequate security guarantees, economic iniquities, and derogation from EU-wide human rights norms, with reservations about the viability of the proposed federal state and the status of mainland Turkish settlers important secondary considerations. Turkish-Cypriots approved Annan not least because they would have done conspicuously better out of it, compared to the South.

Most ominously, the Annan Plan retained the Treaty of Guarantee in toto, and required Cypriots to completely **disarm** themselves – including the South's painstakingly prepared air defence systems – and accept indefinite stationing of up to six thousand Greek and Turkish troops on the island. Turkey would have been largely responsible for air traffic control, and could exercise a veto on exploration for undersea oil in the Karamanian Straits (offshore oil-drilling rights was also suspected as a factor in the UK's retaining some base territory). The Plan also in effect required the South to subsidize the **costs** of remedying the consequences of Turkey's 1974 intervention, a sum estimated at ten billion euros and, even allowing for some EU largesse, clearly beyond the capacity of the island's total economy (the North is one-tenth the size of the South) now or in future. Neither Turkey, Greece, the UK or the US – all variously culpable for the situation – were asked to stump up any money to bring the North's infrastructure up to scratch, or to create a slush fund to compensate refugee property-owners who can't return home.

The Annan Plan **limited population resettlement** in either direction to three percent annually of the total refugee population in either community, thus stringing out the process of theoretical resettlement for up to twenty years – something which rankled on the Greek Cypriot side as a brazen opt-out from internationally accepted norms, but was designed to prevent Turkish Cypriots in the North from being swamped. Although the Greek Cypriots paid, and still pay, full lip service to freedom of movement, far more Turkish Cypriots would have come south to reclaim now-hyper-valuable property than the reverse process. Thus the **potential of losing** what one had gradually accumulated over three decades loomed large. Tourism bigwigs in the South would hardly welcome a massive shift of clientele to the manifestly superior beaches of the North. Greek Cypriots who had been given, or squatted, abandoned Turkish Cypriot properties in the South faced the prospect of the original owners reclaiming them, with no compensation for any improvements made during the interim, and naturally voted "no". And as in the Turkish Cypriot community, there's a significant minority of ultra-nationalists – perhaps four percent – who prefer to continue living separately.

Annan also allowed 45,000 Turkish **settlers** to remain, to compensate for the like number of native Turkish Cypriots who have left the island since 1974; Greek-Cypriot maximalists want most or all settlers to leave, but the

North admits that it "naturalized" 64,000 settlers up to 2003, who then voted in the 2004 referendum. An accurate, island-wide **census** should have been conducted before the poll, and will be mandatory before any new attempt. **Cross-voting**, whereby critical office-holders in the mooted federal republic would have to receive a majority of votes from both ethnic communities, was expressly ruled out by Denktaş during negotiations, so the civic arrangements of Annan merely reprised the disruptive tribalism of the 1960 Constitution. Moreover, it committed the new federal state to back Turkish entry to the EU in future, no matter how Turkey behaved meanwhile, thus depriving the Greek Cypriots of one of their major diplomatic levers for inducing the Turks to leave the North.

2005–08: Last Chance Saloon?

The hangover from the April 2004 fiasco lasted well into 2007, and what tentative settlement initiatives occurred were hostage to unusually volatile domestic politics in Turkey, who as ever will hold the key to approving any solution. The UN kept its head down except for a **July 8, 2006** meeting between Turkish-Cypriot leader Mehmet Ali Talat and Papadopoulos, mediated by new UN envoy Ibrahim Gambari, which among the usual pious platitudes, agreed to set up seven bicommunal **"Technical Committees"** and six **"Working Groups"** to address the tough nuts-and-bolts issues of any peace agreement. Thanks in part to Papadopoulos' foot-dragging, nothing was really done over the next 18 months, other than introducing a reduction in mandatory military service in both communities to 12 months, making significant progress in clearing both Greek-Cypriot minefields and the UN ones in the buffer zone – and UN's **Committee for Missing Persons** reducing the number of post-1974 disappeared by the painstaking discovery and exhumation of many mass graves with over four hundred victims from both communities. Those with guilty consciences – either witnesses or perpetrators of atrocities – are finally speaking out, and it seems that a South-African-style Truth and Reconciliation Commission could, or should, be part of any settlement, replacing the partisan victims' memorials which are the rule now.

Tassos Papadopoulos' surprise first-round elimination from the South's three-way February **2008 presidential contest** finally ended these doldrums. Within hours of his runoff victory, AKEL President Demetris Christofias affirmed his long-standing commitment to finding a solution, and quickly got in touch with Mehmet Ali Talat. The first tangible result of the thaw was the early April **opening of the Lídhras/Lokmacı crossing** in central Nicosia, long anticipated but long delayed by "technicalities" (including Turkish Army interference with UN minesweeping). After the technical committees and working groups made their final report in late July, the two leaders resumed face-to-face negotiations on September 3. Talat and Christofias, both notionally from the same side of the political spectrum, have long been on friendly terms, meeting clandestinely overseas during the bleakest years when Denktaş's regime forbade such contacts.

Outlines of a settlement

Everyone involved privately admits that any settlement will resemble every UN plan presented since 1992. This means a **"United Cyprus Republic"** comprised of two federal units, with a single international personality and EU membership throughout. Border adjustments will closely resemble those of Annan, this being one aspect about which few complaints were heard. There will be a rotating presidency drawn from members of a six-person executive council of four Greek Cypriots and two Turkish Cypriots, and a two-chamber parliament, with the upper house containing equal numbers of Greek Cypriot and Turkish Cypriot "senators". A Supreme Court would be ethnically balanced, with three foreign judges casting tie-breaking votes as necessary. Ercan Airport on the federal border would be legitimized and upgraded as Nicosia's designated airport, with separate access to North and South (the way Geneva has French and Swiss exits).

The devil, as ever, will be in the details, especially concerning **property rights**. To outsiders it can seem that Greek Cypriots especially are fixated on the economic and real-estate aspects of the problem and pay little heed to its civic aspects, but Cyprus is traditionally an agrarian culture, to which land is central – if lately to build on rather than cultivate. That said, few refugees – setting aside town-dwellers from Mórfou, Varósha, Larnaca and Limassol – would return to pre-1974 rural properties, even for use as a weekend home; life has changed too much since then, and they now have a taste for urban comforts. As a counter to this increased urbanization, the establishment of **national parks** in Akámas and Karpaz – one for each federal unit – has been proposed as some token atonement for the rape of the Cypriot coasts, as has the **reconstruction** of ruined Varósha on **bioclimatic** principles.

What refugees want, however, is legal title to their original properties and the right, if not to occupy them, to sell them at market prices (Annan envisioned risible compensation). In the past, partition advocates argued that there would be no need for any settlement if a title swap were arranged, with all refugees laying de jure claim to what they occupied, or if all refugees were paid market-rate compensation for property they lost. But estimates differ wildly as **abandoned property** values – Turkish-Cypriot real estate in the South is vastly undervalued officially compared with Greek-Cypriot property in the North – and integral to any new solution is the establishment of just assessments and a corruption-free property board to oversee compensation, long-term leases, swaps and the like.

Lacking until now any orderly formulae for dealing with this issue, both Greek and Turkish Cypriots have pursued property feuds with **court litigation** or other (extra-)legal maneouvres. In 1995, for example, Denktaş threatened to distribute full, rather than provisional, title deeds of Greek-Cypriot properties to Turkish Cypriots and Anatolian settlers, a ploy which provoked various governing-coalition collapses. In 1989, a refugee from Kyrenia, Titina Loizidou, took Turkey to the European Court of Justice, asserting that her human rights were being violated by her inability to return home, while a Turkish-Cypriot family from the South, long resident in the UK but retaining Cypriot citizenship, sued in Cyprus to regain possession of their land near Limassol, which had been used for building refugee housing after 1974. The European Court eventually awarded Loizidou substantial damages – which Turkey grudgingly paid (plus interest) in 2003, with the proviso that no more embarrassing cases be heard in Strasbourg, but only on Cyprus itself. The ongoing building boom on Greek-Cypriot land in the North will, failing a prompt settlement, doubtless result in a new wave of cases.

As for **freedom of movement**, there will probably be some artificial protection (ie restrictions on Greek-Cypriot ownership and residence) of a Turkish-Cypriot state in the medium term, to guard against token representation and forced buyouts of Turkish-Cypriot businesses; the number of major tourist enterprises kept by Turkish Cypriots before 1974, for example, could be counted on one hand, and – always the poorer community even before the enclave era – they indisputably faced de facto discrimination in the unitary republic. Any delays in Greek Cypriots exercising such freedoms in the North would also serve for those personally involved in EOKA and EOKA-B atrocities to pass away – though since "Good Wednesday" such individuals have kept a low profile, in the North at least.

One can't overestimate the degree of **bitterness** which used to divide Greek and Turkish Cypriots until the millennium year. It could be said that for Greek Cypriots, 1974 was the beginning of history – for which read invasion, dispossession and expulsion while for Turkish Cypriots, 1974 marked the end of history – which for them had meant attacks, enclaves and disenfranchisement. Memorials to those killed by whomever between 1954 and 1975 remain lovingly tended in every village; grandiose, post-1994 monuments glorify EOKA as part of a ratcheted-up Hellenic climate in the South. Children of each community were long raised to believe that their opposite numbers come equipped with horns and a curly tail – the fault of **objectionable history textbooks** used in both the South and North which, as elsewhere in the Balkans and Middle East, fuel ill-feeling. The Annan Plan provided for establishing a mutually agreed version of the truth, complete with shared symbols and institutions, and indeed "Joint History Workbooks", compiled by sixty Balkan scholars, have already appeared in Greek and Turkish.

Particularly since "Good Wednesday", bitterness has been partly replaced by **cautious hope and goodwill**, though these won't substitute for the hard graft of making an improbably complex state function. Southern reconciliationists realize that **time** – perhaps a couple of years more before countries begin recognizing the North – is **not on their side**. The example of Kosovo's February 2008 UDI, with the connivance of much of the international community, has concentrated minds. A solution must come within the lifetime of those who can remember living in an unsegregated society. Those born since 1960 or so have never known anything else, and those not displaced by the 1974 events have become habituated to a truncated realm, and regard change with indifference unless it's really made attractive to them.

In **the North**, time is also seen to be of the essence, as it faces the unenviable choice of being swallowed up by Turkey – it is already a colony in all but name – risking renewed domination by Greek Cypriots, or being saved by the more benign embrace of the EU from a situation where mainland Turks own all the multi-star hotels, mainland Turkish universities open campuses to squeeze out the local diploma-mills, and the trade deficit swells as the only exports to Turkey are a few oranges. Among Turkish Cypriots, the age dynamic is reversed: it's the under-40s who marched at anti-Denktaş and reconciliation rallies, while their elders who lived through EOKA were (and are) warier. Ask older people who suffered pre-1974 at the hands of Greek-Cypriots if they hate them, and you may be told, "I don't hate the Greeks any more. But I still don't trust them." To which Greek Cypriots reply that they have no reason to trust (mainland) Turks. Accordingly, any settlement would rely on EU- or UN-staffed security forces, as NATO forces (including mainland Turks and Greeks) would be anathema to the opposite community.

Prospects for a deal have never looked better, not least because it would be generated by Cypriots rather than imposed by outsiders, benign or otherwise. Any **new plan** would also be submitted to approval by referendum, but this time it would be aggressively advocated by its two architects to their respective communities.

The events of summer 1974: personal accounts

T he following accounts are intended mainly to illustrate the personal impact of events during July–August 1974. Their authorship – a Turkish Cypriot, a Greek Cypriot and an American expatriate – constitutes no endorsement of any position, nor do they imply that any group suffered more than another.

Dana Davies's story

Dana Davies is the daughter of the late American ambassador to Cyprus, Rodger Paul Davies. She now lives in California.

I was a 20-year-old sophomore at Mills College in Oakland, California, in March 1974 when I first learned that we would be moving to Cyprus; I was also attending a Middle Eastern history seminar at UC Berkeley, where by coincidence we were actually studying Cyprus. My father was considered an Arab specialist and had spent most of his 28-year diplomatic career working in the Bureau of Near Eastern and South Asian Affairs, having been stationed in Saudi Arabia, Syria, Libya and Iraq. A Mediterranean island seemed spectacular by comparison, so when Dad asked me if I could take time off from school to serve as his hostess, I jumped at the chance. But a one-day crash-course in Washington DC on the protocol of running an ambassadorial residence hardly prepared me for what actually lay ahead.

As of July 15, I had lived in Nicosia for just sixteen days. The summer stretched before me with promises of new friends, diplomatic functions and learning to speak Greek. All that changed at 8.30am that day, when dull thumps accompanied by firecracker-like pops awoke me in the embassy residence. I wondered briefly if I was hearing gunfire from the Green Line; during the past two weeks we had heard several brief bursts. This cacophony, however, continued, and sounded much closer than downtown. I had nearly convinced myself that the sounds were coming from a building site across the street when the phone rang. In short, gruff phrases Dad informed me that a coup was under way. I was to get my brother John and move quickly to the den, which was the only room with no windows facing the street, and wait for further instructions. He answered my pleas for more information with "We just don't know anything. I'll call when we do."

For the next several hours we were alone in that room with little contact with the outside world. The television was useless: loud military music played over a frozen image of the Cypriot flag, broadcast continuously. The BBC and British Armed Forces stations were equally frustrating; news of the coup had not reached the rest of the world, judging from continuous talk of dreary London fog and ongoing reports on the Watergate scandal. From now until our evacuation on July 22, I was able to leave the embassy compound only twice, so my understanding of events relied heavily on what Cypriot embassy employees, foreign service officers and Marine guards told me.

My initial worry was for our household staff. Andreas lived in a village south of Nicosia and drove into town every Monday morning, stopping downtown to do our shopping; I was certain he must be trapped by the fighting. We also had two housekeepers who lived in Nicosia, whom we imagined must be in some danger out on the streets. We called downstairs and were told that they hadn't heard from anyone who wasn't actually in the building before 8.30am. Shortly before noon Antoinette Varnava, a Maronite Cypriot from Kormakíti village who was an administrative assistant for the embassy, came upstairs to help us prepare a tray of sandwiches and fruit for embassy personnel on the floors below. John and I had been obediently avoiding windows all morning, but "Toni" – already one of our favourite people there – was determined to view the city from our living room, the largest in the residence, so we joined her. From the waist up, three walls were actually windows, from which we could see most of Nicosia and the Pendadháktylos range to the north. To our horror, the eastern window revealed a mushroom cloud rising from the skeleton of the presidential palace's domed roof. [*NB Ms Davies, along with many observers, was mistaken; the archiepicopal palace had been attacked, while Makarios was actually in the intact presidential palace.*] I heard Toni swallow a sob and followed her gaze to the archbishop's residence; its majestic arcade had jagged black bites in the stonework and we could see flames licking at the yellow-and-white masonry. "How could they!" she cried. "Not a man of the cloth! He didn't have a chance." I clumsily tried to comfort her: "But Toni, I thought you were a Maronite Christian, not Orthodox." "Orthodox, Maronite, it makes no difference. Even if one does not agree with the politics, it is not right to kill a man of the cloth!" Later that night, when we learned that Makarios had escaped to Páfos, even those embassy staff who had opposed some of his policies expressed relief that he had not been killed.

Later that afternoon both Andreas and our housekeeper Anna made it to the residence. Andreas had been taking his two children to summer school when he found himself trapped for hours behind a road-block near the presidential palace, watching pillars of smoke pour from the building. After settling his children in a small room off the kitchen, Andreas set to whipping up meals for the 45 employees and embassy dependants we would be feeding three times daily for the next week. Embassy officers defied the curfew to accumulate cooked chickens from the Hilton, bread from a favourite restaurant and a freezer full of meat from one of their own houses, defrosting since the power had been cut. Nicos, another assistant, also managed to run regular errands; much to our alarm, he drove Dad out to Béllapais to meet with the UN forces commander – which let us know that most of the trouble was confined to the capital. They also managed to find an open market selling fish and fresh vegetables.

Our other housekeeper, Anna, lived close by and so was able to go home sooner than other employees; it wasn't until she returned to work on Thursday that we learned she hadn't seen her son, a young National Guardsman, since Monday morning. From her we had our first accounts of trucks full of bodies driving out of the city. Also trapped in the embassy on Monday were two men – one a Turkish Cypriot, the other a member of Makarios' palace guard – who often travelled with my father as bodyguards. As John and I brought food to the buffet table in the living room, we saw these two huddled together, whispering about the situation; only later did I understand that these men in particular would both have been in extreme danger had they left the embassy before Wednesday or Thursday and been caught by EOKA-B members.

Dad stood by his promise of keeping us informed on developments; shortly after lunch he rang and told me to turn on the television. The coup leaders were expected to make an announcement naming their leader and declaring the status of their military exercise. The onscreen visuals had not changed from the static flag, but the martial music was now punctuated every thirty seconds with a brusque announcement. Dad and two of his officers who spoke fluent Greek arrived shortly, and translated the announcement as a reiteration of one on the radio instructing the public to stand by for important information. It was nearly half an hour before the big announcement came, but during that time these three gave me a good outline of the morning's events, learned in turn from an American staff member trapped at home near the palace when the coup erupted. He had a portable two-way radio, and despite repeated orders to take cover, had spent the morning on his apartment building roof, relaying detailed reports of the attack, thus giving the embassy much-needed information about possible open roadways and enabling foreign service officers to reach Americans and embassy dependants stranded across the city.

As time wore on, conversation turned to jokes about the coup leaders, and their lack of forethought as to who would assume leadership; one even wondered if they were trying to bribe someone to take the position, and who might actually become the interim head of state. Their jokes halted when the blaring music stopped and a new voice filled the room with angry sounds. All three men leaned towards the set, and I watched my father straining to catch the rapid words in his newest language. Periodically the Greek statements were punctuated with American curses; finally the broadcast ended, and the quiet was interrupted only by a groaned "Oh, God!" from the room and sporadic sounds of fighting from outside. Once the men had collected themselves, they gave us a quick summary of the broadcast and let us know that Nikos Sampson – the designated leader – would never be acceptable to anyone concerned. Also mentioned for the first time was their fear that this would guarantee Turkish intervention.

As it soon became evident that the coup against Makarios was not going to finish swiftly or neatly, our residence became an extension of the embassy itself. A strong sense of solidarity developed among this community of people who had been virtual strangers a week before. Over our daily group meals for up to 45, we learned of life beyond our compound. Pairs of foreign service officers ventured in cars out into Nicosia and beyond, asking, pleading or even demanding at the various curfew checkpoints for permission to pass. They made the rounds of hotels to check on American citizens, called on two Americans wounded during the second day of fighting, and moved their own family members to safer lodgings.

When Dad managed to get away from his downstairs office, he would settle into the study by the living room, usually with two or three other officers, for informal discussions. He always invited me and my brother to join them, tolerating our interruptions and always answering our questions. With constant talk about the shuttle diplomacy that American envoy Joseph Sisco undertook between Greece, Turkey and Great Britain during the week after the coup, it seemed natural for us to discuss possible American involvement in the current crisis. Dad said bluntly that, except for diplomatic efforts aimed at influencing these three guarantors of Cypriot independence, America had no legitimate role at present. From watching the actions of my father and others, I firmly believe that the US took what diplomatic measures possible to prevent a Turkish intervention during the week after the coup. Relations between the US and Turkey were at low ebb during summer 1974, owing partly to a Turkish decision to resume growing opium poppies, and in the waning days of America's involvement in Vietnam, there would have been little political support for military action on Cyprus to stop the Turks.

I remember clearing dishes from that study long after midnight on the morning of Friday, July 19. Dad and several others were loudly discussing the best possible wording for a radio announcement. Nicosia airport was scheduled to reopen at 6am, and they were desperately trying to phrase the message in a way that would encourage American visitors to leave the island without creating panic, while simultaneously ensuring that any public utterance would not in any way influence – or be interpreted as influencing – Cypriot politics.

I don't think I fully understood the nuances of diplomatic statements or gestures until a number of years later, when I read in Christopher Hitchens' *Cyprus* that "In Nicosia, Ambassador Rodger Davies received [coup participant] Dimis Dimitriou as 'Foreign Minister' – the only envoy to do so." I can't be sure if it was that same night or the preceding one, but it was during the only supper that Dad managed to have with John and me. We had just sat down when someone rang Dad from downstairs. I had never seen him so angry before; he was yelling at the person on the other end of the phone. Finally he calmed down and said he would go downstairs, but to have whoever was waiting to remain in the lobby, at the Marine guard's desk – he did not want him in the office. The visitor standing at the front gate was Dimis Dimitriou, demanding to see the ambassador. Most of us at the table were acquainted with Dimitriou, whose brother was the Cypriot ambassador to Washington, and by showing up he had put all the foreign service officers present in a compromising position. Dimitriou had just been appointed foreign minister of the EOKA-B regime, which no country had recognized. After several minutes of consideration, Dad felt he had no choice but to go down to the lobby and speak to him as briefly and informally as possible, without inviting Dimitriou to official premises. Unfortunately his actions were misconstrued.

***

I was not actually present on August 19, 1974, when at least two men fired into the embassy from the building site across the street, killing my father and our friend Toni Varnava, but I have had extensive interviews with those who were actually there, and possess photographs of the bullet holes. So it amazes me to still hear – from Glafkos Clerides, among others – the theory that their deaths were accidental, a result of random shots from the ground-level riot. The only two locations to be struck by gunfire were my father's second-floor office, and his third-floor bedroom, precisely where he would most likely have been. The one random aspect of the deed was that Ambassador Davies chose to step into the hallway and phone Clerides to demand protection as the fighting outside escalated; the fatal bullets passed through the thick wooden shutters and glass of the office window, cleared the official reception room, and went out into the hallway. One struck my father in the heart, and shortly after another hit Toni in the head as she ran to his aid. The identity of the assassins is in fact known; one actually served time in prison for a token charge of illegal firearms possession, and is now a security guard at the main Cypriot race track near Nicosia.

George Demetriades's story

George Demetriades, originally from Skoúlli village in Páfos district, was 18 and on holiday from the American Academy in Larnaca when the events of summer 1974 took place. His father was for some time personnel and payroll manager at the Límni mines, working with many Turkish Cypriots. George has his own restaurant at the Páfos-Yeroskípou municipal boundary, which he runs with his son Ben. Some names have been changed in this account to protect individuals now living in the North from reprisals.

It is so difficult to begin, almost impossible in fact. Where does one start to tell about such catastrophic days on such a beautiful island? In my mind these events are still intensely vivid, like a movie. I have strenuously tried to write down my memories and not my opinions. I have also refrained from being overtly political, but at the same time I am a Greek Cypriot who has been through these difficult times, so they are inextricably part of my life.

I had just returned to Skoúlli, in Paphos district, near Pólis on the north coast, for the summer holidays. My involvement in politics was not considered of any importance by my elders since, back then, 18-year-olds didn't have the vote, but I could understand a few things. I told my mother early in July that something bad was going to happen in Cyprus. Over the past year or so, EOKA-B had, with the full cooperation of the Greek junta, increasingly stepped up its activities. Makarios continually warned the Cypriot public about impending dangers which, unfortunately, most Cypriots could not (or would not) see.

On Monday morning, July 15, the inevitable happened. The National Guard, commanded by mainland Greek officers and EOKA-B cadres, carried out a coup d'état. Their main target was Makarios, the lawfully elected president of Cyprus, but also the combined presidential palace and Archbishopric, plus the *efedhrikó*, a special auxiliary police force which Makarios had formed to combat EOKA-B. The first thing I heard on the CyBC [Cyprus Broadcasting Corporation] radio station, after my mother woke me up in a panic, was that Makarios was dead. The CyBC was already in the coup-plotters' hands, and soon they had taken over the presidential palace, having overwhelmed the guards with tanks. By the evening of the 15th, the putschists had gained control of the whole of Cyprus, except for Paphos district. Paphos, overwhelmingly pro-Makarios (it was his birthplace), refused to surrender and continued resisting. I went down to the Pólis central police station in order to help. The station was in uproar, with some EOKA-B members from the area under arrest; others had managed to escape.

Suddenly some people started shooting in the air, smiling and laughing – word had come that Makarios was alive. He had managed to escape from Nicosia and was in the monastery of Kýkko, heading towards Paphos. An impromptu militia was formed by policemen and civilian volunteers, in order to go to Nicosia via Limassol to help counter the coup. But in Limassol they were ambushed, with many wounded and some killed, and had to retreat. By then Makarios was in Ktima Paphos, at the Bishopric. His first act was to order everybody to put their guns down. He did not want bloodshed or worse, an all-out civil war; resistance meant casualties. The most important thing at the moment was that Paphos was still free, and it had a radio station operated by Nikos Nicolaides, which was powerful enough to be heard across much of the Mediterranean. Makarios going on the air was the best evidence that he was still alive and well.

Eventually it was decided that to guarantee Makarios's safety, he had to leave the island. He was smuggled abroad through the Akrotiri Sovereign Base to continue the fight to restore the legal government of Cyprus. That happened unexpectedly quickly, not necessarily through Makarios's efforts, but rather as a result of Turkey's invasion on July 20.

I would like to backtrack a few days to say one or two things about the activities of EOKA-B and the mainland Greek officers. Paphos eventually surrendered, the legal government was formally dismissed, Nikos Sampson was appointed President of Cyprus, and a band of his adventurist cronies were installed in the various ministries. Sampson had begun his career during his 20s as a fighter in the original EOKA against the British; he was now the owner-publisher of the extremist *Makhi* and *Tharros* newspapers, and above all a fanatical supporter of *énosis* (union of Cyprus with mainland Greece), a utopian vision which has cost the island dearly in many ways.

Around Skoúlli EOKA-B was now in full swing. They began going around arresting people and collecting all weapons from absolutely everybody. I remember seeing one of them with a Kalashnikov hanging on his shoulder, and one in his hands. They came to our house in the village, found one of my uncles there, and arrested him. I think it's important to stress that at this point no hostilities were directed against the local Turkish Cypriots.

On July 20 Sampson's "reign" was rudely interrupted by the initial Turkish invasion, which took place around Kyrenia, a considerable distance from where I was living. I remember sitting under the shade of the mulberry tree in our yard with my parents, Uncle George and Aunt Christina, and my cousin Steve from Australia – he was visiting Cyprus to avoid being drafted and sent to Vietnam, though ironically here he was stuck in another war. We could hear the bombs, most probably rockets or napalm clusters. The sky had a very different colour during those days, which I can still visualize: sometimes grey, other times white, while at night it turned a golden crimson from the burning of the beautiful forests of the Pendadháktylos and Tillyrian mountain ranges. The CyBC was continually broadcasting war bulletins, most of them untrue as it turned out. In a few days the Turks had managed to establish a bridgehead between Kyrenia and Nicosia. During this same time most of the Turkish-Cypriot enclaves in the southern part of the island were compelled to surrender to the National Guard, after pitched battles and casualties on both sides. These enclaves served a purpose by tying down Greek-Cypriot forces, thus allowing the mainland Turkish army to get on with its job. To be frank, though, the battle for the enclaves was a sideshow, and didn't really influence the outcome. The bulk of the Greek-Cypriot forces were in a state of chaotic disorganization. Antonis, a reservist from my village, and a number of others had to return to Skoúlli having seen no action, because they were taken to the front at Kyrenia to fight without guns.

On either July 21 or July 22, I remember an enormous black cloud forming slowly over the sea southwest of Paphos. From the explosion of shells in the air, I realised that a naval-air battle was raging. Later on I learned that Turkish jets had bombed some of their own ships and sunk one. An Israeli ship picked up numerous survivors, but a lot of sailors were killed.

On Tuesday July 23, Sampson was replaced by Glafkos Clerides, the legal successor to Makarios and still [this account was written in 2001] president. He resumed talks with Turkey in Geneva and by month's end a ceasefire was established. A new round of August talks collapsed after a few days owing to Turkish intransigence; as the victors, they could dictate terms. On August 14 the mainland Turks resumed their self-described "peace operation". Everything went according to plan: having secured their bridgehead during the ceasefire, the few days after the 14th saw nearly forty percent of Cyprus fall into their hands, with the well-known consequences in refugees and fatalities. With the second-largest standing army in NATO after the US, it was like running over a mouse with a road roller.

Over the next seven months or so there was a population transfer, with scenes painful to recall. The Turkish Cypriots did not have any choice about leaving, and it is true that some had to be forced into waiting lorries and buses bound for the North. One day during the transfer, a bus full of Turkish Cypriots going to the North from a nearby village stopped outside our house. Binaz stepped off it for a moment, put her arms around my mother and would not let go. In tears, she said "We do not have an alternative. We must go, but I hope we come back soon." Redif kissed my dad and said, "How can we leave our property, our house, the place we were born? We are being forced to move."

Another woman came to our house with two boxes containing glassware and a couple of cooking pots. She said to my mother, "Please take these. I do not want anybody else to have them." The articles are still in those boxes; my mother kept them for her. If this woman ever returns, she will get them back. [She did in fact come to visit in 2003, but insisted George's mother keep the utensils.]

I believe that the Turkish Cypriots lost a lot more than just kitchenware, especially taking into consideration today's conditions in the northern part of the island. The number of native, resident Turkish Cypriots has diminished; where have they all gone? In spite of the self-imposed isolation and numerous provocations by Denktaş, ordinary Turkish Cypriots and Greek Cypriots have kept in contact.

Based on my personal experience, I want to elaborate on this central aspect of our pre-1974 life, the everyday relationship between Greek and Turkish Cypriots. After late 1963, the Turkish Cypriot TMT-based internal regime had prohibited commerce and indeed any kind of transaction with Greek Cypriots, as a deliberately political ploy leading up to formal partition. But how can you stop personal exchanges between people who used to live next door to each other, ate together and worked together? The mining company that my dad once worked for had a mixed staff of just over three hundred people, one-third of them Turkish Cypriots. In 1965, my entire family was invited to a wedding in a Muslim village. It was already an enclave but we were allowed in; my father and the bridegroom Kâmil were very good friends. When that family came to bid farewell to us in 1974 the atmosphere was like a funeral.

My Uncle George's village house had been built by Turkish Cypriots. He had a bulldozer, and used to terrace fields and open farm tracks. Many Turkish Cypriots employed George for this kind of rural work. Jemal, from a nearby village, owed him C£125 for a job like that. Forty-eight hours before leaving for the North, Jemal came by with a giant load of wheat as payment. He too had tears in his eyes; he did not want to leave his home. Jemal could have gone off without paying, but he didn't. This was typical of the respect and friendship which existed between Turkish and Greek Cypriots. In and around Skoúlli at least, we lived in harmony in spite of the violence and political machinations elsewhere.

I would like to ask anyone who reads this memoir not to consider it a domestic political account – and to also bear in mind that it is very difficult to elaborate enough in a few paragraphs so as not to be misunderstood. We all agree that the Cyprus Question cannot be analysed in a few words; this complex issue involves a mountain of facts, centuries of history and many states with enormous political and financial interests. Of course there were Cypriot extremists on both sides who did a lot of damage, but the larger powers have the lion's share of the blame. They should start thinking about human factors as well – in this case the Cypriots, Turkish and Greek – and revise their policies which blight the lives of people in small nations.

Küfi Birinci's story

Küfi Birinci, a businessman and former TKP politician in North Cyprus, was 16 at the time of the Turkish landing on Cyprus. While he was experiencing the events described below, his future business partner and his twin brother both narrowly escaped death before an EOKA-B firing squad in their home village, only through the intervention of a widely respected Turkish-Cypriot policeman.

At 7pm on July 19, 1974, I heard on the BBC news that the Turkish fleet had "sailed towards an unknown destination". I didn't know exactly why, but this time I was sure that Turkey was really coming. Early next morning, my uncle came by, in a really excited state, shouting: "Wake up, they came!" I didn't even have to ask who "they" were. Within a few minutes we were all in the streets, singing and dancing, as we watched the Turkish parachutists landing on the fields of Hamitköy [Mándhres, a village just north of Nicosia]. It crossed nobody's mind that this was the start of a fierce war; we only came back to earth after the shooting started, and our great joy gave way to panic as people started thinking about the safety of their loved ones. (I myself had no news of my twin brother, trapped in our home village of Áyios Nikólaos, until after August 1.)

Caught up in the general excitement, I was nearly half a mile from home when I decided to go back, but it was too late. A police Land Rover stopped next to me and a police sergeant told me to jump in; I replied that I had to go home, but he said that he knew better where I should be going. So we went around the streets of Turkish Nicosia, collecting some other young lads who were not old enough to fight, but suited for other service.

On the first day our job was easy; we filled potato-sacks with sand for use as cover for Turkish-Cypriot fighters against gunfire from the Greek-Cypriot National Guard. But on the second day we were taken to Tekke Bahçesi, site of a Turkish-Cypriot martyrs' cemetery, given hand tools and ordered to start digging. There were about twelve of us, all teenagers except for one older, partly disabled man unfit for military service. Over the next two days and nights, we dug countless graves; we weren't given proper food, and had to sleep rough in the building site of what is now the Vakıflar Çarşısı. A new sergeant, very rude and cruel, was in charge of us; perhaps he felt he had to be like that in order to keep us under control.

On July 23, while we were having a short rest at lunchtime, an open lorry pulled into the cemetery and turned around; with it came a horrible, unbearable stench. I could see that the back payload area was covered with a white sheet, now stained a dirty mud-and-blood colour. On top of the sheet was somebody we all recognized: Hami the sandwich-maker, who sold sandwiches next to the Zafer cinema. Sitting with his legs crossed, he had in each hand cigarettes which he was chain-smoking, looking really nervous. When he jumped off the lorry and pulled the dirty sheet off, immediately a huge swarm of flies and a horrible smell spread out. I'd never smelt anything worse, anywhere, in my entire life, but the stink was nothing compared to the scene before my eyes. The lorry was full of dead soldiers who had been killed during the landing [near Kyrenia]; the driver used the lorry dumper to sling them off as if the corpses were sand or pebbles at a building site. The bodies were in an awful state: three days old, and all blown up like balloons in the July heat. Some of them were without heads, or sometimes the head was lying separate next to the body; others had hands missing; and some were badly burned.

Hami the sandwich man sat by the pile of corpses and started to take their boots off with a huge knife; since then I've never been able to buy a sandwich from him, imagining he still uses the same knife. According to Muslim belief, war martyrs (şehitler) go directly to heaven and can be buried with their clothes on; however their shoes must be removed to make them more comfortable. After removing their boots, Hami emptied the soldiers' pockets of their personal belongings and put them in a nylon bag together with their künye [ID dogtag worn around the neck]. We just watched him, astonished, holding our breath; we couldn't breathe that stinking air anyway. Hami and everyone else who'd arrived with the lorry had cologne-drenched handkerchiefs to hold over their noses – we didn't. We just stood there terrified and shocked, not knowing what to do next; I was praying to God to get out of there, without knowing how I might do so. While we waited in that state, the sergeant ordered us to go bury the soldiers. He shouted at us but we still wouldn't move, so he came over and hit us one at a time. Those whom he hit snapped out of it and ran to bury the bodies. I thought to myself, "We'll have to anyway, better to do it before the bastard hits you," so I ran off to bury them before he got to me.

There was a *hoca* [Islamic prayer leader] present, reciting the necessary last rites for the dead soldiers and ensuring that they were buried in accordance with Islamic rules. My first body was the most difficult; I tried, together with another boy, to carry and bury it, but since we were both so disgusted, not wanting to touch the corpses, we couldn't get a proper grip. I was trying to grab him by the end of his trousers, while my companion was trying to hold the soldier by his shirtsleeves; it was a difficult task because the swollen body weighed much more that it would have when alive. We just managed to bring it to a ready-dug grave, and threw him inside. The *hoca* saw us and shouted angrily: "You must not *throw* him in, you must *put* him in gently." He then came and inspected the body in the grave and said: "You laid him out in the wrong direction. His head is not facing towards Mecca. Jump in and do it right." So I had no choice but to jump into the grave and turn the corpse to the right orientation. Neither Turkish nor English is adequate to describe my feelings at that moment.

Lorries and transit vans arrived one after the other that day; the pile of dead bodies got bigger and bigger. We hadn't dug enough graves to bury them all, so on the advice of the *hoca* we started putting three corpses to a hole. Soon this wasn't enough either, so the *hoca* gave us permission to make it five in each grave. In the end I recall being allowed to bury them eight to a grave, and still we didn't have enough space to bury them all. We spent that night next to a pile of unburied corpses, plus those in the many open graves which we hadn't had time to cover with soil.

The next morning someone brought a bulldozer abandoned by the Greek Cypriots. We were very happy to see it, because we were really at our physical and psychological limits. The 'dozer made things much faster, and helped us finish the job – I would guess that by that second afternoon, we boys had buried almost 1500 corpses.

My grandmother had a house with one door opening onto this cemetery, and another looking towards Girne Caddesi [north Nicosia's main commercial street]. I pointed out her house to the sergeant, and got permission to go get a handkerchief for the smell; he gave me fifteen minutes' leave. So I entered my grandma's house through the back door, and immediately ran out the front door to my own house, which was about a mile away. When I got home, I went straight to our basement toilet, where I hid for 48 hours until I was convinced that the sergeant was not following me.

I write of this terrible experience to show everybody how war and nationalism are the worst enemies of mankind. Why do we Cypriots have to distinguish ourselves as Turkish or Greek? Cyprus our homeland has more than enough for both communities; all we have to do is recognize that it's our country and that we can share everything it offers. We must stop running after other countries as our motherland; if we deny our real home in favour of other nations, then the day will come when we won't have a motherland of our own. Didn't the Turkish Cypriots already lose one part of it and the Greek Cypriots the other? If we don't come back to our senses, one day soon we will lose all of it.

Wildlife

Cyprus's location has made it a "collecting basket" for wildlife from Asia Minor, Africa and the Mediterranean countries, offering a rare chance to see plants and animals otherwise only findable by making separate journeys further afield. Cyprus escaped the ravages of the Ice Ages, which eliminated many species in northern Europe, and there's a broad diversity of rock types and natural habitats. The island supports over 1300 different species of wild **flowering plants** – comparable to the total number in Britain, but concentrated within a Wales-size area.

The current political division of Cyprus has parallels in the island's **geological history**. Until around one million years ago, the Tróödhos to the south and Kyrenia range to the north stood as the cores of separate islands, with the primordial Athalas Sea in between. This became silted up to form the central plain (Mesaoría) during the most recent ice age. Today, wherever winter streams cut through the plain, they expose fossil shells which look like modern scallops, mussels and oysters.

Long-term isolation from neighbouring land masses such as Turkey meant that some plants evolved into **distinct species**; over ninety plants rank as endemics. To a lesser extent this is true for animals, and there are insects, birds and rodents particular to the island. Even the separation of the southern and northern mountain ranges has been long enough for plants in the Tróödhos and the Kyrenia hills to have evolved separately from a common ancestor – for example, purple rock cress (*Arabis purpurea*) abounds on volcanic rocks in the South, while the similar Cypriot rock cress (*Arabis cypria*) grows on the northern limestones.

Human activity has changed Cyprus as it changed the rest of the Mediterranean. Eratosthenes (275–195 BC) writes of a very different island where innumerable streams flowed year-round and even the Mesaoría was thickly forested. From the Phoenician up to the Venetian era, traders were attracted to the island by abundant timber suitable for ship-building; the destruction of forests has contributed to drastic local climatic change since antiquity. From the early days of British administration, Cypriot forestry departments have established and managed new forests throughout the island. Thus, about eighteen percent of the land area is covered with "forest", albeit more open, park-like woodland than in northern Europe. The commercial and colonial history of Cyprus has resulted in horticultural exotics such as the palms, agaves, cacti, mimosas, eucalyptus and citrus trees which are a familiar part of today's landscape. Even the olive (*Olea europaea*) originated in the Middle East, and today its range broadly defines the limits of Mediterranean vegetation and climate in Europe.

Birdlife is diverse, especially in the hills, with the island straddling spring and autumn migration routes. While possessing comparatively few **mammals**, Cyprus is rich in **reptiles and amphibians** – in spite of the age-old association of snakes with evil, which seems to require that every snake crossing a road be run over. Away from intensive cultivation and use of insecticides, the **insect fauna** is as diverse as the flora.

To sample the most varied wildlife, the **hot summer** months should be avoided: the ground is baked solid in the lowlands, sensible life-forms are hidden away from the sun, and there's no birdsong – though crickets and cicadas make up loudly for this absence. However, many native flowers persist in the mountains through early summer, bulbs start to flower with the first rains in late autumn, anemones bloom by Christmas, while lowland orchids appear from February (December in some years) to early April (into May on the heights).

Habitat types

Geographically, the island can be split into three regions: the **northern mountains**, which are mainly limestone; the **southern mountains** of igneous rock, which has erupted from deep in the earth through younger sedimentary rocks, leaving volcanic heights with chalk and limestone flanks; and the **central plain** of comparatively recent deposits, with conical schist hills at its edges. This geological diversity creates **four main habitat types**: coastal habitats, cultivated land, low hillsides less than 1000m and mountains above 1000m.

Coastal habitats

Some coastal **flood plains**, such as those in the north around Güzelyurt (Mórfou) which extend up to Cape Koruçam (Kormakíti), and those in the south stretching westwards from Limassol, stay moist much of the year. Until the British planted thirsty eucalyptus, these were open malarial swamps. Water arrives from the mountains in seasonal streams or from deep wells, enabling the plains to support vast citrus orchards and, more recently, avocado groves. Reedy river mouths are rare nowadays, since inland reservoirs capture much of the winter rainfall, reducing some watercourses to little more than a trickle year-round.

Steadily shrinking **coastal wetlands** exist north of Famagusta near Glapsídhes, in the Güzelyurt and Pólis hinterland, and east of Xylofágou, near Ayía Nápa. Little of the Asómatos marshland, north of the Akrotíri salt lake, remains because of drainage for the local citrus orchards. There are also two coastal **salt lakes**, at Larnaca and Akrotíri, though in current drought conditions they are usually just crusted-over salt pans.

Natural beaches along the west coast from Coral Bay to Lára and beyond include some interesting fossil-rich chalk (shark's teeth and sea urchins), which the sea has eroded into a stark lunar landscape. In the north, excellent beaches stretch from Famagusta to İskele (Tríkomo) on the east coast, intermittently east of Kyrenia, and along the Karpaz (Kárpas) peninsula. Coastal plantations of funeral cypress or Aleppo pine form extensive **open woodlands** – the grove by Hala Sultan Tekke, for example – rapidly colonized by various insects, birds and plants.

Much of the coastline, however, consists of **low cliffs** of clay or limestone with rocks plummeting down to the sea; high cliffs occur between Episkopí and Pétra toú Romioú. Coastal rocks at first sight seem to provide an inhospitable environment, but especially near Cape Koruçam (Kormakíti) fleshy-leaved stonecrops grow in crevices together with another succulent – *Mesembryanthemum crystallinum*, a relative of the colourful Livingstone daisies grown in gardens. The most unspoilt limestone coastline, however, fringes the **Akámas peninsula** at the western tip of Cyprus.

Cultivated land

Most **cultivated land** is kept clinically free of weeds and insect pests by deep ploughing and application of insecticides and fertilizers. But smaller areas on the Mesaoría – orchards near villages, olive groves and carob groves – can be very colourful in the spring, with numerous annuals. The diverse plant life supports a rich population of insects, lizards and occasional snakes; in the early morning orchards are also good places to spot small migrant birds.

Numerous flowering species thrive in badly tended mountain vineyards and even at the edges of well-tended ones. One well-represented family of plants is the *Leguminosae* (vetches and wild peas) – which also includes many important food plants such as peas, chickpeas, lentils and assorted beans. These crops often host a curious red parasite, the Cyprus broomrape (*Orobanche cypria*), a highly damaging pest.

Low hillsides

Low hillsides (up to 1000m) occur over much of Cyprus, their character depending on whether the underlying soil is limestone (alkaline) or volcanic (neutral to slightly acidic). The Akámas peninsula is unusual in its mixed geology, with limestone cliffs and deep gorges of limestone in addition to serpentine and other igneous rocks. **Aspect** also greatly affects the vegetation present because it determines how much sun and, on higher hillsides, how much rain the land will get. There's an obvious change when you cross either mountain range and forsake the almost lush vegetation of the north-facing slopes for the dry southern slopes, their xerophytic (drought-adapted) species clinging to life in the "rain shadow". Over-grazing by **goats** is another key factor; these voracious animals leave pastures with only the tall spikes of white asphodels, one of the few plants they shun. Government policy in the North has allowed Turkish mainland settlers to import their flocks, so that meadows which were formerly ablaze with flowers now have the goat-grazed look of their southern counterparts.

Hills are covered with a dense, low scrub of often thorny shrubs, a type of vegetation widely known as **garrigue** – in the Greek-speaking world it's called *frýgana* (often written *phrygana*), literally "toasted". Many garrigue plants are **aromatic** and, on a warm day, their oils vaporize to scent the air. Anyone brushing against shrubs like thyme, oregano or sage will find their clothing takes on minute amounts of their fragrant essences.

On limestone or chalk, shrubby herbs and wickedly spiny plants form an often impenetrable scrub; numerous bulbous plants grow between and below the bushes, sheltered from the sun and protected from all but the most determined goats. As you climb higher in the Tróödhos foothills the ground changes from white chalks to a range of brown soils derived from underlying serpentines and pillow lavas, with corresponding shifts in vegetation. Whatever the underlying rock strata, garrigue can slowly evolve into dense **maquis**, with bushes and low trees a few metres high; the two habitats often blend into one another on the same hillside. Typical maquis species include **lentisk** (*Pistacia lentiscus*), **terebinth** (*Pistacia terebinthus*), **storax** (*Styrax officinale*), **myrtle** (*Myrtus communis*) and several evergreen oaks, more like holly bushes than the stately oaks of Britain.

The final, or "climax", stage of vegetation is the evergreen forest which once covered the island. **Woodlands** on the northern limestone hills mainly comprise **funeral cypress** and **Calabrian pine** (*Pinus halepensis* ssp. *brutia*) grading into maquis, a pattern also repeated on the Akámas peninsula, where scattered pine groves constitute the nearest thing to virgin forest on the island. The best of these is the **Péyia forest**, a cool place high above the sea that has become a haven for small birds and an astonishing variety of orchids.

Extensive open pine forest of two varieties covers the lower Tróödhos, with less lofty specimens of red-barked **strawberry tree** (*Arbutus andrachne*); its wood has an attractive natural sheen and was traditionally used for making village chairs. Another characteristic small tree is the endemic evergreen **golden oak** (*Quercus alnifolia*) – the leaves have a dark-green upper surface but are golden-brown on the lower side.

The High Tróödhos

Although the core of the Tróödhos range is igneous, chalks were deposited on top when seas covered the land. Upheavals then pushed the underlying serpentines and pillow lavas through the chalk, and one can move rapidly between the two types of strata, noticing the dramatic changes in plant life. In open areas there are low bushes of ankle-tearing **gorse** (*Genista fasselata*), spiny **vetch** (*Astragalus echinus*) and **barberry** (*Berberis cretica*). The native **cedar** (*Cedrus libani* sp. *brevifolia*) is now extensively propagated after being largely confined to the so-called "Cedar Valley" since the 1890s, especially after destructive fire-bombing of the forests by the Turkish air force during the 1974 war.

The **High Tróödhos** – land over 1000m – is extensively forested and much reforestation has relied on both native and introduced species. Lower-altitude woods of Calabrian pine yield to **black** or **Caramanian pine** (*Pinus nigra* var. *caramanica*) mixed with **stinking juniper** (*Juniperus foetidissima*) and, near Khionístra summit, trees of both species appear gnarled as a consequence of their age, attained in a rigorous climate of long, dry summers and cold, snowy winters. On Khionístra there are also specimens where the trunk is violently twisted or split – the cause is lightning strikes which boil the sap to vapour. Such incidents are seldom fatal to resilient trees and they continue to grow, albeit with an unexpected change of direction.

Flowers

Even though something, somewhere, is in bloom throughout the year, things begin in earnest when the first autumn rains relieve the summer drought. It only seems to take a few drops percolating into the hard-baked soils of the plains to activate the bulbs of a tiny, light-blue **grape hyacinth** (*Muscari parviflorum*), or the delicate, white **autumn narcissus** (*Narcissus serotinus*). In the mountains, under golden oak bushes, grows the **Cyprus cyclamen** (*Cyclamen cyprium kotschy*), officially the national plant since 2006, with distinctive pink "teeth" on otherwise white flowers. The blooming sequence continues with **friar's cowl** (*Arisarum vulgare*), a curious candy-striped arum. The first of the **crown anemones** (*Anemone coronaria*) appears at Christmas time near the coast, followed by pink, then red varieties. Growing close by will be highly scented **polyanthus narcissus** (*Narcissus tazetta*) and royal purple stars of the **eastern sand crocus** (*Romulea tempskyana*).

Cyprus is justifiably famous among **orchid** enthusiasts for its unique mix of species – a good example of the island's "collecting basket" role. Cypriot orchids propagate by seed and take up to fifteen years to develop flowering stems, needing a certain soil fungus as well as soil structure. The underground corms may skip a year after flowering or even move so it's rare to see the same orchid in the same place in consecutive seasons. The robust, metre-high spikes of the **giant orchid** (*Barlia robertiana*) bear pinkish flowers like tiny "Darth Vader" figures and give off an iris-like scent. By late December these are blooming near Hala Sultan Tekke, along with the fleshy-stemmed **fan-lipped orchid** (*Orchis collina*). The Akámas peninsula supports the endemic **tongue orchid** (*Serapias aphroditae*) and the rare yellow-flowered **punctate orchid** (*Orchis punctulata*), also found in the Kyrenia range.

By late February to early March the season is in full swing, with numerous bee orchids including the remarkable endemic **Cyprus bee orchid** (*Ophrys* *kotschyi*), the pick of a fascinating bunch of insect mimics – this one has a fat black and white lip forming the insect "body". It occurs in scattered populations near Larnaca, but is more common in the North, especially around Alevkaya, accompanied by the **Lapithos bee orchid** (*Ophrys lapetheca*) or the **yellow bee orchid** (*Ophrys lutea*). Bee orchids produce scents which are pheromones with the power to fool tiny male wasps into thinking they have found a female – each orchid produces a subtly different chemical cocktail to delude a particular species of wasp. When they land they try to mate with the flower, eventually get frustrated and fly off in disgust, carrying pollen to the next orchid flower; fortunately for the plant, memory is not an insect's strong point.

In the **lowlands**, especially on the northern slopes of the Kyrenia hills, the Akámas and Karpaz peninsulas and the southern Tróödhos, the early **spring wildflower** display is staggering, with **turban buttercups** (*Ranunculus asiaticus*) in multi-hued – even occasional bi-coloured – forms. Higher up in the Tróödhos grow two **endemic buttercups**: *Ranunculus cyprius* var. *Cadmicus* and, immediately around Kýkko monastery, *Ranunculus kykkoënsis*. Less obvious to the eye, but equally diverse in colour, are over 170 species of small pea and vetch family members, many endemic to Cyprus. Two in particular stand out: the **veined vetch** (*Onobrychis venosa*), with white flowers and marbled leaves spreading over dry limestone, and the yellow-and-violet **crescent vetch** (*Vicia lunata*) which flourishes on volcanic soils – around Asínou church, for example.

Snow melting on the **Tróödhos heights** reawakens one of the island's three endemic **croci**, the **Cyprus crocus** (*Crocus cyprius*), followed by a **pink corydalis** (*Corydalis rutifolia*) and endemic **golden drop** (*Onosma troodi*). Cyprus also supports the winter-flowering **late crocus** (*Crocus veneris*), frequent in the Kyrenia range, and **Hartmann's crocus** (*Crocus hartmannianus*), encountered in early spring on **Mount Adhélfi**, along with chionodoxa (*Scilla lochiae*).

By mid-March, many bulbous plants will already be dying back. The **annuals**, however, more than make up for the loss by providing sheets of colour, often created from surprisingly few species: scarlet **poppies**, a delicate royal-purple poppy (*Roemeria hybrida*), golden-yellow **crown marigolds** (*Chrysanthemum coronarium*), **corn marigolds** (*Glebionus segetum*), pink **Egyptian catchfly** (*Silene aegyptiaca*), perhaps tempered with white camomile (*Anthemis chia*). In the days before intensive cultivation and deep ploughing, **field gladiolus** (*Gladiolus italicus*) made corn fields magenta with its stately spikes, and people still recall looking down on a Mesaoría scarlet with tulips.

Today, in the South, **wild tulips** (*Tulipa agenensis*) still survive under fruit trees near Stroumbí, north of Páfos, but the endemic **Cyprus tulip** (*Tulipa cypria*), with its dark red, almost purple flowers, most reliably inhabits bean fields near Koruçam (Kormakíti) and cornfields around Çamlıbel (Mýrtou), or the wilder, less grazed parts of the Akámas peninsula.

Two **coastal wildflower displays** are not to be missed. First appearing in late January and February, the **Persian cyclamen** (*Cyclamen persicum*) cascades over north-slope rocks of the Kyrenia mountains. You will also find them forcing their way through cracks and crevices around the Tombs of the Kings in Páfos, but the most spectacular venue is the natural rockery of the Akámas peninsula, where their white, pink and magenta tints contrast with an azure blue sea below. Towards the beginning of April, there's another display: the **three-leaved gladiolus** (*Gladiolus triphyllus*) with scented pink-and-white flowers, growing in countless thousands, virtually all around the coast of the island.

The unmistakable, two-metre-high **giant fennel** (*Ferula communis*) – *anathríka* in Greek, *şeytan otu* ("devil's weed") in Turkish – with their umbrellas of yellow blossoms are everywhere in March, but have largely disappeared by April. In legend, Prometheus hid the fire he stole from the gods in one of their stalks; the slow-burning pith inside is still used as tinder. Shaded limestone cliffs of the **Kyrenia range** are the places to look for endemic plants such as St Hilarion cabbage (*Brassica hilarionis*), an ancestor of the cauliflower, which was supposedly first bred at nearby Değirmenlik (Kythréa) during the seventeenth century.

In the **Tróödhos mountains** things are slower off the mark. Travelling uphill, however, two new orchids – the yellow **Roman orchid** (*Dactylorhiza romana*) and the pink **Anatolian orchid** (*Orchis anatolica* ssp. *troodi*) – appear as soon as the soil changes from chalk to volcanic. From late May onwards, an unusual saprophytic orchid, the **violet limodore** (*Limodorum abortivum*), with purple stems flowers, is a common woodland plant, usually growing beneath pines or close to them. It abounds not far from Tróödhos resort itself, with three other orchid companions: **Cyprus helleborine** (*Epipactis troodi*), **Holmboe's butterfly orchid** (*Platanthera holmboei*) and **red helleborine** (*Cephalanthera rubra*).

When the plains are burnt dry, **pink oleander** (*Nerium oleander*) brings a welcome touch of colour to dried streambeds, or when planted as a flowering roadside "hedge". Few other flowering species now relieve the dull shades of a dessicated landscape, except thistles like the spectacular **cardoon** (*Cynara cardunculus*), a wild artichoke growing several metres tall, and **aromatic inula** (*Dittrichia viscosa*), a yellow dandelion relative forming sticky-leaved bushes. You see this plant everywhere but rarely find in field guides; in this case "aromatic" does not mean pleasantly so.

At middle elevations of the Tróödhos, en route to Pródhromos, May is the season of white, lupin-like **Lusitanian milk vetch** (*Astragalus lusitanicus*), with **purple rock cress** (*Arabis purpurea*) in pink cushions hanging over rock faces above. Late in the day, sunlight on an open glade between Pródhromos and Khionístra might illuminate scarlet **peonies** (*Paeonia mascula*), almost making the flowers glow. During April or May acres of **French lavender** (*Lavandula stoechas*) flower on the pillow lavas, the blossoms sticky to the touch, and whole hillsides burst into bloom with one or another of the local **rock roses**: white (*Cistus salvifolius* and *C. monspeliensis*), pale pink (*C. parviflorus*) and deep pink (*C. creticus*). By July, even plants in the mountains find it too hot, and only spiny gorses, brooms and barberry provide a bit of colour.

In only a few places in the Tróödhos does water run all the year round, but there in early summer – especially around Caledonian Falls – dwells the rare **eastern marsh helleborine** (*Epipactis veratrifolia*), the **marsh orchid** (*Dactylorhiza iberica*) and an indigenous **butterwort** (*Pinguicula crystallina*), a plant that traps insects on its sticky leaves. Surprisingly, it's only when the sand gets too hot to stand on that delicate white **sea daffodils** (*Pancratium maritimum*) bloom; they were once so numerous on the east coast that they were called Famagusta lilies, though almost any undisturbed dune, however modest in size, supports a colony. They survive their arid environment by having a bulb buried so deeply that it would need an excavator to get to it.

Under these same "desert" conditions, in coastal and other lowlands all over the island, tall spikes of starry-white flowers emerge leafless straight out of bare ground. These are **sea squills** (*Drimia maritima*), the product of the huge bulbs half-pushed out of the ground which in spring are topped by long, leathery strap-leaves. The bulbs were once used to make both rat poison and a cough remedy. When little else blooming near the sea, you'll find **carline thistles**, favourites of flower arrangers for their long-lasting flower heads. The tiny one with scarlet, daisy-like flowers found near beaches is yet another endemic – the **dwarf carline thistle** (*Carlina pygmaea*).

Exotic and edible plants

Exotic plants play an important part in the island's **food production**. The climate has favoured introduced subtropical species which are now widely cultivated: **palms** (from North Africa, Asia and the Americas); **agave**, **avocado**, **prickly pear**, **tomatoes**, **potatoes**, **peppers** and **aubergine** (the Americas); **mimosa** and **eucalyptus** (Australasia); **citrus** (originating in Asia) and **pomegranate** (Iran). The British administration introduced flowering trees from other colonies which, in maturity, have become a colourful feature of the parks and gardens in towns and cities: **orchid tree** (*Bauhinia variegata*), **bougainvillea** (*Bougainvillea spectabilis*) and **silk oak** (*Grevillea robusta*).

Cypriots are essentially pragmatic when it comes to natural resources, readily recognizing **edible "weeds"** while remaining indifferent to or disparaging of less "useful" plants. Even town-dwellers head for the countryside in spring to gather shoots of *agrélia* (**wild asparagus** – *Asparagus acutifolius*) or of the **bladder campion** (*Silene vulgaris*) – see the *Traditional Cypriot food* colour section and guide for more details. In autumn, the slightest of bumps in woodland leaf-litter lead the sharp-eyed and knowledgeable to edible wild **fungi**.

Birds

Cyprus no longer has the numerous **birds of prey** that it once had, thanks to the mania, North and South, for the gun, plus the use of poisoned carcasses by misguided goatherds, anxious to protect their flocks. Vultures in particular are scavengers, only feeding on animals already dead. The black vulture had become extinct across the island by the mid-1990s, and the North's small population of **griffon vultures** were all shot by hunters in 1996. Griffons have fared little better in the South: 37 of the colony of 40 in the Xerós valley were poisoned by laced carcasses in 1998, and only three nests have been recorded more recently in the Akámas area, and just six nests in the cliffs west of Episkopí. Assisted by a local conservation programme, numbers have since climbed from a low point of 24 to about 45, but breeding may not be viable and individuals may have to be introduced from Greece and Spain.

Kestrels are still common, but **peregrine falcons** only survive in remote strongholds in the Kyrenia range and offshore on the Klidhés islands beyond the Karpaz peninsula. They breed in March or April and are fast and strong enough to prey on doves and pigeons for themselves and their ever-hungry nestlings. The same islets are also one of the few places where shag and Audouin's gull can nest undisturbed. **Eleonora's falcons** breed late in the year in colonies on the protected Akrotíri cliffs within the Episkopí Sovereign Base. They favour Cape Gáta at the tip of the peninsula and time the hatching of their chicks to coincide with the autumn migration of exhausted hoopoes, orioles, swifts and sandmartins. Once you have witnessed their mastery of flight, as they scythe through the air, you may forgive their opportunism.

Bonelli's eagle is rare nowadays in either northern or southern mountain ranges, whereas it used to even nest in the walls of Buffavento castle. Other raptors seen over the island are usually migrants on passage to nesting grounds in spring, returning in autumn. They tend to be glimpsed over reservoirs and salt lakes hunting prey to sustain them on their journey, or flying over the

Akámas and Karpaz peninsulas. Species regularly observed include the **red-footed falcon** and the **hobby**, a small falcon which looks like a large swift and takes swallows, martins and even swifts in flight. Broad-winged raptors such as **marsh harrier**, **common buzzard** and **black kite** can also be seen soaring above scrub-covered hills or hunting over reedbeds.

In the Tróödhos massif there are permanent populations of familiar species such as **raven**, **jackdaw**, **rock dove** and **wood pigeon**. Less familiar to northern Europe birders will be **crag martin**, **Cretschmar's bunting** and the colourful **hoopoe** with pink body, black and white crest and a far-carrying cry. In the North, Kantára and Buffavento castels have always been favourite places for spring birdwatchers, who anticipate seeing **blue rock thrush**, **alpine swift**, **black-headed bunting** and **spectacled warbler**.

The **chukar**, an attractive rock partridge which prefers to run for cover rather than fly, survives as a ground-nester in dense scrub, especially in the Kyrenia hills, in spite of its being the favourite target of hunters everywhere. The **black francolin**, exterminated in much of southern Europe by hunting, managed to recover from the brink of extinction in Cyprus when the British administration revoked gun licences during the EOKA troubles. For some years it was still shot in its main Karpaz stronghold east of Dipkarpaz (Rizokárpaso), though recently a protective reserve has (in theory) been established here.

Orioles, rollers and **bee-eaters** are the most colourful spring migrants, the Akámas peninsula and the long "panhandle" of the Karpaz peninsula providing "flight paths" into the island; the latter two species may breed locally, choosing suitable holes in sandy riverbanks or soft cliffs for the purpose. Being vividly coloured, they attract the attention of hunters, and have been regarded as food items. Cyprus suffered habitually in the past from depredation by **locusts** – government reports for 1878 and 1879 record how villagers were expected to catch locusts to be bagged and weighed. Failure to comply with the directive or even to collect minimum weights brought fines and sometimes imprisonment. Ironically, locusts form much of a roller's diet – if these insects are around then they will eat nothing else. Rollers are a familiar sight, perching on utility wires before taking off with a distinctive buoyant flight; they get their name from their aerial somersaulting, part of their courtship displays.

Salt lakes provide both food (tiny brine shrimps) and a resting place for hundreds of **greater flamingoes** at Akrotíri and Larnaca. They're present after the first good rains (if any), adults arriving first, with juveniles following later from Turkey, Iran and even further afield. They start to leave by March, in small low-flying flocks; the last stragglers quit in June for their nesting areas. **Reservoirs** – on the rare occasions when they're full – are important sites for over-wintering **water birds**, with a changing profile over the course of a year. They also attract smaller lowland and mountain birds throughout the year, since insects always hover near water. There are various ducks (**mallard**, **shoveler**, **teal** and **wigeon**), **black-necked grebe** and larger birds such as several members of the heron family (**squacco heron**, **night heron**, **little bittern**, **little** and **cattle egrets**). Shallow water at the edges of reservoirs and salt lakes provides mud in which waders probe incessantly for their food. Occasionally, **glossy ibis**, **black-winged stilt** or **black-tailed godwit** can be seen.

Cyprus has several endemic birds, distinct enough from their nearest relatives to be considered true species. The best known of the endemics is the **Cyprus warbler**, with a wide distribution in scrubby areas, where it stands sentinel on bushes. It closely resembles the Sardinian warbler but differs in having black underparts – it also lacks the red ring around the eye and the red iris which are the trademarks of the Sardinian species. Only one other endemic, the **Cyprus**

Scops owl, is widespread, with its repetitive 'pook' cry heard more often than seen; the others – **pied wheatear**, **coal tit**, **jay**, **crossbill** and the **short-toed treecreeper** – are confined to the high Tróödhos pine forest.

Both **demoiselle** and **common cranes** spend the winter months in Sudan but migrate via Cyprus – en route to the demoiselle's breeding sites in Asia Minor and southern Russia in March and April, while the common crane flies in the opposite direction, leaving the Balkans, Turkestan, Asia Minor and northern Europe in August and September. They are often seen following the line of the Akámas peninsula in spring, but particularly evocative are hot, late-August nights over Nicosia: the birds are far out of sight, only the wing beats and trumpeting metallic calls identifying their passage.

Mammals – past and present

Geological evidence shows that the Mediterranean Sea has dried out on several occasions, enabling plants and animals to migrate to mountain peaks which have since become islands. The **Mediterranean basin** formed about 40 million years ago, but until around 20 million years ago it was open at either end to the Atlantic and Indian oceans respectively. First the eastern channel closed up, isolating sea life but still allowing land animals to cross between continents, and then the western outlet closed, effectively sealing it off.

Some six million years ago this land-locked sea **evaporated** almost completely; the Mediterranean became an arid basin with a few shallow salt lakes on its floor and some of today's islands standing as **forested oases**, in which animals congregated and developed. When the Atlantic eventual burst through the present-day strait of Gibralter it isolated the forested hilltops and their inhabitants. Excavations on the Mesaoría have revealed **fossil bones** showing that Cyprus, in Pleistocene times, was home to pygmy elephants and hippopotamus, ibex, genet and wild boar.

Today the largest mammal on the island – and stylized as the tailfin logo of Cyprus Airways – is the **Cyprus moufflon** (*Ovis musimon*); the exact origins of this wild sheep are uncertain but remains have been found in Neolithic settlements from eight thousand years ago. In Greco-Roman times, moufflon were plentiful in both mountain ranges, but hunting, especially during the Middle Ages, reduced the population drastically. In 1878, the first year of British rule, only twenty animals were counted, and the situation did not improve until 1939, when game laws were strengthened, the Páfos forest became a game reserve and goat-grazing was banned there, removing competition for food. Since then, numbers in the wild, augmented by a captive breeding programme, have increased steadily, to about a thousand by the millennium.

The moufflon is very agile, shy and not readily glimpsed; for most visitors, the only specimens seen will be several bored-looking ones kept penned at Stavrós tís Psókhas. Its closest relatives are other insular wild sheep in Sardinia and Corsica, which live in open, rocky territory. The Cypriot race, however, has found its niche as a forest-dweller, although for fodder it prefers grasses to bush or tree shoots. When the uplands are under snow, it descends to lowland valleys, always relying on the cover provided by the forest. Mating takes place in November, when competitive males become aggressive: the dominant male of the group sires the lambs, and the gestation period is five months. In both males and females the summer coat is short and pale brown, becoming white on the underparts; in winter they grow a coat of dense brown hair.

Although **foxes** are rarely seen in the open, they are not uncommon in the Akámas and Karpaz peninsulas. They have paler coats than elsewhere and blend easily with the browns and greys of the landscape. **Cyprian hares** (*Lepus cyprius*) can sometimes be seen as they break cover, but they are justifiably shy creatures barely able to sustain small populations between successive hunting seasons. Other small animals include the **Cyprian shrew**, a race of **spiny mouse** and **brown tree rats**, enormous (for rats anyway) arboreal beasts which live by preference on almonds and carob pods. **Long-eared hedgehogs** look like the animal equivalent of an old Renault 4, their long back legs keeping their rear end higher than the front. For years, hedgehogs were persecuted because they supposedly entered chicken coops to have their spiny way with the hens, a laughable but strongly held superstition that did these creatures – which forage mostly for insects and snails in ground litter – no good at all.

Of the eight bat species in Cyprus, the **fruit bat** (*Rousettus aegyptiacus*) is the most spectacular, with a powerful bird-like flight. They can sometimes be seen at dusk on the outskirts of Pólis and other north-coast villages, when they feed on ripe fruit. The animals live and breed in limestone caves, so are confined to near Neokhorió and Andhroulíkou on the Akámas peninsula, and the Kyrenia mountains. Their visits to orchards have made them a hunting target, but in the wild these bats have played an unwitting but essential role in the propagation of trees, because fruit seeds pass undamaged through their digestive systems.

Reptiles and amphibians

Saint Helena, mother of the Byzantine emperor Constantine, apparently visited Cyprus on her return voyage from Jerusalem to Constantinople after a successful venture to discover the Holy Cross. She found (*plus ça change ...*) an island gripped by drought and infested with snakes and lizards. Her answer to the latter problem was returning with a shipload of cats, disembarked at the tip of the Akrotíri peninsula, henceforth known as Cape Gáta (*gáta* means "she-cat"). Although feral cats in cities continue to take an enormous toll of lizards (and small birds), **reptiles** and **amphibians** still occur in vast numbers.

Spring and autumn are the season to see the island's eight endemic species of snake: in winter they hibernate and in summer they hide, virtually comatose, from the unremitting heat. Looking like a glossy earthworm, the **worm snake** is the smallest; at a length which can easily exceed two metres, the large **whip snake** just qualifies as the longest, edging out its cousin the **Cyprus whip snake**. The former is easily recognized by its almost black back – it wriggles away when disturbed in vineyards or at field edges and will also climb trees. The **coin snake** has distinctive lozenge markings on its back; it and the 1992-rediscovered but still endangered aquatic "**grass**" **snake** are harmless. The latter's last known habitat is the Xyliátos reservoir in the Tróödhos foothills, where it's threatened by the practice of stocking with trout (the fish eat the juvenile snakes). The **cat snake** and **Montpellier snake** feed on small lizards and produce venom which can dispatch their prey in a matter of minutes. Humans fare better if bitten by either, since the inward-pointing fangs are set far back in the throat, but a large Montpellier snake can still inflict a slow-to-heal wound, with local swelling and headache. The **blunt-nosed viper** (*Vipera lepetina lepetina*), fortunately quite rare, is the only really dangerous serpent on Cyprus. Called *koufí* locally, it has a distinctive yellow, horn-like tail and can inflict a highly **poisonous** bite; infant vipers are, if anything, more toxic as

their venom is more concentrated. In autumn 2000 they were proven to be hatched from eggs rather than, as was long believed, born live from the mother's body where eggs are incubated. In Cyprus all snakes have a bad press, based almost entirely on superstition – none of the island's species is aggressive and individuals will only bite to defend themselves.

Small lizards, especially agile **sand lizards**, are ubiquitous, since chalk, with its high reflectance of light and heat, proves particularly attractive to reptiles. The largest lizard in Cyprus is the **starred agama** (*Agama stelio*), up to 30cm long with a disproportionately large head. They are shy creatures, often seen scuttling into cracks in walls or the trunks of ancient olive and carob trees. The politest of the local names means "nosebiter", inspired by the oversized head. If your eyesight is particularly acute, you might spot a **chameleon**; they are fairly common in the Limassol foothills, but remain well camouflaged. By contrast, tiny **geckos** come out at night to feed on insects attracted to wall lights.

In summer, **tree frogs** (*Hyla arborea*) are usually heard rather than seen when they call, often at night and far from water, with a volume out of all proportion to their small size. In winter, they return to water to breed and can be found on bushes or reeds close to streams, ponds and rivers, where you might be lucky enough see their acrobatic climbing. **Marsh frogs** and **green toads** are considerably larger and correspondingly easier to find.

The stream valley above Kakopetriá is one of the last habitats of a curious, olive-green, freshwater **crab** (*Potamon fluviatilis*), once common around the island, especially in brackish streams near the coast. Sadly, agricultural-chemical pollution of streams has sent numbers plunging. Here crabs survive by hiding under stones but emerging at night onto the bank to feed. Locals regret their disappearance since the crab was considered an excellent *mezé*. **Stripe-necked terrapins** can still be found, even in surprisingly murky pools, though they too have suffered badly from agricultural-chemical runoff. A plop into a muddy pool as you approach will usually be a large frog – or just occasionally a terrapin, which will surface several metres away to survey you with quiet confidence.

Sea turtles

Cyprus is one of the few places in the Mediterranean where two species of **sea turtles** still come ashore to breed at certain sandy beaches east of Kyrenia, the western Akámas peninsula, the Pólis area and both sides of the far end of the Karpaz. Tourism has driven them from the sands of the south coast and around Famagusta, though a few may still nest on "Lady's Mile" beach near Limassol. Since 1978, the Fisheries Department has run a camp at Lára bay on the Akámas with the express purpose of raising survival rates of hatchlings; simultaneously, a running battle has pitched conservationists against developers who see the obvious tourist potential of this superb, sandy beach.

Both **loggerhead turtles** (*Caretta caretta*) and less common **green turtles** (*Chelonia mydas*) nest at Lára; in the North more greens than loggerheads come ashore to lay eggs. Both species mate at sea, typically every two to four years,

Wildlife field guides

Cyprus falls just outside the loose definition of Europe used in **field guides**, other than those for birds. Thus, it's not easy to find good illustrations of its special plants or butterflies, let alone for insects, snails and other less glamourous creatures. Since a significant proportion of the flora and fauna is pan-Mediterranean, you can make considerable headway with popular guides, but identifying endemic species is often difficult.

Many of the better natural history works are now **out of print**, but fairly easily available through online book dealers or specialist second-hand booksellers. One in particular to aim for is A. C. Campbell's very useful *The Hamlyn Guide to the Flora and Fauna of the Mediterranean*; this was also published as *The Larousse Guide to the Flora and Fauna of the Mediterranean*. That said, there were massive changes in taxonomic conventions during the mid-1990s, so anything with an imprint before that will be out of date in that respect. In case of difficulty obtaining titles listed below from conventional booksellers, try UK-based botanical field-guide specialists **Summerfield Books** (☎017683/41577, ⓦwww.summer fieldbooks.com).

Flowers and plants

Marjorie Blamey and Christopher Grey-Wilson *Mediterranean Wild Flowers* (o/p). Comprehensive field guide with colour drawings that includes the lowlands of Cyprus; taxonomically up to date.

🏃 **Karl Peter Buttler** *Field Guide to the Orchids of Britain and Europe*. A wealth of colour pictures and modern nomenclature.

Lance Chilton *Plant Checklists: Akamas & Cyprus*. Personal and literary records for this peninsula – order from ⓦwww.marengowalks.com.

Yiannis Christofides *The Orchids of Cyprus*. Covers all the endemics, with full descriptions, flowering-season and habitat charts, phylogenetic minutiae and lavish colour photos justifying a fairly high cover price.

Anthony Huxley and Oleg Polunin *Wildflowers of the Mediterranean*. A classic Mediterranean flora guide; coverage is general but surprisingly useful; nomenclature has been updated.

🏃 **R. Desmond Meikle** *Flora of Cyprus*. Pricey, two-volume work for the serious plant freak. A model of clarity and erudition – whatever you'll find is in here. No colour pictures, but plenty of line drawings.

Gizela & Karlheinz Morschek *Orchids of Cyprus* (Steijl, The Netherlands). Bilingual (English/German) text describing all known species on the island, with colour photos; affordable paperback.

V. Pantelas, T. Papachristophorou and P. Christodoulou *Cyprus Flora in Colour: The Endemics*. Good photos of endemic plants; cheaper in Cyprus than in Britain.

with females producing several clutches of white, ping-pong-ball-like eggs over the summer laying season. The smooth-shelled green turtle, feeding on sea grasses and seaweeds, is the larger of the two species, with mature adults attaining a length of some 100–140cm. Loggerheads, reaching 75–100cm in length, have a tapered shell or carapace, a short muscular neck and powerful jaws which can crush the shells of the molluscs – one part of the varied diet, along with jellyfish, crabs, sponges and aquatic plants. Many die yearly from mistaking plastic carrier bags floating at sea for edible jellyfish.

Popular belief maintains that turtles will only lay on the two nights either side of the full moon, and it's certainly true that female turtles everywhere prefer to

Loucas Savvides *Edible Wild Plants of the Cyprus Flora* (self-published, Nicosia). As it says; gives the common Greek names, harvesting seasons, some recipes, and traditional medicinal uses as well as photos and descriptions.

Takis C. Tsintides, Georgios N. Hadjikyriakou, Charalambos S. Christodoulou *Trees and Shrubs in Cyprus* (A. G. Leventis Foundation, Nicosia). Not exactly portable, but useful photos and authoritative text.

Deryck E. Viney *The Illustrated Flora of North Cyprus* (vol 1, Koeltz Scientific Books, US; vol 2, Gantner Verlag, Germany). Two-volume, affordable paperback series with line drawings. Vol 2 has corata for Vol 1 grasses and ferns.

Birds

Lucas Christophorou *Birds of Cyprus* (Nicolaou & Sons, Nicosia). Brief, not overly technical text; excellent, numerous colour plates.

Peter Flint and Peter Stewart *The Birds of Cyprus*. A thorough checklist with details of good sites for birdwatching.

Dave Gosney *Finding Birds in Cyprus*. Inexpensive, fairly recent (1994) handbook.

Hollom, Porter, Christensen and Willis *Birds of the Middle East and North Africa*. Very thorough, with good illustrations and distribution maps.

Lars Jonsson *Birds of Europe with North Africa and the Middle East*. Very good coverage, useful descriptions and excellent illustrations.

Arthur Stagg, Graham Hearl and James McCallum *Birdwatching Guide to Cyprus*. With 92 illustrations by McCallum and a modest price tag, a good choice for specific coverage of the island.

Insects

Lionel Higgins and Norman Riley *A Field Guide to the Butterflies of Britain and Europe* (o/p). A very detailed, if old classic which contains most of the Cyprus butterflies except the handful of indigenes.

Christodoulos Makris *The Butterflies of Cyprus* (Bank of Cyprus). In large coffee-table format and weighing in at several kilos, this isn't your average handy field guide but it's a gorgeous, erudite volume, with a reasonable price tag and ideal for either casual or expert use.

Reptiles, amphibians and marine life

Arnold, Burton and Ovenden *A Field Guide to the Reptiles of Britain and Europe* (o/p). Most, but not all, species – again this stops well short of the Middle East.

Jiri Cihar *Colour Guide to Amphibians and Reptiles* (o/p). Selective in coverage, but has many species from Asia Minor and is useful for Cyprus.

B. Luther and K. Fiedler *A Field Guide to the Mediterranean Sea Shore* (o/p). Very thorough, and includes much of what occurs around the Cyprus coast.

emerge on bright, **moonlit nights**. The laborious journey up the beach, the digging of a nest to 50–70cm depth, followed by egg-laying and then covering with sand, is an exhausting business which takes several hours. Turtles disturbed as they come ashore will simply return to the sea, but when laying has started they carry on until nearly exhausted.

Hatchlings appear about seven weeks after egg-laying; in Cyprus most nests are established in June or early July, with baby turtles emerging throughout August into September at different rates, a batch each day from the same nest. Immediately after biting and wriggling their way out from the egg, they still have part of the yolk-sac attached and must wait beneath the sand until that has been absorbed into the body. The young then struggle the final distance to the surface and make directly for the sea between dusk and dawn when it's cool. For further details on sea-turtle life cycles, and local conservation programmes, see the boxes on p.175 and p.332.

Insects

As soon as the sun comes out, butterflies are obvious flying over patches of open ground in scrub or hotel gardens. Here, often for the first time, visitors see the glorious **swallowtail butterfly** (*Papilio machaon*), rare in Britain yet common here, where its larvae thrive on fennel plants. Strawberry trees along the coast are the food-plant of the magnificent **two-tailed pasha** (*Charaxes jasius*), a powerful flier which defends its territory against infiltrators by charging at them. Seen at close quarters, a complex, beautiful underwing striping is revealed. As the **southern white admiral** (*Limenitis reducta*) sups nectar from its preferred food-plant, the tree honeysuckle, you'll see its open wings, with two rows of large white spots relieving the jet-black surface.

Cyprus has several unique species of butterfly, including the **Paphos blue** (*Glaucopsyche paphia*) and **Cyprus festoon** (*Zerynthia cerisyi* ssp. *cypria*), a swallowtail relative with scalloped margins to the wings. Its curiously spiked caterpillars feed on a plant with a similarly bizarre appearance, the Dutchman's pipe (*Aristolochia sempervirens*), found throughout the island's hills on chalk and volcanic soils. **Cleopatras** (*Gonepteryx cleopatra*) fly through sunny glades in the mountain woods, especially upstream from Kakopetrá, heralding the arrival of spring; the males are a deep sulphur-yellow, with a splash of orange just visible on the forewings in flight. In summer, numerous species referred to collectively as "browns" (*Satyrids*) and "blues" (*Lycaenids*) are found wherever weeds grow.

In spite of heavy use of insecticides, enough weeds remain for **caterpillars** to thrive. Some larvae are very particular and restrict their diet to one plant species, while others are virtually omnivorous, even resorting to cannibalism if there is nothing else to eat. Noticeable on pine trees are hanging nests of gossamer, spun by **caterpillars** after they hatch. They feed on tender pine needles within the nest and then drop to the ground in a wriggling mass until one sets off and the others attach themselves in a nose-to-tail migratory arrangement. So successful are these processionary caterpillars of **pine beauty** and **gypsy moths** that they've become a major forest pest, causing serious damage to trees across the island; they arrived on Cyprus late in the 1980s, and no drastic measures were then taken to control them. Neither they nor any surface they've recently crawled on should be touched, as the caterpillars are covered in hairs secreting a highly irritant substance.

Many moths could be classed as "small, brown and boring", but **hawkmoths** rival butterflies for colourfulness, and are superbly equipped for fast, powerful flight with strong forewings and small hindwings. Their caterpillars are often more gaudily coloured than the parents and can assume a curious posture to frighten off predators – a habit which has given them the common name of **sphinx moths**. In Cyprus, the most common member of the family is the **hummingbird hawk** (*Macroglossum stellatarum*), which can be cheeky enough to approach on whirring wings and, with long, thin tongue, sample the liquid from the edges of your glass as you enjoy an evening meal outdoors. Less frequently seen are the beautiful **oleander hawk** (*Daphnis nerii*) with olive-shaded wings and the **death's-head hawk** (*Acherontia atropos*) whose large yellow-and-violet-striped caterpillars feed on potato plants and were quite common crop pests before the use of insecticides. **Praying mantids** are curious creatures and, in Cyprus, range from the small brown species to the larger **crested mantid** or *émpousa*, named after ancient Greek, shapeshifting demonesses who visited sleeping men and made love with them until they expired: the insect males have to be fast to avoid becoming the main item in the post-coital breakfast.

Not strictly insects, but under the general heading of "creepy-crawlies", most Cypriot **spiders** are small, except for the **European tarantula**, which lives in hillside burrows, venturing out to catch any passing suitable prey. **Scorpions** are not as common as previously, owing to destruction of habitat and to the use of agricultural chemicals. They are shy, pale-coloured creatures, but in defence of their brood they will inflict a very painful sting. Large black **millipedes** are harmless, but orange **centipedes** pack a nasty, venomous bite: when in rural areas, shake out your shoes or slippers carefully in the morning, and your bedding before retiring.

Marine life

Sea turtles are merely the most celebrated of the marine creatures regularly seen in Cypriot waters. Although **dolphins** are infrequently sighted off the north coast, their true haunts are much closer to Turkey's southern shore where there are more fish. The lack of tidal movement, coupled with very few streams providing nutrients to enrich the coastal water, keep plankton levels low. Consequently, fish numbers around the coasts are not as high as expected, but there is still a surprising diversity of colourful species – scuba-diving is very popular partly because the absence of plankton makes the waters very clear.

A visit to a quay when a fishing boat comes in is also recommended. As the catch is unloaded you see a great mixture of fish, including **peacock** and **rainbow wrasse**, **parrot fish**, **red soldier fish** and **red** or **grey mullet**. Many of these are visible from the surface if you're lazily snorkelling, in addition to the ubiquitous **sea urchins**, **starfish**, **anemones** and the occasional **octopus**. Further out to sea are small, harmless **sharks** and several species of **ray** (including electric and thornback), making a total of around two hundred offshore species. However, owing to overfishing and high tourist levels in the South, taverna squid usually comes from southeast Asia or the North Sea, and nowadays boats have to sail almost to the Libyan coast in order to catch swordfish.

Conservation

After the trauma of the 1974 invasion, many islanders felt that they could not afford the luxury of being Green. Thanks to the joint efforts of comparatively few Cypriots and resident foreigners, people have finally become conscious of the environmental damage caused by unbridled development since 1974 and, moreover, that remedial action has to be immediate and drastic. Dedicated **conservationists** in the Cyprus Biological Society, Cyprus Conservation Foundation, Cyprus Wildlife Society, the UK RSPB, Friends of the Earth, the Green Party and BirdLife Cyprus, as well as individuals in governmental education, fisheries and forestry departments, have all fought an often uphill battle to highlight what is in imminent danger of being irrevocably lost.

Exhibitions, lectures, sets of stamps and broadcasts of David Attenborough's locally shot TV series have all been part of the exercise to increase **public awareness**. Although it's still not officially a national park, such campaigns have until now saved the Akámas peninsula from an unholy alliance of the Orthodox Church and big business hoping to develop it. One of the main rationales of opponents to any Akámas conservation venture was that the Pafiot villagers, like their counterparts in Ayía Nápa, had an inalienable right to make money. To try and ensure local prosperity but simultaneously avoid the seemingly inevitable destruction of the last wilderness in the South, the **Laona Foundation** was set up to encourage **sustainable tourism** (see p.176).

The impact of **hunting** on birds, particularly migrants, is devastating. Its sanctity is inviolate: this, not Christianity or Islam, is the national religion, the main thing held in common in both communities, with the "kill" secondary to the social aspect of a Sunday in the country with the boys. The right to have a hunting licence – 47,000 of them at last count – is passionately defended, and although the Southern government ratified the Bern Convention on endangered species, two weekly days of shooting are allowed during the autumn migratory season.

Cypriots sometimes claim that it was Latin Europeans, in particular the Templars, who introduced **bird-liming** to the island. Until 2002 an alleged 12 million small passerines were indiscriminately trapped each year in nylon mist nets and on sticks coated with the sticky "lime" (actually a glue made from various boiled and treated tree barks). The pickled carcasses of fig-eating blackcaps and thrushes – known as *ambelopoúlia* or *tchíkla* in Cyprus – have long been a much-sought-after taverna *mezé*. Cyprus is certainly not alone among offending Mediterranean states, and the South has at least outlawed lime sticks and the import and use of mist nets. It is now far less socially acceptable than it was, and since Cyprus's accession to the EU is in fact completely illegal (in the SBAs as well), with the annual "harvest" down to about a million. But there is still a ready market for *tchíkla*, with the main centre of pickling now shifted from Paralímni to Yenibouaziçi (Áyios Séryios) in the North, near Salamis. At over €3 per bird in a taverna, there's a tangible cash incentive, and it is now one of the main contraband items smuggled from North to South.

In the North there's an active North Cyprus Society for the Protection of Birds (its initials KKKKD in Turkish). Besides hunting, another pressing concern is the level of **grazing** by the enormous herds of goats brought in by Anatolian settlers. Visiting botanists mapping the orchid flora have deplored drastic changes observed over a short time: once flower-filled hillsides now host little but grass, thistles and white asphodels. The only portion of the Karpaz (Kárpas) peninsula which enjoys any protection from hunting or over-grazing is the far tip, near the monastery of Apóstolos Andhréas.

Books

A s befits a former Crown Colony, there are a huge number of books on Cyprus in English. Many classics have been reissued, and out-of-print but still worthwhile books (indicated o/p) are available through online rare book-dealers like Ⓦwww.abe.co.uk/.com or www.bookfinder .com. Where a title is published in Cyprus only or web-sold only, the imprint/ website is given; titles marked ✻ are particularly recommended.

One knowledgeable and well-stocked specialist **UK outlet** for books on all aspects of Greek Cyprus is **Hellenic Bookservice**, 49–51 Fortess Rd, London NW5 1AD (Ⓣ020/7267 9499, Ⓦwww.hellenicbookservice.com). **Moufflon Books** (Ⓦwww.moufflon.com.cy) in south Nicosia should stock almost everything listed below, particularly Cypriot-published titles, and also publishes its own reprints. Other useful **bookstores in Cyprus** are detailed in the town listings for Larnaca, Limassol, Páfos, Kyrenia and Nicosia.

Travel and impressions

Sir Samuel White Baker *Cyprus as I Saw it in 1879* (o/p). By turns scathing, rapturous and appalling (eg proposals to raze what remained of old Famagusta), from the first year of British administration.

Oliver Burch *The Infidel Sea* (o/p). North Cyprus in the mid-1980s, before tourism had become a significant factor; excellent as a portrait of the Northern community.

Anne Cavendish (ed) *Cyprus 1878: The Journal of Sir Garnet Wolseley* (Marfin Laïki Bank, Nicosia). The memoirs of the first British High Commissioner, republished at a modest price.

Claude Delaval Cobham *Excerpta Cypria, Materials for a History of Cyprus*. Pithy snippets from travellers' and local protagonists' views of Cyprus from biblical times to the nineteenth century, diligently mined by all subsequent writers on Cyprus.

Lawrence Durrell *Bitter Lemons*. Durrell's lyrically told spell as an English teacher, minor colonial official and bohemian resident of Bellapais village in the EOKA-shadowed mid-1950s has aged remarkably well.

Sheila Hawkins *Back of Beyond; Beyond our Dreams; Beyond Compare; Anthology from the Akamas* (Cyprus Mail Publications). Naïve expat and husband set about living in a rustic village of the Akámas peninsula; beach-reading that's spawned many copycat memoirs.

Giovanni Mariti *Travels in the Island of Cyprus*. Wonderful eighteenth-century account; reprint edition includes Umberto Foglietta's useful seventeenth-century *The Sieges of Nicosia and Famagusta*.

✻ **Kyriacos C. Markides** *The Magus of Strovolos; Homage to the Sun; Fire in the Heart*. Markides became involved in the circle of the late mystic and spiritual healer "Daskalos", in the Nicosia suburb of Stróvolos; the resulting, late-1980s trilogy is rather sounder than Castaneda's Don Juan series, to which it's been compared.

David Matthews *The Cyprus Tapes*. Unashamedly pro-North memoirs by a former BBC producer, long a regular columnist for the North's *Cyprus Today*; intimations of Greek-Cypriot skulduggery, and good detail on UN operations.

Colin Thubron *Journey into Cyprus*. Account of a three-month trek round the island during 1972 – and in terms of history in context, and a finger on the pulse of (then) contemporary Cyprus, one of the single best books on the place ever written.

Art, architecture, photo albums

Lucie Bonato, Haris Yiakoumis, Kadir Kaba (eds) *The Island of Cyprus: A Photographic Itinerary from the 19th to the 20th Century* (En Tipis, Nicosia). Fascinating period photos sorted by locale and topic, with excerpted commentary from contemporary travellers.

Cyprus: Memories and Love – Through the Lens of George Seferis (Marfin Laïki Bank, Nicosia). The Greek Nobel-laureate poet was also a keen photographer, and this well-priced album contains 288 photos from his mid-1950s sojourns here.

Philippe Delord *Cyprus: In the Footsteps of Louis-François Cassas*. Retracing, by a talented young artist, of Cassas' 1785 visit to the island; additional captions by Christine Damillier. Widely available on Cyprus.

Michael Radford *The Railways of Cyprus* (Marfin Laïki Bank, Nicosia).

Updates Barry Turner's amazing photo-illustrated monograph of all the railways extant on the island 1905–51, including those used for archeological digs.

Rita Severis *Travelling Artists in Cyprus, 1700–1960*. Watercolours and sketches from the beginnings of the Grand Tour to modernity.

Andreas and Judith Stylianou *The Painted Churches of Cyprus* (o/p). The last word on the Tróödhos country churches, especially, by a couple who made this subject their life's work; only to be faulted for the scanty number of colour reproductions.

John Thomson *Through Cyprus with the Camera in the Autumn of 1878*. Among the first photos of the island, showing how exotic it was at the start of British rule.

Archeology and ancient history

Jane Fejfer (ed) *Ancient Akamas: Settlement & Environment*. Two-volume, illustrated account of a 1988 Danish archeological expedition to the peninsula.

Einar Gjerstad *Ages and Days in Cyprus*. Anecdotal record of travels, personal encounters and site digs by the head of the Swedish Cyprus Expedition (1927–31).

Vassos Karageorghis *Early Cyprus: Crossroads of the Mediterranean*. Definitive,

well-written introduction by one of the foremost Cypriot archeologists, long director of the island's Antiquities Department, who has just published his memoirs, *A Lifetime in the Archeology of Cyprus*. Other lavishly illustrated titles wholly or partly by the same author include *Kition: Mycenaean and Phoenician Discoveries in Cyprus*; *Salamis in Cyprus: Homeric, Hellenistic and Roman* (o/p); *Cyprus Before the Bronze Age: Art of the Chalcolithic Period*, with Edgar Peltenburg; and

Paphos: History and Archaeology (o/p), with Franz Georg Maier.

Demetrios Michaelides and W. A. Daszewski *Mosaic Floors in Cyprus.* Part I covers the magnificent Roman mosaics of Paphos; part II describes the mosaic floors of Christian basilicas across the island. Michaelides' *Cypriot Mosaics* (Cyprus Department of Antiquities, Nicosia; o/p) is a lot cheaper if not easy to find, and adequate for most levels of interest.

Louis (Luigi) Palma di Cesnola *Cyprus: Its Cities, Tombs and Temples* (Star Graphics, Cyprus; o/p). A reprinted classic – the rogue diplomat and archeologist/plunderer in his own shameless words, including fascinating vignettes of everyday life on the eve of British rule.

Louise Steel *Cyprus before History: from the Earliest Settlers to the end of the*

Bronze Age. Slightly misleading title to excellent 2004 survey, which incorporates recent archeological finds and effectively pushes back "history" by some centuries.

Veronica Tatton-Brown *Ancient Cyprus.* Illustrated introduction to the island's past, from Neolithic to late Roman times, by a distinguished archeologist with years of dig experience on Cyprus. Organized by topic ("Jewellery", "The Human Form in Cypriot Art") rather than chronologically, and extremely readable. She also edited *Cyprus in the Nineteenth Century: Fact, Fancy and Fiction*, which entertainingly chronicles all the late-Ottoman, European and American visitors to Cyprus, eager to find a treasure, locate an acropolis or demonstrate a connection with Bronze Age Greece.

Pre-1955 history

Benjamin Arbel *Cyprus, the Franks and Venice, 13th–16th Centuries.* Complements Edbury (see below) well, covering society, economics and politics up to the Ottoman arrival.

Peter W. Edbury *The Kingdom of Cyprus and the Crusades, 1191–1374.* Plumbs the intricate power struggles of the relatively little-known Lusignan period.

Ahmet C. Gazioglu *The Turks in Cyprus: A Province of the Ottoman Empire (1571–1878)* (Kemal Rüstem, Nicosia). Useful, if tendentious history, convinced of how beneficent and tolerant the sultan's rule supposedly was, and how perfidious and deserving of their defeat were the Venetians. That said, full of

fascinating data, and worth the price for C. F. Beckingham's reprinted essay, "The Turks of Cyprus".

Sir David Hunt (ed). *Footprints in Cyprus, an Illustrated History.* Lavishly illustrated anthology covering all eras, far more literate than the usual coffee-table book.

Ioannis D. Stefanidis *Isle of Discord: Nationalism, Imperialism and the Making of Cyprus.* Diplomatic history by a respected Greek scholar, focusing on the period 1945 to 1954. Shows how British and American bungling, together with nationalist extremism on the island and in Greece, precluded a peaceful compromise and fuelled the rise of EOKA.

Independence and after

Many new titles since the early 1990s analyze events from independence to the millennium, often taking advantage of documents released from British archives under the thirty-year rule.

Rebecca Bryant *Imagining the Modern: The Cultures of Nationalism in Cyprus*. Quite recent (2004) and incisive, if controversial, dissection of the topic as stated.

Cynthia Cockburn *The Line: Women, Partition and the Gender Order in Cyprus*. Patriarchy, nationalism and militarism have been instrumental in keeping women at the margins of power in Cyprus; this is documented here, as is the pre-2003 role of bicommunal women's groups in breaching the divide.

Clement H. Dodd (ed.) *The Political, Social and Economic Development of Northern Cyprus* (o/p). Collection of scholarly articles on everything you could possibly want to know about the "nonexistent" TRNC. Objective, and frank about the North's problems, though made partly obsolete by the events of 2000–04.

David Hannay *Cyprus: The Search for a Solution*. Hannay was Britain's special envoy to Cyprus from 1996 to 2003, and pulls no punches in this assessment of the failed 2002–03 negotiations and 2004 referendum.

🏃 **Christopher Hitchens** *Hostage to History: Cyprus from the Ottomans to Kissinger*. Given a new preface in 1997, this lively, provocative, 1984 polemic is essential reading, whether you agree with Hitchens or not. Similar conclusions to Stern (see p.443) as to responsibility for the 1974 catastrophe, but Britain and Cypriot extremists get their share of blame as well.

Robert Holland *Britain and the Revolt in Cyprus, 1954–1959*. Now considered the benchmark account, treating events as an instance of decolonization; Holland had access to all the pertinent archives.

Keith Kyle *Cyprus: In Search of Peace* (MRG, UK). Compiled in late 1997, one of the excellent series of Minority Rights Group pamplets.

William Mallinson *Cyprus: A Modern History*. Very even-handed history from 1878 to modern times, relying on interviews with key players and current source material, brought even more up to date with a new preface to the 2008 edition.

Diana Weston Markides *Cyprus: From Colonial Conflict to Constitutional Crisis 1957–1963* (Moufflon, Nicosia). A post-mortem on what went wrong early on, but one of the best such; explodes the myth of the Turkish-Cypriot community's monolithic-ness, and shows how ethnically separate municipalities were the seedbeds for partition.

Pierre Oberling *The Road to Bellapais: The Turkish Cypriot Exodus to Northern Cyprus*. Useful, if rather lenient on mainland Turkey, written just before the 1983 UDI; Hitchens (see above) characterized it as "the most naïvely pro-Turkish account of the Cyprus problem yet published".

🏃 **Brendan O'Malley and Ian Craig** *The Cyprus Conspiracy: America, Espionage and the Turkish Invasion*. If you've absorbed Stern and/or Hitchens, this presents it all as one coherent thesis: NATO's numerous electronic surveillance facilities on Cyprus, dating back to the 1940s, sealed the island's fate. The conspiracy in question is that, following the UK's relegation to second-division status after the Suez debacle, and its inability to guarantee an abiding presence on the island, US policy was to ensure that these spying devices remained out of the hands of any pro-Soviet or even neutral Cypriot regime – first by encouraging Greek moves to undermine Makarios, and when the junta proved unreliable, by designating the Turks to take their place. If partition was the price for keeping NATO's grip on the island, so be it; Kissinger (who gives a grudging, paraphrased interview) again emerges in a bleak light. Even if you disagree with the thesis, footnoted UK/US government documents are all there to consult.

🏃 **Martin Packard** *Getting it Wrong: Fragments from a Cyprus Diary 1964* (Ⓦ www.authorhouse.co .uk). A distinguished British officer, Packard was head of a tri-national mediating group which successfully reduced intercommunal tensions by visiting flashpoints, and even oversaw some communal re-integration – before being expelled from the island on spurious charges. The title derives

from American diplomat George Ball's disparagement of Packard's efforts: "But you've got it all wrong, son. Hasn't anyone told you that our target here is partition?"

🏃 **Laurence Stern** *The Wrong Horse* (o/p). The "wrong horse" which the US "bet on" was the 1967–74 Greek military junta and parastate, which under its last leader Ioannides engineered the July 1974 coup resulting in Cyprus's partition. Makes clear just how loopy and self-destructive Ioannides was, and good on the blinkered American Foreign Service/CIA culture in Athens at the time, but written too soon (1977) after the events described to benefit from declassification of critical papers. Still, he's barking up the right tree, and despite being relatively polite towards villain of the piece Henry Kissinger (compared to Hitchens, O'Malley and Craig), it provoked the globe-trotting Doctor into buying up and destroying most of the press run. Thus a rare antiquarian item.

Cypriot viewpoints

Especially after 1974, Greek Cypriots were quite successful in monopolizing historiography; titles selected below are some of the more durable, objective sources. For decades, the North got less of a hearing in the international arena, but after the early 1990s there was considerable output, sadly much of it already unavailable.

🏃 **Michael Attalides** *Cyprus: Nationalism and International Politics*. Wide-ranging and readable, if slightly dated, discussion of all aspects of the problem, by a former Cypriot diplomat (ambassador to the UK and France); still considered by many to be the best summary of all the issues.

🏃 **Peter Loizos** *The Heart Grown Bitter: A Chronicle of Cypriot War*

Refugees (o/p). Describes Argáki (lately Akçay) on the Mórfou plain, and the fate of its inhabitants after the Turkish invasion; moreover an excellent introduction to the complexities of Cypriot communalism and politics, by a London professor with roots in Argáki. His *The Greek Gift: Politics in a Cypriot Village* demonstrates how Greek-junta meddling impinged on Argáki party politics, while *Iron in the Soul* continues to follow *The Heart Grown Bitter* refugee community.

Stavros Panteli *The History of Modern Cyprus*. Most recent (2005) and objective reworking of this scholar's two previous comprehensive histories of the island, with especially good material on the colonial period.

Yiannis Papadakis *Echoes From the Dead Zone: Across the Cyprus Divide.* In which a Greek Cypriot, steeped in the nationalist stew of his upbringing, first goes to İstanbul to learn Turkish and then returns to the pre-2003 island (especially Nicosia), on a voyage of discovery of self and the demonized Other. Revealing and often humourous.

Sevgül Uludağ *The Untold Stories* and *Oysters With the Missing Pearls.* Courageous Turkish-Cypriot woman journalist, recently given a forum (in translation) in a Greek-Cypriot newspaper; the "untold stories" are personal accounts from both sides of the Line, while *Oysters …*, now in its fifth printing in Turkish, English and Greek, collects a growing number of oral histories from the families of the missing, also delving into the hitherto taboo subject of mixed marriages.

P. N. Vanezis *Cyprus: The Unfinished Agony* and *Makarios: Life and Leadership* (both o/p). Relatively balanced works, the best of a late-1970s batch by this author.

Specific guides

Bank of Cyprus (Nicosia). A series of excellent, affordable guidelets for various archeological sites and indoor attractions, often written by the supervising archeologists and collection curators. Places covered so far include Amathus, Khirokitia, the Paphos mosaics, the Hadjiyiorgakis Kornesios mansion, Kalavasos-Tenta, Lemba, Palea Paphos, Kourion and the churches at Asínou, Galáta, Platanistássa and Kalopanayiótis.

Lance Chilton *Walks in the Akamas Area* (Ⓦ www.marengowalks.com). A 2007-current guide to the best hikes out of Pólis, Latchí and Neokhorió, together with a colour folding map.

Eileen Davey *Northern Cyprus: A Traveller's Guide.* Somewhat misleadingly named – actually an excellent archeological survey of Northern sites and monuments from all periods, with useful site plans and potted histories; especially good for the medieval monuments.

Gwynneth der Parthog *Byzantine and Medieval Cyprus: A Guide to the Byzantine and Latin Monuments.* Obsessively detailed guide to churches, castles and other monuments in the South; excellent plans, sketches and colour photos, far superior to the *Blue Guide.*

Sophocles Sophocleous *Panagia Arakiotissa, Lagoudera Cyprus: A Complete Guide* (Centre of Cultural Heritage, Nicosia). Well-priced, compact guide to one of the best of the UNESCO Tróödhos churches.

Cypriot fiction and memoirs

Many Cypriots have chosen to write in English in the first instance, but since 2004, EU grant money has also produced abundant Greek- or Turkish-language material in translation. The following – easiest available from the recommended bookshops – is just a sampling.

Taner Baybars *Plucked in a Far-Off Land. (Moufflon, Nicosia).* Lyrically retold World War II-era boyhood near Kyrenia and Nicosia, by a Turkish-Cypriot poet-novelist now resident in France. Vignettes of folk remedies, comfort foods, brandy-fuelled family feuds, pre-pubescent sexuality, Nicosia–village contrasts, and his first steps as a writer.

Christakis Georgiou *Archipelagos: Twenty Years in Labour* (o/p). With a backdrop of miners' strikes and insurrection as Cyprus lurches towards independence, this chronicles a Tróödhos–village girl's rise from grinding poverty and the cabaret demimonde to become – through marriage to the heir of the American-managed mines at Léfka – the most powerful and wealthy women in the land. The prose is staccato and amateurish, but the atmospheric tale itself – the thinly fictionalized story of Zena Gunther, for whom a street and cinema are named in Nicosia – would make an excellent film script.

Andriana Ierodiaconou *Margarita's Husband: A Fable of the Levant* (Armida, Nicosia). The husband is Homer Kyroleon, self-made pillar of society and womanizer, overtaken by historical events, *amour fou* and family tragedy in the 1920s. Deceptively low-key prose and just a smidgen of magical realism combine to make an unexpected page-turner.

Andreas Keleshis *Maïstro-tramountána: A Kyrenia Sea Story.* (Moufflon, Nicosia). Until World War II, Kyrenia was a working fishing port and boat-building centre; this part-autobiographical tale describes a clan of sea-farers, in particular a father and son caught in a *maïstrotramountána* or monster storm. A glimpse of a vanished world, loads better than Hemingway's *Old Man and the Sea*.

Andreas Koumi *The Cypriot.* It's 1974: Andonis the tailor is grimly exiled in Britain, shunning his village past near Larnaca, revealed slowly in flashback – the EOKA rising, sectarian murder, family tragedy, forbidden love across the communal divide. More than a tip of the hat to Louis de Bernières' Aegean epics, and a ties-it-all-up ending that strains credulity, but still essential reading.

Costas Montis *Closed Doors: An Answer to Bitter Lemons.* A self-described attempt to "re-appropriate the narrative" concerning Lawrence Durrell's colonial era and milieu, from a former EOKA operative.

Nora Nadjarian *Ledra Street* (Armida, Nicosia). Thirty-five (often very) short stories, some slight, others poignant, exploring love, adultery, disillusionment, the immigrant experience, racism and familial estrangement, by a younger writer best known for her poetry.

Food and wine

Yiannos Constantinou *The Cyprus Wine Guide* (Wine Products Commision, Limassol). 2006–current coverage of the 25 best wineries in the South, with top picks from each and extensive coverage of Commandaria and *zivanía*.

Gill Davies *The Taste of Cyprus.* Seasonally organized and well illustrated, with easy-to-follow recipes set in cultural context.

Amaranth Sitas *Kopiaste: the Cookbook of Traditional Cyprus Food* (Loizou, Cyprus). Overview of island cuisine and culinary customs, preceding a selection of recipes.

Films

S ince the 1990s, Greek- and Turkish-Cypriot film-makers, often working together in difficult conditions, have been the surprise heroes of film festivals across Europe. Rather revealingly, the first two works listed are effectively banned from screening in both North and South for telling the unvarnished truth about the events of 1963–67 and 1974 (they have only been shown at the UN's Ledra Palace).

Our Wall (Panicos Khrysanthou and Niyazi Kızılyürek, 1993). Superb, unflinchingly honest feature-length documentary directed by two instructors at the Cyprus University in south Nicosia. Besides the experiences of the two film-maker-narrators, it follows the effect of post-independence events on the bereaved of the 1974 war, and on two Turkish Cypriots – Hasan Mustafa and Fatma Mehmet – who elected to stay in the South, and who effectively steal the show.

Parallel Trips (Derviş Zaim and Panicos Khrysanthou, 2002). Initially shot with Zaim (resident in the North) and Khrysanthou having to work separately, this documentary contains some unflinching personal testimony about atrocities committed by both communities, together with some humbling attitudes of forgiveness from those directly affected. After "Good Wednesday", Zaim and Khrysanthou were able to edit together and made only small changes. The natural outgrowth of this was their equally controversial feature, *Mud* (Çamur), an allegory

about a conscript soldier's search for a cure to the "Cyprus disease", which won the UNESCO Prize at the 2003 Venice Film Festival but also fell foul of Cypriot censors.

Living Together Separately (Elias Demetriou, 2003). Account of somewhat fraught bicommunal living, after a fashion, in Pýla.

Which Cyprus? (Rustem Batum, 2003). Courageous film which exposes the links between the cynical Denktaş regime and military/intelligence figures in the Turkish "deep state", who have together prolonged the island's agony far longer than necessary; banned from, of all places, the Thessaloníki Film Festival as the Greeks were keen not to offend Turkey.

Akamas (Panicos Khyrsanthou, 2006). Full-length feature loosely based on the life of Hasan Mustafa, in which a Turkish-Cypriot shepherd boy is taken in by a Greek-Cypriot family, and falls in love with their daughter during the EOKA rebellion – with explosive results. A hit at the Venice Film Festival, unscreened on Cyprus.

Language

Language

Greek

I asked in Greek and was answered in English. I asked again in Greek and was once again answered in English. It was a long moment before I recollected why. I was in the presence not, as I thought, of Turks who either knew no Greek, or would not condescend to speak it: no, I was in the presence of *babus*. To lapse into Greek with anyone who was not a peasant would involve a loss of face. It was rather sad.

Lawrence Durrell

D urrell's experience still applies, and to a great extent, in the Turkish-Cypriot community as well. Speaking English in Cyprus is a badge of sophistication and, despite Greek's official pre-eminence in the South and similar rank for Turkish in the North, the road to advancement in tourism, education and the private professions, if not the civil service. In touristed areas, your Greek or Turkish will have to be nearly perfect to get a reply in kind. Most tourists can and will get by on the island without learning a word of either local language; leave the beaten track, however, especially in the North, and you'll be surrounded by a monolingual culture.

Both Cypriot Greek and Cypriot Turkish are strong dialects – some might argue almost separate languages from the standard phrasebook fare – and familiarity with the latter is not as much of an advantage as you'd think. You will be understood if you utter Athens or İstanbul pleasantries, but you may not catch the reply the first time round – and you won't be alone, since before the homogenizing effect of metropolitan Greek and Turkish television, islanders could carry on conversations virtually incomprehensible to visitors from the "mother" country. About fifteen percent of the day-to-day vocabulary of each community is still peculiar to Cyprus, and the distinctive island accent tends to make Cypriot Greek and Turkish sound almost identical to the untrained ear.

Greek

So many Greek Cypriots have lived or worked abroad in Britain, and, to a lesser extent, North America and Australia, that you will find **English-speakers** even in the remotest village. Add to this the fact that any adult over 60 grew up under British administration, that English is all but compulsory at school, and the overriding importance of the tourist industry, and it's easy to see how many British visitors never bother to learn a word of Greek. You can certainly get by this way, but it isn't very satisfying, and the willingness and ability to say even a few extra words in Greek will upgrade your status from that of dumb *tourístas* to the honourable one of *xénos*, a word which can mean foreigner, traveller and guest all rolled into one.

Learning basic Greek

Greek is not an easy language for English-speakers – translators' unions in the UK rate it as harder than German, slightly less complex than Russian – but it is a very beautiful one, and even a brief acquaintance will give you some idea of the debt owed to it by western European languages.

Greek **grammar** is predictably complicated: nouns are divided into three genders, all with different case endings in the singular and in the plural, and all adjectives and articles have to agree with these in gender, number and case. To simplify life for beginners, all adjectives are arbitrarily cited in the neuter form in the boxed lists on pp.453–454. **Verbs** are even more complex; they come in two conjugations, in both active and passive voices, with passively constructed verbs often having transitive sense. As a novice, it's best to simply say what you want the way you know it, and dispense with the niceties.

Teach-yourself-Greek courses

Alison Kakoura and Karen Rich *Talk Greek* (book and 2 CDs). Probably the best in-print product for beginners' essentials, and the confidence to try them.
Anne Farmakides *A Manual of Modern Greek, 1, for University Students*. If you have the discipline and motivation, this is among the best for learning proper, grammatical Greek.
Hara Garoufalia et al *Read & Speak Greek for Beginners* (book & CD). Unlike many quickie courses, provides a good grammatical foundation; new in 2008.
David Holton et al *Greek: A Comprehensive Grammar of the Modern Language*. A bit technical, so not for rank beginners, but it covers almost every conceivable construction.
Aristarhos Matsukas *Teach Yourself Greek* (book and optional cassettes or CDs). Another complete course, touching on idiomatic expressions too.

Phrasebooks and dictionaries

Rough Guide Greek Phrasebook Current, accurate and pocket-sized, with phrases that you'll actually need. The English–Greek section is transliterated, though the Greek–English part requires mastery of the Greek alphabet.
The Pocket Oxford Greek Dictionary, by J. T. Pring. A bit bulky for travel, but considered the best Greek–English, English–Greek paperback dictionary.
Collins Pocket Greek Dictionary, by Harry T. Hionides. Very nearly as complete as the Pocket Oxford and probably better value for money. The inexpensive *Collins Gem Greek Dictionary* (UK only) is palm-sized but identical in contents – the best day-pack choice.
Oxford Greek–English, English–Greek Learner's Dictionary, by D.N. Stavropoulos. For a prolonged stay, this pricey, hardbound, two-volume set is unbeatable for usage and vocabulary.

Idiosyncrasies of Cypriot Greek

Cypriot **consonants** are often at complete variance with those in metropolitan Greece. The "b" sound of standard Greek (ΜΠ, μπ) is frequently delivered as a simple "p": thus *parpoúni* for the tasty reddish fish, not *barboúni*; *tapélla* for "sign, placard", not *tabélla*. The letter pi (Π, π) is in turn rendered as "b" rather than "p", as in *baboútsia* (shoes) rather than *papoútsia*, Báfos town rather than Páfos. Kappa (Κ, κ) before an "e" or "i" type vowel will sound like the "tch" of Crete rather than "k", as in *Yerostchípou* for Yeroskípou. When initial before "a" or "o", kappa sounds more like "g"; the letter tau (Τ, τ) often sounds more like "d" than "t"; thus *káto* comes out more like *gádo*, *tavás* as *davás*. Where it's intended that the initial tau be pronounced "t" not "d", the letter is doubled (eg Ttákkas Bay

– also done with kappa in this word to make it a "k" rather than a "g" or a "tch" sound.

Strong **sibilants**, lacking to most peninsular Greek-speakers, are also a feature of the dialect: the letter combination sigma-iota (ΣΙ, σι) is pronounced, and transliterated (though no longer in officialese), as "sh" rather than "si". The letter khi (X, χ), when medial, is often pronounced the same way – *éshi*, not *ékhi*, for "there is" or "he/she/it has". The combinations delta-iota-alpha (ΔΙΑ, δια), theta-iota-alpha (ΘΙΑ, θια) or delta-ypsilon (ΔΥ, δυ) have unpredictably bizarre results in sound and accent: the first two, as in the bridge of Roúdhias, come out as *thskiá*, while the latter, as in dhýo, "two", emerges as *thskió*. Iota after rho (PI, ρι) becomes a "g" sound: eg *horgó* rather than standard Greek *horió*, "village", or *Tillyrgá* rather than Tillyría, the remote western region. Especially in Páfos district, **Turkisms** abound: *chakí* instead of the standard *souyiás* for "pocketknife", *chatália* (literally, "forks") for "trousers". Many final iota-ni (IN, ιν) syllables, not found in metropolitan Greek, have been added to words of Turkish or Venetian origin.

If you know Greek at all, there is one small learning aid designed for continental Greeks: Konstantinos Yiangoullis's *Lexiko-Etymoloyiko ke Ermineftiko tis Kypriakis Dhialektou* (Etymological and Interpretative Dictionary of the Cypriot Dialect), available in the South, listing thousands of words derived from ancient Greek, medieval French, Italian, Turkish (and even English), often with short examples of use in folk ballads or poetry. There is unfortunately nothing in print to assist the English-speaking novice – the local dialect is considered beneath serious consideration by the linguistic powers that be.

The Greek alphabet: transliteration and accentuation

Besides the usual difficulties of learning a new language, Greek has an entirely separate **alphabet**. Despite initial appearances, this is in practice fairly easily mastered – a skill that will help enormously in getting around independently (see box below). In addition, certain combinations of letters have unexpected results – especially compared to peninsular Greek; see the preceding remarks on Cypriot dialect. This book's transliteration system should help you make intelligible noises, but remember that the correct **stress** (marked throughout the book with an acute accent or sometimes dieresis) is crucial. With the right sounds but the wrong stress people will either fail to understand you, or else understand something quite different from what you intended. There are numerous word-pairs with the same spelling and phonemes, distinguished only by their stress.

The **dieresis** is used in Greek over the second of two adjacent vowels to change the pronunciation that you would expect from the table below; sometimes it can function as the primary stress. In the place Kaïmaklí (near Nicosia), the dieresis changes the sound of the first syllable from "kay" to "Ka-ee", but in this case the primary stress is on the third syllable. It is also, uniquely among Greek accents, used on capital letters in signs and personal-name spellings in Cyprus, though for simplicity our city street maps are unaccented.

The Greek alphabet, the system of transliteration used in this book, and a brief aid to pronunciation are set out below.

Greek	transliteration	pronounced
A, α	a	a as in father
B, β	v	v as in vet

Γ, γ	y/g	y as in yes, except before consonants, α, o or ου, when it's a breathy g, approximately as in gap
Δ, δ	dh	th as in then, except before i/y; see note p.451
E, ε	e	e as in get
Z, ζ	z	z sound
H, η	i	i as in ski
Θ, θ	th	th as in theme, except before i/y
I, ι	i	i as in ski
K, κ	k	nominally k sound, usually 'tchí if medial, 'gí if initial, unless doubled
Λ, λ	l	l sound
M, ∝	m	m sound
N, ν	n	n sound
Ξ, ξ	x	x as in box, medial or initial (never z as in xylophone)
O, o	o	o as in toad
Π, π	p	p sound
P, ρ	r	xr sound
Σ, σ, ς	s	s sound, except z sound before μ or γ; note that single sigma has the same phonetic value as double sigma
T, τ	t	t sound, but more like d unless doubled
Y, υ	y, i	y as in barely
Φ, φ	f	f sound
X, χ	kh	harsh h sound, like ch in loch, but often sh when medial
Ψ, ψ	ps	ps as in lips
Ω, ω	o	o as in toad, indistinguishable from o

Combinations and diphthongs

AI, αι	e	e as in hey
AY, αυ	av/af	av or af depending on following consonant
EI, ει	i	long i, exactly like ι or η
EY, ευ	ev/ef	ev or ef, depending on following consonant
OI, οι	i	long i, exactly like ι or η
OY, ου	ou	ou as in tourist
ΓΓ, γγ	ng	ng as in angle; always medial
ΓΚ, γκ	g/ng	g as in goat at the beginning of a word; ng in the middle
MΠ, μπ	b/mb	b at the beginning of a word; mb in the middle, but see note p.450
NT, ντ	d/nd	d at the beginning of a word, nd in the middle
ΣI, σι	sh	sh as in shame
TΣ, τσ	ts	ts as in cha-cha
TZ, τζ	tz	j as in jam

Greek words and phrases

Essentials			
		No	Óhi
		Please	Parakaló
Yes	Né	OK, agreed	Endáxi
Certainly	Málista		

Thank you (very much)	Efharistó (polý)
I (don't) understand	(Dhén) Katalavéno
Do you speak English?	Miláte angliká?
Sorry/excuse me	Signómi
Today	Símera
Tomorrow	Ávrio
Yesterday	Khthés
Now	Tóra
Later	Argótera
Open	Anikhtó
Closed	Klistó
Day	Méra
Night	Níkhta
In the morning	Tó proï
In the afternoon	Tó apóyevma
In the evening	Tó vrádhi
Here	Edhó
There	Ekí
This one	Aftó
That one	Ekíno
Good	Kaló
Bad	Kakó
Big	Megálo
Small	Mikró
More	Perisótero
Less	Ligótero
A little	Lígo
A lot	Polý
Cheap	Ftinó
Expensive	Akrivó
Hot	Zestó
Cold	Krýo
With (together)	Mazí (mé)
Without	Horís
Quickly	Grígora
Slowly	Sigá
Mr/Mrs	Kýrios/Kyría
Miss	Dhespinís

Other needs

To eat/drink	Trógo/píno
Bakery	Foúrnos, psomádhiko
Pharmacy	Farmakío
Post office	Takhydhromío
Stamps	Gramatósima
Petrol station	Venzinádhiko

Bank	Trápeza
Money	Leftá/Khrímata
Toilet	Toualéta
Police	Astynomía
Doctor	Yiatrós
Hospital	Nosokomío

Requests and questions

To ask a question, it's simplest – though hardly elegant – to start with *parakaló*, then name the thing you want in an interrogative tone.

Where is the bakery?	Parakaló, o foúrnos?
Can you show me the road to…?	Parakaló, ó dhrómos yiá…?
We'd like a room for two	Parakaló, éna dhomátio yiá dhýo átoma
May I have a kilo of oranges?	Parakaló, éna kiló portokália?
Where?	Poú?
How?	Pós?
How many?	Póssi, pósses or póssa?
How much (does it cost)?	Póso (káni)?
When?	Póte?
Why?	Yiatí?
At what time…?	Sé tí óra…?
What is/Which is…?	Tí íne/Pió íne…?
What time does it open?	Tí óra aníyi?
What time does it close?	Tí óra klíni?

Talking to people

Greek makes the distinction between the **informal** (*essý*) and **formal** (*essís*) second person, as French does with *tu* and *vous*. Young people, older people and country people often use *essý* even with strangers, though it's best to address everyone formally until/unless they start using the familiar to you, to avoid causing offence. By far the most common greeting, on meeting and parting, is *yiá sou/ yiá sas* – literally "health to you". As across most of the Mediterranean, the approaching party utters the first greeting, not those seated at *kafenío* tables or doorsteps – thus the occasional silent staring as you enter a village.

Hello	Hérete
Good morning	Kalí méra
Good evening	Kalí spéra
Good night	Kalí níkhta
Goodbye	Adío
How are you?	Tí kánis/Tí kánete?
I'm fine	Kalá íme
And you?	Ké essý/essís?
What's your name?	Pós sé/sás léne?
My name is ...	Mé léne ...
Speak slower, please	Parakaló, miláte pió sigá
How do you say it in Greek?	Pós léyete avtó stá Elliniká?
I don't know	Dhén xéro
See you tomorrow	Thá sé dhó ávrio
See you soon	Kalí andámosi
Bon voyage	Kaló taxídhi
Let's go	Páme
Please help me	Parakaló, ná mé voithíste

Greeks' Greek

There are numerous **words and phrases** which you will hear constantly, even if you rarely have the chance to use them. These are a few of the most common.

Come on, let's go!	Háde!
Literally, "Indicate!"; in effect, "What can I do for you?"	Oríste!
Standard phone responses	Embrós! or Léyete!
What's new?	Tí néa?
What's going on (here)?	Tí yínete?
So-so	Étsi kiétsi
Whoops! Watch it!	Ópa!
Expression of dismay or concern, like French "o là là"	Po-po-po!
My boy/girl, sonny, friend, etc	Pedhí moú
Literally "wanker", in mainland Greek; rarely heard in Cyprus and best not used by foreigners	Maláka(s)

A nutcase, a loony – much more used in Cyprus than *malákas*, and more socially acceptable	Palavós
Take your time, slow down	Sigá sigá

Accommodation

Hotel	Xenodhohío
Inn	Xenón(as)
A room ...	Éna dhomátio ...
for one/two/three people	yiá éna/dhýo/tría átoma
for one/two/ three nights	yiá mía/dhýo/trís vradhiés
with a double bed	mé dhipló kreváti
with a bathtub	mé baniéra
with a shower	mé doús
Hot water	Zestó neró
Cold water	Krýo neró
Air conditioning	Klimatismós
Fan	Anamistíra
Can I see it?	Boró ná tó dhó?

On the move

Aeroplane	Aeropláno
Bus, coach	Leoforío, púlman
Car	Aftokínito, amáxi
Motorbike, scooter	Mihanáki, papáki
Taxi	Taxí
Bicycle	Podhílato
On foot	Mé tá pódhia
Trail	Monopáti
Bus stop	Stássi
Harbour	Limáni
When does it leave?	Ti óra févyi?
When does it arrive?	Ti óraftháni?
How many kilometres?	Póssa h700ómetra?
How many hours?	Pósses óres?
Where are you going?	Poú pás?
I'm going to ...	Páo stó ...
I want to get off at ...	Thélo ná katévo stó...
The road to ...	O dhrómos yiá ...
Near	Kondá

Far	Makriá
Left/Right	Aristerá/Dhexiá
Straight ahead	Katefthía, ísia
A ticket to ...	Éna isitírio yiá ...
Beach	Paralía
Centre (of town)	Kéndro
Church	Eklissía
Monastery	Monastíri
Sea	Thálassa

Days of the week, months and seasons

Sunday	Kyriakí
Monday	Dheftéra
Tuesday	Tríti
Wednesday	Tetárti
Thursday	Pémpti
Friday	Paraskeví
Saturday	Sávato

You may see *katharévoussa* (formal Greek) forms of the months written on schedules or signs; these are the spoken forms.

January	Yennáris
February	Fleváris
March	Mártis
April	Aprílis
May	Maïos
June	Ioúnios
July	Ioúlios
August	Ávgoustos
September	Septémvris
October	Októvrios
November	Noémvris
December	Hekémvris
Summer schedule	Therinó dhromolóyio
Winter schedule	Himerinó dhromolóyio

Numbers

1	énas/éna/mía
2	dhýo
3	trís/tría

4	tésseris/tésseres/ tréssera
5	pénde
6	éxi
7	eftá
8	okhtó
9	ennéa (or enyá)
10	dhéka
11	éndheka
12	dhódheka
13	dhekatrís
14	dhekatésseres
20	íkossi
21	íkossi éna
30	triánda
40	saránda
50	penínda
60	exínda
70	evdhomínda
80	ogdhónda
90	enenínda
100	ekató
150	ekatón penínda
200	dhiakóssies/dhiakóssia
500	pendakóssies/ pendakóssia
1000	hílies/hilia
2000	dhýo hiliádhes
1,000,000	éna ekatomírio

Time

What time is it?	Tí óra íne?
One/two/three o'clock	Mía íy óra/dhýo iy óra/ trís íy óra
Twenty minutes to four	Tésseres pará íkossi
Five minutes past seven	Eftá ké pénde
Half past eleven	Éndheka ké misí
In half an hour	Sé misí óra
In a quarter of an hour	S'éna tétarto
In two hours	Sé dhýo óres

Turkish

It's worth learning as much Turkish as you can while you're in North Cyprus; if you travel far from the tourist centres you may well need it, and Cypriots always appreciate foreigners who show enough interest and courtesy to learn at least basic greetings. The main advantages of the language from the learner's point of view are that it's phonetically spelt, and (98 percent of the time) grammatically regular. The disadvantages are that the vocabulary is completely unrelated to any language you're likely to have encountered, and the grammar – relying heavily on suffixes – gets thornier the further you delve into it. Concepts like vowel harmony further complicate matters.

Vowel harmony and loan words

Turkish usually adheres to the principle of **vowel harmony**, whereby words contain either so-called "back" vowels a, ı, o and u, or "front" vowels e, i, ö and ü, but rarely mix the two types. Back and front vowels are further subdivided into "unrounded" (a and ı, e and i) and "rounded" (o and u, ö and ü), and again rounded and unrounded vowels tend to keep exclusive company, though there are further nuances to this. A small number of native Turkish words (eg, *anne*, mother; *kardeş*, brother) violate the rules of vowel harmony, as do compound words, eg *bugün*, "today", formed from *bu* (this) and *gün* (day).

The main exceptions to vowel harmony, however, are foreign **loan words** from Arabic or Persian, and despite Atatürk's best efforts to substitute Turkish or French expressions (the latter again failing to follow vowel harmony), they still make up a good third of the modern Turkish vocabulary. Most words beginning with f, h, l, m, n, r, v and z, or ending in d, t, b or p are derived from Arabic and Persian.

Dictionaries and phrasebooks

For a straightforward **phrasebook**, look no further than *Turkish: A Rough Guide Phrasebook* (Rough Guides), which has useful two-way glossaries and a brief and simple grammar section. For an **at–home course**, Geoffrey L. Lewis's *Teach Yourself Turkish* still probably has a slight edge over Yusuf Mardin's *Colloquial Turkish* (o/p); or buy both, since they complement each other well. Alternatively, there's Geoffrey Lewis's *Turkish Grammar* (o/p), a one-volume solution.

Among widely available Turkish **dictionaries**, the best are probably the Langenscheidt/Lilliput in miniature or coat-pocket sizes, or the *Concise Oxford Turkish Dictionary*, a hardback suitable for serious students. The Redhouse dictionaries produced in Turkey but marketed by Milet in the UK are the best value: the affordable 11.4-centimetre pocket version or the 12.5-centimetre *Minisözlüğü* have the same number of entries as the 24-centimetre desk edition and are adequate for most demands.

Idiosyncrasies of Cypriot Turkish

Pafiot Turkish in particular, while it lasts as a separate sub-dialect, shows the effects of long cohabitation with Cypriot Greek. There is no indicative tense as in standard Turkish, the indefinite mood being used on most occasions; nor are there interrogative particles as in Turkey, a question being indicated by voice inflection as in Greek. Moreover, refugees from Páfos (*Baf* in Turkish,) frequently use *etmek*, only an auxiliary verb in Anatolian Turkish, in place of *yapmak* for "to do, to make". Slurred pronoun constructions are common and confusing: *ba* for *bana* (to/for me), *sa* for *sana* (to/for you), *gen* for *kendin'e* (to/for oneself). *Na'pan*, the standard colloquial greeting, is an elision of *Ne yaparsın* (approximately, "Whaddya up to?" or "Whatcha doin'?").

That last translation gives a fairly accurate idea of the casualness of Cypriot linguistic mores; the islanders derive some amusement from the painfully precise diction of İstanbul people, who in turn consider the island dialect just plain slovenly. However, Turkish television plus over three decades of army occupation, mainland settlers and refugee status are steadily eroding these peculiarities, which could disappear over the next generation unless there's a solution which permits substantial social mixing with Greek Cypriots.

Pronunciation and accentuation

Pronunciation in Turkish is worth mastering, since once you've got it, the phonetic spelling and regularity helps you progress fast. The following letters differ significantly from English pronunciation.

Aa	short a, similar to that in far	Çç	like ch in chat
Ee	as in bet	Gg	hard g as in get
İi	as in pin	Ğğ	generally silent, but lengthens the preceding vowel, and between two vowels approximates a y sound
Iı	vowel resembling the vestigial sound between the b and the l of probable		
Oo	as in note	Hh	as in hen, never silent
Öö	like ur in burn	Jj	like the s in pleasure
Uu	as in blue	Şş	like sh in shape
Üü	like ew in few	Vv	soft, between a v and a w
Cc	like j in jelly		

The **circumflex** (^), found only over the letters a, u and i in loan words from Arabic or Persian, has two uses. It usually lengthens (and stresses) the vowel it crowns, eg Mevlâna sounds like "Mevl**aa**na", Alevî is pronounced "Alev**ee**", but when used after the consonants g, k or l the affected vowel sounds as if it's preceded by a faint y, and distinguishes words that are otherwise homonyms: eg *kar* (snow) versus *kâr* (profit). Although its meticulous use is dwindling over 'i', news of the circumflex's demise has been greatly exaggerated, and you still commonly see it in media as diverse as airline publicity and newspaper headlines.

Turkish words and phrases

Basics

Mr; follows first name	Bey
Miss; precedes first name	Bayan
Mrs (literally lady) polite Ottoman title; follows first name	Hanım
Half-humorous honorific title bestowed on any tradesman; means "master craftsman"	Usta
Honorific of someone who has made the pilgrimage to Mecca	Hacı
Good morning	Günaydın
Good afternoon	İyi Günler
Good evening	İyi Akşamlar

Good night	İyi Geceler	With/without (milk)	(Süt)lu/(Süt)suz
Hello	Merhaba	With/without (meat)	(Et)li/(Et)siz
Goodbye	Allahaısmarladık	Enough	Yeter
Yes	Evet		

No	Hayır	Left/Right	Sol/Sağ
No (there isn't any)	Yok	Straight ahead	Doğru, direk
Please	Lütfen	Turn left/right	Sola dön/Sağ'ta dön
Thank you	Teşekkür ederim	Parking/No parking	Park yapılır/Park
	Mersi/Sağol		yapılmaz
You're welcome,	Bir şey değil	One-way street	Tek yön
that's OK		No entry	Araç giremez
How are you (familiar/	Nasılsınız?	No through road	Çıkmaz sokak
formal second	Nasılsın? Ne	Slow down	Yavaşla
person)?	haber? Na'pan?	Road closed	Yol kapalı
I'm fine (thank you)	(Sağol) İyiyim/	Crossroads	Dörtyol
	İyilik sağlık	Pedestrian crossing	Yaya geçidi
Do you speak English?	İngilizce		
	biliyormusunuz?		

Common signs

I don't understand	Anlamadım/	Entrance/exit	Giriş/Çıkış
(Turkish)	Türkçe	Free/paid entrance	Giriş ücretsiz/Ücretlidir
	anlamıyorum	Gentlemen	Baylar
I beg your pardon, sorry	Affedersiniz	Ladies	Bayanlar
Excuse me (in a crowd)	Pardon	WC	WC/Tuvalet/Umumî
I'm English/Scottish/	İngilizim/İskoçyalım/	Open/closed	Açık/Kapalı
Irish/Welsh/	İrlandalıyım/Gal	Arrivals/departures	Varış/Kalkış
Australian	'liyim/	Pull/push	Çekiniz/İtiniz
	Avustralyalım	Out of order	Arızalı
I live in …	… de/da	Drinking water	İçilebilir su
	oturuyorum	To let/for hire	Kiralık
Today	Bugün	Beware	Dikkat
Tomorrow	Yarın	First aid	İlk yardım
The day after tomorrow	Öbür gün/Ertesi gün	No smoking	Sigara İçilmez
Yesterday	Dün	Don't tread on	Çimenlere basmayınız
Now	Şimdi	the grass	
Later	Sonra	Stop/halt	Dur
Wait a minute!	Bir dakika!	Military area	Askeri bölge
In the morning	Sabahleyin	Entry forbidden	Girmek yasaktır
In the afternoon	Öğleden sonra	Please take off	Lütfen ayakkabılarınızı
In the evening	Akşamleyin	your shoes	çıkartınız
Here/there/over there	Burda/Burda/Orda	No entry on foot	Yaya giremez
Good/bad	İyi/Kötü, Fena		

Requests and questions

Big/small	Büyük/Küçük	Where is the …?	… nerede?
Cheap/expensive	Ucuz/Pahalı	When?	Ne zaman?
Early/late	Erken/Geç	What/What is it?	Ne/Ne dir?
Hot/cold	Sıcak/Soğuk	How much (does	Ne kadar?/Kaça?
Near/far	Yakın/Uzak	it cost?)	
Vacant/occupied	Boş/Dolu		
Quickly/slowly	Hızlı/Yavaş		

How many?	Kaç tane?
Why?	Niye?
What time is it? (polite)	Saatınız var mı?
(informal)	Saat kaç ?
How do I get to ...?	... 'a/e nasıl giderim?
How far is it to ...?	... 'a/e ne kadar uzakta?
What time does it open?	Kaçta açılıcak?
What time does it close?	Kaçta kapanacak?
What's it called in Turkish?	Türcesi ne dir? or Turkçe nasıl söylersiniz?

When is the next bus/ferry?	Bir sonraki otobus/ vapur kaçta kalkıyor?
Where does it leave from?	Nereden kalkıyor?
How many miles is it?	Kaç mildir?
How long does it take?	Ne kadar sürerbilir?
Which bus goes to ...?	Hangi otobus ... 'a gider?
Which road leads to ...?	Hangi yol ... 'a çıkar?
Can I get out at a convenient place?	Müsait bir yerde inebilirmiyim?

Accommodation

Hotel	Hotel/Otel
Do you have a room?	Boş odanız var mı?
Single/double/triple	Tek/çift/üç kişilik
Do you have a double room for one/two/ three nights?	Bir/iki/üç gecelik yataklı odanız var mı?
For one/two weeks	Bir/İki hafta için
With an extra bed	İlave yataklı
With a double bed	Fransiz yataklı
With a shower	Duşlu
With a bathtub	Havuzlu
Hot water	Sicak su
Cold water	Soğuk su
Can I see it?	Bakabilirmiyim?
I have a booking	Reservasyonım var

Travelling

Aeroplane	Uçak
Bus	Otobus
Shared minibus-taxi	Dolmuş
Car	Araba
Taxi	Taksi
Bicycle	Bisiklet
Ferry	Feribot
Catamaran	Deniz otobüsü
On foot	Yaya
Bus station	Otogar
Ferry terminal/jetty	İskele
Harbour	Liman
A ticket to ...	... a bir bilet
What time does it leave?	Kaçta kalkıyor?

Days of the week, months and seasons

Sunday	Pazar
Monday	Pazartesi
Tuesday	Salı
Wednesday	Çarşamba
Thursday	Perşembe
Friday	Cuma
Saturday	Cumartesi
January	Ocak
February	Subat
March	Mart
April	Nisan
May	Mayıs
June	Haziran
July	Temmuz
August	Ağustos
September	Eylül
October	Ekim
November	Kasım
December	Aralık
Spring	İlkbahar
Summer	Yaz
Autumn	Sonbahar
Winter	Kış

Numbers

1	Bir
2	İki
3	Üç
4	Dört
5	Beş
6	Altı

7	Yedi
8	Sekiz
9	Dokuz
10	On
11	On bir
12	On iki
13	On üç
20	Yirmi
30	Otuz
40	Kırk
50	Elli
60	Altmış
70	Yetmiş
80	Seksen
90	Doksan
100	Yüz
140	Yüz kırk

200	İki yüz
700	Yedi yüz
1000	Bin
100,000	Yüz bin
500,000	Beşyüz bin
1,000,000	Bir milyon

Time

(At) 3 o'clock	Saat üç (ta)
2 hours (duration)	İki saat
Half hour (duration)	Yarım saat
5.30	Beş büçük
It's 8.10	Sekizi on geçiyor
It's 10.45	On bire çeyrek var
At 8.10	Sekizi on geçe
At 10.45	On bire çeyrek kala

A Greek and Turkish food glossary

In the following lists, the words are given in this order – **Greek/Turkish, English**. If the dish or drink is not found in the particular community, or there is no known Greek or Turkish equivalent, a dash is shown.

Basics

neró/su	water
aláti/tuz	salt
eliés/zeytin	olives
pítta/pita	flat Arab bread
psomí/ekmek	bread
elióti/–	olive bread
piláfi/pilav	cooked rice
pourgoúri/bulgur	cracked wheat
makarónia, fídhes/ şehriye	(thin) noodles
yiaoúrti/yoğurt	yogurt
gála/süt	milk
méli/bal	honey
voútyro/tereyağ	butter

Appetizers (mezédhes/mezeler) and picnic items

talatoúra/talatur, cacık	yogurt, cucumber, garlic and herb dip; Turkish-Cypriot *talatur*

	has more mint and cucumber, less garlic
taramás/tarama	pink fish-roe paté
húmmos/humus	hummus
tashíni/tahin	sesame seed paste
–/eşeksiksin	tahini with lemon juice or other souring agents
loúntza/–	smoked pork loin slabs
shirómeri/–	cured local ham, like parma or prosciutto
tsamarélla/samarella	lamb- or (better) goat-based salami
halloúmi/hellim	minty ewe's or goat's cheese, often fried
anarí/nor	soft, crumbly sweet cheese, byproduct of above
fétta/beyaz peynir	white goat's or ewe's cheese
kasséri/kaşar	kasseri cheese
moúngra/moungra	pickled cauliflower

tsakistés/çakistes	split olives, usually green, marinated in coriander seed, lemon and garlic

Meat and game entrees

kléftigo/küp kebap, fırın kebap	lamb/goat baked in an outdoor oven
souvláki/şiş kebap	meat chunks grilled on a skewer
rifi/–	whole lamb on a spit
–/kuyu kebap	meat baked in an underground vessel
sheftália/şeftalya, şeftalı kebap	grilled mince-and-onion pellets in gut casings
keftédhes/köfte	meatballs
pansétta/–	pork spare ribs
pastourmás/ pastırma, sucuk	greasy sausage or cured dry meat
glykádhia/–	sweetbreads
zalatína/–	brawn
kotópoulo/piliç, boulí	chicken
gourounópoulo/–	suckling pig
peristéri/güverçin	pigeon
kounélli/tavşan	rabbit
ortítchia/bıldırçın	quail
ambelopoúlia, tchíkla/amberobulya	pickled songbirds
karaóles/salyangoz	land snails
lougánigo/bumbar	skinny home-made sausages, the latter often with a high proportion of rice filling

Soups

avgolémono/düğün	egg and lemon
trakhanás/tarhana	grain, yogurt, spices
patsás/işkembe	tripe

Preparation terms

tís óras, stá kárvouna/kömürde, ızgarada	grilled
tiganitó/yağda	fried
stifádho/yahni	stewed in a sweet onion-and-tomato sauce

parayemistá/dolması	stuffed
plakí/pilaki	vinaigrette, marinated
xydháta/turşu	pickled
oftó/fırında	baked

Fish and seafood

péstrofa/–	trout (farmed)
parpoúni/tekir	red mullet
koutsomoúra/ barbun	dwarf red mullet
sorkós/sargoz	bream
ballás/–	large-eyed dentex
melána, melánes/–	saddled bream
lithríni/mercan	red bream, pandora
marídhes/smirida	picarel
wóppes/küpes, woppa	bogue
parakoúdha/–	barracuda
lakérdha/lakerda	white-flesh bonito, marinated
mayátiko/mineri	amberjack
lagós/lahoz	small (golden) grouper
rofós/orfoz	large (dusky) grouper, rather bony
stýra, vláhos/vlahos	stone bass, wreckfish
skáros/ızkaroz	parrotfish
kourkoúna/sokan	leatherback
fangrí/mercan	common bream
spáros/karagöz	two-banded or ringed bream
skathári/sarıgöz	black bream
tsipoúra/çipura	gilt-head bream
synagrídha/sinagrit	dentex
khános/asıl hani	comber
smérna/merina	moray eel
karídhes/karides	small prawns
khtapódhi/ahtapod	octopus
kalamarákia/kalamar	small squid
karavídhes/ karavidler	crayfish
kolokythás/–	"sea mole", a meatier crustacean than crayfish

Greens

saláta/salata	any salad
tsayíri/çayırı	mixed-greens garnish

maroúli/marul	lettuce
koliándhros/kolandro	coriander
maïdhanós/maydanos	parsley
glystírga/semizotu	purslane
sélino/kereviz	celery
lapsána/lapsana	wild mustard greens
rókka/rokka	rocket greens
molóha/gömec	mallow greens
louvána/–	pea-plant leaves
strouthoúthkia/–	bladder campion
khristangáthi/–	dockweed
pangáli/–	eryngo; another Lenten green
hostés/hostes	wild artichokes
molehíya/molohiya, mulihiya	a mint-like leaf used as meat flavouring, or served steamed on its own, mostly in the North
kírtamo/kırtama	rock samphire
agrélia/ayrelli, kuşkonmaz	(wild) asparagus
kappariá/kapa, gebre	pickled caper plants
angináres/enginar	globe artichokes

Other vegetables

krambí/lahana	cabbage
domátes/domates	tomatoes
kremídhi/soğan	onion
skórdho/sarmısak	garlic
repánia/turp	radish
kouloúmbra/ kouloumbra	kohlrabi
(kafteró) pipéri/ (acı) biber	(hot) pepper
manitária/mantar	mushrooms, often wild
spanáki/ispanak	spinach
patátes/patates	potatoes
tsíps/çips	guess …
kolokássia/kolokasa bules, yer elması	taro root
kolokythákia/kabak	courgettes
bámies/bamya	okra
bezélia/bezelye	peas
fasólia/fasulye	beans
goutsiá/bakla	broad beans
gounoupídhi/ çiçek lahanası	cauliflower

louviá/börülce	black-eyed peas
óspria	generic for any pulse

Typical dishes

davás/dava	sweetish stew, usually of lamb, with onions
afélia/–	pork cooked with red wine and coriander seeds
réssi/–	cracked wheat and meat dish, served at weddings
moussakás/musaka	aubergine and potato slabs overlaid with mince and white sauce
–/karnıyarık	similar to preceding but no sauce or potato
kolokótes/–	turnovers stuffed with pumpkin, raisins and bulgur
koupépia/yaprak dolması	vine leaves filled with rice
koúppes/–	torpedo-shaped fried turnovers filled with onions and mince meat
pourétcha/börek	turnovers filled with meat or cream cheese
–/laz böreği	meat-filled crepas topped with yogurt
–/mantı	ravioli, filled with mince and served with yogurt and chili
–/tatar böreği	similar meat-stuffed pasta, served with cheese and mint
–/pirohu	ravioli, filled with cheese

Nutty snacks

soushoúkou/ soudzouki	almond string dipped in rosewater and grape molasses
–/köfter	as above, but with no nuts
pastelláki/–	sesame, peanut and syrup bar
fistíkia/fıstık	peanuts

halepianá/şam fıstığı	pistachios
amýgdhala/badem	almonds

loukoúmi/lokum	"Cyprus" delight: varying proportions of sugar, pectin, gelatin, rosewater or citrus extract, nuts, boiled then solidified
pagotó/dondurma	ice cream
baklavás/baklava	filo pastry layers with nut-honey filling
kataïfi/kadayıf	same as above but with "shredded wheat" instead of pastry sheets
katméri/katmer	crepe stuffed with banana, honey and clotted cream (kaïmáki or kaymak yağ)
loukoumádhes/ lokma	deep-fried batter rings
halvás/helva	grainy paste, semolina- or tahini-based
shamísi/şamişi	semolina-based granular sweet
mahallcbí/muhallebi	cherry-pit flour and rosewater pudding
palouzé	grape-must pudding
kalopráma	yoghurt, semolina and citrus-rind cake
shamáli	as above, with nuts
glyká/macun	sweet preserved fruit

Types of glyká or macun include:

výssino/vişne	sour morello cherry
kerási/kiraz	Queen Anne-type cherry
petrokéraso/–	dark red cherry
kitrómilo/neranci	Seville orange
vazanáki/patlıcan	baby aubergines
sýko/incir	fig
karýdhi/ceviz	walnut

fráoules/çilek	strawberries
moúsmoule/ muşmula	medlars
méspila/yeni dünya	loquats
kaïsha, khryssómila /kayısı	apricots
rodhákina/şeftali	peaches
bastésha, batíha/ karpuz	watermelon
gouáva/guava	strawberry guava
pepóni/kavun	dessert melon
paraméles/erik	plums
kerásia/kiraz	cherries
papoutsósyko/ frenk inciri	prickly pears
finícha/hurma	dates
sýka/incir	figs
stafýlia/üzüm	grapes
míla/elma	apples
akhládhia/armut	pears
portokália/portakal	oranges
lemónia/limon	lemons
mandarínia/mandalin	mandarins
gréypfrout/grepfrut	grapefruit
banánes/muz	banana

kafés/kahve	Oriental coffee, served:
pikrós/sade	unsweetened
métrios/orta	medium sweet
glykós/şekerli	very sweet
tsáï/çay	tea
spadjá/spaca	sage tea
býra/bira	beer
krasí/şarap	wine
áspro/beyaz	white
mávro/kırmızı	red
kokkinélli/roze	rosé
aïráni/ayran	diluted yogurt with herbs
khymós/meyva suyu	fruit juice

L

LANGUAGE | A Greek and Turkish food glossary

Glossary

Archeological, artistic and architectural terms

Acropolis Ancient fortified hilltop.

Agora Market and meeting place of an ancient Greek city.

Amphora Tall, narrow-necked jar for oil or wine.

Aniconic Abstract, non-figurative, dating from the Iconoclast Period – see "Iconoclasm" below – when the Orthodox Church forbade figural representation.

Apse Polygonal or curved recess at the altar (usually east) end of a church.

Archaic period Era (c.750–475 BC) when Cypriot artistic expressiveness was most developed in its own right, though heavily influenced by the Middle East.

Ashlar Dressed, squared masonry in an ancient structure.

Atrium Open, inner courtyard of a Hellenistic or Roman dwelling.

Basilica Colonnaded, "hall"- or "barn"- type church adapted from Roman public buildings, common in Cyprus.

Bronze Age Early (2500–1900 BC) to Late (1650–1050 BC); the latter eras show marked cultural influence of the Mycenaean migration from the Greek Peloponnese.

Byzantine empire The Greek-speaking Christian state, ruled from Constantinople (modern Istanbul), which developed out of the eastern Roman empire after its division from the west. Byzantine rule on Cyprus ended in 1191.

Capital The top, often ornamented, of a column.

Chalcolithic period Cultures (3900–2500 BC) distinguished by advanced ceramic and worked-stone artefacts, and by the first smelting of copper – from which Cyprus probably takes its name.

Champlevé In architecture, the technique of chiselling reliefs onto a flat stone surface; the recesses so created might be filled with glass or coloured wax for contrast.

Classical period In Cyprus, from the start of the fifth century BC to the rule of the Macedonian kings late in the next century; a period of destruction at the hands of the Persians, and thus poor in home-grown artefacts.

Conch Curved surface at the top of an apse.

Dromos Ramp leading to the subterranean entrance of a Bronze Age tomb.

Frigidarium Cold plunge-pool room of a Roman or Byzantine bath.

Geometric Archeological era (c.1050–750 BC) so named for the abstract designs of its pottery.

Hellenistic era Extending from 325–50 BC, this meant for Cyprus rule by the Ptolemaic kings, based in Alexandria.

Hypocaust Underfloor space in baths, with brick supports, for hot-air circulation.

Iconoclasm Eighth- and ninth-century Byzantine movement whereby the veneration of icons was forbidden as idolatrous; during this time many figurative frescoes were destroyed as well.

Ierárkhi The Church Fathers (codifiers of Christianity and monastic life), a common fresco subject.

Ierón Literally, "sacred" – the sanctuary between the altar screen and the apse of a church, reserved for priestly activities.

Katholikón Central church of a monastery.

Krater Large, usually two-handled ancient wine goblet.

Lusignan dynasty Mostly French, Catholic nobility who ruled Cyprus from 1191 until 1489, a time typified by monumental Gothic architecture, the introduction of feudalism and the suppression of the Orthodox Church.

Machicolations Openings at the edge of a castle's parapet or above its doorway, usually between corbels, for dumping noxious substances on invaders.

Mandorla An almond-shaped or sometimes star-shaped aura often used by fresco-painters to emphasize the sanctity of the risen Christ.

Mitrópolis Orthodox cathedral of a large town.

Naos The inner sanctum of an ancient temple; also, any Orthodox Christian shrine.

Narthex Vestibule or entrance hall of a church, traditionally reserved for unbaptized catechumens; also exonarthex, the outer-most vestibule when there is more than one.

Nave Principal lengthwise limb of a church.

Necropolis Concentration of above-ground tombs, always outside the walls of an ancient city.

Neolithic period Earliest era of settlement on Cyprus, divided into Neolithic I (7000–6000 BC), as at Khirokitiá, and Neolithic II (4500–3800 BC).

Nymphaeum Fountain-wall in the form of a shrine.

Odeion Small Hellenistic or Roman theatre, used for performances councils.

Opus sectile Roman technique for wall or floor mosaics, using thin, translucent pieces of marble, mother-of-pearl or glass set in adhesive.

Orans Term for depiction of the Virgin with both arms aloft in an attitude of prayer.

Pandokrátor Literally "The Almighty", but generally refers to the stern portrayal of Christ in Majesty frescoed or in mosaic in the main dome of many Byzantine churches.

Pediment Triangular wall space between roof and wall of a chapel.

Pendentive Any of four triangular sections of vaulting with concave sides, positioned at a corner of a rectangular space to support a circular or polygonal dome. In churches,

often adorned with frescoes of the four Evangelists.

Rhyton Vessel, often horn-shaped, for libations or offerings.

Rib vaulting Series of projecting curved stone ribs marking the junction of ceiling vaults; common feature of Lusignan monastic and military architecture.

Roundel Decorative painted medallion in a church, on flat or curved surface.

Soffit Inner surface of an arch, often frescoed.

Stele Upright stone slab or column, usually inscribed; an ancient tombstone.

Stoa Colonnaded walkway in ancient marketplaces.

Synthronon Semicircular seating for clergy, usually in the apse of a Byzantine church.

Témblon Wooden altar screen of an Orthodox church, usually ornately carved and painted and used to display icons.

Temenos Sacred precinct, often used to refer to the sanctuary itself.

Tepidarium Warm anteroom of a Roman or Byzantine bath.

Tesserae Cubes used to compose a mosaic, made either of naturally coloured rock or of painted or gilded glass.

Tholos Conical or beehive-shaped building, especially a Bronze Age tomb.

Transept The "arms" of a church, transverse to the nave.

Tympanum In Orthodox use, the semicircular space over a church door reserved for dedicatory inscriptions, dates, frescoes, etc.

Xenon Hostel for pilgrims at an ancient shrine; the tradition continues at Cypriot Orthodox monasteries, though such inns are called *xenónes* in modern Greek.

Yinaikonítis Women's gallery in an Orthodox church, almost always at the rear.

L

Common Greek-Cypriot terms

Áno Upper; as in upper town or village.

Áyios/ayía/áyii Saint or holy (m/f/pl). Common place name prefix (abbreviated Ag or Ay.), often spelt AGIOS or AGHIOS.

Exokhikó kéndro Rural taverna, often functioning only in summer or at weekends.

Kafenío Coffeehouse or café; in a small village the centre of communal life.

Káto Lower; as in lower town or village.

Kinotárkhis See *múkhtar*, below.

Mesaoría The broad plain between the Tróödhos and Kyrenia mountains.

Moní Monastery or convent (formal Greek).

Múkhtar Village headman.

Néos, néa, néo "New" – a common part of a town or village name.

Paleós, paleá, paleó "Old" – again, common in town and village names.

Panayía Virgin Mary.

Paniyíri Festival or feast – the local celebration of a holy day.

Platía Square, plaza; *kendrikí platía*, central square.

Common Turkish-Cypriot terms

Ağa A minor rank of nobility in the Ottoman empire, and still a term of respect applied to a local worthy – follows the name (eg Ismail Ağa).

Bahçe(si) Garden.

Bedesten Covered market hall for textiles, often lockable.

Bekçi Caretaker at an archeological site or monument.

Bey Another minor Ottoman title, like Ağa, still in use.

Cami(i) Mosque.

Çarşı (sı) Bazaar, market.

Dağı, dağları "Mount" and "mountains", respectively.

Eski "Old" – frequent modifier of place names.

Ezan The Muslim call to prayer.

Halk plajı /plajları Free-of-charge public beach(es).

Hamam(ı) Turkish sauna-bath.

Han(ı) Ottoman-era hostel for travellers, or tradesmen's hall.

Hastane(si) Hospital.

Hoca Teacher in charge of religious instruction of children.

İmam Usually just the prayer leader at a mosque, though it can mean a more important spiritual authority.

Kale(si) Castle, fort.

Kapı(sı) Gate, door.

Kervansaray(ı) Strategically located "hotel", for pack animals and men, on main trade routes; in Cyprus few survive, mostly heavily modified. Some overlap with *hanı*.

Kilise(si) Church.

Konak Large private residence, also the main government building of a province or city; genitive form *konağı*.

Kule(si) Tower, turret.

Mabet Temple, common signpost at ancient sites; genitive form *mabedi*.

Mahalle(si) District or neighbourhood of a larger municipality.

Mesarya Turkish for the Mesaoría; officially renamed *İçova*.

Meydan(ı) Public square or plaza.

Meyhane Tavern serving alcohol and small platters of seasonal delicacies on an equal footing; similar (but often superior) to the *mezé* houses of the South.

Mezar(ı) Grave, tomb.

Mihrab Niche in mosque indicating the direction of Mecca, and prayer.

Mimber Pulpit in a mosque, from where the imam delivers homilies.

Minare Turkish for "minaret", the tower from which the call to prayer is delivered.

Muhtar Village headman; *muhtarlık* is the office, both in the abstract and the premises.

Namaz The Muslim rite of prayer, performed five times daily.

Paşa Ottoman honorific, approximately equivalent to "Lord"; follows the name.

Sarniç Rain cistern, often partly subterranean and domed.

Sufi Dervish – an adherent of one of the heterodox mystical branches of Islam.

Tabya Bastion (on walls of north Nicosia or Famagusta).

Tapınak Alternative term for "temple" at archeological sites; genitive form *tapınağı*.

Tarikat Any one of the various Sufi orders.

Tekke(si) Gathering place of a Sufi order.

Vakıf Islamic religious trust, responsible for social welfare and religious buildings; holds extensive property, often donated or willed posthumously by believers, across Cyprus.

Vizier Ottoman minister of state, responsible for the day-to-day running of the empire; in Turkish *vezir*.

Yeni "New" – common component of Turkish-Cypriot place names.

Travel store

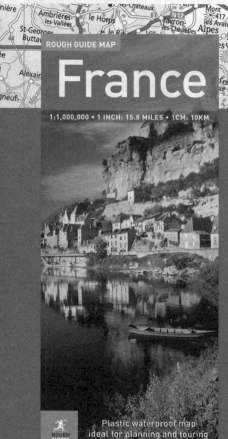

Small print and Index

A Rough Guide to Rough Guides

Published in 1982, the first Rough Guide – to Greece – was a student scheme that became a publishing phenomenon. Mark Ellingham, a recent graduate in English from Bristol University, had been travelling in Greece the previous summer and couldn't find the right guidebook. With a small group of friends he wrote his own guide, combining a highly contemporary, journalistic style with a thoroughly practical approach to travellers' needs.

The immediate success of the book spawned a series that rapidly covered dozens of destinations. And, in addition to impecunious backpackers, Rough Guides soon acquired a much broader and older readership that relished the guides' wit and inquisitiveness as much as their enthusiastic, critical approach and value-for-money ethos.

These days, Rough Guides include recommendations from shoestring to luxury and cover more than 200 destinations around the globe, including almost every country in the Americas and Europe, more than half of Africa and most of Asia and Australasia. Our ever-growing team of authors and photographers is spread all over the world, particularly in Europe, the USA and Australia.

In the early 1990s, Rough Guides branched out of travel, with the publication of Rough Guides to World Music, Classical Music and the Internet. All three have become benchmark titles in their fields, spearheading the publication of a wide range of books under the Rough Guide name.

Including the travel series, Rough Guides now number more than 350 titles, covering: phrasebooks, waterproof maps, music guides from Opera to Heavy Metal, reference works as diverse as Conspiracy Theories and Shakespeare, and popular culture books from iPods to Poker. Rough Guides also produce a series of more than 120 World Music CDs in partnership with World Music Network.

Visit www.roughguides.com to see our latest publications.

Rough Guide travel images are available for commercial licensing at www.roughguidespictures.com

Rough Guide credits

Text editors: James Smart, Tim Locke, Lucy White and Monica Woods
Layout: Jessica Subramanian
Cartography: Alakananda Bhattacharya
Picture editor: Sarah Cummins
Production: Rebecca Short
Proofreader: Susannah Wright
Cover design: Chloë Roberts
Photographer: Suzanne Porter
Editorial: London Ruth Blackmore, Alison Murchie, Andy Turner, Keith Drew, Edward Aves, Alice Park, Jo Kirby, Natasha Foges, Róisín Cameron, Emma Traynor, James Rice, Emma Gibbs, Kathryn Lane, Christina Valhouli, Mani Ramaswamy, Joe Staines, Peter Buckley, Matthew Milton, Tracy Hopkins, Ruth Tidball; **New York** Andrew Rosenberg, Steven Horak, AnneLise Sorensen, Ella Steim, Anna Owens, Sean Mahoney, Paula Neudorf; **Delhi** Madhavi Singh, Karen D'Souza
Design & Pictures: **London** Scott Stickland, Dan May, Diana Jarvis, Mark Thomas, Chloë Roberts, Nicole Newman, Emily Taylor; **Delhi** Umesh Aggarwal, Ajay Verma, Ankur Guha, Pradeep Thapliyal, Sachin Tanwar, Anita Singh, Nikhil Agarwal

Production: Vicky Baldwin
Cartography: **London** Maxine Repath, Ed Wright, Katie Lloyd-Jones; **Delhi** Jai Prakash Mishra, Rajesh Chhibber, Ashutosh Bharti, Rajesh Mishra, Animesh Pathak, Jasbir Sandhu, Karobi Gogoi, Swati Handoo, Deshpal Dabas
Online: **London** George Atwell, Faye Hellon, Jeanette Angell, Fergus Day, Justine Bright, Clare Bryson, Áine Fearon, Adrian Low, Ezgi Celebi, Amber Bloomfield; **Delhi** Amit Verma, Rahul Kumar, Narender Kumar, Ravi Yadav, Debojit Borah, Rakesh Kumar, Ganesh Sharma
Marketing & Publicity: **London** Liz Statham, Niki Hanmer, Louise Maher, Jess Carter, Vanessa Godden, Vivienne Watton, Anna Paynton, Rachel Sprackett, Libby Jellie, Holly Dudley; **New York** Geoff Colquitt, Nancy Lambert, Katy Ball; **Delhi** Ragini Govind
Manager India: Punita Singh
Reference Director: Andrew Lockett
Operations Manager: Helen Phillips
PA to Publishing Director: Nicola Henderson
Publishing Director: Martin Dunford
Commercial Manager: Gino Magnotta
Managing Director: John Duhigg

Publishing information

This sixth edition published February 2009 by
Rough Guides Ltd,
80 Strand, London WC2R 0RL
345 Hudson St, 4th Floor,
New York, NY 10014, USA
14 Local Shopping Centre, Panchsheel Park,
New Delhi 110017, India
Distributed by the Penguin Group
Penguin Books Ltd,
80 Strand, London WC2R 0RL
Penguin Group (USA)
375 Hudson Street, NY 10014, USA
Penguin Group (Australia)
250 Camberwell Road, Camberwell,
Victoria 3124, Australia
Penguin Group (Canada)
195 Harry Walker Parkway N, Newmarket, ON,
L3Y 7B3 Canada
Penguin Group (NZ)
67 Apollo Drive, Mairangi Bay, Auckland 1310,
New Zealand

Cover concept by Peter Dyer.
Typeset in Bembo and Helvetica to an original design by Henry Iles.
Printed and bound in China

488pp includes index

A catalogue record for this book is available from the British Library.
ISBN: 978-1-85828-993-9

The publishers and authors have done their best to ensure the accuracy and currency of all the information in **The Rough Guide to Cyprus**, however, they can accept no responsibility for any loss, injury, or inconvenience sustained by any traveller as a result of information or advice contained in the guide.

1   3   5   7   9   8   6   4   2

Help us update

We've gone to a lot of effort to ensure that the sixth edition of **The Rough Guide to Cyprus** is accurate and up to date. However, things change – places get "discovered", opening hours are notoriously fickle, restaurants and rooms raise prices or lower standards. If you feel we've got it wrong or left something out, we'd like to know, and if you can remember the address, the price, the hours, the phone number, so much the better.

Please send your comments with the subject line "**Rough Guide Cyprus Update**" to ⓒ mail@roughguides.com. We'll credit all contributions and send a copy of the next edition (or any other Rough Guide if you prefer) for the very best emails.

Have your questions answered and tell others about your trip at
ⓦ community.roughguides.com

SMALL PRINT

Acknowledgements

The author would like to acknowledge, on the ground in the South, the managements of Cyprus Villages and Latchi Watersports for various facilities; Angela Richardson at Sunvil Páfos for the SIM card and assorted update material; Yiannis Christofides for his usual gracious hospitality and insights (for five editions now); George and Ben Dimitriades for their usual excellent meals and laying on the wild-foods safari; Ruth Keshishian for book updates, restaurant tips and good company; Christofis Kykkas for his unique perspective; and Stavros

Stavrou Karayanni for another great night out. In the North, many thanks to Steve Abit and staff at Bellapais Gardens for their hospitality, and yet again Küfi and Şirin Birinci for another year of nocturnal safaris and the next installment in the Secret History of Cyprus. Back in London, thanks once more to Dudley der Parthog at Sunvil Travel for helping arrange the trip.

Thanks also to Róisín Cameron, Ainhoa Barrio, Irene Charalambous, Aggeliki Orphanidou and everyone at the London CTO.

Readers' letters

Thanks to all the readers who have taken the time to write in with comments and suggestions (and apologies if we've inadvertently omitted or misspelt anyone's name):

Ulla Alfredsson, Anne Allan, François Andreeff, Trevor Baines, Stephen, Patsy, Stephanie and Daniel Balmforth, Ted Barnes, David and Susan Beale, Susan Bell, Stuart Bostock, John Burton, A. P. Byrne, Lesley Chamberlain and Pavel Seifter, Jane Chesters, Adam Clark, Robert Clements, Michael Coleman, Anne Coney, Joan and Rodney Craig, Robin Dixon, Alastair Drummond-Forbes, Jan Farrar and Jeff Backhouse, Clare Furneaux, Peter and Jill Glover, Dylan Hayes, A. Indart, Ruth Jackson, R. Pritchard Jones, Hugh Kingwell, Mike Leggett, Duncan Mitchell, Peter Mohr, Richard Nelson, Kate Nicholls, Terry and Anita Nicholson, Keith Ougden, Francesca and Richard Peterson, Kevin Platt, Jan and James Randle, Charlotte Spink, Andy Szebeni, Susan Tesei, Alex Thompson, Matthew Tomich, Don Wagstaff, Judy and Bill Webster, Mike Woodroffe.

Photo credits

All photos © Rough Guides except the following:

Introduction

Orthodox Church, Yerakies, Troodhos Mountains © Doug Pearson/Photolibrary.com

Restored Inn © Marc Dubin

Walker standing above a cliff in the Besparmak Mountains © David Robertson/Drr.net

Things not to miss

03 Avgas Gorge © Naki Kouyioumtzis/Axiom

06 St Hilarion Castle © Stuart Black/The Travel Library

07 Divers swimming above lifeboat deck of Zenobia © Gavin Newman/Alamy

08 Buyuk Han in Lefkosa © David Robertson /Drr.net

15 Hala Sultan © Rainer Jahns/Alamy

19 Newly hatched Green Turtle © h2o-images/ Alamy

Traditional Cypriot food colour section

Bladder Campion, Mushrooms and Wild Leeks © Marc Dubin

Sacred art and architecture colour section

Sacrifice of Abraham, Ayios Mamas © Marc Dubin

Black and whites

p.159 Tomb of the Kings © Marc Dubin

p.387 New President of Republic of Cyprus, Archbishop Makarios, Cypriot George Christopoulus and British Ex-Gov. of Cyprus Sir Hugh Foot speaking Dr. Fazil Kucuk at Independence Ceremony © David Lees/Time Life Pictures/Getty Images

p.433 Starred Agama Lizard, Akamas Peninsula © fotolincs/Alamy

SMALL PRINT

Index

Map entries are in colour.

INDEX

INDEX

INDEX

486

Map symbols

maps are listed in the full index using coloured text

− − −	Chapter division boundary	∴	Ruins
▬ ▬ ··	District boundary	⚊	Campsite
═════	Motorway	⊼	Picnic area
════	Main road	🅃	Toilets
═══	Minor road	🅿	Parking
═╪═	Blocked road	★	Transport stop
────	Dirt road	⊕	Phone office
⊞⊞⊞⊞⊞	Steps	ⓘ	Information office
════	Pedestrianized street	⊠	Post office
- - - -	Path	⊞	Hospital
────	River	🛆	Lighthouse
- - - -	Ferry	⛫	Mosque
✦	Point of interest	⚑	Monastery
✈	Airport	⚑	Church (regional)
⊐⊏	Bridge	◉	Accommodation
▲	Mountain peak	▣	Restaurant
⌐⌐⌐	Cliff	▬	Building
⋀	Spring	⊞	Church (town)
⚘	Waterfall	▦	Park/national park
⚲	Beach (regional)	▦	Beach (town)